OWNING IT

BRAD SMEELE

Pro wakeboarder turned quadriplegic

OWNING IT

THE RIDE THAT CHANGED MY LIFE

ALLEN&UNWIN

SYDNEY·MELBOURNE·AUCKLAND·LONDON

First published in 2022

Text © Brad Smeele, 2022

Allen & Unwin
Level 2, 10 College Hill, Freemans Bay
Auckland 1011, New Zealand
Phone: (64 9) 377 3800
Email: auckland@allenandunwin.com
Web: www.allenandunwin.co.nz

83 Alexander Street
Crows Nest NSW 2065, Australia
Phone: (61 2) 8425 0100

A catalogue record for this book is available
from the National Library of New Zealand.

ISBN 978 1 98854 727 5

Design by Kate Barraclough
Set in Adobe Garamond Pro
Printed in Australia by Griffin Press

1 3 5 7 9 10 8 6 4 2

In loving memory of friends lost:

Mark Kenney
Richie Wells
Gareth Jones
Jarrad Wade
Scott Sherill
Brett Hargrave

I want to acknowledge that while some were taken in their prime, some of these friends chose their early exit from this life. So, this book is dedicated to anyone going through shit, anyone struggling or having a rough time, anyone dealing with chronic illness or injury no matter how severe in comparison to others. This is for anyone feeling lost or stuck in a situation they can't see a way out of. For those grieving the loss of a loved one, going through a breakup, losing their job, having financial struggles, or any dramatic life changes leaving them feeling lost. It is my hope that through sharing my story, sharing my own struggles and my journey back to owning my happiness, I can pass on some tools that you may be able to use to find peace in your own life.

CONTENTS

PREFACE

I'm Brad Smeele, and I was a world champion wakeboarder. Born and raised in New Zealand, I left school aged 17 in 2004 and headed for the world wakeboarding stage in Orlando, Florida. I based myself there for successive northern hemisphere summers to increase my training opportunities and surround myself with the best in the world.

I claimed my first world title at the end of that first year, and what followed was a dream run of 21 summers back to back, packed full of adventures, world travel, contest wins, prize money, pro tours, filming trips, sponsorships, road-trips, lake days, babes in bikinis, booze, drugs, partying with great friends and with gorgeous women, and so much more. Best of all, I was living my dream of being on my wakeboard practically every day.

It wasn't all good times — along with the highs came plenty of lows: uncertainty, injuries, contest losses, heartbreak, financial struggles, sponsors letting me down, homelessness, more injuries, surgeries and even a near-death moment or two, but I persevered because I truly loved the sport.

By mid-2014, with the help of the all-new mega-ramp, I landed a world-first double backflip variation that propelled me to new heights, both literally and in terms of my career, even earning me the prestigious Trick of the Year award. But in an attempt to repeat the same trick for cameras just weeks later, I lost control and flipped through the air, not knowing my life was about to be turned upside down too.

When I tumbled head-first into the landing ramp, my C4 vertebra was completely shattered — along with every hope and dream I'd ever had.

On 6 July 2014, in an instant, I went from being a pro athlete on the verge of global success to being quadriplegic — completely paralysed from the shoulders down. All feeling and movement, just like everything I'd ever worked for, were gone.

Thankfully, my friends and teammates saved me, and I was airlifted to hospital. What followed was almost an entire week in ICU that I don't remember.

I underwent a nine-hour surgery to stabilise my neck with titanium-alloy hardware, as well as a tracheotomy to put me on a ventilator. I developed pneumonia and experienced wild and terrifying hallucinations. I finally awoke to be told something even more terrifying: that I would never use my limbs, let alone walk, ever again.

I couldn't fathom life without my physical abilities — no wakeboarding, no exercise, no adventures, no sex! A huge part of me wished I'd died. The following month in ICU was absolutely hellish and it was only the love and support of those around me that persuaded me to be positive and fight to get my life back.

But that was just the beginning of a long and gruelling recovery beginning with five weeks in ICU learning to breathe on my own again, three months in a spinal unit to learn how to exist in a wheelchair, followed by another three months in a spinal unit back in New Zealand.

When I finally moved into my own home, the real issues started to rear their heads. Although I now had full-time physical rehab to keep me busy, the mental struggles were just beginning.

Back out in the real world, it hit home how everything was the same except me. I was *so* changed. I began to feel alienated, like I was a burden on my friends and family, like I was missing out on all the fun. I experienced feelings of total inadequacy, imagining that I'd never be good enough to be wanted and loved by a woman again.

These emotions weighed on me like a ton of bricks. I channelled every bit of anger and frustration into my daily rehab, giving everything I had to get my arms working again — to get my life back. As time went on, my lack of recovery only fuelled my frustrations even further, sending me on a steady downward spiral.

What saved my sanity was the help, knowledge and guidance that came in the form of weekly visits from Susie — my guru, my life guide, my Yoda. Susie's weekly chats helped me understand the emotions I was dealing with. She patiently taught me to sit with them and learn about them, and what underlay each emotion. Susie's visits continued through the years as I struggled to come to grips with my new life, with the lack of hoped-for recovery, through numerous hospital visits, failed relationships and emotional breakdowns — and eventually to the breakthroughs.

As I look back now I am a changed man — someone who has not only accepted but *owns* the changes and the new life thrown at him. A man who understands what he does and does not have control of, and drives his mentality from a place of gratitude. Because, although I still have not regained movement in my limbs, I am in fact grateful for the journey I've been on and everything I've learnt along the way.

I invite you to read on and join me on my journey along a road to an unexpected destination I'm proud to have reached. I'm honoured that I get to share it with you — honest . . . raw . . . real . . . this is my story.

ONE: TESTING THE WATERS

It's Easter 1999. I'm 12 years old and I'm sitting on the beach at Lake Tomarata, watching as Dad, Boyd and Tiff enjoy whipping their kids around the lake on an inflated inner tube, sometimes sending it skimming through the reeds at the edge of the lake. At one stage Simon and Monique are riding doubles, gripping the tube with all their might, and when Tiff whips them into the reeds they connect with a section that's been pushed down into the shape of a ramp. Monique, Simon and the tube go flying through the air, then come crashing down in the swampy shallows. They scream with delight and I can see our dads grinning on the boat, but I have no interest in riding that floating donut. Let myself become some sort of life-sized pinball for their entertainment? No thanks.

These summer school holidays we're staying at nearby Pakiri Beach with our family friends, the Swinburns and the Days, at the Swinburns' bach. When we arrived, Boyd Swinburn swiftly dropped the boat in the water and fired up the outboard. The other kids were absolutely fizzing to have turns behind it, but I'm hesitant. I've still got six stitches in my knee from an accident a few weeks ago. Apparently it's not a great idea to pull a trampoline up on a 25-degree slope, then try to do a backflip on it. I ended up flying off the side, clipping my knee on the steel frame and splitting the top of my knee open to the bone.

All up, there are seven of us kids: my sister Monique is 13 and our brother Alex is nine. Simon Day is 13 and his brother Andy 11. Joe Swinburn is 13 and his brother Sam is 16 or 17. And while the tube might have failed to capture my attention, it's a different story with Sam's new toy — a plastic board with sandal-strap bindings on top that looks like a cross between a surfboard, a snowboard and a water ski.

'It's called a wakeboard,' Sam tells me.

'Can I have a go?' I ask. I know how to water-ski, and I've tried standing up on a kneeboard, but I've never tried one of these.

'Of course, dude!' says Sam. 'I'll just take it for a quick spin first to show you how it works.' He picks up the wakeboard and wades into the water towards the waiting boat. Tiff Day guns the outboard and I watch as Sam effortlessly stands up on the board, then starts carving back and forth doing awesome jumps off the outboard's wake. As he finishes his fourth lap he whips back in towards the beach, throwing a cartwheel-style front flip that he nearly lands. I'm amazed — and I'm itching for a turn.

Several minutes later I'm in the water with my life-jacket on, strapping my feet into the bindings. I float there awkwardly, fumbling for the handle at the end of the towrope while Tiff and Sam give me pointers. The boat takes off . . . and I fail miserably. The handle pops straight out of my hands and I stay floating in the water.

The same thing happens on my second attempt. And the third.

'It's too hard to hang on to the handle,' I say, frustrated. I thought I'd pick this up easily.

'Make sure you keep your knees bent,' Tiff says. 'Don't try to stand up straight away.'

Next time I do better . . . until I crash into the water. Again and again and again. By now I've been pulled almost halfway around the lake on my failed attempts. Finally, on what must be about my tenth go, I stand — and I'm away! Standing sideways, I cruise around the lake, gradually figuring out how to control the board beneath my feet. At first it feels foreign and shaky, but by the second lap I'm starting to feel more comfortable. I know how to skate and snowboard so I soon get the hang of staying balanced and start to steer from side to side between the wakes.

Then I get a little bit too ambitious and my turns become uncontrollable wobbles. The water grabs the board and sends me straight into a faceplant, ejecting me from the bindings. My face stings on impact with the water. As I roll onto my back and wait for the boat to come back I notice that a couple of my stitches have come out of my knee, but I don't care.

I just want to do this again!

After a couple more laps around the lake I drop the handle deliberately and crash into the water. I emerge with a huge smile and I can hear cheers coming from the beach where everyone is watching.

That's it. I'm never water-skiing again.

I'm hooked on wakeboarding.

•

We're back home in Auckland and school has started for the year. I've got my first girlfriend. Her name is Ashleigh, and we met at the Jetsonic disco, a community dance put on for kids aged 11 to 13.

A few weeks earlier, at another Jetsonic, I gave away my first kiss to a girl I wasn't even remotely attracted to. I was so nervous that I just wanted to get it out of the way. After that, I figured, I would be more confident about doing it again. And it worked, because when I saw Ashleigh I went straight up (with a nudge from my friends) and started dancing with her, and before I knew it we were 'pashing'. At 10 p.m. the last song started up — Céline Dion's 'My Heart Will Go On' from *Titanic* — and, while everyone was frantically searching for someone to slow-dance with, I pulled away from Ashleigh and nervously asked for her phone number. She wrote it on a piece of paper.

After waiting the mandatory three days I dialled her number. We talked for hours, and the next weekend we went to the movies together. My first movie date. For the first half we sat holding hands, then we started pashing again and kept it up for the rest of the movie.

Afterwards, I told my friends all about it.

'Did you get to second base?' one of them asked.

I was confused.

'You know,' he said. 'Did you feel her up?'

'Er, no,' I answered bashfully.

So the next time my girlfriend and I were making out in the cinema I slowly, nervously, slid my hand up her shirt. She kissed me deeply. Safe at second base!

●

I only have a couple more opportunities to go wakeboarding through 1999, but I've been begging Mum and Dad all year to get us a wakeboard.

Sure enough, I wake up on Christmas morning to find a big, long present tucked under the tree, for me, Monique and Alex. We tear off the wrapping paper to reveal what we already know is inside. This wakeboard is a newer version than Sam's. Instead of plastic it's made of fibreglass and foam, and rather than sandal straps it has big rubber bindings that can be adjusted to fit different foot sizes. The brand is Hyperlite and the model Fusion. It has a red-and-orange graphic featuring skyscrapers and it's the most awesome thing.

I'm so excited I slip my feet straight into the bindings and stand there in the lounge, pretending I'm behind the boat.

A couple of days later we pack up the boat and head off on our summer holiday. First stop is back at Pakiri Beach, where we spend a few days with our friends and celebrate the countdown to the new millennium. Then we drive a couple of hundred kilometres north to Bland Bay, where we have a block of land we share with the Days.

We've spent our summers at Bland Bay for as long as I can remember. It's where all of my summer memories of camping, fishing and playing on the beach have been formed. A two-minute walk in one direction takes you to the white-sand surf beach, and two minutes in the other direction is the harbour, with a black-pebble beach. It's a perfect combination, the best of both worlds: surf and sand on one side, and calm water for skiing on the other.

On our property are two caravans for the parents to sleep in, while we kids are in tents. The kitchen, shower and toilet are all outdoors. The shower has a tank mounted above it that we fill with bore water and heat using a coil element that hangs in the tank. The toilet is a longdrop — a deep hole in the ground with an outhouse over the top that Dad built. I've always marvelled at the skill and ingenuity of my father. He seems to be able to make or build anything we need, and he and Tiff have turned this place into a camping paradise. Dad was diagnosed with Parkinson's disease when I was about 11, but at this stage it hasn't affected him working as a builder.

When we pull up at Bland Bay, the Days have just arrived and the boys are busy setting up their tents. I leap out of the car, bursting with pent-up energy from the long drive. Never before have I shown this much enthusiasm for unpacking the boat, but I'm really only digging out the bags and tents so I can get my hands on our new wakeboard and show it off to Simon and Andy.

I'm desperate to get the boat in the water, and as soon as we do I'm the first one out behind it. From the moment I stand up on our new board I'm in love with it.

We spend three weeks at Bland Bay, and every opportunity I get I'm on the wakeboard. As I get better at controlling it, I start doing jumps off the wake. On one of the last rides of the holiday, I accidentally figure out how to add some height and start getting about half a metre of air. On the long drive home I can think about nothing else. I want to learn more. I want to jump higher. I want to do more tricks!

•

Starting high school in February 2000 is intimidating. Auckland Grammar School is a melting-pot of egos and hormones. Only a few friends from intermediate have come here. We're streamed according to how we did in our introductory exams and I fall somewhere in the middle — Class G. Partway through the year the classes are reshuffled and I slip to Class J. Needless to say my parents are not thrilled, but I'm not all that fazed. Aside from hanging out with my friends, I don't care much for school. I'd rather be outside, learning from experience.

On the weekends I hang out with my friends Sam and Matt. Matt lives just down the road from Newmarket, so from his place we wander down the street to loiter around the shops, check out the girls and play arcade games outside the movie theatre.

At Sam's we watch car shows with his older brother, John, who is in his last year of school. John is our protector — if anyone at school tries to mess with me or Sam, John and his friends take care of them. John also has a really sweet ride. It's an old turbo Nissan Skyline that he affectionately calls the Slideline because of his love of drifting sideways around corners. Sometimes he gives us a lift home from school or takes us joyriding at night, and I've never been so fast in a car. I love the rush of drifting. John shows off doing burnouts and donuts and it feels like we're out of control. My heart is in my throat and I'm clinging on for dear life, but I can tell that John is in complete control.

Sam and I learn a lot from his big brother. He teaches us about girls — what they like, and where and how to touch them. Ashleigh and I broke up before I started at Grammar and I haven't progressed much further than kissing and a boob grope since, so I listen eagerly to everything John says. Learning about girls is much more interesting than anything I learnt at school, and a whole lot more relevant.

•

'We need to do something about our boat's wake,' I tell Dad one day while I'm reading an issue of *Wakeboarding* magazine. 'It should be bigger, with a clean ramp shape to it, like this one.' I point to a picture in the mag.

I'm constantly hounding my parents to take us out on the Waikato River or nearby Ōrākei Basin, but the wake on our little 5.5-metre fizz-boat with its 85-horsepower Suzuki outboard leaves a lot to be desired. It's small and washy, and riding it is like surfing broken waves. I need a wake that's more like the big clean waves out the back, where the actual surfing happens.

'Well, do you have any ideas for improving it?' Dad asks.

'Yeah, there's an article in here about adding ballast bags to the boat to make your wake bigger.'

'Interesting,' he says as he reads over my shoulder.

Next time we get out on the water, Dad opens up the bungs to the buoyancy tanks in the hull, letting water rush in. Once they're full, I get out on my wakeboard. The boat struggles to get up to speed, then Dad starts playing around with the trim of the motor, changing the angle of the boat as it moves through the water. He angles it up a little more, and in front of my eyes the wake turns from mushy whitewater to a nice clean little ramp. It's not huge, but it's a whole lot better than it was. It makes a massive difference to my jumps. I'm able to actually ride up the wake and get a decent amount of air, enough to reach down and do my first grab on the edge of the board.

I spend the summer trying to get my jumps big enough to clear the wake from one side to the other, but just can't seem to do it. Near the end of summer the family head out on Auckland's West Harbour with some relatives in their new 6-metre Bayliner. As I watch my cousins ride behind the boat I admire its wake, and as soon as I get the opportunity I jump in the water and strap the board onto my feet. My first hit of the wake pops me much higher than I'm used to, but I still land in the middle of the wakes. I cut out wide and edge in harder, and the wake launches me higher and further than I've ever gone, but I case the second wake and crash hard.

As the boat comes back around to bring me the rope, I hear my cuzzies calling, 'You've got it, Brad! Just a little bit further and you'll clear the second wake!'

On my next attempt I cut hard again, but I'm a little spooked after the crash I just took. My legs go a bit soft on takeoff and I case the wake again. I keep trying and it keeps happening. The landings are hard and some take me down. After a handful of tries I'm fed up so I give myself a pep talk: 'Come on, Brad, cut harder and jump harder! You're clearing that wake today!'

I get up again, edge out wide, turn in and lean back against the rope. I speed in and ride up the wake, then push hard with my legs. It sends me flying — the highest I've ever gone — and as I come down perfectly on the second wake it's like landing on the softest cloud. It barely feels real, unlike anything I've ever felt before. Smooth, easy, perfect!

The boat erupts in cheers, claps and whistles and the biggest smile spreads across my face. I cut back across and do it again, and again. I've got this — I'm the wake-to-wake master!

Then I jump again and come up short, bouncing off the second wake. The board catches the water and I faceplant. I'm expelled from the bindings and come back up to the surface with my face burning from the slap. Okay, maybe I got a bit cocky there, but I'm still absolutely buzzing. The pain is nothing compared with the feeling of accomplishment I have.

•

Unfortunately my parents sell the boat over the winter, so when the weather starts to warm up again I do most of my riding at the Ōrākei Basin ski club. They hold wakeboard nights on Tuesdays and Thursdays, and the first time I go along I see a rider with a hard-charging style bust big backflips off the wake. Mum has come with me, and she introduces me to a man she knows from back in her water-skiing days.

'Kevin is here with his son Brant,' she says.

I smile and say hi, but I can't take my eyes off the dude on the water. And when he comes in, he walks straight over to Kevin.

'This is Brant,' Kevin says to me.

I immediately want to ask Brant to tell me everything he knows about wakeboarding. Specifically, I want him to tell me how to do a backflip. But I'm just a shy little 13-year-old in an overwhelming new environment, speaking to a fully grown dude with long hair and an earring, who's really good at wakeboarding, so all I manage to squeak out is, 'That was a pretty cool backflip you did!'

'Thanks, man,' he replies, smiling. 'But in wakeboarding a backflip like that is called a tantrum.'

'Oh . . . well . . . cool tantrum!' I say.

It's nearly my turn so I take my gear down to the dock and get ready. The boat drives past the dock and the blond guy riding behind it comes whipping in, finishing up in style by slowing, then turning around to stop and sit, perfectly, on the side of the dock. As he takes off his board he looks over and says to me, 'Hey, dude, have fun out there!'

The boat pulls up to the dock. It's one of the best ski boats I've seen. It's even got a sky pole, which stands about 1.8 metres high in the middle of the boat with the towrope connected to the top of it — the idea being to stop the rope from pulling you down when you do jumps. The boat also has a bunch of plastic tanks in the back, presumably filled with water as ballast to make the wake bigger.

'Hey!' the driver says. 'You ready?'

I get a 10-minute rip back and forth in front of the ski club, the driver giving me tips the whole time, then my ride is over. I didn't want to stop. I can't wait for the next club night.

Every Tuesday and Thursday I'm there, and I get to know a bunch of awesome people. As well as Brant Hales and Richie Wells, the blond guy who rode just before me that first night, there's Andrea Fountain, our country's top female wakeboarder, Hayden (Haydog) Maguire and Antony (Ants) Colling. As the weeks go by, I start to feel more and more like part of the club. Even though I'm younger than most of them by about five years, they seem to have taken me in. My riding is improving and I'm also learning more about the sport, the equipment, the trick names and the world's best boarders.

Wakeboarding has become my new favourite subject. My obsession. Well . . . that and girls.

•

Earlier in the year at a party I met Stephanie, who became my second girlfriend. She was the life of the party, but that wasn't the only thing that got my attention. She was almost a whole year older, with breasts that suggested she was older still. Her bubbly personality was in stark contrast to my relatively quiet and shy one, and I liked that about her. I took her to the movies, and this time I made it to third base.

One weekend Stephanie invites me to stay at her parents' holiday house. I've spent a bit of time with her family but never slept under the same roof. I'm intimidated by her dad and brother so I try to stay out of their way and out of trouble, but that's a challenge because Stephanie is nothing but trouble. It's in her nature to push boundaries and I'm always along for the ride.

After dinner with her family, everyone goes their separate ways to bed. I tiptoe upstairs to Stephanie's room and within minutes we're kissing and touching each other. Slowly I make my way down her body, until I end up between her legs and, for the first time, I reach third base.

When I'm done, she thanks me. 'Tomorrow night it's your turn,' she says.

I can't believe it. I've had a hard-on for the last hour. Why can't it be my turn right now? I want to ask. And then we can both have *another* turn tomorrow night . . . Instead, I conceal my boner in my shorts and sneak back downstairs.

The next night I lie awake fantasising about my first blowjob while I wait until the parents are asleep. The next thing I know, I'm opening my eyes to daylight. God dammit — I fell asleep!

The whole drive back to Auckland, I can't stop thinking about what I missed out on.

•

The 2000 school year ends and it becomes clear I haven't been paying anywhere near as much attention to my studies as I have to other pursuits.

When my parents sit me down, looking serious, I know they're about to drop a bombshell. 'Brad,' Mum says, 'your grades have slipped so much. You've dropped down several classes. So your father and I have decided to send you to weekly boarding at King's next year.'

'No!' I'm devastated. 'Please, don't do that to me! I can't be a King's boy. All my friends are at Grammar!'

But Mum and Dad are not budging. Their minds are made up.

King's College is a private school, and a very expensive one at that. I guess my parents are hoping that paying for my education will somehow improve my grades. King's also happens to be one of Grammar's main rivals. When my friends find out, I'll never hear the end of it.

The day before term starts, Mum and Dad drive me out to South Auckland. We pass through the school's front gates, then pull up in front of Averill House, which will be my new home during the week. The housemaster greets us and I can already tell we're not going to get along. After showing us around he takes us to my dorm room, opening the door to a large room with eight beds lined up along each side wall. A few guys are unpacking their belongings into the small closet at the head of their bed or the drawers underneath it. Aside from your bed, there's no personal space in here, no privacy except under the covers. It feels like an army barracks, and the housemaster is the sergeant major. Most of the other boys turn out to be returning for their second year so they know each other. They know the school, and they know the drill. I get introduced to a few of them, then my parents kiss me goodbye and drive away.

They really did it . . . Shit!

The next morning, on the way to breakfast, I get talking with one of the other new guys from my year, a squeaky-voiced kid named Jeremy. We get along straight away, both grateful to find an ally in this daunting new environment. As we approach the dining hall I spot something I immediately like: there are girls here! Originally, King's was a boys' school but several years ago they started admitting girls for the two senior years.

I like having older girls to look at but I'm way too shy to go up and talk to any of them. Jeremy and I find a table with some of our dorm mates and we sit around talking about the girls. I talk a big game and the others do the same. We soon identify the 'hot group'— a table of gorgeous young ladies eating their breakfast and gossiping away. The bell rings, snapping us out of our female fixation, and we all scatter to our first class of the day.

Changing schools is tough. I have come from a rival school to a place where everyone else has already had a year together to form friendships. On day three I get my first dose of bullying. As I'm walking back to the boarding house after school I hear a group of guys in my year crooning the words to the melancholy ballad 'All By Myself'. It might be just words, and I can see how they find it funny, but it does a great job of making me feel alienated. I try not to take it to heart but that particular group of guys keep poking fun and coming up with insulting nicknames and other ways to tell me I'm not welcome. I can already tell that if this shit continues there will come a point where it's going to get physical, because I won't put up with it. I won't be their victim.

•

My only respite during the week is when Dad comes to pick me up most Tuesdays and Thursdays for wakeboard nights at the ski club. As soon as the bell rings at three o'clock I rush back to the boarding house to get ready. Those evenings feel like an escape from prison. Ten minutes on the water is all I need to reset the balance and make me feel whole again.

I've decided that wakeboarding is where I'm going to put my focus, but it has required some sacrifices. I've been playing rugby for as long as I can remember and I picked up roller-hockey a few years ago. I really enjoy both, but since their practices clash with wakeboard nights, I had to choose. Wakeboarding was an easy choice.

For my 14th birthday in February 2001 Dad takes me in to the Ballistics shop in Takapuna and buys me the wakeboard I've been dreaming of. A wakeboard of my own! A Hyperlite Premier. I chose it because that's what one of my heroes, Danny Harf, rides — and he makes everything look so stylish and easy. I also like the board's graphics — it's got a weird robotic-looking character on it, and it looks great with the blue Hyperlite high-back boots on it. When Dad and I carry it up to the counter and he is settling up, I summon the courage to ask Jay, one of the store owners who I'd met at club nights, if Ballistics would sponsor me.

'Not yet, little dude.' Jay shuts me down. 'Just keep working on that riding!'

So that's exactly what I do. Specifically, I try to pull off a tantrum, even though I haven't tried — much less perfected — a lot of the basics you're supposed to master before doing a flip. But I can already do a standing backflip on the ground, so I figure I should be able to do it on a wakeboard. At club nights, Brant and Ants have been giving me tips, including pointing out that the correct term for flipping upside down is 'getting inverted'.

On my first attempts I only get halfway around and land on my head, but with every club night my skills improve. I hear about an upcoming event called Boardstock being held at Lake Ohakuri, near Taupō, which draws wakeboarders from all around the country. As soon as I hear about it, I beg my parents to let me go. Mum calls Kevin, Brant's dad, and arranges for me to stay with them down there, and she and I also strike a deal: if I land my first 'invert' at Boardstock, she'll buy me the pair of wakeboarding gloves I've had my eye on.

When the time comes, Brant has already headed down to the lake so it's his sister, Mandy, who comes to pick me up from school on Friday afternoon. It's a three-hour drive and I'm super excited the whole way. Ants is going to be there too, and besides hanging out at club nights I haven't really had a chance to get to know him and Brant. I get that a kid who only just turned 14 could be a bit of a drag on a couple of 19-year-olds geared up for a weekend of riding and partying, but I have no intention of cramping their style. I'm just so stoked to get some riding in.

It's right on twilight when we arrive at the lakeside campground. The last few boats are making their way in, and the keenest riders are squeezing in one last session before it gets too dark. There are so many boats here — everything from small fizz-boats with outboard engines to fully kitted-out ski boats with inboard motors. They all have sky poles, many of which are home-made.

One boat instantly captures my attention. It's a specially designed wakeboard boat called a Malibu Wakesetter and it has a big steel frame mounted on top that looks like a roll cage.

'Wow,' I say to Kevin when I see it. 'That's so cool.'

'Yeah, that steel tower is the latest in design,' he says. 'No sky pole necessary.'

I can't stop staring at the Wakesetter. It's bigger than the other boats — longer and taller.

'It's all about the depth and shape of the boat's hull,' Kevin explains. 'By having more freeboard, you can add more ballast to the boat to sink it lower in the water. The deeper the hull sits, the more water it displaces. The more water it displaces, the bigger the wake.'

I think about Dad opening up the buoyancy tanks in our old boat. Same principle, but this boat is so much more sophisticated, with specific ballast tanks that fill with the push of a button. I desperately want to have a go at riding behind it.

'Pushing through that much more water requires a big, powerful engine,' Kevin adds. 'That thing has a 360-horsepower V8 driving it.'

The next morning I get to see it in action. While we're heading up the lake in Kevin's racy red outboard boat, the Wakesetter passes us going in the opposite direction. The guy riding behind it charges into the wake and launches higher than I've ever seen anyone go, then does a trick I can't even comprehend. It's like some sort of spinning Superman manoeuvre. I didn't even know that kind of thing was possible on a wakeboard. I'm pretty sure my mouth is hanging open.

Kevin's boat is better suited to ski-racing than wakeboarding, but as soon as we put up the sky pole and Brant gets out behind it, I realise it's not always about having the fanciest equipment. I watch Brant landing all kinds of flips and spins. If he can do it, then surely so can I. As soon as it's my turn I leap in the water absolutely pumped to get inverted, but I just keep crashing.

'Hey, I know the wake isn't huge, but you're still leaving at the bottom of it,' Brant says to me after my first few attempts. 'To give yourself the time to rotate, you need to wait a little longer so you really get the pop you need.'

It's such a strange concept to wrap my head around. He's telling me I need to wait longer before flipping, when my instinct is to do the opposite in order to make the flip come around more quickly. On my next attempt I try it his way. I wait a little bit longer; then, when I stand tall and throw my head back, I feel the punch from the wake send my board up and over me. It's like doing a backflip on the trampoline, where the springback from the mat has its own energy that actually contributes to the rotation. Suddenly it all clicks. I've been thinking of it as like doing a backflip on the ground, where I have to create the force all by myself, but the wake has its own energy I can use. I flip all the way around and, for the first time ever, I land on my board. I crumble into the water — but at least I landed on my board, not on my head!

It takes me a few more goes but finally I land my first invert. My first tantrum!

With my fist in the air, I listen to the cheers and whistles from our boat and another one cruising past. But I'm not done yet. I need to prove to myself that it's not a fluke, so I cut back out, carve and edge in hard at the wake. I land another one. Two in a row!

Mission accomplished.

As we head back in, I think about what Brant told me. His words helped me land my first invert, but they've also got me thinking about something else: I've realised that sometimes I feel I need to rush things to make them happen, but those are the times when I really just need to be patient.

•

At the end of the day we take the boat up a small arm that branches off the main part of the lake, putting along at 5 knots for a few minutes before I notice steam rising from the water. As we round a bend I see a whole bunch of boats parked in a narrow cove. The Wakesetter is there, pumping the tunes through the speakers mounted on the tower. Dancing on the back is a small dude with long hair, big plastic earrings and board shorts that reach down past his knees. He's got a drink in his hand, as does everyone around him.

'That's Mark Kenney,' says Brant. 'He's the guy you saw riding behind the Malibu earlier. He's from Australia, and is probably one of the best riders in the world.'

We find a spot to park up, then jump into the water. It's hot — actually hot, like a bath.

'Someone tapped into a natural hot spring,' says Brant, pointing to a large pipe sticking out the side of the hill with hot water flowing from it. 'They call this place Paradise!'

I can see why. As Brant and I swim over to join everyone else, I hear a whistle from over by where the hot water is flowing. I turn to see a guy put his hand up in the air and yell, 'Kenney!' The Aussie rider flips open the storage locker in the back of the Wakesetter, revealing that it's packed full of ice and beer. He tosses a frosty refreshment and it lands perfectly in the guy's outstretched hand.

'Yo, Kenney!' Brant pipes up. 'Hook us up!'

Kenney lobs him a beer, then grabs another, but he pauses before throwing it to me.

'Are you old enough to be drinking, kid?' he says.

'Ummm, er, I . . .' I stammer.

'I'm just fucking with you!' He laughs, tossing me the beer. 'I'm not either!'

As night falls, everyone returns to the campground and carries on the party there. The stereo is blasting dance music, the campfire is blazing and everyone is pumped for a good night. I've only had a couple of beers and I'm aware of being the youngest in this new crowd, so I mostly stay sitting beside the fire, soaking it all up.

Ants comes over and ruffles my hair. 'First invert for the grommet!' he says. 'I believe that calls for a celebration.' I've heard that term before — a young wakeboarding newbie.

He pours me a shot of tequila. I've only tried it once and I really didn't like it, but there's no way I'm turning this shot down in front of the crew. I knock it back and, even though I feel like I want to hurl, hold it down and let out a cheer: 'First fucking tantrum!'

Everyone erupts around me and in no time we're all up and dancing on the patch of grass between the music and the fire. Another shot is handed to me so I force it back and keep dancing. A circle forms and everyone takes turns to break it down in the middle. I pick my moment and jump in, busting a couple of dance moves then leaping into a standing backflip. Again, I'm rewarded with loud cheers.

I'm having the best time with this cool older crowd. I don't feel I need to be shy around these guys any more. It's like my shell is starting to crack and break away. I've found my tribe.

●

For the Easter school holidays my parents book me into a wakeboard camp hosted by Ballistics down in Ātiamuri, a tiny little town parked beside the Ātiamuri Dam. There's no store and no petrol station, just a cluster of 30 or so houses and a pristine lake that's protected from the wind by hills covered in tall pine trees.

I head down there with a family friend, Justin, and we're greeted by the camp coach and manager, who introduces himself as Azza. I'm excited to see that Mark Kenney is also here. He's been helping out at the camp for the past few months. 'It's my way of getting away from all the politics and bullshit,' he tells us. 'I just want a quiet place to ride, and I've found it here.'

The few days we spend riding at the camp are the most fun and productive I've ever had. Kenney and Azza are both great coaches and fun dudes to be around. We spend all day out on the water, only coming in to refuel the boat and our bodies. In the evenings, Justin and I unwind on the couch and work our way through the stack of wakeboard videos on offer. I decide US rider Parks Bonifay is my favourite.

Here at the camp I start learning the basics I skipped in pursuit of getting upside down, but really all I want to do is land my tantrum again and the guys give me pointers on how to take it bigger. On day two I launch a tantrum that sails across both wakes and I land cleanly down the second wake. I also leave the camp having mastered a backroll — a sideways rolling invert off the heels.

Nailing these tricks is definitely a highlight, but it's not the most incredible thing I get from the camp. While Justin and I are having a break one day, Kenney takes to the water and puts on an absolute clinic. He cuts out as wide as possible, then hooks a sharp turn, leans right back and burns in at the wake at lightning speed. He explodes off it and sends an outrageously large trick out into the flats. It's like a Superman barrel roll that he lands backwards with his hand behind his back.

'Woah! What was that?' I ask Azza.

'That's called an S-bend to blind,' he replies casually. 'Kenney's one of very few people in the world who can do it.'

Kenney made it look easy. Flipping and spinning, spinning while flipping — it's all so smooth yet so powerful. Azza explains that landing blind means landing while facing backwards — riding away with the handle behind your back.

'That's a whirlybird,' Azza says when Kenney does a spinning flip thing that looks so awesome I immediately decide I want to do it one day too.

Then he cuts back across on his toes, casually doing another underflip-looking trick that I can't even comprehend, landing about 5 metres past the second wake.

'And that's a Pete Rose,' says Azza. 'It's named after a baseball player who was famous for sliding into home base on his stomach, which is how you usually fall if you mess up that trick.'

Kenney cuts back in on his heels and does another whirlybird, but this time he lands blind.

'Whirly-five,' Azza says.

Kenney's display lasts about 40 minutes without a single fall. Justin and I are speechless. The power possessed by this small, hyperactive Aussie string-monkey is incredible.

Kenney gets back on the boat for a rest, then, just as he's about to jump back into the water for another set, Azza says, 'Okay, dude, no inverts this set.'

'All right,' Kenney grins. 'No worries!'

And for another 45 minutes he blows our minds all over again. Azza tells us the name of each trick, and I learn that what I've been calling a Superman — when a rider sticks their board out behind them with their arms stretched out in front, like they're flying through the air — is actually called a raley. Kenney just goes so huge on everything, takes everything to the flats, lands blind, and spins frontside and backside, both flat and off-axis. He's peeling open my mind, enlightening me on the vast array of possibilities for a fibreglass board with a couple of rubber boots attached.

Mark Kenney has just put himself in the running against Parks Bonifay as my favourite. I want to be like him. He rides for CWB, so I want to ride for CWB. He rides for Oakley, so I want to ride for Oakley. He rides for Ballistics, so I'm going to ride for Ballistics.

•

A week after the camp, I attend my first New Zealand national wakeboarding championships. It's a fun experience, but I barely make it through the first day of competition on the Saturday, squeaking through the last-chance qualifier. In my finals run I manage to land both of my inverts, but my weaknesses are blatantly revealed. My toeside wake-to-wake jumps are still below par, so my run consists of all heelside tricks, and between them I just do a small jump or 180 into the middle of the wake. I'm what's dubbed a heelside hero, the nickname given to those who haven't put the work in to learning to jump the wake off the toes.

I just miss out on a podium finish with fourth place. The winner of the junior division is a kid named Ben, who is actually a couple of years younger than me and absolutely rips. He looks really comfortable both heelside and toeside, and has inverts both ways. I vow that I'll take his spot next year, but I'm also looking way beyond next year. I've been watching the guys in the open men's division, and they've inspired me to look to the future.

A rider called Jeff Weatherall ends up winning the weekend with his rock-solid technical game and his combination of hard-charging raley tricks and smooth spins. If I want to become the best in the country — and I've already decided I do — Jeff's the man I have to beat.

•

As the weather starts to cool, so does my relationship with Stephanie. We've been together almost a year. I still love her and enjoy her company, but with wakeboarding and school I'm struggling to find time for both her and my friends. Besides, it's been months since we were at the beach house together and she still hasn't delivered on her side of the exchange.

I decide my friends take priority, so one night after school I call her from the hostel pay phone. It takes me a while to build up the courage, but I finally tell her I think we should break up. She's crying, and so am I, but I've already made up my mind. Time to move on.

•

Near the end of 2001 I head down to a wakeboarding competition in Hamilton and this time I take the win in the junior division, thanks in large part to pulling off the biggest raley I've ever done. With some instruction from Richie and encouragement from the rest of the crew at the club I finally managed to master the raley just before winter kicked in. The first time I got my board kicked out behind me so I was fully extended, but then I didn't know how to bring it back in so I let go while I was still in the air and swan-dived into the salty water.

'That was perfect,' Richie said when I came back up, 'until you let go. This time I want you to pull the handle down towards your knees to bring the board back under you.'

I tried and got close to bringing the board under me that night but after a few spankings I'd had as much as I could take, so I called it quits. I was back at it a few nights later, and finally claimed my first raley.

At the competition in Hamilton, I charge into the wake provided by the Malibu Wakesetter, which is much bigger than the one behind the ski boat at the club. When I take off and stretch out into my raley it's like I've set sail. It's an incredible feeling, flying through the air with so much more time to play with. I am addicted.

Part of my prize is a free week at the next Ballistics camp, and when the guys hear about my competition win — my first — I get a call from Rich, the other Ballistics owner. 'Hey, buddy, nice work at the Hamilton event!' he says.

'Thanks!' I reply.

'Look, we've been approached by a magazine that wants to do a story on the next big up-and-coming rider. They're giving it away for free at every McDonald's in the country. Would you be interested?'

'Hell yes!' I respond.

'And we would love to have you as our newest Ballistics team rider.'

I thank him profusely.

'Just mention the camp in your interview, and you're welcome to go down and spend time there to get some riding in.'

After I hang up the phone I do a quick celebratory dance on my bed. Then I rush downstairs. 'I got my first sponsor!' I tell Mum and Dad. They're both stoked for me.

•

Before the end of the year I bag my second sponsor.

I'm down riding at Ōrākei Basin when Ants and Brant introduce me to a dude named Brent. He's the rep for CWB New Zealand ('C-dub'), the wakeboarding brand they ride for.

'You want this kid on C-dub,' Brant says.

'Yeah, he's the next big up-and-comer!' adds Ants.

It's awesome to hear them talking me up, and Brent looks interested.

'Here, give this board a demo,' he tells me. 'It's mine.'

'Sure!' I reply. 'But the boots are a bit smaller than mine.'

'You should be able to squeeze into them,' Brent says.

As I squeeze some lube — actually detergent — into the bindings to make it easier to slip my feet in, Brent tells me, 'A good set of bindings should be nice and tight. Difficult to get into, and firm but comfortable once you're in. That way you have more control and responsiveness with your board.'

With a bit of a struggle, I manage to get my first foot into the binding. Then I push down hard with my second foot and it slips in too. Except that a rip has appeared, running all the way down the side of the boot.

'Ah shit!' I say. 'Sorry, dude.' I feel terrible. This is not the way to impress a potential sponsor.

Someone grabs some duct tape and I wrap that around the boot to keep it together. Then I get out on the water, and I love this board immediately.

When I come in, Brent's smiling. 'Great work out there! Welcome to the team, Brad,' he says, shaking my hand.

I'm stoked. Not only do I have a board sponsor, but it's the same one that Ants and Brant ride for. And, based on their grins, they're pretty happy with themselves for helping to hook me up.

•

As soon as the summer school holidays start, I head straight down to Ātiamuri and take Rich up on his offer for me to stay on at the camp for a while after my free week.

Azza is still the head coach, and for part of the summer Richie Wells joins him. Since I'm the youngest I basically become the 'camp bitch'. I help clean the boat, make sure it's got gas, cook dinner, fetch beers for campers while they're in the hot tub and so on. Whenever we're out on the boat, I soak up everything I can about coaching. It's not just about learning new tricks any more. Now, I want to learn to teach others and explain how it's done.

I love riding with Richie. He seems to have taken me under his wing and is great at teaching me new and more difficult tricks because he can actually do most of them. Azza is also a good coach but he's more of a cruiser on the water — he mainly does grabs and spins but doesn't go upside down like Richie does. Azza knows the theory behind most tricks, though, and he's helping me think about style and making my tricks look good.

•

When I head back up to Auckland for Christmas, I receive the best gift I could have wished for: my Auckland Grammar jersey!

'I'm going back to Grammar?' I ask Mum.

She's smiling at me. 'You're going back to Grammar,' she says.

I can't tell if she's smiling because I'm so happy or because she and Dad won't have to pay private school fees any more. Probably both.

As for me, I've never been so happy to be given an old woollen sweater.

Back at Grammar not much has changed in the year I've been gone. In French class I'm seated beside a skinny kid named Doug. We quickly find mutual enjoyment in making fun of our elderly teacher and his very obvious toupee. There's a rumour that some of the senior students once ran a piece of nylon fishing line across the doorway at the teacher's head height, so that when he walked into the room the rug was peeled from the top of his head. Doug and I picture it and laugh whenever he enters the room. We don't learn much French.

It's not just in French class that I don't pay attention. Before long, my lack of interest in my studies is made apparent by the fact I'm sliding down the classes once again. Economics and accounting don't interest me at all, and although I'm good at basic maths, the teacher has lost me with statistics and calculus. Science is okay — I love doing experiments in chemistry, and I'm pretty good when it comes to understanding basic physics.

I'm all right in English, and I enjoy technology because we get to play around with wood and metal, but my favourite class is physical education. I love playing sports and I'm also into learning about the body — the muscle groups, the skeleton, the cartilage, tendons and so on. Basically, I'm drawn to anything I can apply to wakeboarding — the laws of physics and the way the body works. I don't really bother with the rest. For me, school is really just about hanging out with my friends.

One day while Doug and I are having lunch together he introduces me to one of his best friends, Jordan Lewis. He and Doug went to primary school together, and Jordan and I soon discover we have quite a lot in common. We're both athletic and love to skate, we're into the same music, and we both love chicks!

On the weekends the three of us blast music from Jordan's DJ setup in his basement, then we wander into Newmarket to scope out the cute girls. I really envy Jordan's confidence in particular. He seems to be able to walk up to any girl and deliver the perfect line. Sometimes he doesn't even say anything. On one occasion he simply walks up to a ridiculously attractive girl at McDonald's and eats a few fries off her tray, then next thing she's his girlfriend.

I'm still way too afraid of getting rejected to ever do something like that.

•

Only a matter of months after getting me hooked up with CWB, Brant and Ants decide to jump ship — they've been approached by Hyperlite Wakeboards. I'm gutted, as I loved being on the same team as my friends.

Not long after, the Hyperlite New Zealand team manager asks if I'll cross over too. I hate the idea of letting down the C-dub guys, as they've been really good to me, but Ants and Brant convince me to do it. Hyperlite, as well as offering to supply all the gear I need, are also promising other perks, including a boat we can use whenever we want to. And of course some of my heroes ride Hyperlite, including Parks Bonifay, Danny Harf, Chad Sharpe and Erik Ruck.

So I call Brent from C-dub and tell him I'm going to Hyperlite as well. Needless to say, he's not thrilled. Just a couple of hours later I get a call from Rich at Ballistics, who gets straight to it. 'Look, Brad, if you leave CWB that will seriously jeopardise your sponsorship with Ballistics.'

I can't believe it. I feel like I'm being blackmailed.

Rich goes further: 'I don't think you should associate yourself with the likes of Ants and Brant either,' he said.

It's true that Ants and Brant have a bit of a reputation as the bad boys of the local wakeboarding scene. They're seen as loose units, hooligans, and they have copped the blame for some dodgy happenings. I've never believed they were responsible — it's always seemed they were just convenient scapegoats — but not everyone is convinced. To me, Brant and Ants are good friends who motivate my riding. I look up to them — and, yes, that's partially because they *are* bad boys who like to party hard and show up to contests with hot chicks. They always make wakeboarding look fun.

But at the end of the day, I don't really have much choice. Ballistics want me to keep riding for CWB, and I don't want to lose Ballistics. So I stay — but I also make it clear that they have no say in who I ride with, or who I'm friends with.

•

I invite my friend Sam to come down to Lake Karāpiro with me for the wakeboard nationals. He doesn't wakeboard himself but he enjoys watching, and I'm stoked to have him supporting me. At the campground we set up beside Brant and Kevin. There are heaps of others there — it's going to be a big weekend!

I ride well in my first round, and book myself a spot in the finals. As soon as I'm done riding, the pressure is off for the day. This year's event sponsor is Corona, and they've loaded the clubrooms up with case upon case of Cerveza. I manage to sneak a bucketful from the Ballistics tent, and Sam and I spend the rest of the day sinking cold ones, even though we're still three years shy of being legally able to purchase it for ourselves.

By the time darkness falls, I've got a good buzz going and the party is just getting started! This year, instead of sitting on the edges, I'm all amongst it. With some Dutch courage, I'm much more confident than usual. People keep coming up to introduce themselves and compliment me on my riding, and I love it. By the end of the night I've drunk more beer than I've ever had in one sitting and I feel great. I cut shapes on the dance floor with no thought of people watching me. I have conversations with strangers who then become friends.

I tap out and crawl into my tent while the party's still raging outside, and the following morning I feel surprisingly fresh. After a breakfast of bacon, eggs and baked beans, I'm ready for battle on the water. For a moment, I wonder if I might have sent it a bit too hard last night considering I have a final today . . .

but I'm feeling good, feeling loose, feeling ready. I warm up and watch my competitors ride before me. They're landing some good tricks but their runs are scattered with falls. I know that with all the work I put in at the Ballistics camp over summer, I've really stepped up my game. When I get out on the water I'm ready to show it.

My first pass includes a few inverts off both sides of the wake, as well as a heelside 360, then I open my second pass with a raley, and it feels awesome. My confidence is through the roof, so I turn and burn into the wake as hard as I can, sending myself soaring through the air and stomping the landing. The crowd cheers from the shoreline. A bit further through my run I bust out a whirlybird. I've only just recently learnt this move, which is a tantrum with a 360, and it's by far the hardest and most visually impressive trick I can do. I've wanted to do it ever since seeing Kenney do it. I make it all the way around to the point where I spot my landing, but I'm a little slow on the rotation and end up crashing so hard I get thrown from my bindings. Regardless, I'm stoked with my run. Everyone else had a fall too, so that won't rule me out.

Sure enough, my performance is enough to win me my first national title — junior champion!

I stick around to watch the open men's final, and I notice that Jeff Weatherall is not here this year, apparently because of knee surgery. His absence opens things up for the other riders — Richie bags the top spot and Brant comes second.

As I stand on the podium to claim my title, I'm filled with pride to have a medal around my neck and a trophy in my hand. I like this feeling — the feeling of winning. It's like landing a new trick for the first time, and it's another feeling I could get addicted to.

It's around now that I pick up additional sponsorship from Oakley and complete my vow to be sponsored by the same brands as Mark Kenney: Ballistics, CWB and Oakley.

•

At home, I start to notice some tension between Mum and Dad. They don't really fight in front of us kids, but it's obvious that they're not getting along as well as usual. Things just feel a bit strained. One night they disappear into their room and close the door much earlier than they usually go to bed. In the past, I might have suspected something else was going on in there but this time I know it's because they're arguing. I stand outside the closed door until I've heard enough, then I run downstairs to my room, slam the door behind me, jump onto my bed and scream into my pillow.

A few weeks later they sit me and my siblings down at the table.

'We're going to spend some time apart,' Mum says.

I never thought my parents would split up. They tell us it's just a trial separation, but I know the chances are they won't be getting back together. It all happens so quickly that I don't really have time to process it.

They rent an apartment nearby and take turns staying there and with us in the house. One week Mum is with us and Dad's in the apartment, the next Dad is here and Mum is gone. Then, after a couple of months of this back and forth, the decision is made that Dad will live in the apartment permanently. I can tell that Dad's not thrilled about it, but he's going along with it to keep Mum happy. The apartment only has one bedroom so Monique, Alex and I will stay at home with Mum. I actually think the apartment is pretty cool — it's a loft-style space above a homewares store, and it's only a five-minute walk from school. At least I can still pop in to visit Dad on my way home. It sucks that this has happened, but I'm old enough to know that it's got nothing to do with us kids.

•

In late August, I stop off to see the crew at Ballistics. As I'm browsing through the winter gear I see Jenny, who works in the shop. She's also one of New Zealand's top female riders and we've spent a bit of time together at the camp.

'Hey,' I say, then I notice the sad expression on her face. 'What's up?'

'I guess you heard about Kenney?' she says.

'No. What happened?'

She looks like she's fighting off tears. 'He died. A couple of days ago.'

I pause, trying to make sense of what she's just said. 'Wh-what? He *died*? But how?' My heart drops; I'm trying not to cry too.

'We haven't heard exactly what happened, but he died in his sleep,' she says. 'He had an injury and it might've been a reaction to the painkillers he was taking — no one's really sure.'

I can't believe it. Poor Jenny. I know she and Kenney were hooking up over summer, so she must be utterly heartbroken.

When I get home and see Kenney's poster on the wall, I finally let the tears stream. He was just 18, and on an absolute streak in the US — he'd started winning pro tour events, was showing the world a new way to ride and stomping his mark on the sport. The tears don't relieve the pain, so I knock my dartboard off the door and proceed to punch a hole right through a panel of the door. My knuckles throb, but something about it makes me feel better, like I've transferred the pain to the outside of my body. I sit on the edge of my bed looking at the poster of my hero, taken well before his prime, and I vow to do everything I can to make him proud.

•

I spend most of the summer down at the Ballistics camp, and my riding is steadily improving. I come back home to Auckland just in time for the start of another school year, and not long after that it's Valentine's Day.

Mum tells me she's going out with her new man, Gordon. I've only met him a couple of times and I don't really like him — or maybe I just don't like the idea of Mum seeing another man. I still haven't really got used to the fact that my parents have split up.

'I won't be home till the next morning,' Mum says.

I decide it's the perfect opportunity to have a party in the park across the street. Our house is at the end of a cul-de-sac that finishes at a small cove called Judges Bay, and the bottom of the park goes right down to the water's edge, while at the top are the Parnell Rose Gardens. Rows and rows of different-coloured blooms stretching the length of a rugby field — what better place to take a girl for a romantic little Valentine's make-out session?

I tell all my school friends to come. 'Invite as many girls as possible,' I say, 'but not too many guys.' The less competition the better, I figure, and I've also learnt from experience that this sort of thing can get out of hand if word spreads too far.

As soon as Mum's out of the house, Jordan, Doug and another one of my close friends, Rory, turn up dressed in their best jeans and polo shirts. I'm wearing a brand-new white Prada polo that I got for my birthday, and my black-and-white checked Vans. We stroll across to the park with my boom box, and once the tunes are pumping we crack open our first beer of the evening.

'Cheers!' I say. 'Here's to a good night!'

Within a couple of hours more than 40 teenagers — some friends of ours, some acquaintances and some complete strangers — are bustling around the park, drinking and mingling and dancing. Sitting on a park bench with my boom box, I proudly survey the party I've pulled together, then I get up and wander down to a large group of people hanging out nearby. A girl I don't know hands me a perfect long-stemmed red rose. 'Happy Valentine's,' she says. It's clearly not stolen from the gardens up the hill, which probably means another dude gave it to her, but I don't care. I still feel pretty special.

Then I see a familiar-looking group of guys walking down the street towards us — and they're not familiar in a good way. It's Sean, a guy from school, and some of his wannabe gangster friends. I'm instantly on high alert because it's obvious from the way they swagger into the park that they're here to cause trouble.

Sean and I had a fight after school towards the end of last year. It started over nothing, but our friends and classmates hyped it up until next thing we're face-to-face throwing punches, surrounded by bloodthirsty teens eager to see a good scrap. I kicked his arse, but broke my thumb in the process, so I showed up at school the next day with my arm in a plaster cast and my tail between my legs. Which actually turned out to be a blessing in disguise, as exams were coming up and I'd broken my writing hand, so I was given compassionate consideration and passed without sitting a single test.

I'd suspected there might've still been some tension there, and it appears I was right, because now he's here with his whole crew.

I frantically scan the partygoers for my friends and soon spot Doug. As I start moving towards him, Sean and his crew set eyes on me and veer eagerly in my direction. I keep my eyes down and I get halfway to Doug before I hear one of the guys call out loudly, 'Hey, who's that faggot with the rose?'

I stop, and turn to face them. 'Believe it or not, a girl gave this to me. Don't be jealous!'

The guy with the smart mouth responds by stepping forward and swinging a right hook that catches me on the cheek. It's not a knockout punch but it stuns me for a second. I don't retaliate. Instead, I race over to Doug.

'It's on, bro!' I say as soon as I get to him. 'Where are Jordan and Rory?'

He scurries away to get Jordan, and I'm soon joined by Rory and several other friends, including a girl called Liv who I've known for years. Doug returns with Jordan just in time and I'm really glad I've got my three guys with me. I know they've got my back. Words are thrown, then it's Liv who steps forward first, shoving the smart-mouth. He pushes her, knocking her back a couple of steps, and that's all it takes.

Fists are flying in all directions, and I'm swinging wildly, but there are too many of us for anything to land clean. Amid the chaos, I see Jordan grab hold of one guy and toss him down the hill, then Sean is straight on Jordan and they tumble down the hill together. Meanwhile, Smart-mouth and I are taking swings at each other, but nothing significant connects. I do manage to throw him down the hill in the direction of the main action, where I see Rory tussling with another guy. Sean throws a bottle at Jordan from close range that bounces off his head and onto the grass. He picks it up and returns fire, and the bottle smashes across Sean's face and drops him. Time to bail.

Where's Doug? I wonder, then I see him. He's making a beeline towards my house with the boom box. I take off after him. Jordan is running too, and we're both fighting people off as we go. It's absolute mayhem.

I get to the house just as Doug closes the door behind him. Within seconds I'm surrounded, and kicks and punches start raining down on me. I put both arms up to cover my head, and get my back up against the door. As soon as there's a gap in the flurry, I swing a couple of heavy blows and crack the guy directly in front of me a good one to the cheek. He wobbles, and I cover my face again, expecting retaliation. I block a few punches but then I cop a bottle to the side of the head. It breaks on impact, shattering on the tile porch. I'm stunned, but I stay on my feet and keep my guard up.

'Motherfucker, making me bleed!' I hear a voice yelling over the commotion. 'Fuck you!' It's Sean and he's got blood dripping down his face. I pop up and hurl a right jab that knocks him off his feet and splatters blood all over me, my shirt, my shoes and the front porch. His friends catch him just in time to stop him from hitting the deck.

As I brace myself for the next wave, I'm grabbed from behind and pulled inside the house. It's Doug.

'Thanks for finally letting me into my own house!' I say furiously. 'Fuck, man!'

Then Rory rushes inside. 'That was fucking crazy!' he says through a mouthful of blood — his braces haven't been too kind to his lips.

We head upstairs and find Jordan standing outside on the balcony. I open the door to let him in.

'Oh my god, that was nuts!' He's breathing heavily. 'I ended up running right around and then had to scale your house and get on to the balcony to get away.'

Once we know our attackers have departed, skulking off down the driveway, we go outside to inspect the damage. The front of the house is trashed, and someone has kicked in the ranch-slider door on my sister's room. Down on the street we hear yelling, swearing, bottles smashing. It's madness, with all the partygoers wandering around trying to figure out where to go and what to do.

We go back inside. I get a bag of frozen peas, and while I'm on the couch holding it to the side of my head I hear sirens. We all rush out on to the balcony, expecting to see a squad car, but instead a paddy wagon pulls up and six officers jump out in full riot gear. Then three squad cars screech in, blue and red lights flashing, lighting up the entire park. I hear the front door swing open, then footsteps racing up the stairs. The cops! They're about to take me away in handcuffs! But it's so much worse than that.

'GET THE FUCK OUT OF MY HOUSE, YOU FUCKING ANIMALS!' Mum screams as she bursts into the lounge. I have never heard her sound so ferocious.

Gordon is right behind her. 'Yeah, get the fuck out!' he pipes up.

My blood boils. Who the hell does this 50-something silver fox think he is? This isn't even his house. I leap to my feet, staring him down. 'You can't talk to my friends like that! *You* get the fuck out of *my* house!'

But Mum just yells, '*All* of you get the *hell* out of *my* house!'

My friends scatter and I'm left fuming, the bag of frozen peas still held against my head. I start to clean up all the broken glass and blood on my own.

●

The next day, after apologising profusely to Mum, I try to explain what happened.

'All I did was arrange a gathering in the park,' I say. 'I was trying to keep everyone away from the house. Then Sean and those guys showed up looking for trouble.'

'Who's Sean?' she asks.

'Some kid from school who thinks he's a bad-arse,' I reply. 'He only came so he could pick a fight. All of this is his fault.'

'I'm going to call Sean's mother and invite her and her son over here so we can put this all behind us. And Brad,' she adds, seeing my look of reluctance, 'this meeting is not going to be about pointing fingers or blaming anyone. You are going to shake hands and move on. Understood?'

I nod.

A couple of days later Mum and I sit down at our dining table with Sean, who has a line of fresh stitches across his cheek, and his mother. She immediately takes the floor. 'Your son is the bully here,' she says to Mum, then she even makes me and Sean stand beside each other to demonstrate her point. 'Look at how much bigger he is! My little bunny rabbit would never hurt a fly!'

I have to fight so hard to keep myself from bursting out laughing, and I desperately want to defend myself, but I hold my tongue. I let Mum play mediator and, even though I can tell she's getting frustrated too, she does a good job of calming things down. After just 10 minutes, Sean and I are shaking hands and making peace. Then as soon as they leave, Mum turns and says to me, 'Sheesh, that bloody woman was a handful!'

'Yep,' I reply. 'And I can't believe she called him a bunny rabbit in front of me!'

I start laughing and I'm delighted when Mum has a bit of a chuckle too. I know I'm not yet forgiven, but I can see she's a little more on my side now.

During lunchtime at school the next day, my friends and I are playing rugby on the main field when Sean appears, and starts walking directly towards me. 'Fuck you, faggot!' he says, trying to look staunch.

I'm dumbfounded. 'You've got some balls, dude, I'll give you that much,' I say. 'But I have no desire to kick your arse again. Just walk away, little bunny rabbit.'

He stalls, then does as he's told.

I turn and get back to the game. I've realised I've got absolutely nothing to prove by fighting this guy.

•

Having won the junior title at last year's wakeboard nationals, I decide it's time to step up into the open men's division this year, even though I'm only 16 and could ride in juniors for another couple of years. It's a fun contest and I ride reasonably well, squeaking into seventh place. Jeff Weatherall reclaims the top spot, and there's a new name in the mix: a South Islander called Tony Evans who's around my age. He's a solid rider, not just in his style but also in stature. He's slightly shorter than I am, a similar build and we even have similar tricks. I can tell we're going to be good friends, with a healthy rivalry. He beats me this time. Even though I don't end up on the podium, it feels good to be in the big league. I'm excited to be putting myself up against the best in the country.

A month later, Dad surprises me by telling me he's looking at a new boat so I can keep training through winter. It's a Bayliner that belongs to a friend of his from way back. Since this friend's kids are into wakeboarding, he installed a tower and ballast system and the wake is pretty good. It's definitely an upgrade from our old outboard, and I'm super stoked to be getting a boat, but part of me is a little gutted that it's not one of the new wakeboard-specific ones.

'I wish we could afford one of those, Brad,' Dad says. 'But with an $80,000 price tag and the way things have turned out between your mother and me, things have tightened up, so this is what you've got for now.'

A couple of times a week Dad picks me up from school in his Isuzu truck, the boat hitched to the back, and we drive over an hour south through the traffic and over the Bombay hills to Tūākau, a small town on the banks of the Waikato River. Sometimes I get Sam, Matt, Jordan or Doug to come as support crew, as having the extra weight in the boat increases the wake. Dad tweaks the trim on the motor to get the wake as clean as possible, and he does his best to drive perfectly, but more often than not I end up frustrated and criticising his driving, occasionally even throwing the handle in anger, and the set ends with the two of us bickering. I know he's doing his best but I just get so frustrated when all I want to do is learn new tricks and the conditions aren't good enough. Being a hormonal teen probably doesn't help the situation.

As we move further into winter and the water gets colder I stop taking breaks between sets. Instead, I just do one long set, and the moment I get back in the boat, that's it for the day.

Midway through winter I hear there's a new MasterCraft dealer, and he's just landed a new X2 — the best wakeboard boat in the country. I give him a call and get myself invited down to Lake Ōkāreka, near Rotorua, to go out with him. Dad comes with me. But even though the sun is out, there's an ice-cold breeze blowing across the lake and by the time I get back on board my teeth are chattering and my hands are aching to the bone. It's worth it, though. I loved riding behind the X2.

I don't need to explain the difference to Dad. On the drive home I do my best to convince him that we need to upgrade.

'It's just out of our price range at the moment,' Dad says. 'Maybe down the track a bit we can sell the Bayliner and put the money towards an upgrade.'

At least it's not an outright no.

•

I'm realising that if I want to carry on wakeboarding I need money — and that means I need to find a job. I get turned down by the first few places I try, then one day on my way home from school I stop in at the Lone Star restaurant in Newmarket. When the bar manager, Clinton, asks me what kind of job I'm looking for, I simply say, 'What have you got?'

'Well, I could use some help behind the bar,' he says. 'You're too young to serve alcohol, but I could use a glassy a couple of nights a week if you're interested?'

'That sounds great!' I reply. 'What does a glassy do?'

Clinton laughs. 'You just help collect, clean and put away the glassware. You also stock the fridge and replace anything that's empty, then help clean the bar at the end of the night.'

'Cool! When can I start?'

He throws me a T-shirt. 'We could use you both nights this weekend.'

I fumble my way through my first night, trying to get into the swing of things as quickly as possible. On my second night, after the restaurant and bar close around 11 p.m., there's a staff party. I join in, even though I feel like an outsider, and everyone is really warm and welcoming. The majority of the staff, I can't help noticing, are attractive young women.

Even though I can't legally drink myself, Clinton teaches me how to make drinks for everyone else. I get talking with a girl called Kate. She's slightly older than I am, and she's outgoing, confident and hot! When the party starts to wind down around one in the morning, it doesn't take much to convince her to come home with me. It's the first time I've ever sneaked a girl into my bedroom, and I feel pretty proud of myself. It's a big boost to my confidence. To top it all off, she disappears beneath the covers.

I think I'm gonna like this job!

•

I might have only placed seventh in the open men's division at nationals earlier this year, but I'm still named as one of the invitees to represent New Zealand at the International Water Ski Federation (IWSF) world championships being held in October 2003 in Penrith, near Sydney. (The IWSF will become the International Waterski and Wakeboarding Federation (IWWF) in 2009.)

When Dad and I arrive at the comp venue I find it all a bit overwhelming. It's huge. Riders from all over the world have flown in for the event, and I start to get nervous. I'm in the junior men's division, and on the first day I don't have the best ride, placing fourth. Thankfully, I get another shot the next day. This time I ride well, winning my heat, which sends me through to the semi-final. On day three, though, I have an absolute shocker. I fall apart and come dead last in my heat, bringing my first worlds campaign to an underwhelming end.

They're long days hanging around at the competition site, but I enjoy watching all of the incredible riding going down — especially getting to see the legendary Parks Bonifay in action. He's riding in the pro men's division, as is Jeff Weatherall. Jeff absolutely slays his first run, and Parks is up next. He charges in his run too, blowing me away when he ollies up to the top of the floating flat bar, which must be at his shoulder height. But then we find out that he has been disqualified because he cut inside the buoy at the start of his second pass, which is against the rules. He protests, but the judges won't budge. Rules are rules, but everyone I talk to thinks it's pretty ridiculous.

Thankfully, he has another shot later in the afternoon. Dad and I find a position halfway down the course to get the best view of the action, and as soon as Parks is up the entire crowd edges closer to the shoreline to see how he will come back from his earlier mistake. To start his run, he goes to cut out wide around the buoy, but then he turns an aggressive edge back in towards the wake, purposely cutting *inside* the buoy and doing a big wake carve. Murmurs ripple through the crowd — some onlookers are wondering what's going on — but there are a few cheers from those who know what he's up to. His slash of the wake is basically a big 'Fuck you!' to the judges, event organisers and the IWSF. Parks is using this run to make a very public protest. He does a few impressive tricks, but he's not taking this seriously at all. When the boat turns to give him his second pass, he once again goes to cut out around the buoy, but this time he ollies straight over it.

His display does not go down well with the officials.

For me, it's the best thing to happen all weekend. The spectators are losing their minds. Some are completely confused — they can't understand why he would blow his world title hopes like that. Others, like me, are in hysterics. I love his display of rebellion. He would rather make his point than make the podium. Seeing him stick it to the man like that has only increased the respect I already had for him.

Jeff continues his dominant run to take the top spot and world title. Our junior girl, Jane King, wins her division, and team New Zealand places third overall.

To top it off for me, I manage to score a ridiculously attractive blonde Swedish 23-year-old named Annette at the after-party. We end up making out all night, but that's as far as we get since I don't have my own room to take her back to. But pulling such a hottie, especially one so much older than me, gives me a huge boost in confidence. I've only recently grown into my six-foot-two (1.88 metres) stature

— Ants and Brant call me the man-child — and I'm starting to realise that I can attract older women. What a way to top off the trip!

•

Back at home, Brant and I talk about my performance at worlds the next time we go riding at the river.

'I really want to take my riding to that next level,' I tell him. 'But how? What do I need to do? Do I need to go to Florida, like you guys did?'

'Yeah bro, if you want to take this seriously, then Orlando is where you need to be,' he replies. 'It's so much easier to get more quality riding there. Everyone lives on a lake, the weather is perfect, and the water gets so warm it makes the wakes bigger and the crashes softer. It's where all the best riders are and where all the magazines are based.'

It sounds like wakeboarding heaven.

Brant's already done a couple of seasons in the States, but unfortunately he was denied entry last year when he tried to get back in after having just used up his three-month visitor visa. He got sent home the long way round, via London and Singapore, and the worst part is he's not allowed back into the US for 10 years.

'Orlando is where it's at,' he says, then adds, 'but be careful. It's so good it can also ruin you.'

I have no idea what he means by that, and I don't ask. I've already made up my mind.

•

Near the end of the year Dad decides to sell the Bayliner. At the same time, I manage to line up a summer job working at the MasterCraft dealership down in Rotorua. Dad's considering upgrading boats, depending on how much the Bayliner fetches, and my plan is to try to arrange a sponsorship deal with MasterCraft that would help to make an X2 more affordable.

With the newfound freedom of a driver's licence and a car I can commute between school and my two jobs, and — most importantly — I can get to where the riding is. Some weekends I work a night at the bar before heading downtown and sneaking into clubs using a fake ID, then I wake up early to drive to Rotorua in time to open the MasterCraft shop at 9 a.m. Needless to say, I'm always hung over and running late, and the speeding fines are beginning to pile up.

Dad puts the boat out on the road across from his apartment during the day, with a big FOR SALE sign hanging from the tower. At night he backs it into a corner beside the apartment, and locks it behind the truck. Then, one morning, he calls me to tell me that the boat's gone.

'What? It sold?'

'No, I mean, when I walked outside this morning it was gone,' he says. 'It's been stolen.'

'What?! How on earth did that even happen with the trailer behind the truck?'

'I really don't know, Brad. I have no idea how they broke off the lock, let alone got the trailer out. I've contacted the police, but there's not much else we can do besides keeping an eye out.'

I can't believe it.

Several days later I find out the really bad news: the boat wasn't insured. It's cost Dad about $35,000 and me any possibility of a new boat. To say I'm pissed off is an understatement, and it's not even my money that was lost. I can only imagine how gutted my dad must feel.

•

By the time the 2003 school year comes to an end, I've already decided I don't want to go back for Year 13. All I want to do is wakeboard. After getting a taste of the international competition scene in Australia, I want more. I want to go back to the world champs next year a different rider. I picture myself at the top of the podium, and I know there's only one way to get there. I need more quality time on the water, all year round, and that means spending the New Zealand winter in Florida.

I break it to Mum one evening at the dinner table.

'Brad,' she replies, looking serious, 'I appreciate that you're passionate about wakeboarding, but you can't just do that. How are you going to earn a living? You've got to think about your future.'

'But I think I *can* earn a living out of wakeboarding,' I say. 'There are plenty of pros out there who seem to be doing well for themselves.'

'Okay, but you've still got to think about plan B,' Mum counters. 'What if it doesn't work out the way you want it to?'

'I can always study and get a real job later,' I say, even though I have no intention of ever working a 'real' job. 'But I've got to do this while I'm still young, Mum.'

She sighs. 'I understand where you're coming from. And maybe school isn't the best option. Maybe there's a course you could enrol in at uni instead?'

I'm relieved. She's much more receptive to the idea than I thought she would be. When I tell Dad, he also seems pretty cool with it.

In the end we find a one-semester course at Auckland University of Technology that will accept me. It's a certificate in sport and recreation — basically a bullshit paper that means nothing on its own, but it would give me the option to go into a sport-related career later if that's what I want. If agreeing to do the course means I can drop out of school, I'm more than happy to sign up.

●

Once school's done, I shift down to Rotorua to continue my job at the MasterCraft dealership, working every day now. At first it seemed like a pretty sweet deal: I don't have to pay rent, as I can live with the shop owner, and I get to ride behind an X2 for free. The job itself is pretty boring — it mainly involves sitting around and waiting for a customer to come in to look at the boats or buy some gear. And it soon turns out that living and riding with the owner and his family, although they're nice enough, is not exactly a thrill. He and I are like chalk and cheese.

Ants is working there too, but he gives up on the job within a few weeks of me moving down here. Part of his reason for quitting is that the shop's X2 just sold, and Ants happens to have made friends with its new owner. He's a large, somewhat intimidating Māori guy named Daz who has a lakeside house about 10 minutes away, in Ōkawa Bay, a sheltered cove on Lake Rotoiti. Ants moves in there when a spare room becomes available, and soon there's another one available, so Brant jumps at the opportunity and comes down to join the house.

Daz keeps the boat sitting permanently on the dock, meaning it's ready for us to ride at a moment's notice. There's no towing the trailer and dropping the boat in, no filling and draining ballast. It's the first time I've ever had such easy access to a boat, let alone one with a wake this good.

My first ride behind the fully loaded X2 changes my life. Daz isn't afraid to let us load the boat with as much ballast as it can handle and the wake is bangin'! Once the boat is finally up on plane, I cut out and, for the first time, I'm actually scared to cut in at the wake. It's an excited kind of scared, though — the sort where your heart starts pounding, the adrenalin pumping. This is a wake on steroids, standing above my knee height, and my first jump off it makes me giddy. I'm sure a look of disbelief mixed with pure stoke bursts across my face.

All I did was a basic wake jump, but in that moment I've had a taste of everything that's possible with a wake like this. It's like a cheat code that has just unlocked the next level of the wake game for me.

TWO: TOTAL IMMERSION

The guys and I are sitting on the deck, enjoying the warm morning sun while nursing our hangovers and reliving the events of the night before — including bragging about who got action from who. It's the first day of 2004, and we couldn't be in a better spot to welcome in the new year: this bach, which Mum has rented, is right by the beach at Whangamatā, close enough to hear the crashing surf and the squawking gulls.

Then Mum walks out in her underwear. My friends avert their eyes and I'm momentarily embarrassed, until I see the look on her face. She's holding a newspaper.

'Brad . . . Richie Wells just died,' she says.

I'm speechless.

'I'm so sorry, darling,' she says. 'I just read about it now.'

Somehow I manage to swallow down the horrible feeling rising from my gut and stammer a response. 'What? How? What happened?'

'They're saying he drowned in a swimming pool while on the Gold Coast,' Mum replies, then she hands me the paper.

My eyes skim over the words but I can't take it in. I was riding with Richie down at the Ballistics camp less than a month ago. How can he be gone?

I'm with my friends from school, and none of them knew Richie. They'd only heard me talk about him, and they do their best to be comforting. 'Oh, I'm so sorry, bro. That's terrible,' they say, but I barely hear them.

I need to be alone so I head down to the beach. At the top of a sand dune I sit down and stare out to sea. I'm absolutely crushed. I can't hold the emotion back and I burst into tears. This is so fucking unfair! First Kenney, now Richie. Memories of Richie flash through my mind — riding on the Waikato River together, him teaching me to do off-axis spins, partying together at worlds in Australia, our countless days together on the water at the Ballistics camp. He was such a good guy.

For the rest of the day it feels like I'm in some kind of trance. Mates get in touch to make sure I've heard the news, and that's how I learn that he drowned in

Jeff Weatherall's pool. The two of them had been hanging out, practising holding their breath, and made a friendly competition of swimming laps underwater. Then, while Jeff, Andrea and the others disappeared to make dinner, Richie stayed in the pool and must have decided to carry on doing it on his own, but he must have blacked out. Andrea found him later, at the bottom of the pool. When I hear this, I can't even imagine the horror. My heart breaks for Jeff, and Andrea, and for all Richie's family and close friends.

A week later I stand alongside the majority of the Kiwi wakeboarding fraternity and try to hold myself together while Richie's casket is carried out and into the back of a hearse with his wakeboard strapped to the roof.

Richie took me under his wing. He truly believed in me. He thought I would become New Zealand's next top wakeboarder. So I decide that's exactly what I'm going to be. That's how I'm going to honour him.

•

Now that summer is in full swing, I want nothing but time on the water. When I'm not working at the MasterCraft shop, I'm out riding behind Daz's boat with Ants and Brant, or I race across to the Ballistics camp to ride with Haydog, who now runs the show there.

We have a great arrangement with Daz: in exchange for putting petrol in his boat and coaching his seven-year-old son, we get to use the X2 whenever we want. Ōkawa Bay is a relatively short cove, but it's well protected from the wind so the conditions are always good. Once the X2 is up to speed we can usually get in about five tricks before we need to turn around. One of the good things about the short bay is that every time we turn the boat it presents an opportunity for a double-up — the moment when two wakes come together to form a massive single peak that will send a rider flying. I've always loved watching videos of the pros hitting 'dubs', but I'm pretty inexperienced with them myself. Ants and Brant, on the other hand, love nothing more than absolutely boosting off a well-timed double. It requires precision on the part of the driver and the rider's timing is crucial, and before long I'm mastering both sides.

Spending time with Ants and Brant does amazing things for my riding, and over the summer our friendship flourishes. I'm no longer the grommet they have to look after — at almost 17, I've become one of the guys. They introduce me to new music, including a punk-rock band with a hip-hop flavour called hed (p.e.), who just don't give a fuck. We crank them loud in the car or on the boat, smoking spliffs — another thing Ants and Brant have introduced me to — and generally having a good time. I feel really at home with these guys, although I do notice that hanging with a couple of dudes who are in their twenties sees me behaving like I'm older too.

•

When my AUT course starts at the beginning of February I keep the job at MasterCraft by arranging to work longer weekends instead of during the week. And, as much as I don't want to be at uni, I'm pleasantly surprised to find I actually enjoy the course. Every class involves sport and the human body — two things that I'm actually interested in learning about. Also, there are girls here! A definite improvement on school.

As summer draws to an end I head down to Lake Karāpiro for nationals, eager to improve on last year's seventh-place finish. For me, last year was about throwing myself in the mix to gain some experience, but this year I'm out to make a statement. I get through to the open men's finals, and just before riding we all pay an emotional tribute to Richie. Arms adorned with black bands, the other open men's finalists and I watch the boat run a contest pass with a rope trailing behind while the crowd sits in silence. I have to hold back the tears. This tribute is followed by an eruption of cheers and applause.

Then my focus is firmly back on the final. I'm nervous to be up against the big guns, including Ants, Brant and Jeff. Tony Evans, who beat me last year, is there too and we're the youngsters of the field. Jeff puts on an absolute clinic and once again takes out the top spot. Tony beats me again to come in second, while I land third place, meaning I get to stand on my first-ever open men's podium. I'm pretty happy about this. My ranking also earns me a spot on the team going to Spain for the world championships later in the year.

I soon hear from my boss at MasterCraft, who congratulates me on being selected for worlds and sets me a very enticing incentive. 'If you come back from Spain with a world title, I'll organise a sponsored boat for you.'

After the competition I get chatting with Kurt Robertson, an older South Island rider. When he says he works at The Wakeboard Camp in Florida, I tell him I'm keen to go there for the upcoming US summer. 'If a job opens up at the camp, keep me in mind,' I tell him, and he promises to do so. About a month later he emails to say there's a coaching position available. 'It's yours if you want it. We'd need you here in two weeks.'

I'm elated. The Wakeboard Camp is supposed to be the best camp there is, with some amazing coaches. There's just one slight problem: I've still got a month left at uni and then my final exams. When I tell Mum, she wants me to stay and finish the course.

'Look, I could stick around and finish it,' I say, 'and I'll end up with a piece of paper that says I can kinda sorta coach any sport maybe . . . or I could take this opportunity to learn to coach wakeboarding from the best coaches in the world.'

Mum can see the sense in my argument.

'What if I come back afterwards and sit my exams then, with the next course intake?' I suggest.

'Okay,' she says. 'But that's the deal.' Amazingly, AUT agrees to this.

•

The day I fly out to the US, my whole family comes to see me off. I've got my tickets in my hand and I turn to say goodbye and I can see Mum is starting to get emotional. I can tell she's both proud and sad to see her 17-year-old son go off to see the world.

I give her a big hug. 'Love you, Mum.'

'I love you too,' she says as I let go of her. 'Have an amazing time, and please keep in touch.'

As I disappear through security, I can see her still waving.

I'm equal parts excited and nervous. Mostly, though, I just can't wait to get to Orlando and take the next step on my wakeboarding journey. I'm also really glad I'm not travelling alone. My mate and rival Tony Evans is here, as is the New Zealand women's champion, Andrea Fountain, who I first got to know at the Ōrākei club nights. Tony and Andrea are also chasing Orlando's warm weather and wakeboarding, and will both be working at wakeboarding camps too. Tony's going to the World Wakeboard Center (WWC), which is only about 15 minutes' drive from my camp in Clermont, 40 kms west of Orlando. Andrea will be at O-Town in Orlando.

It's the first time in the US for all of us, and we're eager to see if this wakeboarding mecca is really as good as everyone says.

•

More than 48 hours later we finally arrive in Orlando. Belinda, a fellow Kiwi I know from the Ballistics camp, is there to pick me up and drive me to the camp. I say goodbye to my friends and we all go our separate ways.

Belinda and I arrive in Clermont 45 minutes later, pulling up to a big old wooden building painted bright blue with yellow trim on the edge of Lake Minneola.

'We're here!' Belinda says. 'Welcome to your new home for the summer.'

Belinda — or Bee, as she's known — is the receptionist, cook and one of two 'camp mothers' at The Wakeboard Camp. I follow her into the big open common room and kitchen. There's nobody in here so I wander around looking at all the old wakeboards fixed to the rafters and checking out the wall posters featuring some of my favourite riders, several of them coaches here.

The room is filled with couches, stacks of wakeboard magazines on every side-table, and there's also a ping-pong table and a pool table. The big glass ranch-slider doors in the front wall open right out onto the lake. The sun is just starting to set and I see a boat pulling up onto the front beach. Everyone aboard starts unloading their gear.

Feeling a little overwhelmed at the prospect of meeting so many new people at once, I head over to introduce myself to the other coaches, the people I'll be spending all summer with. There's Bo, Joey, fellow Kiwi Lance and two Norwegians, Egil and Dan. As it's starting to get dark, we head inside together to eat.

I immediately get along with Bo. He's a super chill and friendly dude who looks like he'd be more at home tucking into barrels in the Hawaiian waves than being towed behind a boat in Clermont. Built like a surfer, with dark-tanned skin, he's close to my height but a few years older. I can also tell that Joey Arcisz and I are going to get along. He's much shorter than me, with sun-bleached blond hair, but he seems closer to my age than the others — maybe only a year or two older.

I'm feeling wrecked from my flight, so when I next spot Bee I ask her if she can show me where I'll be sleeping.

'Sure, follow me,' she says, and leads me to a house across the street.

Hey, this doesn't look too bad! I think.

We go inside and head upstairs, but at the top of the stairs, rather than opening the door to a bedroom, she pulls back a curtain that's really a bed sheet and says, 'This is you for now.'

The tight little corner, wedged in beside the bathroom, is just big enough to fit my bags alongside a single air mattress. It's definitely not what I was expecting but I'm so excited just to be here, working with some of the best coaches in the world, that I'd be happy sleeping on a couch, on the trampoline — anywhere, really. I drop my bags, unpack my sleeping bag and crash out on the partially inflated air mattress.

•

When I wander into the common room the following morning it's bustling with people. All the coaches are here, along with about 20 enthusiastic campers, here to learn as much as they can about wakeboarding over the next five days. There's a new intake every Monday.

I'm immediately introduced to the four senior coaches, although there's no introduction needed — I know exactly who they are. The head coach is Kyle Schmitt, an absolute legend in the industry, and I also meet Ben Greenwood and Aaron Reed. Ben — or Benny G, as the other coaches call him — has an amazingly smooth riding style that I admired in many of the films I watched at the Ballistics camp, and Aaron is one of the main innovators in wakeskating, which is like skateboarding on water. The fourth senior coach is Kurt Robertson, the guy I have to thank for being here.

Junior coaches like me don't get paid to work at the camp, but our accommodation and food are supplied, and we get to ride heaps for free. Senior coaches get paid.

The camp kicks off after breakfast with a theory session in the common room. Kyle stands up front beside a blackboard, with the campers gathered around him on the floor.

I sit at the back with Dan and Egil, soaking up every word that leaves Kyle's mouth and memorising everything he draws on the blackboard. He talks about body position, edge control, loading the line, using the energy of the wake — all stuff I know and understand, but he puts it in a way that's so clear and will make it so easy to teach.

After class finishes, everyone scatters to get ready for the first practical session. I'm not sure what I'm supposed to be doing so I ask Kurt.

'This first week, we're going to get you shadowing the senior coaches,' he replies. 'You'll basically be sitting in the boat with us and hearing how we teach, what drills we run with the beginners, watching how we drive the boats and so on. Sound good?'

'Sounds good!' I can already tell that I'm going to learn a lot here, and I'm eager to get stuck in and prove myself.

•

Within a couple of weeks I'm in the swing of things. Today I'm heading out on the boat with Joey, Dan, Egil and a couple of campers who are hanging out for the weekend. Since it's the weekend, Lake Minneola is crazy busy with boats and jet-skis ripping all over the place, making the conditions terrible for us.

'Cherry Lake will be calm,' Joey says, as we cruise slowly under a bridge that's barely high enough for us to fit under. 'Not many people take their boats all the way out here so we should get the good stuff!'

Cherry is part of the Clermont chain of lakes all connected to Minneola. As we race through the maze of narrow canals cut through marshlands, I can't help wondering about alligators . . .

It takes about 20 minutes to get to Cherry Lake, and Joey rides first. He blows my mind with his warm-up run — the moment the boat gets on plane, he's linking technical tricks back to back as if they're nothing. They're all tricks I'm envious of, and he's doing them both regular and switch stance too! His fluid style is super inspiring, and I hope I'll get to ride with him a lot more this summer.

I'm up next. After my warm-up — which feels pretty pitiful after Joey's performance — I start linking some spins together but end up taking a fall. As the boat drives slowly past to bring the rope back to me, Joey pops his head up over the windshield and says enthusiastically, 'Bro! You should try to take that toe five to seven! Have you ever tried?'

'Nah, man, never,' I reply, 'but I'll give it a shot!'

'You've got it, dude! Just try to keep the handle close and then pull it in to your lower back.'

I get around on the first attempt, but I'm miles away from landing it. I try a few more times and start to get a bit closer, then submit to the fact that trying is as close as I'm going to get today.

'Another day!' I say to Joey as he drives the handle back to me once more.

'No way, dude! You're landing this today! If you're tired, just take a breather. We're in no rush.'

Taking a breather is a foreign concept to me. Back home, there's not really any such thing. We'll go from one rider to the next, then get the boat out of the water — maybe because there's a boat full of riders to get through, or it's a long drive to get home. Also because sometimes it's cold and you don't want to be out in it any longer than you have to. But here in Florida, on this particular day, none of that is a problem. The day is hot, the water is warm and we're in zero rush. So I kick my feet out of my bindings and just float in the water for a few minutes, while Joey gives me a few extra pointers.

Once I'm feeling refreshed, I get back up on the water and straight back to work. Attempt after attempt, crash after crash, I'm getting closer. It's within my grasp. After what must be about 45 minutes on the water I pop off the wake, pull the handle across my body, pass it behind my back and across my body again, then place the handle behind my back for a perfect blind landing. I did it! I landed my first 720! Everyone on the boat cheers, and a wave of satisfaction rolls over me as I throw the handle in celebration.

Back on the boat, I throw a high-five Joey's way. 'Thanks so much for your coaching, bro,' I say. 'I would've given up if you hadn't pushed me.'

The drive back to the camp just feels sweet. I sit in the front of the boat, basking in the buzz as we speed through the canals, the wind blowing through my hair, and I watch the sun setting over the horizon. I love this feeling, and I love this place.

•

When I get back to the camp I message Tony: 'Landed my first toeside 720 today!'

The next afternoon he replies to tell me he just landed his first one.

A couple of days later he tells me he's learnt a backroll to blind, so the following day I land one of my own.

All season it goes like this. The rivalry between us is as strong as ever but always friendly. Tony's always beaten me in competition, so I know I need to step up my game — especially since he's currently revelling in the same perfect learning environment as me. Knowing this fuels my hunger to learn as many new tricks as I possibly can. I barely see him, but he soon ends up being one of this summer's biggest influences on my riding.

As the weeks roll by, I'm constantly getting my fix, with new tricks almost every day. And, as much as the other coaches are teaching me new moves, I'm starting to be able to teach myself as well. I'm a sponge, soaking it all up. My coaching is helping my riding, and my riding is helping my coaching. The more I learn, the better I teach. And the more I teach, the better I learn.

•

I've been here a few weeks before I have my first encounter with the local wildlife.

It's my turn to do gas duty so I drive the camp Suburban to a nearby gas station, with a trailer hitched on the back loaded with empty five-gallon tanks. After filling them all — and marvelling at how cheap petrol is over here — I return to camp and load the tanks back into the shed. The next morning I unlock the shed and grab some tanks to fill up the boats. I have to do a few trips, and I use each one as a miniature workout — one full tank in each hand, I shrug and curl and lunge from the shed to the shoreline. Then, as I reach to grab two more tanks from the shelf, I feel something on my hand. I glance down to see a gigantic hairy spider.

'*Aaaarrrrggghhhh!*' I drop both tanks and start shaking both hands, dancing around like a big sissy.

'Hahahahahaha!' A bellowing laugh erupts from behind me. It's Bo. He was setting up a board nearby and saw the whole episode. He's now rolling on the ground in hysterics.

'Dude! There was a fucking tarantula on my hand!' I say frantically.

'It was a wolf spider, bro,' he says, still chuckling as he stands up and dusts himself off. 'We don't really have tarantulas here.'

'Well, whatever it was, it was fucking *huge!*' I bend down to pick up the tanks I dropped. 'It looked like it could kill me.'

'They can bite, but they're not deadly,' Bo says. 'The brown recluse, on the other hand? You'll want to watch out for that one. Those fuckers are evil! They're brown with a small violin-shaped mark on them. Much smaller than that wolf spider you just threw across the shed.'

'I don't think I'll be taking the time to pull out my magnifying glass and look for violins the next time a spider crawls across me,' I reply. 'So what else do I have to watch out for around here?'

'Well, obviously there are alligators in the lake,' he says. 'They won't usually bother you. They like to keep to themselves.'

Yeah, right, don't worry about the alligators, says Bo. I'll definitely be keeping my eyes peeled.

'Then there are the snakes,' Bo goes on. 'Water moccasins are the worst. A bite from one of those guys could potentially kill you, and they can be found both in and out of the water. Then there's rattlesnakes, copperheads and coral snakes. I doubt you'll encounter any of them, but basically you want to watch where you're stepping.'

He says all this way too casually. From now on, my eyes are constantly scanning not just the ground but my entire surroundings for any sign of Florida fauna.

•

As we hit the peak of summer, the camp gets super busy. Loads of people are here for their dose of summer-holiday action.

Lance recently left, and Joey not long after, meaning I've graduated to a large bedroom with a double bed and a view to the lake. I miss hanging with Joey, but getting his room isn't the only silver lining to his departure. It also means there's less competition for the cute girls!

One week a couple of girls around my age arrive and one of them in particular catches my eye. Her name is Meg, and she's slim and fit. We start talking at the start of the week, and by Thursday night I've got her back to my bedroom. We're making out in my bed and she feels so good in my arms — not just because she has an incredible body but also because being with her makes me feel pretty proud. The other guys had their eyes on her too, but she chose me.

Our clothes are coming off and our hands are exploring each other's bodies. As I start to pull down her panties she stops me. 'Have you got protection?' she whispers.

'Yeah, hang on a second.' I start rummaging through my bag. Thankfully, that's something I optimistically threw in before leaving New Zealand. I've only slept with one other girl since losing my virginity 18 months ago, but within seconds I'm hitting home base for the first time in the US. Any nervousness I felt as a result of my lack of experience quickly vanishes as I become engrossed in Meg — in her green eyes, her lips, her body. She feels so good.

The next evening Meg leaves the camp. I'm a little bummed out but my disappointment is short-lived. On Sunday night, Alyssa arrives for a week. She's a shy little blue-eyed beauty with curly blonde hair, and by Wednesday she's invited me into her bunk bed. The following week it's a dark-haired girl named Chelsea. She plays a bit hard-to-get and it's not until Friday night that we venture back to my room. There, for the third time in a month, I'm digging through my bag for a little latex pleasure pass.

That's the end of my run. It was good while it lasted!

A few weeks later I'm hanging out in my room with two very flirty older girls. They must be in their mid- to late twenties and they keep referring to me as an Abercrombie model, but my luck runs out when I propose a threesome. My hat-trick has made me cocky, so a dose of rejection is just what's needed to keep me in check.

I'm checked again when I hear laughter bursting from behind the curtain to my old room. It's Cathy Williams, Jeff Weatherall's girlfriend — the two of them are here for a week — and she heard every word of the final exchange. I'll never hear the end of it now.

•

Since we coaches can only ride outside of coaching hours, I've started getting up early to sneak in a morning set before the day gets going. I've been going with an Aussie chick named Amber Wing, one of our new coaches who just transferred over from the camp Tony is at.

Although the lake is like glass this early, mornings aren't the best for doing harder tricks, since the body is still waking up. It's hard to get things moving quite as snappily. So Amber and I use our morning sets to get back to basics and work on our weaknesses. She's working on being the first woman to land a toeside seven, and I'm working on getting mine consistent, so we focus on our toeside threes and switch backside 180s — awkward tricks for both of us.

I've never really put enough effort into my switch riding. I tend to get carried away and skip fundamentals, so I've been struggling with blind landings. For this reason I must've landed no more than a handful of toeside 720s since that first one I popped on Cherry Lake. I find it much easier to spin a toeside five than to slow it down to a 360 and land blind. But concentrating on nailing the basics will help me build a more solid foundation and make those harder tricks more reliable.

After a few of these morning training sessions I'm out riding during the lunch break with a handful of students watching. The wake is perfect today — we've got the boat maxed out with ballast and with people, so it's about as good as it gets. And I'm feeling it! I've figured out exactly how the takeoff on my seven should feel, and it makes the landing come around perfectly, especially with my newly honed skills in landing blind.

After landing two toeside sevens in a row, I hit my third, then fourth. Deciding to take advantage of being on, I throw a seven every toeside hit of the wake. After 13 toeside sevens in a row, I throw the handle up in the air in celebration.

Proof that sometimes taking a step back to work on the basics really does make the hard stuff that much easier.

•

A few days later Amber and I both have the day off so we take a drive into Orlando to visit Andrea at O-Town, owned by Kiwi rider Glen Fletcher and his American wife. They've got some fun rails there, so we take turns riding and driving the ski.

Afterwards, while I'm sitting on the dock, one of Glen's students shows up for his coaching session. He's a lean but strong build with dark blond hair, about the same age as me. He strides confidently down the dock, and he's got a hot girl with him. My first impression is of a cocky jock. I watch him ride and he's pretty good.

But I'm better, I think, feeling like I might be looking at a future competitor.

When he's back on the dock, Andrea introduces us. His name is Alex Brown, and I soon realise my first impression was way off. He seems like a genuinely nice guy. What I thought was a cocky swagger was, I realise now, actually just excited anticipation about getting out on the water, which I can totally relate to.

The following weekend Amber and I drive up to Alex's place to go riding with him. He lives with his parents in Mount Dora, a small city about 40 minutes away. As soon as we arrive at the dock I see he's got his priorities sorted: waiting to get on the boat with us are three bikini-clad girls.

I like this dude's style, I think as we all jump aboard. If there's one thing that makes pretty much any good situation better, it's girls in bikinis.

Once we're done riding, we head back to his parents' place to play pool and drink a few beers. It's the first of many excursions to Alex's place — sometimes to ride, sometimes to party, usually to do a bit of both.

My weekends in Florida settle into a fairly reliable pattern. I've made friends with a local rider named Cory, and after he and I smoke a bowl — a small blown-glass pipe for smoking weed that I've recently been introduced to — we jump in his VW beetle and boost to Alex's place to ride and party. And they're some great parties! They're so similar to what I've seen in movies like *American Pie*. And, since Alex is still in high school, they include lots of hot girls around my age. I'm the token foreign guy, and the girls can't get enough of my accent, which makes it really easy for me to break out of my shell and talk to anyone.

Near the end of my season at the camp, Alex celebrates his 18th birthday. Since his parents are away for the weekend, he decides to have a huge party. I arrive early, and within a couple of hours there are close to 50 people in the house, with more arriving all the time. Alex has set up all sorts of drinking games: beer pong, quarters, various card games, and Alex's custom-made spin-the-wheel game, Fuck Your Liver.

I pass out on the couch at some small hour, and wake the next morning to a scene of carnage. Things got pretty debauched last night and there's a massive mess to clean up. The house is trashed. There are cans and bottles everywhere. The white carpet looks like it might be ruined. There are muddy footprints all over the tiles. And the trampoline's broken.

Alex emerges, takes a look around and immediately starts panicking. 'Shit!' he says. 'My parents are due home in a few hours!'

With a huge amount of help from Alex's now ex-girlfriend, we clean that house up so fast and so thoroughly that I reckon it's cleaner than when Alex's parents left, which is surely a telltale sign. I'll be very surprised if they don't instantly know there was a party. But maybe they won't mind, since the place is now spotless? I don't hang around to find out.

•

On my last day at the camp, I stand on the shoreline of Lake Minneola and it's as calm as glass. I've had one hell of a first season in the US.

As well as learning so much that's going to be incredibly valuable to my wakeboarding future, I've made new friends and new connections. I've gained more confidence — within myself, with riding, with coaching . . . and with girls. I feel very grateful to have had this opportunity.

But now it's time for the next adventure: the world championships in Spain. I'm flying over with Tony and Andrea, and once we land in Seville we link up with our other teammates — including my bros Ants and Brant, who have just spent the season in the UK, where they both had jobs at wakeboard parks near London. It's great to see them again, and I'm excited to show them how much I've improved.

The next evening, after checking out the competition site during the day, the whole team heads out and finds a quaint little place to eat dinner. The cobblestone roads and brick buildings are so beautiful — as are the women!

•

Tony and I make it through the first two days of riding and advance to the finals, but Ants and Brant both miss out on their semis on day two and drop out of the competition.

The contest site is on the Guadalquivir River, which runs straight through the middle of Seville, with the course set between two bridges that span the river. On the morning of our finals, Tony and I decide to take a leap from one of the bridges into the river. As I stand on the edge and look down at the water far below, I think it's probably higher than anything else I've ever jumped off. But, as I'm standing there contemplating the plunge, Tony simply backflips off the bridge. I follow him, but I go for the more traditional pin drop.

We haul ourselves out of the water, then head back up onto the bridge to do it again. Once more, Tony flips perfectly.

I climb over the railing and turn around. You can do that too, I tell myself. I leap off, throwing my head back to initiate the flip — nice and slow, unlike flipping on the ground — but as I look over to spot the water I realise I've completely misjudged it. I over-rotate the flip and land on my back. The impact when I hit the water instantly punches the air out of my lungs and my entire back stings. For a moment I'm sinking, then I manage to swim back to the surface, where Tony is waiting for me. I gasp for air.

'Dude! I thought I was about to have to David Hasselhoff myself down to save you!' He sounds relieved.

'Yeah, I completely misjudged that one,' I say, still trying to catch my breath.

I get out of the water, and the stinging slowly becomes a burning sensation but my back remains bright red. For the next hour I lie on my board bag, trying to rest before I have to ride. The whole time I'm thinking: *That was really stupid. You've probably just screwed yourself for the biggest and most important final of your life.*

But by the time I'm standing on the dock with my feet in my bindings, my back is not too bad. Just a dull muscle ache. I open my run with an aggressive glide into the flats, then follow it up with some of my more consistent tricks, including a whirlybird, crow mobe and a tantrum to blind. My second pass is solid too, and I pull off a toeside 720 followed by an off-axis backside 360, then a toeside backroll — which was supposed to be a Pete Rose but I backed out at the last minute when I missed my timing. Then there's just the double-up left — my opportunity to end my set with a bang. The boat passes back in front of the crowd, then drives its double-up pattern. I edge out and spot my roller, then I cut in at the wake. My timing is perfect. The roller boosts me twice as high as a normal wake jump, and I pull on the handle to start spinning. It all happens in slow motion: I pass the handle once . . . twice . . . and I'm reaching, waiting for the third pass to complete the 720. I feel it hit the palm of my hand and I grip on tight as I drop down for a perfect, buttery-smooth landing. Not bad for the first heelside 720 I've ever landed off a double-up!

Back on the dock, I'm flooded with relief. My job is done. Now it's in the hands of the judges.

It's a few hours before the results are posted. Even though I'm confident I'll be on the podium, I feel anxious as I approach the noticeboard. I scan the list for my name . . . and find it sitting right at the top of the Junior Men's category.

'No fucking way!' I turn to Tony, who's there to check his results too. 'I WON!'

Tony finds his name. 'And I'm third!' he says.

We high-five each other.

'Kiwis on the podium! Hell yeah, bro!' I say, attempting to hide that I'm quietly stoked about beating Tony for the first time ever.

'Nice work, B-rad!' He cracks a big smile, looking more excited than I've ever seen him. B-rad ('Bee-rad') appears to have become my nickname. We're also both stoked to be sharing the podium with our mutual Aussie friend, Hank.

Later, as I'm standing on the podium with my friends alongside me and a gold medal around my neck, I think of Kenney and Richie. I hope that somehow they know they have had a hand in me getting this world title. I beam with pride and hold the New Zealand flag high. It's surreal to have made it here. I can't believe the dream of being a world champion has become a reality.

And, to make this even sweeter, I've just earned myself a boat!

•

I get back to New Zealand at the end of 2004, just as the summer is heating up. I enjoy a bit of media attention after my win, but mostly I just want to get back to riding.

I return to my job at MasterCraft in Rotorua, and I immediately ask the owner about that boat he promised me.

'Yeah, I'm following up with MasterCraft International about getting a team rider discount on an X2 for you,' he says. 'I'll get back to you.'

The following week I ask again and he gives me the same answer. When I ask again the week after that, I can tell from his expression that it's not good news. 'I'm really sorry, Brad,' he says, 'but MasterCraft International won't give us a discount so I'm afraid I can't afford it.'

To say I'm disappointed would be an understatement. I'm angry, crushed, heartbroken — and I want to punch him. Why did he promise me something he couldn't deliver? I had my hopes set on that boat — and now, when I have finally earned it, he's snatching it away. I walk out of the shop and sit on a boat trailer out the back, trying to calm down. I'm so gutted I want to quit the job but I can't — I need the money. I decide I'll stay till the end of the summer.

Fortunately, I get a bit of work doing private coaching, and most evenings after work I drive to the Ballistics camp to ride and hang with Haydog. Unfortunately,

Ants and Brant aren't living with Daz this summer. Ants moved to the Sunshine Coast in Aussie, and Brant brought a girlfriend back from the UK for the summer, so although we still ride together, he's off showing her around the country. It's not the same without all three musketeers together, but it's given Haydog and me a bit more of a chance to bro down, and thankfully I can always count on quality riding on a good wake at the camp.

On the days out riding with Daz, his extra 100-plus kilos always makes the wake noticeably better. Then one day he invites a couple of mates to join us, and when I show up after work my eyes light up — not just because his friends include some cute girls, but also because of the other dude who's come along.

'This is Tiny,' says Daz, introducing us to a big Māori guy. And when I say 'big', I mean fucking huge. He must be almost 2 metres tall and at least 200 kg.

When Tiny steps into the boat, the hull sinks visibly deeper in the water. The boat's so heavy it struggles to get on a plane even with every factory tank empty and everybody sent to the bow. Once we're up, though, we have the most epic session on the biggest wake I've yet to ride.

Days at Daz's place are the best.

THREE: THE SACRIFICE

A couple of years ago, when I was about 15, my sister invited some friends over before they headed to the school ball. They were all dolled up and looking stunning, but there was one petite brunette in particular who caught my eye. I passed Charlotte in the hallway and we locked eyes briefly. That glance lasted less than a second, but in that time her captivating blue eyes took my breath away.

Now, over two years later, it's 2005 and I've reconnected with her. I'm stoked, but I know Monique won't be if she finds out so I've kept it from her. Anyway, nothing has happened between us. Yet.

In January, Jordan and I decide to go to an event in Tauranga called Blues, Brews and BBQs, and I manage to convince Char to come with us. Daz and some of his mates are also going, so I catch a lift from Rotorua with them — and, even though I'm a tall, well-built athlete, I'm somehow the smallest person in the car. I end up squished into the middle seat in the back. The whole hour-long drive to Tauranga, we're seriously low-riding in Daz's already lowered ride and, with Tiny in the front, I'm surprised we're not scraping the road. And not long after we arrive, Jordan and Char arrive down from Auckland.

The event is awesome, and it proves handy to have Daz and Tiny nearby, as some dudes try to step to Jordan and me in our drunken states, but all it takes is calling out for Tiny to stand up for the aggressors to flee, tails between their legs. But by the time it finishes I've lost Daz and his crew. Jordan, Char and I are at a loss. We haven't organised anywhere to stay, so we don't know where to go.

'We could go back to Daz's lake house in Rotorua,' I say, 'but it's an hour's drive away.'

'I'll drive,' says Charlotte.

So the three of us pile into her little red Honda Civic and start the journey. Not long into the drive, I reach across and take Charlotte's hand. It's the first time we've shared any sort of intimacy, and it feels good when she squeezes my hand gently and smiles over at me. We're both so smitten that we refuse to let go even when she goes around a sharp corner and almost veers off the road. I'm now realising she's probably way too drunk to be driving, but we're already in the middle of nowhere, so we're committed.

We make it back to Daz's just after one in the morning, only to find that he's not there and the house is locked up.

'Shit! He must've stayed somewhere in Tauranga,' I say. 'There's no alarm, at least. We'll have to break in somehow.'

I circumnavigate the house and find a bedroom window with one of its two latches unlocked. I pull the unlocked corner of the window open and use a thin piece of wood that I find beside the house to try to flick the other latch open. But I can't quite reach, so I pull harder on the window frame to open it up a little more, then — *SMASHHH!* The window shatters and I fall to the ground in a shower of broken glass.

'Are you okay?' Charlotte asks.

I check myself over, secretly enjoying the concern she's showing for me. 'Yep. Just a couple scratches.' Then I look up at the broken window. 'Well, shit, that's not okay though! That's gonna cost me. But at least we're in.'

Inside, I suggest that Charlotte take my bed. 'I'll sleep on the couch,' I say gallantly. But she insists that I stay with her — which is exactly what I was hoping for. So I cuddle up in bed with her, and it's there that we share our first kiss. But it's so much more than just a kiss. I've wanted this for so long that the anticipation only adds to the sparks that fly the moment our lips touch, and my chest is instantly filled with butterflies. After our lips part, I hold her in my arms as we drift off to sleep.

●

We take our time to rise the next morning, and by the time we're finally up Daz has just got home. I explain about the window and call the glazier straight away to get it replaced, but thankfully he's not fazed about it.

Later in the afternoon we head out on the lake for a ride. Charlotte has never seen me ride before, and it's been a couple of years since Jordan came out on the Bayliner, so I'm excited to have them both on the boat.

I start my ride with some cruisy grabs and basics to blow last night's dustiness off. Once I'm feeling loose and warmed up, I step it up a notch with some tech and a couple of big glides — they're always the crowd-pleasers. Then I signal for Daz to drive me a left double-up, which he does to perfection. I line up the third roller and edge in on my toes to connect perfectly with the peak, then I pull hard on the handle and start spinning — through 360, 540, 720, 900. And I land it! No, I stomp the absolute piss out of it!

It's my first successful 900. What's more, I'm the first Kiwi to land one. It's the biggest spin anyone is currently doing, besides the 1080 that Parks Bonifay landed back in '99, and landing it has just secured me a place as one of the sport's elites.

I'm so stoked that I throw the handle and take my board off, even though I'm only 10 minutes into my set. Daz is cheering and pumping his fists in the air, and Charlotte and Jordan are clapping and cheering too. The smile is wide across my face, and I can't wipe it off.

As Jordan and I drive back to Auckland later in the evening, I'm still grinning. My mind's full of my 900 and my girl: holding hands with her in the car, cuddling up with her in bed, sharing our first kiss. My phone beeps, and I pick it up. It's a text from Char: *Brad, I think I'm falling for you.*

I reply immediately: *I'm falling for you too.*

•

It's my 18th birthday at the start of February 2005, and a couple of days later I'm off to Aussie to compete in two stops of the pro tour for the first time. Char and I are still seeing each other, and it seems to be getting more serious, so by now Monique knows and has accepted that I'm dating her friend. Before I leave Char treats me to the most glorious birthday sex. I'm sad to be saying goodbye to her for the next few weeks and it's not just about the sex. Our intimacy is unreal — unlike anything I've ever experienced before. I feel like we have a real connection. I'm well and truly in love with this girl.

It's evening when I land in Sydney, and a guy called Kris Bower is there to meet me. He's the editor of *Wake Magazine* and is following the pro tour to write about it. I don't know him well, though we've met a couple of times — when he was commentating nationals, and once at the Ballistics camp. I'm still pretty shy and can take a little time to open up, especially as the youngster mixing with older crew, so it was decent of Bower to offer to take me with him on tour. I toss my wakeboard bag in the back of his van and jump in.

For the first couple of hours of our long drive up to Port Macquarie, Bower and I chat about everything wake. I like how real he is — no bullshit, no sugar-coating. He also has some good advice for me to propel myself into the limelight a bit more.

We stop for a break and Bower pulls a scrunched-up piece of tinfoil out of his pocket. My first thought is that it's a tinny containing some green for us to smoke, but I'm mistaken.

'We've still got a couple of hours ahead of us,' Bower says. 'This is just a little something to keep us awake and alert.'

'Okay, cool,' I say. 'What is it?'

'Speed.' He takes a small amount on the tip of his finger. 'Usually we'd snort it, but this is a little damp. If you want some, just take a little bit and do this,' he says, then rubs his finger back and forth behind his bottom lip.

Besides smoking weed I've never done any drugs, but I'm curious.

'Yeah, can I have some? I'm keen to try it,' I say, taking the piece of tinfoil and looking more closely at the dry, off-white paste in it. 'What exactly does it do?'

'Well, at first it'll make your gums a bit numb, and then you should feel a rise in energy and focus.'

I take a little chunk and rub it behind my lip like he did. My mouth fills with an acidic, chemical taste and my gums start to go numb almost instantly. Within a few minutes my eyes widen and I feel my awareness of everything around me heighten. It's like I see everything more clearly than ever — every passing car and licence plate, every road sign, every bit of wildlife, living or roadkill. A kangaroo hops across the road in front of us and Bower pumps the brakes, and that's enough to get my heart racing more than it already is. The rest of the drive literally speeds by. Our conversations get deeper, and I'm speaking faster. We dance to music I've never heard before, switching from funky old-school hip-hop to high-energy electronic dance music that pulses through my whole body.

When we finally get to Port Macquarie some time after midnight, I feel like we've packed a year's worth of getting to know each other into one five-hour drive. Bower picked me up as slightly more than a stranger, but now we're best mates.

•

The next day we pick Tony up from the train station. After a quick scout of the competition site at Stoney Park we race five minutes up the road to Bower's friend Tallun's place. When we pull up I see that he's dug a long ditch on his property and it's filled with water. At one end there's a ledge-seat cut out of the dirt, and at the other there's a makeshift dock. In the middle, in the water, there's a 15-metre flat bar — a type of rail. Tony and I leap excitedly out of the van just as Tallun pulls up in the most beat-up, shitty-looking ride. It looks like it got saved halfway through being scrapped — there's no roof, no windows, no windshield, no doors.

'This is your tow vehicle,' he announces with a wide grin.

And here I was thinking we'd be getting pulled by some sort of winch.

Minutes later, I'm strapped into my board and being pulled along the water behind the beater car. When I get to the seat at one end of the ditch I sit down, still holding on to the handle, while Bower rips a 180 in the car to take me back the other way. As soon as the rope comes tight again I'm pulled back up onto the water and past the flat bar for another hit. At the other end I hop up onto the dock while Bower spins the car around again.

It's an amazingly efficient system. I get in so many more laps and rail hits than if we were winching, which would require me to get out of the water and run the rope back to the start of the ditch for each lap. After half an hour I toss the handle to Tony and take over at the wheel of the shit-box. Driving the car is just as much fun as riding behind it! I never thought I could have so much fun — and do so much quality rail-riding — in a ditch with a beat-up piece-of-junk car. I haven't had a huge amount of opportunity to ride rails but this was a great way to get more confident hitting a flat bar.

We head to the competition the next day. Unfortunately I get knocked out in the first round, but it's a fun event. I get to see Jeff, who's also here competing, and meet a bunch of other pro riders from Australia and further afield. As soon as we get the chance, though, Tony and I are out of there.

We head straight back to Tallun's place for more ditch-riding.

•

Our next stop is the Gold Coast. Tony joins Bower and me for the drive this time, and after six hours on the road — with more great tunes, deep conversations, wide eyes and numb gums — we pull up at Jeff's parents' place. He's living here at the moment, and it's a beautiful home right on the waterways. I wander through some sliding doors to the back of the house, and as I step outside I spot the swimming pool. I freeze. I'm hit with a feeling I was not expecting.

Fuck, I think. *That's where Richie drowned.*

For the next hour I sit on the pool's edge with my legs in the water. I'm sad, but I also feel like it's helping me connect with Richie on some level.

After a little while, Tony, Bower and Jeff come out and join me. We sit around and share stories about Richie. It feels good to talk about him, to remember the good times, but it's also surreal to know that it happened right here.

•

We have a week on the Gold Coast before the next event, and in the meantime there's Jeff's 23rd birthday to celebrate. We're just about to head into Surfer's Paradise for a big night out when Jeff asks Tony and me if we want a pinger.

'A what?' I ask.

'A pinger. Ecstasy. We're all getting on it tonight!'

Tony and I look at each other, then back at Jeff.

'Sure!' we reply at the same time.

Once we're at the bar, I knock back my little party pill and wash it down with a beer. There's a slight chemical taste, similar to the speed. Half an hour later I've got a warmth in my belly that starts to intensify through my body. It feels incredible. I feel incredible! My energy spikes in a similar way to the speed but better. This just feels like love. I'm touching the upholstery and the wallpaper and my clothes, revelling in the texture and sensation of everything. When I look over at Tony I see that he's feeling the same. I can see why they call it ecstasy.

I also notice that I'm loosening up and having conversations with everyone. I was a little bit hesitant when we first got to the bar, because I'm the new kid among a bunch of guys who know each other really well, but that's well and truly gone now. I get chatting with a random girl. She's cute, so we step outside to get some air and so we can hear each other better. After a while we decide to head back inside but the bouncer stops us at the door.

'Lockout is in effect, sorry, guys. I can't let anyone in,' he tells us.

'But we were just in there,' I say. 'And all my friends are still in there!'

'Sorry, mate. You're not going back in.'

'Aah, shit.' I turn back to the girl. 'What do we do now?'

'We could get a drink at the casino?' she suggests. 'They're open all night.'

So next thing I know, we're sitting at a couple of slot machines but we're not playing them. We're too busy talking. And that's when I notice, thanks to the casino's bright lighting, that her pupils are the size of dinner plates. They've basically taken over her irises. Her eyes look like mine do.

'Wait,' I say. 'Are you on pingers right now?'

'Yesss! You are too?'

I laugh. 'No wonder we've been chewing each other's ears off!' But as I say it, I realise it's my jaw that I'm chewing off. I can't stop moving it.

'Do you want some gum?' she asks, and I nod gratefully.

Eventually I decide it's time to head home.

'Why don't you come to mine?' she says, and I'm tempted. But then Charlotte pops into my head. 'I can't. I've got a girlfriend,' I say.

When I step back outside, it's into a burst of hot sunshine. It burns my eyes and I instantly squeeze them shut. What the fuck? How long were we in there?

The girl — whose name I now realise I can't even remember — is standing next to me.

'Well, bye,' I say. 'It was cool to hang out.'

As I go in for a hug, she plants a kiss on me in a last-ditch effort to entice me to go home with her. But I'm in love with a girl back in New Zealand. I have no intention of fucking that up.

•

Soon, it's time to head back home again. I fared only slightly better at our second stop on the pro tour, scraping through my first head-to-head matchup, but then I got taken down in the next round. Tony was taken out just as quickly but Jeff went on to place second in the overall pro tour. I might not be bringing home any medals this time but I had a blast in Aussie. I'll definitely be back.

It's not long before the New Zealand nationals come around again. I invite Charlotte to come down for the weekend to support me and she happily agrees. This year I'm out to beat Jeff in the open men's. I want that title! But Jeff's not my only competition — I've obviously got to keep an eye on Tony too, and I can't sleep on Ants, Brant or Haydog either. In reality, I also know that my biggest competition is myself. I can't control what any of the others do. I can only control my own performance.

On the dock for the finals, I'm riding third-to-last. Tony and Jeff are up after me.

'Go nuts B-rad!' Jeff laughs as I'm about to jump off the dock, and I turn to see that he's hanging his balls out the leg of his shorts in an attempt to throw me off my game. It doesn't work. My run goes well. I hit most of my tricks, and even with a fall towards the end of my second pass, it's still enough to take the lead and put some pressure on Jeff.

But when he hits the water, he does it in classic Jeff style. He lands all his standard competition tricks and that's all he needs to better my run.

I'm stoked to get my first silver medal, but I'm still one step down on the podium from Jeff. Haydog's there with us, in third place. As per tradition, the winner's cup is filled to the brim with beer and I watch enviously as Jeff sculls it, everyone cheering him on until it's empty. Someone times him — 35 seconds.

I can't wait to do that, I think. *And I'm going to do it faster.*

•

There's no way I'm sticking around for another New Zealand winter. I'm going back to Florida, and I can't wait.

The only thing that makes leaving hard is Charlotte. We spend my last night in Auckland together, and it's a night full of intense lovemaking and deep conversations about whether or not we can make it work long distance. Our connection is so strong that I really want to try. I'm confident I can go six months until I see her again but she's not so sure. She seems hesitant to trust me completely, no matter how much I try to reassure her. Eventually, we agree to give it a go. It's going to take a lot of effort but I'm up for the challenge.

As soon as I step off the plane and into the arrivals area at Orlando airport I'm greeted by two smiling girls.

'Hey, are you Brad?' one of them asks.

'Yeah.'

'We're here with Alex,' the other replies. 'He's just doing laps in the car outside so he sent us in to find you.'

Not a bad welcome, I think — right before Charlotte pops into my mind.

This season, instead of going back to The Wakeboard Camp to work, I've decided I'll just wing it. I haven't even really planned where I'll be living, beyond arranging to crash on Alex's couch to begin with.

As soon as we arrive at Alex's parents' place, we start drinking. After a couple of hours Alex disappears into his room with one of the girls, leaving me and her friend alone. This was obviously his plan but I have zero interest.

'I'm just going to step out and call my girlfriend to let her know I got here okay,' I say.

As soon as Charlotte hears another girl's voice in the background of our call, her fears rear their heads. I manage to salvage things by reiterating my feelings for her, and she seems reassured. Sort of.

Phew, I think when I hang up. *One night down. Only about 179 to go.*

•

Alex's couch is super comfortable and his parents are cool about letting me stay, but after a month I start to feel like I'm wearing out my welcome.

Alex and I ride every day, and when we're not riding we're either working out, playing chess (which he almost always beats me at) or pool (where we're more evenly matched), or partying. Almost everything is an opportunity for a bit of friendly competition between us, and that's something that really fuels our riding. If there's a trick he can do but I can't, I'm going to learn it. And if I learn a new trick, then it's his mission to land it too.

But when his parents start asking what my plans are, I figure it's time to move on. Jeff Weatherall and his girlfriend, Cathy, also a pro wakeboarder, are living 45 minutes away in Sanford with a few of the Aussie dudes, and when they offer to take me in I gratefully accept. But after just a few weeks there they decide to move because of the lake. It's barely big enough for the boat to get up on plane and cram a few tricks in before you have to turn around, plus it's kinda shallow, so it affects how big the wake can get. Jeff finds a new place on the much bigger and better Lake Jessamine — only this time it's the house that's tiny, only two bedrooms, so the Aussie lads find another place elsewhere. The tiny house is actually an old cabin that's been added as a second dwelling, while the property owner lives in the main house.

The cabin is pretty shitty, but it's a place to live. It's also got a nice dock where Jeff keeps the Malibu Wakesetter that has just arrived from his sponsor. The wake behind that thing is the biggest I've ever ridden — and I get to ride it every day! The lake itself is a million times better. It's deep, long and well sheltered, with a cove at each end to get a few extra tricks in or throw a double-up without the rollers affecting the main lake.

A couple of weeks after we move in, Andrea joins us. She'd already arranged to take the second bedroom before I turned up, so I'm back in the lounge. This time I'm on an air mattress and there's barely enough room for it. On my first night out here a huge cockroach crawls across my pillow and onto my face as I'm trying to fall asleep. 'Arghhhh!' I squeal as I swat it across the room. It's harder to get to sleep after that.

I'm just thankful to have somewhere to stay. I feel bad that my lack of a plan has meant I've had to rely on my fellow Kiwis to take me in, but it's cool that they have. Even if the living situation is a bit shitty.

. I'm living off my savings, but they're dwindling rapidly. I haven't arranged any coaching work this season, as I was confident that I'd win more prize money and get paid by sponsors — but that hasn't worked out. Mum's given me her credit card with strict instructions to use it for 'emergencies only', but as my savings dry up I find myself pulling it out more and more often for everyday expenses. I start to realise I have grossly underestimated just how much it actually costs to live and ride here.

•

One morning Jeff tells me he's taking me to an event for the day.

'We're going to "Parks' Double or Nothing",' he says and my face lights up.

I've heard about this event. It's an invite-only jam-style double-up contest hosted by none other than Parks Bonifay. You have to be in wakeboarding's inner circle to even know where it's being held.

From the moment we arrive I'm completely star-struck. All of the sport's biggest names are here. There's the Pointless Posse, of course — Parks, his brother Shane, Danny Harf, Chad Sharpe, Shawn Watson and Erik Ruck. There are the Aussie legends: Daniel Watkins, Josh Sanders and Brett (Ike) Eisenhauer. And I spot Andrew Adkison, Rusty Malinoski and Phil (Froggy) Soven — who just won Wake Games. Legendary American rider Erik 'Gator' Lutgert is already out on the water when we get there.

Jeff and I hitch a ride on a boat out to where the double-ups are going down and, as we putt past, Gator launches an insanely large heelside front flip, then crashes hard, ending his run in the contest.

While Jeff and I are watching the rest of the competition we get chatting to some of the other guys, including Oakley team manager Matty Swanson, and I notice a familiar scent in the air. It's coming from the next boat over. Jeff notices it too.

'Shall we?' I say, and he nods.

We follow the sticky-sweet smell and hop over to the boat. It's Shane Bonifay's, and he's just sparked a bowl. Jeff doesn't usually smoke but he takes a hit and introduces me to Shane. Next thing I'm smokin' weed with several members of the Pointless Posse. I talk a little but I'm feeling incredibly shy around these guys who I've idolised since I first learnt wakeboarding was a thing. Before long I'm super stoned so I mostly just sit back and listen, and watch the action on the water.

The riding is incredible. By the end of the day I've witnessed some of the most insane double-ups I've ever seen. Parks wins biggest air with a massive batwing to swan dive, and Danny Harf takes best trick with a cab (switch) 900 — the first ever to be landed in contest. But the 1080 attempts are the most exciting. Parks is still the only one to have landed the trick, and that was about five years ago.

Andrew and Shane almost make their heelside 1080s, but Danny and Phil Soven come the closest on their toeside attempts.

After the contest is over, Jeff tells me we're heading over to his buddy Darin's place.

'Cool. Darin who?' I ask.

'Darin Shapiro,' he replies, and I'm pretty sure my jaw literally drops. Darin is one of the godfathers of wake.

The first thing I notice is how rad Darin's place is. Jeff introduces us and I manage to squeak out, 'Hi, it's really nice to meet you!' Darin is short — barely up to my chest — and he's built like a tank.

He's a really friendly guy. 'Come in!' he says, and we follow him into his music room, where he and Jeff start chatting away and we all crack open a beer.

We hang out at Darin's for the rest of the night, shifting every now and then to a different room or out by the pool or even down to the dock. Jeff and Darin are talking away all night, but I barely say a word. Darin soon bestows me with a new nickname: The Ghost of Christmas. It's mainly because I'm still a little stoned, but also I'm just trying to soak it all in. I'm still processing the fact that I've spent the day at Parks Bonifay's invite-only event, where I hung out with the best in wake and got stoned with Shane, then came and spent the evening hanging out at Darin Shapiro's house. It feels like a dream.

This has been one of the best days of my life.

•

There's just one little cloud darkening the otherwise clear skies of my second summer here in Florida: I'm really missing Charlotte.

We talk every couple of days but it's hard not being with her, and I know she's wondering what I'm up to over here. She imagines me hanging out with loads of girls and having fun without her, but that's really not how it is. This summer I'm firmly focused on my wakeboarding. It's pretty much all I do.

Then, one evening when I'm talking to her, about two months in, she says, 'Brad, I'm really sorry, but I can't do this any more.' It's just been too hard, she says.

Her words feel like a punch to the gut.

I plead with her to reconsider. 'You can trust me,' I say. 'You don't need to worry.'

But my efforts are in vain. She's made up her mind.

'Maybe we can revisit things when you come back to New Zealand,' she says, but that's little consolation.

I hang up, a tight ache in my chest, and then the tears come. I can't hold them back. I'm utterly heartbroken.

I feel torn between two loves. It seems I can't have both. My dedication to becoming a pro wakeboarder has cost me the girl I love the most in this world. As I dwell on that thought, I decide I'd better make the sacrifice worth it. If that's the cost, then it would be idiotic not to make the most of my time on the water.

I turn my focus to hitting all the competitions I can while I'm in the US. Around the same time I moved in with Jeff he took me to the first event of the year, Wake Games, but I didn't even make it through to the second run.

The next contest is in Texas. I ride well in the junior pro heats, landing back-to-back 720s in my run, but unfortunately I take a fall and that's enough to see me eliminated.

After that, Jeff, Cathy and I make the six-hour drive in Cathy's truck up to Georgia to the USA Masters. It's an invite-only contest and I've managed to qualify with my win at worlds last year. Cathy makes it through to the pro women's final, but Jeff and I both come up short and miss out on ours.

I'm starting to get frustrated and wonder what it is that's causing me to ride so badly in every contest, as it's a different trick that gets me every time. Maybe it's just the pressure, or maybe the other riders are simply better than me. I really need to work on consistency.

After he's out, Jeff comes up to me and says, 'Bro, I'm over it! Fuck sticking around here for another day. Let's boost back to Orlando.'

'Yeah, good plan,' I reply, 'but what about Cathy — you're not going to stick around to watch her ride?'

'Na, I'd much rather get back and get some riding in than sit around here tomorrow. She'll get a ride back with someone else.'

Jeff tells it as he sees it. When he tells Cathy we're taking the truck and heading back to Orlando it's obvious she's not happy, but that doesn't stop him.

•

On our way out of town we stop in at the cabin where Parks and a few other guys are hanging out. The room is a haze of smoke. Parks, who has a history of rebelling at Masters, was escorted off the contest site earlier in the day, causing a bit of a scene. I'm told it all started a couple of years ago when he hit the ski jump during his contest run and was disqualified, so he followed up with a swan-dive from the roof of the pavilion into the lake. It was his way of sticking it to the water-ski federation, which runs the contest.

Jeff takes a hit on the bowl, then passes it to me. We don't stick around for long, and about an hour into our road-trip the munchies kick in. So we pull into a McDonald's drive-through, then get back on the road. When we're almost at the Florida state line, an officer at a checkpoint signals to us to pull over. Jeff parks the truck and an officer and his canine companion start circling us. As they reach the driver's door, the dog sits down.

'Step out of the car, please, both of you,' the officer orders.

Next thing, we're both up against the truck with our legs spread and hands wide, getting a pat-down.

'Go and sit on the grass over there,' the officer tells us.

We do as we're told, as six officers proceed to tear the truck apart. There's one at each door and two at the back, going through the tray, pulling out everything that can come out. They go through our bags. They check under the seats. They look in every pocket and compartment, every nook and cranny.

Jeff and I glance at each other nervously, but it's mostly just paranoia from still being a little stoned, as we know they're not going to find anything. There's nothing for them to find.

Fifteen minutes later we're allowed back in the truck.

'All right, you're free to go,' the officer says.

'You might need to feed that dog of yours,' Jeff says cheekily. 'He probably just smelt the Maccas.' He points to the empty fast-food packaging on the floor.

'Get out of here,' the officer barks, clearly unamused. 'Now! Before I find a reason to keep you here.'

Jeff puts the truck in gear and takes off.

A few minutes down the road I say, 'They never searched the hard-shell luggage case on the roof. It could've been packed with kilos upon kilos of drugs.'

Jeff laughs. 'We could've been transporting a dead body in it, for all they knew.'

We have ourselves a good chuckle over that, relieved the whole incident is safely in the rear-view mirror.

•

A few weeks later we head up to Canada for Wakefest. It's held in Kelowna, BC, and it's one of the biggest pro tour stops of the year in terms of the size of the crowd. It's also notorious for the terrible conditions on Okanagan Lake, which is big and open with a concrete sea-wall shoreline that bounces every wake, every bit of wind chop and every ripple back out across the course. I'm less than excited to ride in such choppy conditions, but I suppose they're terrible for everyone.

I make it through my first heat, and head out for a couple of drinks with some of the Aussie riders that night, but I decide to call it quits around 11 p.m. so I'm fresh for the following day. The next morning I'm woken by my phone. I'm confused because it's still pitch black — who's calling me in the middle of the night? It's Bill, the C-dub junior team manager. 'Brad, where are you? Your heat's about to start.'

I leap out of bed and tear back the curtains to let bright daylight pour into the room. 'Fucking black-out curtains!' I yell.

I race to the contest site but I'm too late. I've missed my heat. I'm out because I slept in.

Fuck!

•

Back in Florida, we head to a party at Lake Holden, which is the next lake over from us. There, I'm introduced to a pro rider called Dallas Friday. I already know all about her. Back when I was at high school I used to use the school computers to look up pictures of her. I've had a huge crush on her ever since. She's about my age, and, as well as being one of the best there is, she's also really cute. Her blonde hair, sweet face and petite athletic body are all very appealing. We get chatting, then she excuses herself to head outside for a smoke.

I see her step outside a few more times, and eventually summon up the courage to follow her out the next time. I want to get her alone so we can talk some more.

'Mind if I join you?' I ask.

'Sure,' she says, and holds out a menthol. 'You want one?'

'Thanks.' I light up, even though I don't smoke cigarettes, and I sit there with her, looking out over the glassy lake and the lights of downtown Orlando sparkling in the distance. It's hard to read Dallas, but as we chat more I feel like we're making a connection. I just can't tell whether she likes me too.

Around midnight, Andrea comes to tell me she's ready to call it a night. Jeff and Cathy have already left, so Dallas offers to drop us both home, as it's only five minutes down the road, so the three of us jump into her bad-arse GMC Denali. As Andrea is getting out of the truck I turn to Dallas and say, 'Do you think the party will go for much longer? I don't know if I'm ready to call it a night.'

'I'm sure it'll still be going for a while,' she replies. 'Do you want to come back?'

'Yeah, fuck it! Let's go back,' I say.

'Sweet, well, thanks for the ride,' Andrea says, shooting me a quizzical look before shutting the door and heading into the cabin.

We're only about halfway back to the party when Dallas says, 'So do you really want to go back to the party? We could go to my condo instead. It's right up the road.'

'Let's go to your condo,' I say, keeping a cool exterior while inside I'm ready to bust out a celebratory dance. Is this really going where I think it is? I sure hope so.

Just then, I think of Charlotte. How will this affect that? But then again, she broke up with me. I'm single now, and I am not going to miss this opportunity.

As soon as we enter Dallas's condo, she excuses herself and disappears into her bedroom. Moments later she emerges wearing nothing but some short shorts and a white tanktop that shows off her perky new boobs.

'Just had to put on something more comfortable,' she says.

Within a couple of minutes that tanktop is on the floor.

We're making out on the couch, hands all over each other, and the rest of our clothes soon come off. She has an immaculate body, and she knows it. Before long we're in the bedroom, and she's both confident and intrepid sexually. When I wake up in her bed the next morning and she's cuddled up naked beside me, all I can think is that 15-year-old Brad would be so proud.

We take our time enjoying more of each other before she drops me home.

As well as continuing to see each other, Dallas and I also start riding together. She's asked me to keep our relationship as discreet as possible, and that's fine by me. Our arrangement is pretty sweet — not only do we have a lot of fun off the water, but Dallas absolutely rips on the water and I love watching her ride. After a while, though, things start to peter out, but I enjoy it while it lasts.

•

My wakeboarding has really been thriving in this environment.

I arrived here at the start of the season with a few good tricks that were good enough for me to hang in the junior men's division, but now I've levelled up to where I can start to hang with the best in the world. I've got my heel and toe 720s dialled in. I'm pulling my toeside 900 off the wake now, without a double-up. I'm also taking my whirlybird to 540, and I've just learnt to drop my toeside backroll to blind — a new trick that only a handful of guys in the world can do. It's amazing what a season of quality riding can do.

Riding every day with Jeff, in particular, has really pushed me to step up my game. And my progression appears to be pushing his riding too, because his competitiveness won't allow me to surpass him that easily.

Jeff and I have been going out together for riding sessions on our own lately, and it's been better than ever. It's come off the back of a bit of a meltdown that Jeff had after getting frustrated at watching the girls crash over and over on the same tricks. So the new arrangement is that Jeff and I take the boat out to ride, then we come back in to recover and refuel while the girls ride, and then we're ready to take another set by the time they're back. Most days Jeff also invites a different pro over to ride with us. I've never ridden so much in a day, every day, as I have here. So although it started because of a meltdown, the change has actually ended up being really good for our training. At least, it has for mine!

By this stage my savings have well and truly run out. I'm living as cheaply as possible, but I'm now swiping Mum's 'emergencies only' credit card for every petrol run, food shop and flight booking. I shudder to think how much I've ticked up already.

•

My season in Orlando is at an end, and although things were not especially successful on the competition front, it's been an incredibly productive summer for my wakeboarding. I've added a bunch of new tricks to my repertoire, I'm much more consistent, and I've also got to meet most of the big-name pro riders.

Riding with Jeff in particular has done wonders, and we've also become much closer friends. The five-year age gap between us has always meant I felt a bit like the kid he took under his wing — and the kid he liked to give a hard time — but that gap seems to have faded into insignificance. He still gives me a hard time pretty frequently, but now I know it's just tough love. It's his way of making me step up in order to shut him up.

I'm leaving Florida, but I'm not heading straight back to New Zealand. First, I'm off to Moscow to defend my world junior men's title at the IWSF worlds. Tony and my roomies are coming too, and Mum is flying over to join us as the New Zealand team manager. As soon as I step off the plane, I realise that my Orlando wardrobe is nowhere near appropriate for the cold here in Russia. Thankfully, our team uniform includes a warm hoodie, and Mum brought mine over with her.

The first thing I notice about Russia, aside from the cold, is it seems like everything is either one extreme or the other. The buildings are either completely run down or super fancy. It's the same with the cars . . . and the women. They're either incredibly attractive or not at all. The only exception, apparently, is the food. It's universally terrible.

Our accommodation situation is pretty sketchy. Unlike other places where you book a room and get a key and that's it, here we get given a small piece of paper that we must trade for a room key every time we come and go. On each floor of the hotel there's a woman sitting behind a desk to facilitate this whole process. A lot of the competitors speculate that the Russian mafia has a hand in the local wakeboard and water-ski federation, and that's why the whole accommodation set-up is so dodgy. Whatever the reason, I don't feel like my room is a safe place to leave anything valuable so I keep my passport with me at all times.

The contest site is a long and straight man-made rowing lake, and a cold wind constantly blows down the course. It's miserable and I really don't want to be here. The food is shit, the hotel is shit, the weather is shit. I am not stoked to be competing in Russia. I'm only here to defend my world title, so that's what I focus on, even though I was recently told by my board sponsor that it's also shit. While we were in Texas, I tracked down the CWB junior team manager and asked to be added to the team. 'Sorry, Brad,' the manager told me. 'Unfortunately, there's no room for you at the moment.' When I asked what would get me on the team if not a junior world title, he replied, 'Look, an IWSF world title isn't really recognised by the industry. They're not the legit world champs. The World Wake Association champs are.' I was baffled, and it still bugs me. It feels so unfair.

I don't do much to hide my negativity and Mum soon has me on about it. '"This is shit, that is shit,"' she says. 'You've got to sort out your attitude, Brad. The conditions are the same for everyone.'

But all that comes of her pep talk is that I have one more thing to be sour about: my mum's here lecturing me at worlds.

When it's time for my first heat, I stand on the starting dock and scowl at the wind. I hope it will drop off slightly for my ride but it does the opposite. As I'm tightening my bindings I think bitterly, *You've got to be fucking kidding me.*

On my first pass I'm riding right into the wind. I charge into my first trick — the nuclear glide — but I get overextended and hung up in the wind and I slam hard onto my back, getting turfed out of my bindings. After shaking it off and getting back on my board I fumble through the rest of my first pass, but each trick is at least a 180 less than I had planned. My second trick of pass number two takes me down. And, to make things worse, I bomb in the last-chance qualifier, coming dead last. With that, my hopes of holding on to my title for another year are dashed.

From top of the world to dead last . . . Great.

Of course Mum has me on about my attitude again.

'Did you not see the wind chop I was dealing with?' I say. 'There were practically waves. And don't tell me the conditions were the same for everyone, because they weren't. The driver even told me I got the worst of it.'

'Okay, but you've been so negative since you got here,' she replies. 'That type of mindset won't get you anywhere. It's so unlike you.'

'Well, it's pretty hard to be enthusiastic about this event when my sponsor says it doesn't even mean anything!' I retaliate. 'How am I supposed to be positive when I'm told my world title isn't actually legit? Why should I stay motivated for the "fake" worlds?'

My eyes have welled up, and Mum understands what's going on. Winning that world title in Spain was my greatest accomplishment, and to have it trashed by the CWB junior team manager damaged me more than I've let on. Mum gives me a hug, which I pretend not to like, but it definitely helps. I decide to make an effort to be a positive supporter for the rest of my team for the remainder of the contest.

Jeff takes his second world title and Andrea takes the top spot in the women's division. I'm really proud of my friends — but I'm also well and truly ready to say goodbye to Russia.

●

It's so good to see Charlotte again, but it's only for a couple of months because she's going to Australia for the summer to work at a resort on Hamilton Island. After talking it through we decide to stay together, as she'll be gone for just one season. I'm planning to head over to Australia for the pro tour in the new year, so I can fly in to see her after the final stop.

Being home also means I have to front up to the money issue. Mum tells me I clocked up a solid $18,000 on her credit card. My heart drops.

I knew it was going to be bad, but I had no idea would be that bad.

'Brad, that's a serious amount of money!' she says. 'But, look, I'll cover this last season. I guess it's only fair since I've contributed a similar amount to your sister's university costs this year. But I can't continue to bail you out, so from now on, you're on your own.'

I'm extremely grateful — and relieved that I don't have to pay her back. I guess I was pretty naïve about just how much it costs to do a season in Florida. And, though Mum might not think that my seasons in the US are of similar value to my sister's studies, I feel like I am earning a master's in wakeboarding.

Right now, though, I have to figure out how to earn enough money to keep this wakeboarding thing going. I'm done working for MasterCraft, but I signed up with a modelling agency a couple of years ago so I let them know I'm back, in the hope they'll have some work for me over the summer. I don't really like modelling work, especially not for underwear catalogues, but the money is good and there are plenty of worse jobs out there.

Same goes with my other occasional gig: promo work. On the good days I'm basically paid to go around giving out free stuff. I usually have to wear some kind of cheesy outfit, but it's easy money. The worst jobs — and the ones I usually try to turn down — involve standing in a supermarket aisle giving people product samples and trying to get them to buy it.

Along with the promo and modelling work, I also manage to pull together a couple of coaching camps and that brings in some extra cash.

Then, just a few weeks after getting back to Auckland, I'm leaving again. This time it's to attend the World Wake Association (WWA) world champs — aka the 'real' worlds — on the Sunshine Coast. It's the first time they've been held outside the US, and having them in Aussie means Dad and my brother can come along as my support crew. There's no official New Zealand team, but Brant and a couple of other Kiwi riders also take the opportunity to set themselves against the world's best.

The contest site is perfect. It's a super-deep man-made lake sheltered by trees that ensure the water stays perfectly calm. The depth means big wakes, and the best part is that the boat of choice for this event is the Malibu Wakesetter.

I feel super comfortable on the water and advance easily through to the finals, finding myself up against riders like Adam Errington, Austin Hair and others who have consistently beaten me all year. My final run starts out as usual, with a large nuke glide out into the flats, then a whirlybird, Pete Rose and a tantrum to blind. Midway through my second pass I unleash an off-axis 720 from the heelside, snag the handle and land it perfectly.

Oh yeah, I'm on!

I follow that up with the same trick but off the toeside, nailing another perfect landing. I finish my second pass without taking a fall, except I come up short on my 900 off the double-up and case the wake, which takes me down.

Nevertheless, it's enough to earn me the win. When I hear the announcer call my name as the WWA Junior Men's World Champion, I step up on to the podium absolutely brimming with pride. I'm ecstatic!

'Our next award,' the announcer continues, 'is given only to the most outstanding up-and-coming rider . . . and I think that, after seeing that back-to-back 720 combo, we can all agree it can be awarded to no one else. Brad, congratulations! You are the recipient of the 2005 Mark Kenney Memorial Award!'

The crowd erupts and I'm holding back tears as the presenter hands me the trophy. Winning this competition was already massive for me, but the Kenney award is the greatest honour I could ever wish for. Later, I'm introduced to Mark's parents, who are here to witness his award being handed out, and I get to tell them about riding with him at the Ballistics camp. I tell them I wouldn't be here today without the inspiration that he gave me.

Today was as good as it gets.

FOUR: DAMAGE CONTROL

After my victory at the 2005 WWA worlds, I fire off an email to the C-dub team managers:

> *I'm so stoked to finish the year on such a high note, after such an average US season. Since I've won both IWSF and WWA worlds, can I please get on the team now?*

It takes over a week for a reply to come back.

> *Congratulations, Brad! A promising start.*

I keep reading and come to this sentence:

> *Unfortunately, we still don't have room for you on the junior team.*

'Oh come on!' I yell at my computer screen.

So they're still having trouble 'finding room'. I'd almost prefer it if they'd just said, 'We don't want you on our team.' And I'd understand if they said that because I did sleep in and miss my ride in Canada, and bomb pretty much every other event this season. It would be better than this bullshit excuse.

•

In early January 2006 I head back over to Australia for the pro tour.

Kris Bower again meets me at the airport, but this time in his home town, Melbourne. We hit the road for the next month. With competitions each weekend, it means pretty much everyone on tour moves up and down the coast together. It's cool because we can ride together in between stops, but it's also dangerous because it means we party together — a lot!

These Aussie lads are completely loose and the entire tour is an absolute blast. By the end I've done more partying, drinking and drugs than ever before. I've also snapped three boards, wrecked a set of bindings and lost a bunch of my belongings along the way. When it comes to my riding, I've done more than enough to make myself known as someone to look out for, while Jeff has claimed his first overall title.

At the end it's time for me to catch a flight out to Hamilton Island to see my girl! I'm damned excited about reuniting with Charlotte, and proud of myself for not giving in to the considerable amount of female temptation I've been exposed to over the last month. Although, to be honest, it wasn't all that difficult knowing I'd be seeing Char at the finish line.

As soon as I see her I pick her up and give her a big squeeze. She's working a bit during the three days I'm here, but when she's off we go on hikes, she shows me around the resort where she works, and she takes me for drinks with her staff mates. And, when we're alone in her little room, we make love. She only has a single bed but we make it work. Thankfully, her roommate is away for the whole time I'm here.

On my flight home I think about how incredible it was to see Char after months apart, but I know something just wasn't sitting right. She seemed a little distant, slightly standoffish. I push the thought to the back of my mind and remind myself that it's just a couple of weeks until she'll be home.

•

Two days later I get a message from her. She's breaking up with me.

I'm crushed, and I don't understand. She gets home in a few days. Why now? And it's my birthday tomorrow.

But I don't have any time to sit around and dwell on it because my shift at my latest promo gig — repping a bank at the start of semester for Auckland unis — is about to start. So I finish getting ready, then head out the door with a broken heart.

On campus I meet Courtney, the girl I'll be working with for the next couple of weeks. She's five years older than I am and she seems cool. She's also stunning. My heart is in pieces over Char . . . but Courtney's beauty and her company provide a welcome distraction. We get along really well and I end up telling her about the breakup. She's very sweet and supportive.

A few days later, when I know Charlotte is back, I decide to drive past her house on the off-chance that she's home, hoping I can get her to talk to me. Ever since sending that message she's completely shut me out. All I want is an explanation. I just want to understand why she ended it.

I park on the road beside her drive but I can't get out of the car. I'm frozen. What do I even say to her?

Then I see a car driving out of her driveway. It's Charlotte. She sees me and stops but she doesn't get out.

I walk over to her and she rolls down the window. 'Brad,' she says, 'what are you doing here?'

'I just want to talk. But you won't message me back or answer my calls.'

'I don't know what to say, Brad,' she replies. 'I'm sorry, but I can't talk.'

Then she rolls up her window and drives away, leaving me standing on the roadside awkward and confused. I'm at a total loss. I came here hoping we might be able to work things out face-to-face, or that I could find out what had suddenly gone wrong, but I got neither.

•

The next day, at the end of our shift, I tell Courtney about what happened. She confesses that she's in an unhappy relationship situation too.

'What are you doing tonight?' she asks. 'I think we could both use a drink.'

'I could definitely use a drink!' I feel my mood lift instantly.

We head out to a local bar, and as we're chatting, I can't take my eyes off her. This girl is ridiculously stunning! A couple of hours later we're back at my place, fooling around in my bed.

Courtney is the perfect rebound. She completely takes my mind off the breakup. And, since she's using me as an excuse to end her relationship, neither of us is looking for anything serious. We're both on the same page: happy to be friends with benefits.

•

Newly single, I make the most of Auckland's balmy summer by going out with my mates and blowing off steam at all the huge raves and foam parties we can find. While the electronic dance music pulses through me and I ride euphoric ecstasy-induced waves, I appreciate the tiny shorts and tanktops of the local talent. There's nothing like a rave for getting hot girls to leave the house in minimal clothing.

Then, it's time to hit the road. I spend some time down at the Ballistics camp in Ātiamuri with Jeff, Ants, Haydog and Aussie rider Chris O'Shea (Chris-O). A young Australian videographer called Josh Robinson, affectionately known to his friends as Carnie due to his small stature and tiny hands, is here filming us for his new project, *Playback*.

Riding with these guys is so motivating, but I also feel pressure to perform in front of the camera. We're pressed for time for good light and gas, especially as Carnie's filming from a chase boat, so we crank it up. After a couple of sessions on Lake Ātiamuri we boost over to Rotorua and hit Lake Tarawera and Lake Tikitapu to mix up the scenery.

Then Brant, Ants and I leave to chase the New Zealand contest series around the North Island. First we hit Tairua Pipe Masters, an all-rail event where I snag second place behind Jeff, while Ants takes third. The after-party absolutely goes off, and after escaping from a girl who freaks me out by swooning over my eyes — 'You have glacier eyes!' — I'm approached by a woman who wants to introduce me to her extremely hot blonde daughter. I don't think she knows what she's getting her daughter into, but the daughter certainly does. I take her back to my accommodation and we fuck all night. I emerge the next day with my back and chest covered in scratches. That girl was vicious!

Next stop is the North Island champs, and since Jeff isn't competing, I have no trouble taking the win, while Ants and Brant come second and third respectively. After that we're down to the Hawke's Bay for an event called Wake Up, where Ants beats me, then on to the capital city for X-Air to put on a demo in Wellington Harbour. The water is far too rough to ride in so we park the boat and truck in a high-foot-traffic area of the event, then start drinking and chatting up girls, inviting them to sit in the boat and drink with us. Things take a messy turn when we get our hands on some of the new legal party pills.

The next morning, having basically owned every town we've competed in and raked in a fair bit of prize money along the way, it's time to get back up to Auckland. No sooner do we arrive than I'm off again, this time to Melbourne to continue filming for *Playback*. I head out on a houseboat with Chris-O and another Aussie rider, Troy Mackey. Bower and a *Wake* photographer come along too, and get some awesome shots for the mag.

As it happens, Courtney is in Melbourne at the same time so she joins us on the boat, which is great for me because it means we get the master bedroom. It has mirrors all over the walls, which we definitely make good use of.

When I get home there's no time to get cosy, as I get invited to feature in another film. And the best thing about this one? It's set in Tahiti. The producer, Christian Fitzpatrick, gave me my first spot in a wakeboarding movie last year. It was called *Accidental*. This latest one, his second major wakeboarding film, is *Deliberate*.

I feel like everything is beginning to take off for me. Since claiming my second world title and meeting the awesome crew on the Aussie pro tour, the wins just seem to keep coming. Contest placings, magazine shoots, filming trips — it's all coming together. And I owe so much of my success to Jeff Weatherall and Kris Bower. Between them, they've helped me break into the Aussie and US wakeboarding scene by introducing me to all the key people. These guys accepted me, and as a result the rest of the industry seems to be accepting me too.

•

Jeff is there to meet us at the airport in Tahiti, a couple of dudes on either side practically holding him up. He got here a few days ago, and there are no prizes for guessing what he's been up to: hanging out and drinking with the locals.

'You look like you've been having a great time,' says Christian the film producer.

'Yeah, it's fucking sweet here, bro,' Jeff replies, then introduces us to the two dudes holding him up. 'This is Arnaud and Ojip.' He pronounces their names *Are-nu* and *O-Gee*. 'Let's go. The van's out this way.'

The next morning we head straight down to the wakeboard school to meet the guy who owns and runs it. He's also called Arnaud, and we've arranged to use his MasterCraft X2 while we're here. It's an awesome spot this guy has, with a beautiful old building right on the water's edge. It would be a dream to live and ride here every day.

When we hit the water I realise it's even better than a dream. It's a tropical paradise. The water is calm and crystal clear, while in the distance huge waves crash at the reef's edge. I strap in and jump into the water for my maiden ride, and for the first few minutes after I'm up I'm not even interested in hitting the wake. I'm completely enthralled by my surroundings — coral reefs and sea life passing by under me, palm trees and sandy beaches scattered along the shoreline. We even pass a local out for a paddle in his little outrigger canoe.

How did I even get here?

•

I get home from the most awesome time in Tahiti just in time for nationals and, while I put up my best fight yet, I once again end up the bridesmaid to Jeff, while Tony comes in third.

Not long after, I head back to Orlando. I'm feeling a bit guilty about leaving. Dad's Parkinson's disease has progressed to the point where he can no longer be a builder. He's found another job that's less physically demanding, but it's definitely noticeable that he's not as able as he once was. I can't help wondering how far it will progress while I'm gone.

Alex Brown picks me up from the airport, with two blondes in tow. Again, I didn't plan much coming into this season, but thankfully I can rely on Alex to let me crash on his couch until I figure something out. The riding is always so good at his place.

'This is Gemma and Laura,' he says, introducing me to the two girls.

Back at his place it's straight into the drinking games and not long after that I'm in the spare bed with Gemma. She's just my type: petite, athletic, with small boobs and a phenomenal arse. And, just like that, I'm right back into the swing of things — riding, partying, hooking up with girls.

•

A few weeks later we're due to leave on the Junior pro tour. The day before, Alex heads out to run an errand. I stay at his parents' house with the three other friends who are here — Nick, Robby and Wade. We're out the front of the house when Wade spots a black racer snake in the garden right beside us. It's big, but harmless. I'm spooked enough that I begin to back away, but Wade goes in after it. These Florida boys are something else! He emerges with the snake in his hands, and soon we've hatched a plan.

When Alex gets home, the rest of us take turns making subtle comments to him about his body odour. 'Maybe you should take a shower, bro,' I say.

He soon heads off to his ensuite bathroom and we all crowd around the door, listening out for his reaction. Minutes go by and all we hear is the sound of running water. Eventually the door opens and Alex walks out to find us all huddled together, staring at him bewildered.

'What?' he says. 'What are you guys up to? What are you looking at?'

We push past him into the bathroom and I open the door to the shower.

'It's empty!' says Robby.

'Where the hell did it go?' Wade says.

'There's no way it could've got out!' Nick adds, scratching his head as he surveys the shower, which is over a bathtub completely enclosed by frosted glass doors.

'No way *what* got out?' Alex is suspicious. 'What the fuck did you guys do?'

'Well,' I say, 'there *was* a four-foot black snake in your shower . . . but I guess it went down the drain.'

'*Ohhhh!*' Alex starts laughing. 'That's fucked up, you guys!'

We road-trip up to Acworth, Georgia, for the first stop of the Junior pro tour. I go into the event feeling confident but I go down twice in my run. Alex flops as well, so unfortunately neither of us qualifies for the tour. There's not much point sticking around so we boost back to his place to get some more riding in.

First thing the next morning we're out on the water. Towards the end of my set I ask Alex to roll me some doubles. On a left double, I attempt a toeside roll-to-blind. It's a trick I can do easily off the wake, but the plan is to take it bigger off a double-up so I can eventually add an extra 180 to it. On the landing, while my back is still arched from passing the handle behind it, I case the second wake hard.

I instantly feel a sharp pain in my lower back. When I get back into the boat I'm struggling to stand upright and any movement makes it worse. Back at Alex's, I recline on the couch. After handing me an ice-pack to lie on, Alex disappears to his room, closing the door behind him.

About five minutes later I hear some kind of commotion. A near-womanly squeal is followed by a deep thud, then the door swings open and Alex emerges wide-eyed and wrapped in a towel.

'You all right in there, bro?' I ask.

'Dude! I completely forgot about that fucking snake!' he says. 'I was mid-shower and I felt something around my leg . . .'

I burst out laughing but am forced to stop by the pain in my back. 'Hahaha — *oowww!* Oh my god, dude! So I assume that thud was you busting your arse on the tiles?'

'Yeah, man, I was outta there! That thing was coiling its way up my leg like it was going for the family jewels!'

'That's the stuff of nightmares, right there,' I say. But it's still some seriously funny shit!

•

For the next week I focus on resting up. Alex is training for a competition — as was I until I tweaked my back — so I drive for him when he wants to ride. By the time competition day comes around my back is feeling good enough for me to enter. It's just an amateur event at the Malibu boats dealership, but the 'outlaw' division is usually stacked with up-and-coming talent so it's worth entering. And it pays off — with a standup run, I take the win!

It comes at a cost, though. When I'm called up to the podium to receive my trophy I can't even stand up straight and have to hobble over, using my board as a crutch. The win feels good but I'm regretting riding because the pain's even worse now.

I make an appointment with a chiropractor who treats a bunch of other wakeboarders. The walls of Dr G's office are lined with autographed photos of all sorts of top athletes, particularly pro golfers.

He asks me about what happened, then takes an X-ray of my lower back.

'Okay, your injury is most likely a pinched nerve,' he says. 'See this here?' He points at the X-ray. 'Your hips are tilted because your back muscles are overdeveloped, and your abdominals aren't strong enough to balance it out.'

He then gets me to lie on the table and proceeds to twist and crack my spine, bringing me back into alignment.

For the next month I see Dr G twice a week. He also instructs me to stay off the water.

Fortunately, I've got Alex to help me find constructive ways to pass the time. One thing we focus on is developing stronger abs, challenging each other to do a hundred push-ups a day. We amuse ourselves with chess and pool. Alex even hatches an ingenious plan for getting ridiculously good at drinking games while actually being kinder to our bodies. Basically, we replace the beer with water. It starts with water quarters, then we progress to water pong. I don't think either of us has ever been so hydrated in our entire lives. And the next time we play actual drinking games it's almost unfair how good we are.

•

Thankfully, after a month my back feels good enough for me to start riding again, just in time for Christian's arrival in Orlando. He's here to finish off filming for *Deliberate*, so I'm glad to be fit enough to perform for the camera. I put in a solid couple of weeks, alongside Jeff, Chris-O, Dean Smith, Troy Mackey and the rest of the Aussie crew, and I'm stoked to get my first wake-to-wake 900 down on film too.

Once again, I've reached the end of my time on Alex's parents' couch, so Alex and I find an apartment to move into with two friends. For the first few weeks after we sign the lease it's just me, as the others aren't quite ready to make the move.

The next stop on the pro tour is coming up, and I've been waiting to hear whether I can get a wild-card entry. Finally, with just two weeks to spare, the email comes through and I'm in. I'm excited and want to celebrate but I'm all alone, so I head outside and kick it with a few of the local kids, one of whom I've befriended because he's my neighbour.

I'm the only white dude in a group of black kids — that's the general demographic of this apartment complex — but they're all cool with me. One of the shorter kids starts showing off with some gymnastic-style backflips and, in my wild-card joy, I decide to join in and show him that the tall white kid can do it too. Only I overshoot my landing and come down with my left foot on the corner of a concrete base to a power box.

Oooouch! What the fuck have I done?

The next day I limp in to Dr G's office and ask him to X-ray my foot.

'You've broken one of your metatarsals,' he tells me. 'It's not too bad but you need to stay off it for a few weeks.'

A few weeks? The junior tour is less than a fortnight away.

I spend the next week with my foot iced and elevated, and the swelling goes down enough that I'm able to hobble about on it without crutches. So, with just a week to go before my event, I decide to start riding again. It hurts, but I discover the injury has an unexpected positive side-effect. Usually when I do a 900 off the wake, I land it best by taking off with a bit of an extra stomp off my front foot. That's my sore foot — so, if it hurts, then I know I've done it right and I can commit to the full spin. My 900 becomes much more consistent thanks to my broken foot.

The day before I'm due to fly out, I go to O-Town to get in some final training on their transfer box. There's one on tour, and I know it's the part of my riding that needs the most work.

Jimmy, one of the O-Town staff, drives the ski for me. I take a handful of laps hitting the transfer box and another rail, dubbed 'Hillary' for its hill-like contours — up, flat, up, flat, then a long decline.

On my next hit of the transfer, I crash.

'One more,' I tell Jimmy as he pulls by.

On the way out of my final lap I go for a frontside boardslide-up Hillary, but I slip out and get taco-ed over the rail, taking it to the stomach. Then my board hooks an exposed post and swings me suddenly into the side of the feature. My lead leg smacks into the four-by-four post and I'm spat off the rail and into the water.

Jimmy races back to see if I'm okay.

'Yeah, I think so. Just feels like a dead leg,' I reply hopefully.

I get on the back of the ski for the ride in, and at the dock I hobble back and forth.

It's just a dead leg, I tell myself. *You just need to walk it off.*

But the pain's not going away. In fact it's getting worse. I lie down and rub my leg, which does nothing to help.

I call Dr G, who sends me to the hospital.

Another X-ray. Another broken bone.

This time I've put a big crack through my fibula. Thankfully, it's the smaller, less load-bearing bone in my lower leg, and it's just a crack, so I'm sent home with crutches. But there's no way I'm going to my competition. I'm out of the Junior pro tour, likely for the rest of the season.

•

It takes a month for my leg to heal enough for me to ride again. In that time I drive the boat for Alex and the guys, I work on my core strength to prevent further back injury, and I continue to see Dr G for adjustments. My single-life antics also continue. I've been hanging out with a blonde I met at a recent lake party called Floatstock and, now that I've upgraded from the air mattress to an actual bed, I'm able to bring my core-strengthening exercises into the bedroom.

It's amazing to finally get back on the water. I feel fit and healthy, and I set my sights on the 2006 WWA world champs in Fort Worth, Texas, which are coming up at the end of September, less than a month away.

But it's not just bones I've been breaking this season. Even having spent more days off the water than on it, I've still managed to break more boards this summer than any other. My stature is probably a contributing factor, since I'm bigger than most top wakeboarders, who tend to be shorter, lighter and built more like gymnasts. But also CWB have been making their boards lighter and more rigid. For the first half of the year I kept snapping them like twigs, going through a board every week or two. C-dub was good at sending me fresh ones but after a while they got fed up. So they custom-made two boards for me, reinforced with extra fibreglass. Although much heavier, these boards have lasted much longer. I've only just broken the first one after having it for a couple of months.

So I call my US contact to get a couple more boards sent out.

'Sorry, Brad,' he says, 'we just can't send you any more.'

'Wait, what? Why not?'

'You've been through so many this season, and we even sent you those two custom boards to get you through the rest of the summer. That's all we've got for you.'

'Well, I just broke one of the customs, so I'm down to my last board.' I reply.

'Sorry, Brad, I just can't send you any more boards.'

'So if you're not going to supply me with boards, then why am I even sponsored by you?'

'To be honest, Brad, we actually don't sponsor you,' he replies. 'We've just been helping out our New Zealand distributors by getting you boards while you're here.'

So, just like that, my five-year relationship with CWB appears to be at an end. I stood on the podium and lifted their boards high at two world championships, so I'm pretty gutted. But I need to talk with the guys back in New Zealand to see if there's anything they can do from their end. I think back to them repeatedly telling me there isn't 'room' on the junior team for me, even after I won two world titles.

●

If I do need to find myself a new sponsor, the timing couldn't have worked out better. Surf Expo, the world's largest and longest-running board sports and beach-lifestyle trade show, is held right here in Orlando, and it's almost upon us. All of the biggest and best wakeboarding brands will be there. I'm excited to see if I get any bites.

A rumour has been floating around that the owners of Hyperlite have left the company and taken some of the brand's top riders to start something new. But when we get to Expo I don't see any new board brands here. Some other riders we bump into say they reckon there's a stand over at Orlando Watersports Complex, so after an hour at Expo we race over there.

Ronix Wakeboards the banners read.

Inside the marquee, a TV up on the wall instantly catches our attention.

'No fucking way!' Alex says, eyes glued to the screen.

'Holy shit!' My jaw drops. 'That was a 1080!'

For the next few minutes we're fixed to the spot, enthralled by footage of Danny Harf stomping a perfect switch heelside 1080 — the first trick of its kind — on repeat. And the board he's riding? His new Ronix pro model, the One.

We finally snap out of our trance and I spot Chad Sharpe from the Pointless Posse — I met him at Parks's Double or Nothing. We get chatting and he introduces me to Herb O'Brien, who founded Hyperlite back in the early nineties, and his son Paul. This duo are the ones behind Ronix, and I'm a bit nervous to meet them. Herb especially is something of a legend in the water-ski and wakeboard industry. It's only a brief encounter, as they're busy guys with hundreds of people to meet.

After parting ways with them I turn to Chad. 'Hey,' I say, 'I heard there's some sort of try-out event to pick riders for the team. Is that right?'

'Yeah, bro,' Chad replies. 'It's being held after worlds.'

Agh! That's after I'm scheduled to fly home. 'Do you think there's any chance I could ride for you guys some time before I leave Florida?' I ask hopefully, explaining about my flight.

'Yeah, man!' He glances outside, then looks around like he's trying to spot someone. 'Have you got your stuff with you? We could go right now.'

My heart almost stops. 'Er . . . ye — yeah, bro. I'll go grab it now.'

'Cool,' he says casually. 'I'll just grab the guys and we'll meet you down at the dock.'

I am not mentally prepared for this, but there's no way I'm passing up the opportunity.

Outside, the sun has dropped below the horizon so we're running on the glow that dusk provides. Down at the dock, Chad's waiting by the boat with 'the guys' — none other than Danny Harf and Parks Bonifay, the other two legends who have come with Herb and Paul to start this epic new board brand.

Is this really happening? Holy shit.

I step into my old CWB bindings, feeling slightly embarrassed since the new Ronix boots are a hundred times cooler, while the others climb onto the boat. Alex follows them, and shoots me a look as if to say, *No pressure, bro.* He knows exactly how I'm feeling. Then he smiles and nods as if to add, *You've got this! Fucking crush it.*

Feeling more nervous than I've ever felt at any tour stop or world champs, I take a deep breath to clear my thoughts and pull myself into focus.

The throttle goes down and I leap onto the water.

For the next 15 minutes I crush one of the best rides I've had all season. I land everything, including my tantrum to blind, Pete Rose, roll to blind, whirly-five and toeside roll to blind — which I know Danny will appreciate, since he's the one who invented it. I stomp both heel and toe 720s, then send a huge nuke glide into the flats — that one's for Chad — and then I send another one but drop it to fakie — a grabbed version of one of Parks's signature tricks, the buttafuoco. I keep going until it's so dark it's hard to see the wake, and finish up with a toe 900 that I just drop the handle on.

My three biggest heroes in wake give me props, so I'm pretty chuffed.

On the drive home, Alex fills me in on what they had to say while I was riding. Apparently, Parks got especially stoked on the nuclear buttafuoco.

'Shit, man,' Chad apparently said. 'I didn't realise this kid rides so good!'

•

A few days later Alex and I are out with a few others on East Crooked Lake. It's the next lake over from Alex's, and it's much better to ride on due to the shelter provided by the surrounding small hills. It's deep and calm with a nice, long shoreline. Perfect conditions.

I ride after Alex, who's been working on grabbing his moby dick properly. It's a trick I haven't done in years, and I don't even recall why I stopped doing it since I had it consistent and big. So I get a little cocky and decide I'll show my friend how it's done.

After warming up quickly I cut out wide, then turn a hard edge in to send a moby dick into the flats. I get upside down and pass the handle behind my back, then reach down for the grab, but, as I spot the water, I realise I'm behind on my flip rotation. So I tug the handle across my body and only just get my board down. The momentum of the late rotation crumples my upper body, and my chin smacks straight on top of my knee as I continue down into the water.

I'm met with a familiar pain. I know instantly that I've broken my leg again. I can also feel blood dripping from my split-open chin.

What a way to end the season.

And as if to rub extra salt in the wound, when I go to check into my flight home, I realise I've left my passport on the previous connecting flight and it's now off to Hawaii on its own. Thankfully I bump into a guy named Mouse who is on the same flight. He's friends with Ants and Brant and, since I'm flat broke, he kindly saves my arse by giving me $100 to get me through till the next day when my passport returns and I can fly home.

•

I move back into Mum's to learn that my brother Alex has been splitting his time between her place and Dad's, and Monique's gone flatting. Dad is still independent — he can still drive and has been doing a bit of work — but his health is definitely on the decline, and I feel renewed guilt for being away for so long. I resolve to make up for my absence now that I'm back.

Within a week of getting home I'm off my crutches and have lost the cast. After checking my X-rays, the orthopaedic surgeon seems pretty unconcerned. 'It'll heal on its own,' he says. 'And you're good to walk on it. Just give it a month before you start wakeboarding again.'

But, while I'm pleasantly surprised to have been able to ditch the crutches, it seems like my whole body is out of whack from limping and hobbling around. I decide to spend the few weeks until the end of the year focused on rehabbing my body.

One afternoon Alex and I head around to the small townhouse in Remuera that Dad's now living in, and we find the place in a bit of a state. Dad's lying on the floor all cramped up, and there are multiple holes and dents in the walls from where he's punched or kicked them, likely through frustration at trying to get himself moving. It's clear that he's not okay, not just in physical health but also mentally. Though he tried to hide it, I don't think he took the divorce well. He did have a girlfriend for a while, but she recently returned to her ex. I think Dad's held on to the hope that he and Mum might get back together. While I admire his refusal to give up, I also know it's futile. It's just never going to happen.

Once we've got him up off the floor, Alex and I sit with him and he hesitantly opens up to us. He tells us how he's struggling with the fact that he's slowly losing control of his body. He just gets so angry at being in this situation, he says, especially when his life seemed to be on such a good path. I try to imagine what he went through when he and Mum split, and I realise he must have felt like he was almost losing us kids too. We couldn't live with him in his old studio, and the spare room at this new place isn't exactly ideal either — it makes me admire my brother's efforts even more.

I can see how, to Dad, it must've felt like he lost everything, and now his health was packing up too. It's got to be especially hard for a man who has always been so capable with his hands. After we've been sitting for a while his movement returns — the meds must be kicking in, and his mood lifts with it. He's always been an optimist and it's good to see that start to return to him now that his body is cooperating.

Alex and I go down to the garage and grab some putty and gib off-cuts, then get to work repairing some of the damage to the walls. Before we leave, Dad tells us he's decided to seek some anger-management counselling. 'It's not fair on you to have to come over and fix my mess,' he says. 'So I'm working on being better.'

I admire him for coming to the decision to seek help on his own. It must be a difficult thing to come to terms with. It's not the last time we find our dad in a frozen, cramped-up state, however.

Then I give him a big hug and we both pat each other firmly on the back. It's our way of saying, 'I love you.'

•

I start working to make a dent in the debt I've accrued while in the US. As well as promo work, I pick up some gardening work for a friend of Mum's.

I still haven't heard anything from Ronix after my ride at OWC, but I'm not happy about how CWB cut me off in the US so it's obvious that a change is needed. After my leg has healed, I test out Jeff's pro model J-Star board and fall in love with it instantly. The next day I send an email to CWB NZ:

> *I am not jumping ship to another sponsor, but for now I've just decided to ride a board that I enjoy riding. I'm open to discussing the possibility of getting me back on your boards, but I'm not happy with how I've been treated in the States, so things would need to change there. Thank you for everything you've done for me so far, I really appreciate it.*

The response makes no offer, in fact I think it's a rather unsavoury email that solidifies my departure from CWB and leaves me as a free agent.

•

At the end of November, Mum gets my siblings and me together. She won't tell us why, only that she needs to talk to us about something.

When we're gathered, she finally delivers the news — and it hits us like a ton of bricks.

'I've been diagnosed with breast cancer,' she says. 'They found a lump in my breast.'

My mind immediately starts racing.

'It seems like they caught it early,' she goes on, 'but I have to have a mastectomy.'

'What's a mastectomy?' Alex asks.

Mum explains that the surgeons will be removing her breast. 'But I'm going to be okay,' she says reassuringly.

Teary-eyed, we all give Mum a big hug.

Just a few days later she undergoes surgery, and she recovers surprisingly quickly. In fact I'm blown away when, less than a week after the operation, she and Gordon fly down to Wellington for an Elton John concert.

When she arrives home, she gets us together for another talk. I'm a bit nervous after our last sit-down conversation, but this time she's smiling.

'Gordon proposed,' she says. 'We're getting married.'

Honestly, this news is almost as unexpected as the first lot. I feel a little conflicted to begin with, but of course it's great. I'm so happy for her. I'm happy for both of them, actually. Gordon is great for Mum, and I can tell he really loves her. I just can't help worrying about how Dad will take this news.

●

At the end of December I head down to Mangakino to celebrate new year with Brant and Ants, who both spent the New Zealand winter over in the UK.

Brant's dad, Kev, has a place in Mangakino, and it's awesome to have a base for the summer. The town itself is a bit notorious for having a gang presence, but they've put a lot of effort into cleaning it up in recent years. Mangakino sits on the shores of Lake Maraetai, which is surrounded by huge pine trees and, thanks to its boomerang shape, provides great water conditions in almost any wind. There's just one problem: we don't have a boat. So we hitch rides with whoever we can, always making sure to bring along Ants' three fat sacks for ballast and the huge pump that quickly fills them. Kiwis generally seem to have an aversion towards loading their boats, but with the three of us and the fat sacks on board, we can usually get a good wake out of almost anything.

Early on New Year's Eve the three of us are sitting around the table playing cards and sipping on special batch Jack and Coke. We've got a big sack of weed and we take turns rolling spliffs, making sure the next one is rolled before the one previous is extinguished. I pride myself on rolling the perfect tapered cone-shaped doobie, but I am yet to master the back roll — where it's rolled with the paper inside out, so that any excess paper stays on the outside and can be removed — the guys are teaching me.

A few hours, a handful of drinks and just as many spliffs later, Brant's British girlfriend calls out that dinner is ready. But when I stand up the world starts spinning and I have to sit straight back down. I spend the next couple of hours sitting with my head in my hands, feeling super nauseous. I can't even sit up, let alone eat. When I finally get myself outside to the back of the house, I puke all over the grass.

I'm in bed and passed out by ten, completely missing the countdown to the new year.

It's a fitting end to what has been a less than spectacular year.

FIVE: ON THE UP

The Aussie pro tour in January 2007 doesn't go well for me in terms of contest results, but as usual it's an absolute blast riding, hanging and partying with the Aussie crew. Back to Auckland and it's straight into a hectic New Zealand series. First off, we road-trip down to Napier for an event called Wake Up: Bower is commentating and Ants and Brant and I are competing.

I manage to take my first win for the year, swapping places with Ants after he beat me last year.

Afterwards, we head to Brant's bach for a few days, then it's on to Tairua for Pipe Masters. On the way, I stop at Hamilton airport to collect a stunning girl I met while in Australia. Her name is Hannah, and she was one of the trophy girls — as in, she literally presented the trophies at the awards banquet at the end of the pro tour. As soon as I set eyes on her I wanted her — and she was *my* trophy that night. Afterwards, I lay in bed looking at her and could barely believe she was beside me. When I floated the idea of her visiting me in New Zealand she said yes but honestly I wasn't sure she'd come. I'm very happy that she has.

As soon as she's safely strapped into my Honda Prelude I put my foot down. The guy I've been doing gardening work for has let me use his holiday place in Tairua, and I want to get Hannah there ASAP! We arrive just after one in the morning and we waste no time getting jiggy. I have the next morning off since the tide won't be high enough for us to ride till later on, so Hannah and I don't leave the bedroom and can barely prise ourselves apart. Eventually, though, we take a break and go to the beach for a swim, only to end up having sex in the ocean too. I literally can't keep my hands off this girl.

In the main Pipe Masters event the next day I ride well enough to make it to third place. On the podium I'm once again standing just below Jeff, who's won the top spot. The after-party's solid, and the next morning we're off to our next stop: Lake Karāpiro. There I win the North Island championship, and I'm extra stoked to have Hannah there to witness my triumph. She's staying for a couple more days, so we head down to Mangakino together with Ants and Brant.

On her last night, the guys and I are hanging out in the lounge, passing around a spliff while she takes a shower.

'So what's the go with the sweetheart once she goes back to Aussie?' Ants asks.

'I really don't know, dude,' I reply. 'She wants us to be together, and I really like her, but I live between here and the US, and she lives in Aussie. I just don't see how we would make it work.'

'B-rad's not a one-woman man!' Ants laughs, and Brant and I have a bit of a chuckle too.

Not a minute later, Hannah walks out of the bathroom in her bathrobe. She keeps her head down, not looking at me or anyone else as she walks straight through the lounge to our bedroom.

I follow her a minute later, and find her crying on the bed.

'I heard you guys laughing about you not being a one-woman man,' she says between sobs.

Aah shit.

'It's not really that . . .' I try to explain. 'It's just that the distance between the places we live is a challenge.'

In actual fact, the challenge for me right now is attempting to even have this conversation. I'm super stoned and I'm struggling to string the right words together.

I hold her in my arms. 'Look,' I say, 'I think you're incredible, and I wish we could be together, but I just think the distance is too much of a hurdle.'

The sobbing subsides and she stands and wipes her eyes. 'I was just excited to show you this,' she says, taking off her robe. Underneath, she's wearing the most mind-blowingly sexy lingerie, complete with a corset and everything. I've never seen such sex appeal standing right in front of me, close enough to actually touch.

Oh god, she's making it so hard to let her go!

I can't resist. So we have some epic goodbye sex before she goes home.

Later on, when I drop her at the airport, we say an emotional goodbye. Just before she disappears she stops and looks back at me one last time. Her blue eyes are sparkling with tears.

•

The following weekend it's the wakeboard nationals. They're being held earlier this year, as they're in the South Island for the first time.

We road-trip down to Wellington with the competition boat in tow, then take the ferry across Cook Strait and drive to Blenheim, where the event's being held. The river is shallow, making the wake small, but the challenging course is offset by the fact that my two major rivals won't be here this year. Jeff's gone back to Australia to have keyhole surgery on his knee, and Tony's also out with a blown knee.

But I don't get away with zero competition. Brant rides really well, and Ants puts the pressure on by absolutely killing it in his finals run. After my two passes, it's too close to call between Ants and me, with my double-up to come. Once again, Bower's on the mic and, with him amping me up, I cut in and connect perfectly with the third roller and stomp the first 900 ever done at New Zealand nationals. That's all it takes for me to claim first place. Ants comes in second, with Brant third.

Standing atop the podium, I watch as the trophy is filled to the brim with beer. Not only am I thrilled to finally get to drink from it, but also I couldn't be more stoked to have my best friends standing on either side of me. It doesn't feel like a complete victory, though, because the one man who always beats me isn't here.

With everyone cheering, and a timer going, I scull the trophy's liquid contents in 11 seconds flat. Take that, Jeff!

•

We head further south to Christchurch, where we're catching up with Mouse at his family's private ski lake. It's great to see him again after he saved my arse at LA airport, and to have a chance to return the favour: Ants, Brant and I are here to put on a demo at his family's pro-am water-ski event.

While we're here, Ants introduces me to a guy named Duncan Hancock, who's the new Ronix dealer for New Zealand. I let him know I'm a free agent.

'I'd love to ride for Ronix,' I say.

'Done!' he replies. 'But I don't have any boards for you to try, unfortunately. I'm still awaiting our first shipment.'

'No worries,' I say. 'I'll just spray-paint Ronix across the bottom of my board for now, but if you could get Ronix US to have some gear waiting for me in the States, that would be awesome.'

I know I don't need to test-ride anything. If Danny Harf can stomp a switch heel 10 on the One, then I already know that's the board I want.

'Easy as, big fella,' Duncan says happily. 'Welcome aboard!'

And just like that, I'm in with the ultimate board company. I'm unbelievably stoked.

The summer is coming to an end but I have one more mission I want to accomplish before I take off back to the US. A couple of years ago Brant showed me a concrete spillway near Mangakino that's about 4 metres high.

'You could do a step-up from the bottom to the top using a big kicker,' Brant said, and my eyes lit up.

I haven't been able to stop dreaming about it since. We see it done all the time in snowboarding and motocross but it's never been done before in wakeboarding. Since wakeboarding is limited to a flat surface of water, and since what goes up must come down, wakeboarders have always been somewhat limited in terms of how high they can go. Lately we've been seeing more spillway drops and creative riding thanks to the inclusion of the winch-pull system, but I still haven't seen anyone go up a step-up.

I plan to be the first.

I know I'll need an extra-large kicker to pull it off, so I source a freestyle motocross kicker from a friend. After adding a plastic surface to the ramp, I organise a jet-ski and an extra-long rope, to account for the fact that the jet-ski will have to start in the lake at the top of the wall, while I'll be starting at the bottom. Then I set a date, round up some helpers and invite the crew from MTV to film it. Even Mum drives down to watch nervously.

It takes weeks of prep, days of errands, hours of set-up and a couple of practice runs, but finally I'm ready to go for it. Brant takes off on the jet-ski as I leap onto the water and start accelerating towards the large kicker. But I'm going too fast and practically collide with it, and the ramp turns out to be way too steep. It sends me up and completely out of control, flipping me upside down. I brace for impact, but thankfully I make it the necessary 4 metres up and 20 metres across the gap and clear the spillway, taking a heavy crash into the lake at the top.

Well, so much for that, I think. But I can't back out now.

Next time I get Brant to drive more slowly. I manage to stay upright but the rope is pinged out of my hands mid-air, as it gets caught on the piping that was supposed to stop it from dragging over the concrete.

Attempts three, four and five are not much better but I don't want to stop until I land this thing. I went to so much effort to make it happen, the TV crew are here, and I just want to nail this challenge. I step up for another go.

Then Mum steps in and calls it quits before I end up seriously hurting myself.

Although I'm not happy about it at first, I come to accept that it was the right move.

'I'll be back!' I tell the wall as we drive away.

•

Once again, I'm flying to the States without much of a plan. I don't know where I'll be living, and up until a couple of days ago I didn't even have a ride from the airport, since Alex is away for the weekend. Instead, I've arranged for a girl I don't really know to pick me up.

I hear a car horn honking and look up to see her head hanging out the window of a black truck. I wave and carry my bags over. I've never actually met her in person before but we became friends on Myspace a few months ago and have been talking a little since. Her name is Molly and she's just my type with her blonde hair and blue eyes. She's a total hottie. The fact that she's into wakeboarding only sweetens the deal.

We roll to a mutual friend's place where there's already a small party going on. I jump in on the next game of beer pong with Molly as my teammate, and I quickly realise how cool she is. She's not one of those prissy girls, but more like one of the guys — just inside a ridiculously attractive girl's body.

I still don't have a place to crash tonight, so I ask Molly if I can stay at hers.

'Yeah, no problem,' she says. 'The only thing is that my mom is staying with me at the moment, but it should be fine for you to crash on the couch.'

We arrive at her place and I meet her mum. She seems pretty cool, and is welcoming of me.

After her mum goes to bed, Molly and I put on a movie, and it's not long before we're cuddled up on the couch. Then we start making out. This whole winging-it approach to accommodation is working out better than expected!

We don't take things any further, though. After the movie finishes, Molly goes to bed and I pass out on the couch.

The next day she gives me a lift to scoop up my new Ronix setup: two beautiful crisp-white One boards, with stylish silver accents and subtle pinstripes, and a matching pair of One boots. Then we head to a coaching session that Molly has booked with pro rider Sean O'Brien. I'm pleasantly surprised to see that she's actually pretty good out on the water, which makes me even more attracted to her.

When she's done, I ask Sean if I can take a quick set.

'Yeah, go for it,' he says.

I slip my feet inside my new boots and I'm blown away. They are unbelievably comfortable — soft yet firm, flexible yet supportive; they're levels above anything else! And my first ride on the One is even better than I expected. I feel instantly connected with the board, which responds to my every command and pops off the wake like a dream, and the landings feel really solid. The final touch comes at the end of my set, when I get Sean to roll me a double-up and I stomp my very first heelside 900. I've spent all summer back in New Zealand trying to master this trick, but never stuck it.

I couldn't be more sold on this board. I'm Ronix all the way!

•

By the time we get back to Molly's apartment it's just after midday, and her mum is drunk. The welcoming woman I met yesterday has disappeared, and this one is spoiling for a fight. She engages Molly in a screaming match, although I can't see any real reason for her anger, and all Molly can do is try to defend herself.

It also happens to be Mother's Day. Earlier this morning Molly gave her mum a teddy bear that says 'I love you' when you squeeze its belly. Now, her mum is wielding the teddy like a hostage. She grabs one of the spare sharp fins from her daughter's board and starts stabbing the teddy bear, while screaming all sorts of abuse at her daughter. Then, as if on cue, the teddy bear says, almost mockingly, 'I love you.'

I'm frozen stiff. I want to help Molly, but it's not my place to get in the middle of this.

Eventually her mum seems to be calming down, but then she suddenly grabs the car keys and storms out. We rush out after her.

Okay, I think, *now it's time for me to step in.*

I stand between her and the driver's seat. There's no way I'm letting her drive in this state. I manage to get the keys off her, and help Molly regain control of the situation.

Half an hour later we're driving her mum to the airport to fly home to New York. Her flight isn't until later that night, but she can figure something out to pass the time. Or not. We just want to make sure she at least gets to the airport safely. Once we've dropped her off we say goodbye and leave her there to sort herself out.

Back in the apartment, it feels eerily calm after such chaos. That's when Molly tells me that her mum suffers from bipolar disorder, and is also an alcoholic.

She explains that they're really close, and get along well most of the time, but occasionally she has bad episodes. Molly has become used to it.

She is exhausted. She curls up on her outdoor chair and is soon asleep. As I sit there watching over her, I'm filled with a feeling of protectiveness. No one should have to put up with that shit, especially not from their own mother. I admire her strength and bravery. Plus, she looks adorable sleeping. This is all so new, but I think I'm falling for her.

That night Molly invites me into her bed. She's sweet and naughty, and the sex is incredible, but it goes beyond the physical act. The intimacy between us is something special.

It's barely 24 hours since I met this girl in person, and I'm already hooked.

•

A few days later, Alex is back so I link up with him at his parents' place. His girlfriend's family just bought a new Malibu Wakesetter and we're excited to ride behind it. We head over to their home on East Crooked Lake and get out on the water with our girls, Molly and Michelle, and Michelle's younger brother Cole. He's a cool kid and actually rips behind the boat, plus the girls hit it off straight away. We've ended up with a super-fun boat crew, and being on my favourite lake and riding my favourite wake means this feels pretty close to perfect.

Every day for the next few weeks we're out on the lake with our babes in bikinis and my mix CDs pumping the best tunes, from my favourite hip-hop to amping punk rock to funky electronic dance music. I feel like things have come together to make for the best training conditions possible and I know it's benefitting my riding. The vibe is consistently high. The water conditions are always prime, as the lake is deep, flat and sheltered. The wake is big, and the driving's consistent since I've always got Alex at the helm when I'm riding. The days often end in a party, bringing our friends together with Molly and Michelle's friends.

After so many ultimate lake days it's finally time to head up to Atlanta for the first tour stop. I'm pumped and nervous this year, as I've stepped up into the pro division — making it my rookie year as a pro. This stop is my first of two opportunities to qualify for the whole tour, and I'm looking forward to seeing how I fare against the best of the best. I'm also feeling pretty honoured to be one of only a few people repping for Ronix.

Unfortunately the pressure proves too much and I'm knocked out of the comp in the first round. I'm really having trouble with consistency under pressure.

Back in Orlando, I move in with Jeff and Cathy. They're back on Lake Jessamine this summer, but this time we're in an actual house. It's much more homely than the shack we were in a couple of years ago, and I even have my own room. We're living with a rad English couple who bought the place because they love wakeboarding. Jeff's brother Greg, a photographer, is also living with us, so we take advantage of that and get out on the lake for shoots that make the most of that golden-hour light at the start and end of the day.

Within a couple of weeks I get my next opportunity to qualify for the pro tour and Jeff and I fly up to Texas. The venue is perfect and the spectators come out in force — it's by far the biggest crowd I've seen. The night before the main event they hold a rail jam pulled by a winch and there's $500 cash up for grabs. My broke arse leaps at the chance of some cash and I snap up the win.

The following day I pull together a good enough run to get me through the first round, but a second-round knockout has me missing the cut.

I've failed to qualify for the pro tour.

I'm gutted, as I had planned my season around it. I'll just have to see what other opportunities are out there for me.

Before we leave Texas we hear about a qualifier event being held right here the day after the tour stop. And the event it's for? Parks's Double or Nothing! Even though I can't exactly afford to stay in Texas longer, I call the airline and change my flights. There's no way I'm missing this opportunity.

The first rider out is Texan Joey Bradley, who sets the bar high with a huge heelside 900. There are only 10 qualifying spots open for the main event, and just two spots are being given away today, as it's the first of five qualifier events throughout the summer. So unless another rider can somehow better Joey's effort — which won't be easy — he's got his name on one of them.

By the time it's my turn to ride, Joey is still holding the top spot. The next likely contender is Jeff or one of the other guys who, like him, has landed a backside 720. Parks Bonifay is in the boat judging.

My first hit off the toes is a 900, which is more of a warm-up for my next toeside hit. At the other end of the lake I'm served a heelside double and I spin a heel 900, pleasantly surprising myself when I land it clean. It's not huge like Joey's was, but there's a chance it's bumped me up the list. For my remaining hits, I start going for the toe 1080 — especially since Parks is the judge, as I know it'll get him pumped up. He was the first to land a switch toeside 10 back in '99, and since then only two others have proof of landing the holy grail of wakeboarding: Danny with his clean switch heel 10, which was the Trick of the Year winner last year; and contest powerhouse Canadian Rusty Malinoski, who claimed his own switch toeside 10 earlier this year.

I'm determined to become the next, and started trying it a couple of years ago, but so far I've only just started actually getting close.

My first 1080 attempt isn't super close. Then on my next attempt I hit roller number three and start spinning like a top, turning a full 1080 degrees before landing on my board with the handle in my grasp behind my back. *Yessss!* I turn my head to see Parks raising both hands in the air in celebration, but before I can reclaim control, I slip out and fall onto my back. *Nooooooo!*

For the next few hours I watch the rest of the guys, unsure where I stand because some good tricks have been landed. After the final rider is done, Parks gathers us together.

'The winner of today's qualifier,' he says, and everyone's hanging on his words, 'is Joey Bradley!'

Loud cheers and claps, even though Joey's not actually here — he had to leave early.

'And the second person to receive an invitation to Double or Nothing is . . .'

Everyone falls silent, and Parks pauses for dramatic effect.

'Brad Smeele!'

Holy shit. I got it!

I run up and shake Parks's hand.

I'm going to Double or Nothing!

•

When I get back to Orlando, I begin looking around for other events that are worth attending. There's one coming up in Oklahoma with a couple of grand up for grabs, and it's the same weekend as the next pro tour event, so the best riders won't be able to attend. I register, book my flights, and a week later Molly drops me at the airport.

'Good luck, and have fun!' she says, then kisses me goodbye.

The event MC picks me up in Oklahoma, then takes me to the event site to meet the organisers. The competition starts tomorrow, so they're just finishing setting everything up. I do a little pre-press with the local media, which involves a quick ride and an interview, and they make out that it's a big deal I'm here. I go along with it. It's the first time I've been treated like some kind of wake star, and it's actually pretty cool.

Then a couple of Red Bull 'Wings' girls arrive. It's their job to hand out cans of energy drink during the contest, and they've come to set up their branding. The MC knows one of them and takes me over to say hi.

'Hey, I'm Leah,' she says, smiling, 'and this is my friend Dawn.'

My jaw drops. Dawn is unbelievably beautiful. She's tall with blonde hair, and is wearing mirror sunglasses and a long, flowing white summer dress that hugs her body in all the right places in the slight breeze. Big boobs, slim waist, long legs, perky booty . . . She's absolute perfection! I can't take my eyes off her.

I snap out of my little trance for long enough to introduce myself. 'H-hi . . . I'm Brad.' I shake Leah's hand, then gently take Dawn's. 'It's a pleasure to meet you.'

'Oh my god! You have an accent,' Dawn replies. 'That's so cool. Where are you from?'

'New Zealand, but I'm currently living in Orlando.'

She lifts her sunglasses and deals me another blow with her piercing blue eyes. And her face! Her bone structure is like something straight out of a fashion magazine. Perfect jawline, perfect cheekbones . . . I can't believe how stunning this girl is.

'Hey, dude,' the MC says, tapping me on the shoulder as though to bring me back to the real world. 'How about we take these girls out for lunch?'

'Sounds good, bro,' I reply, trying to play it cool when I'm melting on the inside. 'I'm starving.'

Over lunch, the four of us chat and enjoy a few beers. I do my best to spread my attention evenly, but I'm really only interested in talking to Dawn. I am so besotted that I've pretty much completely forgotten about Molly. I know it's bad, but that doesn't stop me.

When we're finished eating, I turn to the MC. 'Hey, why don't you take Leah back to the site with you?' I say casually. 'I'm gonna roll back with Dawn.'

We jump into her racy little roadster. On our way, we stop at a red light, and we're chatting the whole time. There's a car in front of us that doesn't move when the lights change.

'Come on!' Dawn yells through the windscreen. 'If it was any greener, you could smoke it!'

I burst out laughing. 'I've never heard that one before,' I say. 'I'm gonna steal it for later.'

Turns out she loves smoking weed as much as I do. When we arrive back at the event site she pulls out a bowl and loads it with sticky green, then fires it up. We sit in the car, smoking and chatting. The more time I spend with this girl, the more I like her.

'I've got a few things to do this afternoon,' she says. 'But, if you want, I can come back later to take you out and show you around?'

'Cool,' I say. 'That'd be great.'

We exchange numbers, and true to her promise she comes back. We head to a nightclub, and leave around midnight. I've been told there's an RV at the contest site for me to sleep in, but when we get there I discover it's full of sleeping people. There's no bed spare. I need a Plan B.

'Come this way,' I say, and I lead Dawn over to where all the display boats are set up for the next day.

It's not hard to sneak past the lone security guard. I pick a boat and we climb in underneath the cover. The moment we're inside the clothes come straight off and we get busy. Once we're done, we realise we should probably find a motel. The boat's not exactly suitable to sleep in, and we definitely need an actual bed to do that again.

•

The next morning in the motel, after Dawn and I have just finished going another round, I check my phone to see I've missed a call from Molly.

'I've just got to make a quick call,' I say to Dawn, then I head outside.

When Molly picks up, I make an excuse for missing her call. I pretend everything's normal but the moment I hang up I feel extremely guilty. I've never cheated on anyone before. I never thought I would be capable of betraying someone's trust like that, but I'm helpless around Dawn. I find her addictive, intoxicating and I just can't resist her — no matter how bad I feel about Molly.

•

In the afternoon I win my heat easily with a solid run. It turns out there are actually some really good riders here, including Joey Bradley, the Texan who won the Double or Nothing qualifier, and later in the evening we hang out together at the official competitors' party. Joey is a rad dude and I also know he's going to be my toughest competition in the finals tomorrow.

Dawn comes to meet me at the bar, and she's even brought her mum. We're introduced over a shot of Patrón tequila . . . then another, and another. I'm a bit of a lightweight when it comes to hard liquor so I'm soon pretty wasted. Then Dawn and I head to a house party, where we each take a rip from a bong. The room starts spinning. I'm totally fucked up — I can't even speak. Dawn is sitting on my lap, and she's just as paralytic as I am.

'Someone must've laced the weed with something,' she slurs, but I know this feeling. It's the same one I had at new year in Mangakino. We're greening out. A rookie error.

'Gotta remember the rhyme,' I mutter to Dawn. 'Beer before grass, you're on your arse. Grass before beer, you're in the clear.'

By the time we make it back to her place we've sobered up enough to have sex. Then we pass out.

•

Next morning I have the worst hangover I've had in a long time. My head is pounding and my whole body is weak. I shower, attempting to pull myself together, but I'm still struggling when Dawn drops me at the contest.

By the time of the final, the wind has picked up and is carving up the water. What was a nice, smooth course yesterday is now a battleground. My biggest competitor today is no longer Joey — it's the combination of my shaky legs and the wind chop. Usually I'm pretty good in choppy water, as my size allows me to power through it, but the brutal hangover has made my legs feel so weak that every wave just bounces me around.

Somehow I manage to pull together a good enough run to take second place behind Joey, earning myself a welcome $1200.

After a quick thank you speech at the prizegiving I race away. I'm running late for my flight back to Orlando and arrive right on check-in time. I sprint to the gate.

'We're not boarding the plane just yet,' says the woman at the counter. 'There's been a slight delay. We'll make the boarding call shortly.'

Phew. I grab the closest seat and put my feet up but I'm so shattered that I fall asleep. When I jolt myself awake, I'm the only person in the boarding area. Everyone is gone — including the woman behind the desk. I look out the window and see the plane pulling away from the gate.

What the fuck?!

I'm fuming. Why the hell didn't that lady wake me up? She knew I was supposed to be on that flight. What a bitch!

I run back to the check-in counter and unload on a different woman who is unfortunate enough to be standing there.

'Unfortunately your bags have gone with the plane,' she says. 'And the next flight we can put you on is tomorrow.'

Fuck!

I call Molly to let her know what's happened, but my phone beeps while I'm talking to her, meaning the battery's running low.

My charger is in my bag, which is on the plane.

'I'm sorry, I've got to go,' I tell her. 'I need to save battery so I can call someone to come and pick me up. I need to find somewhere to stay for the night.'

I neglect to mention that I know who I'm going to call — and, hopefully, exactly where I'm going to stay.

•

Dawn is only too happy to swoop by and grab me. We go straight from the airport to her place, and spend the rest of the day and night in her bed. I'm actually stoked I missed my flight, because it means I can spend more time getting intimate with this babe. We don't get drunk or go partying. We enjoy being wrapped up in each other and, as much as we've had fun fucking each other's brains out previously, now it's more like we're making love. We go for hours on end, only breaking for water and a shower before getting right back to it.

•

The next day's flight is delayed and my phone is dead so I can't let Molly know. When I land two hours late, I call her from a pay phone and she's already halfway back home. She's pissed off, but she turns around and comes back for me.

As soon as I get in the car, she starts grilling me about why my flight was late. She's super mad.

'And how did you manage to miss your flight yesterday?' she asks.

I explain about the woman at the boarding gate, but she's still suspicious.

'Okay,' she says. 'It's just that Michelle told me Alex said he missed a flight once, and she found out later that he was really staying an extra day with some girl.'

Dammit, Alex!

'Look, I really didn't mean to miss my flight yesterday,' I say. 'I'm telling the truth.'

And I am — I truly didn't intend to stay an extra night. I feel guiltier than ever, but I can't bring myself to confess. I really like Molly. I love having a girlfriend, and I especially love that she's into so many of the same things I am. Admittedly, I've been feeling a bit unsure about the longevity of our relationship, since I'm going home at the end of the season (and my previous failed long-distance attempt with Char has me reluctant to try again) but I'm also not ready for this to end just yet.

So I lie to her. I reassure her I wasn't with another girl.

By the time we get back to her place she seems to believe me.

•

I get straight back to training, and it's such a relief to have a little extra cash from my recent wins. In past years, and even earlier this season, my riding has been limited by what I can afford. When money is tight, I sometimes have to choose between eating and riding — there have been days where I've gone to bed hungry because I chose to put the money towards petrol for the boat instead of food for my stomach, and other days where I have to skip my ride so I can afford dinner. But, with a bit of money in my pocket, I'm able to ride multiple times a day and eat well too.

As well as riding at home with Jeff and driving out to Mount Dora to ride with Alex and co, I've also started going to Lake Hiawassee with Chad Sharpe and the Aussie lads. Chad is someone I've looked up to for years. As well as riding for Ronix, he's a part-owner in the company. It's especially cool to get to know him better.

In early July I'm headed to a competition in Wales that Ants told me about. Wakestock is Europe's largest wakeboard music festival, with a first prize of £2000.

Ants picks me up from Heathrow and takes me to the nearby Princes cable park where he lives and works. When we get there, I catch up with Dunc Hancock, the Ronix New Zealand distributor, who's managing the club here during the New Zealand winter, and Mouse, who also lives and works there. I spend a couple of days hanging out and riding at the club, then Ants and I hit the road. It takes most of the day to drive to Pwllheli on the north-western coast of Wales.

We link up with the other riders: one of them is Aussie rider Scotty Broome, and I get introduced to some of the UK crew I haven't met yet. It's rad to get together with the lads I've ridden against at worlds over the years, including the likes of Marc Rossiter (Rossi) and Jonty Green. Everyone gets amongst the party on the first night, and there's a bunch of drugs going around, but I stick with just a few drinks. I want to be fresh for my qualifying ride tomorrow.

When I wake up, it's to absolutely shit weather. It's cold and rainy. We're supposed to ride in this? The contest is being held in a small harbour so Ants and I roll down to check it out. When we get there, I'm a little confused. The harbour is practically dry. The tide's so far out, there's hardly any water at all. Standing awkwardly on the exposed sand are a couple of huge sliders — one's an A-frame with a step down to the down-rail section, while the other's an incline to decline with a large gap in between. As I'm busy examining the sliders and visualising how I'm going to hit them, I notice the harbour has started to fill up.

'Yo, check out how fast that water's coming in,' I say to Ant.

'Yeah, there's something about this area that makes a couple of metres of tide come in and drain out in just a few hours,' he replies. Apparently, the depth changes so rapidly that it drastically affects the size of the wake across the course of an event.

'You want to ride in the middle of the order so the wake is bigger,' Ants tells me.

At that moment it starts absolutely pelting down. It's truly miserable. I really don't want to ride today.

We hang around for a while, and Ants introduces me to the contest organiser, who eventually agrees we can skip riding today and just have a straight final tomorrow. I manage to snag myself a spot around the middle of the field so I'll get the biggest wake possible. It won't come remotely close to the size of the wakes I ride back in Orlando, but this is what all my years of riding in New Zealand have got me used to: small wakes and salty water!

Back at the festival site we join the huge crowd and rage out to some grimy UK electronic tunes. The continuous rain soon turns the grassy field into a muddy bog and the site is a mess. Thankfully, a friend of Ants has loaned me some 'wellies', as they call gumboots over here.

As we party into the night, some kid who looks about 16 comes up and offers us some pills that I assume are ecstasy. Whatever he's dishing out, he's got a bag full — there must be hundreds of the colourful little pingers. Ants is all too happy to partake. He's on a bender, and stays up all night. I'd love to join him, but I decline. I don't want to blow my chances tomorrow by partying too hard tonight.

There's one reason I flew all this way: I'm here to take that prize money.

•

Overnight, the music festival site becomes such a mud pit that it's cancelled.

Thankfully, the wakeboarding contest is still on, and the rain has eased to a light sprinkle that clears up by the time we get to the harbour. My ride goes reasonably well, considering how small the wake is. I link together some basic but reliable tricks but unfortunately my two hits at the sliders are less than ideal as I don't quite make it all the way along. Then, at the end of my pass, I go down on a toeside 720, which screws me for the double-up at the end of the course.

On the way back to the dock, though, I've got room for three more tricks. I take a 360 out to the flats and follow it up by stomping the 720 that took me down, then I finish with a tantrum to blind. The combo has the crowd cheering.

As I'm getting back into my warm clothes, I watch the rest of the competitors. UK rippers Rossi and Jonty ride really well. Jonty in particular slays the rails and puts together a solid run with no falls, a crow mobe and a huge off-axis backside 360 off the double-up. After seeing him on the water, I resign myself to the fact that he's probably beaten me. I'm pretty sure I've done enough to be on the podium, though.

The awards ceremony was meant to be held on the main stage at the music festival, right before the headline act — meaning the winners would have been cheered on by a crowd of 30,000-odd wasted festival creatures — but since the festival has been cancelled, it's now being held right here by the harbour. And, instead of a podium on stage, they're using a fire-escape stairwell. Not quite the epic rock-star vibe.

The MC, Matty Crowhurst, starts reading the results. 'Third place goes to James Young,' he announces, and I'm just reaching down to grab my board so I can carry it up with me when he calls out, 'And in second place: Jonty Green!'

My heart sinks.

'What the fuck?' I mutter quietly to Ants, who's standing beside me. Did I really not even make the top three?

He shrugs and gives me a look as if to say, *Sorry, bro, I guess you got screwed.*

I put my board back down.

'And your 2007 Wakestock champion is . . .' Matty pauses, then continues, 'Brad Smeeleeeeeeee!'

A rush of excitement hits me, and Ants slaps me on the back. '*Yeeeaaahh!*' he yells.

I grab my board again, and make my way to the top step on the fire escape.

Matty hands me a big wooden trophy, and when I read the plaque I see a familiar name: Mark Kenney. He won this very event five years earlier, just months before his death. I'm filled with pride to know that I'm fulfilling my dream of following in his footsteps.

Someone hands me a bottle of champagne. I pop the cork and spray the contents in the air as the crowd cheers. And, even though I'm standing on a fire escape in front of 200 people instead of a stage in front of thousands, I'm feeling totally elated. Having my name on the same plaque as my idol means even more to me than the win itself. Although, that £2000 is a very welcome bonus! At about $NZ6000, it's the most I've ever won.

'You get a triple-A pass for next year's festival too,' says Ants.

'What's that?' I ask.

'Access all areas,' he replies. 'It means you can go wherever the fuck you want! VIP, backstage — hell, you can even go *on* stage if you want.'

Later, as I'm packing up my gear in the riders' area, I find Jonty.

'Sorry, man,' I say to him. 'I totally thought you had me beat! You killed it out there.'

'Oh, cheers, man,' he replies in his soft Cockney voice. 'But, nah, man. That toe seven to tanny to blind combo was mad! You deserve it.'

We slap hands and hug it out.

•

Back in London, Ants and I join Matty and Scotty for a filming session at Thorpe Lakes cable park. To begin with, it's all good fun, sessioning the kickers and sliders. But when I get too lazy on an air roll to blind, I'm instantly whiplashed into the water as my back edge catches. I come to with my head ringing and a pain in my neck. I'm underwater, and I open my eyes to see the surface above me. Instinctively I go to swim to the surface — but I can't move my arms.

I try not to panic. Thanks to my buoyant wetsuit and life-jacket, I float to the surface anyway. Once my face reaches the air I take a huge breath and lie there immobile, waiting for the rescue boat.

Then, after a few long, scary moments, I feel movement returning to my limbs. By the time the boat gets to me, I'm able to pull myself up into it.

I got my bell rung so good that my neck is aching and I'm out of it for the rest of the day. I sit on the dock watching the others ride and asking people how I got hurt, because I keep forgetting.

From the UK I'm off to Canada, to compete in Wakestock in Toronto. Weirdly, although it's got the same name as the UK event I've just been at, the two are not in any way affiliated. I don't have quite the same success at this event, as all of the best pro riders are there, but it's fun anyway.

Molly arrives at the end of the event. Her minivan shat itself, so she flew to her family home in upstate New York to pick up an old car they're giving her, then drove up to Toronto to get me. For the whole month before I left Florida, she and I spent almost every day together, and things were good. Our relationship is filled with fun, laughs, intense passion and the occasional argument that fizzles as soon as we have make-up sex. And she's always down for an adventure. It helps that she has wheels, doesn't have a job and is also pursuing wakeboarding.

Just before I left, though, she hadn't been riding much due to an injury. I'd noticed she seemed to get injured easily, and when I asked her about it, she ended up telling me how, a few years earlier, she woke up one day completely blind and unable to move. She was diagnosed with Guillain-Barré syndrome, a rare disorder where your body's immune system attacks your nerves. Thankfully, she regained her vision after about a week and full movement after a couple of months, but it sounded like one of the scariest things imaginable. I can't think of anything more terrifying than being paralysed and becoming a prisoner in your own body.

It's good to see her again, and she looks good. She always does.

After a six-hour drive we pull up at her grandparents' place. It's great to meet them — they're really sweet and make me feel very welcome — and their home on the shore of the picturesque upstate New York lake is beautiful. I'm staying in a small cabin in the woods beside the main house. Molly's family won't let her stay there with me but of course she sneaks out to join me.

It's so nice to have a break from riding and competing and to be able to relax and put my feet up. I even read a book, something I haven't done since I was at school. Molly and I spend our days exploring the lake in kayaks, adventuring through the woods and even playing a few games of tennis. When we're alone, though, you know exactly what we're doing: giving free rein to our mutual lust.

After a week it's time to head back to Florida. Molly wakes me at five in the morning and I pass out again as soon as I'm in the car, waking up a few hours later. We stop for petrol and lunch, then I take over the driving to give her a break. For the rest of the 22-hour drive, I sit behind the wheel. It's only thanks to good tunes and several energy drinks that I manage to stay awake and keep my eyes on the road ahead.

A week later Molly flies back up to spend a week with her family, and while she's gone I get this overwhelming feeling that something needs to change. So I shave off my long locks for a fresh new feel in the heat of summer. I also decide to call Molly and break up with her. I've been feeling guilty about my infidelity with Dawn, but also I didn't expect to fall into a relationship as hard as I have, so I use our physical separation as an opportunity to end it. It helps that Molly being away means I'm not instantly drawn back in by our undeniable sexual chemistry.

•

Jeff and I had to move out of the Jessamine house, as the owners needed it to be vacated, so we've been crashing with the Aussie lads at their place on Hiawassee. There's not much room, as there's already nine inhabitants, so Jeff and I crash in the garage on air mattresses.

Christian Fitzpatrick has just arrived in Orlando to start work on his latest film project, about the Aussies and Kiwis who come to live and ride in the US. There's definitely something super cool about our crew over here, which has grown to include a bunch of riders from both countries. We're all out to help each other in whatever way we can, and I'm very lucky to have such a great group of friends. They've pretty much become family.

We get straight into filming out on Lake Hiawassee, and the following days are filled with the most fun and progressive sessions I've ever had. Everyone is riding so well, especially Deano and up-and-coming ripper Mitch Langfield, who both blow our minds with brand-new tricks. My riding is going well too, really well, and I get most of my best tricks captured on film. I even land my first toeside 720 way out into the flats, which very few other riders can do.

On one pass down the lake, I'm going for my signature overturned stalefish batwing to blind. It's a trick that requires a really late handle pass, and Deano is driving the chase boat so that Christian can shoot a cool angle. I manage to pull the late backside 180 around, but when I land, the handle pings out of my hand. I remain standing on top of the water, but my momentum carries me away from the wake and into the path of the chase boat.

As I come to a stop and start to sink into the water, I can see the chase boat coming — and it's not slowing down. Deano isn't looking where he's driving, and he's coming straight for me. By the time Christian cottons on and yells at Deano, they're so close it's too late to turn.

Oh, fuck, I think. *This is it — he's going to run me over!*

There's no time to swim out of the way so I take the only option available: I stand as tall as possible to sink my board as deep as I can. With the bow of the boat coming up fast, I wait for my moment. Then, just as I'm about to get run over, I scoop the water with my board to pull me under. I pull myself as far down in the water as possible, then curl up into a ball and hold my tuck, expecting at any moment to feel the hull or the fins or — worst-case scenario — the propeller.

I wait, and wait and wait . . . but I feel nothing. So I pop up out of the water.

I'm now behind the chase boat, and it's slowly turning around.

'Holy shit, B-rad!' I hear one of the guys yell. 'Are you okay?'

'Oh my god!' I yell back. 'How did I not just die?'

My heart is beating like crazy and the adrenalin is pumping. I'm feeling both relieved and incredibly spooked.

Then I see Deano, his forehead creased with concern. 'Are you okay, B-rad?' he asks soberly.

'Yeah, dude. I'm fine. Just a little rattled. I was curled up waiting to feel the prop hit my back or something.'

'Fuck, I'm so, *so* sorry, mate. I thought you still had the handle when you landed, so I looked down to change the music . . .' He's clearly shaken.

I can see how he missed me dropping the handle. From his perspective, since I landed with my back to him and stayed on my feet, it must've looked like I was still riding.

'It's okay,' I say to him. 'Cheers for the quick reactions, bro.'

It all happened in a matter of seconds, but as I was ducking under the water I noticed that Deano had spotted me and pulled the throttle back. Based on the way the boat was now drifting to the left, I imagine that means he turned slightly right, then left towards me, before pulling the boat out of gear, which made the back of the boat — where the propeller is — turn away from me. I'm lucky he's such a master, because a less experienced person would have instinctively done the opposite — and I would have been toast.

'Let's go have a beer, mate,' Deano says. 'Glad you're still with us in one piece.'

For the rest of the afternoon I can't shake the thought of just how bad that could've been. I count my lucky stars that I'm okay.

•

Molly is arriving back in Orlando today, and I'm nervous since I'm picking her up from the airport in her car. When I pull up to the kerb, I barely recognise her. She's gone from platinum blonde to black hair and she looks insanely sexy! She's cold towards me, and shows some sass, which I probably deserve.

I've been looking for a more permanent place to live, and my friend Austin Hair is about to sign the lease on a house on one of the end coves of Jessamine, so I claim a room there. Austin is away, so Molly and I roll over there to get the key from owner Josh Sanders. I'm sitting on the only piece of furniture, an outdoor chair, when Molly decides to sit in my lap. She knows exactly what she's doing to me, and as soon as Josh has left us with the keys and the house to ourselves, we proceed to fuck in every room, on every countertop, against every wall and on every surface possible. I'm completely powerless when it comes to her. My willpower is no match for the sexual chemistry between us.

Molly moves into one of the other rooms, and just like that it's as if nothing has changed. We're back together.

Filming with Christian continues, and I'm racking up tricks on film. There's a new trick I've been working on all season, the wake-to-wake heel 900 — without the extra help of the double-up. Only a few people have landed it and I'm determined to be the next. Molly sets me a sexual incentive to add to the motivation.

After a filming session in Mount Dora, the guys and I gather back at Shane's place, where Chris-O is living. When Molly arrives to pick me up, I ask her to watch the clip on Christian's camera. Her jaw drops as she sees the footage of me landing my first wake-to-wake heel 9, partially in amazement at the trick, but mainly because she knows what it means. So we head home for me to claim my prize.

•

Late one night a few weeks later I get a message I have been waiting for. A message that only I and 19 other specially selected riders are receiving: the secret location for Parks's Double or Nothing — and it's on tomorrow!

I'm so full of nerves I barely get any sleep. The next day Molly and I drive west towards Polk County. Our destination: an old sand-mine lake that's perfect for double-ups.

At the rider briefing I look around at the other 19 competitors and take a moment. Here I am, sitting with the best of the best, the cream of the crop, the guys I've been looking up to since before my balls dropped. Two years ago I was just some shy, wide-eyed kid watching this event . . . and now I'm riding in it. It's absolutely insane.

'And don't even think about bringing out your heel 9 today,' Parks warns us at the end of the briefing, 'because I can promise you, it won't win!'

Almost all of us qualified with a heel 9, so that makes sense. I plan on landing my 1080 today, and, if I manage that, I'll go for a 1260. That's why I've chosen 12 as the number on the back of my Double or Nothing jersey — to amp me up to go for it!

The day gets going and it's an absolute huck-fest. Riders are going for all sorts of double flips and 1080s and backside 900s, but no one has much success actually landing anything. When my turn comes up, I'm feeling it. On my first couple of attempts I make the spin but miss the handle pass. The next few times I get the handle but don't land in control. Then, on my last attempt I get the handle and land in control . . . but then the handle is tugged out of my hand.

It's frustrating not to get the result I wanted, but just being here is really fucking cool.

•

One afternoon, not long before I'm due to head back to New Zealand, I get another message — and this time it's one I was hoping I might dodge.

I'm on my way with Alex to his place for a ride when I get a text from Molly.

'You know that Justin Timberlake lyric, 'I'm tired of using technology'?' she's written. 'Who does that make you think of?'

I instantly know what she's getting at. I've been busted.

Dawn and I have stayed in touch since we met, messaging on Myspace. Molly's obviously been on my laptop and found some of our conversations.

I call my girlfriend. 'You already know the answer to that question,' I say as soon as she answers.

She's pissed off, understandably.

'Look, I'm sorry,' I say. 'I know I lied to you, and you have every right to be mad, but can we talk about this when I get home?'

I hang up and grimace at Alex. He doesn't say anything. He doesn't need to. He's been through this all before so he knows what I'm in for.

When I get home, Molly and I argue. I finally confess to cheating on her, and

I tell her how guilty I've been feeling. She's really mad, but she only stays that way for a few days. Eventually she stops giving me the cold shoulder and things become good again for a while. But on my last night in town, we talk properly about what's going to happen with us when I leave. I have to be honest with her.

'I just don't think it can work long-distance,' I tell her. 'I think it's over.'

We both get emotional. I really like this girl, but it's obvious that's not enough. If I cheated on her when I was away for just a weekend, how can I possibly trust myself when we're half a world apart for several months? How can she trust me? Although I know it's hurting her, I have to tell her the truth. If I tell her what she wants to hear, I know I'll only end up hurting her more later on.

Surprisingly, she still wants to be with me for my last night. We make love, we laugh and we cry . . . and then I have to let her go.

•

Before heading back to New Zealand, I fly over to Doha, Qatar, for the IWWF world championships. I'm not overly enthused about it. I win my first heat but narrowly miss out on advancing to the semi-final.

When I finally arrive in Auckland I'm looking forward to a little bit of downtime to reflect on a long and hectic northern season. It feels like all the hard work is starting to pay off. I'm really happy to have gained some good results and avoided any real injuries, and to return with the promise of some increased financial security. Just before leaving Orlando I hit up the Oakley team manager, Matty Swanson. After congratulating me on my success this season — which was gratifying all on its own — he said, 'I know I've turned you down in past years, but we love what you're doing. I don't have much room to work with, but let's start by getting you on our international team. I'll have to take a look at what we've got in the budget, but we'll get you on a starting rate and I'll have a contract sent out to you soon.'

I was ecstatic.

Granted, I haven't heard anything from him since, despite chasing him up several times, but just knowing a contract and a salary are in the works is a win.

It feels like my career is on an upward trajectory.

SIX: THE HOLY GRAIL

The New Zealand season fires up with Tairua Pipe Masters just a couple of weeks into 2008. For the first time I come away with a win, stoked to be starting the year on a high note.

As usual, it's a wild weekend of partying and hitting the gnarliest rails found in this country. Mouse is here, and he's staying with a super-cute blonde he met at the end of the year. It was actually Mum who made the introduction — I was out with Ants, Brant and Mouse when she messaged to say she was at a Christmas party and had met some girls she thought we'd like. We showed up half an hour later to find her standing with three gorgeous blondes in Santa outfits — the party's festive promo squad — and a fourth who wasn't working but was just as cute. 'Nice work, Mum!' I said.

Mouse and I have been hanging out a bit since I got home, including spending new year together down in Wanaka. It's just as well he lives in the South Island, otherwise we'd be partying a lot. We've discovered we're a pretty dangerous duo when we're out together — we're as alike in our pursuit of pretty girls as we are in our ability to pull them.

The blonde he pulled at that Christmas party is called Casey. She's a charismatic bundle of joy who's super sweet and lovely to everyone. She's also very flirty. She might be hooking up with Mouse, but I swear she's been giving me eyes all weekend. I thought maybe that was just her bubbly personality but I discover otherwise when we get back to Auckland and catch up for a drink. One thing leads to another . . .

•

It's good that I made the most of the short break at the end of last year, because pretty soon I'm back to both riding and promo work. Even with almost $NZ10,000 in prize money from my northern season, I still managed to come home with a maxed-out credit card. Riding and competing in the northern hemisphere is not cheap. Accommodation, food, petrol, travel, plus a bit of fun — it all adds up.

Not long after Pipe Masters, it's time to head across the Tasman. I've actually already attended the first event of this summer's Australian pro tour, as it was held at the end of 2007. This time the tour's not a month of back-to-back events, but one event every month. It's really changed the dynamic — the tour's no longer one big road-trip, more of a fly-in, fly-out affair. The first stop was Brisbane, where the water conditions were terrible and I finished fifth equal.

Now I'm off to Sydney for the second stop. At the airport I meet up with Alex Brown, who's just landed from Florida, and we head to Penrith together, where I smash my way through several rounds of competition, only to have my run brought to an end in the semi-final by a 14-year-old phenom by the name of Harley Clifford. I first came across Harley at my first worlds in Aussie, when he must have been only about eight or nine. Everyone's had their eye on him over the years, knowing it was only a matter of time before he started beating us all.

He absolutely rips on the water, pulling the most insane run of tech tricks to perfection and blowing everyone's minds. He's officially put us all on notice, and he's coming for the US pro tour too. I bag third place, though, and I'm super pleased with that.

After a week or so road-tripping to Melbourne with the guys, I jet over to the Gold Coast for Planet X. It's my first time at this event, and there are two parts to it — the boat event here, then a rail section next week in Melbourne. Harley takes the win again, solidifying himself as a very real competitive threat.

Two days later, and just in time for my 21st birthday, I return to Melbourne. Alex, Bower and I hit the bars to celebrate, and I'll party with my mates in New Zealand once I get home.

•

Then the weekend comes around, and it's time for the second Planet X event, out at St Kilda in the world's biggest portable three-pool arena.

Riders start down the far end of the setup, on a raised platform with a down-rail into the first pool. Then, between the first and second pool, there's a flat bar that's long enough to get a nice press on. The second pool leads us to the main attraction: a 20-metre-long fun box, but it's such a monster that it's been dubbed 'the slaughter box'. It's a much more appropriate name given how big and gnarly it is, with its huge kicker into a flat-to-down-rail specially designed for huge transfers.

Last week when we first got to session the slaughter box, we all took some big spills. Then, while I was practising on it earlier today, I managed to pop my shoulder out as I landed on the down-rail. As soon as there was some slack in the rope, my shoulder popped back in, but it hurt. I was gutted, but 20 minutes' icing it seemed to do the trick and it's now feeling good enough for me to ride in the main event.

We're competing in front of thousands of spectators, and I am feeling really on. I advance through the heats to the final, where I'm up against Aussie wake veteran Brett 'Ike' Eisenhauer. On my first of three hits, I link together a back-lip 270 on the flat bar to a transfer to back-lip over the slaughter box, narrowly putting myself ahead of Ike. On my second hit, I crash out on my 270 transfer — but so does Ike. As I splash into the end pool, I soak the crowd and the girls squeal with delight. So it all comes down to the final run.

After watching Ike successfully land a technically difficult 180 to switch 50–50 transfer, I decide I'm going to have to throw my pride out the window. Since this event's being filmed for TV, I've noticed the judges are scoring better for the tricks that are the biggest crowd-pleasers rather than the ones that necessarily require the greatest skill, and I realise that if I don't go big, it won't be me heading home with that gold medal and the $1000 in prize money.

So I tell the driver, 'When I land in the second pool, gun it and go full speed.'

He does exactly as he's told, and when I feel the pull on the rope I accelerate in and send a big un-grabbed tantrum easily 4 metres into the air, sailing over the slaughter box and missing it altogether. When I stomp the landing, I pump my fists triumphantly in the air, egging the crowd on. But they need no encouragement — they're already going crazy over my 'backflip'. Little do they know, it was much easier to do than any of the rail hits. Sending a big one over the entire 20-metre gap is more about balls than skill.

Moments later, I'm standing on top of the slaughter box rail, raising my board above my head in front of thousands of cheering fans. My stunt paid off. I'm going home with a Planet X gold medal!

Deano, who's one of the judges, comes up to me laughing. 'That's the one and only time you'll win with an un-grabbed tantrum on my watch!' he says, high-fiving me. 'But I could tell you were hungry for that win. Congrats, mate.'

•

Alex and I get just a couple of days' rest back in Auckland before we're on our way down to Hamilton for the next comp. It's actually the third stop of the Aussie pro tour, and it's the first time there's been a stop in New Zealand. I'm looking forward to putting on a good show for the home crowd, as lots of my friends are making the drive down to support me — including Casey and a couple of her cute friends. Afterwards, we're all going out to celebrate my 21st and hit the pro tour after-party.

My shoulder has been giving me grief since last weekend but a physiotherapist friend straps it up for me. I advance through the first couple of rounds, easily disposing of my early match-ups. Then, in the semi-finals, I find myself up against Harley Clifford once more. The teenager has been almost unbeatable so far this season, and he's ranked above me so I know I have to put the pressure on.

The conditions are pretty challenging, with the water moving swiftly downriver and the sea wall bouncing the rollers back out across the course, but my ride goes well enough. Just at the end of my run, though, I fall on my heel 720, leaving the door wide open. This kid is too good and too consistent to waste an opening like that — but, if I've learnt anything from my fellow countryman and longtime adversary Jeff Weatherall, it's that there's more to competing than just doing tricks.

Back at the starting dock, Harley is strapped into his board, moments away from taking off. As I go past, I tap my hand against the nose of his board. 'Come on, board,' I say, 'you've gotta break for me. It's my only chance of winning!'

I know there's very little chance his board will really break, but that's not the point. The point is that now I'm in his head. By saying his board breaking is my only chance, I've implied that I think there's no chance he'll fall. My hope is that, feeling the extra weight of my expectation, he might just make a mistake, and that's all I need. A classic bit of reverse psychology.

Out on the water, Harley backs out of several tricks, then takes a fall towards the end of his set, handing me the semi-final.

In the final I'm up against Jeff. A Kiwi vs Kiwi showdown for the very first New Zealand tour stop — it's like it was meant to be. I ride well enough to put a good amount of pressure on Jeff, but I take a fall at the end of my run. It's my career-best finish on the Aussie pro tour, and I'm super happy with that — but I'd be lying if I pretended it wasn't ever so slightly tainted by another defeat to Jeff.

I just can't seem to beat the guy here in New Zealand!

•

The after-party goes off, and it's so cool to have my Kiwi and Aussie friends together, but the night's not without its dose of drama.

As things are starting to wind up, Mouse and I butt heads over Casey.

It was only a matter of time. He knows that she and I slept together in Auckland, but the way I see it, neither he nor I are in it for the long haul: he lives at the other end of the country, and I'm heading back to the US in a few months. And Casey doesn't seem like she's looking for anything serious.

I assume things will fall in my favour, since Casey and I got together more recently and we also live in the same city. But Mouse has made it clear that he sees himself as still being in the running. Casey, for her part, has spent the whole night avoiding the situation. She's up on stage, dancing with her friends, and neither of us can get near her.

As we're standing at the bar, Mouse declares, 'She's staying with me tonight!'

I just start laughing. As if he has any say over where she sleeps. That's on her. Plus, it's pretty obvious she's not sleeping with anyone tonight. Looks like she's staying with the girls.

The next day a few of us head down to Lake Ohakuri to ride in the country's most picturesque locations while Carnie catches it all on film. In the evening the rest of the gang head to some nearby natural hot springs for a few beers, but I stay behind at the bach.

I call Casey and we spend a bit of time talking. She apologises for the drama with Mouse.

'You're the one I want,' she reassures me.

I feel conflicted. Mouse is my friend, but I can't help but be attracted to Casey. And it's not just because she's gorgeous. She's also a sweet and lovely person. Honestly, I'm smitten.

After hanging up, I stay sitting outside for a while. The others still aren't back, and the crickets are singing as twilight begins to blur the edges of everything. I immerse myself in my surroundings — the sights and sounds and feelings — and I think about what I'm going to do when it's my turn to ride tomorrow. Usually, I wouldn't put much thought into it. I'd just get out there and ride. But we're going to be behind Andrea's boat, which is a Wakesetter but has a smaller engine, so it doesn't produce a wake that's big enough to do anything crazy off. Since the boat won't be slammed with weight it'll be easier for the driver to manoeuvre and shape some perfect double-ups, so that's what tomorrow's going to be about.

I'm going to use the opportunity to try to land a 1080. Over the past two years I've tried the trick hundreds if not thousands of times but so far it's eluded me. If I manage it, I will be the fourth person in the world to do so, after Parks, Danny, and Canadian rider Rusty Malinoski. It's said that Mark Kenney might've landed one, but it's not official without any footage to prove it.

I slip into something of a dream state, visualising myself riding away from a 1080. I become a spectator, watching myself complete the three full rotations. I can also feel the punt of the double-up, the handle passing from hand to hand, the stomp of the landing.

Over and over, I see it. I feel it.

It's so real.

•

Early the next afternoon, on glassy water that reflects the surrounding green hills, I'm up behind the boat. Straight away, I get stuck into some toeside double-ups, served up beautifully by Deano, who's behind the wheel. From the chase boat driven by Scotty, Carnie shoots my every attempt on film, while Jeff's taking photos.

I'm getting closer and closer to landing that 1080. Every time, I land on my board with the handle behind my back, only to either fall back over my heels or tip over my toes. When you've been wildly spinning through the air, timing your landing so you're perfectly balanced is an incredibly fine art, which is why the 1080 club is so exclusive.

By my fifth attempt, I'm really feeling it. The boat circles around to cross its own rollers and I line up the third one, timing my approach to connect with it. Up into the air I go. To initiate the spin, I pull the handle hard across my body with both hands. Next, I start passing the handle from right to left behind my back, then left to right in front of me — I do this four times, spinning through three full rotations. Then I plant the handle into my lower back and brace for the blind landing. Before I know it, I'm riding away with my fist up in the air.

It all happens so fast, in less than two seconds.

For a moment I'm stunned . . . then I'm overcome with a rush of pure elation like nothing I've ever felt before. I throw the handle in celebration, then turn towards the boat just in time to see Deano and Alex leaping into the water, cheering.

'*YEEEEAAAAAHHH! WOOOOOHOOOO! FUCK YEAH, B-RADDDD!*'

I hear yelling from the chase boat and see Ants, Jeff and Scotty leaping into the water too. All my mates swim over to me, meeting me with splashes, high-fives, hugs and more cheers. They're every bit as stoked as I am.

I can't believe it.

Finally, today — 19 February 2008 — I've conquered the 1080, wakeboarding's holy grail. What's more, I'm the first to land the trick in a regular stance. For whatever reason, Parks, Danny and Rusty all did theirs switch.

I'm brimming with pride, and I know it's about more than just nailing a new trick. My overwhelming sense of achievement is a direct product of the time, effort, blood, sweat and tears that have gone into this. Nothing has ever felt so good. Not taking ecstasy, not winning worlds, not having sex. Nothing!

And now I get to celebrate with my friends, in the water, knowing that Jeff and Carnie both caught the proof on film.

It seriously could not be more perfect.

•

I'm still dripping wet when, less than 15 minutes later, the first of many calls comes in.

'Brad, congratulations!' It's Craig from Urban Rider, who I picked up as a sponsor last year. As well as chucking a little cash in my account, he's also promised to give me a good deal on getting my own wake-winch.

'Thanks, man!' I say, asking how he found out so quickly. Jeff sent a text to his brother Greg, who immediately posted an update to his website, and that's where Craig read the news.

The congratulatory calls keep coming for the duration of our filming mission south, and the one I least expect comes from Matty at Oakley. For six months now I've been trying to get hold of him about the salary and contract he promised me, but he hasn't replied to any of my calls or emails. I've seen no money, no contract. It's great to hear him pumped at my achievement, but once he's done praising me I cut to the chase. 'So, Matty, what's the status on that contract you were sending out?'

'Yeah, my bad, dude,' he replies. 'Sorry I haven't got back to you about that . . .'

He pauses. 'Unfortunately, due to the dive the economy has taken, my sponsorship budget has dried up. I have nothing left for you. I'm really sorry, Brad.'

I've been riding high on my 1080 but Matty's news punctures my elation. My heart plummets. When I heard his voice I half hoped maybe he was calling to offer a bonus, but in fact he's telling me I'm getting nothing at all. What a let-down.

'We might be able to figure out some sort of incentive package,' he adds.

Yeah, yeah.

I'm sure he's telling the truth about the sponsorship budget, but I also can't help feeling like it's personal. This just seems to keep happening. I'm fed up with being strung along, and I'm sick of working so hard in this sport for sweet fuck all.

So I say, 'I'm sorry, Matty, but that's not good enough. I've been with Oakley for six years, and it's at a point now where I can't keep your stickers on my board if you're not going to pay to have them there.' It feels good to finally stand up for myself. 'Especially not when my other sponsors are paying to be there,' I add for impact, even though that's not entirely true. I only get a small amount of financial support, in the form of things like flights here and there, from my other sponsors.

'Look, let me see what I can do,' he says. 'I'll get back to you.'

I'm not holding my breath.

When Paul O'Brien from Ronix calls me, it goes pretty much the same way. He's extremely pumped for me, and I'm stoked to have made enough of a splash to hear from the boss man himself, but it would be nice to get better news.

'I really wish we could pay you, Brad,' he says. 'You truly do deserve it. But starting a new company in this economy has been extremely challenging, and we simply have no money for you.'

At least I'm getting noticed, I guess, but overall, I'm gutted. I put in so much work to land that 1080. It was my ace in the hole that I thought might bring tangible benefits, but here I am with little more than warm words to show for my efforts. I need more than high-fives and 'well dones' to live on. I need an income.

•

Our filming trip comes to an end at Mouse's family's place, where Ants, Alex and I are earning a bit of extra cash for putting on a demo at their water-ski contest. I'm pretty relaxed about the demo, to the point that Alex and I add a drinking component to a game of Frisbee golf beforehand and I get a little tipsy. Alex, meanwhile, is drunk.

The demo goes well, and we get straight back to drinking afterwards. By this time, Casey has also arrived, invited by Mouse. We're all drinking together at the party Mouse's family has put on for the event. In the middle of a drinking game we run out of beer, so Mouse asks me to go and get a round for everyone. I wander into the marquee where the bar is, and when the bartender asks me what tab to put it on I say, 'Mouse's.' I just assume that these drinks, like everything else so far, are on him.

But his sister, who's standing nearby, overhears me. 'Put it on your own tab!' she says firmly.

'Sorry, I didn't even know I had a tab,' I say, then my inebriated logic kicks in. 'Actually, do you know how much I'm getting paid for the demo? So I know how much my tab is?'

It doesn't come off well. I appear to have hit a nerve because suddenly I have the entire family in my face. They're all having a go at me — even Mouse. I've clearly screwed up and I'm being reamed about all sorts of things, including stuff I don't recall ever being responsible for. I'm so confused. I try to defuse the situation but I can't get a word in. When they all finally pause for long enough to take a breath, I simply turn and leave. As I make my way back down the road towards the house, I'm absolutely fuming. Tears of frustration fill my eyes.

Once I'm back in my tent, my thoughts turn to Casey. No one's addressed the tension caused by having her here but I get the feeling she's part of the reason Mouse joined in. And, as much as I want her here with me now, I actually think it's better that she's not. I honestly can't deal with any more drama.

Next morning I apologise to Mouse's parents. They're pretty receptive, and everything seems cool between me and Mouse. I think we all just had too much to drink.

•

Just before I head over to Melbourne for the final pro tour stop, Alex returns to Florida. It's been epic to play host to him after he's been so good to me in the US over the last few years.

A decent crowd turns up for the final tour event at Melbourne's Caribbean Gardens, and I'm going into it sitting in third place in the overall rankings. I make it through the semi-final head to head, where I'm bested by my opponent, and I finish third equal with Jeff. Overall, I hold on to my third place, making this easily my best Aussie tour finish yet.

Back in New Zealand, Jeff and I face off in the only contest remaining for the season: nationals. Once again, I cannot beat this man, who always seems to one-up me on home turf.

•

I spend the next few months either working or with Casey. What was supposed to have been some good fun and great sex until I left for the US has become a bit more than that.

Our feelings for each other have definitely deepened. Her energy is infectious and she's incredibly driven, which inspires me to apply myself even more fully to wakeboarding. The truth is, I have well and truly fallen for her, to the point that I'm dreading leaving. We discuss the possibility of a long-distance relationship, but ultimately agree that it's better to just let it be. We'll see if we can pick things back up when I return.

•

Not long after I get back to Orlando, Alex tells me his parents are getting rid of their little Chevy S-10 truck. I figure that now's as good a time as any to get some wheels of my own here in the US, so I put some of the funds I've earnt towards buying a vehicle. The instant freedom is incredible. Any time I want to go shred with Alex or the Aussies, I can just pick up and roll out. The tray in the back is perfect for my gear and petrol cans.

I move back into the rental on the shores of Lake Jessamine with Austin Hair and two other guys — Nick Jones and Brazil's top pro rider, Marcelo 'Marreco' Giardi. Since I'm the last to move in, I'm relegated to a small mattress in the corner of the living room but I'm not worried — I'm just happy to have a place to stay for the season. I'll get a bedroom when Marreco moves out in a month.

It's a fun dynamic in the house. Austin is seeing a girl who brings her cute friends over all the time, so we all go on lake cruises while drinking and listening to music. We have Austin's sponsored Supra boat on the dock outside, but the wake is trash so I really only ride it as a last resort. It's not worth the $15 spent on petrol. Thankfully, Jeff is back living in our old place on the main section of the lake, so he swings by and picks me up when either of us wants a decent ride.

I'm pumped up to ride the wave of momentum after the most successful year of my career. Within my first two weeks back, Jeff swings me a juicy double-up and I stomp my second 10, first try! Jeff and I have a moment where we stare at each other in disbelief before we both burst out laughing. It's going to be a good season!

The contest season kicks off towards the end of April with the first event in the King of Wake series in Orlando. I finish up 19th equal, which is an average start but I can't be totally disappointed — I've made the top 20!

A couple of weeks later a bunch of us are up in Acworth, Georgia, for the second King of Wake event, which is also the first of two qualifiers to get on to the US pro tour. With 72 competitors from all over the world here and just 24 spots up for grabs, competition is fierce. The conditions are typical of Lake

Acworth: choppy, with loads of rollers produced by the hundreds of boats going to and fro. To begin with I manage a respectable run, but them I'm knocked out of contention. While Jeff, Chris-O, Alex and Austin all advance, I'm left with a salty 41st-equal finish.

Thankfully, I get another shot a couple of weeks later in Fort Worth, Texas, where I manage to beat out some stiff competition to progress all the way through to the quarter-final. The night before the big day, I swing by my hotel to change before heading out to dinner, but while I'm there I discover that my laptop's missing. Everyone else's computers are still there but mine is definitely gone, along with the charger. I don't get it. Why would someone steal my Sony Vaio and leave all the Apples? I'm gutted. I try to put it out of my mind ahead of the quarter-final.

The next day I link together a good run in my heat — although I take one fall, I still get in my sevens and the rest of my tech tricks. My score comes through at 85.0 and I finish with a career-best 11th equal. Not bad out of a total of 72 of the world's best. And — the thing that really matters — I've qualified for the pro tour!

I follow this up by advancing through to the quarter-final at the third stop in Twin Cities, Minnesota, bringing me a 16th-equal finish.

•

This season I get to compete in a location I've always wanted to visit: Lake Powell, which runs across the border of Utah and Arizona. I first saw it in the wakeboarding movies I watched as a kid at the Ballistics camp, and it's basically wakeboarding heaven, with high red cliffs and glassy green water. In order to get here, we have to fly in on a small propellor plane over the dramatic canyon-scored landscape, and to say it's magical isn't an exaggeration.

I'm here for Brostock, and I'm with fellow Ronix riders Chad Sharpe and Adam Errington. Our little plane lands by the lake and we hitch a ride to the event site in a boat with a random couple. The guy is friendly and is clearly a fan of wakeboarding as he recognises Chad instantly, and his girlfriend is hot — she looks like a *Playboy* model with oversized implants and a bunny tattoo on her hip. Since she's clearly off the market I do my best to avert my eyes for the 20-minute ride.

When we get to the sheltered cove we see half a dozen houseboats parked up — apparently this is our accommodation. Loads of the guys are already here and all the beds are taken, so we inflate our air mattresses and set up on the top deck of one of the boats.

Although the party's pretty mellow on the first night, I find out in the morning that several guys have already slept with *Playboy* chick. I guess her boyfriend couldn't compete against a bunch of pro wakeboarders.

By late morning it's time to get on the water but it's far from smooth, with boat rollers coming in from all directions. I completely botch all three double-ups and get knocked out in the first round. So I just start drinking. For the rest of the day, I sling back beers and watch the competition.

•

From Brostock, Adam, Chad and I fly up to Spokane, Washington, then drive down and across into Idaho, where we join the rest of the Ronix team for the brochure shoot for next year's product. It's a bit of a drive, but we finally pull up to a cabin on the edge of a valley overlooking a narrow section of Snake River. It's a cool little quiet spot to have our team getaway, and the fresh air is a welcome change from the thick humidity of Florida.

This is my first Ronix team trip and I'm both excited and nervous. There are only eight riders here — as well as me, Chad and Adam there's also Parks, Danny, Emily Copeland, Deano and wakeskater Reed Hansen — as well as a handful of reps, product guys, photographers and the boss man, Paul. I'm stoked to be invited, but I'm not totally at ease among all these guys yet. It's not that I'm starstruck nervous like I used to be; I just feel like the new guy who's been invited to hang with the cool group for the first time, and I don't want to start off on the wrong foot. They've all known each other for ages, so, to begin with, I just sit back and observe.

It doesn't take long for me to loosen up, though. We all spend the afternoon driving golf balls across the river, then in the evening we bond over a few beers and a game of Texas Hold 'Em. Then some of the guys excuse themselves and invite me to join them. Next thing, we're passing around an apple that's been affectionately named Bonita Apple-bong. I'm much less on edge after that, and by the end of the trip I feel much tighter with the whole crew.

•

For the next month or so I spend almost all my time travelling. First, I head to Portland, Oregon, for the Tigé Pro-Am Wakeboard Championship. It's not part of the pro tour but does count towards the overall King of Wake standings. It also includes a 1080 contest offering $10,800 for the rider who can land the trick within four attempts. I come frustratingly close to getting my hands on that cash. But the event's not a total waste — I'm pumped to come out with my best US pro finish of fifth equal, and that's enough to snag me a little prize money.

Then, after a fleeting rest back in Orlando, I'm off to Phoenix, Arizona, for the fourth stop of the pro tour. This event is held on a lake in the middle of a raceway and the dry heat is intense. With the temperature hovering over 40°C we're all sweating bullets as we wait around on the hot tarmac to ride. The water is much saltier than the ocean so it's challenging for everyone; the salt content makes the water so buoyant that the wake is much smaller than usual. In the scorching heat, the salt dries onto the plastic surface of the sliders, making them grip — and that's what catches me out. I don't even make it through my heat.

The next flight I'm on takes me all the way to the UK to return to defend my title at Wakestock in Wales. Ants isn't here this year so Dunc snags me from the airport and I spend a couple of days kicking it around the cable park but mostly resting. My back's been giving me trouble and my shoulder has been niggling me as well — it's slipped out several times since the first time at the beginning of the year.

The night before driving up to Wales I meet a cute girl called Jessica. We hit it off over a spliff and a couple of beers. She invites me to come out with her but I've got an interview early tomorrow and I'm also completely broke, so I politely decline. The next morning — a typically cold and drizzly London day — she gets in touch to tell me she's heading to Wakestock too. Do I want to roll up there in her Mini Cooper? Of course I do!

The first night of Wakestock gets a bit messier than I planned. By the time darkness falls I'm completely blitzed, thanks to the free drinks in the VIP area and multiple hash spliffs. A bunch of us cram into Jessica's Mini to burn another one down, but in order for everyone to fit I have to take my board bag out and wedge it under the rear bumper. That spliff puts me on another level. I lose control and lose all sense of time, so it's not until I retreat to my tent that I discover that Jessica has moved her car. My board bag is nowhere to be seen. I need my gear for the contest tomorrow so I spend a while searching for it, but end up crashing out, hoping it'll turn up.

It doesn't.

I end up riding on someone else's board. It's a Ronix One like mine, but it's smaller, with bigger fins and bigger boots — the size 14s feel like gumboots. Needless to say, my ride doesn't go well and I finish up in fourth place.

I take full advantage of my AAA pass, including getting myself onto the side of the stage while one of my favourite groups, The Streets, are performing. They put on an incredible show, and it's awesome to be right there on stage for it.

This year the prizegiving goes ahead up on stage like it's supposed to, and I'm asked up to stand beside the podium in fourth. While everyone else proudly holds up their boards, I brandish a cardboard sign that reads, 'Pikeys stole my wakeboard.' I know it's my fault for not looking after it, but I'm still pissed off that some opportunist decided to swipe it.

•

I let Ronix know about my board bag getting stolen (although I decline to mention the circumstances), and not long after I get back to Florida they send me a whole new kit, which is amazing.

After a hectic six weeks of back-to-back contests and travelling, it's great to be back in Orlando. The final pro tour stop is in Reno, Nevada, this weekend, but I've decided not to go. There are two main reasons for this: my back, and my finances. Wakeboarding is a cut-throat sport, and if you're not making the top five then you're probably spending more than you're earning. My recent fourth and fifth-equal placings haven't come close to meeting what I've been spending.

Every year I've come over to the US with significantly less money than it costs to be here, let alone to do it properly. The expenses just never end: there's the cost of riding multiple sets a day, of eating properly and of things like physio and the chiropractor, and then there are all the flights, accommodation, entry fees and so on.

Before leaving New Zealand this year I actually sat down and plugged my predicted expenses for the season into a spreadsheet — it included all of the above plus other costs like insurance, and the total came out at around four times what I actually had at my disposal. My credit card has been catching the overspend, and it's now maxed out.

Admittedly, I'm not great at planning ahead. Rather than booking my flights and entries in advance, I've got into a bit of a habit of leaving it late, and travel costs more if you do that. I'm not just procrastinating because I'm lazy or disorganised; it's more that I'm never quite sure if I can afford things, so I always leave it to the last minute to decide. Then I feel so bad about asking for help that I end up putting it off some more, until I become desperate.

I've been fortunate to receive support from several quarters. As well as getting me to the team shoot and the pro-am, Ronix helped me get to a couple of the pro tour stops. Bower (who sponsored me with his underwear brand) and Craig have also both chipped in where they can, and Dunc Hancock helped me get to the UK for Wakestock. But even with all that assistance, I'm still broke. I had to borrow money from Jeff to get to the Phoenix stop. I hated having to ask him, but it was that or fall off the top 20 on tour, and then I dropped my ranking anyway. And I end up having to call Mum, tail between my legs, to ask for yet another bailout loan to keep me going for a little while longer.

It's pretty demoralising constantly having to ask for money. It actually makes me feel like a beggar, even when it's my sponsors I'm asking. When I think about how I'm going to get through the next three months I feel completely overwhelmed. I'm flooded with anxiety and end up curled in a ball on my bed in tears. At least now, thanks to Mum, my rent is paid for the rest of the season, so if nothing else I've got a roof over my head and a set of wheels to get me places. Food and riding I can figure out as I go.

Then there's my back. Ever since I put it out a couple of years ago, the pain in my lower back has come and gone, and my recent hectic schedule has really taken a toll. I know I should have had it looked at sooner, but I've chosen to spend my available money on riding and the essentials. Then, to add to that, my shoulder's been bothering me ever since I put it out in Australia. My body just isn't performing the way it should. I'm starting to feel a bit like I'm falling apart.

I go back to see Dr G, who twists and cracks me back into shape. I leave feeling much better but I know not to rush back into riding. It's going to take more than one visit to get me properly straightened out and I have some big goals for what's left of the season. As well as landing a few more 1080s, I've decided I really want to be the first rider ever to land a 1260.

So, as much as missing Reno is definitely going to screw up my top-20 ranking, there's not much choice. For the same reasons, I also decide not to go to US nationals. Instead, when Carnie arrives to finish shooting his new film, I stay and focus on completing my section — which already includes the 1080 banger. We spend every day on the water, mixing up the locations and the crew. We go from hitting double-ups in Mount Dora to sessioning the rails at the projects to charging Jeff's monster wake on Lake Jessamine.

Since I'm still wary of pushing my body beyond what it can handle, I'm not on the water every single day, but Carnie has a handful of other riders to film, so sometimes I drive the boat or the chase. It's awesome to watch the other guys in action. At the end of it all I'm really happy with what we've achieved and excited to see the finished product.

•

September rolls around and I'm headed to Oklahoma for the WWA world champs, the last event on the 2008 calendar. This is where I met Dawn and I immediately get nostalgic, but she's not here any more. We've kept in touch so I know she's moved down to Dallas, which is a bummer because I'd love nothing more than another weekend of debauchery with her, guilt-free this time.

In the quarter-final I'm facing my toughest competition of the season, possibly of my career. I'm up against both Rusty Malinoski, one of the current tour front-runners, and Danny Harf, four-time X Games gold medallist, legend and my Ronix teammate. (As an aside, it's an interesting coincidence that the three of us are the second, third and fourth riders ever to land a 1080.) The fourth competitor is a really good young rider from Brazil named Deco Rondi.

Only two of us will advance through to the semi-final, so I'm really feeling the pressure to put a strong run together. Even my best might still not be enough if Danny and Rusty hit their runs. My best hope is to apply some pressure and hope someone has a fall.

Then, while I'm warming up in the riders' area, I get a message from home. It's Monique, letting me know that our grandfather, Pieter, has passed away. 'We weren't going to tell you until after worlds, but I thought you'd want to know,' she's written.

I know you're not supposed to have favourites but Dad's father was definitely my favourite grandparent. I really enjoyed hearing his stories from the Second World War when he was part of the Dutch underground. He still had the cabinet in which all of the communications equipment was hidden. He and my grandmother came by boat to New Zealand, moving their whole family from the Netherlands. My grandfather and I got along especially well and he was always interested in my sporting achievements.

This was heavy news to get but I'm glad Monique let me know. I would've been pissed off if they had withheld such big news from me simply because of a wakeboarding contest. It warms my heart to hear that a lot of family were with him when he passed, as he'd just turned 90 and they'd had a bit of a celebration.

I channel my emotions into my ride, and I feel pretty good about how I go. As I wait for the results I'm hoping it's enough. There's no question that Rusty took the heat, but it's going to be close between Danny and me. When the scores are released, I've just edged him out with 85.25 to his 83.25. I can't help but feel that maybe Pieter was there in spirit, cheering me on and helping me sneak through.

The next day, though, I bomb my run in the quarter-finals and come last in the heat. Fortunately, I still come away with a 13th-equal finish at worlds, bringing me to 22nd in the King of Wake standings, and 24th overall on the pro tour.

Which, when you consider that I missed the final tour stop and nationals, is not bad at all for my first season qualifying for the pro tour!

•

With a little extra financial backing and a bit more hard work, I reckon I could be pushing for a top 10 finish in the US next year. So I set my sights on trying to get some fresh sponsors on board. Back in Orlando, I head along to Surf Expo, but every brand I speak to and every sponsor I approach says the same thing: 'We would love to work with you but our budgets are too tight due to the recession. Any funds are already allocated. Sorry.'

It's so disappointing. There have been so many highlights this year, my 1080 being the most obvious, and yet I'm still struggling to get decent financial support. What the fuck do I have to do to get paid?

The only possibly good prospect came while I was still in Oklahoma. Just before I rode in the semis, Alex introduced me to his new sponsor, a short, stocky dude called Jay who owns a wakeboarding shop in Texas. After Jay commended me on my 1080 we got chatting for a while, then Alex suggested maybe I could ride for the shop too. Jay was open to the idea and we agreed to keep in touch. So that's something, at least.

•

Fortunately, the *Wakeboarding* magazine annual Wake Awards soon come around, reviving my enthusiasm. As I sit in the crowd, I'm frothing to see all the Trick of the Year nominations, as I have no doubt my 1080 will be among them. But, as the highlight reel runs through all the nominees, there's no sign of my 10. It's not included at all.

'I don't get it!' I say to the guys I'm sitting with. 'Why isn't my 10 in there?'

'Did you submit it?' Deano asks. When he sees my crestfallen expression he adds, 'It's on you to nominate it, bro.'

Bugger! *I really wish I'd known that sooner*, I think, feeling like a bit of an idiot. But surely *Wakeboarding* mag could've just added it into the mix since they printed the photo sequence? I'm feeling a little sorry for myself.

But my disappointment is soon erased by what comes up on the screen next: this year's Trick of the Year winner is Danny Harf, with the world's first-ever 1260!

The room absolutely explodes. People are completely stunned — me included — not just at the achievement but at what a well-kept secret it was. No one had any idea that was coming. How did they manage to keep such big news under wraps?

And, while I might be a little gutted it wasn't me who conquered the trick, I'm beyond stoked for my teammate. It's an incredible achievement.

•

After a US season that's been equal parts challenging and awesome, I'm looking forward to getting home. In the past six months I've gone from feeling on top of the world one moment to panicking about how I'm going to afford to live the next, so I'm ready to take some time to unwind.

Most of all, I'm excited to see Casey. While I've definitely been living up the single life in the US, she's always been at the back of my mind. And although we've kept in touch a bit, we've also given each other some space and the freedom to make the most of our careers and opportunities without worrying about what the other might be up to. But I'm keen to see how things go once we're in the same city again.

•

Not long after I get home, I join Dad's side of the family at a West Auckland beach to farewell my grandfather. I'm relieved to see that Dad's not looking too bad. I was worried his father's death might have hastened his decline, but things seem to have remained steady.

This beach is the one where, so many years ago now, I first landed a wake-to-wake jump while my cousins cheered from the boat. After a simple but beautiful service, we scatter Pieter's ashes into the sea.

I'm sad for Dad and his siblings, and for my grandmother Lise, and I shed more than a few tears. But I also find myself reflecting on how much living Pieter did in his 90 years. Whenever I went to see him, he always seemed really chill and content, like he'd lived a full and rich life. Rather than a day for mourning, this feels like a celebration of that life.

•

October in New Zealand is not great for wakeboarding — it's still a bit too cold — and anyway I need to work to start paying off my credit card and repaying

Mum. So I get straight back into the promo work, and it's the kind I hate. Instead of wandering the streets handing out free stuff that people actually want, I'm stuck in a supermarket aisle trying to get people to take samples of something I know nothing about and they don't want. Plus the uniform is goofy as hell!

But it's money — I desperately need to get out of the red and start saving for next season. I have no wish to face yet another US summer where I'm cripplingly broke while up against dudes who have everything at their fingertips.

The shining light amid the slog is Casey. The moment I see her she leaps straight into my arms and I enjoy the embrace I've been missing for too long. We quickly settle back into how things were before I left, spending every possible moment together. I love being with her. She's every bit the bundle of warmth and energy that I first fell in love with, but it's also just so nice to have someone to cuddle up with as we fall asleep, someone to wake up beside, someone who loves me as deeply as I love her.

As much as I've been enjoying all the travelling and partying and living the single life, the flipside is that sometimes the unsettled nature of that lifestyle — the being broke, the injuries, the highs and lows, the procession of women — just gets too much. While the entanglements satisfy an immediate need, the constant pursuit of more can get exhausting, and the moments in between can be quite lonely. I have to admit it's incredibly comforting to come home to Mum's place and have a quiet life with the girl I love. Just lying with her feels good — so stable and calm. It feels right. I open my heart up to her fully.

We have six months before I leave again. That feels like enough time to see if what we've got is solid enough to last long-distance — because I know now that I want this to last.

•

Ronix Australia flies me to Melbourne for the premiere of Carnie's film. He's called it *Canvas*, and I'm blown away to see I've got the opening section. Carnie's put together a year's worth of my best tricks and it's awesome. I'm feeling proud before my section even finishes, when the place erupts in cheers and applause that makes my grin even wider.

As always, it's epic to see Carnie and the Aussie crew. They really know how to party and we get pretty loose afterwards. A couple of girls come over to ask me to sign their boobs. I don't honestly think they're very big fans, but who am I to deny them?

Then I'm home again searching for more work. Not only is the sporadic supermarket stuff draining my soul but it's not bringing in enough cash. My brother Alex hooks me up with a second job behind the bar at a fancy inner-city restaurant where he's been working as a waiter. It's called Cibo, and it's conveniently just down the road from Mum's place.

It takes me a while to get into the swing of things. To begin with there's the matter of learning (and remembering) how to make all of the fancy cocktails the well-heeled customers have a penchant for ordering, but the most difficult part is memorising the incredibly long wine list. My years of partying and drinking American beer and cheap liquor have not turned me into much of a wine connoisseur, even if the fancy black-tie attire makes me look the part.

●

Casey comes over one day and she's bursting with excitement.

'You should enter *Cleo* Bachelor of the Year!' she tells me, as though it's the best idea ever.

A *bachelor* contest? I thought we were together . . .

But she's so excited I feel like I can't outright dismiss the idea. And it might be good publicity.

A few days later she calls sounding much more downbeat. I soon find out why: she's breaking up with me.

'You need to focus on your wakeboarding,' she says. 'And you'll be travelling all the time. I just don't see how it can work with both of our careers.'

I'm devastated, and shocked, and I can't hold back the tears. I plead with her to reconsider.

'We can find a way to make it work,' I say, but her mind's made up.

'Look, I'm really sorry,' she says. Then, 'I have to go.' She hangs up.

I'm sobbing and I feel like a pitiful, desperate idiot.

Eventually I find out there was more to it than she let on. She's been seeing some other guy since before I got back. I feel betrayed, and my heartbreak and sorrow turn to anger.

I'm done. Done with trying to make a relationship work. Done with opening up my heart, falling in love. I don't want to feel that pain again.

From now on, my focus is solely on my career.

From now on, I'm strictly single.

●

It doesn't take me long to find the perfect antidote to my heartbreak.

One Sunday, while I'm sitting around bored at home, I get chatting online with a girl I met recently through a friend. Her name is Sarah, and she's a stripper. I've never actually seen her at work, but she's got to be one of the hottest strippers in town. She's tall, blonde with dark roots, and has arm tatts, nice perky tits, great legs and a phenomenal ass. Her whole look just oozes sex appeal.

What are you up to? I type.

Just having a chill day, she replies. *Didn't get home from work till 6 a.m.*

You must be wrecked! I reply, and my fingers hesitate only briefly before I add: *Sounds like you could use a massage.*

Less than an hour later I'm at her place.

She's lying face down on her bed, wearing only a pair of jeans, and I'm straddling her hips and running my hands over her incredibly sexy back. As I work my way slowly down from her shoulders to her arms and then lower, I admire the line of Asian symbols tattooed along her spine. Finally, I dig my thumbs into the trigger points at the top of her glutes, and then she turns over. Her breasts are perfect, perky and totally natural, and both nipples are pierced. She reaches up and pulls me in to kiss her. Her tongue is pierced too. I wonder what else is pierced . . . and just thinking about it gets me so turned on I'm ready to fuck her immediately. But instead I slap her on the butt.

'Get back on your stomach,' I tell her. 'I haven't finished your full-body massage yet.'

She gives a mischievous smile and does what she's told, helping me to pull her jeans down.

And holy shit, she's not wearing any underwear. Keep it together, Brad . . .

She's so sexy I'm having to work hard to stay composed as I moisturise her butt and her legs, working my way down to her feet, which I rub with my palms, since I know she spent last night dancing in heels. Then my hands start working their way back up, and the sensual massage finally morphs into full-on foreplay . . . And yes, she has another piercing, one that might as well act as a giant sign that says 'Lick here!'

The sex is intense.

This girl is a savage, and she tells me exactly how she likes it.

Once it's all over, we lie facing each other and catching our breath, and I'm feeling pretty happy with myself.

Then she says, 'We need to teach you some better self-control techniques, boy,' and my face falls. There I was thinking I'd done a good job . . . but my ego's only bruised for a moment before I realise there's an opportunity here. Sarah is seven years older than me and she knows what she's doing. If all my escapades have left my abilities in the bedroom in any way lacking in some crucial areas, then this smokin'-hot siren is just the mentor I need. She can coach me to become a better lover, and I'm ready to get some guidance from a pro.

We continue seeing each other, and every time we're together I learn something new. She teaches me stall tactics to control myself so I can go for longer, and shows me what positions best hit the spot for her. She loves it rough, and even more so when she's drunk, so I happily oblige when she begs me to do things like spank her arse, pinch her nipples and pull her hair.

It's a fine balance, this combination of pleasure and pain. Some days she likes to dominate me and be in full control, and others she just wants to be dominated and fucked . . . It's about communicating and learning to read what she, or any sexual partner, wants in the moment.

I thoroughly enjoy my sessions learning from this vixen, and I'm getting better at satisfying her with each interaction. And when I happen to finish first, at least I know to go down and finish the job. Because there's no faking it with Sarah. And there's nothing complicated about our arrangement — we're just friends who have loads of sex and loads of fun together. Casey couldn't be further from my mind.

SEVEN: UP IN SMOKE

I start 2009 by getting back to the promo work. My sister Monique is working at the same agency now, so she ropes me into all sorts of jobs — including more than a few that I really don't want to do.

One I'd rather forget involved donning a superhero costume to promote some new juice company. At first I didn't mind the idea of wandering around in a muscly superhero suit, until they told me I couldn't wear a mask. 'We need your face showing as it makes you more approachable,' they said. I had to visit different inner-city businesses and hand out free juice samples. *Ah well*, I thought, *how bad can it be?*

Pretty bad, I realised as soon as I arrived at one of the nominated businesses and discovered it was one I visited a month or so earlier to ask for sponsorship. They said no.

Maybe they won't recognise me, I tried to reassure myself as I walked in.

They did.

I'm definitely not getting paid enough for this, but I need the money so I persevere. I also make a brief foray into topless waiting. A stripper friend of Sarah's gets in touch to ask if I'll work a hen party one weekend, I'm hesitant until I learn how much it's paying: $300 for three hours' work. I can't turn that down. I walk around in nothing but board shorts most of the time anyway so, aside from the fact that I'll be serving a bunch of drunk women, this isn't really that different. Right?

The day before, Sarah's friend drops by to give me a quick rundown. When he hands me some full-on Chippendale-style cuffs, collar and bow tie to wear I'm not stoked but I'd have to do 15 hours of bartending to earn the same amount. Then he hands me a little apron. 'Wear this over the top,' he says. 'And underneath you can wear either black dress pants or this.' He holds up a black G-string.

I laugh. 'Er yeah, I'll wear the pants, thanks.'

When I arrive at the hen party, the bride-to-be wanders over to introduce herself and I realise — my worst nightmare — that I recognise her.

Top left Me as a kid, asleep on Dad's shoulders after a day at the beach.
Top right On the podium at the 2004 IWSF World Championships after winning the junior men's division. Michael Hancock came in second place and Tony Evans in third. **Bottom** Performing a backside lipslide in front of the snow-capped Southern Alps (photo by Luke Thomas).

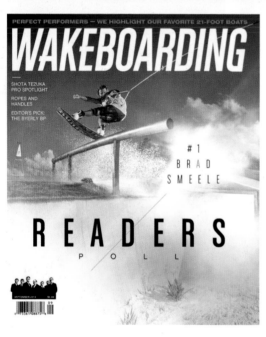

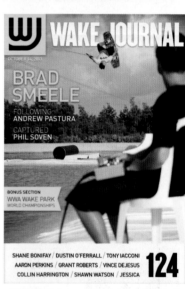

Top 19 February 2008: the moment I made history with the world's first regular-stance 1080 (photo by Jeff Weatherall). **Bottom** A small selection of wakeboarding mags featuring me on the cover. Clockwise from left: *Wakeboarding* (photo by Chris 'Flash' Garrison); *Wake Journal* (photo by Joey Meddock); *Wake Magazine* (photo by Joey Meddock).

Top left Modelling for *New Zealand Weddings* magazine (photographer unknown). **Top right** Kitted out in double denim for a modelling assignment (photographer unknown). **Bottom** The main beach at Lake Ronix, aka wakeboarders' paradise.

Top Yarning with Paul and Ruck on my newly made bench seats, built and positioned around the fire pit on Wake Beach, Lake Ronix. **Bottom left** A rattlesnake at Lake Ronix that didn't make it. **Bottom right** Holding my niece Mila for the first time, alongside my brother-in-law Jonny and niece Maisey.

Top A hero's pose – the iconic photo that spread around the world after my accident (photo by Josh Letchworth). **Bottom left** Performing a frontside boardslide during a moonlight session at Lake Ronix (photo by Bryan 'Bear' Soderlind). **Bottom right** The hard life of an MC: on stage with the promo girls from Rockstar Energy.

Top The lads taking a lunch break on top of the wall we were building at Lake Ronix (photo by Erik Ruck). **Bottom** A transfer to frontside lipslide on the finished wall (photo by Bryan 'Bear' Soderlind).

Top The Lake Ronix bi-level setup, complete with mega-ramp.
Bottom Resting between hits on the mega-ramp (photo by Bryan 'Bear' Soderlind).

Top Competing at the Red Bull Rising High event in Hamm, Germany. This image shows the sequence of my toeside indy double backroll over the mega-ramp (photo by Steffen Vollert). **Bottom** Jeff (left) and Alex, with support from team Ronix, accepting my Trick of the Year award at the 2014 Wake Awards (photo by John Lipscomb).

'Hey,' she says, looking at me closely. 'I know you — we met at Cibo, didn't we? When my band was performing? You're the wakeboarder!'

'Yeah, that's right,' I reply.

'Oh cool,' she says. 'Hey, I actually know your mum through work.'

'Oh right,' I say. 'Haha . . . um, how embarrassing!'

We chat for a little longer, then I awkwardly say, 'Okay cool, so I'd better get to work. I'm just gonna go take my shirt off.'

When I walk back into the bar in my Chippendale cuffs and collar and little else, I'm greeted by the ecstatic cheers of 30 horny ladies. For the next two hours I'm the sole waiter, strolling around topping up glasses. The only other guys in the room are behind video cameras, and they seem to be getting a good laugh out of it all.

I'm mortified, as I had no idea this would be recorded. As I walk by one woman, she reaches out and grabs my arse, then gives me a fluttery little wave. For the first time I start to understand what it must be like for girls in bars, getting groped and hit on by horny men. I don't enjoy it.

At long last Sarah's friend arrives to put on his strip show, and I get a welcome break. I don't know how he does it. While the $300 cash feels good in my hand at the end of the night, I'm not sure I'll be doing this again. Later, I find out that topless barmaids get paid two-thirds of what I earned. Why should I make more when they have to expose more? It makes no sense to me.

•

Since deciding to be single, I've been enjoying all the benefits that come with it. On the weekends I hit downtown Auckland with my old mates Jordan, Doug and Rory. Some nights, we pop pingers and absolutely rage to drum and bass. Other nights, Jordan and I get stoned and hit the small dubstep gigs.

Every night, I'm on the hunt for the hottest thing I can drag home — and I have plenty of success.

I've never wanted to be labelled a player but I know I'm dancing a fine line. The way I see it, though, a player is someone who misleads women to get them into bed, and that's not what I'm doing. I'm totally upfront about things. With all my sexcapades, I'm crystal clear about the fact I'm not looking for a relationship, and for most of the girls I pick up that doesn't seem like much of an issue. I certainly don't want to leave any woman feeling used or mistreated. I only want to make them feel good.

I'm starting to realise what Brant meant when he warned me that Orlando would ruin me. The New Zealand wakeboard scene feels pretty stagnant in comparison. The contest calendar isn't nearly as packed, and we've just lost two of my favourites — there's no more Pipe Masters and no more Wake Up, which means there's $1500 less prize money up for grabs. I snag a cheeky grand when I once again take out the North Island champs, but I need more than that. So I start MC'ing wakeboarding events. As well as being a pretty enjoyable way to make a few extra bucks it gets me free entry, but they're long days on the mic.

It's hard to get quality riding here also without a boat of my own, and having to work so much means I have less time for wakeboarding. My riding rarely improves while I'm back here — it's really just about maintenance, making sure I don't lose any of my tricks, and trying to keep them consistent until I get back to Florida and can ride daily again.

My final competition of the season is nationals, which are held down at Mouse's family's place in the South Island. It's the first time I've seen him since last year's run-in, so it's great to catch up and know it's all in the past, and we're both glad we didn't let a fight over a woman ruin our friendship. The contest on the water becomes the most epic battle yet between Jeff and me. After putting together the best pass I've ever done at nationals — a run that would easily beat any of his previous year's runs — I know I've put the pressure on him. But, in typical Jeff fashion, he throws down two solid passes and even pulls a crow five on a small wake out of his arse.

Once again I'm the bridesmaid.

●

Before I head back to the US there's one challenge I'm determined to conquer: the step-up on that concrete spillway near Mangakino. It got the better of me last time because I didn't have the right-shaped kicker. So Ronix have thrown a grand my way to build just what I need.

Brant and I rope in a few mates to help. Together, we construct a super-kicker that's 9 metres long and around 2.5 metres high at its peak. As I stand back to admire our handiwork, I get a proper sense of its scale and realise it's a monster! It's comedically large when compared with what riders usually hit on a wakeboard. I've always wondered what it might feel like to soar off the top of something this big — and I'm about to find out.

I've managed to secure the support of a local crane company, and the next day they send a Hiab truck to lift and transport the kicker 20 minutes up the road to the spillway. I've also brought in Carnie to take photos, with the goal of nailing a magazine cover shot. Ants, Doug and a handful of others make the trip down from Auckland to support me, including helping with the rest of the setup and the filming.

First, I take a couple of warm-up runs to make sure I've got enough speed and the kicker angle is on point. It all feels good, and it definitely looks much friendlier than the steep booter from last time. It's time to go for the step-up.

As I wait for the 100-metre-long rope to come tight behind Brant on the jet-ski, my veins are pumping with nerves and excitement. The moment I feel the pull, I clasp the handle and hold my line into the super-kicker, which smoothly launches me heavenward. I've only ever gone bigger once in my life: off a huge wave in Tahiti while doing tow-ins on our wakeboards. Still holding the handle, I watch the concrete spillway fly past below me, then enjoy a fast but super-soft landing on the top lake. My friends and supporters applaud and cheer (most likely because I didn't splatter myself on the spillway, which I'm pretty glad of myself).

For the next hour I session the step-up. Each time, I get more comfortable and start trying different grabs. I make sure I get a good backside indy grab up the gap and, when I check the shot that Carnie got, it looks epic. It's hard to see properly on the camera's small screen, but it definitely looks cover-worthy!

It's gratifying to have made wakeboarding history yet again, and once word spreads I get props from pretty much every rider I know. But I don't get the cover I hoped for. When we send the best shots off to the mags, they're pretty stoked with them, but the best ones were taken in landscape format and they need portrait format. I'm gutted, but *Alliance* ends up running a spread inside the mag.

•

By the time I head back to the US I've cleared my credit card and saved a couple of grand, which I know is not enough. I'm stressed about entering another US season with far less than I need. The harsh reality is that I just don't have the financial backing required to compete properly in this career I've chosen.

It's not for lack of effort. I've worked so much all summer that it's cost me quality training time. I even brought on a manager to help find me some sponsorship but didn't have much luck on that front. Wakeboarding is a niche sport in New Zealand, and the few wake-related brands don't have the money to pay riders.

But I'm undeterred. I'm hopeful that 2009 will be the year I get my big break.

I make an overnight stopover in Dallas to see Dawn. She swoops me up in her little sports car and we spend the night together in her downtown apartment. It's incredible to see her again. The attraction and passion are still just as intense, and I immediately wish I was here for more than just one night.

The next day I fly to Miami, where I meet up with Jeff, Deano, Scotty and a few others for Board Up Miami. It's the first event on the US calendar and there's $10,000 up for grabs. Since most of the best are away competing at Wake Games in Orlando, the odds are better than they might be — but the rough water conditions prove too much for me and I bow out in the semi-finals. Jeff grabs third, and Deano takes second.

After the contest I'm exhausted. It's not just the solid few days of riding that have me spent — it's also the loose partying every night. On the drive up to Orlando I realise that in just four days I've managed to blow almost a quarter of my tiny savings for the whole season.

Brad, you're an idiot! I berate myself. *What have you done?*

I can't believe I've been so careless . . . I just get so caught up in the moment. These guys love to get amongst it, and I didn't want to miss out on the fun that Miami had on offer: drinks, cocaine and women. Something has to change.

●

Once again, for the first few weeks I crash at Alex's. His parents have moved into a new place on a different lake. The house is a huge upgrade, and there's a spare room for me right beside Alex's. As always, it's epic to be back hanging and riding with my brother from another. We link up with some of the guys who moved out to Lake County last year, and we're a competitive bunch. Everyone is super talented, so I feel pretty lucky to have found such a motivating crew to ride with. I really notice the positive influence it has on my own riding. Whenever I see one of my comrades do something rad, it just motivates me even more.

The first month flies by, then we're off to Fort Worth, Texas, for the first stop of the pro tour. I ride well in the qualifying round, winning my heat, but end up getting knocked out of the action in the second round. Alex's sponsor Jay is here, and I'm keen to try to solidify this sponsorship deal we discussed briefly last year.

After the event, I go back to Jay's place in Mineral Wells for a couple of days of riding. After dinner with his wife and kids one night he takes me upstairs to his man-cave, which boasts a bar with beer on tap and a wall lined with guitars. I take down one of his Taylors and strum my fingers across the strings. It sounds beautiful. I've always wanted to learn to play the guitar properly.

Jay gets straight to the point. 'Brad, I'd love you to ride for my shop. And I also want you to help promote my new website.'

'Thanks, man!' I'm stoked, but before I can agree, I have to be up-front with him. 'There's just one thing. If you want your website to be successful, you're going to have to change the name.'

'Why? What's wrong with WOLY Wake?' Jay seems a little put-out. His shop and his website are both named after the church he goes to, Walk of Life Youth.

'I don't mean to insult you,' I say, 'but it's just that it reads as "wally", and in most places that's a word used to describe someone who's a bit of a kook on the water. You know, the guy driving circles around the lake, making the conditions terrible for everyone else — like a weekend wally.'

'I've never heard that,' Jay replies.

'I wouldn't be bringing it up if I didn't really believe in the potential of your website with another name. And honestly? I don't know how stoked I would be to have a WOLY sticker on my board.'

Jay still looks pretty confronted but he thanks me for my honesty.

We have a couple more beers together, and as we talk I can see he's slowly coming around to the idea. We even start throwing alternative names around.

That night I struggle to sleep. My mind is busy with ideas of what we could do to create something awesome and different — some kind of social media platform for wakeboarders. As well as featuring an online shop, Jay's website allows users to create a rider profile and upload videos and pictures. It's got a bunch of users from around Texas, and with some tweaks — including the name — I reckon it could become an international thing.

After breakfast I share some of my ideas with Jay and he's really receptive. We also settle on a new name: iwake. By the end of our chat, Jay's grabbed a napkin and written up a 'contract', granting me dividends in the future sale of the website if it's successful. We also shake hands on our sponsorship agreement. It starts at $500 per month, but since I'm not allowed to earn money in the US we make it a travel budget.

On the way to drop me at the airport, Jay pulls in to an Apple store.

'I just have to grab something,' he says.

While I wait for him, I browse the shelves.

After a while, Jay comes over to me. 'Looking for a replacement?' he says. The previous night I'd told him about my laptop getting stolen.

'Yeah,' I say, 'but I can't afford any of these!'

He has a white box tucked under his arm and heads over to the counter to pay. As we're on our way out the door he hands the box to me. 'Here you go, dude,' he says, grinning. 'Here's your new laptop.'

'You can't be serious!' I'm completely stunned.

He just nods, still smiling.

'Really? I don't know what to say! Thank you!' There are no words to show how grateful I am. I never expected him to buy me a computer — let alone a brand-new MacBook Pro. It's the first time I've felt like a sponsor has gone above and beyond for me. I've got a good feeling about this relationship.

•

Having my truck means I can move around a bit while I'm in Florida, and I make sure I spread myself around so I'm not always at Alex's, getting on his parents' nerves. More often than not, I kick it with the Aussies at Mitch Langfield's place in Clear Lake. His parents bought him a house here, and he's good with letting the likes of myself crash on his couch. Maybe it's because he wants to help others who don't have the same support as he does, but he's also just a good dude. There's no boat, but there are some fun rails on the lake that we session behind a jet-ski. I also head back to Texas and stay at Jay's for a while, after a rather terrible showing in Wisconsin that has me out of the top 40 and off the pro tour.

Even though crashing on couches is definitely helping on the money side of things, by the time I pass the halfway mark of this trip the funds are drying up. With no winnings this season I've done well to make the money last this long. I'm resorting to a diet of ramen noodles and $5 foot-longs from Subway so I can still afford to ride.

•

One afternoon just after a storm has passed through, I head out on East Crooked Lake with Alex, Cole Chapman and a bunch of other mates. We've got the boat completely packed out so the wake is monstrous. I get my blood pumping with some warm-up carves — leaning hard and digging my board's edge into the mirror-like water before powering in to slash hard at the wake. After that I start on some tricks. First, I charge in for a nuclear glide and I get so much height I know I've got time to add a 180 and drop it to fakie. I'm on my game today: my timing is on point, everything is flowing well, I feel strong. I'm firmly focused on the present moment. It's time to shred!

As we plane up and down the lake, I work my way through my trick list. At the end of each run, Alex swings me a double-up. I boost a clean heel 900 off the first, then play around with some different grabs on basic spins on the way back down the lake before cutting out as wide as possible then charging in on my heels. It's this freedom of expression, and being able to make tricks my own, that I love about wakeboarding.

Being on the water is the one thing that makes me forget all about my money troubles. The moment my board is gliding across the water's surface and I feel the wind on my face, everything melts away. For the next half an hour, nothing else matters. None of my troubles exist. And it's not just the worries I leave behind. The constant noise of my thoughts quietens. The meaningless chatter goes from my head. There's no future or past. When I'm riding, there's just what's happening now.

Next, I send a huge mute grab to late backside 180 right out into the flats. I land heavily, but can't power through it. My back edge catches and I crash into the water. I get spanked. The whiplash rattles my brain, and as I pop up out of the water I take in a big breath and try to shake it off. Some bails are easier than others, and it always seems to be the ones I expect least that hurt the most. But, as long as I'm not injured, I actually don't mind crashes. It's all part of the learning process — sometimes a heavy crash leaves me feeling more alive.

Towards the end of my set, Alex rolls me a left-hand double-up right in front of the dock. I line up the third roller with a 1080 in mind. I've been trying at least one 1080 whenever I'm riding a good wake with someone who can drive double-ups, and I've learnt that my usual mistake is to let the wake kick me into the spin. So this time I focus on holding my body position and standing tall all the way through the double-up. The moment I feel the vertical punch I start spinning . . . and this is the one! After the three full rotations, I absolutely stomp the landing, smoothly passing the handle behind my back as I ride away.

A wave of elation washes over me as I hear the cheers erupting from the boat. I've conquered my third 1080! I feel like the king of the fucking world. I ride away so smoothly, so easily, and in that moment every single crash is more than worth it. I'm absolutely buzzing. Yet again, all it's taken to refill my cup is one good set. My soul is overflowing with immense pride and utter fulfilment, my money troubles a worry for another time.

I really don't know what I would do if I didn't have this as my outlet.

•

In August I head to South Korea for the 2009 IWWF World Championships. I arrive three days before the event kicks off, with time to recover from the long journey.

Most of the top riders are at the WWA worlds in Orlando right now, and I'm gutted I can't be there with them. But if I can make it onto the podium here, it'll be a big payday for me. Not because there's any prize money on offer — there never is — but because this event is recognised by Sport and Recreation New Zealand as world wakeboarding's pinnacle competition, even though riders and the core industry know that it most certainly is not.

I don't really care about winning the title, but I could definitely use the $15,000 Performance Enhancement Grant (PEG) that's on offer from Sport and Rec if I place in the top three. And, since the IWWF worlds now run biennially, any grant rolls over for a second year, meaning a grand total of $30,000. I can't afford to turn my nose up at that.

I meet up with some of my fellow New Zealand team members for dinner at a local restaurant. It's a dingy little hole-in-the-wall establishment, with a bunch of skinny stray dogs lingering on the street outside. They're so miserable-looking that I want to feed them, but there's way too many of them for that, even if I did have something to offer.

As I step inside, I can't help wondering whether the food on offer will be safe for Western stomachs, but I'm here and I'm hungry so I point at the most familiar-looking thing I can find on the menu. It's a kind of beef shank stew, and when it comes out I'm relieved to find it's actually pretty tasty. The meat is so well cooked it practically falls off the bone. But I'm halfway through devouring my delicious meal when I suddenly have a sickening thought: what if the dogs outside — the ones I wanted to feed — are actually feeding *me* right now?

I've heard about Korean dishes containing dog meat, but I don't think eating dogs is exactly a mainstream practice, especially not in recent years. Is it? Dog definitely has no place in my diet. I do my best to banish the thought and finish my meal, but there's no chance of that now.

As soon as I get back to my hotel room I crash out, only to wake the next morning feeling pretty average. My body aches, I've got a sore throat and I'm feeling a headache coming on. I get up out of bed and rush to the toilet.

Ughhh, my guts! My stomach is not happy. I don't think it likes whatever I ate last night.

I shower and get ready, then head down to the lobby to meet up with the team to go and check out the event site. It's a good-looking venue with terraced seating along the shoreline for plenty of spectators. The lake is a bit too big and open for my liking, though. The water is calm now, but if the wind picks up it will get really rough and the conditions won't be easy.

As the day goes on, I feel more and more unwell. No one else seems to be affected but I need to lie down so I excuse myself and head back to the hotel. By the time I get there I'm beginning to get the sweats. I don't think this is food poisoning — it feels more like flu.

Shivering and coughing, I wrap myself up in my blankets, feeling sorry for myself. Jeff's arriving later tonight — having won the IWWF championships twice before, he's back for more — and he's supposed to be rooming with me, but I don't think it's safe for him to be anywhere near me. I don't think it's safe for anyone to be near me. Hopefully I'll feel better tomorrow.

Hours pass, and I hear the door open. It's Jeff.

'I'm not sure you want to get too close, dude. I'm sick as a dog!' I call out from my bed.

'You and me both, bro,' I hear him reply in an uncharacteristically flat tone.

'Ohhh, no way! You got it too? So it's definitely not something I ate.'

'Nah, bro, this is something else,' he mutters as he crawls into his bed.

We both try to sleep but without much success. It's a night filled with sweats and regular bathroom visits, and my crook gut amps up from diarrhoea to include vomiting.

When the morning finally dawns, I feel like death. I'm much, much worse than yesterday. Worse than I've felt in my entire life. My sheets are soaked with sweat and my entire body aches.

Jeff's no better.

I message our team manager that there's no way either of us will make the practice or the opening ceremony today.

For the next 24 hours, Jeff and I take turns in the bathroom, spewing out of both ends and taking cold showers curled up on the floor in the foetal position.

'I think we've got swine flu,' Jeff proclaims.

I remember at the airport we all had to pass through an extra screening point where they checked people for signs of illness. There were signs everywhere warning people of the H1N1 outbreak. Maybe he's right. This is without a doubt the most horrible sickness I have ever experienced.

'So much for that $30k, hey, bro?' I say to Jeff.

•

The next day is the first of competition but Jeff and I wake up well and truly steamrolled. We're meant to be competing in the first round of the men's division this afternoon. By an extraordinary effort of will, we both make it to the contest and ride in our heats. We each place third, just missing the top-two cut-off to advance to the next round.

Mentally and physically defeated, we return to our quarters and continue to purge anything and everything we have in us. Thankfully, we'll get one more chance tomorrow — there's a last-chance qualifier — so we eat some plain rice and hope for the best.

The next morning dawns and we're both feeling a little better. We grab a quick breakfast, glad to feel like it won't be instantly ejected.

This time we each perform better in our heats, both taking the top spots.

Phew, we're still in this!

On day three I advance through my quarter-final round, placing second in my heat, and Jeff does the same. Part of me is stoked that my friend is also advancing to the semi-final, but a tiny part of me regrets that my biggest rival is still in the running. Best-case scenario: we both make it to the podium and both get a PEG. Worst-case scenario? Jeff knocks me out of the money.

•

The last day is here and I'm feeling almost human. The conditions, though, are less than ideal. The wind has picked up and made the water choppy and challenging.

Jeff rides his semi-final heat ahead of me, and he falls apart. Flu fatigue and the rough conditions have got the better of him and his run has come to an end.

With a solid but conservative run I manage to place second in my heat. I'm through to the final — and, with Jeff out of the equation, things are looking much less dangerous.

A few hours later I'm back on the starting dock. The wind is blowing even harder and the conditions are the worst they've been all week. Physically, I'm wrecked. But mentally I'm feeling good. I get myself amped up listening to some pumping tunes and start stretching while I wait for the riders ahead of me to finish.

The first rider off the dock is Australian Sam Thomson. He crashes out in his run.

Next up is American Adam Fields, who links together two solid passes and punctuates his run by stomping a huge front mobe off the double-up. The bar has been set!

The third guy in the final, Italian Giuliano Molli, also falls.

As I'm stepping into my boots, I'm calculating my plan of attack. Adam's run is beatable, and if I can top his score I guarantee myself a spot on the podium — and a possible win. Then I check myself. I don't need to win, I just need to make the top three to get a PEG. I don't need to go too hard.

I jump off the starting dock. My body's spent. Running purely on the prospect of bagging myself that payday, I cruise through my first pass, linking my tricks together smoothly, taming the rough water with power, landing with precision. I find a couple of gems in the rough, lining up the wind-chop rollers as I cut into the wake and using them like miniature double-ups to launch into my manoeuvres — I'm finding ways to turn these horrible conditions to my favour.

As soon as I finish pass number one and the boat starts to turn, I suck in a couple of deep breaths only to end up coughing and dry-heaving. The 30-second break I get before my second pass barely gives me enough time to catch my breath.

But I'm on the home stretch: one pass, five tricks away from possibly bagging the biggest payday of my career.

One trick at a time, I remind myself.

I make my way through two solid tricks, then for trick number three I launch into a heelside 720. It's the riskiest trick in my run, as I have to pass the handle three times while spinning through the air. I almost miss the third handle-pass, just getting my fingertips to it in time, then gripping the handle and dropping out perfectly over my board.

Cha-ching!

I cut back in on my toes and pop a toeside 720.

Cha-ching!

I hit my last trick: a backroll to blind.

Cha-CHING!

Just one double-up left and my work here is done. As the boat circles around to cross its own rollers, I eye up my target: roller number three. In spite of the wind chop, I manage to spot my line. Time for my final banger: the toeside 900. I cut in hard and feel the punch of the double-up send me upwards. I pass the handle once . . . twice . . . three times. I pull myself into position to land — and then I see I'm coming up half a metre short. I case the top of the wake and crumple into the water.

Dammit! I had it!

Back on the dock I feel relieved and proud, but that last bail means I probably won't top Adam's score, and there are still two riders to come.

American Austin Hair, my former roommate, is halfway through his ride, and it's looking solid, but on his second run he backs out of a couple of tricks in order to avoid succumbing to the rough conditions. Like me, he falls on his double-up.

The last man off the dock is Thai ripper Padiwat Jaemjan, aka Bomb. He comes out charging — in typical Bomb fashion — and goes huge into the flats. Then, not far into his first pass, I see a big splash. He's down! He gets back up and finishes his first pass, only to go down again in the second.

I'm in the top three! I've done it!

As I dry myself off and change into some warm clothes, I do my best to contain my excitement. I have to wait for the official results to know my placing, but on the inside I'm already celebrating. I'm getting 30 grand! *Yeeeeeeeow!* I've never had that kind of money. It's the break I've been waiting for, the cash injection I need to propel my career forward. And I've earnt it after coming back from what felt like my deathbed, battling challenging conditions.

I take a moment to let it all sink in. Damn this feels good!

Just then, I feel a tap on the shoulder, and turn to see an IWWF official standing there with Adam.

'Brad,' he says, 'I need you and Adam to stick around for a minute.'

'Okay,' I say. 'What for?'

'We just need you both to do a drug test,' the official replies. 'Follow me.'

My elation is erased by a wash of dread.

As the three of us walk towards the main building, Adam and I linger slightly behind our babysitter.

'Dude,' Adam says softly, leaning towards me, 'when did you last smoke?'

'I had a couple of puffs of that blunt we smoked together on the first day of Expo a couple of weeks ago,' I mutter. 'You?'

'Same. I think we should be sweet, but I'm drinking as much water as possible before pissing in that cup, just in case.'

'Good idea.'

The official hands me a little plastic cup, and I tell him I don't need to go yet. I grab my bottle and chug the water back. Then I refill it, and do it again. And again.

Before long my bladder feels like it's about to burst, so I go into the bathroom with the official and fill the cup while he watches. I hand him my sample and make my way to the awards ceremony.

Moments later, the official results are announced and I'm called up to the podium to take second place and a silver medal. With my gold medal from '04 and my team bronze from '03, I now have a full set.

But, even though I stand proud on the podium, inside I'm freaking out. The drug test results won't be known for some time.

•

By the time I get back to Orlando after the long haul across the Pacific, the main competitive season is over for the year and I'm looking forward to having some free riding time.

The spare room at my friend Dieter's place on Lake Holden has come up for rent, so I move in. He's a six-foot-three (1.9 metres) South African wakeskater who I've got to know over the years at IWWF events, and he's been living here for several years with his gorgeous blonde girlfriend, Vee. It's nice to have a home base again, and it's a fun household to be part of. All up, there are seven of us, and we regularly throw pool parties or host Sunday Fundays out on the lake.

Jay flies me and the rest of the iwake team up to Texas for a quick filming trip, and while we're there he and I get chatting about ways to increase the content on his website.

'I could get some of my adventures on film,' I suggest. 'Then you could use the video to promote the site.' He's into that idea, so on the way to the airport he stops off and buys me a camcorder. I can't wait to start playing around with it and creating some cool content. Back in Orlando, Alex and I head out to Lake Saunders to ride with Canadian Anthony Hollick and some of his mates in Anthony's Malibu Wakesetter. It's a beautiful, calm day and I get to ride first. Anthony drives while Alex films me, linking together lines of my consistent tricks. At the end of one run I call for a left double-up. Anthony does as requested, and as I cut out from the wake I spot my roller, then time my toeside cut back into the double-up before boosting a wild 1080 attempt — but I case the second wake hard, crashing into the water.

'Hey, bro,' I call out to Anthony once the boat's close enough, 'could you put a bit more meat on the next one?'

He drops the throttle to get the boat up on plane, and as we gradually pick up speed I'm pulled back up on to the water. Once we've reached a speed of nearly 30 kph and the raging torrent of displaced water has formed into a crisp knee-high wake, I connect a few tricks. As we near the other end of the lake I signal another left double-up. Anthony spins the steering wheel, which abruptly turns the boat to the right, washing off speed in the process. The 410-horsepower beast in the back roars to get back up to speed, while Anthony gives a short and slight turn to the left, creating a line of larger rollers that push together in an open V shape and form a triple-up.

By the time we're fully turned around, we're approaching a chunky set of rollers. Anthony ploughs the boat straight through them.

Thud! Thud! THUD!

'How do ya like *that*, bitch?!' Anthony yells, half out of excitement at crafting me these thick and juicy rollers and half to teach me a lesson for complaining about the last double-up.

I charge in on my toes with another 1080 in mind but, as I reach the double-up, it rears up in front of me like a hydro-monster ready to feast on my body. Slightly spooked, I flag the 1080 and decide to just see how high I can get punted. This thing sends me nearly 5 metres up in the air. I grab my board indy and let it drift out behind me, then at the peak I pass the handle behind my back to drop a backside 180 as gravity kicks in.

I land heavily in the slight trough on the outside of the wake — the 'hard spot', which riders generally try to avoid. The impact causes my 95 kg body to crumple into the water while my board shoots out to the side.

SNNNAAP!

My right knee bends sideways and I feel something pop on the inside.

Oh god, that didn't feel good.

I emerge from the water clutching my leg and groaning in pain.

Cheers and hoots and hollers are coming from the boat, then as they get closer Alex pipes up.

'Dude,' he says, 'are you all right?'

'*Faaarrk*, man — my *knee!*' I try to straighten it but an excruciating pain shoots up my leg.

The guys help me up onto the swim platform. Once I've got my bindings off I climb into the boat but I can't put any weight on my right foot.

'Are you okay, Brad?' Anthony asks as I hobble to my seat. 'Do you think it's blown?'

'I'm not sure, dude. I've never blown a knee before but this certainly doesn't feel good.'

'Do you need to go in?'

'Ummm . . .' I think back to when a friend injured his foot while I was in the boat. He'd also been the first to ride that day, and the wake was absolutely pumping. He'd insisted on getting to hospital, so the rest of us had to leave without riding. I'd been gutted. If I've blown a ligament or broken something now, I figure it's not going to make much difference whether I go in straight away or in a few hours. So I say, 'Nah, I'll just put it up for now. But maybe we can stop at the dock between rides for some ice?'

'Are you sure?' Alex seems surprised, but also somewhat relieved.

'Yeah, I'll be fine. Pass me the camera! Who's up next?'

But as I sit there filming my friends, the blaring throb deep in my knee is joined by a whirlwind in my mind.

Fuck! What if I've done my anterior cruciate ligament? I don't want to get surgery — that would be my New Zealand summer gone. Will I be able to bounce back from this? Please, please don't let it be my ACL.

•

I didn't go to hospital in the end, and after a week the swelling around my knee has come down and I'm walking on the leg fairly normally. Maybe I just tweaked it? It still gives me pain when I bend it to around 90 degrees, it's pretty unstable and I'm miles away from being able to ride, but I'm starting to feel better about it. With more rest and rehab I might be back on the board in time for summer in the Southern Hemisphere.

Near the end of September, a week before I fly home, my roommates and I invite a few friends over for one last Sunday Funday on the lake. Dieter and I have just come back up to the house when I receive a phone call. It's Craig Gibson, the New Zealand team manager from the IWWF worlds. Craig starts talking and within just a few words my heart drops to the floor. I no longer hear what he's saying, but I'm certainly aware of his angry and disappointed tone. It rips straight through me.

I hang up and grab my laptop. Sure enough, there at the top of my inbox is an email from the IWWF.

No! There's *no way* this is happening!

'What's up? You all right?' Dieter asks.

I look over at him, then back down at the screen as the tears start to well up. I say nothing, but I know my face says everything.

Dieter reads aloud over my shoulder:

We regret to advise that you have received a positive result from the drug test carried out during the World Wakeboard Championships in Korea . . .

•

He looks at me in disbelief. 'You've got to be kidding!'

I smile sarcastically through the tears. 'Yep. I've been disqualified. I just lost 30 fucking grand.' I'm fuming. I feel it bubbling under the surface and I don't think I can contain it — the anger, the frustration, the utter disappointment. 'How is this possible? I smoked weed a couple of *weeks* before the event. How could that possibly have had any impact on my performance in the competition? *Fuck!* This is absolute bullshit.'

Dieter shakes his head. 'That sucks, dude.'

'If anything, they should bump me up into first place since I was competing with swine flu!'

Then I remember Adam. I wonder if he got done too? We smoked that blunt together, so if I'm getting screwed he must be as well.

I pick up the phone. 'Bro, those motherfuckers got me!' I blurt out as soon as Adam answers.

'What are you talking about? Who got you?'

'Those IWWF pricks! The drug test! They've disqualified me for having weed in my system. Did you get an email?'

'Oh shit. Hold on, let me check.' He's silent for a few moments, then he says, 'I don't see anything, man. Maybe they haven't sent it yet?'

'Maybe you passed, bro,' I reply. 'You did chug a shitload of water. Fingers crossed for you.'

Of course I'm hoping for my friend's sake that he's somehow passed the test, but I also don't want to be the only one getting disqualified. If he fails too, maybe we can fight this together.

I head out to the swimming pool. The rest of my friends have already heard the news. 'Dude, that's such bullshit!' they're saying, but I barely hear them. I'm pissed off at the IWWF and I'm ashamed of myself — I should've stopped smoking earlier — but mostly I'm numb. I dragged myself halfway around the world, fought through the most hellish sickness, battled the elements and still managed to come out on the podium, only to have it snatched from me. I feel like I'm being robbed.

I stand on the edge of the swimming pool and flop into the water. Blowing all of the air out of my lungs with a big underwater scream, I sink to the bottom, where I drift, weightless, lifeless. I don't want to go up for air. I just want to hide right here. It's so fucking unfair.

•

By the time I land back in Auckland, I've almost forgotten about my knee. It gives me no pain aside from the occasional twinge. Then, a few weeks later, I'm skating down Parnell Road, a beautifully smooth hill to bomb. I get past the shops, and the road turns left and starts to get steep. Intimidatingly steep. I glance behind me.

Great! No cars coming.

I pull into the middle of the lane and start carving from side to side to wash off some speed, but I just keep accelerating. Soon I'm going so fast I can't carve any more. I point straight down the hill and hang on for the ride, praying I don't hit a rogue stone or get speed wobbles. The wind is blowing in my face and the adrenalin is flowing.

I'm three-quarters of the way down when I see the traffic lights at the bottom. They're red. I place my back foot on the road to brake, but the moment I apply pressure my knee buckles sideways and I go down hard.

After donating some of my skin to the road, I pick myself up.

It's time to go see a doctor about my knee.

•

Dr Mark seems young for a surgeon. With his slicked-back hair and tailored suit he looks more like a Wall Street tycoon, but I saw his name on the parking space right by the hospital entrance — and the black Maserati slicker than his hairdo filling it — so I figure he's gotta be good at what he does.

He gets me to sit up on the examination table. 'Bend your knee up at a 90-degree angle,' he says, 'and keep the sole of your shoe flat on the table.'

I do as instructed.

'This might hurt a little,' he says, 'but try to relax.'

He grabs my leg right below my knee and wiggles my joint a bit, then gives it a hard yank straight forward.

'*Aghhh!*' I cry.

'Unfortunately, it feels like you've ruptured your ACL,' he proclaims. 'Your anterior cruciate ligament.'

'How can you tell that just from pulling on my leg?' I ask.

'If your ACL was intact,' he says, giving my leg another pull, 'your knee would be much tighter and would stop your tibia from pulling forward this much.'

Damn. Deep down I've known all along it was more than a tweak, but I've done such a good job of convincing myself otherwise that the news hits me almost as hard as the crash that caused the injury in the first place.

'You'll need surgery,' he goes on. 'Let's get you booked in for our next available date.' He crosses to his computer. 'Looks like it'll be . . . December.'

'That's not for two months!' I say. 'I can't wait that long. I need to get this thing fixed in time for next season.'

'Unfortunately, that's the soonest we can do,' Dr Mark says. Then he delivers another blow: 'And, with a minimum of six months' rehabilitation, I'm afraid you won't be wakeboarding until June at the earliest.'

Oh man. I'm feeling pretty sorry for myself now. 'That sucks.' Then I think of something else. 'I injured my shoulder a while ago, and it's been popping out more frequently this last season. Can I maybe get that done at the same time?' If I'm going to have to take all that time off the water, I figure I might as well kill two birds.

Dr Mark takes a look at my shoulder. 'You can go and see a specialist about it,' he says, 'or you can concentrate on rehabbing it at the same time as you rehab your knee. That way you might be able to avoid shoulder surgery altogether.'

'I guess I'll have to smash the rehab then,' I say. 'Is there any way of shortening the rehab time?'

'Look, the best thing you can do is to start now, so you're as strong as possible before surgery. You'll still need six months post op — and I wouldn't recommend getting back on a board any sooner — but you'll recover better if you start now.'

I leave his office, head straight home and do what I'm told.

Thankfully, Gordon has a stationary bike at home. I ride it until my clothes are drenched in sweat and my legs feel like jelly under me.

•

I'm still bitter about being disqualified by the IWWF — I can't shake the sense of unfairness and I want to fight their decision. As it happens, Mum's next-door neighbour Mike is both a family friend and an amazing lawyer. So I tell him about it and ask what he reckons.

'They kicked me out for having weed in my system, but I've ridden stoned before and it's definitely not easier,' I say.

Mike chuckles. 'Yeah, weed is more likely to impair your performance than enhance it,' he says. 'But if we're going to beat this we need something else. Let me take a closer look at the rule book and get back to you.'

He comes over a couple of nights later holding a thick folder. I'm eager to hear how he got on.

'I've gone through the IWWF anti-doping rules and highlighted a few sections that appear relevant,' he says. 'I've also read the World Anti-Doping Agency's list of prohibited substances, and carboxy-THC, which is what they identified in your system, is one of the substances they class as "prohibited in competition".'

'But I wasn't using it "in competition",' I say. 'I hadn't smoked in two weeks. There's no way it could've affected my performance after so long.'

'Yeah, it seems the testing system might be flawed,' Mike replies.

'What do you mean?'

'Well, if they're testing to make sure you're not using something as a performance-enhancer in competition, that would require them to use a method that will show whether you've used the substance in the past few hours or days. Something like a mouth-swab test.'

'And not a piss test which will show traces weeks or even months later?' I ask.

Mike nods, and I feel my frustration rising.

'It's *completely* flawed!' I say. 'That's like a cop pulling me over and telling me I can't drive because I was drunk a week ago!'

'You're absolutely right, Brad,' Mike says, 'but I don't think the IWWF will drop the disqualification because of that. If we want to challenge the testing methods, we need to take it up with WADA, not the IWWF. WADA makes the rules.'

Mike flips through a stack of paper until he finds the one he's looking for and shows me. 'The rules are pretty clear, and you agreed to abide by those rules when you got your competitor's licence and signed the entry form for the event.'

'Wait, what the hell is a competitor's licence?' I can't recall ever signing anything.

Mike points to one of the sections he's highlighted. 'It says here, "To be eligible for participation in IWSF events, a competitor must have a competitor's licence," and that the licence "will only be issued to competitors who have personally signed the Appendix 2 consent form". In that consent form it states: "I will abide by all anti-doping rules."'

(The IWSF was the forerunner of the IWWF.)

'Mike, this is the first time I have ever heard of a competitor's licence,' I say. 'I've never had one. I don't know of anyone who has had one.'

Mike pauses to think. 'Okay,' he eventually says. 'We just might have something here.'

I feel a glimmer of hope.

'If you were never officially made aware of the rules, and if you never signed anything, then you never agreed to abide by them. The only problem, of course, is that if you never signed anything or agreed to their rules then you'll probably be disqualified anyway.'

'But wouldn't that mean they would have to disqualify everyone? If no one had a competitor's licence?'

Mike starts arranging his papers and putting them back in the folder. 'So, that's the angle we're going to take, then, and it seems pretty strong,' he says, and he sounds confident. 'We'll get a hearing date, probably in a couple of months. In that time, I need you to ask as many other competitors as you can whether or not they had a competitor's licence.'

'Consider it done,' I reply.

I'm feeling upbeat as Mike leaves. Surely they won't be able to take my medal away when we drop this bomb on them.

•

The weekend before my ACL surgery I head down to an event at Lake Crichton where there's $5000 up for grabs. This is the most paid at any event in New Zealand wakeboarding, so I strap on my knee brace and go for it. I can't miss the chance to go after one last payday before I'm out of commission for a while.

It's not going to be a walk in the park, though. My mate and former rival Tony Evans is here, along with a kid from Australia called Ryleigh Pfitzner, who won the junior Aussie tour earlier this year. I make it to the final, and so do they. Tony rides pretty well, but I should be able to beat him. Riley's run, on the other hand, is strong enough to put him in the top spot. I'm the last rider off the dock, and I put together a solid but safe ride, knowing that my toe-seven and Pete Rose will bag me the win if I just make it to the end. But on my last trick, a pretty simple tail-grabbed roll to blind takes me down.

As we head back in to shore I plaster a big smile on my face and say to the judges, 'Phew! Should be enough, eh, boys?'

I've seen tactics like this used before, and usually I wouldn't resort to such a stunt, but I could really use that dosh. So if planting a seed in the judges' minds helps them decide, then why not?

I have no idea whether I would have won anyway, but I head home and onto the operating table with $5000 in my pocket.

●

I don't feel too bad after my knee surgery, but then again I am on strong pain meds. I can't bend my knee at all, and any movement hurts, but it's not as bad as I thought it would be. I have crutches to help me hobble around the house, and before long I slowly start putting more weight through my leg.

One afternoon just over a week post op, I accidentally straighten my leg too far as I'm getting up off the couch and I'm delivered an agonising dose of pain up the back of my leg. Dr Mark harvested some of my hamstring tendon to reconstruct my ACL, and it feels like a bunch of fibres just tore away from the scarred area that he took it from. I flop back onto the couch and drop my crutches to the floor. Looks like I'll be stuck with them for a while longer.

I might be out of action on the water but I find other things to keep me amused. Not long after getting back to New Zealand I met a girl at a bar. With her model-like figure and stunning smile, she caught my eye instantly. She comes to visit after my surgery, with an enormous sunflower from her garden.

'I thought this might brighten your day,' she says.

It's our first time hanging out since we met, so we sit and chat for a while before getting cosy in front of a movie.

She leaves after dark, and I really don't want her to go. I like this girl. And it's not just a physical attraction. She's a sweetheart and I find myself wondering what it would be like to have her as my girlfriend . . . Then I remind myself that I can't have a relationship right now. And she seems like the quality, wholesome girlfriend type, so that means I can't have her at all. I can't do that to her, or to myself. So I decide to let her go.

●

Since I have free time on my hands I decide to learn a new skill. I put some of my recent winnings towards a beautiful new Takamine guitar. At $1800 it's a big investment, but I figure spending the money on it will force me to learn.

It's awkward at first, learning to bend the fingers of my left hand into chord shapes, and my fingertips hurt from pressing against the steel strings. I also didn't realise I'd feel so gumby strumming with my right hand! But before long, it starts to feel more natural and the skin on my fingertips toughens up.

Brant comes over and shows me how to play a few Metallica tunes, and for the fundamentals I turn to the internet, teaching myself by watching YouTube videos and reading guitar tabs.

Within a couple of months I've got a few songs under my belt, but the moment I open my mouth to sing along, my strumming turns to shit. Multi-tasking! It's like patting your head and rubbing your stomach at the same time but I stick at it, and after only a week or so I'm getting the hang of it. I love this new skill I'm learning, and it feels good to overcome that beginning phase where nothing sounded good and finally be able to play a few actual songs. Now to find a girl to serenade!

●

I can't do any of the paid work I've done in previous summers but I really need to make some coin so I need a plan. Last summer, even with all of the extra work I picked up, I still didn't have enough to get me through the US season. I need to step things up.

Instead of buying the odd 50-bag of weed for my own use, I start buying it by the ounce. Then, armed with some digital scales, I divide each ounce into 10 small ziplock baggies, with a little left over for myself. I do this every week or two, and it's not a big operation — I just supply a handful of my friends — but I make about $250 each time. I know it's a bit dodgy, but needs must.

EIGHT: REHAB-RECOVERY-REPEAT

I really hate being off the water, but I spend the early months of 2010 channelling my energy into my knee rehab. The intensity of it gives me the outlet I need.

I've gone back to the physio friend who strapped my shoulder in Hamilton just over a year ago, and she's had me cycling, rowing, on the leg press, hopping on and off a balance pad, balancing on one leg, hamstring curls and more. Many of the exercises focus on my injured shoulder as well as my knee, and by February my basic mobility is back to normal.

There's something else that's been demanding a lot of my attention, and that's my anti-doping hearing. It's scheduled for 19 February — two years to the day since I pulled off my first 1080. As I sit in front of the computer with my lawyer, waiting for the IWWF to answer on Skype, I think about that moment and realise I'm about as far from it as I could get.

Mike and I are in his beach house on the Coromandel peninsula. We've discussed our plan and submitted several supporting documents. Once the IWWF panel is assembled, the hearing starts, and I'm up first. After explaining that I never wanted to bring negative attention to the sport I love, I go on to plead my case: I mention the swine flu, I point out that cannabis is not performance-enhancing, I describe the funding struggles I've faced during my career. 'If I can keep my IWWF title,' I finish, 'I'm eligible for the biggest funding boost I've ever had. It will make a huge difference to me as a professional wakeboarder.'

Then I hand over to Mike, who hits them with some legalese. Basically, he outlines how the IWWF's failure to provide me with a competitor's licence means I was never given the opportunity to read or understand the anti-doping rules — let alone sign anything to confirm I had understood and agreed to those rules. 'Technically,' he concludes, 'you have no jurisdiction to disqualify Brad or take his medal.'

After the hearing's finished and we're off the call, I shake Mike's hand.

'Thanks for all of your help and hard work,' I say, before adding tentatively, 'I think that went as well as it could have.'

'Yeah, me too,' he replies. 'You did well, Brad. All we can do now is wait for their decision. Unfortunately, in this case the IWWF are their own judge and jury, so let's just hope we did enough to get them on your side.'

I spend the entire three-hour drive back to Auckland wondering what the verdict will be. I've done everything I can and it's out of my hands now. I decide that whatever happens, whatever the outcome, I'm going to put the whole thing behind me as soon as their decision is announced. I need to move on. I need to focus on my rehab — and on the future.

•

Nine days later I receive an email with the subject line: *IWWF — Smeele decision.*

I open the attachment, holding my breath as I begin reading. It seems to be a transcript of the hearing. Then I notice the document is 10 pages long so I scroll straight to the last page, where I read: . . . *the panel therefore finds that Mr Smeele has violated the rules by testing positive for the presence of a prohibited substance . . .*

'*Fuck!*' I yell at the computer screen. 'This is such shit!'

I continue reading: *Mr Smeele's individual results . . . are therefore disqualified with all consequences, including forfeiture of all medals . . .*

Good luck getting that medal off me, I mutter.

Mr Smeele shall also be subject to a 90-day period of ineligibility . . .

Fuck them. I don't care if they ban me for life. I'll never enter another IWWF event.

I skim-read the rest, and there's a note saying I've got a right of appeal. But Mike and I already discussed this, and he said it'd most likely end up costing me more than the grant money I'm missing out on.

I start typing a reply.

I acknowledge receipt of this decision. I do not intend to appeal.

Then I press send and shut my computer.

Goodbye, $30,000.

This chapter is now closed.

•

Even though I can't ride, I stay involved in wakeboarding by commentating the North Island champs again. It's frustrating having to sit back and watch, but it's great to be with the crew in Mangakino.

I'm back for more the following month, and by now my knee is strong enough for me to feel confident getting behind the boat again. I'm not quite back on the wakeboard yet, but I do enjoy some wakesurfing sessions, which are actually a really good, low-risk workout.

While in Mangakino I also start building a rail with my friend Jesse James and his brother. We're being paid to construct it for nationals and we only just finish in time, towing it up to Lake Karāpiro. Even though I'm not competing in nationals this year, Dad loves the sport so much he's come down to watch.

Finals day arrives, and I commentate the whole event. An up-and-coming rider called Nick Gibson rides before Jeff, and does pretty well, but I'm guessing it'll be an easy win for Jeff. Then he takes to the water and completely falls apart in his run, basically handing the win to Nick. I'm so mad! Every year, no matter how well I ride, Jeff always one-ups me. The *one* year I'm not riding, he crashes and burns, getting himself beaten by an 18-year-old!

I don't let Jeff hear the end of it.

The after-party kicks off in epic fashion and I find myself on the dance floor opposite an attractive blonde who lives nearby. We soon sneak off to find somewhere a bit quieter to talk and get to know each other. She's super cute and I'm rapt to have met her. After making out lakeside for a while we head back to the party, and that's when I notice Dad's car is still parked up where he left it earlier in the day. Then I see he's sitting in the driver's seat.

'Hey, Dad,' I say, opening the door. 'Are you okay?'

He's completely frozen. He can't move at all. I know straight away what's happening, as it's a symptom of his Parkinson's — instead of shaking, he locks up when the disease is at its worst.

'Yeah,' he says, 'but I've, ah . . . I've wet myself.'

Poor Dad.

'No worries,' I say. 'Here, lean on me.'

I help him out of the car and he's able to stand. It's mainly his arms that don't want to work right now. He hobbles alongside me to the clubroom showers, where I help him get cleaned up. It's the first time I've ever had to do something like this for him, and I feel awkward washing my naked father, but I figure he and Mum spent years of their lives doing the same for me so I just get on with it.

Once he's clean, I get him dressed again in some of my spare pants.

It's a hefty dose of reality for me. Of course I've noticed Dad's condition gradually getting worse over the years, but this has forced me to confront exactly what he is dealing with. I hate that he has to face this shit day after day, but he's handling it amazingly. I mean, he could have stayed home and hidden away in order to avoid embarrassing situations like this, but he hasn't. Instead, he drove all the way down here just to support me and the wakeboard scene.

I wish I knew how to express to Dad what I'm feeling right now, but I don't. So I just give him a big hug and pat him firmly on the back.

He really is my hero.

•

I head out to a dilapidated two-storey waterfront house on the outskirts of Auckland to shoot a TV commercial for Mountain Dew. The softdrink brand has sent a bit of sponsorship money my way over the past few years, and this time I've cut a deal to appear along with two of their other athletes, BMX rider Haimona Ngata and skater Brett Band.

The house is due to be demolished in a week, and the three of us scope it out for places where we can show off our respective sporting talents. The vibe's a bit like we're flatmates trashing the house. In the second-floor lounge, I eye up the gap from the balcony to the ocean. The gap's big, but I reckon it's doable. There's a stretch of lawn in between and a decent drop. The run-in through the lounge is long enough to get the speed I'd need, but it'd require a landing ramp to soften the landing and clear the rocks.

I start getting excited about the idea — then I remember my knee. I'm only five months out of surgery and there's no way I should risk injuring myself again with a stunt like this — but it's a once-in-a-lifetime opportunity so of course I'm considering it.

I run my idea past the production crew and they love it. But, rather than actually build a landing ramp so I can do it properly, they start brainstorming ways to use stunt rigging so it would just *look* real. I'm pissed off. I don't want to fake it! But the producer is set on it, and I guess it would be better not to take the risk with my knee.

So the crew film me being pulled through the lounge on my wakeboard, giving the coffee table a quick tap on my way past. Then I'm put in a stunt harness and launched off the balcony, only to end up dangling from a crane above the lawn. Next, they move the crane so it's extended over the water. As I swing out, the jet-ski pulls me until a quick-release drops me to the ocean, then I am meant to ride away. It's a soft enough landing for my knee, but the moment I hit the choppy water my left shoulder is pulled right out of its socket.

Fuuuck!

After all that rehab, my shoulder's screwed again. I'm furious that I didn't just go ahead and get it operated on at the same time as my knee but it's too late now.

It's only a couple of weeks before I fly to the US. I'll just have to make the most of the US season, even though it's now crystal clear I won't be competing.

•

I arrive in Orlando and move back in with Dieter and Vee. This year, though, it's a slightly different vibe. They've made it clear they don't want this to be the 'party house' that it was last summer — and that's fine by me, because I just want to focus on my riding and getting my tricks back.

I love being back in the Florida heat, and I'm just in time for the Ronix team shoot. For the third year in a row I'm asked to ride the Vault — the Ronix beginner's board — and again I say thank you, even though I wish I didn't have to. I'm so out of practice I'm riding below par anyway, and throwing me on a beginner's board has me feeling like a total rookie! Especially with the old knee brace I dug out to wear for extra support.

The good news is that the knee itself is feeling strong and stable, thanks to all that rehab. My shoulder, on the other hand, is feeling sloppy, but I do enough to get the shots needed for the brochure, then set my sights on restoring my riding fitness.

It's crazy how much just six months off the water have set me back. I might have spent that time getting fitter and stronger, but riding fitness is something that can really only be achieved on the water. The one thing I haven't lost, thankfully, is the knowledge of *how* to do my tricks — I spent much of my time off visualising them and trying to keep that muscle memory strong. I soon get fitted with a custom knee brace, which is a huge improvement on the old one. It's half the weight and fits perfectly, so it gives me much more confidence while I'm riding.

I love living with Dieter and Vee but it's not the best for my riding, since my roommates are all wakeskaters and there's no boat on the end of the dock. But, as always, I'm on a very tight budget so it's not like I could afford to ride daily anyway. I occasionally catch rides with Dallas Friday or with Aussie rider Harley Clifford, who both live on the same lake — but mostly I watch as Harley's boat does laps back and forth across the water all day. He rides a crazy amount, and he's quickly becoming one of the best. I'm in the boat filming one day when he lands two of his first 1080s in just a couple of sets. I feel a wave of frustration — I've only landed three in the space of two years! And, after all my time off, I'm not even close to trying another one yet. Harley is incredibly talented, but it also shows what a difference it makes having a boat and the budget to ride.

One of my favourite things about Dieter's house is the mini-ramp in the garage. Although I've been skateboarding since before I learnt to wakeboard, I've mainly skated for transport and can only do a handful of basic tricks. I spend hours in the garage every day, pumping back and forth, ending up drenched in sweat with my legs burning. As well as learning loads of fun new tricks, I find it's an awesome exercise for my legs, particularly for strengthening the finer balancing muscles that support my recently reconstructed knee.

And I might not be back to riding at the level I have in past US summers, but I do get straight back to the same style of partying, venturing out with the guys whenever the opportunity presents and making the most of the local talent. One night I bring home a stunning brunette. It's the early hours of the morning but we jump in the pool in our underwear and start making out, then retreat to my bedroom. The next day, Diets and Vee don't seem super impressed. Their room is right by the pool, so I guess the commotion woke them up.

A week later I bring not one but two sexy girls home. They're both platinum blonde, and they're giving off a vibe like they're looking to get laid tonight.

'Let's go for a swim,' I say when we get back to the house. 'But we need to be quiet. Can't wake the roomies.'

They just start giggling. I should have known better than to expect two drunk girls to keep quiet for more than 10 seconds.

'We don't have our swimsuits,' one of them replies.

'Oh no, what a shame,' I say hopefully.

That's when Vee emerges glowering from her room. It's after 2 a.m. and I can tell Vee is not happy. *I'm sorry*, I mouth at her.

Then one of the girls pipes up, 'Hey! Would you mind if we borrow some swimsuits?'

'Okay,' Vee replies, surprising me. 'But try to keep it down.'

We go for a quick swim, then in an effort to take the noise elsewhere I snag Dieter's jet-ski and take the girls for a joyride out on the lake. When we get back we head to my room and the three of us get in bed together, only for me to be told I won't be getting any action after all. I can think of worse ways to end the night than having a sexy girl cuddled up on either side of me, but the sexual frustration is real.

Later the next day I'm chilling in the lounge with Kallas, one of my roommates, when Diets comes in and completely blows up at me. I know he has every right to be mad at me — he and Vee did tell me they didn't want this to be the party house, and I also took his jet-ski in the middle of the night without asking. It's not like they're party-poopers — they both love to get amongst a good house party or a night out when the occasion calls for it — but this is their place and I'm a guest. So I sit there and take what he's dishing out.

When I see Vee later on, I apologise. And, after giving Diets a chance to cool down, I apologise to him too. He and I are good mates so we quickly put it behind us. Everything is cool again, but I've learnt my lesson.

•

I haven't seen much of Alex this season, as he's moved to Texas to live near Jay and run coaching clinics. We finally get to catch up in Redding, California, when the whole iwake team converges on a bad-arse three-level houseboat complete with hot tub and slide-off-the-top deck.

Twelve of us pile aboard and cruise out on beautiful Lake Shasta, nestled among the Cascade mountains. With its steep tree-covered shores and multiple arms splitting off in different directions, this place reminds me a little of Lake Ohakuri back home, only this lake is much, much bigger. The crystal-clear and rather cold water is a refreshing change from the warm lakes of Orlando, and the change of scenery makes it feel like a bit of a holiday.

We're all up at dawn the next morning and I'm the first rider on the water. Since this is just the first of several sessions I concentrate on my more solid moves, planning to step things up for the camera after that. All goes well until my shoulder pops out. Again.

In truth it's happened a handful of times since I got back to the US and, while it hurts, I'm usually able to ride again within an hour. I came prepared with rolls and rolls of strapping tape, and I ask Alex to help me strap it up. Although the result is not pretty, it makes my shoulder feel more secure.

By day three I've dislocated my shoulder on every ride. I feel like I'm falling apart, and riding for the cameras just feels like a chore. It's at the point where I'm enjoying the downtime between rides much more than the riding itself.

I'm going to have to get my shoulder fixed when I get home. I've basically wasted a season, and I'm pissed off.

•

More frustration awaits me when I get back to Orlando. My truck is right where I left it, parked on the road, but the back is completely smashed in.

I ask Dieter if he knows what happened.

'Yeah, bro,' he says. 'I got woken up in the middle of the night by the sound of a crash, so I went out and saw your truck like that.'

There were no other cars around but he followed a trail of fluid down the road all the way to the culprit's car, which was still steaming from its smashed-in front end.

'I got the driver's details for you,' Diets says, handing me a piece of paper.

So I contact this guy's insurer, hoping I'll be able to either get my truck fixed or receive a payout. They tell me that the damage is more than my truck is worth, so they'll pay me out what I paid for the little Chevy pickup in the first place — just $800. The extra cash couldn't come at a better time. I can actually go grocery shopping, rather than relying on $5 meal deals from Subway or Burger King.

But I'm pretty gutted about losing my truck.

•

One stormy afternoon, wrecked after a couple of hours skating on the mini-ramp, I'm kicking it in the lounge with Kallas and Carnie. We're playing *Skate 2* and smoking spliffs when one of the guys pulls a bag of magic mushrooms out of his pocket.

'You guys down to join me for a trip?' he asks, jiggling the bag at us.

'Yeah, bro,' I reply. I've never done shrooms before, and I figure there's not much else to do today.

It turns out none of us have much idea about how best to eat them. We eventually decide to just place two or three on top of a granola bar and chomp it down. It doesn't taste great but I manage to get it down after chewing for some time. While we wait for things to start, we carry on playing. Time goes on, and I'm still not really feeling anything. Then I find myself staring at the tie-dyed T-shirt our little skater character on the screen is wearing. It's mesmerising.

'Yooo!' I laugh. 'Is that dude's shirt spiralling around? Or is it the mushrooms kicking in?'

'I don't know,' Carnie replies, 'but, dammit, I can't stop looking at it now! I'm sure it's moving . . .'

The three of us burst out laughing, and those magical little mushrooms hit us all at once.

With each game, I feel myself being drawn more and more into the digital world inside the TV screen. It begins to feel as real as the world I'm sitting in.

'Do you reckon our little tie-dyed T-shirt man just sits there waiting for us when we're not controlling him?' I ask the guys. 'Or does he go home to his pixilated girlfriend?'

The three of us are soon in hysterics, coming up with random scenarios and backstories for our character.

Then a large electric storm rolls over, booming and flashing ferociously, and things get a bit intense. There's just a pane of glass between us and the furious weather, but I feel safe looking out from inside these walls. Before long the storm is moving away over the lake, towards the sunset. We sit on the patio, watching it roll into the distance. I'm transfixed by the tall clouds and the bright orange sky. I've never seen colours so bold. The contrast between the hectic purple storm and the calm orange sunset is like nothing I've ever seen — or maybe I have seen it, but I've just never appreciated it as deeply as I do right in this moment. I feel small, sitting here before the full force of nature. I'm a tiny observer on this enormous spinning rock alive with chaos and beauty.

I look over at my two good mates. Being here with them, on the same level, provides me with the feeling that we're all connected in some way. Everything is connected.

My mind drifts to the feelings of jealousy and envy I've experienced over the years. The way I've felt about riders who have been more successful or had more good luck than me. The sense of being hard done by in this sport because I never have enough — not enough money, no right boat, not enough sponsors — and because things keep going 'wrong' — my knee, my shoulder, my truck.

And a simple truth strikes me: other people's journeys have nothing to do with me or mine. All that competitiveness over winning and sponsorship and coverage and girls is misplaced. It's not me versus them. It's me against myself. In order to find success in this sport I need to change my focus. I need to concentrate on bettering myself, not beating others. And that feeling of being worse off needs to go! Dwelling on my difficulties won't make my future any easier. Envying what others have won't get me the things I want.

As the intensity of the trip begins to fade, the boys and I retreat back into the lounge, melting into the couch, laughing and playing games for the rest of the evening. But my epiphany sticks with me. I'm keen to flex my new perspective and give wakeboarding another good crack — but before I can do that, I need to get home and get fixed up. Since my shoulder's preventing me from making any real progress here this season and my funds have dried up, I bring my flight home forward.

●

Before I leave the US, I head to Texas with Carnie and Chris-O to do some filming with some of the local pros. While we're there we decide to catch a wakeskate movie premiere. During the day, before the party kicks off, we head down to the beach for a surf.

My shoulder won't handle the paddling, so while the others hit the waves I go and make friends with three girls I've spied a little way off. After all, it's a hot day, they've got a cooler full of beer and they're all wearing bikinis. How could I not?

'Hi,' I say as I approach them. 'Mind if I join you?'

'Oh my god!' one of them says excitedly. 'You have an accent!'

Another hands me a beer. 'Where are you from?' she says.

'New Zealand,' I reply.

The third girl pipes up. 'Wow, that's so friggin' cool!' Then she pauses, as though she's thinking about something. 'Wait, so . . . did you drive here?'

I burst out laughing, as do the other two girls. I can't believe she really just asked me that.

One of the others sets her friend straight. 'Of course he didn't drive here,' she says confidently. 'New Zealand is in Europe, you dummy!'

Oh my god. She's so sure of herself it just makes me laugh even harder. And she's still giggling at her 'dummy' friend.

I explain that you can't drive from New Zealand to anywhere, and the girls just giggle some more. The stupid questions continue, and while all three of them are good-looking I feel the attraction draining. They're just too ditzy. One of them proudly shows me her brand-new fake boobies, but even that's not enough to persuade me.

I know my mind is set that I can't have a relationship at the moment, but I'm also starting to tire of the random hookups and their lack of depth and connection. The girls I meet might be hot, but when a hot girl opens her mouth and says something just plain dumb, I'm finding it such a turn-off.

I thank the girls for the beers and say goodbye, then head back to my friends.

●

On the way back to Auckland I've arranged a stopover in LA to spend a few days with a girl I recently met through Facebook.

We've been texting and calling each other for the past few weeks and, as well as being really sweet and great to talk to, Jenna is unbelievably gorgeous. Perfection in every aspect! She's blonde with blue eyes and a smile that would light up the darkest room. And her figure is to die for — slim but with curves in all the right places, strong but still petite and feminine. And, as if all that's not enough, she also plays the guitar. To say I'm excited to finally meet up with this sweet thing in person is an understatement.

The moment I touch down I flick her a message, as she's promised to come and pick me up. I wait eagerly out the front of LAX but after about 20 minutes she still hasn't replied. I try calling her. No answer. I leave a message. I wait around for another hour before I finally give up and grab a cab to a nearby cheap motel — neither of which I can really afford.

The next day Jenna still hasn't got back to me. I'm starting to wonder if she's feeling a little overwhelmed about having invited someone she's never actually hung out with to stay in her home. I check out of my motel and grab a cab to Brentwood, where she said she lives.

Hey, I message her, *I'll be chilling and playing my guitar outside the Brentwood library this afternoon if you want to come and hang out there.*

I figure that proposing to meet in a public place might take the pressure off for her. For the next few hours I sit there quietly playing the guitar. Since I'm still pretty shit and definitely not confident enough to busk in public, I don't play loud enough for anyone else to hear, but that doesn't stop several people from trying to give me money.

As the sun sets, there's still no word from Jenna.

I resign myself to the fact that she's not going to show. Once again, I need to find somewhere else for the night. I drag all my stuff — backpack, laptop bag, suitcase, board bag and guitar case — several blocks in search of another cheap motel. It's a struggle, especially since I've barely eaten anything all day, but I've only got enough money for the motel and a cab to the airport tomorrow. I'm going to have to go hungry until I'm on the flight. I'm pretty gutted.

Finally, just before I fall asleep, I get a Facebook message from Jenna's best friend explaining that Jenna has been in hospital. When I ask what happened, she says it's something to do with an infection and internal injuries from a car accident a while ago. It's not until I'm at the airport the next day that I hear from Jenna herself.

As soon as I answer her call, I hear that she's crying. 'I'm so sorry,' she sobs. 'I should've called! I collapsed at home, my stomach got infected, that's why I've been so sick. And I know I should have called you from the hospital, but I dunno, I thought maybe you'd be mad that I didn't show at the airport to pick you up.'

'Holy shit, are you kidding? Of course I'm not mad,' I say. 'I mean, I was a little gutted you didn't show, but I would've totally understood if you'd just explained. Are you okay?'

I feel so sorry for this sweet girl. She's obviously had a hell of a time.

'Yeah,' she sniffles. 'I'll be okay. I had surgery yesterday to clean the infection and redo the stitches. I'm so sorry and bummed that I didn't get to see you.'

'I'm just glad you're all right,' I say. 'You had me worried there for a minute! And, look, it's not the end of the world that we didn't see each other. Maybe you'll just have to come to New Zealand.'

'Oh my god, yes! I'd love that!' she replies, and I can hear in her voice that she's smiling.

Although it's been a shitty couple of days, it feels good to hear her voice. I really am happy she's okay. I say goodbye and board my flight back across the Pacific — and, let me tell you, I've never been so happy to eat an in-flight meal.

•

As soon as I get home I reconnect with Sasha, a hot blonde babe I was hooking up with just before I left for the US.

'Come over,' she says. 'I want to welcome you back properly.' She doesn't need to ask twice. After my LA letdown I'm looking forward to some action.

Sasha's a stripper so she looks absolutely incredible naked and, damn, does the girl know how to move her body. The sex is great, but afterwards I'm left feeling a little flat. Usually I'd be raring to go for round two, but for some reason — and it's definitely no fault of Sasha's — I'm just not feeling it.

So I head home to my own bed. In the car on the drive back I try to work out what's changed. I absolutely loved sleeping with Sasha before I left. I've been loving the single life. But now I keep thinking about Jenna, and the idea of being with her has me less enthusiastic about being with anyone else. I guess, deep down, I'm still looking for that relationship worth having, and Jenna has me wondering if maybe she's the one.

Jenna and I continue talking pretty much every day, and she's still planning to come and visit me in New Zealand — but, she says, there's just one problem. Her parents won't let her fly to see someone who's not her boyfriend. 'Well, how about you be my girlfriend then?' I ask, and an hour later we're Facebook official. It's a big step, especially considering we've never actually met, but we've been talking so much that I feel I know this girl well enough.

●

A year to the day after my knee surgery, I'm back on the operating table. This time it's Dr Bruce, and he's reconstructing my shoulder.

When I wake up I instinctively go to move my arm and receive an excruciating burst of pain. Thankfully, there's a morphine button beside my bed that gives me near-instant relief. The next day I head home with my arm in a sling. The slightest movement still hurts like hell so I'm glad I've been given a pump that delivers morphine straight into my shoulder. That button gets regular use.

I can't really start on any intensive rehab for about two months until my shoulder is healed enough, but Jenna tells me she's booked her tickets and she'll be here just before Christmas. That timing works perfectly, as it'll be while I'm recovering and I won't have much else to do, I figure I might as well use the time to show her this beautiful country of mine.

I come up with a plan to put the road-trip to good use on the work front, doing a bit of coaching across various parts of the country. As well as providing an opportunity to make money along the way, it might also help me rake in some sponsorship. The only problem is I don't have a boat — or a truck to pull my non-existent boat.

I reach out to the main boat companies, but no matter how much I try to sell them on the idea that I'll be bringing plenty of potential customers aboard, they're just not interested in lending me a $100,000 boat. I meet the same resistance from vehicle companies and my road-trip starts to fall apart before it's even begun.

And that's not the only thing that seems to be unravelling. A week before Christmas, on the day she's meant to fly out, Jenna calls.

'I've lost my passport!' she tells me, in tears. 'I've looked everywhere but I just can't find it. I'm going to have to delay my flight. I'm so sorry.'

The next day she still can't find it. The day after that she tells me her mum has found it — back at the family home in Florida.

'Mom's sending it to me in LA,' she promises. 'Then I'll reschedule my flight.'

But of course that's too late for Christmas. As much as I know shit like this can just happen, and I try to be understanding, I'm pretty gutted. I console myself that at least she'll still be here for New Year's Eve.

Except, a few days later, she's back in hospital with another infection. It's another two weeks before she's finally cleared to travel again and then, just hours before she's meant to be leaving for the airport, she calls me, crying hysterically. 'It's my brother,' she eventually manages to say, between sobs. 'He tried to kill himself. He's in the ICU.'

I can't believe it. This girl really is having a bad run. My heart breaks for her and her family but it's starting to seem like maybe this just isn't going to work. When I mention this to her she tries to reassure me that she still wants to come. 'I want to see you. I need to get away from it all,' she says.

'No way,' I tell her. 'You have to go back to Florida. You need to be with your family.'

Reluctantly, she agrees.

And I close out the year wondering how I've suddenly found myself embroiled in a rollercoaster relationship with this dream girl I still haven't even met.

NINE: KEEP ON TRUCKIN'

Once again, I find myself spending the New Zealand summer unable to wakeboard, and once again it sucks.

My number one focus as 2011 kicks off is rehab. I want my shoulder as strong as possible as soon as possible so I can get straight back on the water when I return to the US. I'm not going back till July this year, because I want to make sure I'm completely physically ready.

I get started on the rehab as soon as I can after surgery. After a few weeks of basic exercises using an elastic therapy band, I'm feeling ready for more. I carry on attending physio sessions a few times a week, but I also get back into Pilates and I return to another gym I went to last year for my knee. I go there for gut-busting one-on-one workouts with my trainer Chris. It's called bodywall, and it's all done in a small room with a Velcro wall and floor, and involves obscure exercises like running back and forth on super-soft pads, or pushing against the wall in different directions while wearing Velcro gloves. The Velcro means nothing ever budges, so the workouts are intense and I finish up drenched in sweat and on the verge of puking. Bodywall was one of the best things I did for my knee last year, and as the weeks go by I can definitely feel my shoulder getting stronger.

I start playing the guitar again as soon as my shoulder is up to it. As well as being an enjoyable way to pass time, it's really helped to improve my range of movement, especially with the external rotation of my arm as I'm sliding my hand down the neck of the guitar.

Even though I'm not back wakeboarding, I still get down to Mangakino with Brant and Ants. Neither of them really wakeboards much any more. They have both found a new love — motocross, and Mangakino conveniently has a pretty good moto track. I watch them ride, and whenever I can I head out on the lake to earn some much-needed dosh by coaching.

I also keep myself involved in the wake scene by picking up some more event MC'ing, and I'm starting to feel much more confident with all that time on the mic. I can easily call all the tricks, and it helps that I know how they're done, so I can spot the subtle positives and negatives in each manoeuvre. I've come to know most of the riders and their families personally by now, which makes it easy to talk about them while calling the run. Whenever there's downtime in between riders, I keep the spectators entertained with wakeboarding stories and random wake trivia, and I entertain the kids with sticker scrambles and other free swag. The better I get at commentating, the more I enjoy myself — but it's amazing how drained I am after a full weekend of it.

In terms of pay, it only really covers slightly more than my costs, so I pick up any promo or modelling work I can. I'm also still selling bags of weed when I can, and somehow with all those random sources of income — and thanks to the fact I'm living rent-free with Mum and eating from her kitchen — I manage to make it work.

•

Towards the end of January, I hear from Jenna. Her brother has died and they've just buried him. She says she needs another week or so with her family and then she wants to come to New Zealand.

I have a few reservations this time. First, the timing's no longer ideal. Between my rehab and the need to work whenever I can, I don't have anywhere near as much time on my hands as I did back in December. Second — and possibly most important — I feel like this 'relationship' has become way more of a big deal than it should have, given that we've never even met. And third, as time's gone by I've found myself wondering whether she really has just had a string of awful luck or whether there's more to this. I'm not about to accuse her of faking anything, but some things just don't feel right.

I decide it's time to back out, and I tell her I want to just be friends for now.

She's not happy but reluctantly agrees. 'I'd still really like to see you when you come back to the States,' she adds.

•

One evening I get a call to say Dad's in an ambulance on his way to hospital. He recently sold his place and bought himself a caravan, and is living in a holiday park about 45 minutes north of Auckland. The paramedics tell me he had frozen up and been stuck like that, alone in his caravan, for hours until a passer-by found him.

Once he comes right he is discharged and heads back to the campground.

This episode reinforces my concern about his living situation. He says he just wants a bit more freedom — to be able to move from campsite to campsite, to wake up at a beach every morning, to live a simpler life, and to one day travel around the country. He's made some cool friends at the campground and seems to be enjoying his new lifestyle. So, although I worry about him on his own up there, I'm not about to try to take all that away from him. He needs to live his life.

•

One night in early April, just as I'm getting ready for bed, a message chimes on my shitty old Nokia. It's Sasha.

Brad! Come downtown!

I've been hanging at Brant's place and I'm pretty stoned, so bed is looking pretty inviting.

Nah, next time, I reply. *I'm going to bed now.*

My phone immediately pings again.

Seriously, Brad, trust me! You NEED to come downtown.

I'm only halfway through typing a response when my phone rings.

'Nooo, Sasha!' I answer bluntly.

'Braaaaad! Seriously! You *need* to come downtown! Pleeease,' she begs.

'Where are you?'

'At Flight Lounge,' she says. 'Brad, believe me, you want to come and join us.'

'Us? Who are you with?'

'Just some friends,' she replies coyly. 'I'll introduce you when you get here. Come on! If there's ever a time to trust me, it's now, Brad. I promise, you will *not* regret it.'

'Ah, fuck it.' I cave. 'I'll be there soon.'

Fifteen minutes later I'm stepping out of a cab in downtown Auckland. Sasha is waiting for me at the entrance. As we head down the stairs I let go of her hand and wrap my arm around her fit body.

'You see those girls over there?' Sasha points to two gorgeous blondes standing in one corner, and I nod. 'We're going to fuck the shit out of them tonight!'

I look back at her and she grins at me mischievously.

'Oh, okay.' I glance back at the girls. 'If we have to.'

Sasha hits me playfully on the chest and I laugh. I'm stoked. 'Okay, Let's go and meet your friends.'

I stop at the bar and order two whiskeys. To snap myself out of my stony haze and into game mode I scull the first one, then carry the second one over to meet the girls.

'Brad, this is Kendra,' Sasha says, and one of the blondes waves. I smile at her. 'And this is Lara.' Sasha gestures at the other.

I do a double-take. *Wait a minute*, I think. *Is that . . .? Holy shit! It is!*

I recognise Lara from the posters my friends had on their bedroom walls back when we were teenagers. She's a model here in New Zealand and, with her incredible body and rather large fake jugs, she looks damn good. And I'm about to have a foursome with her? I'm still struggling to believe it.

Just then, another hot blonde comes over and joins us. 'Hi,' she says to me. 'I'm Annie.'

Okay, make that a . . . fivesome? I don't know if I've got enough hands, stamina or self-control to take on four girls by myself, but, dammit, I'll sure as hell give it a go!

And so, less than half an hour after entering the club, I'm exiting again, with two gorgeous blondes on each arm. Dudes look at me with envy as we pass.

When we get to Annie's car — she's the designated driver for the night — I climb into the back seat and sit in the middle, while Sasha and Lara hop in on either side and Kendra nabs the front. As soon as we start driving, Sasha begins kissing me, then she pulls Lara in too. Game on! While I'm making out with Lara, Sasha strips her clothes off, then straddles me and steals Lara's lips from mine. I sit back and watch the two of them making out. It's such a turn-on — especially with Sasha's phenomenal tits right in my face.

On the way, we pull into a McDonald's drive-through to grab a round of midnight munchies. As we pull up to the window and the dude working the till reaches down to hand Annie our takeaways, he catches a glimpse of Sasha, who's still naked, straddling me in the back. He smiles and shakes his head as if to say, 'You lucky motherfucker!'

Annie drops us at Sasha's, then says goodbye. Turns out she's heading home, which at least makes things slightly less daunting for me.

As soon as we get inside, I'm led to the bedroom. My shirt is torn off and I'm shoved onto the bed. While Sasha ferociously unbuckles my belt and removes my jeans, I watch Lara and Kendra undress each other. Then all three naked women jump into bed with me, and I'm practically swimming in blonde hair, long legs and perfect tits.

Kendra lies down beside me, and I let one of my hands wander down her body at the same time as kissing Lara's neck and breasts. Meanwhile, Sasha's head is between Kendra's legs. I guide Lara up my body, kissing my way down hers until I've got her straddling my face and my lips and tongue are treated to her for the first time. Several minutes later, she and Sasha start taking turns blowing me, then Lara positions herself over me and looks questioningly at Sasha.

'You're all good,' Sasha says. 'He's a good boy.'

Lara slides me inside and begins riding me.

I can't believe this is actually happening. Not only have I one-upped every guy's threesome fantasy, but this foursome is with some of the most desirable women I can think of. It doesn't get much better than this.

It's hard to say exactly how much time passes. All I know is it's long enough for several partner swaps and multiple position changes. I've never had to practise such coordination: I'm thrusting my hips back and forth while my hands touch and feel and massage and spank, and most of the time my lips and tongue are working too. I want to please all three girls at once — I want to make sure everyone is included and satisfied — but there's only so much I can do.

Once the girls are satisfied — and with some serious self-control on my part — they turn their attention to making me come. After all of the excitement, it doesn't take much.

After a 10-minute break to catch my breath, drink some water and take a piss, I'm ready for another round. Kendra has passed out in a corner of the bed, but both Lara and Sasha are ready and eager to go again. Round two is more intense. Faster. Harder. It's like the first round was simply a warm-up.

When I wake up some time later, the light is peeking through the blinds. One girl's arm and another's leg are draped across my chest, and I lift them out of the way so I can sit up. Strewn around me is the aftermath of last night's escapade — blonde hair, naked bodies, discarded clothes. It's a glorious sight.

The boys are never going to believe me.

•

It's June and now the furthest into the New Zealand winter I've been in seven years. As well as doing some promo work for Mountain Dew, I've picked up a job running a giant skate park that was built for an ad campaign and has now been opened to the public.

I also recently met a cute blonde girl called Soph. She lives near the skate park so I go back to her place each night after work. I feel a little awkward at first, because she's only 18 and I wonder what her parents think about a 24-year-old guy coming over to sleep with their daughter. But I soon meet her family, and they turn out to be super cool and welcoming. One of the things I like most is that they don't have a TV, so in the evenings after dinner we all sit around the fireplace and have actual conversations over a glass of wine.

I've taken quite a liking to Soph. She's super sweet and we have loads of fun together. While we also have great chemistry, this feels much more pure and authentic than many of my flings — the moments I most enjoy are the laughs we have while snuggling in bed. Right from the very start she's felt familiar and comfortable in my arms. When I'm dozing on my stomach, she climbs onto my back and wraps her arms around my neck, then nestles her cheek into mine. We call it the spider monkey and I love it.

I've been up-front with her about my work and travel situation, and we both know that this can't go anywhere serious, but I realise pretty quickly that if I let my defences down I could easily fall in love with this girl. If only I weren't already committed to my first love, wakeboarding. The thought kinda scares me. I simply can't afford to fall in love right now, and I don't want a big drama when I leave.

So, with my departure just a few weeks off, I do the only logical thing — I slowly stop going over to see her as much.

•

I leave New Zealand in mid-July, by far the latest I've flown out to the US. I'm excited to get away from the winter cold and into a North American summer.

This season I'm taking a completely different approach. I've learnt the hard way that I don't have the funds to just live and ride in Orlando for the next four months, so the plan is to meet up with Jay in Texas, then fund my trip down to Florida with a coaching tour that should also leave a bit of coin in my pocket for the rest of the season.

On the way to Texas I stop off for a couple of weeks in LA. I catch a train to Encinitas, the beachside city where Jeff is living this season. He's a block back from the beach, so he can surf daily. Every morning we begin with a sunrise stand-up paddle across the nearby Carlsbad lagoon and out into the surf and back. That's followed by an acai bowl for breakfast, then either a surf or a wakeboard with California rider Chad Lowe.

It's my first time behind a boat since surgery, and my shoulder is holding up really well. It feels strong and stable, and I manage to land a bunch of my tricks, but it's clear that I need to work on my riding fitness, as I take a few crashes and

I'm exhausted and puffing hard after only 10 minutes. We usually wrap up the day with another paddle if we can squeeze it in. I've never been so incredibly active day after day!

Before I left New Zealand, Jenna asked if we could catch up while I'm in LA, and I'd be lying if I said my California stopover wasn't slightly influenced by the idea of finally meeting her. But, after the last few times, I'm not about to make any plans around her. I tell her I'd like to see her, and leave it at that. If she wants it to happen, then she needs to make the effort.

Near the end of the month Jeff and I cruise up to LA for X Games. I've been watching X Games on TV for as long as I can remember, and ever since I started wakeboarding I've dreamed of winning gold here. I remember watching Parks and Danny battle it out in 2003, and seeing Danny win his fourth gold medal in '05, but that was also, unfortunately, the last year wakeboarding was included in the X Games. Since it can't fit into a stadium or the surrounding parking lot, like the other sports, wakeboarding got dropped. It was a real bummer for the sport, decreasing its visibility and some of the sponsorship dollars it attracted. And don't I know about that struggle.

This is my first time actually attending X Games, so I'm as excited as a kid at Disneyland. I want to see everything! And, thanks to Jeff and his hook-ups, we've got passes to go everywhere. My favourite attractions are the freestyle moto best trick, and the gigantic mega-ramp for both BMX and skateboarding.

By the end of my California trip I've had a blast. The only let-down is Jenna. Yet again, I'm leaving LA without having seen her. I'm still curious about her, and especially about why she's so elusive, but I've had enough. Time to put that girl in my rear-view!

•

I land in Texas late in the evening and I'm picked up by a girl I met here last year. The next morning, after she's given me a pleasant welcome to the state, I get her to drop me at a used-car dealer I found online. An hour later I'm driving away in my new ride: a green '98 Ford F-150 that I got for $1800. The air-conditioning isn't working, but I'll get that fixed when I can afford it.

I've lined up my coaching tour, and have locked-in clinics with a few Ronix dealers. As well as being a way to earn some money, it'll also give me a tour of much of the south-eastern United States. I'm staying at Jay's for the week or so before I'm due to head east.

I drive my truck to a nearby cable park, where I meet up with Jay and the Texas iwake crew. Since I'm still fresh back into it, I mainly use my turn on the water to cut a bunch of laps in order to improve my riding fitness — and cool off in the Texas heat. The next day we head out on the river with Joey Bradley and a couple of his buddies, including Clay, whose XStar we're riding behind. And the wake is huge! Clay has a place here on the river and he's not afraid to slam his boat with as much weight as it can handle. When it's my turn to ride I make the most of the air time and am loving the way all my tricks seem to be coming back to me. I cruise through a grabbed 720 off the toes, but on the landing I get a little lazy and fall back into the wake.

It's a very mellow fall, and one I've taken plenty of times before, but this time when my body hits the water I'm dealt a stab of pain on the left side of my ribcage. As I surface I let out a loud groan, then struggle to take a breath. With every inhale, it feels like there's a knife twisting between my ribs.

'You've got to be fucking kidding me!' I mutter once I'm back onboard. 'I seriously can't catch a break.'

'Bro, are you okay?' Jay asks. 'Do you need to go in?'

'Nah, I can wait,' I groan, clutching my ribs and on the verge of tears. 'I'll stick it out until everyone has had a ride.'

I spend the next couple of hours sitting in the boat hugging myself and trying to breathe as shallowly as possible, but I can't get comfortable. I feel every bump and every little roller the boat drives over. By the time we're finally back in the truck I'm completely falling apart. I'm in so much pain the tears start streaming down my face and I begin to sob uncontrollably.

The guys have never seen me like this before. I'm embarrassed about it but it's out of my control. It's not just the pain that's chipping away at me; it's everything. After two years of injuries, surgeries and rehab, not to mention the constant battle just to afford to be here, one thing has kept me going: the prospect of being fit, healthy and riding at my best again. This new injury, just five rides in, has absolutely shattered my spirit.

I spend the hour-long drive back to Jay's place contemplating my future in this sport. Was blowing my knee just the beginning of the end?

•

For the next few days I'm bedridden. The only time it doesn't hurt is when I'm not moving, so that's what I do.

Jay offers to take me to a doctor, and even offers to pay, but from what I know of rib injuries there's not a lot they can do besides check to make sure I haven't punctured a lung. I think I'd know if it was that bad.

After a quick google I'm pretty sure I haven't actually broken a rib. I think I have a separated rib, as I have a prominent lump matching the one in the diagram. According to the internet, separated ribs tend to heal on their own over a couple of months, and besides getting as much rest as possible and taking pain medication there's not much else to be done. So I guess that means I'm off the water while I recover — again.

Everything I do aggravates the pain: talking, breathing, coughing, sneezing, hiccups, laughing. I've still got a few days before I leave on my road-trip so I keep myself occupied playing one of Jay's guitars, but even that is a challenge without making the pain intolerable.

One day while I'm chilling in bed I get a couple of messages from Jenna. She's apologising for not seeing me while I was in LA, and in my weakened and sorry state I call her. At first I find comfort in talking to her, but it doesn't take long for me to realise it's just more of the same. There's a pattern here, and I'm finally seeing it. When I'm not around she constantly wants my attention, but when we're in the same city she mysteriously vanishes. The moment I leave, she's back again, full of apologies and empty promises.

I tell it to her straight: 'Look, I don't know what your deal is. But you and me — we're done.'

To confirm her exit from my life, I de-friend her on Facebook.

•

Jesse calls. He's working as a counsellor at a summer camp up in Maine. He was supposed to be up there for another month but he just got fired. It turns out the camp operators weren't so pumped on him giving a bunch of the campers Mr T mohawks.

'Yeah, that didn't go down so well,' Jesse says, laughing. 'But can I help it if those kids all wanted the same hairdo as me?'

'Book a ticket to Dallas, bro,' I say. 'Join me on the road for the next month!'

Three days later, with my ribs feeling slightly better and all my gear packed in the back of my truck, I swing by Dallas/Fort Worth Airport to snag him. I'm stoked — having one of my best mates with me is going to make this road-trip so much more fun. It's got me feeling a bit more upbeat about things.

Jesse throws his gear in the back, jumps in beside me and we hit the road. Destination: Hot Springs, Arkansas, a six-hour drive away.

I love my new truck. She's running smoothly, and the V8 roaring under the hood provides me with instant power under my right foot. This midsummer Texas heat is something else — over 37°C — so we cruise along Interstate 30 with the windows down and hot wind blasting through the cab. And we chug water. After a couple of hours I notice that I'm not even sweating — but then I wipe my hand across my forehead and realise that actually I have been, but the wind has been instantly drying the sweat to leave little salty crystals all over my face.

Not long after crossing into Arkansas we pull into a McDonald's in a town called Arkadelphia. When we return to the truck, it won't start. Since it's really struggling to turn over, my first thought is that it's the battery. Thankfully, there's a mechanic nearby and it's still open. So Jesse and I push the truck out of the parking lot and down a grass embankment to get it there. They're just about to close but agree to take a quick look. Turns out the battery is fully charged, so they try replacing the old terminal connectors but the thing still won't start.

I might have considered sleeping in the truck but I have to get to Hot Springs for a coaching clinic tomorrow. So there's really only one option: I call a tow truck to pick up the truck and drive us the final hour to Hot Springs. It sets me back $280. The tow truck drops us outside a mechanic's, where we'll hopefully be able to get her fixed tomorrow.

The rider from the shop hosting tomorrow's coaching clinic comes to meet us.

'Are you guys down to go for a beer at Buffalo Wild Wings?' he asks.

'Shit yeah!' Jesse and I say simultaneously. After a massive day on the road we're both hot, sweaty, sticky and could do with a shower, but damn, a cold beer sounds good right now.

The following morning I'm dropped off by a very hospitable young *Playboy* model I met at BWW who kindly let me sleep in her bed.

Jesse's already here, and so are most of the students for today. I introduce myself with a pep in my step after last night's antics, and once everyone's arrived we load up and head out on beautiful Lake Hamilton. The boat is packed and the riders are all super cool and motivated. By the end of the day everyone's landed something new, so I'd call it a successful first stop for the B-rad coaching tour!

Jesse and I head back to the mechanic's to find out what the damage is with my truck.

'It's the air-conditioning compressor,' the mechanic tells us. 'It's completely seized, so it's restricting the starter motor from turning over as it's on the same belt loop.'

Replacing it isn't a major job but it's out of my price range, so I opt for a bypass pulley to be put in instead. That, plus last night's tow, sucks up most of the $700 I made from today's class. Talk about a bump in the road.

●

We continue east, next stop Nashville, Tennessee. En route we stop outside the Graceland gates to sing Marc Cohn's 'Walking in Memphis'. Jesse gets excited every time we see a billboard with Elvis on it, or anything he can reference to a song or movie.

We arrive in Nashville late in the evening. As we drive down the main strip we see a couple of places that still seem to be poppin', even though it's a Tuesday, then we round a corner and spot a Hooters. 'Let's start with dinner there,' I say, because who knows where things might lead? We don't have anywhere to be until tomorrow afternoon, so if we happened to meet two gorgeous girls who wanted to take us home with them we would be okay with that . . .

We fill up on wings, deep-fried pickles and beer, but leave without girls.

On the way here we spotted a live music bar on the main strip that I've been to before, so that's where we go next. Beers in hand, we turn our attention to the music. The band on stage is incredible, but that's hardly surprising — this is Nashville, where every man, woman and their dog is a talented musician.

The bar's not that busy, so at first I don't spot much female talent, but then a tall blonde catches my eye. I go over and spark up a conversation, and she seems really cool. Her name is Tiffany, and before the night is through I'm in her bed. But she turns out to be one of those hypersensitive girls who twitches and jolts and moans at the slightest touch, so that's as far as she lets me go.

Jesse ends up crashing on the couch downstairs, where he is joined by Tiffany's friend. Her male friend, who is gay. He has clearly taken a liking to Jesse but the feeling is not mutual, and my poor friend spends the night fending off unwanted advances. He's pretty disappointed when he learns that he went through all that for me and I didn't even get laid. He earns wingman of the year for that one.

The next day we have a bit of time to kill, so when Tiffany suggests over breakfast that we head to the lake we're keen. We jump in her car and 10 minutes later she's racing down the freeway at 160 kph, swerving between cars and crossing multiple lanes at a time. At first we beg her to slow down, but she laughs and ignores us. Jesse turns to me and says, 'Hey, bro, if we don't make it, I just want to tell you I love you, man.' He's only half joking.

•

We spend a couple of days with my buddy Scott at his place in Winchester, Tennessee. His family home is nestled in the trees on the shores of Tims Ford Lake, and the first day here I don't have any coaching lined up so we spend it chilling on the water. It's a little over a week since I separated my ribs and they're still tender. I'm not ready to be riding again yet, but for the sake of getting wet I opt to take a wakesurf. It's still a little much for my ribs, but just being behind the boat is refreshing for my soul.

The following day I pass on more wakeboarding knowledge in exchange for more cash. And, while I know I've put in the years to be able to charge for lessons, it's still a pretty fucking awesome job — I get to hang out on the lake all day, meet a bunch of rad new people and teach them to wakeboard. My favourite part is seeing a student learn something new. Whether it's getting up for the first time, landing their first flip or finally understanding how to ride away from that 720, the stoke is always so real.

From Winchester, Jesse and I have a solid drive up through the mountains to east Tennessee and South Holston Lake.

'Brrrro!' says Jesse as we walk out onto Lake View Dock, our base for the next week. 'This place is insane!'

'Yeah,' I reply. 'I couldn't believe it either the first time I came here.'

We walk along the marina, and even though it's familiar to me I know he's right: this place *is* insane. Bobbing on the water and connected by wide pathways, Lake View Dock is essentially a floating village, complete with cottage-style accommodation, general store, restaurant and more. All around lies the glassy water of South Holston Lake, its shores bordered by deep green forest. It's like a postcard.

The guys from the local pro shop and boat dealership, CBK, are there to meet us, as are the Slagel family, who own the docks. I introduce Jesse and they show him around, then we head to our cabin and start crushing beers while the burgers are on the grill. Sitting out the back on the water's edge, it's so good to catch up with these guys. They're an awesome bunch and I always have a blast with them — that's why I've allocated more time to hang here.

The next morning when I go to meet the day's students, I'm a little hung, but they're a fun crew and it's awesome to see them all leave happy and having learnt something.

The best rider of the lot is a teenager named Austin Pratt — his is a really nice style to watch. At the end of the day his parents come to pick him up. After introducing themselves, they ask me what their son needs to do in order to go pro. He's already hooked up on a grassroots level by Ronix, they tell me.

'He seems like he could do well if he dedicates himself to it,' I say, then I give it to them straight. 'The best chance you could give him is to upgrade your boat, and Orlando really is the place to be.'

They seem grateful for the advice and we agree to stay in touch.

•

My friend Levi has been going on at me about this girl he wants me to meet.

'You'll fall in love with her instantly,' he promises.

When I finally meet her, I realise he was not exaggerating.

Jesse, Levi and I are at Hooters in Johnson City, sitting at the bar, when I hear a voice say, 'Hey, Levi,' in a super-cute Southern drawl.

'Joelene,' Levi says, grinning, 'I want you to meet my friends from New Zealand.'

For a moment I'm lost for words. The blonde, blue-eyed waitress is unbelievably gorgeous.

'Oh, erm . . . hi,' I stutter, then I manage to snap myself out of my trance and smile at her. 'It's a pleasure to meet you.'

She blushes. 'Oh my . . .' She turns back to Levi. 'You weren't lying . . . and that accent!'

'What did I tell you, buddy?' Levi replies.

It appears he's been telling her about me, too, and his matchmaking is on point. Joelene and I are both instantly infatuated with each other. For the next two hours, as we eat dinner, I can't take my eyes off her. We exchange smiles and glances at every opportunity, and every time those blue eyes lock on mine I feel my heart skip a beat. She has the most beautiful face, her rig is befitting of where she works, and her arse is unbelievable. I've only just met this girl but I want to take her straight back home to New Zealand and wifey her up!

Levi interrupts my daydream to mention something he probably should've brought up sooner. 'Yeah, she's engaged to a buddy of mine,' he says.

'*What?*' I'm confused, even a little pissed off. Why the hell has he done this? But, to be honest, the information goes in one ear and I let it sail right out of the other. I couldn't care less that she's engaged. I want this girl more than anyone else before.

We arrange to meet up with Joelene once she finishes her shift. Jesse has scored digits from a gorgeous brunette he's been chatting up, so she'll be joining us too. While we wait for the girls we grab a room at a nearby motel so we can shower and change for a night out. Joelene conveniently arrives right as I'm getting out of the shower, so I stay in my towel for an extra minute or so, peacocking a little before getting dressed.

We head out to Capones bar, named after the infamous gangster Al Capone, who's said to have frequented the area back in the 1920s. Jesse toasts Capone with our first drinks. He and Levi then start playing a round of pool, so Joelene and I jump into a nearby photo booth to get some pictures together. We pull all kinds of funny faces, and I want to kiss her, but the ring on her finger causes me to hesitate. An hour and a few more drinks later, we dip back into the photo booth and she grabs my face and starts kissing me before the first flash goes off.

I'm not the only one who's chosen to forget for the night that she's engaged.

The following morning, hungover and ready to write the day off, the guys and I go over to Joelene's place. We all laze about on the couch while her one-year-old daughter plays and coos on the floor.

I really want to snuggle up on the couch with Joelene but her fiancé is due home any minute, so I keep my distance. Next thing, in walks an absolute tank of a human. He's not tall but he's absolutely jacked. I can practically smell the steroids seeping from his pores. He doesn't try to hide the fact that he's on the juice, popping something right in front of us that he says is supposed to stop him from getting 'bitch tits'.

He then goes on to tell us that he injects himself with some sort of skin pigment darkener. Up until this moment I was feeling a little guilty about last night with Joelene, but this guy is an absolute tool. I have no qualms about taking his girl.

We all go for a late breakfast and I have to consciously remind myself not to stare at Joelene the whole time. As everyone is about to pay, I'm feeling like I've done a pretty good job at hiding the chemistry between us, but when I pull out my wallet I almost let the previous night's photo-booth shots fall right on the table. I catch them and shove them back in place just in time.

With a few days left to spare before we move on to Kentucky, we head to a house party for a friend's 21st birthday. Joelene is there and I'm happy to have another chance to see her.

We go for dinner first, and later on at the party, once we've had a few drinks, she pulls me into an empty room and we screw on the carpet, then again in the ensuite. Joelene is as sexy as she is sweet, and I'm seriously wondering how I can go about stealing her back to New Zealand. There are just two obvious things in the way: the ring on her finger, and her child to the guy who gave her the ring. But I can tell she's not happy with him — if she was, why would she be here with me?

●

My compadre Jesse and I depart Tennessee having built great friendships, got laid and had an absolute blast. Back on the road, we crank 'Wagon Wheel' by Darius Rucker as we drive west through the Cumberland Gap and up towards McDaniels, a small town in Kentucky. It's after 11 p.m. when we pull up outside Nick's Boat Dock on the shores of Rough River Lake, but owner Mike Brown is up and waiting to greet us.

'Come in!' he says, ushering us into his huge garage, where — along with a bunch of trampolines and gym equipment for the kids — there's a bar. We sit down and he pulls out what at first glance looks like a handle of Jack Daniel's.

'This right here,' Mike says proudly, 'is a little homemade wine I call Raisin Jack.' He unscrews the cap in a fashion befitting a Kentucky man about to serve bootleg booze, then tosses it out the door. 'It'll put hair on your balls! And we're sitting here till we finish the whole dang bottle!'

'Can't argue with that,' Jesse says.

The three of us clink glasses and knock back the first one. Jesse and I immediately start coughing and gasping.

'Pheee-ew!' Jesse sputters.

'Geez!' I exclaim. I can feel it burning all the way down my throat. 'The name wine is a little misleading. This shit kicks more like hard liquor!'

While the three of us sit there sharing stories, cracking jokes and laughing our arses off, the bottle slowly empties. It's around 1.30 a.m. when the last drop is poured, and I'm pretty well smashed. We all are. But Mike walks over to the freezer, pulls out another handle of Raisin Jack, and takes the cap off and tosses it out the door. Jesse and I give each other a worried look, but this is Mike's place. We can't turn down his Kentucky welcome — it would be rude.

By the time the second bottle is empty it must be close to 4 a.m. We stumble blindly inside and crash.

•

It's already afternoon when Jesse and I begin to regain consciousness.

My head is absolutely pounding, and when I open my eyes I instantly close them again. I appear to be sleeping in a pink bedroom in a pink bed with pink fairy sheets. I curl up in the foetal position.

I hear Jesse groan. I slowly reopen my eyes and see him on a pull-out bed beside me. He also has fairy sheets, and looks as bad as I feel. He also looks as confused as I am about where we are. Squinting, we both look around. Everywhere there are Barbies and unicorns. Mike put us in his daughter's room.

We lie there for a long time, trying to summon the energy to drag ourselves out of bed. This is officially the worst hangover I have ever experienced. When we finally manage to stumble downstairs, we meet an equally hungover Mike.

Nobody talks. We just laze about on the couch for a while, until we can manage to eat. That brings us back to life just in time for Mike's kids to get home from school. They barge in the door, eager to get out on the river for some coaching.

Initially I had hoped to do a full day with a boatful of students while I was here, but now I'm really relieved that didn't happen. Coaching Mike's kids I'll still make enough for the trip to be worthwhile, and Jesse and I both feel so welcome. This awesome family has taken us two random Kiwis in and made us feel right at home. Southern hospitality!

•

Our last stop before heading down to Orlando is Knoxville, Tennessee. I'm here for the pro tour stop — not to compete but to help Jay at the iwake booth. I also spend some time helping out at the Ronix booth.

I notice that the commentator, Dano, is solo on the mic. I've got to know Dano over the years — he's a cool guy and kills it on the mic. I go over and tap him on the shoulder. 'Hey, bro, do you need a hand? I can jump on the other mic and help if you want.'

'Yeah, thanks!' he replies. 'That'd be awesome.'

I'm nervous at first but I soon feel more comfortable. I know the riders and the tricks, I can break down the runs, and Dano and I bounce well off each other. It's less than an hour before his co-announcer returns and I hand over the mic, but as I step away from the stage I'm surprised to have a bunch of people stop me to compliment me on my commentary skills. Who knows — maybe I've got a future on the mic?

Austin Pratt has made the trip down too. He and his parents come over to say hi, and his parents tell me they've purchased a better boat and they're moving to Orlando in a couple of weeks.

'We wondered if you might be interested in living with us for a while?' they say. 'If you were happy to coach Austin, we could give you free board and riding time behind the boat.'

'That sounds perfect!' I say. 'Thank you!'

The timing couldn't be better as I have nowhere to stay in Orlando as yet. Austin is a cool kid and I see a lot of potential in him, so I'm excited to ride and hang with him. It's really kind of them to invite me to live with them.

Our girls have come to Knoxville to join Jesse and me for the after-party. The following day Joelene and I are floating in the hotel pool and talking about running off together. Then she checks her phone and her face drops instantly.

'He knows,' she says.

I realise I've really fucked up. My total lust for her overpowered my deep-down acceptance that she and I were never going to run off together. Her daughter, my unstable lifestyle and financial situation — it was all a pipe-dream.

She's going home to face the music.

•

After more than a month of full-on adventures, coaching and partying, Jesse leaves and I'm about ready to get back to riding. My ribs feel fully healed.

I get word from Austin Pratt that he and his family have settled into their new place out east of Orlando on Lake Brantley. It turns out they're renting it from Adam Fields, the American rider I competed against at the IWWF championships a couple of years back.

Living with a family and respecting their rules is a bit of a change from my partying life but I'm just glad to have a home base until I fly back to New Zealand in a couple of months. They've set up bunk beds in the laundry room by the garage, which means I have my own space, and on the canal out the back of the house sits their new Axis A22, just begging to be ridden. And, every day after Pratt gets home from school, that's exactly what we do. The kid not only rips, but we get along super well. It's not long before we're basically brothers.

When we're not riding at home we race out to Mount Dora — just half an hour away — to ride on East Crooked Lake with Alex, Cole Chapman and Cole's friend Mike. Alex has his Malibu at the Chapmans' dock and Mike has an XStar at his parents' place just across the lake, so we're spoilt for boat choice — we get to ride two of the best wakes out there on one of my favourite lakes! Before long, my riding is almost back to where I left off two years ago, and life finally feels like it's getting back on track.

•

One evening when his parents are out, Pratt calls me into the garage.

'Check it out!' he says, holding up one of Adam's bongs. 'I found it in a cupboard. Wanna hit?'

Pratt's only 17, so I haven't even spoken to him about smoking, let alone smoked with him, but he's busy packing the bong with some green so of course I oblige. An hour later we're still in the garage, cracking each other up and goofing around, when his sister wanders in to grab something. 'Hey,' she says, glancing at the bong, then she leaves without saying anything else.

The following day Mrs Pratt pulls me aside and gives me a bit of a growling.

'I really apologise,' I say. I want to defend myself, but I also don't want to drop Pratt in it. 'I know I should be a better influence on him than that.'

I really do mean it — but I also feel torn between respecting the Pratts' rules and bro'ing down with my bud. So, a few days later when Pratt suggests we go for a drive to blaze, I agree. While we sit in the car in the Taco Bell parking lot, I introduce him to his first spliff.

•

At a Halloween party, a girl who's just my type — petite, blonde and gorgeous — catches my eye and we hit it off right away. Her name is Bianca. One night, while I'm over at her place, playing the guitar and serenading her with Pink Floyd's 'Wish You Were Here', I notice a cop car pull up outside the window. It's stopped right behind my truck, which is parked out on the street. I go outside to see what the deal is.

'Evening, officer,' I say to the cop, who's closely inspecting my licence plate. 'Is there a problem?'

'These are dealer plates,' he says. 'From Texas.'

'Yeah,' I reply, 'I bought the truck in Texas, and drove it back here. I'm planning on getting Florida plates but I only just got back.'

Which is almost true: I've been back almost a month.

The cop is not convinced. 'I'm going to need to take these,' he says, grabbing the temporary plates.

Shit. My truck is no longer legal to drive on the road. How am I going to get it back to Pratt's place half an hour away?

I figure that problem can wait till the morning, because right now I've got a hot little blondie waiting for me to join her inside.

The next morning I drive five minutes down the road to Mitch's place to get the guys to help me figure out what to do. Without plates, I'll be an instant target for the police.

Mitch himself has returned to Australia, but some of the other lads are still living here. After pondering for a while, the only solution I come up with is borrowing the plates from Mitch's Cadillac Escalade. I slap them on my truck and make it back to Pratt's without getting pulled over.

That next afternoon Pratt and I jump in my truck and head for Mount Dora, planning to go to the DMV for new plates, then for a shred with Alex. We're halfway there when a cop pulls up behind me at a red light. I hold my breath in hope but he flicks his lights on.

I pull over and he walks up to my window.

'Sir,' he says, 'do you realise that running stolen plates is a criminal offence?'

What the . . .? My mind runs through all the worst-case scenarios. Am I about to be arrested? What will that mean for my visa? Could I be deported?

'I'm really sorry, officer,' I reply, 'but I assure you the plates aren't stolen. They're from a friend's car. I was just trying to get to the DMV without getting pulled over.'

I show him the folder of paperwork on the dash but he issues me a ticket anyway, requiring me to go to court in a few weeks. I don't mention that I won't be here in a few weeks. I'm flying home in three days.

•

The next day Alex picks me up and we head back to his place. I've been coming out to Mount Dora a lot to hang and ride with him and the guys. Today, though, Molly is here.

It's been a few years since we've seen each other or even spoken, but she and Alex have remained close friends. The three of us used to be inseparable and always had a blast, but my contact with Molly petered out not long after our relationship ended.

But we have a great day and it's such a relief that everything is cool again. I'm still so attracted to Molly. She's gorgeous and has a bangin' body, but she's also such a rad human. We vibe so well.

The chemistry is definitely still there, because eventually we're having sex in the bathroom. I go for an evening ride on the lake with the guys, then Molly and I drive back to my place in her car. And when we pull up at the house we are straight back at it, and take things inside, doing our best not to wake anyone.

The next morning I pack my bags and throw them in the back of Molly's car. On our way up the road for breakfast we start bickering. I think maybe she's feeling conflicted about us sleeping together again, especially right before I'm leaving. And, honestly, I'm feeling a little conflicted as well. I doubted we'd ever speak to each other again, let alone end up sleeping together. It's brought up a whole lot of feelings I wasn't expecting.

After spending the night with my ex, I feel I need to be up-front with Bianca. There's one slight issue: I'm meant to be staying with her for my last night in Florida and she's agreed to take me to the airport in the morning. I just hope she's okay with me crashing on the couch.

She takes it surprisingly well. So well, in fact, that as I'm busy making a bed for myself on the couch, she comes out and invites me into her room where we enjoy each other's company for one last night.

•

On my flight home the next day, my thoughts turn to my scheduled court appearance. Before leaving, I did everything I could to postpone it to when I'm next due to be back in the US but it was impossible. I sit stressing about the consequences of failing to show up. It's quite possible I'll return next year with a warrant out for my arrest.

Oh well, there's not much I can do about it right now. I'll just have to write a letter explaining my situation and hope for the best.

TEN: FINDING MY VOICE

I decide I'm going to start 2012 right.

It's been a tough couple of years recovering from injuries, and I'm aware that wakeboarding as a sport has moved on without me. I'm now playing catch-up, and I need to give myself the best shot possible. So I'm going to use the New Zealand summer to get in prime shape for the US season.

As I discovered a couple of years ago, summers in New Zealand are not what they used to be for wakeboarding. The scene has become somewhat stagnant, with fewer contests and less prize money, meaning there's not much competition for me any more, and the quality of riding isn't really enough for me to learn any new tricks.

On top of that, Ants and Brant both have jobs, and Brant's had a girlfriend for the past few years, so the guys don't really ride much any more, if at all. I still try to ride as much as possible, but it's more about maintaining my riding fitness than mastering anything new. Basically I only come back because I'm out of money. I can crash at Mum's while I get my shit together and save for the next US season.

So, as well as getting back to the usual lines of paid work, I charge full steam ahead into my physical conditioning. I quit drinking alcohol, smoking weed and eating fast food. I run 6 km almost every day. I'm not a great runner, but I enjoy the feeling of moving fast through the fresh air and there's something soothing about the way my breathing becomes synchronised with my shoes hitting the pavement. I go to Suna Pilates with Mum's friend Susie Turner, who lets me attend morning sessions for free since — in her words — I'm eye-candy for her and all the mums who come in after dropping their kids at school. I'm totally fine with this arrangement. I've actually been coming to Susie's Pilates classes for a few years now, and I really feel the benefits.

My buddy Ricky is a boxing trainer, so I also start working with him too, and I rope myself into two early-morning sessions a week at a high-intensity circuit-training gym called Ludus Magnus.

I realise very quickly how unfit I am.

Ricky works me hard, leaving me completely spent and drenched in sweat. I love the intensity of our sessions and it's fun getting in the ring for a few rounds of body sparring. Ludus is just brutal. Some of the All Blacks train here, so whenever we're put in groups I try to end up with them to really push myself and see if I can keep up. By the end of an hour and a half of circuit training — including hill sprints, sit-ups, push-ups, chin-ups, burpees, lizard crawls, flipping tyres, battle ropes, kettlebells, sledgehammers and more — I feel like I'm about to puke, and some days I actually do.

•

In January I reconnect with a girl I met while I was home last year. Her name's April, and she was a contestant in a bikini contest I judged at a V8 supercars race in Hamilton. Another girl won that contest but April got my vote — and, when I told her so afterwards, she gave me her number.

As I'm on my way home from a weekend in Mangakino, I invite her over to watch a movie. Seeing her again is an extremely pleasant reminder of her breathtaking beauty. She's just wearing casual clothes, her blonde hair tied back and with no obvious make-up and I just love that. From the first embrace I'm intoxicated by her sweet fragrance. Everything about this girl is alluring.

On Valentine's Day I surprise her with breakfast in bed. Her face lights up when I appear with a tray of pancakes, coffee, orange juice and a bunch of red roses. The smile on her face makes the small effort it took well worthwhile, and the enthusiastic kisses she bombards me with are a welcome bonus.

In a few short weeks I've grown really fond of April and want to spend as much time as possible with her. She makes me realise how much I've missed having someone around. How nice it is having love in my life. Over the last few years I've been filling the void of loneliness with sex. Whenever I have let a girl get close to me it's because I've felt love for her, but even then I've kept her at arm's length to protect myself. That wall I built around my heart when Casey broke up with me is still firmly in place.

But having April around reminds me what I'm missing out on, and it slowly begins chipping away at that protective wall. I love the freedom of the single playboy lifestyle, but I'd be lying if I said I didn't sometimes wish I could keep one of the good ones. And April is a good one.

We continue to spend almost every day together, and we have a lot of fun. Although April is an absolute stunner she's also down to earth and even a little rough around the edges — and I mean that in the best way. Like, she doesn't care what people think of her. She's just herself. She keeps me guessing.

We both know I'm leaving soon, so our time together is limited. I've been honest with her about wakeboarding being my first love, and I've told her I'm going back to the US no matter what. But, along with all the things that make me excited to be leaving, she's the one thing that makes me want to stay. I do my best to keep things in perspective, but I think I'm falling for this girl. I try to bury the feelings. They will only make it harder when the time comes.

•

By the end of March I've been sober and healthy for three months, and I'm really happy with the results.

The boxing and running and intense Ludus sessions, along with eating well and resisting the temptation to drink or smoke while hanging with friends have paid off. I've trimmed down from my usual 96 kg to 91, and my power-to-weight ratio has significantly improved. I'm really proud of what I've achieved, and I'm so ready for the upcoming US season.

Before leaving, I throw a little get-together at Mum's, to share some laughs and quality time with my closest friends before I disappear for another six months. Charlotte, my ex, even pops along for a while, which is cool. When she heads home, I walk her up the drive to say goodbye, but soon April finds out and is pissed off at me. She grabs her stuff and heads for her car before I'm able to reassure her that I was simply saying goodbye to Char. Nothing else.

April calms down and comes back inside, but her outburst tells me that she's probably struggling with my imminent departure more than she's letting on. I get it. Saying goodbye to my friends sucks, but at least I know I'll see them when I get back. April, on the other hand? I can't be so sure.

That night we discuss the possibility of rekindling things when I come back, but reluctantly agree that it would be foolish to hold on to that hope for half a year. Neither of us knows how the next six months will play out. Some tears are shed, but we make the most of our last night, fucking like there's no tomorrow.

The next day I try to ignore my feelings for her. The only way I know to deal with saying goodbye is to look forward and move on.

•

As I stand outside LAX, a dark blue Chrysler 300 pulls up to the kerb in front of me. The driver winds her window down.

'Welcome back to the States!' she says.

I cram my board bag and suitcase into the back seat, then jump in the front with her. She leans over and gives me a kiss.

'How could I not be stoked to be back with a welcome like this?' I say as she pulls away.

Amanda is a professional dancer I met two years ago. She's from Tennessee, but came to LA to pursue her career. She's tall, gorgeous, brunette and, damn, can the girl move her body! I've arranged to spend a couple of days with her before heading to Texas to meet up with Jay.

As usual I'm arriving in the US practically broke — probably the most financially strained I've ever been at the start of a season. So I'm hoping to keep this stopover fairly cheap.

After unloading my gear at Amanda's condo we meet up with a friend of hers and hike the popular Runyon Canyon loop. From the top, the view across the city of angels is impressive: an ocean of buildings and homes filled with actors, athletes, musicians, gym junkies, beach babes, cops, crooks, crazies, thieves, drug dealers, drug addicts, suits and everyone in between stretches as far as the eye can see. People pursuing their dreams side by side with those who have already given up on them. It's the land of opportunity, but it can just as easily swallow you whole.

The next morning, after a night of hot lovin' where Amanda showed off her impressive flexibility, she goes out to run some errands. I stay at hers to make use of the air-conditioning and the wifi and get some work done. Once I've sent a handful of emails — some chasing money I'm owed and others setting up money to earn — I log on to Facebook, planning to let my US friends know I'm back, and I see a message from a Texas sweetheart I met a couple of years back and have stayed in touch with.

Hayley is in a league of her own. If I believed in a divine creator, I'd give him a round of applause for his impeccable work. Not only does she look incredible, but she's incredibly sweet too. When we first met she had a boyfriend, but the message I'm reading right now tells me they've broken up. *Do you want to come and visit me in San Diego?* she's asked.

Do I?! I want to go right now! I want to sweep her off her feet and make her mine! If I had a car, I would get in it and drive the 200 km down to her. If I had the money, I would catch a taxi and then a train. I would have no second thoughts about disappearing on Amanda. Quite frankly, I've just stopped off for some fun with her — we're not about to start a relationship. But Hayley? Hayley I would date long-distance. Hayley I would settle down with. Hayley I want to see so badly.

I'm due to fly out to Texas tomorrow but I call the airline to see if I can delay by a day or two. I can't afford the change fee so I try to charge it to Jay's card, which was used for the original booking, but it doesn't work. I can't change my flight.

So I sit in Amanda's apartment, messaging Hayley. She's telling me all the things she'd like us to do to each other if I could just get there, and I can't do anything but type my own ideas back to her and it's pure torture!

The next day when we get to the airport in her Chrysler, Amanda asks me for petrol money.

'I'm really sorry,' I reply, 'but I don't have any cash.' I want to add that, personally, I wouldn't ask anyone who was visiting my home for petrol money, let alone someone I was sleeping with. Instead, I say non-committally, 'I'm expecting some through soon, so I'll transfer it to you if you really want me to.'

She's not happy, but I don't care.

•

I spend a few days in Texas with Jay and his family before he and I endure the 18-hour overnight drive down to Florida. It's around nine in the morning when we finally pull up at local pro rider J.D. Webb's place on Lake Ariana, and it's already hot and humid. JD and his roommates Kyle and Scott have just come in from a shoot, and it's good to catch up with the guys again. And it's damn good to be back in Florida!

I crash out on the couch for a solid nap to recover from the drive. I'm glad this couch is super comfortable, because it's where I'm sleeping for the next few weeks. Before leaving New Zealand I had actually arranged to go back to the Pratts', but just days before I flew out they dropped the news on me that 'plans had changed' and I could no longer stay there. Maybe it was the smoking weed with their son. It's just lucky I found another option so quickly.

Over the following weeks the days are busy. We typically start with an early-morning photo shoot, then come back to the house for breakfast. After that, we're in the back yard working on a new feature — an incline rail to wall-ride — that will go on the end of JD's dock. Since in New Zealand we only get to hit what we build, I have a fair amount of experience with these sorts of projects, and I love having the skills to really help.

After lunch and a run to fill petrol tanks for the boat, we're back out on the water, enjoying the ridiculously large wake behind JD's Nautique G23. It's a brand-new model and the wake is about 30 per cent bigger than any wake I've ridden before. It's completely changed the game. Late afternoon generally brings thunderstorms that roll in and out in just a couple of hours, giving us some rest time while we sit back and enjoy the lightning show, then we're back out on the lake for a photo shoot beneath fiery sunsets that will hopefully grant us access to the pages of wakeboarding's best magazines. We finish huge days like this with dinner, beers and playing the guitar.

These are the perfect days that I fly halfway around the world for.

•

The first major event of the year is Wake Games at the Orlando Watersports Complex (OWC). It's also the first event being towed by the G23, so everyone is frothing to get behind it and throw down. I ride pretty well in my first round, but get beaten and don't advance.

A few days ago I heard that one of the commentators for the pro wakeboard tour and King of Wake series has left. I immediately wondered about trying to take his place. At Wake Games I notice there's already a new guy on the mic with Dano. He's okay but I feel like I could do better. So I approach Dano and let him know I'm interested.

'Why don't you come up and have a go when my offsider goes for a lunch break?' he suggests.

So that's what I do. For half an hour Dano and I bounce off each other, and we gel instantly. He hypes it up, I break it down — I'm the more mellow, analytical dude. My low, smooth New Zealand accent perfectly complements his higher Illinois voice.

For the rest of the day I'm complimented about my commentary by friends and strangers alike. Then Chris Bischoff, director of the pro tour, asks if I'd be available to announce alongside Dano at the next event. 'We'll cover your entry, sort your accommodation out and we have $150 for you,' he says. 'If it goes well, we'd continue it for the rest of the season.'

'Done!' I reply, stoked. 'I'll be there. Thanks for the opportunity, Bisch!'

•

One evening JD and Jay return from a round of golf. Jay has had a few beers. 'Get up!' he proclaims. 'We're going to the strip club! And you're driving!'

Reluctantly, I get up and throw on a change of clothes. Some guys my age might be into strip clubs, and I'm sure my liaisons with strippers might suggest otherwise, but I don't really frequent them. It's never really been my thing. I've only ever gone when I'm with a group of dudes who are keen after a few drinks, or if a girl I'm out with suggests it. Tonight, I really have no desire to drive 45 minutes just to pay to see some tits — especially not when I've already got plenty of nudes on my phone from the likes of April and Sasha back home — but my sponsor has spoken. JD isn't coming, as he lives with his girlfriend.

In town, Jay and I wander into the first strip club we find, but they turn us away for being too casually dressed. I guess it's their loss, because we wander across the road to another doll house, where Jay drops two grand on stripper dollars and gets us a booth and a bottle of vodka. As soon as we sit down we're joined by four girls, and Jay splits the stripper cash into four $500 wads and hands one to each girl.

Rookie error!

Two of the girls disappear and we hardly see them again, but the other two hang around and show us a good time. I'm mildly entertained, thanks to the vodka. But mostly I can't get past the fact that my sponsor just dropped two grand to see some titties and have his ego stroked for a couple of hours while I'm struggling to get more than $500 a month out of him.

I'm starting to feel like this sponsorship might not last.

•

Alex has invited me out to Mount Dora for the night, and when he picks me up he has a sly grin on his face. He flashes a little ziplock bag at me. 'Bro!' he says. 'Are you down for some mushrooms tonight?'

'Shit yeah, dude!' I reply.

I haven't done shrooms since the time I took them with Kallas and Carnie, when the storm rolled through and we were mesmerised by the incredible sunset that followed.

Alex and I cruise over to the Chapmans' house. Everyone except Cole is away, and his friend Ashley comes over to join us on our journey. Alex puts his bartending skills to work, dicing the shrooms into tiny pieces then throwing them together with lemon and who knows what else, and serves us each a shot of his cosmic concoction.

'Cheers!' I say as we clink our glasses together. 'See you on the other side!'

We down our shots, but the mixture is hard to swallow. Alex definitely could've diced the mushrooms more finely, and the lemon isn't quite powerful enough to mask their earthy taste. The sun's about to go down so we wander down to the lake and take a perch on the Chapmans' dock, talking and laughing while we wait for the trip to start.

Before long I feel it kicking in. I'm becoming entranced by the painted sky, the brushstrokes of orange and white streaking across the darkening blue canvas, everything doubled in the mirrored surface of the tranquil lake. I'm always fascinated by a good sunset, but this one is different — pure artistry! I've never seen colours like this before: moving, glowing, three-dimensional colours growing towards me. It's like they're speaking to me, permeating me to my core. I not only see the beauty; I feel it, I absorb it, I *am* it.

I look around at my friends, and their wide eyes and wide grins tell me they're also feeling the euphoric effects of the fungi. We start talking in depth about sunsets — how the beautiful orange colour is due to the sun's light passing through more atmosphere than it does during the day, how the clouds that hold those colours are merely gatherings of water vapour reflecting light from the sun, and how we only get these sunsets because we're on a rock spinning through space and rotating around a ball of flaming gas which brings light and life to us.

'Woah, dude, that's some deep shit!' Alex says.

I feel like I've been teleported out into space to watch our tiny planet.

Cole has such a big grin on his face and looks so full of energy that I tell him I'm going to take a picture of him.

'Stand there so I can get the sunset in the background,' I say.

He does as instructed, maintaining his exuberant expression while I aim my phone at him.

'Oops, hold on, that was out of focus,' I say. 'Let me try again . . . Shit, that one was no good either. Hold that, Cole, here we go! This is looking better . . . Damn! Almost got it.'

I fumble with the phone, trying to check the settings, and all the while Cole keeps the same huge cheesy grin plastered across his face.

'Oh,' I finally say. 'It's on video. I haven't taken a single photo. It's been recording the whole time instead.'

We all burst out laughing, and it's uncontrollable, hysterical laughter that makes my eyes leak and leaves my cheeks hurting.

Once the sun has disappeared, we retreat into the house and soon become obsessed with the chandelier hanging in the kitchen. For at least half an hour we can't get enough of the patterns it casts all over the ceiling.

Meanwhile, my thoughts wander to my truck. While I was back in New Zealand I managed to get my court date shifted, and it's in three days' time. Once that small matter is dealt with, I'll be able to drive my truck again. All going to plan, that small green Ford and its V8 engine will be my transportation and my home for the next few months.

In 10 days I'm due to hit the road for the first stop of the pro tour in Acworth, Georgia, and from there I'll chase the stops around the south-east United States, from Georgia to Texas, then up to Missouri and back to Texas, to then grab a return flight up to Seattle, then to Ohio and back down to Tennessee.

What if my truck breaks down? I wonder.

I can't afford to fix it. I can only just afford the gas to get me to Acworth, where I know there's $150 waiting for me for commentating with Dano. Knowing my money won't stretch, I've organised some coaching stops on the way to Fort Worth to earn some money. But it's a fragile plan. If just one thing falls through, I'm screwed.

My tripping mind picks up this thread and follows it.

I start mentally exploring every possible thing that could go wrong, every way my tour could fall apart. I'm homeless, for starters, so I need this tour to work because I don't have anywhere to live for the next few months if it doesn't. I'm also hung up on the money Jay blew at the strip club. I could've put *half* of that money to much better use. Then there's the looming court case, and I really don't want to think about the worst-case scenario there. What if I get deported?

The thoughts continue to spiral as the trip takes me deeper. I try moving to different parts of the room to improve my vibe, but I can't get out of my own head. It doesn't help that every time I move, one of the others gets up and follows me. I was enjoying the company of my comrades on this journey, but now I'm feeling like a bit of a Pied Piper. I just want to get enough space to rein in my thoughts and save my mind from being swallowed into the vortex.

My chest starts getting tighter. I feel like I'm losing my grip on the positive and I don't like this feeling one bit. I like to be in control, and right now I'm losing it.

Then, right before panic takes hold, I hear Alex say something about being 'along for the ride' and I grab onto it. I suddenly realise that maybe worrying about future things that are outside my current control is what's turning this into a bad trip. Right now I have no control over my upcoming court appearance, or whether my truck makes it through the road-trip, or whether I have somewhere to live. And the moment I realise that is the same moment that I let go and my mind becomes lighter, the downward spiral stops.

Cole calls it a night but the rest of us aren't done yet. Back down by the lake again, I lie on the roof of the dock with Alex and Ashley, gazing up at the stars, and I finally feel good again. I soak in the awe of how big and vast the universe is, and how tiny but connected we are here on earth.

It makes me feel like I'm nothing and everything at the same time.

•

I've never been to court in my life so I have no idea how it goes. I call Jay, who is now back in Texas, to ask for his advice, as I can't afford a lawyer.

'Wear a suit and tie, be respectful and plead guilty,' he tells me.

So that's how I find myself standing in front of the judge wearing my dark grey suit, white shirt and black tie.

'Mr Smeele, you have been charged with operating a vehicle while displaying incorrect licence plates, which in the state of Florida is deemed a criminal offence,' the judge says. 'How do you plead?'

'Firstly, I'd like to apologise for wasting your time today, your honour,' I reply. 'I feel I had good reason for driving my vehicle with someone else's plates on it, but I am guilty of the stated offence so I guess I plead guilty?' I say this last part hesitantly.

The judge looks at me with a confused frown. 'Mr Smeele, what, if I may ask, was your good reason for taking a licence plate off another vehicle, then driving around with it displayed on your vehicle?'

'Your honour, while I won't argue that what I did was wrong, my intentions were in the right place. I just went about it the wrong way. On the day in question, I was actually on my way to the DMV to get a new registration and plates, but I didn't want to be a target by having no licence plates. So I borrowed my friend's plates to get me there, but unfortunately I got pulled over on the way.'

The judge pauses for a second before responding. 'You know, I'm really not supposed to do this,' he eventually says, 'but there's a public defender just there to your right who could probably work out a deal to reduce your charge. You're currently facing a criminal charge, which would go permanently on your record and potentially restrict you from coming back to the United States. Now, I'm not supposed to tell you *not* to plead guilty but I will give you a chance to reconsider your plea.'

'Er . . . okay. I'd like to plead not guilty! Thank you, your honour.'

I have a feeling the judge is only being lenient because I'm literally the only person besides the lawyers who's in a suit. At least some of Jay's advice was worth taking.

After I've spoken to the public defender, I'm called to stand in front of the judge once more. This time, he tells me the court has agreed to drop my charge to a civil suit. I have to pay a $350 fine plus the public defender's $80 fee, and I must provide the court with evidence that my truck is registered and road-legal. It's basically a slap on the wrist.

My relief as I walk out of the courtroom is enormous — especially when I think of how close I just came to being barred entry to the US.

•

JD and the rest of the guys are leaving today for a filming shoot up in Alabama, which unfortunately means I'm on the street as I can't stay at the house while they're away. It's a bit frustrating but I certainly appreciate JD's hospitality so far — I've been crashing with them for over a month.

I am a little stuck, though, as they didn't give me much warning. I need to find somewhere else to go at short notice, but my truck is about an hour away at the Pratts' — where I left it at the end of last summer — and I can't go and get it until I've got new plates.

I scroll through my contacts, trying to find someone I can call to come and pick me up. Alex would be more than happy to help, but he's busy. I'm starting to stress. My options are pretty limited, as I'm not just asking for somewhere to stay — I also need someone who'll be happy to drive 45 minutes out to Polk County to get me, then turn around and drive me back to Orlando. Oh yeah, and I'm completely broke, so I can't even offer petrol money.

Eventually I get hold of Tammy, a girl I met at Floatstock. Although she can't come and get me she says she'd love for me to come and stay. We have history but it's always been good with her — whenever we get together it's just fun, no attachments, good sex as good friends. She lives with my old roommate Austin Hair, so I give him a call. He can't come and get me either, but he arranges for his other roommate to collect me.

I feel really bad. My disorganisation is putting others out, and it leaves me feeling low.

But as soon as I get back to Tammy and Austin's place on Clear Lake, the stress lifts. I'm relieved to be among friends again. For the next few days I stay here and try to sort my life out. I make a few calls to a guy back in New Zealand who told me he'd hook me up with a monthly sponsorship deal but has since gone silent. He's not answering and I'm getting desperate — Ronix have already told me they don't have any money for me, and I've exhausted every other avenue. Then I remember I've got his wife's number, so I call her and she picks up straight away, but when she puts her husband on he finally tells me what I really already know: he's decided not to sponsor me. I'm gutted.

It's an incredibly lonely and panicky feeling having no home, no transport, no money, and relying so heavily on the generosity of others. I feel ashamed. I feel like I'm a burden. And the more I try to figure out my next steps, the more the anxiety tightens in my chest. I can see how people are led to beg, steal and borrow when it feels like there's no end in sight.

I pin my hopes on making it to the first tour stop. From there, everything should fall into place. I hope.

•

Four days later my green F150 is registered and up to date. With a fresh set of plates, a full tank, everything I own in my bags in the back, and just enough money for food and one more full tank, I hit the road. I'm not at all religious, but you bet I'm praying the entire seven-hour drive up to Acworth that my baby gets me all the way.

I'm up bright and early the next morning to join Dano on stage and on the mic for the first heats of the day. It goes well, and I ride okay too — well enough to advance through the first round, but the next day I get knocked out in the semi-finals. The great thing about this pro tour stop is that I leave with more money than I arrived with, which is definitely a first!

My next stop is Tri-Cities, Tennessee, where the CBK guys have lined up some coaching for me. It's always a blast catching up with these guys, and South Holston is one of my favourite lakes to ride, with its multiple different arms that always provide flat water conditions. After that, I head to Winchester, where Scott and the Pirates Cove guys have arranged more students for a couple of days out on Tims Ford Lake. By the time I'm done in Tennessee, I've earned more than enough to get me to the next tour stop, an 11-hour haul away in Fort Worth, Texas.

The Texas tour stop is a blast as always, but my riding isn't up to scratch and I don't even get out of the first round. It might just be an off day, or it might be that the amount of time I've spent on the road instead of riding has affected my performance, but either way I need to step my game up if I'm going to make this pro tour worthwhile.

I haven't had much success on the wakeboarding front so far, but Dano and I are becoming quite the MC duo and I'm beginning to think I could possibly make a career out of this. For now, though, I'll settle for the free accommodation and $150 cash in pocket.

After the comp I end up crashing in Arlington with fellow iwake rider Joey Bradley. I first met Joey when he beat me at the Double or Nothing qualifier in Texas in 2007, and over the last couple of years we've hung out a bit. I hadn't made a plan for this point in my trip, figuring I'd land on my feet as usual, and it's awesome to be able to stay with Joey until I work out my next move.

Joey's up early in the mornings to head off to work. Like his dad, he's in the pool-cleaning and maintenance business. To me it sounds like a pretty mediocre job, but Joey obviously does well from it, as he's got his own house, boat and bad-ass truck. When he gets home from work just before noon each day, it's time for us to get out on the lake and shred! He has a Nautique 230 that pumps out a really good wake. It's not as big as the new G23, being more like the new XStar that tows the pro tour, so it's perfect for training. He keeps it a few blocks away at a friend's dock on Lake Arlington. Riding with him is fun. Our riding styles are quite different, so we both push each other.

After a few days of riding and hanging with Joey, we take a road-trip with his best mates Cliff and Clay up to Branson, Missouri, for stop three of the pro tour. Branson's a small town right on the edge of Table Rock Lake, which provides a prime location for the event. On event day I hold it together enough to take second in my qualifying round and advance through to the quarter-finals — but that's as far as I get.

I'm really not happy with being a heat-filler. It appears I have some work to do on the water.

But even if I'm not making the finals, I'm still making my presence felt. Commentating with Dano, I've become one half of the voice of the tour, and one of the key faces that the fans will remember. And I am having an absolute blast. Dano and I command the crowd with each word, building up the hype as the riders throw down. We're like the conductors of this crazy orchestra, bringing a swarm of people to the stage whenever we've got free swag to give away. The punters go crazy for free shit!

It's wild to think that I'm becoming an integral part of this travelling circus.

•

Back at Joey's, after a few days of sleeping in and waiting for him to come home from work I decide I need to quit being lazy and get up and help him.

On our first day on the job together he shows me the ropes.

'Here,' he says, handing me a brush. 'Take this and scrub the sides of the pool while I check the pH levels and add chemicals.'

I do as he says.

'Don't bother scrubbing all the way down the sides, bro,' he tells me. 'Just get the top two feet. The pool vacuum will get the rest.'

Once that's done, we empty the leaves out of the skimmer baskets and do a quick sweep with the net to gather any extra leaves.

It's hot work — the Texas summer leaves us drenched in sweat, and the ice-cold air-conditioning in Joey's truck between pools provides welcome respite. After a few pools I start to get the hang of it. We become a well-oiled machine, getting through Joey's round much faster than he does on his own, which means we've got more free time.

One morning, on our last pool of the day, Joey sticks his hand in to grab the skimmer basket, then suddenly whips it out at lightning speed.

'*Woahhhh!* Holy shit, that was close!' he cries at the same moment a snake races out of the skimmer basket and across the pool. 'And that right there,' he adds, 'is why you *always* check the skimmer basket before you reach your hand in.'

He grabs the leaf net and casually scoops up the snake, removing it from the pool. 'This one's not venomous,' he says, seeing my appalled expression, 'but there are plenty of nasty ones around.'

At the end of the week, Joey hands me a small wad of cash. 'Thanks for your help this week, bro,' he says.

'Oh, thanks!' I reply. 'I wasn't expecting that. I just wanted to do my bit to contribute and say thanks for letting me stay.'

'It's all good, bro,' he says. 'You earned it!'

•

When it's time to organise my trip to Washington for the next pro tour stop, I call Jay, telling him I'd like to use the rest of my travel budget for the month to book my flights to Seattle. 'Can you sort that for me?' I ask.

'Sorry, Brad, I'm not able to fly you up to that stop,' he replies. 'I'm tapped out!'

I'm annoyed, and not just because he's not honouring our sponsorship agreement. I'm missing out on stop four of the tour, but he still flies his promo girls up to hand out stickers!

•

I only ever intended to stay with Joey for a week or two but it's turned into a couple of months. We've become tight friends and I'm really grateful to him for taking me in, showing me around, introducing me to his friends and family and helping me earn some much-needed cash.

My career focus remains wakeboarding, but based on my latest earnings I'm really more of a pool boy, commentator and coach. And, much to my disappointment, not once in my time as a pool boy did a lonely housewife invite me in for a glass of sweet iced tea and hot sex!

It's time to leave Texas and head back east. I thank Joey and hit the road. I have a little cash in my pocket but I'm still nervous that something might go wrong with my truck. Halfway across Arkansas, as I'm cruising in the fast lane at around 130 kph and passing an 18-wheeler semi, my tyre blows out, sending me swerving out of my lane towards the truck. I grip the steering wheel and manage to avoid getting flattened by the semi, then pull off on the side of the road.

There's a rest area just over a kilometre ahead so I crawl along the shoulder until I reach it. Once I've stopped, I discover that although I have a spare wheel I have no jack. Fortunately, a friendly elderly couple pull in and lend me theirs. I change my wheel and get back on the road. That was a close call.

I drive carefully the rest of the way to Nashville, making it in one piece.

After the coaching session I've lined up is done, I head to the airport to catch a flight back to Texas. I'm being flown all the way I just drove to commentate a cable contest at Texas Ski Ranch. It's my first cable comp, and the first time I have to hold it down on the mic on my own in the US. I pull it off and have an awesome time.

Back in Nashville, my road-trip continues to Johnson City, where I reunite with my bro Jesse James. He's been with friends up in New York and flew down a couple of days ago to hang out with the woman he met here last year, but he's already massively over it and is stoked when I pick him up.

'Look out, America!' he yells out the window once he's in the car. 'The boys are back on tour! *Yeeehawwww!*'

It's so good to have him on the road with me again.

After a couple of great days in the Tri-Cities area with the CBK crew we head across to Knoxville for the final pro tour stop. This time, I make it through to the final — only to blow it and land in tenth place. It's still my best result so far this season, plus, making the top 10 means I've made the payout — a couple of hundred bucks. A few days later in Ohio for the US nationals I make it to the semi-finals and leave with a better result of fifth equal.

My results are showing an obvious improvement, and I reckon it's from being under less financial pressure. In the past I entered each event knowing I had to make it into the top 10 for the winnings. Now, thanks to picking up the mic, I know that I will at the very least break even at each stop. This small change in my material situation has led to a big change in my mentality, attitude and performance. I truly feel at home on tour now. I'm no longer an outsider. I'm one of the main personalities, and I'm becoming a real top-10 contender!

Jesse and I hit up the Cincinnati cable park. By the end of our session, after taking an absolute beating time after time, I ride away from my very first double flip — the half-cab double backroll! It's not a pretty landing, but I'm just stoked to ride away from it.

●

After tearing up Wisconsin for the world champs, and plenty of other antics along the way with my wingman Jesse, it's finally time to get back down to Orlando. I drop Jesse at the airport in Nashville as he's off to visit his dad in San Francisco, and set off on the drive back alone. I'm actually lucky my truck even makes it the whole way back because, thinking I was being smart and saving money, I put E85 ethanol gas in my F150 and ended up burning out a couple of the cylinders, converting my V8 into a V6.

I'm still homeless in Orlando but Mitch lets me crash on his couch. In fact, right now I'm one of several. It's easy to get lost in the vortex with the amount of weed we smoke and video games we play, but it's nice to have a place to base myself until I go home.

Surf Expo provides nothing in the way of new sponsors, which is incredibly disheartening. I also talk to Jay and express my frustration with his refusal to pay my way to Washington.

'I felt like I was being shuffled to the bottom of the pecking order,' I explain. 'You even put me below your promo girls!'

I haven't forgotten that I was one of the first guys Jay picked up. I played a big hand in the initial changes to his brand, but when word got around that he was paying riders, the bigger names started to swarm around and made Jay feel like a big dog. He forgot about his original riders — like me. But I don't see it lasting much longer for him anyway. I know he's been sinking loads of money with little return. So I decide to stand up for myself.

'Look, I really appreciate everything you've done for me so far,' I say, 'but I think the iwake stickers have to come off my board.'

I'm glad it ends with no bitterness between us. And maybe it's a bit strange that I'm parting ways with my last remaining sponsor, but I have to be true to what I know I'm worth.

My board is now looking emptier than ever.

Maybe a fresh start is just what I need.

●

After Expo's done and dusted, and Jesse has returned, I get a call from Lisa Chapman, mother of Cole and Michelle, who is super cool, always feeding and watering us when we're riding at their place at Mount Dora.

'You and Jesse are meeting me for drinks tonight at Rocco's, where Michelle works,' she tells me. 'I have a friend from work you have to meet.'

That night, I'm introduced to the most alluring little Argentinian babe. Her name is Camilla and she's a true natural beauty. We hit it off instantly. Her smile is mesmerising, and her personality is ticking all the boxes: friendly, intelligent, witty, ambitious and a little bit sassy, but one of the most genuinely sweet girls I've ever met. Within an hour I'm wondering if I've already fallen in love with her.

After a few drinks we hit the dance floor and she starts teaching me to salsa. I don't tell her that I already know a little, so she thinks she's just an extra-great teacher and I'm an extra-great dancer. When it comes time to part ways, we exchange a kiss and our phone numbers. But the timing really couldn't be worse, as I'm leaving the country in a matter of days.

I can't go without seeing Camilla again so I invite her over the night before I fly home. I'm sleeping on the couch at my buddy Cody's place, so Camilla and I head down to the lake and take a little dip in our underwear, then spend some time making out. I really want this girl, but the couch I'm sleeping on doesn't even fold out, so we can't really spend the night together. Anyway, I get the vibe she would make me wait — and that's exactly what I like about her! While she's sexy as hell, she's also got some class.

●

I arrive back in New Zealand just in time for the birth of my brand-new niece, Maisey. She's the most precious little thing, and it was especially nice of her to wait a few extra days for her Uncle Brad to get home.

My sister, brand-new mum Monique, hands her precious creation to me. I'm holding Maisey in my arms and I'm blown away by the thought of such a tiny little ball of meat and bones eventually growing into a fully functioning member of society. I imagine I'll have one or two of my own one day, but that's not on the cards any time soon. For now, I'm happy to stick to being the fun uncle who can give the kid back when I'm done. And I'll continue practising how to make one until I find a girl I want to make one with. I even stop for a second to imagine an Argentinian-Kiwi mix with Camilla.

Before leaving the US I sold my truck for $800 to a guy who planned to fix it up a little. I would've liked to get more, but since I had almost killed the engine I had to take what I could get. Short on cash as always, I get straight back to work in New Zealand — more of the same promo, modelling, acting stuff. Anything I can hustle to put some money back in my pocket. I even manage to land a quick job taking a van full of scooters to sell at the markets around Auckland. One morning, while I'm sitting around not long after 6 a.m. without much to do because no one seems interested in buying a scooter at this hour, I get a Facebook message from Jenna. In a moment of weakness, I friended her again yesterday and sent her a message saying, *Damn you for popping back into my head . . . I thought I was doing so well at forgetting you. I hope all is well in your world.*

Her response has thrown me a curveball: *I don't know who you are*, she has written. *What are you talking about?*

Is she fucking with me?

Are you seriously going to act like that? I reply.

To which she responds: *Look, if this is your way of picking up chicks, I'm not down with it, dude. Go mess with someone else.*

Okay, something is definitely awry.

I apologise and ask a few questions, trying to work out what's going on. It soon becomes clear that this Jenna is not the same person I've spent so many hours talking to. I dig back through my messages in search of our old conversations. The profile picture is the same, but I notice a slight difference in the profile names: I was messaging a Jenna Marie G, but now I'm messaging Jenna Marie Grayson. Two different profiles for the same girl . . . I look more closely at this Jenna's profile, I see it's much more complete and active than the other one.

That's when it finally dawns on me. I've been catfished!

I'm dumbfounded. How could I have been so gullible? We spoke on the phone almost every day and she sent me loads of gorgeous pictures, but, come to think of it, she could never seem to get her webcam working and got upset whenever I questioned why. The thought did cross my mind at the time that something was amiss. I don't understand what this faux Jenna had to gain from pretending to be someone else. It's not like I sent a single dime her way. She never, ever asked for anything from me. It makes no sense. I feel confused, but most of all I feel betrayed.

I forward the fake profile to the real Jenna so she can report it, then I remember I've still got the fake Jenna's phone number. I haven't had any contact with her in a long time, but she picks up.

'Hi, Jenna,' I say. 'How are you doing? It's been a while. How's life in the world of Jenna?'

'Umm, hi, Brad,' she replies awkwardly. 'Er . . . what's up?'

'Oh, not much, Jenna. I just thought I'd let you know I know everything.'

'Huh? What do you mean?' she says, playing dumb.

'I know everything,' I reply firmly. 'Time to fess up!'

'Oh, er . . .' she stammers. 'Now is really not a good time. Can I call you back in half an hour?'

I'm more than surprised when my phone rings an hour later and it's her.

'You're right. I'm not who I said I was,' she confesses.

'I don't get it,' I say. 'Why did you do it? What was in it for you?' I just can't work out what her point was. If it was for the attention, getting compliments while pretending to be someone else isn't even real attention. Like, when I told her how beautiful she was, that compliment was meant for the real Jenna, not this imposter. I'm baffled.

But she has no explanation. She tries to tell me who she really is, giving me her real name and sending me real pictures. These photos are more believable — while she's not bad-looking, she's also not as ridiculously stunning — but I can't help feeling this is probably all bullshit too. It's probably just the next one down in her list of fake personalities.

'I appreciate you telling me,' I say. 'But now, please lose my number.'

•

The single life continues for me. While I was gone, April got herself a boyfriend, so there'll be no rekindling there. To be honest, I'm really just thinking about Camilla. We've kept in touch, but I'm months away from being back in Florida so I might as well enjoy myself while I can — and I do.

As the year draws to a close I get a call from the head of WWA.

'Do you want to host the video coverage of the WWA Wake Park World Championships in Abu Dhabi?' he asks. 'We'll fly you over and put you up.'

A free trip halfway around the world to wakeboard somewhere I've never been? And, as well as getting to compete, I'll also get paid? Of course I'm in!

The flight to Dubai takes about 17 hours, and that's topped off with a 90-minute bus ride to Abu Dhabi. In Dubai, I'm surprised to see how green it is — I thought this was supposed to be the desert. But the moment we get out of Dubai the greenery disappears and I spot the reason it's there in the first place: a huge desalinisation plant that turns seawater into fresh water. I had no idea it was even possible on such a large scale! I suppose lack of water isn't a problem when you've got all the money in the world — and the reality is we'll never have a water problem so much as a salt problem.

This is my first opportunity to host in front of the camera, which is vastly different from dribbling on the mic all day. I struggle through the spiel while filming the opening clip, running a bunch of takes to get it right, but I eventually get the job done, meaning I can turn my attention to riding.

I'm stoked to get some good time on the cable here, because I really want to push myself in that realm of the sport, especially now that I'm landing a double flip.

I'm feeling confident going into the first round, but then I get schooled and I'm knocked out of the competition. It's clear I've got some work to do. My mate Windsor wins both pro sections.

Regardless of my early finish, the trip is one I'll never forget. Wakeboarding really has taken me all over the world!

ELEVEN: RIDERS' PARADISE

For the first three months of 2013 I once again quit drinking, smoking and fast food. It made me feel so good last year. That means more running, more boxing and more circuit-training at Ludus.

I've also just reconnected with an old sponsor from years ago. Rip Curl used to flow me free wetsuits and life vests, and now they want to clothe me as well! Since my Oakley clothing deal is long gone, I'm more than happy. What's more, they're not expecting a sticker on my board because they know they can't pay me. I rock up to the Rip Curl New Zealand head office and catch up with Leon, who is still the main man. He shows me to the warehouse, grabs a shopping trolley and says, 'Have at it!'

This is the most sponsored I've ever felt. I always enjoy receiving a box of new gear: some Spy shades, a new watch from Gshock; and of course unboxing a fresh new Ronix board is always exciting, as is getting flown somewhere for an event or filming. But taking a shopping trolley around the Rip Curl warehouse and loading it up with T-shirts, hats, shorts, jeans, wetsuits, bags and anything else I want — this is the real deal. Although a paycheck would be pretty cool too.

•

Dad recently had to move from his caravan in the holiday park. His condition has been deteriorating and there have been multiple occasions when he's frozen up and ended up being taken away in an ambulance. Being an hour away from us kids also made it tough for us to visit and help him out. He's moved into a communal home called Hopper House, where he lives with several other people with different conditions. A woman cooks and cleans for them.

I hate that he has to be there, and it really sucks to watch him gradually lose his independence. His driver's licence has been taken from him. It must be so tough for him. We kids drive him places when we can, and since I got rid of my car last year, I'm able to use his car most of the time.

Today I'm making the two-hour drive up to Ruakaka to ride the System 2.0 cable to complete a mission that began a month ago. I decided I was going to bring the double flip home to New Zealand, since it hasn't been done here yet. But to do that I had to build a kicker that would give me enough lift to get both flips in.

With Jake behind the lens we allocated two days to film the building, transporting, anchoring and riding parts for an *Airtime* episode. Unfortunately the build didn't go smoothly — as I was laying the sheets of ply across the top surface of the ramp, I was using a smaller offcut of 2 x 4 to bunt the ply into place. As I got to one of the last sheets of ply, I reached behind me, grabbed the offcut and smacked my palm against the end to knock the ply into place.

'*Aaaggghhhh fuck!*' I screamed in pain, realising I'd grabbed an offcut that had a nail sticking out the end, which was now firmly impaled in my palm. I lifted my hand and the 15-centimetre-long piece of lumber just hung there. It must've reached the bone at the base of my palm because it hurt like hell and took quite an effort to remove. This brought the day's work to an end, but thankfully I didn't need a tetanus shot as I had had one a couple of weeks earlier after splitting my chin open while riding the cable.

The next morning I managed to finish the build, transport the kicker to Ruakaka and anchor it in the lake. Then it was time for a quick test ride. But the pain and weakness in my punctured hand meant I was unable to hold the grab on my board so I couldn't tuck properly for the double.

Now, a month later, my hand has healed and I'm back at the park ready to huck some doubles. Even after a bit of extra work on the kicker to give me enough height and time for the double, time after time I come up short and slam on my face. Eventually I tuck into a good one, pull on the board to tuck into a small ball, speeding up my rotation enough to bring me all the way around, and I stomp my first double on New Zealand water!

A tremendous wave of relief rolls over me and I feel incredibly satisfied on the drive home.

•

My name as a commentator must be getting out there because in late January I'm invited back to Penrith, New South Wales, to commentate for — and compete in — Boardstock and the Team Rider Cup. I'm back there a month later for the Wake the Line qualifier. I narrowly miss out on one of the two qualifying spots to win a trip to Germany for the Wake the Line event later this year.

As I'm preparing to leave for the US again, I sell anything I can to make some extra coin: boards, my guitar, other stuff. I've been selling weed all season to bring in a little extra. I'm starting to get rid of everything because I've decided I actually need to move to the US. I've been thinking about why I'm not getting any love from sponsors and I reckon that in order to give myself a real shot at being a pro rider I have to base myself there full-time.

I realised years ago that New Zealand does nothing for my career besides providing stunning backdrops for photos and videos. So I've started looking into visas and what else I need to move there in 2014.

As if to reinforce this decision I receive a message from Mike Ferraro. He's one of the most respected coaches in the game, involved with Ronix product development. He and I have been keeping in touch as I have been giving him feedback on a new Ronix board I've been riding. But this message has nothing to do with that. Ferraro tells me that Ronix has just purchased a section in Florida with two private lakes on it, and it's to become the team training facility.

'There's a lot of work to do so if you can be here to lend a hand, that would be a huge help and I'm sure it would go down well with Paul and BG,' he says. Brian Gardner is the president and part-owner of Ronix.

'I'm totally going to buy a van and park it on the side of the lake and live there!' I tell him.

'Sure, why not?' he replies. I'm not sure if he knows I'm serious.

•

A few weeks later I touch down in Dallas, where Joey, Cliff and Clay are waiting to pick me up. It's much colder than I expected, but I'm here earlier in the year than usual, catching the end of their winter.

Over the week that I'm in Texas, Joey helps me find a vehicle. As usual my budget is pretty small, and the type of van I can get for my money is pretty crap. I may as well spray-paint *Free Candy* down the side of it. So we widen our search and come across a few Chevy Tahoes that are in my price range. With the back seat folded forward there's plenty of room for an air mattress, so it's a better option than a shitty van. We look at a few and eventually find one that test-drives well. Joey looks under the hood and gives me the thumbs up, so I buy it on the spot for $1800.

A couple of days later, I pack my bags into the back of my new ride and get ready for the long haul to Orlando. I pre-roll myself eight spliffs — that's almost one for every two hours of driving. I pack a cooler bag with water and Red Bull to help me stay awake for the drive through the night.

The last two hours of the drive are the hardest. It's early morning and the sun is just starting to make the horizon glow. My eyelids are really heavy, each blink becoming slower, until I'm suddenly awoken by the rumble strips on the side of the road. I'm sure I was only out for a couple of seconds, but I'm certainly awake and alert now. I down my last energy drink, roll down the windows and turn the music up to keep me awake the rest of the way.

I arrive in Orlando and pull up outside Austin Pratt's new place on Lake Hiawassee, where I've arranged to live. But the guy who's in the room I'm taking only moves out today, so I inflate my air mattress in the back and pass out for a few hours.

I wake around noon and go inside to kick it with Pratt. It's great to see him again. He's become like a little brother to me after I took him under my wing a couple of years ago. Of course the first thing we do is smoke a spliff together.

The following day we drive to East Orlando towards Titusville. Just past Bithlo we pull off onto a gravel driveway, drive through a farm gate and there it is right in front of us — the body of water freshly purchased by Ronix. Up ahead we see where all the action is happening at the corner of the lake. I'm just so excited to be here.

I take a moment to drink in the surroundings before wandering over to catch up with the team. Pretty much everyone on the team is here, as well as Ferraro and Paul O'Brien. I recognise a bunch of others, but some are strangers. A bobcat is finishing off the freshly graded bank that wraps around the corner of the lake, and a small excavator is digging holes along the border between the driveway and the bank.

After a quick catchup with the lads, I ask Ferraro what I can do to help. He fills me in on what's happening today.

'As you can see, we've just had the bank along the edge of the lake graded. That's becoming a beach. We've got truckloads of sand arriving tomorrow, so the guys are about to lay down some weedmat to get it ready. Then we've got trailerloads of palm trees arriving — those holes are being dug for them. This guy from Puerto Rico, over there,' he says, pointing him out, 'is Amiel. He's supplying the palms, and he and his guys are building tiki huts around the property too, starting with a large one in the corner there.' We walk over to the open-sided hut with its thatched roof.

Ferraro walks me over to a shipping container beside the fenceline. 'In here is where we keep tools, hardware, wakeboards and anything else that needs to be locked away.' We drive around the rest of the property, Ferraro showing me where beaches will be put in, and talking about the plans for the second, smaller, lake out the back of the 85-hectare property.

After the tour I join the guys on the beach and help them roll out the weedmat. It takes several huge rolls to cover all 100 or so metres of shoreline. I've noticed there's a small team of guys out building a rail on the lake, so I ask Ferraro, 'Is there anything specific you'd like me to do? If not, there's something I'd like to do that I think will help.'

'I think we're okay for now,' he replies, so I tell him I'll be back soon. After taking a couple of measurements I jump in my truck and race to the nearest hardware store. On my return, I measure and cut some of the 2 x 4 planks which I knock together to make a couple of sawhorses. I then measure up the rest of the 2 x 4s and plywood, cut them to size on the sawhorses and screw it all together to produce a work bench that fits perfectly across the end of the container, complete with shelves for power tools and a pegboard to hang hand-tools on. Ferraro is suitably impressed.

A few more days and this corner of the property looks completely different. What was a boring dirt shoreline is now a bright white sandy beach complete with palm trees and a really dope tiki hut! And now they're are setting up the System 2.0 cable!

A storm rolls in and the rain buckets down. I love Florida rainstorms — they come in fast and hard, absolutely pour down, and then they're gone just as fast as they arrived. Right now it's pouring and most of the crew are seeking shelter by standing under the 20 x 10 tiki hut.

This gives me an idea. I do a quick google search, make a list of materials and I'm back off to the hardware store. By the end of the day I've built a picnic table. As I'm driving the last screws through the hefty 2 x 6 planks, Ferraro and Paul wander over.

'Holy shit, Brad, that is one bad-ass picnic table!' Paul says enthusiastically.

'At least one of these guys knows what he's doing!' Ferraro proclaims. 'Hey, Brad, where did you learn to build a picnic table?'

'I've never built one before,' I reply. 'I just did a quick search online. But I learnt to build from my dad.'

Paul looks astounded.

Then Ferraro says, 'We might need a couple more of these things around the property.'

'I thought you might,' I say, 'so I've got enough materials to build another one. I've already pre-cut it so I'll knock it together tomorrow. And I'm thinking maybe a third one, twice as long, under the tiki?'

I'm feeling pretty good about the reaction I'm getting from the big boss-man.

That evening, before we go home, Paul and I are sitting at my freshly built picnic table under the tiki hut.

'Man, how cool is this hut!' says Paul.

I look around at the size of it and reply, 'So cool. Put four walls on it and I'll live in it!' He laughs it off.

The following day, after I finish the second picnic table, Paul approaches me and says, 'Hey Brad, I know we were kidding around last night, but would you seriously consider living out here as like an on-site manager?'

I look him in the eye. 'Consider? Didn't Ferraro tell you? I've already decided that's what's going to happen!'

We discuss various options for the living situation and decide the best idea is to find a trailer for me to live in. So I start the search for my new home.

•

Camilla and I have kept in touch and I'm excited that tonight I finally get to see her. She comes over to Pratt's house and we sit outside, her comfortably in my lap, catching up and watching the colours shift as day turns to night over Lake Hiawassee. After the sun has disappeared and the mosquitos start to bite, we head inside and start making out on the couch. I want to take her to my bedroom but I literally only have my small air mattress in the corner of the room — not the most inviting setting. But once we're both grabbing at each other's clothes ready to tear them off, I really have no choice . . .

'I'm sorry my room currently looks like a homeless person just moved in. I've got an actual bed coming later this week,' I explain awkwardly.

'It really doesn't bother me,' she replies. 'I just want you right now!'

Half on the mattress and half on the floor, we work out six months of built-up sexual tension. To finally have this exotic little Argentinian beauty naked and in my arms is something I've wanted since the moment Mrs Chapman introduced us at Rocco's. Her body is more perfect than I'd imagined, her slim figure accentuated by her perky natural breasts. I kiss her nipples and run my fingertips down her sides, following with my mouth. Making my way south to go down on her, I notice a small surgical scar beside her hip bone. I take a moment to kiss it, as if to acknowledge the slight imperfection as just another part of what makes her beautiful. I want all of her exactly as she is — there's nothing about her I would change.

The sex is incredible, especially considering the setting, but I think it's the passion between us, the intense chemistry, that makes it so amazing. However, I cannot pretend it's not a little tricky trying to be smooth and sexy on a deflating air mattress.

•

Our first job at the lake each day is to water the palm trees and bamboo plants that surround the beach. Pratt and I grab a bucket each and make our way along the beach, filling the buckets in the lake. Eventually I figure out that it's easier and more efficient to carry two buckets, because although I'm carrying twice the weight, it's easier if my body is balanced with a bucket in each hand, and it means half the number of trips. This becomes part of my daily workout, and I soon add shoulder shrugs and lunges. It's also a great way to warm up for a quick shred on the glassy-calm lake as we wait for the rest of the guys to arrive.

We're only a few weeks away from the team brochure shoot, so there's a lot of work to do to get the System 2.0 cable park ready and loaded with features for us to hit. There are plenty of hands to get the job done, and it's so rad to be working with such an eclectic group of multi-talented humans. We split into groups to work on different features. A team led by Parks, Danny and Chad gets started on a huge vertical wall-ride 18 metres long and 4 metres high.

Pratt, Rossi and Keenan Allen take charge of building a PVC multi-pipe rail.

I float between the two teams, helping out and giving guidance where I can, but I'm careful not to overstep. Even though Paul asked me to live here and help manage the place, I don't feel like I'm the 'team leader' and I'm not about to start bossing anyone around. The rest of the time I focus on other jobs that I can do, like helping Sam and Bdahl from Sesitec, the cable wakeboarding company, put the unit kicker and quarter-pipe in the water and anchor them down.

•

Wake Games is on this week, so I'm at OWC on the mic with Dano for four days straight, while the rest of the team continue working at the lake when they're not competing here. It's a long event, but I really enjoy my new role as a commentator for all of the King of Wake stops. I ride well, but get stuck at the quarter-final round after taking a fall on my toe 900. Harley Clifford takes the win, while my Ronix teammates Deano and Shota from Japan take second and third respectively.

Next, I head straight to the OWC cable to announce the new Wake Park contest that's been added to Wake Games. By the end of the weekend I'm absolutely flogged.

Back at the lake it's all go with the brochure shoot. The finishing touches are being put on the wall, including an A-frame rail running across the face of it, partially to strengthen the wall at the deep end. The new pipe rail — aka Wesley Pipes — is complete and it's starting to look like a pretty dope wake park!

The team shoot is a solid week of action, involving riding next year's product, photo shoots with Bear and Flash, filming with Mariano and product videos talking about the gear. The whole Ronix team is here, along with the product developers. I'm really impressed at how Pratt's riding has improved in the park. Last year he told me he was feeling a bit lost and really wanted to get on the Ronix team . . . and I know his struggle! So I suggested he spend the off-season riding cable because I knew they were looking for park riders, and it's really impressive how good he's become.

When day turns to night we grill out and sit around the fire pit, watching Chad Sharpe load more and more wood on the fire while listening to Parks and Erik Ruck jam out on their guitars. It feels special to me knowing I built the seats we're all sitting on. The vibe is always great with this crew but something about this shoot just feels better. Maybe it's because we're at our own private facility, maybe we've become closer over the years, maybe it's that my new role makes me feel more a part of the crew — whatever it is, we've all become pretty tight over the last month.

The combination of work and riding had me feeling pretty sore, and during the team shoot I manage to put my lower back out again. This injury rears its head from time to time, and when it gets to the point where it's a sharp stabbing pain I'm usually out for several weeks and making multiple visits to the chiropractor.

This time I take Alex's advice and instead visit a sports massage therapist who works with Olympic athletes. Mona is a big and strong-looking woman from Haiti who's super friendly and cracks jokes as she begins digging into my muscles. I'm lying face down on the massage table while she uses her knuckles and even her elbows to get into some of the knots. Bending my leg up to a 90-degree angle, she digs her elbow into my hamstring while slowly straightening my leg. The pain is agonising, so I grip the legs of the massage table. I'm immediately beading with sweat. *'Arrrgghh fuuuck!'* I grunt through the hole in the table, and I get a slap on the back and I'm told off for cussing. This woman is absolutely brutal!

After my hour is up and she's worked through my back, glutes, hamstrings, hips and more, I'm sweating and aching but I can feel that the tension around my back has released a bit. She tells me to take an ice bath when I get home, so I pick up some bags of ice, fill the tub and slowly lower my aching body into the frigid water.

The following day my back is feeling immensely better, and on the second day after seeing Mona I'm back on my board and feeling great! I can't believe how quickly that's helped me heal up. If I'd known about her years ago I would've saved many visits to the chiropractor and been back on the water much sooner.

●

In the middle of May, after the team shoot, it's time to head to Atlanta for the first pro tour stop of the year. After a fun weekend on the mic and an average weekend competing, I meet up with Pratt and our friend Sam Baker and head to Lake Lanier where we hear there's a sick handrail to hit. We link up with another car load of riders and when we arrive there's a Nautique G23 full of crew on the water, along with a jet-ski that we'll use to tow past the handrail. It's been raining heavily and the water level is really high. It's about a waist-high ollie-on, so the guys who ride before me struggle a little to get right up on the railing for a decent slide.

I get my best hit of the session, but as I'm about to finish, Sam spots a state trooper approaching. It's like he spots us at the same time because he flicks his lights on to signal that he's after us. We immediately scatter, aware that the boat and jet-ski are in trouble for operating so close to the shoreline in a 5-knot zone. Sam jumps into the water and starts swimming to the boat, while the rest of us gap back through the trees to the trucks in the parking lot.

As Pratt and I emerge from the trees by his truck, dripping wet and with wakeboards under our arms, the state trooper is right there on us. I figure we're fucked, but he just races straight past us — he didn't even see us! Thankfully the Bishops, who own the boat and ski, live on the lake, so they're already racing back there. We toss our boards in the truck and hightail it out of there. It's an added rush of adrenalin on top of what riding already gave me.

We crash the night at the Bishops' place and then the next day get on the road across to Texas. It's a long haul so I've left my truck at Lake Lanier and I'm riding with Sam and Pratt. We arrive in Waco after a full day on the road, ready for the first stop of the Wake Park Triple Crown. A few days of practice before the event takes off, and once again I'm doing double duty on the water and on the mic.

After getting back to my truck at Lake Lanier, I boost up to North Carolina for the next pro tour stop. I get stopped in the quarter-finals, then return to the stage to commentate for the rest of the event.

•

I'm back home on Lake Hiawassee and Camilla is with me tonight. It's only the second time I've seen her this season and over a month since our first rendezvous. My time out at the lake and on the road, combined with her work and college schedules, have made finding time a challenge. But this time I have an actual bed! I splashed out on a pillow-top California King bed, an investment that is already proving its value now that I'm snuggled up with this Argentinian beauty.

We talk and kiss and nothing more, but I'm more than okay with not having sex because as I lie here looking into her brown eyes, I feel the connection growing, I feel myself falling for her.

'I'm sorry I've been so busy but I'd love to spend more time with you,' I say. I feel like our second time hanging out is too soon to be talking about dating or getting too serious — besides, I want to take time to get to know this girl before getting too excited. It's been about five years since I've really let anyone in. Given that I plan to base myself in the US in future, I feel like I'll finally be able to have a relationship as I'll be anchored in one place for the first time in 9 years. I'm very aware of the wall I have built to protect myself, but as Camilla looks me in the eyes and brings her lips to mine, I can feel her beginning to pull that wall down, brick by brick.

Then, just a couple of days later, I receive a text from Camilla as I'm chilling on the couch and playing the guitar after another long day of work at the lake. I messaged her earlier about catching up, but her response has thrown me a curveball.

C: I'm really sorry Brad, but I've met someone, and since he's actually interested in a relationship, I'm going to see where this goes.

My heart aches just reading her words. But the part that gets me the most is her assumption.

> B: *What do you mean 'he's actually interested in a relationship'? You assume I'm not?*

I thought I was doing the right thing by not moving too fast.

> C: *You're a single pro wakeboarder travelling the world, and you never said you wanted anything more!*

> B: *Dammit Camilla, I told you the other night I wanted to spend more time with you. I just didn't feel like we were at that stage where I could ask you to be my girlfriend. I mean we've only hung out twice in the six weeks I've been back. I was hoping for more time with you before telling you I was falling for you.*

> C: *I'm so sorry, Brad. I didn't know.*

I'm so frustrated that I put down the phone and pick up Pratt's guitar. I've always found the guitar to be a good outlet when I've got shit on my mind. I sold mine to pay for my flights back here, and even though Pratt's guitar is a bit of a beater compared with what I had, it still sounds pretty good.

I recently learnt to play 'For What it's Worth' by Buffalo Springfield, so I begin strumming the chords, but instead of singing the original lyrics, I start putting my own words to the chords, and change the melody so it's not a total ripoff.

Within an hour I've written, recorded and sent Camilla a song.

It goes like this:

I never told you how I feel . . . but, well, I thought you knew,
That when I hold you in my arms and kiss you, I thought . . . I thought you
*   felt it too.*
Now you're telling me there's someone else and that they're into you,
You say they want something more and I don't, well, or so you assume.

Chorus

You're tellin' me that you're leavin' now, I hope I can change your mind
  somehow.
Knowin' everything that you know now what can I do to bring you back
  around?
Cos I want you back around.

Her reply comes back quickly.

C: Shit, I honestly didn't know you felt that way. Did you really write that
just now?

B: Yeah, I mean I didn't predict this and pre-record a song.

C: Well damn, I'm impressed! And that kinda changes things. Can I sleep on it
and make a decision tomorrow?

I can't help feeling a bit guilty for putting the pressure on, and I'm still pissed off
that she chose someone else over me. So eventually I reply:

B: Look, maybe it wasn't entirely fair of me to send you that song. And as
much as this sucks, you've already made your decision and it would be unfair
of me to ask you to change it. I'm sorry. I wish you all the best with him.

I'm upset, but mostly I'm angry for letting myself open up to getting hurt again.

•

I meet Ferraro back out at Lake Ronix the next day, where a storm must've hit and
knocked over a couple of the palm trees. Luckily a small excavator was dropped
off this morning, so I jump in the driver's seat and drop the trees back in place.
Noticing that I'm capable on the controls, Ferraro sends me in the excavator to
the other side of the lake to start work on clearing the weeds along the shoreline
of what will be dubbed Wake Beach.

For the rest of the day I gradually make my way along the beach, clearing out
the weeds and leaving them in piles as I go. Ferraro shows up late afternoon to
take photos and videos of me working. He's good at that. Everyone gives him

crap about how his clothes still manage to get dirty by the end of the day, even though he never does any actual work. In fact he's a big part of everything getting done around here, running things for Paul who's back home in Seattle. So I'm kinda stoked that he's here snapping away, because I know the photos will be sent straight to the boss.

By the time the sun has set, Wake Beach has unobstructed lake access along its whole width. By the time I get the excavator back to the front of the lake it's dark, and after grabbing some takeaways on the 30-minute drive home, I crash on top of my bed without even pulling back the covers. It won't be long until my trailer arrives and I can live there, avoiding all this daily travel.

When I pull up the next day, Ferraro has swapped out the excavator for a bobcat. Excited, I jump in the driver's seat and familiarise myself with the controls before heading back around to Wake Beach. This machine is much faster. I'm racing down the back stretch when, at the very last second, I spot a tortoise out of the corner of my eye. It's only just out of the undergrowth onto the dirt road but it's directly in line with my right track. I pull the joystick to the left but it's too late. I turn back and see that I busted its shell wide open — he's done. I feel terrible for killing that harmless little guy, but there's nothing I can do, so I scoop him up with the bobcat bucket and find a place off the road to dump him.

At the beach I switch back to slow mode and the shape of a turtle lights up on the dash, delivering a jab of guilt. This reminder gets me every time I drive the bobcat.

I spend the day removing the weed piles I left yesterday, adding them to a pile that was started from stage one of clearing the beach.

For the next few days I wake up before sunrise to get on the road out to the lake, grabbing McDonald's breakfast on the way. I'm in the bobcat from sun-up to sun-down, with a couple of pre-rolled spliffs to get me through the day. I've discovered that a little smoke during a mundane task helps get me into a zone where I'm powering through the work and time seems to fly by. I make a deal with Ferraro that if he brings me lunch, and keeps the diesel topped up, I'll work nonstop throughout the day. It's a welcome distraction from my recent romantic frustration.

By the end of the week I've cleared and graded the entire stretch of beach and I'm super proud. That evening Paul calls me.

'Brad!' he says excitedly. '*Duuude!* Ferraro has been sending me updates on the work you've been doing out at the lake. Unbelievable stuff, Brad. Thank you!'

'It's my pleasure, Paul. I'm glad you're stoked on it. I've actually been having a lot of fun in those machines!' I reply.

'When did you learn to drive a bobcat like that? Was that your dad again?'

'No, I just got in it and learnt here,' I reply, laughing.

'*Whaaat?!* No way! That's bad-ass, Brad! Very impressive.'

Then his tone changes. 'Look, Brad, I feel like I owe you an apology. Over the years you've been incredibly loyal to our company, and I feel very guilty that we've never really supported or even promoted you as one of our riders. And now you come in and just completely own shit with everything you've been doing at the lake. I feel like we don't deserve you. So, can I ask why you've stuck around for us?'

I pause for a second, then reply, 'Look, Paul, I've always loved Ronix and everything about the brand and the team. The way I see it, if there's something worth fighting for, then I'll fight for it, and to me, Ronix is worth fighting for.'

'Wow, I'm truly humbled, Brad. Thank you, thank you, thank you! Hearing you say that just gave me chills. It reminds me of when my dad and I left Hyperlite to start Ronix. I told Parks we couldn't offer him anything close to what he would be making if he stayed with Hyperlite, so he should stay. His reply has stuck with me to this day. He told me he would be leaving if he stayed, since the company is not in the name, but in the people behind it. Brad, his response gave me chills just like you've just given me. I'll never forget it.'

We keep chatting — in fact it's the longest and easiest conversation he and I have ever had — until the subject of money comes up.

'I've spoken with BG,' Paul says, 'and obviously we agree that we need to get you paid.'

Finally! I think to myself.

'We're going to get you started you on $500 per month right away.'

My heart sinks. *$500? Are you kidding me? $500 per month is the minimum rate I should have started on after landing my 1080 five years ago, as a team rider. Now I'm managing your property — just one day in the bobcat might've cost $500 or more if you'd hired someone to do it.* That's what I want to say, but I don't. He must sense from my pause that I'm not thrilled.

'Brad, I know you deserve more and we'll work towards getting you what you deserve,' he says.

'Thank you, Paul. I'll be honest and say I am a little disappointed. It's less than

I was expecting, but I appreciate the start, and I'm stoked to be moving out there soon.'

Our conversation ends well but I am left feeling short-changed. I was thinking closer to $1500, or a minimum of a grand a month. But at this point I'll take what I'm being offered. Any regular income is better than none. I'll be saving on rent and riding costs once I'm living out there.

•

To take a bit of a break from Lake Ronix, I drive out to Lake County to ride with Alex and our friend Mike, who has an XStar on East Crooked Lake. After putting work before riding for most of this season, I'm stoked to be out free riding on my favourite lake, especially with my good buddy driving for me. Every moment on the water is a therapeutic escape from reality.

The sun is not far from setting when I punt a big toeside 1080 attempt off of Alex's nicely sculpted double-up. My trajectory is a little too vertical, so I come down on top of the second wake and finish my set with a heavy crash. I pop up unhurt and feeling a rush of endorphins from the crash, so I swim back to the boat, unable to wipe the smile from my face. But when I go to stand up, I feel a twinge in my knee that wasn't there when I was swimming. I try to bend it but it's locked out straight and doesn't want to bend at all. *You've got to be kidding me. Please, not now — not another injury!*

The guys help me out of the boat and we head back to Alex's to put my leg up and ice the knee. I'm surprised to see there's no apparent swelling, and it only hurts if I try to bend it, so I reckon it can't be anything serious. I pop a couple of anti-inflammatories and Alex and I relax with a few hits on the bowl. A few hours later we decide to head out to McGregors for a few drinks. I'm hoping it'll help relax me enough to rid me of this peg-leg limp.

McGregors is a local bar that Alex and I have frequented since long before we were legally allowed to. It's not exactly known for its premium clientele so our expectations are low. I'm not here to pull tonight, I just want a few Jamesons to take the edge off. But when I hobble into the bar I'm pleasantly surprised to see a very attractive young woman with wild blonde hair sitting to one side of the bar.

My immediate thought is *What is she doing here?*

Alex and I sit on the other side of the horseshoe-shaped bar. After I've had a couple of drinks I notice a lady on the opposite side of the bar trying to get my attention. She's not the gorgeous blonde, but she's trying to signal something to us. Alex and I mockingly wave random hand signals back. Next thing she's walked around and comes straight up to me. 'Hi,' she says.

'Hi. Sorry, I'm not great at sign language. What were you trying to tell me?'

'I was saying you need to go over and steal my friend away from the guy she's talking to,' she says, pointing at the blonde woman.

'You don't need to tell me twice!' I say, standing up on my bad leg, which has been locked out straight this whole time.

I limp over, tap the woman on the shoulder and, after she turns to face me, lean into her ear and say, 'Hey, I'm Brad. I was wondering if I could steal you away from this guy and buy you a drink.' She smiles and agrees, before introducing herself as Candice.

'Great, and please excuse my pirate limp — I did something to my knee while wakeboarding today,' I say as we make our way back to where her friend is waiting with Alex. I plonk myself back down on the barstool, then grab Candice by the hips and pull her into my lap.

'Sorry — I'd offer you my seat but my knee is sucking right now. Hope you don't mind if we share.' Her smile tells me she likes it.

We chat over some drinks, and when Candice stands up off my lap and I stand up I'm stoked to find I can bend my knee again! It feels completely back to normal. A song comes on that sparks Candice to grab my hand and say, 'Come on then, let's test out that knee on the dance floor.'

While we're dancing up a storm I try to plant a kiss on her lips but she evades my advance. Later, when we're back at the bar, a guy who's with Candice's group comes up and tells the ladies it's time to leave. I stand up to walk her out but the guy points at me and says assertively '*No!*'

No what? I think. *Who the fuck are you?*

Candice places her hand on my chest and says, 'Don't worry about him, he's just a bit protective. Here, take my number down.'

Then, as they're leaving, she grabs my hand and pulls me with her to the back of the line of her friends. As we reach the door, all her friends having exited before her, she stops abruptly, spins a 180, grabs me by my shirt and firmly pulls me in close for a kiss, her back against the wall. But it's more than just a kiss. She kisses me long and passionately enough to tell me she really wants me. When she pulls away she looks at me with her beautiful blue eyes and says, 'I hope to see you again soon.' Then she walks out the door . . . and I'm hooked!

The following night I'm speeding my way back out to Mount Dora. I'm impatient to see the woman who kissed me so passionately last night and I've got my foot down. Less than two minutes from the country bar I see flashing lights behind me. *Fuck!*

The officer asks me why I was speeding and I figure it's best to be honest. 'Sorry, officer, I got a bit excited about seeing this sexy blonde I met last night.'

He has a slight chuckle and issues me a ticket with a small fine.

After a few drinks and some line-dancing lessons from Candice, we leave the bar with her friend from last night and her husband to head back to their place. Candice stops halfway up the drive, turns to face me and pulls me in for a kiss. Then she says awkwardly, 'There's something I haven't told you.'

'Can I guess — you've got a kid?' I say.

'How did you know?'

'It was just a hunch,' I reply, before kissing her again.

'And that doesn't bother you?'

'Not at all,' I reply, and we head inside to the spare bedroom, where we cuddle up under the covers. She seems a little nervous, and then she opens up that she's never done this before. At first I'm like *yeah, right*, but then she tells me she's recently divorced, and that she and her husband had been together since high school.

'He's the only man I've ever been with,' she tells me. I reassure her that she's in complete control of what we do or don't do tonight. She asks how many women I've been with.

'I don't know if I should answer this,' I laugh, 'but I want to be honest with you. Umm, just under 100. About 97, I think.'

The look on her face makes me regret my honesty at first, but then she laughs and gives me shit about being a man-whore. After a bit more pillow-talk she asks if I've got protection, so I race out to my Tahoe and grab a couple out of my bag.

There's a crazy amount of passion between us and I take pride in doing things to her that her ex-husband apparently rarely or never did.

•

It's late June and I've been working my arse off at the lake. Going into peak summer it's sweltering hot and I'm drenched with sweat in no time, but at least that's helping to keep me in shape.

I'm about to fly to the west coast for the next tour stop, in California. I'm excited because I'll be meeting up with three of my favourite people: Jesse, Courtney and my little brother Alex! They all linked up in LA and are on their way to meet me at San Francisco in a rental car. However, they miscalculate the drive time so I have a few hours chilling at the airport before they scoop me up.

After a night in San Fran with some of Jesse's friends we cross the Bay Bridge to Oakland and on up to the small town of Lathrop — just below Stockton, where the pro tour is to be held. I love having my friends and bro here supporting me. I'm matched up against Harley in the first round. I'm second off the dock in a heat of three, with my Ronix teammate Keenan up before me. Only two of us will advance. Keenan rides well and puts the pressure on me, because I know Harley will smoke us both.

I ride well, but a fall in my run means my teammate has me beat, so it looks like my weekend is about to end in the first round. As I'm packing my gear into my bag, I hear an 'Ooohhhh!' from the crowd, and the boat powers down. I turn to see that Harley has fallen in his first pass. I watch closely and am dumbfounded to see him fall again on his first trick of pass two. Everyone is shocked. Turns out he *is* human after all, which means I'm gifted the second spot advancing into the quarter-finals!

The following day I start off the day on the mic with Dano, then get myself ready for my ride in the quarters. Although I link together a fairly decent run, I'm bested by my former roommate Austin Hair, and Phil Soven. I finish ninth equal, which is not too shabby but not great. I spend the rest of my day having a blast on stage with Dano and the two Rockstar girls, along with my Kiwi crew. I'm feeling so at home on the mic and on stage now and I especially love that my friends and bro are here to see how far I've come.

•

Jesse and Alex and I part ways with Courtney — I'm so glad to have caught up with her over here — and jet back to Orlando. Before I left, I'd helped Pratt pack up the house as we were both moving out. He's moved in with his sister, and tomorrow is the day my trailer finally arrives and I get to move out to Lake Ronix!

Problem is that we've actually got nowhere to stay tonight, so after hitting the downtown Orlando bars I find I can still get into the house, which has a few pieces of furniture left in the garage, so we crash on my mattress and a few couch cushions on the floor.

Out at the lake the next morning we meet the truck delivering my new home.

Before going to California I used a bobcat to clear an area just back from the main beach and that's where my 18-metre trailer is headed. It's a bit of a squeeze between two trees, but only a few hours later it's been levelled and anchored, and I'm moving my bed and other gear into my new home, parked among trees only 20 metres back from the edge of Lake Ronix. It doesn't get much better!

Even though it's a trailer home it's actually pretty nice. It has carpet and a room on each end, a bathroom although it's not operational and a lounge area in the middle. It's a perfect setup for me. I build a bench seat and table for the lounge so at least there's somewhere to sit.

Our first night is hot and humid. Jesse crashes on my air mattress and Alex shares the bed with me. The next day I grab the small generator from the container and Ferraro brings a window air-conditioning unit that's a game-changer.

●

The three of us go out to Mount Dora to hang with Alex Brown, and we share a messy night at McGregors. The following day we celebrate the Fourth of July out on the lake wakesurfing and drinking, then boost back to Orlando to Harley's Independence Day party. I feel old around all these youngsters emerging into the scene, some of whom are already beating me on the water.

Then it's time to bid my brother farewell as he heads to New York before venturing to London, where he's planning to live for a while. It's been a blast having him here and I'm so glad I got to show him what I've been doing over here for all these summers.

That same day Jesse and I drive over to Tampa for the Red Bull Wake Open. Dano has hired me to help him out on the commentary as this event will be live on NBC. I won't actually be on the mic; instead I'll be sitting beside him and feeding him the trick names as they're happening. Dano knows all of the tricks behind the boat, but since this is a new style of Wake Park event with really technical park features, the hits become much more technical and harder to call live, especially keeping track of whether their approach is switch or regular, if they're spinning frontside or backside, and if it's a lipslide, boardslide, nose or tail press or some other variation. Some features lend themselves to really creative combinations as well, so it's easier to have one person watch the tricks closely and call them quietly to the person on the mic.

I'm a bit gutted I didn't get invited to the event because the setup looks incredible. There are quarter-pipes at the far end, and a standalone event features two huge kickers to a mega-ramp landing for the big air event — the first of its kind in the US. Jeff and I spoke a lot about this type of setup, and he even tried to get the backing to do it but it never came about. I thought I might have qualified for an invite by being the first to do something similar back when I performed the step-up, but I guess it was four years ago, and my couple of years off with injuries haven't helped my name recognition. So I'm not one of the 36 park riders chosen, but that said, the lineup features some seriously heavy hitters!

I enjoy watching the big air event, but the whole time watching all I can think about is just how much fun it would be to ride that setup! I hope they hold this event again, and I need to secure an invite if they do! I do really enjoy commentating, but there's no doubt I'd rather be riding.

•

The following day I'm pleasantly surprised to see a bunch of the features from the Red Bull Wake Open turn up at Lake Ronix! This is unreal for the team, and for me to have all this in my back yard is insane! It's a shame the mega-ramp didn't come, but there's really nowhere to put it. The large tech feature is deposited in the corner of the property in pieces, to be assembled and placed in the lake at a later date. But the double handrail and the incline rail are both anchored in no time.

•

I fly up to Seattle for the fourth tour stop, leaving Jesse in Orlando with my truck. To get from the airport to the host hotel in Monroe, I share a rental car with friend and fellow pro rider Oli Derome. I crash early the first night to be ready for the competition start tomorrow.

After making it through the qualifying round and spending the day on the mic with Dano, I catch a ride with Chad up to the iconic Radar Lake. I've seen this place in so many films over the years it's a dream to finally be here. It feels every bit as magical as it seemed on film. The redwoods in the surrounding forest tower up into the sky. I can see why they call this the Ewok forest because it feels like I'm there in that *Star Wars* movie.

Looking along the shoreline of this custom-built water-ski lake, created by Paul's father, the legendary Herb O'Brien, who passed away less than a year ago, I get flashbacks from movies like *PrePop* and *Counterfeit This*, and there's even the leftover framing from one of the features built for *The Parks Documentary* left looking like a skeleton on one side of the lake.

As the sun sinks lower, I sit on the edge of the lake and watch replays in my mind of Shaun Murray and Chad both doing huge 270 transfers onto the monster A-frame, and Parks's ultra-smooth back-lipslide on the C-rail — so many incredible moments that drove me to want to be like those top riders. And finally here I am at Radar Lake, as part of the team with some of those legends who inspired me.

Parks and Danny take me for a tour of the property on quad bikes, and we stop to enjoy a lakeside doobie as the sun is about to set. After dinner back at the main house I sit around the campfire drinking beers with my Ronix family as Parks and Ruck entertain us on their guitars.

When it comes time to crash, I find a couch in the lounge and lie down to rest up for another big day tomorrow. Chad, who didn't make it through today's qualifiers, is passed out on the La-Z-Boy after crushing a bunch of beers. I wake up when he gets up to take a piss sometime around 3 a.m., and I'm dozing off again when he returns and starts telling me to move. 'Brad, get the fuck off my couch!' he grunts in a drunken slur.

'Oh come on dude, you've been sleeping on the recliner all night, and I've got to ride tomorrow!'

'Seriously, Brad, don't make me fire your arse! Get . . . the *fuck* . . . off my couch!'

I know he's not serious about firing me, and even if he is, he doesn't have that power alone, but now is not the time, so I give up and move to the recliner.

The following day Chad apologises, admitting that he thought I'd snaked his couch when he got up to piss. We laugh it off.

•

I'm up against a couple of heavy hitters in the quarter-final. Mike Dowdy wins the heat and Rusty Malinoski takes the second advancing spot, leaving me in third to finish 11th equal overall.

Back at Radar Lake with the team after the event I get chatting with Aarne from MasterCraft. I've been trying for years to get sponsored by them, and this is the most promising chat we've had. I think he sees value in me being at Lake Ronix — hooking me up with a boat is a good way to get one of their boats there. While chatting, we're approached by BG. He's the president and co-owner of Square One, the parent company of Ronix. I met him years ago but we've never really spoken.

'Is this one of your guys?' he asks Aarne, turning to me.

'Nope, he's one of yours!' says Aarne.

'I'm Brad,' I say, shaking his hand. With a surprised expression he says, 'Oh, so you're the guy I keep hearing good things about!'

Part of me wants to reply, *Yeah, and the guy who's been riding for your company for over six years!* but I smile brightly and say, 'Yip, that would be me!'

'Thank you for everything you're doing at the lake,' says BG. I hear you've become a bit of a leader out there. We really appreciate what you're doing.'

I thank him for the opportunity and tell him how much I enjoy it. It's good to have a face-to-face with BG, because he's the guy who controls the budget for the team, and the lake. At least now he knows who I am.

●

I've convinced Candice to come out to the lake. She arrives after dark and I meet her at the front gate to let her onto the property. She must be wondering what the hell she's got herself into, driving through a farm gate at night in the middle of nowhere.

But she plays it cool, giving me shit about having no furniture, but that just means there's not much to do besides head straight to my bedroom. Each time we're together I notice she's more into it, more comfortable with letting her guard down . . . and I fucking love it! She kisses me deeply as our clothes hit the floor and we dive into foreplay. Our love making is scorching hot — it's like all inhibitions are gone and we transition from passionate love making into full-on intense fucking.

Our sexual chemistry is out of this world. I love that I can teach her so many new things. It's like her lack of partners gives her an element of innocence for me to corrupt, but her 12-plus years of marriage means she's completely comfortable in her own sexual skin. Being out in the middle of nowhere seems to trigger something primal in both of us. Several bouts leave us both spent, panting and beaded with sweat, and she falls asleep in my arms.

The following morning she wakes to see the beauty this place holds, and after a tour of my new home she can see why I love the place so much.

●

That very evening, Jesse and I are on the road again. First up, we head to the Johnson City area in north-east Tennessee for a little riding, a little coaching and some golf with our friends at CBK. Then I have to fly across to Texas to host the second stop of the Wake Park Triple Crown at Texas Ski Ranch.

I smash out the two days on the mic and get in some fun riding with the best park riders in the world. I don't hold up so well in the contest, after which I race straight back to the airport to fly to Nashville for an event tomorrow.

This contest is basically a huge raft-up party where houseboats and wakeboard boats all tie up on a long section of the lake. With $4500 up for grabs for the winner, my sights are set on cashing in, especially since most of the top guys won't be here as it's not a pro tour event. But I get to the main houseboat to see JD, Austin Hair and the current pro tour leader, Phil Soven.

My day just got a lot tougher.

I ride well in the first round and make the final. With thousands of spectators across hundreds of boats all amped and liquored up, I'm ready as I'll ever be. JD missed out on the final after an uncharacteristically poor run, and Austin doesn't have a good start. Then out of nowhere, underdog rider Matt Sims absolutely kills it! But I keep my cool and stand up my run to land myself on the podium. I'm named in third place behind Matt in second. Phil takes top honours, as expected. But third comes with a nice bonus of $1500. Not the largest payday, but enough to take the pressure off for a while.

Jesse and I roll up to Kentucky to stay and ride with the Browns for the week. As usual it's awesome to spend the week with them while preparing for nationals, but when it comes time to compete, I only manage a quarter-final finish. We cruise back down to Nashville for a night on the town, then it's back to Lake Ronix, to a welcome-home present from Candice.

•

Jesse flies out a few days later. For the third year in a row we've partied hard, travelled all over, made new friends and caught up with old ones, and created lasting memories. I'm sad to see him go, but it'll be good for me to get back to focusing on my riding and my work here at the lake.

I've only got a few days here before I fly up to Wisconsin for worlds, so while the massive tech feature from Wake Open is being assembled I get to work repairing the wall-ride, which has been damaged by storms. It's hot work and there's not much help around, as many of the guys are travelling at the moment. But that doesn't mean the property isn't still a hive of activity. The earthworks guys are just getting started on the most exciting project to date, the bi-level pool setup on the back lake. This is where there are two bodies of water at different levels.

I land in Chicago with no real plan of how I'm getting up to Pleasant Prairie, but thankfully I'm saved by the Browns, who are on their way through in their RV and can swoop me up.

It's a solid four days on the mic at worlds. I guess the one thing I don't enjoy about my job as an MC is having to be at the full event, which means I'm not feeling quite as fresh as I'd like when I ride in my own event on day three. Dano is good at giving me breaks and taking some of the early shifts, but I do wonder if it is having a negative effect on my riding. Once again I get knocked out in the quarter-finals.

I guess the reality is that I haven't been focused on my contest riding this season because it's all been about the lake. At the Dinner of Champions awards banquet I'm surprised to be called up on stage with Dano to be awarded with microphone trophies for our work over the season. Dano's award is called 'The Dano the Mano Award', while mine is announced as the 'International Announcer of the Year Award'. It sounds fancier, but I know it's more of an appreciation award, since I'm the only international. Nevertheless, it feels good to get some recognition, and I'm totally going to claim it!

•

I decide to skip the final pro tour stop in Michigan, so my contest season ends with me in 20th place on tour and 22nd in the King of Wake series. Another modest finish. One reason for not finishing off the tour is that there's too much to do at the lake before the big reveal during Surf Expo. So far we've had to keep very tight-lipped about the lake. No posting photos or videos, no one allowed out here except our team. People know something is going on and rumours have been circulating, but very few know any details.

Six weeks out, we're finally allowed to share a photo introducing people to our new team facility. We're still not supposed to reveal too much, but I'm so proud to give people a glimpse and announce that it's my new home.

I wake up as the sun is just rising above the horizon. I get out of bed to enjoy the cool, tranquil morning before anyone else turns up. Ever since moving out here I've been going nonstop; I've barely had a moment to sit back and soak it in. Sitting here on the beach with my towel wrapped around my waist, tuning into the ambient sounds of the local birds and insects who are also absorbing the warmth of the morning sun, I'm overcome with immense pride for having landed myself here, through sheer hard work, sacrifice and determination.

I'm the only person in the world who gets to call Lake Ronix home. Looking out across the mirrored lake at the park the team and I have built, I'm grateful to be able to work with my hands, and with such a rad group of humans, building for ourselves and for each other, for our team and for our future, to leave a mark on this sport. A surge of emotion almost brings a tear to my eye as I realise I am finally home — *this is where I'm supposed to be.*

I stand and spread my arms in a big stretch in preparation for my morning rinse. I smile as I realise I've basically become Kiwi trailer trash, yet I'm so content and feel so lucky. Living in a trailer with no power or running water, taking dumps in the outdoor porta-potty and washing myself in the lake every day would not be everyone's picture of success, but here I am, brimming with pride and joy.

I realise it's because I'm living my passion. I'm literally surrounded by it and that's so much more important than material things. In primal ritualistic fashion I drop my towel and stand on the sand in all my glory, as if to symbolically surrender myself to this place and claim it as my territory. I close my eyes and take in a big breath, then step forward and dive into my home waters to bathe before the day begins.

•

Having no consistent power means no fridge or freezer, so aside from a few items like fruit, bread and snacks, I can't keep much food here. So, after throwing on some board shorts and a T-shirt, I drive down the road to grab some breakfast along with a few cases of bottled water and bags of ice for the day ahead. I have a chilly bin (cooler) that I try to keep packed with drinks for me and the team, although I hate going through so many plastic bottles each day.

Not long after I get back, Ruck and Chad pull up ready for the day's work and join me in my trailer, still cool from having the a/c cranking overnight, to chat about our plans for the day ahead. These two are out here almost every day and have pretty much taken on leadership roles. Between us three and Ferraro, we basically run the place. But the vibe is not that we boss anyone around, we're just seen as leaders because we take the initiative to make sure shit is getting done. We lead by example, because we love this place. A lot of the other guys, like Parks, Danny, Rossi, Dominik Hernler and Deano, and more, have moments of leadership as well, but their other commitments mean they're not out here quite as much.

I've always looked up to Chad and Ruck, so spending almost every day with them has been cool and has brought me closer to them as friends. But they're older, and both heading towards the tail end of their careers as top professionals, so I guess that gives them more time to spend out here. For them it's a way to maintain their value to the brand. For my part, I'm looking to increase my value in order to propel myself forward in my professional career.

We all do a bit of everything but we each have our strengths and specialties. Mine is building and general coordination of tasks around the lake, so today I'll be out on the lake doing further repairs to the wall-ride. Ruck is more into the garden and maintenance of the grounds, so today he's planting more bamboo and has some railroad sleepers being delivered to border the back of the beach.

Then there's Chad, who is kinda like the demolition man! He absolutely loves jobs where he gets to use his jacked-up diesel F250. Today he's planning to use it to rip down a dead tree and drag it away. He's all rip shit and bust! But if anything needs dragged, ripped, towed, smashed or burned using an excessive amount of fuel, then Chad's our man!

I notice elements of their riding styles in their approach to their work at the lake. Ruck has good flow and a smooth, mellow, somewhat peaceful style on the water, whereas Chad's all about hard charging, going big and sending it.

Before cracking into the day's work, Ruck and I burn down a spliff as we wander out to the beach. I've always enjoyed smoking weed as a way to unwind at the end of the day. If I smoked before I needed to be productive, I found I lost track of what I was supposed to do. But recently I've found that as long as I know my plan prior to smoking, then it gets me into a zone where I can just work away for hours, especially at a mundane job.

So, as the roach is extinguished I take the pontoon boat out to the wall-ride and get to work. Another section has come loose due to the post not being in deep enough, so I decide to strip the whole wall down to just the four vertical posts and rebuild it like you'd build a wall in a house, with some structural integrity throughout. So our wall-ride shrinks from 12 metres long to 7.5, which will still be long enough for some fun hits on the vertical wall.

Towards the end of the day Ferraro pulls up with his usual box of warm Heineken. He always gives us crap for something — today calling us lazy for sitting around, even though it's the end of a big day and he's just showed up. He asks me if I can replace a belt on his truck for him. It's my own fault for telling him a while back that I'd changed a fanbelt in my own truck. His is a different belt but I say, 'Fuck I'm good to you, Mike!' as I climb under his Tahoe.

'I'll pay you in warm beer!' he laughs.

I escape the lake for the evening and chill with Shane Bonifay at his place. He's been letting me do my laundry there, which I really appreciate. It's a nice change from my usual quiet nights in the trailer to kick it with Shane, Rossi and Dom while chilling and playing Call of Duty.

●

The following day videographer Spencer Norris arrives to do some filming for the 'reveal' of Lake Ronix to the world. Keenan, Pratt and Adam Errington are all here to shred, along with Chad and Ruck. We spend a good chunk of the afternoon riding and filming and the boys are killing it! Especially the young dudes, Keenan and Pratt. Pratt even stomps a huge double tantrum off the kicker, which is a relatively new trick for him.

When it's my turn I play around with different hits on the double handrail, and then —inspired by my bro Pratt — I throw, and stomp, a new double flip of my own: the indy grabbed toeside double backroll. I'm pretty sure I became the first in the world to land this trick off a kicker a few weeks back while riding at OWC, but this is the first time I've done it here at the lake . . . and I land it near perfectly!

This becomes the final banger for the section when it's released and I'm pretty stoked. At the end of the filming session, and after getting a little bit more work done, Pratt, Keenan and I are unwinding. I skin up a doobie and proceed to light it up, but I stub it out instantly when I spot an unfamiliar car driving onto the property. A man hops out and is looking around checking the place out as he walks over to us. I recognise him as the father of a new young rider I've seen at OWC. He asks if Ferraro is around.

'No, it's just us here, sorry,' I say, holding the spliff behind my back. 'Were you supposed to meet him here?'

'No, no, I was just in the area so I thought I'd pop in,' he replies. Aware of the project's privacy, I'm not too happy about this. His son is one of Ferraro's young riders, who put in hours testing boards and boots around OWC, to see how they hold up. But he's not on the team, and has only been invited out here a couple of times.

●

A few days later we find out that someone at one of Ronix's biggest retail accounts has just reported to Paul that he's heard Lake Ronix is a 'drug haven'. Paul is not happy. He knows that many of the team riders smoke at times, and he doesn't encourage it but he knows it's something that tends to go with the lifestyle.

'But it's not a good look when that's the message one of our biggest retailers gets about the place,' he says to me on the phone.

'Yeah, I'm so sorry that happened, Paul, but I know exactly who it came from.'

I explain about the guy who randomly showed up at the end of the day just as I was lighting up. 'But calling it a "drug haven" makes it sound like we're snorting coke and shooting heroin out here!' I continue, attempting to laugh it off.

'Yeah, who the hell does this guy think he is?' Paul responds, laughing awkwardly. 'He invites himself out here unannounced and then goes and talks shit to one of our retailers? Unbelievable.'

'It's pretty low,' I agree, glad that Paul doesn't appear mad at me.

'Well, he just fucked that up for his son — he'll never ride for Ronix now,' Paul says. He tells me he'll be here in a few days to help get ready for Surf Expo.

As soon as Paul arrives, all of a sudden, as if by some force of magic, the whole team starts coming out to the lake every day to work. Most have been pretty good at coming out a couple of days a week — and throughout the middle of the season that's understandable as everyone is busy travelling, training and filming, myself included — but as soon as the boss comes to town, everyone is hard at it!

As comical as I find it, it's great to have the full crew here again. Once again the property is a hive of activity. The huge tech feature from Wake Open has been completed, so a team get to work pouring concrete into some old tyres to use as anchors, then float it into position. Another team are assembling the skateboard mini-ramp delivered by the Stuckys, an awesome family who all ride Ronix. Their two young sons, Trent and Gavin, both absolutely rip, especially for their age.

I spend most of the day out at the wall-ride. Generally, it's a pretty productive day and I crash out as soon as the sun goes down.

By the end of the next day I've got the wall fully reassembled and ready to hit. The digging and shaping of the pool at the back lake is finished so a whole crew help lay out the plastic sheeting to line and seal it. It's another massive day, and again I'm pleasantly flogged by the end of it.

Another load of palm trees is being delivered to line the back of Wake Beach on the other side of the main lake, and Amiel — who Ruck has affectionately dubbed Email and it's caught on — is in charge of planting and bracing them.

I've decided to build a deck that extends out from the back of the Wake Beach tiki hut, with space for a barbecue grill and bench seating around the perimeter.

I sketch it up, crunch some numbers and put together a materials list before making a run to the hardware store. I've never built a deck before, but as usual I enjoy the challenge and use the web to get any tips I need. While I have my head down with this, the rest of the team are either helping Email with the palms, working on the beach for the back lake, or helping Pat, Bdahl and Sam from Sesitec, who are starting to erect the towers for our second System 2.0 straight-line cable.

By mid-afternoon, I've finished the framing and have started laying out the decking planks when Paul brings everyone in for a team meeting. He starts by expressing his appreciation for the work everyone has been putting in.

'Thank you, thank you, thank you. It's incredible to see how this place has changed since the start of the year, and you guys have been, and will continue to be, instrumental in making this place the paradise it's already becoming.'

He singles out Ruck, Chad and myself for taking charge and putting in so much effort. After a motivational talk about his vision for this place, and the concept of being different and standing above the rest, he gives props to the likes of Pratt, Dom and Rossi for their creativity. His talk then turns more serious.

'As I said, you've all been doing great work out here, but I need to bring up the weed smoking, especially after the whole "drug haven" comment.'

I notice a few of the guys shift awkwardly in their seats.

'Now I know that shouldn't have happened and is not really anyone's fault here, but I have seen your productivity drop noticeably after smoking. I'm not telling you that you can't smoke weed, because I know that's not up to me and, as you know, I might even join you on the right occasion, but I do ask that you try not to smoke out here during the day until after the work and riding is done.'

Reed Hanson stands and thanks Paul for providing us all with this amazing property, and hands him a gift. Paul opens the box and pulls out an alligator skull! It's from the first gator he pulled out of the lake at the start of the year. We all think it's a rad gift and Paul seems touched.

As the meeting breaks up, Paul pulls me aside. 'Hey, you know I wasn't meaning you, right? I've seen you smoke a doobie and then spend all day by yourself in the middle of the lake building a giant wall-ride! You clearly can be productive after smoking!' he says with a smile.

I laugh and thank him, but add that I could definitely do better in general if I smoked less, so I'll make an effort and try to lead by example.

Paul spends the rest of the afternoon and evening working with me. I get him started on the bench seats around the fire pit. I mark where to dig and he gets his hands dirty digging post holes while I measure, cut and screw the seat tops together. Ferraro even gets involved, mainly standing back and giving Paul crap, but he does get his hands dirty a little.

When the seats are made and the decking is laid, Paul and I sit and chat, looking out across the lake towards the setting sun. He asks me how it's been living out here, and it's hard to find the words to do it justice. I tell him about feeling like I'm where I'm supposed to be — that I'm home. 'It has its spooky moments with the resident wildlife at night when I'm on my own, but I love it. This is a really special place.'

I thank him for the opportunity to live here.

'Dude, I'm the one who should be thanking you for everything you've done here! You just took control and . . .' he gestures to our surroundings, 'look what you've done to this place!'

'I can't take all the credit, but it's cool to have been involved,' I say.

I tell him my dad renovated or built the houses I grew up in, but his Parkinson's disease has stopped him working. 'So I guess my dad is still building, only through my hands now,' I say.

Paul looks out across the lake and nods his head silently, and it makes me think. Paul is running the company that he and his father created, continuing the legacy of making the best water-skis and wakeboards in the world, started by his father back in the early 1960s. He tells me how much this place means to him as a facility created in his father's honour, after Herb himself created Radar Lake back in 1972. I feel honoured to have been a small part of making that dream become reality.

Paul shares a story about how, after he fluffed around and partied during his first year of college and flunked out, his dad made him spend the summer working for him making skis. He didn't let him use the fibreglass cutting machine to cut multiple sheets at a time — he made Paul cut each sheet individually by hand, as a sort of punishment. That's what taught Paul the value of hard work, because he was so proud of the skis he made painstakingly by hand. I think that's why he loves to get out here and get involved, get his hands dirty, because he's leaving a piece of himself in this place — as am I.

We continue to talk until the sun has almost vanished below the horizon. It's a far cry from our short, awkward interactions of years past. I feel like we've really connected and I've broken through the shell that used to keep me at arm's length.

•

With just one more week until the big reveal, everyone pitches in as we smash out jobs that need to be done. We've got some extra help in the form of the Ronix reps, product guys and others from the head office who are all down from Seattle for the expo — even BG pitches in.

After finishing off the deck I build an exact copy of the System 2.0 box that houses all of the electronics and computer components that operate the cable, complete with roofing shingles and a door that opens at the front. I'm pretty bloody proud of both of my latest builds!

I get back from running a quick errand in the evening and arrive just as a storm is rolling through. I park outside my trailer and then wander over to where Paul, Ferraro, Brett (the Ronix South East sales rep) and few of the other guys from Seattle are sitting drinking beer. As I'm nearing the tiki, I look out to the lake and I cannot believe it — the wall-ride has toppled over and is lying on top of the kicker.

'You're fucking kidding me!' I say as I get to the tiki.

'Yeah, sorry, bro,' says Brett. 'We were sitting here and watched as the wind blew it over about two minutes ago.'

'*Raaaah!*' I bellow. 'I spent *so long* fixing that bloody thing!'

I swim straight out and pull the kicker out from under, then begin to drag the floating wall-ride back to the beach. A handful of the guys give me a hand getting it partly up onto the shore, where I proceed to take out my frustration with a sledgehammer. After weeks of work repairing and then rebuilding that thing, it's been completely demolished in a matter of minutes.

Smashing it to bits makes me feel much better and we all have a laugh about it over a beer.

•

A few days back, a couple of the guys jumped over the back fence into the Amish-owned farmland next door and came back with a bunch of mushrooms that have since been drying in my trailer. Tonight is the night we eat them! I'm cautious after the not-so-fun trip I had over a year ago, but I'm in a good space and I'm confident that this time will be different.

We each munch down three or four mushrooms to send us on our way, then, after pre-rolling several doobies, we wander over to get the fire going and sit around the fire pit on main beach. With the sun setting behind us, it's not long before I feel myself becoming mesmerised by the gentle orange hue it emits across the mirrored lake and into the distance. As the shrooms begin to take me on their journey, I'm overcome with the most gratifying feeling of peace, calm and tranquillity that reflects my surroundings. The twilight dims and the fire burns brighter as we sit around the fire pit. We go from being entranced by the colours in the flames to laughing hysterically at Parks's country comedy tunes on the guitar, and Pratt's wild-child antics.

Pratt has become a bit more of a loose unit since we first met a few years back, and that's part of the reason he's so damned good on a wakeboard. He has us all in stitches when he grabs a fallen palm frond, lays it across the top of the fire and then proceeds to run back and forth across the beach waving it around and screaming like a man possessed.

In the back of my mind I'm thinking, *Great, I'm going to be the one who has to clean that shit up tomorrow*, because I know he sure as hell won't. But I choose to abandon my caretaker role and focus on the hilarity in his performance, because that's what I want to feel right now, and the direction I'd rather the night heads. The positive feels continue to bloom inside me as I'm filled with the most empowering feeling of pure gratitude and love for this place, and for these brothers of mine. Unlike the downward spiral of my last shroom experience, due to my unstable situation and personal insecurities, right now I feel completely elevated; those little fungi are brewing nothing but total confidence in me.

The difference is that this is my domain. All the hard work, blood, sweat and even tears I've poured into this place have given me a huge sense of ownership of this 85-hectare wakeboarders' paradise. The fact that I live here on my own and have walked this beach in my total nakedness, all add together to give me the feeling that I fucking own this place!

I'm sure Parks, Ruck, Dom, Pratt, Rossi and Todd Watson are all feeling the same about this place right now, because it's an ownership we all share. And although this particular episode may take this place slightly closer to being the drug haven that douche-bag made it out to be, I feel like we all deserve this blowout after all the hard work.

After a couple of hours on the main beach, one of the guys makes an excellent suggestion.

'Dudes, we should go over to the other beach and light another fire!' he says.

We're all wide-eyed and mind-blown by this thought, so we enthusiastically pile into a couple of trucks and roll around to the other side. We get the fire started on Wake Beach, and while it's getting going we all wander over to the pool at the back lake, which is now completely full. We stand there for a while, mind-shredding the new down-rails and step-up kicker under the moonlight, talking about how excited we are to finally ride it.

Our second fire is not burning as well as the first one so we decide to return to the main beach, which had better vibes.

It's here that Rossi suddenly starts laughing and says, 'Guys, I just realised Ferraro's motion sensor camera is set up at the other beach.'

We all start laughing as we think about the incriminating photos he will have.

'We really should've done more to fuck with him!' Parks adds, then starts doing impersonations of Ferraro's possible reactions on finding the photos.

My face hurts from laughing so hard, and eventually I go to bed after what was one of the best nights of my life.

●

Expo weekend hits and the lake is a hive of activity. Boats going all day for surf and wakeboard demos, dealers taking laps of the cable even though most of the features are far too advanced for most of them. We team riders periodically ride demos to show off what's available.

I mainly oversee everything, jumping in anywhere I'm needed — host people on tours, fixing any minor problems that arise. I love being able to show VIPs and mates around my pride and joy, and I'm especially stoked to catch up with Dunc and Stu, the New Zealand and Australian Ronix dealers.

'Epic work mate!' and 'Proud of you, big fella!' they say, saying they've heard nothing but good things about what I've been doing.

In the afternoon I'm on the Ronix booth at the convention centre, and running a quick round of sponsorship chats. They're not much more promising than previous years but there's a definite buzz going around about my role as the Lake Ronix on-site manager, so I hope that might lead to future opportunities. Every year I leave Surf Expo hopeful of future opportunities — when will that handshake over a sponsorship deal finally happen for me? When will I finally get to sign on that dotted line? It's getting more and more difficult as the younger riders coming through are better and better.

At the annual Wake Awards night I watch as young gun Mike Dowdy takes out Trick of the Year with a Melon grabbed double backroll to blind, but done with an early backside 180, making it one of the most creative tricks I've ever seen. I've always wanted to win that award but this year was a write-off, and anyway these tricks are getting so insane I don't know what it would take to win it next year! The one saving grace is knowing I'll be moving to the US full-time from next season, to live and ride at the best facility there is.

•

Candice and I see each other sporadically. I love being with her but I've just been so busy I haven't had much time for dating. Today we meet up for a drink and she invites me back to her place. I'm stoked to enjoy the comforts of a real home after being in my trailer so much, but I don't get much of a look before I'm whisked off to her bedroom. After a night of incredible sex I especially love having a proper shower, and by the time I'm dry and clothed, Candice has made me a grilled egg and cheese sandwich for breakfast.

I'm very much drawn to the woman I've been seeing for the past few months, but as I look around her lovely home at photos of her beautiful children I get a bit overwhelmed at the thought of that much responsibility. So, as much as I like Candice, I don't feel like she's the one.

•

After the madness of Surf Expo the compound is back to being quiet. While there are still some small jobs to do, we also get in plenty of riding. It's especially fun to session the huge new features from Wake Open and the brand-new setup on the back lake. Paul has gone back to Seattle but there's always a crew here.

With just a few days until I'm due to be leaving the country, I line up a morning photo shoot with a renowned wakeboard photographer named Joey Meddock. I call on Todd, who lives just up the road at the Projects, to operate the cable for me, and I set my focus on hitting Chad's super-kicker and stepping up into the pool. The kicker sends me over 3 metres high above the top pool, so I launch some big method grabs and work on tweaking out a tuck-knee indy tantrum, getting as torqued as possible for the click of the shutter at my peak.

By the end of the half-hour session Joey has some really sick shots of both tricks. A few days later I hear that Joey plans to use the tuck-knee tantrum as the cover of his mag *Wake Journal*, and apparently my favourite method grab shot is headed for the cover of *Wake Magazine* in Australia. Not a bad morning's work!

From here I'm supposed to be getting flown to Abu Dhabi for the Wake Park World Championships, but my US visa expires the week before, so I buy myself a ticket to London and get the WWA to fly me from there to Abu Dhabi. So after packing up my life once more I say peace out to my friends and teammates, take one last look at the lake, and head for the airport at the end of my 2013 US season.

I've got quite the journey lined up for the next couple of months and I'm frothing for it! After London and Abu Dhabi, I'll stop off in Jakarta for a few days before heading to Bali for the wedding of my friends Jordan Lewis and Emma Davison. After that I'll fly to the Philippines, Australia and Thailand for more Wake Park World events, finally getting home in November.

At Heathrow I'm met by Ants, who is currently living here. He doesn't have any room for me to crash with him so he drops me at his friend Gareth's place. After I've showered up, Gareth suggests we go up the road to the local pub for some beers. Before leaving the house he racks us each up a line of coke to send us on our way. We strike out on the lady front, but we get pretty smashed and bro out all night.

I spend a few more days at Gareth's and we go to watch Ants base-jump an antenna. Ants has been working towards base jumping for the last couple of years, with Jeff's help. Participants jump from any one of four fixed objects — Building, Antenna, Span (bridges) or Earth (cliffs) — with a parachute. It turns out Gareth is quite the experienced base-jumper as well, only he's given it up after a couple of recent near-misses.

We head for an antenna in the country that Gareth knows about, and after jumping a few fences and crossing a couple of fields I watch as both Gareth and Ants scale this antenna structure. Then it's 'three, two, one . . . see ya!' and Ants leaps from the tower while Gareth gives him a PCA, which is where he holds the pilot chute so it tugs out and opens almost instantly. They do this because it's a low jump; after the parachute has opened, it only takes Ants a few seconds to fly down to his landing.

Right then we hear police sirens so we assume the local farmer called the cops. Gareth scurries back down the tower, Ants quickly collects his chute together and we bolt back across the fields.

We don't know for sure that they were coming for us, but it adds to the adrenalin rush of it all!

I catch up with other mates in London, including my brother Alex, before flying out to Abu Dhabi.

●

A bunch of us are here early to help out with the United Arab Emirates champs prior to worlds. In the days leading up to the main event we rise early to ride for promotional photos and videos. On one morning, Colin Harrington and I are riding doubles and he comes up with the idea to cut around the kicker and then back under me as I launch into an indy toeside double backroll. The footage is insane and the way he goes under me makes it almost look like I'm doing a triple. I've got my doubles absolutely dialled now, so I'm pumped to throw it in the contest.

This time around I'm the chief event MC, as they have someone else to host the TV show. Much as I enjoyed being in front of the camera last time around, I'm much more comfortable dribbling over the mic all day instead. I announce for all of the different divisions, which takes up most of the day, but the competitions stop mid-afternoon so I have the rest of the day to ride.

When it comes time for me to compete I reckon I should get through to at least the semi-finals, but I crash out on two doubles and fail to advance. So for the rest of the weekend I'm on beer and mic duties.

●

I arrive in Jakarta for the first time and grab some rupiah for the taxi to my accommodation. The local Ronix dealer is putting me up and I'll hang and ride with them while I'm here. They own Epic Cable Park, so I'll happily kick it here and ride for a few days before I go to Bali.

It's night when I land but as we drive through the streets I'm struck by how dirty and how jam-packed this place is. We pull up at a barrier arm where a security guard checks to make sure I'm allowed into the gated area containing the park. I hand them a piece of paper and we're through.

My accommodation has a really cool feel to it, with a modern interior and Indonesian-hut-looking exterior, and it's right on the water. I'm wiped out, so I take a much-needed bath and crash.

I wake up the next morning to find that the cable is literally right outside my window. I could throw my board into the water from my room. It's a cool setup with plenty of fun-looking features scattered around the man-made cove. And while the hut-style accommodation and palm trees attempt to give it a tropical island vibe, that feel is a bit stifled by the fact that the cove is surrounded by concrete.

I spot the office on the other side of the cove so, after filling up at the buffet breakfast, I wander over to the shop and meet the Epic Cable Park crew. Raf, the owner, is about my age and I'm told his family owns one of the largest mines in Indonesia. He introduces me to some of his crew. Something I've always loved about wakeboarding is that no matter where I go in the world, and who I meet, if they're into wakeboarding then we get along. Soon enough the heat has me eyeing up the cable — time for a rip to cool off!

After cutting some laps, Raf takes me to a restaurant overlooking the park. 'While you're staying here, just come here and order anything you like,' he says. Turns out he owns the restaurant as well. After another ride I hang out on the dock and give some tips to the other riders. It's gratifying to watch them progress with just a few pointers.

In the evening Raf takes me to their Epic Wake Store to meet more of the crew, some of whom have come here just to meet me, which is both gratifying and uncomfortable. I don't like being the centre of attention, but I like to be as close to it as possible! We go out for dinner, after which I hit the town with another guy. We go to a couple of bars and I'm starting to get loose when he suggests we go to the massage parlour.

'Shit yeah, I could do with a good massage!' I say, feeling the aches and pains accumulating from the past weeks of riding and travel.

'Oh, they'll get you feeling good all right!' he says with a sly grin. It turns out he's taking me to a parlour that does the special happy-ending type of massage. At first I'm hesitant, because I've never paid for sex in my life, but I figure *when in Rome* — or *when in Jakarta* — and I would hate to offend my gracious hosts.

'Okay, but I want an actual massage first, because my body is sore,' I tell him.

We enter a shady-looking establishment and he pays the woman behind the desk for us both to have a shiatsu massage. As we're going up the stairs he tells me, 'Don't pay any more than a 50,000 rupiah tip for happy ending,' which equates to about $5 back home. I enter the curtain room where I'm instructed to undress and lie down on my stomach with a towel across my waist.

A couple of minutes later, in walks a small Indonesian lady with a tray of oils and towels. She oils my back and then proceeds to walk up and down my spine, holding on to handles in the ceiling and using her heels and toes to dig into my aching muscles. After around 30 minutes she moves down to my legs, continuing to dig in and give my muscles a good rub. Then suddenly she puts her hands up under the towel and starts tickling my balls. I'm barred up in no time, then she taps me twice on the butt and says, 'Okay, you roll over now.' I do as I'm told.

Now that I'm on my back she moves the towel and proceeds to jerk me off. It feels good with the oil she's using, but I feel awkward lying back doing nothing while being jerked off by a fully clothed girl I don't even know. I let her finish the job and give her the Rp 50,000 tip as I leave to shower up and get dressed.

As we walk out of the parlour I feel relaxed and relieved, but also slightly cheapened and conflicted over what just happened. My new friend pats me on the back and says, 'Welcome to Jakarta!' and we both laugh.

We have a few more drinks and he tells me about a place called Seventh Heaven where he wants to take me tomorrow night. Apparently it's a building with multiple levels, the ground floor being a nightclub, the second floor a strip club, the third a massage parlour, then prostitutes work on the upper levels. Apparently on the top floor you can pick from a lineup of girls of all different makes and models and do whatever you want.

'But we don't want you getting lost there, like your teammate did,' says my friend. 'He loved it so much he was selling his wakeboards so he could afford to go again!'

'I think tonight was enough for me,' I say.

The next day I'm back on the cable ticking up the laps. I bust out a few more doubles and session the more basic features, including a basic mellow rooftop rail leading into the corner at the control tower. I lean right back into a front boardslide on the tail but I slip out and fall off the end — and that's when I feel my left knee pop.

'*Agrrrrhh!*' I yell as I emerge from the water. I know that feeling all too well. I've just done the ACL in my other knee. Swimming back to the starting dock I can feel my knee wobbling as I kick through the water, and back on shore it feels no better. I cannot believe it. Does this mean another surgery and six months' rehabilitation? I don't know if I've got it in me. That might be the end of my career.

I change out of my wet gear and one of Raf's guys takes me to hospital. I hobble into the crowded waiting room, and stand back to let him speak to the receptionist. Next thing, before I even get the chance to sit down, I'm whisked away to the MRI machine. It appears Raf's influence extends even here.

I fall asleep while they're scanning my knee, and wake to being handed a folder containing my results. Raf tells me not to worry about the cost of the MRI — 'I've got you covered, bro,' he says casually. I thank him profusely for his help then head back to my room, where I ice my knee and burst into tears. Why me? After everything I've been through, this can't be happening! I think about last night at the massage parlour and wonder if this is some sort of cruel karma.

I can't call Mum because it's the middle of the night there, so I call Paul. I'm gutted to tell him I've blown my knee and that I'll be out for at least six months, but I assure him that I still plan on being back at the lake as soon as I can, even if it means I finish my rehab there. Paul does his best to console me, telling me he has a gut feeling it might not be as bad as I think it is.

By the end of the conversation I decide to quit drowning in self-pity and start planning ahead. I email Dr Mark, my previous knee surgeon, and send him the scans, hoping I can get surgery as soon as I get home. I consider flying home early but there's no way I'm skipping out on the wedding of one of my best friends. So the following day, after thanking Raf and his crew for their incredible hospitality, I climb in a cab to the airport to fly to Bali.

TWELVE: WHERE I'M SUPPOSED TO BE

I'm straight in to see Dr Mark a couple of days after landing. He does the trick where he gets me to bend my knee up with my foot on the bed, then tugs my lower leg, then says, 'Well, your ACL is still good.'

Phew!

'From the scans it looks like you've actually torn your medial collateral ligament, but the good news is that the MCL will heal up with no need for surgery.'

I'm baffled because I was sure I was going to be out of commission . . . but I'll take that good news! And I let Paul know he was right. I get stuck into rehabbing and strengthening my knee, pumped that I'll be back on a board in no time.

I then dig into the paperwork needed to apply for a five-year performance visa for the US. Becky, an action sports lawyer I met through Jeff, is helping. Ronix have agreed to sponsor me and pay for my visa, so once the application is filed it's just a waiting game.

On a night out in Kingsland, Brant and I meet up with our mate Staples, who is here with some girls. One in particular catches my eye so I spark a conversation with her. She's a rather stunning brunette named Morgan, but although she's very attractive physically, it's more her energy that grabs me. Some hot girls give off a vibe of being unapproachable or too cool, but Morgan seems spritely, friendly and open. We have a great conversation and then hit the dance floor. As we're leaving the bar I ask for her number and she gives it to me.

We text back and forth for a few days, then Jesse and I go along to a play that she's in. She doesn't have a main part, but I can't take my eyes off her the whole time. Afterwards, I join her and some friends from the show at a bar up the road, where Morgan grabs the microphone for some karaoke, and she's got a beautiful voice. I'm more and more attracted to this girl the more I know about her.

When it comes time to leave, I walk her to her car. I hold her door open for her and she sits in the driver's seat. I lean in, place my hand softly on her cheek and she turns to let me kiss her soft lips. She kisses me back and we savour the moment. I can't wipe the smile off my face the whole drive home.

I don't bother to play it cool — I text her as soon as I get home, and she tells me she's having equal trouble removing the smile from her face.

Morgan was raised a Canterbury farm girl, and it's hard not to fall in love with her. I tell her straight up that I'm moving to the US at the end of summer, and I'm relieved when she tells me she still wants to spend the summer with me.

•

In mid-December I'm called to a casting for a TV commercial shooting next week. I go and meet the client, and the next day I'm told they've chosen me for one of three male roles. Two will be extras and one is to be featured. It will pay either $3000 if I'm cast as an extra, or $6000 if I get the lead. I'm driven to Taupō for the shoot, with the two other guys and a stunning blonde girl named Jasmine, who is the other talent in the ad.

On the way down we all start getting to know each other, although none of us guys know yet who scored the main part. My phone beeps and I read a message that says I've been selected for the main role. I keep quiet until an hour or so later when one of the guys says, 'I wonder when we'll find out who got the main part,' at which point I reveal that I got the nod.

The next morning we're up bright and early and on a Taupō dairy farm, dressed in white shirts, beige pants and black suspenders. We're filming for a milk commercial that will only play in China, and we're all supposed to be 'angel farmers'. It's super cheesy. At first we three guys are cutting grass in the distance with our hand-tools as Jasmine picks daisies in the foreground. Then I change into an 'actual farmer' outfit. But, far from what you might expect — Swanndri, tank, stubbies and gumboots — it's a fluoro orange polarfleece top with reflective strips, waterproof pants and a hard hat, which is apparently what Chinese dairy farmers wear. I convince them to let me ditch the hard hat.

In this scene I wander up to one of my cows and say, 'Hi Peggy, it's time for your spa.' I'm super glad this won't be on New Zealand TV. We shoot a bunch of takes, and that's day one done. The others roll back to Auckland in the morning. I'm tempted to knock on Jasmine's door to see if she wants to 'watch a movie' with me in my hotel room, but I resist when I think about Morgan. Even though we're not officially together, I don't want to fuck up a good thing.

The following day we change locations to shoot on a farm in Ātiamuri, which sits right on the edge of the lake where I spent so much time in my younger years at the Ballistics camp. Here I'm to shoot as both the Angel farmer and the actual farmer, and I have to learn some lines about cattle and grass and milk. The first problem is that the script makes absolutely no sense. I think they just ran the Chinese version through Google Translate. So I sit around while the Kiwi producer rewrites it.

We shoot some other scenes that have me shaking my head. I'm lying in the paddock topless, with my fluoro top rolled up under my head as a pillow. They've got me oiled up to look like I'm tanning on my break. I feel terrible that this is the way I'm depicting Kiwi farmers, but I take a deep breath and we smash out the rest of the filming. I'm stoked that I'll be able to pay off most of my credit card with the pay from this one.

●

Back in Auckland I spend more time with Morgan. She has such an uplifting energy that it's impossible not to smile when we're together. It's not until the third or fourth time hanging out that we end up sleeping together. On a night out I introduce her to Jordan, Emma, Rory and a few others. Jordan gives the big thumbs-up just after one look, and Emma gives her approval after they've sat and chatted for a while.

Back at my place, Morgan and I make love for the first time. It's not the most intense sex I've ever had but I'm more than okay with that, as this feels incredibly intimate and genuine. We kiss passionately and hold each other close as we move together and get tangled in the sheets, and I marvel at her perfect form in all her naked glory. We make love several times before we fall asleep cuddled up in my bed.

●

The new year brings new life with the birth of my sister Monique's second daughter, a precious little gift named Mila, born 7 January 2014.

I'm back on my three-month challenge of no booze, weed or fast food. I hit Pilates sessions and Susie helps me put extra work into stabilising my knee with sessions on the reformer. It's harder than it looks but I approach every session knowing that the more effort I put in, the more chance I'm preventing future injury. I'm always drenched in sweat by the time I get back home to Mum's place for a refreshing dip in the pool. Same when I get home from Ludus, and the gym — the pool beckons as that extra incentive to help me push just a little harder.

While I'm still hustling with promo work, coaching and flicking 50-bags to my mates, I've picked up another job working for the family of Ants' flatmate, Anna-

Marie. Her dad has me in their back yard working in the garden spraying and pulling weeds, trimming hedges and tree branches, climbing under their house to clear out any unneeded crap, and trailering all of the waste off to the tip.

I do some handyman stuff as well like installing a new clothesline and fixing up their deck. This all keeps me busy and active and keeps the money coming in. But by the end of each day I'm always covered with scratches and, once again, I look forward to getting home for a swim — and of course seeing Morgan.

•

I'm in the head office of Red Bull New Zealand to meet the new athlete and event manager, an Australian guy who goes by the moniker BT. The former manager, who seemed to have no interest in wakeboarding, has moved on, and since my sponsorship with Mountain Dew is all but a memory, I hope BT will see the value in adding me to the team.

I present a handful of stunt ideas, one of which is a crazy big step-up over a rocky spillway with a cool walking bridge over it. And I tell him I don't plan on just doing a straight step-up; I'm going to be the first in the world to double-flip up a step-up! It would take a lot of preparation and funding but it's got Red Bull written all over it.

He digs the concept, but he doesn't seem to see what I see, and suggests I find a more picturesque *New Zealand* setting to do something similar on — as if step-ups like this are easy to find. He doesn't offer any support, but instead offers the job (paying peanuts) of taking branding and product to Red Bull-sponsored wake events. Then he asks if I know of any up-and-coming young riders that Red Bull could sponsor!

You're kidding, right?

'Look, BT,' I say, 'this might come across as cocky, but there's no one else — I'm it! There's not one up-and-coming rider who is at the level I was at their age. No one as dedicated and no one who will bring stunts like this.' I place my hand on my proposal.

'And I'm sorry but I'm not going to be your events guy, I'm 100 per cent riding-focused now,' I continue. 'I came here to get sponsored, because that's what I know I deserve.'

He apologises and says his hands are tied as Red Bull only want young talent that will last the distance.

I shake his hand and thank him for his time, because he actually seems like a nice guy, and he apologises again for not being able to do anything for me. I leave disappointed that the brand that most aligns with my goals and approach to the sport has turned me down.

●

Morgan and I continue to grow closer despite the imminent end date. In late January, Brant and I take Morgan and two of her friends on a roady up to the Ruakaka cable to take them wakeboarding. I'm really impressed by how quickly she picks it up — she listens to my tips and adjusts well. Her rural upbringing has made her a bit of a tomboy, keen to give everything a go and not afraid to get her hands dirty. She's such a welcome change from the girly-girl type who won't get in the water because it'll mess up her hair and ruin her fake tan.

Of course Brant and I put on a demo for the girls before we head home. On the drive Morgan is so full of energy and constantly smiling. She sings to every song that comes on the radio and she has such a lovely voice, but after several hours of it I'm finding it a bit much. 'Hey Morgan, *shuuuuuddup!*' Brant and I start repeating, only half joking.

After a stop-off at Tāwharanui beach for a swim, and another quick stop at a little-known freshwater swimming hole to wash the salt off, we arrive home, where Morgan and I collapse onto my bed, exhausted after a huge day. Thankfully we have just enough energy to make love.

I'm overcome with a feeling of contentment and comfort with Morgan in my arms. This is what I've been missing. It's not just about being physically attracted to someone, but becoming best friends as well, and Morgan has become one of my all-time favourite people. As I lie here gazing into her pretty blue eyes, I know I'm hooked. Even though I'm consciously trying to keep some distance, to keep that wall up around my heart, she's not just pulling the bricks off, she's bulldozing that wall down! I've fallen deeply in love with this girl but I don't dare tell her, because the more we build this up, the harder it's going to be when I leave. But I have no doubt she can see it in my eyes, just as I can see it in hers.

●

Brant and I take off for a weekend to the Hawke's Bay, where I clean up at an event called Cable vs Wake, combining boat riding and cable riding on a home-made 2.0 cable setup. A couple of weeks later we're at the North Island champs, where I take another pretty easy win. It's fun to be back among the wakeboard community here, a big fish in this small pond, but it's clear that I've well and truly outgrown the New Zealand competitive scene, which reaffirms my decision to move away. I know I'll miss coaching and inspiring the next wave of Kiwi wakeboarders, but if I can earn enough to scrape by in the US then it's better for my career to stay there.

The day after my 27th birthday, Morgan and I swing by and pick up Dad, whose birthday is three days after mine, and we spend the day with my sister and my two little nieces. Maisey gets cuter and cuter every time I see her. And Mila, now one month old, has grown slightly but is still just a very fragile tiny human.

Dad beams as he holds his new granddaughter in his arms. After I get in my cuddles, I hand Mila to Morgan, who gets in some cuddles of her own. She looks so comfortable holding her in her arms, and she's good with Maisey too, which I guess is not surprising since she hosts a kids' TV show. I catch myself imagining her as the mother of our children, but I quickly push the thought from my mind as I know that's unlikely.

On 25 February I receive the news I've been waiting for: my five-year performance visa has been approved. I email Paul, and book my one-way flight for late March.

I do another photo shoot for the agency, and a quick shoot for Susie — a freebie to repay her for all the free Pilates and help over the years. I'm happy with both shoots — I feel confident, strong and powerful; right now I'm in the best shape of my life.

•

At the end of February, Paul calls to ask if I can move my flight forward. MasterCraft are filming a campaign at Lake Ronix for their new boat and they want me there to ride behind it since I have no affiliation with any other boat companies. They'll pay me for it of course, but the kicker is that they're also bringing in the biggest legend in action sports, Travis Pastrana. Another bonus is that by getting to Orlando a little earlier I'd get to go to the Daytona Supercross, which is something I've always wanted to experience.

I can't pass this up, so I change my flights, and then have to break the news to Morgan. She's gutted, because now my flight leaves two days before her 24th birthday. My earlier departure also means I'll miss nationals — for the fourth time in five years. But Jeff can have this one (too).

Mum and Gordon have already left to go on a skiing holiday in Aspen. She's upset that this will be the first time she's not been able to give me a big hug goodbye, but she tells me they'll come to Florida later in the year.

Saying goodbye to Dad is tough. I feel guilty for leaving, especially since Alex is also living overseas, so that leaves just Monique to be there for him, but with her own family now she doesn't have a lot of spare time. I know she'll visit him and help when he needs it, but I feel bad about landing that whole responsibility on her.

I love my dad. He's the strongest and most resilient person I know, and has always been my biggest inspiration. Whenever I'm having a tough time I think of what he has been through and how strong he has been through it all, especially for us kids. I know he struggles to accept his disease, and has moments of frustration, sadness and anger, but he rarely shows it around us. He's doing the best with the hand he was dealt, and I could never ask for a better role-model. Before I leave, Dad gives me a leaving present that I know I'll use almost every day at Lake Ronix: a really nice tool belt and a top-quality hammer.

'Thanks, Dad,' I say. 'I'll definitely make good use of these!' I give him a big, long hug goodbye.

I'm home alone, so Morgan stays with me for the last few days. I have a small gathering of close friends to send me off, and it's a fun but pretty reserved night — a far cry from the raging leaving parties I used to throw. These are the people I'm going to miss the most, but we don't get all sentimental and emotional. We part ways with a hug and a 'See you soon, bro!' because I have no doubt several of them will come and visit, and I'll make a trip home in a year or two.

Morgan is the hardest to say goodbye to. We spend my last night in New Zealand together and I can't stop the tears when I have to say goodbye to this sweet, talented, kind, loving, beautiful soul. As much as I've tried to play this as a fun summer fling, after just three short months this incredible young woman has made a home for herself in my heart.

•

Pratt swoops me up from Orlando airport and we head straight to Lake Ronix. It's a chilly morning for Florida, and the trees are still bare, but this is the earliest in the year I've ever arrived. But damn it's so good to be back! Pratt welcomes me back by rolling up a perfectly crafted spliff.

I spend the first day running errands and settling back in — making sure my truck is running, my phone is activated and so on. I've even got a portable wifi device for the trailer. I send a picture of me and my trailer to Morgan to let her know I've arrived safely.

The next day we're straight into filming with the MasterCraft crew. They've brought Jeff Tremaine from Dickhouse Productions to film a fun video to launch the new boat. Parks and Rossi are here as well and it's rad to catch up with them. With the boat parked up on the beach we're about ready to get on the water. Over the off-season the team picked up a new young member who's an incredible rider and a fun person to be around. Italian rider Massi Piffaretti will add some European flair to the team. He shows up as we're getting on the boat.

Parks is standing beside the driver's seat and there's a Swiss ball sitting in front of him in the walkway to the bow. I go to grab it but he stops me. Massi walks up all full of energy. 'Buongiorno!' he says, standing in front of the bow. Suddenly, in typical Dickhouse fashion, Parks kicks the Swiss ball and smokes Massi in the face, almost knocking him off his feet. We all burst out laughing and Massi takes it like a champ.

I guess that sets the tone for the day. We get some filming done behind the boat, and I go for a quick shred to get some wakeboard footage before heading back in to pick up Travis Pastrana. He arrives late because he's hungover from a big night out with the MasterCraft guys, who took him out downtown. I introduce myself and ask if we can get a photo together. I don't want to fan-boy out but I can't miss this opportunity to snap a pic with one of my heroes. He graciously agrees and throws his signature thumbs-up as I extend my arm. He's in a moon boot, which is no surprise since he's often in the wars, but it's his other foot that draws the most attention today. While out drunk last night he took a dare to get a rather odd tattoo. So here he is with a pink unicorn driving a Trans-Am on the top of his foot.

We get back on the water and it's an awesome fun day. I dare to hope that it might lead to a sponsorship deal.

●

On Monday morning I'm welcomed back by Ruck and Chad, who join me in the trailer to catch up and fill me in on the off-season. Chad is excited to tell me about all the work they've been doing out at the back lake. After a while Pratt, Massi, Parks and Danny show up and we head around back to check it out. I'm blown away at the difference from when I left.

'Dudes, you guys have been busy!' I say.

From the top pool, on the right side they've started on the lower half of a long double-kink rail, and on the left there's a multi-stage platform that runs between the pool and the lake, with a kicker shaped into the lower section.

'We've been working really hard on this one,' Chad says enthusiastically, walking over with me to take a closer look. I walk around it and check out their handiwork.

'What do you think, bud? Not bad, huh?' says Chad proudly.

'I'm really impressed!' I say. Then, taking a closer look, I add, 'I'm impressed you managed to build this whole thing without using a square or anything!'

They all look at me.

'Huh? What do you mean?' Chad asks.

'I mean, I really am impressed with what you've done, but the problem I've just spotted is that none of the framing is square. Which means that when putting the PVC sheeting on, rather than it all matching up nicely, almost every single sheet of plastic will need to be cut to fit.'

I see the stoke drain from his face.

'Sorry, bro, I don't mean to rain on your parade. It's just that having to cut all that PVC means we can't reuse it for anything else. But we'll make it work,' I say, trying to soften the blow.

Chad starts laughing. 'Aaah shit! You're right. We clearly missed you, bud!'

We get to work finishing the framing and the rest of the new setup.

I've got a new project I'm excited to dig into. Danny has come to me with an idea for a new wall-ride that will already be more stable than last year's fail. It will start wider at the base and get gradually more vertical as it goes up, giving us more options when hitting it. He shows me a basic sketch, so I've got an idea of what he wants. I sketch it up so I can put together a materials list, price it and get the approval from the boss.

•

Chad and I take a day off to do a first aid course with the medic from the pro tour. With the responsibility of living on-site and managing this place, it feels appropriate. It's a very informative course and I like knowing that both Chad and I are better equipped for if (when) something goes wrong. Back at the lake we get the whole team together to pass on some of the basic techniques we've learnt.

The other medical thing that we discuss is a snakebite plan. While it's unlikely that anyone will be bitten by a dangerously venomous snake such as a coral snake, rattlesnakes and cottonmouth water-moccasins are not uncommon around here, and both have a nasty bite.

We discuss the idea of keeping antivenin on site but decide that a better snakebite plan is to know exactly where to go for professional help. And while Orlando Hospital is slightly closer, there's less traffic and fewer traffic lights between here and Titusville Hospital.

Aside from the snakes and alligators, the other creature we need to be aware of is the brown recluse spider. Every time I go to sit on the porta-potty I check under the seat! While a bite from one of these guys is not as threatening as a snakebite, it would still be rather unpleasant, especially in that vicinity.

I look into getting a gun to keep out here for the snakes and other critters, but I'm not legally able to get one. So Pratt leaves his .22-calibre AR-15 in my trailer for me, which I keep under my bed.

My trailer is still lacking furniture. I have a nice couch now, but I'm still using a wakeboard coffee table I made last year. So one evening, after everyone has gone home, I pull apart some packing pallets and knock together a rather nice coffee table and a matching bedside table that I'm pretty proud of.

Brett has also dropped off a set of cubby-hole shelves that's perfect to keep my clothes in, so the trailer is starting to look and feel a bit more homely. I still don't have full-time power or running water. Ferraro assures me they're working on getting a well drilled, a septic-tank system, and mains power out to the trailer.

I buy myself a mailbox that I erect at the roadside so I have an actual mailing address. This helps with getting my social security card sent out, along with my phone bills and bank statements. Bank of America turned down my credit card application so I just pay for everything on my New Zealand card, and keep a tally of the work-related purchases so Ronix can reimburse me.

•

Weekends are quiet at the lake, so this weekend Chad has invited me to stay at his place. The first thing I do is take a hot shower, which is a nice change from lake baths. I clearly needed it, judging from the brown water swirling down the drain.

I'm pumped for a night out downtown with Chad. We get pretty drunk and I flirt with a few girls but don't really get anywhere.

•

I've been hard at work with a crew on the wall-ride. We load the pontoon with each of the vertical sections, ferry them out and start erecting them on the base. I tack a couple of bracing lengths along the back, making sure they're all standing perfectly vertical. One of our younger riders, a kid named Jake, who's been out here most days after school, is helping me out. He helps me place a couple of lengths of 2 x 4 across the top of the wall, and I climb up, with my tool belt around my waist, and proceed to screw it in. I run out of screws in my pouch, so I turn to ask Jake to pass me up another handful, but he's already halfway up the wall with a handful ready for me. I don't even need to ask.

He's a pretty quiet kid, but the more I work with Jake, the more I'm starting to realise that he's one of the more onto-it and driven guys out here. I enjoy having him around to help. As time goes on, Jake becomes the next most reliable guy after Chad and Ruck, earning himself the nickname 'Ol' Reliable'.

The following day a truck arrives loaded with 3 x 3 x 3-foot steel-framed cubes, with the bottom halves boxed in and filled with foam. Bdahl tells me they need to be bolted together to make a big floating platform. He disappears and comes back with another truckload so there must be more than 50 of them in all. A few of us get to work.

Less than an hour later the truck is back with three huge bits of kit on the back. They're the three parts to the super-kicker that was at last year's Wake Open. Two more truckloads bring partially pre-built framing, and the last load has a rolled-up mat that must be about 5 metres wide and needs to be craned off!

This is a game-changer for Lake Ronix: we have all the parts to make a fucking mega-ramp! Ferraro mentioned that this might happen but I didn't want to get my hopes up. Now that it's here I'm super excited! Although rebuilding it will be a massive job, that's for sure.

•

I escape from the lake for the day to attend Shane Bonifay's birthday party on Clear Lake on 4 April. I've been so focused on work that it's so good to take a break and have a few drinks. As always, it's a party not to be missed, with loads of girls and good times, and a great chance to catch up with friends I haven't seen since I've been back.

I've been here for about a month now and I really miss Morgan. We've been keeping in touch, and any interactions I've had with girls over here so far have just made me miss and appreciate her more. One night I'm chatting with Morgan and we talk about the possibility of her coming to visit. I love the idea of that, but then she would leave again and we'd be back where we started. As much as it's sucks, we agree that it's probably not for the best.

•

It's all go with the mega-ramp build. Pat, Bdahl, Sam and several of their crew are working with us on piecing this monstrosity together. They pulled this thing apart so they know how to put it back together, so we just try to keep out of the way and help where we can. As it takes shape I realise it must be over 4 metres high and almost 20 metres long.

Some of Pat's guys have also been hard at work welding together the double-kink rail and a single pipe rail for the bi-level. I watch carefully, as welding is a skill I'm keen to learn. It's incredible to see what can be done with the right crew and machinery at hand.

•

Tonight is the premiere of a new wakeboard film called *Al Sur*. I'm gutted to arrive late but I catch the final section, which has to be some of the most mind-blowing riding by the legendary Randall Harris. He is known for going bigger than anyone.

After the film Andy Lazarus (Laz), an old-school rider and a friend of everyone in wakeboarding, grabs me and slingshots me into meeting some girls at the bar. There's one in particular he knows I'll be interested in, so he introduces a girl named Brandi. He's not wrong — she's an absolute stunner: black hair, dark brown eyes and cute freckles across her cheeks and nose. We get a drink and hit it off, so when it comes time for the next round I suggest we go to another bar to get away from the crowd. After another couple of drinks at a different bar we link back up with the others until the bars close at 2 a.m.

Brandi invites me back to her downtown Orlando apartment, where it doesn't take us long to get wrapped up in each other. It's dark in her room, but the downtown Orlando lights shine in through the blinds, casting bars of light across the bed as I explore her exquisite body. It's the first action I've had since getting back stateside, and we make a great team sexually. She's a handful, but I'm more than equal to the challenge.

•

I get back to the lake with a pep in my step, reinvigorated from Brandi's lovin'. Which is just as well because the team shoot starts in just a couple of weeks and there's a heap of work still to be done before then. Danny, Deano, Adam and Shota have not been here quite so much because Wake Games are coming up and they've been training at their home lakes. I should be doing the same, but there's just too much work to do. I squeeze in a few rides here and there, but only short runs where I can fit in four tricks before we turn around. It's good practice for squeezing in the manoeuvres but it's not exactly the quality of riding I should be getting.

When we break for lunch we generally retreat to my trailer to escape the heat and soak in some cool air-conditioning. I usually crank the generator late morning so it's nice and cool for when we need a break. We chip in and roll up a couple to pass around and relax before stepping back out into the heat to get back to work. Even though the park isn't quite finished, we still make time for a quick shred on the main cable, hitting the incline rail, double handrail and the kicker.

After everyone has left for the day, and it's dark out, I throw the generator and a work light in the back of my truck and drive around to the back. With most of the plastic sheeting on the bi-level we've been screwing it down to each beam, but with the framing skewed it's hard to work out exactly where each beam is. So I've come up with the ingenious idea to place the light under the setup shining upwards, which casts shadows of the framing through the plastic, revealing exactly the location of each beam. I spend an hour or so going over the whole thing, counter-sinking screws where needed. It's a little eerie being out there alone late at night, but the constant whirring of the generator drowns out any surrounding sounds so I just focus on getting the job done. The next day I make my way through under the platform and add braces under the unsupported seams. It's a lot of work that wouldn't have been needed if it was all built square, but regardless, it's good to get it finished.

The next evening I've invited Brandi to come here. I take her across the lake in the Malibu and park up on Wake Beach before wandering through to show her everything we've done out here. We're standing at the top of the almost-finished bi-level and we start making out with her leaning against the pipe rail. Part of me wants to fuck her right here to christen this new setup, but instead we christen the Malibu, then retreat back to rock the trailer for the rest of the night.

I'm attracted to Brandi, and our sexual chemistry is on point, but our next date kinda throws me off. We grab dinner and a few drinks, but I haven't had any income since getting here aside from the MasterCraft money and one of my monthly Ronix cheques. I'm still waiting for some expenses from the lake to be repaid. It feels shit to do so but I tell her I'm ballin' on a budget for now. So when she orders two whiskies that together cost more than my weekly food budget, I feel like she didn't quite grasp just how tight that budget is. Thankfully my card goes through, but, although we have another fun night together back in her apartment, I'm left feeling like this girl's tastes are a little out of my league for now. So that's the last I see of Brandi.

Besides, since coming back to the US I've started talking to Dawn again. We've kept in touch and even linked up several times over the years since we first met. I've always had a thing for her, and since she's recently broken up with her NFL player boyfriend and we've been chatting more and more. She's several states away in Oklahoma, but maybe there's a chance of us being together now that I'll be living in Florida full-time. We FaceTime and she sends me video messages as she's getting up early for work at the fitness studio she works at.

But I'm still a single man, so one night when I'm bored and lonely in the trailer I decide to try out this Tinder app that Jesse was using last year. I've scrolled through it a few times but never gave it much of a go. I extend my range so it reaches the University of Central Florida area and I make a few matches. But, while a few messages go back and forth, nothing really comes of it.

•

Wake Games kicks off the next day, so I'm out there early to join my main 'Mano' on the mic. I feel at home up on the stage with a mic in my hand — certainly more at home than on the water this weekend: I'm knocked out in the first round. I didn't really expect any different, since I haven't put any time into training behind the boat. While I'm here at Wake Games for the next few days, I've got a few of the guys working on the wall-ride back at Lake Ronix.

On the final day of Wake Games I'm on stage in between calling the semi-finals when I hear a familiar voice. I look behind me and it's Candice. She's with her new boyfriend, a guy I know well who works in the industry. I say hi to them both, shake his hand and give her a hug. She looks really good. I'm stoked that she seems to have found a good guy.

•

Back at Lake Ronix, with the team shoot starting next week, Paul has flown into town, along with the head product developers Jason, Scott and Ronzie. That evening it's just Paul and me left here at the back lake after I've finished bracing the last of the PVC seams.

'You want to christen it?' Paul asks.

'It would be wrong not to!' I reply, and grab my gear from the back of my truck. Paul drives for me as I cut laps and test out the new setup. Hopping from the top deck and catching the lower transition, then coming the other way, I use it to air back up into the pool. After a handful of laps I'm ready to test the long double-kink handrail as well, which gets my heart rate up and puts a big smile on my face. I know the gang will all be stoked to shred this setup tomorrow.

Paul, seeing my face, can't let me be the only one to have all the fun, so I take the controls and he borrows my gear. After he slips out and splashes into the lake at the bottom of the ramp I realise that although I've seen Paul ride before, I've never seen him on a setup like this. He waves that he's okay so I pull him up and towards the end of the lake. I slow him down on the way back up, as I know he's not going to clear the middle section of the ramp, and it'll be easier to ride through the transitions at a slower speed, but his balance is off and he slips out on the first kicker section and slams hard into the second incline.

He signals that he's okay but he's grabbing his shoulder and wincing as he stands up. I feel bad, but he assures me it's not my fault. His slam actually broke part of the setup, revealing a weak point where I must've missed a seam that needed bracing, so I fix that up the following morning. For the next little while Paul has his arm in a sling. Turns out he separated his AC joint.

•

For the next few days I split my time between riding, helping with the team shoot, and finishing off bits of work that still need doing. Pratt came to me a few days ago with an idea for another addition to the park. Rather than add that to my plate as well, I give him the reins, saying, 'Good idea, bro. You can take lead on this one — grab some of the guys and go for it!'

Next thing I know they've cut down two tall, skinny pine trees and they're using machetes to strip the bark from one side. Then, after driving some posts into a shallow patch under the cable, the trunks are lifted onto the posts and we've got a unique new kinked rooftop tree rail.

Meanwhile, Jake and I lifted each of the coping sections on top of the wall, slotted them together and screwed it all in place. Standing back on the beach, I'm immensely proud of the finished product. A 5-metre-high, 17-metre-long banked wall-ride, complete with a woodgrain finish accentuated by the white Ronix logo and matching white coping along the top. It's a thing of beauty . . . the biggest and best-looking thing I've ever built — the *pièce de résistance*!

We're all pumped to hit it, and also the mega-ramp. By late evening the ramp is anchored in place, so with the whole setup floodlit, I'm the test dummy. My heart is racing. I'm standing at the end of the pool, my feet in my bindings, hands gripping the handle as I visualise my line into the kicker. There are no previous attempts to go off to know how fast to go — this is the first time a mega-ramp has been hit with a step down, since we're taking off from an elevated pool, meaning the top of the kicker is slightly higher than the top of the landing.

With the entire team watching, I tell Dom, who is driving, just to send it full speed. But as I'm cutting at the kicker I can already tell it's too fast, so I soak it up with my knees and send a low flyer, slightly out of control but I just make the downslope of the landing. Everyone is cheering, and I'm stoked to get that first hit out of the way, but it felt super uncoordinated. I slow it down on the next one, and even more on the next, until after a few hits, when the speed is perfect, I launch a big indy guide and land smoothly. This is going to be a *whole* lot of fun — my mind is already buzzing with the possibilities of this new feature. Right now, the rest of the guys are already lining up to have a turn, and we session it into the night.

●

The following day we're shooting on the main beach park, including our first hits on the new wall-ride. The unit XL kicker is lined up at the far end of the wall, so it's set up on the right for a toeside approach. I'd prefer it was at the other end so it was on my heels, but I'll hit it regardless. It's daunting cutting hard and leaning over my toes while charging towards the kicker at a monstrosity of a wall, but I send the first one and catch the coping with a frontside lipslide, then rock back down the wall, exactly as it was intended.

The landing is hard, but I stick it and ride away, hearing Parks and Danny cheering from the shoreline. While Todd films from the side, and Bear shoots from end on, I continue to launch off my toes and the XL kicker sends me on the perfect trajectory to catch the coping. I decide to go for the biggest transfer to frontside boardslide I've ever done. On the first attempt I end up looping out a little and catch myself in almost a blunt slide. Thankfully the very tip of the tail of my board catches the coping and I'm able to save it and ride away.

On the third attempt I get the perfect takeoff and land in a super low crouched front boardslide that feels awesome at first — until suddenly my board grips on a dry patch and I'm ejected out the front. From 5 metres up I'd usually try to dive into the water to avoid getting hurt, but I know it's really shallow where I'm landing so I'm forced to spread out and take a full-on backflop. The slap of the water knocks the wind out of me, and it happens again when I hit the bottom. I really feel the hit that one delivered.

When I pop up, catching my breath, I wave to Danny and Parks, who call out to see if I'm okay. To show them how shallow it is where I crashed, I pull my board under me and stand up to reveal that it's only knee deep.

'*Oooohhh, dude! No waaay!*' I hear from the shore. I want to keep riding, because I was having so much fun, but that hit kicked my arse so I'm done. I'm feeling it on my back and in my ribs. Then I cough and spit blood onto the sand. *That's not ideal*, I think, realising my lungs must be bleeding slightly.

'That one's gonna hurt tomorrow!' I say to the guys who come over to check on me. I cough and spit again, this time there's less blood so I'm not overly concerned. My pain is eased when Bear comes over and shows me an incredible photo of me all pressed out on the tail on the very top of the wall. It's one of the coolest photos I've had taken of me, and I'm stoked it's on top of my pride and joy.

The shoot moves back to the mega-ramp in the late afternoon, so I spend some time stretching, then go back for more hits on the mega. I'm quite timid on my hits, focusing on big method grabs and various glides. Danny is the first to flip it when he sends a huge cab roll. Everyone loses it and cheers for him, then on the next hit he adds a 180 and takes it to mobe, but over-rotates it and ends up slamming his chest and face on the landing ramp. It's one of the heaviest crashes I've ever seen, but thankfully the landing mat has 10 centimetres of padding to absorb some of the impact, so we're all relieved to see him wave it off and he's okay.

Adam is sending it bigger than anyone else, Parks throws a sick half-cab front flip and Pratt is getting comfortable as well, pulling a half cab roll of his own.

We're all having a blast, and although I'm a bit slower starting than some of the others, I plan on grabbing hold of this new direction in the sport and running with it. I've accepted that I'm not going to be a top contender in the boat contests, because more and more young rippers are coming through and absolutely killing it. But this big-air shit — this is what I'm all about and I really feel like I could be the best in the world at this!

The team shoot continues for another couple of days before Paul and the other Ronix guys head back to Seattle.

•

A few days later we start on another super exciting project. One of the best filmmakers in the game, Sean Kilgus, is starting filming for a new movie featuring the best of the best in wake. Kilgus has come to Lake Ronix to scope out the new features so he knows what he's working with. He's even booked a helicopter and phantom camera that shoots super-slow-motion video. It's a big production and there's a lot to organise so I let him know I'm here to help make his job easier in any way I can. He calls me a few times leading up to the first shoot day — coordinating shoots has now become another part of my job.

Early on in the filming Dom has a heavy landing off the wall-ride and breaks his leg. I feel a little guilty since I built the thing, but we all know it comes with the territory. He's okay, but he broke it right below the head of the tibia, so he's done for the season. We're all gutted for him, especially since he's our best and most creative park rider. I know he's gotta be livid.

Kilgus has the helicopter here for the day. We're focusing on the back lake and Chad has brought over one of the XXL kickers that were used when the mega landing was on one level last year at Wake Open. He's placed it where we had his super-kicker last year for step-ups into the pool, only this kicker has slightly more boot to it. Chad starts by launching some huge glides that have him landing right on the very edge of the side of the pool. It looks like too much fun so I jump in on the session and we take turns.

After warming up, I throw a couple of tweaked-out tantrums and drop them to blind, which is scary when landing so close to the edge, but they feel good and I've got loads of time on them. So I pick up my balls and decide to huck a double. I've only tried a double tantrum once — in Penrith last year — and I got around but didn't land it. But I figure it can't be much different to a double toeside backroll. I cut hard at the XXL kicker and straighten out at the last second so I don't end up trimming the edge of the pool like Chad did, then tuck hard into the double. I hold on tight and wait till I feel the second flip rotate before looking to spot my landing, then I open up and land on my board! It's not a clean landing, but I got around!

While Kilgus films from above in the helicopter that's circling above the trees, on my third attempt I flip over the land gap, over the rails and stomp the piss out of my very first indy grabbed double tantrum. And it's up a step-up! Exactly as I predicted when pitching to Red Bull at the start of the year. The gang are hooting and hollering for me, which is an unreal feeling. We really have become like a family. No matter who is riding, if they land a new trick or something dope, we're all stoked for them.

And I'm pretty stoked to have landed my third variation of a double flip — the first in the world to do it up a step-up. But I'm not done yet. That double felt so easy, and with the time I had dropping out of it, I'm confident I can drop a backside 180 on the end and land another world first.

After landing another double, I pick my timing and huck the next one to blind, but with the edge of the pool just two feet away, fear of falling out the front and onto the side of the pool causes me to under-commit and fall over my heels. I try again, but by now I'm clearly getting over-confident. As I take off the top of the kicker, I hesitate and back out of the double, but I've already initiated it so I'm about to over-rotate. I pull on the rope and brace myself for what ends up being one of the heaviest back edges I've ever taken, in the shallow edge of the pool. I hit the bottom and feel my brain rattle against my skull, even through my helmet.

Moments later the chopper lands and Kilgus rushes over to me. I'm a bit dazed, but I'm still in one piece and nothing is broken.

With a mild concussion, I sit and watch as the guys session the mega-ramp while the chopper flies overhead. Just 20 minutes go by before I decide *Fuck it! I'm not missing out on this!*

I shake off the dizziness and join the queue to ride. And with the help of a mild concussion I pick up the guts to flip the mega-ramp for the first time. *Today is a good day!*

•

A 10-day break in filming gives me a chance to chip away at a few jobs around the place. I've noticed that there's an issue with the person driving the cable seeing the rider if they fall at the bottom of the bi-level, so I spend the evening knocking together a 2.5-metre-tall elevated chair for them.

I've kept in touch with Morgan since getting here, but as time has gone on our contact has become less frequent. Dawn and I, on the other hand, have been speaking almost every day and I can't wait to finally see her in person. Our morning FaceTime sessions have me feeling the love for this girl I've known for seven years now.

I've been invited to host the Collegiate Wakeboard Nationals in Shreveport, Louisiana. I ride for some local media on Red River, which winds right through the city centre. I'm a little freaked out after watching a pest-control guy pull at least 10 snakes out of the water from around the dock, but it's fun to put on a display for the cameras, with the goal of attracting more spectators over the next few days of competition.

I'm stoked to run into a couple of guys from CBK here, so we all head out to dinner at Hooters. It wouldn't be a Hooters dinner without pulling some digits from a cute waitress. We're staying in the Margaritaville hotel and casino, so naturally I try my hand at the blackjack table. I haven't been in a casino since the Aussie pro tour in Penrith where I came out on top, but this isn't the case this time around — I blow a couple hundred of the grand I'm being paid for this event. Thankfully I have the smarts to get out before I blow it all.

Competition kicks off on the Friday. Being invited to host this event on my own is an honour and it reinforces to me that I'm a good MC. I'm treated like a bit of a celebrity guest and I receive loads of compliments on both my commentary and my playlist, since I'm doubling as the DJ. I'm jamming my favourite tunes from back home and Fat Freddy's Drop seem to be a real hit, and a cute little brunette bundle of energy starts dancing in front of the speakers beside my tent, and asks me about the music. Others join her, meaning I've turned this event into a party!

Once the first day of competition is done, I retreat back to my hotel room to rest, shower up and get ready for a big night. The after-party is completely dead when we arrive so we bounce around a few bars before heading back later on. I've taken a liking to the local Red Bull rep, who's a fiery redhead. We bar-hop together, and I can tell she likes me but she's playing hard to get. After midnight the after-party is packed with competitors and locals all having a great time. The riders keep buying me drinks, so I'm well on my way and feeling a great buzz.

While mingling and dancing with my newfound friends, I spot a girl dancing and twirling a couple of light balls around like a little festival fairy. It's the little bundle of energy from the contest earlier today. With many glasses of liquid confidence on board I walk straight up and start dancing with her.

'I knew I'd find you here!' she says with a sweet smile. I know I'm taking this girl home tonight. The bartender pours me a whisky and dry, and mixes up her cocktail. After she takes her first sip, I steal the cherries from the top of her glass and drop the cheesy line: 'I hope you don't mind, but I'm taking your cherry'. A mischievous grin spreads across her face. We practically scull our drinks and can't get out of here fast enough!

Back at her place it's all on. She's an absolute pocket rocket and our energy together is like nothing else. I'm sitting up as she's straddling me and we're moving our hips in perfect rhythm. I stop and look her in the eyes and say, 'Hold on, hold on, pause for a second.' Then I hold out my hand and say, 'Hi, I'm Brad.'

'I'm Hali,' she replies giggling, and shakes my hand.

Then we're back into it. By the end we're both so blown away by the fireworks that there's nothing else to do but high-five each other and laugh.

The thing about the Collegiate Nationals is that they basically encourage partying, because the next day's first event isn't scheduled to start until noon, which is just as well. Hali drops me off just in time to get on the mic and amplify my croaky voice for everyone to hear and know that I sent it last night. But I think that's how most of the competitors are feeling today. My voice recovers as the day goes on and the competitors give their all on the water. I even get out there to put on a demo, which goes surprisingly well considering how I feel.

•

I arrive back home to the welcome quiet and solitude of my trailer. We're filming again in two days, so I enjoy the break. But the solitude also brings a feeling of loneliness so I message Dawn to see what she's up to. I don't feel bad about sleeping with Hali because it was just a weekend fling. The way I see it, I'm going to live like I'm single until Dawn and I meet up again and decide whether this is going anywhere — and I hope it does!

The next day Kilgus calls me in a panic. 'Brad, my team and I will be there early tomorrow. It's the last day I've got the helicopter coming but I'm worried about the weather, and how I'm going to manage the riders — who rides when, how many people we have on each feature. I don't know the best way to organise this.' The stress is clear in his voice. I tell him I'll call him back with a plan, which I do 30 minutes later. He's hugely relieved.

It all starts out according to plan. I drive the chase jet-ski to get Kilgus and his camera as close as possible to the boys riding Pratt's tree rail. When we move over to the back lake for the handrail session, I sit out and do what I can to help make it run smoothly. I'm confident on rails, but I'm not as strong as some of the others are. On the wall-ride, Deano has the kicker set up on the opposite end to the last time I hit it, so I'm excited to hit it on my heels. But I struggle — every time I transfer up and drop off the end, I land like a ton of bricks. I figure the wall must be ever so slightly angled towards the cable heading this way, which means less line tension as I land. Deano is struggling to get a clean landing as well. By the end of the session my back ankle is wrecked.

I sit on the beach looking over the lake and feeling sorry for myself. My ankle's killing me, and I'm pissed off because I think I'm going to have to sit out the mega-ramp session. My teammates have already headed over to the back lake, and the chopper is whirring overhead, ready to capture them in action. I should be there with them.

I've already amped myself up to throw my first double tantrum over the mega-ramp. It would be risky — by far the scariest trick I've ever done — but it would be worth it if I pulled it off. But instead I've got a swollen ankle.

Still fuming, I hobble back to my trailer and put my feet up on the coffee table. I look angrily at my ankle. Then I make a decision.

'You know what? Fuck it!' I say out loud. 'I'm not letting this stop me!'

I get up and jump in my truck, then race to the back lake. I limp up to the others, wearing my vest, knee brace and helmet, board tucked under my arm, and join the queue. Above us, the film crew circles in the helicopter, rotor buzzing.

Finally it's my turn. I take a warm-up run first, running through several indy tantrums in a row. I'm both terrified and excited, working up the nerve to throw the double, and each warm-up hit I tuck in my back knee — even though it hurts my ankle — to make it at least visually pleasing. By now it's the end of the day and the sun is low in the sky. I'm the only one left riding. Ruck is driving the cable for me, while the others watch from the beach and two more camera operators shoot from the ground by the pool.

Okay, I tell myself. *I'm ready.*

But next time around I back out and open up instantly. I do the same thing again . . . and again. Each time, I signal up to Kilgus in the chopper that I'm going double on the next one.

'This one!' I say out loud, revving myself up.

I edge hard at the kicker and . . . '*Fuuuccck!*' I yell, after backing out yet again.

Just one more! I indicate to the chopper. I feel bad for wasting Kilgus's time, because I know hiring a helicopter isn't cheap. But as Ruck switches the cable direction and I turn around for my last try, the chopper flies off into the distance.

'*Noooooo!* Come back!' I beg, even though I know he can't hear me.

When I get back up to the starting point my ankle is killing me but I know I'm ready. It doesn't matter that Kilgus isn't filming any more. I'm doing this now, while I'm feeling it. After checking to make sure the camera operators are still beside the pool, I give the nod to Ruck and charge at the kicker. This time I hold the grab. I stay tucked and, after feeling the second flip come around, I spot the landing and ride away. It's not a clean landing so I make a big splash, but I pop up out of the water instantly and ride down to the end of the lake.

On the beach the guys are all cheering like crazy. Ruck is so stoked he forgets to turn the cable around to bring me back. So I just ride straight up onto the beach, then take my board off and start carrying my gear towards my truck. I'm still realising what just happened. I did it! The first ever double tantrum over the mega-ramp! And I rode away on my first try. I can't believe it.

Seconds later, I head back to my friends. They're still losing their minds over what they just witnessed. Their stoke for me is so real, so raw. Deano runs up and gives me a big hug, slaps me on the back in celebration, followed closely by the rest of the gang.

What a moment. This is the shit I live for.

•

While my ankle is recovering, I manage to detour off a Ronix promo event in Kansas City, taking a Greyhound bus on an overnight ride to Oklahoma to see Dawn.

I get off the bus at about 5.30 a.m., and a few minutes later Dawn pulls up in her car and gives me a big hug. It feels so good to have her in my arms again, and I'm looking forward to spending the next three days with her. She drives us back to her place, where I dump my gear and plonk myself down on her couch. She packs a bong — she loves to wake and bake to start the day. She's leaving for work soon, and I plan on going to sleep while she's gone, since I got barely any sleep on the bus.

We're standing in the kitchen as she's about to leave and I pull her in towards me and plant a long overdue kiss on her lips. She kisses me back before heading out the door. After taking a nap I work on my foot a little, then hang out with her two dogs, Willy and Dayday, while sending out emails chasing new sponsorship opportunities.

When Dawn returns we hang out by the pool and swim. She looks so damn good in a bikini! She has the most stunning facial features, with her alluring blue eyes and perfectly sculpted bone structure. Plus she's sweet and way too cool for me, so I feel incredibly lucky that she has strong feelings for me too. After going out for dinner, we chill on the couch and watch TV with her roommate.

When we finally get into bed, I'm excited to finally get intimate with this incredible woman. But I'm surprised that she's not more forthcoming. She turns and faces away from me at first, so I wonder if she's got her hesitations, but I cuddle in behind her and it only takes kissing her neck and lightly running my fingers over her skin for her to turn over and start passionately kissing me. It's different to the wild and free fucking we shared seven years ago — more intimate, more connected, more like passionate lovemaking.

We make love again several times the next night, and I'm gutted to be leaving the next day. She's only working in the morning so while she's out, I hide some notes around the house for her to find when I'm gone. Like under the covers of her bed: 'Where I'd rather be.' Next I tuck one inside the roll of toilet paper in the bathroom, a couple of layers in: 'Oh shit! Sorry to interrupt, but I just wanted to say I miss you!' The last one I place in the nozzle of her hairdryer, folded in a way that it'll shoot out of the end as soon as she turns it on: 'You blow me away!' Although I end up telling her about that one, just in case it doesn't fly out and catches fire instead.

We head out for lunch on the way to the airport, and our waitress exclaims, 'Oh my god, you're the most beautiful couple ever!' We smile at each other because we both love the idea of being a couple, but we haven't really discussed it. I just wanted to have a good time with her while I'm here.

I give her a big kiss goodbye, and tell her I'll see her very soon. I want to get her down to Orlando to stay for a little while. I'd love it if she would consider moving down to be with me because, well, I could never live in Oklahoma.

•

Parks, Pratt and I have been invited to compete in a big-air event in Germany towards the end of the month. It's called Red Bull Rising High, and they're setting up the world's only other mega-ramp for it. With my new trick in my arsenal, I'm going there to win.

The day before I'm due to fly out to Düsseldorf, Kilgus returns to try to capture me doing the double tantrum over the mega-ramp. I was gutted that he hadn't filmed it from the chopper the first time, and when we reviewed the footage from the poolside cameras we decided it would be worth trying again, to try to get it with a clean landing.

My ankle is feeling much better so I'm ready — but I'm still nervous, having only ever landed the trick once before. My heart is racing and I feel the fear rising inside me. It's trying to tell me not to go, not to do it. But the possibilities that the trick will open up for my career far outweigh any fear of injury.

I need this, I think. *Let's do it!*

I wave to check that Kilgus is ready. By now I've gone over the double tantrum so many times in my mind's eye that although I've only actually landed it once for real, I've done it thousands of times in my head. After several warm-up indy tantrums, I commit to the double. It's nerve-racking but this time I don't pull out. I'm relieved to get through both flips and ride away.

That's that out of the way, I think. *Now it's time to nail the perfect landing.*

My confidence is brimming. It takes several more goes but finally I get that sweet, sweet feeling of the buttery-smooth, near-perfect landing I'm looking for. As I ride away I throw up a shaka and I see Kilgus with his hands in the air. He got the shot!

When he shows me the footage, it's a thing of beauty. As I go into the second flip I must be about 4 metres above the top of the landing. I've never gone so big.

I'm well and truly hooked on this big-air shit. And I plan to keep pushing the sport in this exciting new direction.

•

After 13 hours of travel I land in Düsseldorf and am picked up by an event helper, who drives me out to Hamm, the small city where the event will take place.

When we pull up and I lay eyes on the mega-ramp setup, I'm hit with an instant rush of excitement. It's very similar to the one at Lake Ronix, except the landing is slightly longer and mellower. There are two kickers angled towards each other in the middle of the small run-in lake, which is just slightly shorter than ours, and they've also got two cables set up — one on either side, so the landing is in the middle. Unlike our one-sided setup, where the cable is in the centre and the landing off to the side, this setup gives more options. It suits both regular and goofy riders, and works for heelside, toeside and switch hits as well.

It's colder here than I expected, especially after Florida's balmy sunshine. I'm glad I brought my wetsuit. There are four days of practice before the main event on Sunday, and we've been organised into session teams. When it's my team's turn, it only takes me a couple of warm-up hits before I throw a double tantrum. It feels super easy on this setup. I get a few under my belt, then I switch to the other cable to try another new trick.

No one has hit this thing toeside yet — and I don't blame them. With such a short run-in, it's really hard to get a good strong edge on the toes. But I'm going to do it. I've got this new 'fuck it, let's go' mentality towards my riding now, as it seems like the only way I'm going to get anywhere. No risk, no reward, as they say. On my first hit, I loop out and almost get worked. But the landing ramp provides a pretty gentle slide to crash down. Second time, I launch off the top of the kicker and huck a toeside indy double backroll, and just manage to catch the downside of the landing ramp and ride away cleanly, my heart absolutely racing. Another world first!

As I watch the rest of the guys practising, I see I'm not the only one here with a double in my arsenal. A few riders can do double half cab rolls, but I'm the only one with the two double-flip variations. That gives me a bit of an advantage.

By the final practice day I'm dialling in double tantrums. I've got them super consistent, and can throw and land them every time. Parks and another mate, Brenton Priestley, are watching me from beside the takeoff kickers. As I'm between hits, they start calling out to me.

'Take it to blind!' Parks yells. 'You've got it, Shmeez!'

'Get it, bud!' Brenton chips in. 'You've got loads of time!'

Fuck it, I think. I've had it in the back of my mind, but with these guys amping me up I decide to go for it. I focus my gaze on the kicker in front of me, then nod to the cable operator that I'm ready. I charge hard, and as I'm coming out of the second flip I spot the landing. I still have loads of time so I tug on the handle, pull it in to my lower back and rotate into a backside 180. I land on my board, surprising myself, but slip out over my heels, and slide down the landing on my butt. I can't believe I got so close to an NBD (never been done) trick on my first attempt!

All the riders who saw me are buzzing when I get back to the starting dock, as am I. Some are running over with cameras to film my next attempt, and Parks has jumped on a camera crew's boat to get a better angle next time. My confidence is through the roof after getting so close to pulling off such a frightening trick on my first try. I'm ready to do this! But on the next few attempts I fall exactly the same way.

'You're sending it too big,' Brenton points out. 'It's making the landing harder.'

Next time I don't cut quite as hard. It means I won't travel quite as far, but I spring hard with my legs as I'm riding up the kicker so I still have plenty of time in the air.

I tuck . . .

First flip . . .

Second flip . . .

I spot the landing and pull it around to blind . . .

I'm focusing hard on getting over my toes so I don't slip out again . . .

And next thing I know, I'm riding away off the end of the landing with my fist up in the air in celebration. I can't believe it!

I can hear cheering from all around. Parks's voice is the loudest since he's the closest to me. '*Yeeeaaaaahhhh, Smeeeeeeleeeee!*' he's calling.

Did that just happen?

I just landed the world's first double tantrum to blind! And it's a true first: no one has ever done this trick anywhere. Not behind a boat, not off a kicker, not on a mega-ramp. I'm ecstatic.

As the cable turns around, I ride back past Parks and he's still losing his mind over it.

I whip back towards the starting dock and use the end of the pool to air out and land, sliding along the pebble pathway towards the riders' tent. I untie my bindings, step out of my board and turn to face the riders who are coming over to high-five and congratulate me. Others are standing by and clapping, possibly unsure whether to be stoked or gutted.

Parks runs up and gives me a big hug, then shows me the footage on his phone. I'm still in a state of disbelief, but seeing it with my own eyes seals it.

'That . . . just . . . happened!' Parks says.

I give him a big high-five. Nothing could ever top this!

That trick is in line to win me the award I've aspired to my entire wakeboarding life: *Wakeboarding Magazine*'s Trick of the Year. Surely, sponsorship and funding would come along with that. Surely I'd get to reap the rewards of the risk I just took. Finally the financial struggle would be eased and I might actually get to earn a living from the career I've dedicated more than half my life to.

I take a moment to appreciate how far I've come.

•

As soon as I've changed into my dry clothes, I ring Paul to tell him the news.

'No way! For real?!' He asks eagerly.

'Double tantrum to blind — I just stomped the absolute piss out of it. *Yeeheeeew!*'

'*Duuuuude!* That's seriously insane, Brad! Unreal! Congratulations, my friend!'

Then he asks, 'So did you win?'

'The contest is tomorrow. This was just a practice run, but Parks shot it on his phone. I'll get him to send it to you.'

I'm on cloud nine for the rest of the day, and I go to sleep with all the confidence in the world that I'll take out the event tomorrow.

The next morning we have a rider briefing — the format and how the judging will work. They've talked to some of the riders and decided it'll be a combination of best trick and style trick, which is a 360 or less with the focus on grabs and making it look as stylish as possible.

Huh? Style trick? When was that ever part of it? I'm confused, and can't help but think that after yesterday, some of the influential riders must've talked them into including a style trick into the format. For weeks leading up to this event I've been emailing the organisers to find out the format will be, and all I've ever got back was that they were encouraging the biggest, baddest tricks — 'We really want to see a triple go down.'

'You'll get seven hits each in the first round. Two will count for best trick, and one for the style trick,' we're now told. 'Out of the starting 17 riders, only six will advance to the final. In the final you'll get five tricks — one will count as best trick, and one as style trick. The two will be combined to give your total score.'

I'm fuming that we're only just being told this now, after three days of practice. I should've practised some style tricks, but what can I do about it now?

I warm up with a big tuck knee tantrum, then boost a huge indy double tantrum, then move across and land a toeside double backroll for my two best tricks. I then launch a big method grab as my style trick. I try to take one to blind, but it takes me down. Nevertheless, I win my heat and claim one of the spots in the final, where I'm up against Daniel Grant, Nico von Lerchenfeld, Felix Georgii, Chris O'Shea (Chris-O) and Dominik Gührs.

I start with a double tantrum, then drop a toeside double backroll, since I'm not sure which one they'll score higher. Then, after sending a large method as my style trick, I set my focus on the double tantrum to blind. Unfortunately on both attempts I slip out over my heels and end up sliding on my butt and splashing into the lake.

I'm hoping my other tricks will still be enough but the other guys killed it as well, so it's down to what the judges liked the most. Dominik landed a backside 900; Daniel a front 900, going bigger than anyone; and Nico had a sick grabbed backside 720. And they all had solid style tricks.

I feel like I'm for sure on the podium, but when the top three are announced I don't hear my name. Daniel gets third, Nico second, and Dominik takes the top spot.

I'm not happy. I really think the way the format and judging criteria were changed at the last minute was off, and I tell them so. Fourth place gives me a measly $500 in prize money, which is less than it cost to get here.

After having one of the most incredible days of my life yesterday, it's a bitter pill to swallow.

•

The day before I fly to California for the next pro tour stop, I get started on my new project: a three-storey tiki tower, right by the bi-level. A bunch of old telephone poles have been dropped off and we've got a bobcat on site with an auger attachment. I sketched this up a few weeks ago and Paul loved the idea. So after I mark out where each pole will go, I drill holes 2 metres deep into the beach, then, with the help of Todd and Pratt, I lift each pole into place with the bobcat. I have them all leaning slightly towards the middle, then bury their bases. Standing back I can already see how epic this tower is going to be! I'm excited to get to work on it when I'm back from Cali.

Before I fly out, Dawn and I have our regular morning FaceTime catchup. I ask her if she'll visit me in Orlando, which leads to us talking about our possible future together. We both love each other but she tells me she just got out of a relationship where she and her boyfriend lived in different states, and she really doesn't want to do it again. Then she tells me she's not interested in moving to Florida either, so that leaves us in a bit of a shitty position. We finish the call having decided there's no future for us right now. I'm upset, but I've kept myself at enough of a distance that I'm not devastated.

On my way up to San Francisco I get in touch with Lindsay, who I met up here last year. We have an excellent night that helps get Dawn out of my system.

There's a buzz among the athletes about my new trick, and it's a gratifying feeling to have such respect from my peers. I'm stoked to see Jeff too — it's been a while. After neither of us makes it straight through from the first round, we're now matched up in round two, from which only two riders advance. Since I wasn't able to compete against him at the last New Zealand nationals, this is like our own little competition. But that fucker just beats me again! Thankfully we both claim an advancing spot and move on to the finals day.

The following day Jeff and I are in different heats. I ride well, but I take a fall and end up third in my heat. Jeff bombs. So although Jeff won the battle yesterday, I won the war with a ninth-equal finish overall, to his 20th equal. It's my best pro tour result to date. Jeff gives me shit, as he does so well: the friendly rivalry continues.

THIRTEEN: DREAM TO NIGHTMARE

It's Sunday morning, 6 July 2014, and I've just woken up. I look at my watch: 6.30 a.m. I've never been an early riser — not unless I have to be on the water to capture that golden morning light for a photo shoot. But since I moved to Lake Ronix in Florida, I've started to form a new habit: I wake up with the sun, so I can get my day started early and make the most of it before it gets too hot.

I kick off the covers and, still half asleep, sit up and plant my feet on the floor. There's a slight chill in the air from the air-conditioning that was running throughout the night. It's not running now, though — my generator must've run out of gas in the early hours. That's what happens most nights.

I grab a towel and — since I'm still in my board shorts from yesterday — I'm good to go. I basically live in board shorts all day long. I open the front door and step out into a perfect Lake Ronix morning. The air feels cool for a Florida morning at this time of year, but warmer than my air-conditioned trailer. The sun has only just risen above the horizon and the birds are just starting to sing their morning songs.

I'm in love with the mornings here: the peace and tranquillity, the fragrance of the surrounding plants and trees, the way the mist rises from the mirrored surface of the lake, telling me that the water is still warm from yesterday.

In a few steps I'm sinking my toes into the soft white sand of the main beach. I sit down on the bench seat I built last summer and look across to the tiki hut, placed perfectly in the middle of the palm-fringed beach, which wraps around the lake. I gaze out across the calm lake, and all I can think is, *I fucking love this place! I'm exactly where I'm supposed to be.*

I'm also super proud to call this my back yard. It's taken me a long time to get to this point. Years of hard work and sacrifice. Years of riding for sponsors with scant recompense, thousands of dollars of debt ticked up with each year travelling to Orlando in pursuit of the pro tour and chasing my dreams. My pride comes from knowing that I've been knocked down with countless injuries, only to bounce back even more motivated than before.

But mostly, I'm proud of all of the work I've put into making Lake Ronix what it is today. I still don't have much money, I don't have a fancy car or a big house, but I've found my own little paradise.

●

My focus snaps back into the present moment. Something has caught my eye — a movement, out in the middle of the lake. I've been living here long enough to become pretty familiar with the wildlife and can identify most creatures by their tracks or from a partial glimpse at a distance. I instantly know what's in the water: one of our resident alligators out for a morning cruise.

We have a few gators in the lake and a couple of them are getting big enough to be concerning, but for all my time on the water I've only seen a small one up close. I watch the creature make its way across the lake, cutting a line across the mirrored surface like a diamond cutting glass, only the top of its head and the end of its snout visible. From that I can tell that it's about 2 metres long. Thankfully it's not close enough to disturb my morning rinse so I stand up, drop my shorts and dive into the lake.

Before we came along, Lake Ronix was a sand and dirt mine, so the edge of the lake drops off really fast, meaning I can dive nice and deep from the beach. This is great because it's not until I get a few feet down, where the water is much cooler, that I feel refreshed. The downside is that you can't see the bottom. Even though I know that one of the alligators is over in the middle of the lake, I never know where the others are.

I get back out pretty quickly, grab my soap to give myself a quick scrub, then shampoo my hair. Then I dive back in for a rinse. I use as little soap and shampoo as possible, conscious of their impact on the environment.

●

The first car rolls past my trailer, closely followed by a couple more. Pretty soon the gang's all here: Austin Pratt, Dean Smith, Massi Piffaretti, Spencer Norris and myself. Chad Sharpe messages to say he's running a bit late. Spence is going to be the man behind the camera.

I throw my board, vest, knee brace and helmet in the back of my 95 Tahoe and we head for the back lake. The road around the lake is mainly dirt and soft sand and the Tahoe is an absolute beast for getting through the difficult terrain.

Pratt starts up the big industrial generator to power the System 2.0 cable system. Meanwhile, I fire up the small generator that runs the pumps that spray water down the entire surface of the landing, providing a slick surface for us.

Dean and I get ourselves ready to ride and quickly make sure the kicker is sitting at the right angle and in the correct position in the front left corner of the pool. I give it a quick splash of water so it's not dry and grippy for the first hit. The kicker is a nice, poppy ramp that I made earlier this summer, replicating the Unit XL kicker we have under the main cable, which is everyone's favourite-shaped kicker — not too big but with a nice smooth transition that sends the rider as big as they want to go, based on how hard they cut at it.

The plan is for Dean and I to alternate turns to start out with, then Pratt, Massi and Chad will tag in as we finish up. When planning this shoot I had to make sure Chad was going to be here, because he and I recently did a CPR course specific to handling emergency situations in the water, and since he's the only other guy on the team to have completed the course, I like to have him here when I hit the mega-ramp.

I put my life vest on and throw a T-shirt over the top, then I strap my knee brace tightly onto my left knee. A few jump squats followed by some shoulder rotations and I'm ready to go. I step into my boots and tighten the laces so I'm locked in tight. I can feel my legs shaking a little from the nerves that have somehow pushed through my calm confidence. Helmet on and clip the buckle, a few deep breaths with a positive affirmation between each: *You've got this — I've fucking got this!*

Dean passes me the handle while I'm visualising my line into the kicker. I nod to Massi at the controls, then jump forward, put my board to the water and I'm away, accelerating quickly down the pool to approximately 34 kph with just a second or two to pick my moment to start cutting across on my heelside edge towards the kicker: too early and I won't have enough speed to make it over the knuckle of the landing ramp; too late and I'll risk not being able to make it across to the kicker.

I love the sound of my board edging across the glass-calm water — *sssssshhhhhhhhhh* — as I lean back hard against the rope to take a nice strong edge at the kicker. From here it's all about split-second timing as I hit the kicker. I stand tall and get a nice 'boot' up into the air, instantly tucking myself into a tantrum and reaching for an indy grab. Since this is my first hit of the day, I sail through the air doing a nice big and slow indy tantrum. I spot my landing and stomp my board down solidly on the landing ramp. Gliding across the water back to the starting zone, I pass the handle off to Dean for his turn.

'Yeah, mate!' he says, grabbing the handle.

'Get it, bud!' I reply enthusiastically.

While Deano has his warm-up hit, I focus on my next run. Now that I've done my warm-up indy tantrum, it's time to step things up a notch and go for the double. Dean comes flying back and I'm up again. My heart is racing. I increase my edge slightly and as I launch off the kicker I tuck hard, grab my board and hold on tight. Staying tucked, I commit to the double flip and wait for my moment to spot the landing. I land a bit too crouched, which causes me to sketch out on the transition from the landing ramp to the lake.

I still manage to ride away from this one, but I know that won't be a usable trick for *Prime*. Dean is aiming to get a big, grabbed backside 720 over the mega. On his next hit he goes for it, but backs out at 540, and it's not a clean landing.

We go a few more rounds, neither of us quite getting the clean landings we're after. That's the nature of it — some days you're on, some days you're not.

I finally get a good indy double tantrum — not perfect, but good enough for me to feel ready to start adding the late backside 180 to land blind. I jump back onto the water, take a hard edge at the kicker, feel the upward punch as I take off and tuck into the double flip.

This time as I spot the landing, I pull the handle behind my front hip and place it in the small of my back, causing me to rotate into a backside 180. I land blind with my board on the ramp, but with my weight too much over my heels, causing me to fall backwards. I crash into the water and come up to hear cheering from the guys. I look over to Spence pumping his fist in the air.

Dean and I have been riding for about 20 minutes now and I'm starting to feel a little fatigued. Dean must be too, as he decides he's done for the morning.

I'm going to give it one more go. I crouch down and give myself a pep talk. *Come on, Brad, you can do this! You've done it before, you can do it again!*

From behind me I hear a 'Yeah, B-rad!' I turn around to see Pratt getting ready beside his truck. I throw up a shaka and then turn back to focus on the kicker.

I edge hard, take off the ramp, tuck, grab, count the flips in my head — one, two, spot the landing, pull it to blind and stomp it on the landing ramp. The hand behind my back is squeezing the handle as I ride blind to the bottom of the ramp and reach the water. The moment my board hits the water I feel my legs buckle a little from the impact.

Noooooo! I scream internally as I feel myself falling backwards — it's all happening in slow-motion. I give everything to hang on but it's hopeless. I crash on my back into the water — again!

'*Grrrrrrraaaaaaaahhhhhh!*' I yell as I surface.

'What the fuck! That was *so fucking close!*' I hear Massi yell from the tower.

'You've got this, B-rad!' Chad calls out from his seat on the beach, where he and Dean are watching.

'Next one!' I tell them.

I get pulled back up to the starting point. My elbow is bleeding, my muscles ache, but my heart is racing and adrenalin is coursing through my veins. *This is the shit I live for!* I don't mind the pain of minor bumps and bruises, and I love the feeling of crashing, coming up out of the water and shaking it off. It makes me feel alive! These moments of psyching myself up before trying something crazy, something risky — they are what really gets my adrenalin pumping.

I run a quick diagnostic in my head of what I'm doing wrong, then calculate what tweaks I need to make to land this next one. To land a little more over my toes I need to either go slightly bigger, or rotate slightly faster, or wait a split-second longer before I let go of the grab — or a combination of the above.

I wipe the water from my eyes, shake out my arms, suck in a few deep breaths and give the signal that I'm ready. I accelerate down the pool and wait a touch longer before starting my edge at the kicker. I lean hard, feeling the tension of the rope through my arms. I hit the kicker and stand up tall, instantly tucking into the flip. But right away it feels wrong, I don't know exactly why, but I make the split-second decision to back out, just as I have done multiple times before. I release the grab, open my body right up to slow my rotation and do just a single flip. But as I open up and look down at the landing ramp below, only two words come to mind: *OHH FUCK!* I've gone too big. The combination of the slightly later and harder edge, along with standing taller off the kicker, has sent me maybe 1.5 metres higher. I have also untucked a split-second too late.

I'm at the peak of my jump, about 4.5 metres above the landing ramp, still rotating slowly and starting to go into the second flip, but I've already opened up so there's no way to complete it, and there's no stopping the rotation. I know for sure I'm going to land on either my back or my head.

Everything feels like it's going in slow-motion, like I have time to think and react. So as I'm falling towards the landing I pull hard on the handle to try to save it, but in doing this I alter my axis of rotation, from flipping backward to spinning in a backside rotation — similar to what I intended to do at the end of the double flip to take it to blind, only this time I'm completely out of control. I rotate a full backside 270 and have to loop the handle up above my head to avoid getting wrapped up in the rope.

I turn my head to see the dark grey of the landing ramp coming at me fast. I'm tumbling forward but I just manage to touch my board down onto the mat. I have just a split-second to try to alter the way I hit the ramp, and because I'm tumbling forward I choose a break-fall, a pretty common manoeuvre in martial arts like judo. Basically you absorb a forward fall by tucking your head and shoulders under in a forward roll.

I tuck my head under but it's too late . . . *BAM!* The back of my head and top of my shoulders slam into the ramp, forcing my head down into my chest. Everything goes black.

•

I open my eyes and I'm looking up at the sky, the soft candyfloss clouds scattered across the vast blue background catching my attention for only a moment before chaos ensues. My head is ringing like crazy and my entire body is buzzing with a strong tingling sensation as I lie flat on my back in the water, trying to catch my breath.

'We've got you, B-rad,' I hear Dean say. 'Stay with us, mate.' I pick up the frantic tone in his voice and feel water droplets splashing on my face. I try to look at what's going on around me but I can't.

'*Agghhhh*, my neck . . . my . . .' I groan. My neck is rigid, with a sharp burning sensation in the centre.

'Don't move, bud. Just try to relax.' I recognise Chad's voice.

The intense ringing in my head gives way to a mild throbbing. Dean, Chad and Spence are swimming beside me, behind me, dragging me backwards through the water towards the beach. I hear heavy breathing and spluttering all around me, the three of them are clearly struggling.

My mind is spinning out of control and I can't think straight.

'My board — get my board,' I mutter. Like that's the priority.

Dean replies, 'It's right here, mate, it's still on your feet.'

Is it? But I can't feel it . . . come to think of it, I can't feel anything. I can't move anything. *What the fuck have I done?! Oh fuck, I think I've broken my neck.*

Just be patient and wait, I reassure myself. Maybe this is like that time I hurt my neck in London — I'll be able to move again soon. Deep down, however, I suspect this is not the case.

Chad calls out to Massi, 'Call 911 — we need an ambulance.'

Clearly rattled, Massi responds, 'What's the number?' Even I can't help chuckling a little.

Spence holds his arms firmly on either side of my head, with his hands on my shoulders to stop my neck from moving, as the others do their best to get me very carefully onto the sand.

Why can't I move yet?!

I lie there dazed and confused. Why can't I move? Concussion is causing me to drift in and out of awareness of what's happening around me. The sensation in my neck is not painful exactly — it's more of a widespread warm discomfort buried deep, with sharp spurs of consequence for trying to move my head. Like something out of a Jet Li kung fu movie — several precisely placed acupuncture needles in my neck locking my body into paralysis.

The bloody graze on my elbow, previously raw and stinging, is now just the dull ghost of pain.

'My board — take my board off,' I say, feeling like my feet are cramping from being in the bindings too long.

Dean replies, 'It's off, mate. I already took it off for you.'

I swear it's still on my feet — I get Dean to lift my legs so I can see my feet. That introduces a fresh worry: I couldn't feel him lift my legs.

'Just focus on your breathing, Brad,' Spence tells me. 'Help is on the way.'

I'm finding it hard to take a deep inhale. Each breath is shallow, laboured, as if my chest is being squeezed so it can't expand.

Chad is off to my left talking urgently on the phone, pacing back and forth. He's talking to the first-responders, giving them directions on how to get here. 'Hey what's the street address here?' He asks, looking around for an answer.

'33003,' I say, and Chad stares at me in amazement. Where did that come from?

Pratt disappears in a cloud of dust to meet the ambulance at the front gate.

I have no insurance and I know the ambulance is going to set me back at least a couple of grand. But lying in the sand, unable to move or feel anything, or even breathe properly, I sense that this is not the time to worry about that. I probably need that ambulance.

But when I hear Chad talking on the phone with the paramedics and saying, 'Yeah, I think we need the helicopter,' I look across at him and call out, 'Chad, don't you call that fucking helicopter! No way can I afford an ambulance *and* a helicopter! But then I picture lying in an ambulance, going over all the bumps in the road back to the front entrance, followed by the long drive through traffic to the hospital in Orlando. No thank you, I'll take the express sky route, thanks, I conclude.

While I lie there waiting, I ask the guys to squeeze my hands and feet, and move my limbs for me. I want to feel it so bad. I want to feel *something* . . . but I can't feel a thing.

The first-responders, after only 10 minutes, turn out to be from the local fire department. How did they get here so fast? The firefighters introduce themselves while checking my vitals and then asking questions. When they ask me to wiggle my toes and fingers I feel like I'm failing a test.

I'm then prepped for transport by helicopter. A firefighter cuts my T-shirt and life-jacket off before slipping a brace under the back of my neck and fitting it tightly around the front. With my neck supported, they all roll me onto my side, slide a backboard underneath me, then roll me back and strap me down.

I can hear the helicopter coming from a distance — the sound of salvation, the sound of crippling debt. As it gets closer, I'm lifted into the air and carried over to where the helicopter is going to land. Dean runs over and asks me who I want him to call. There are only two people I think of: 'Call my mum, and call Dawn.'

Minutes later I'm in the chopper, which lifts from the grounds of Lake Ronix, leaving behind a scene of carnage and shock. My friends are now left to marinate in the wake of what just happened. Have they just watched their teammate take his final ride?

The generators are shut off and the guys pile into vehicles to race to the hospital, leaving behind what looks like a crime scene — my gear scattered across the beach, my helmet still floating in the middle of the lake.

The man beside me introduces himself as Rob, the flight nurse for AirCare Medevac.

'We're going to take care of you as we get you to hospital, okay? Our flight time is about 10 minutes so we'll have you there in no time.'

His deep voice and his words are relaxing and put my mind at ease. The vibrations and ambient sounds are also soothing as I lie there tucked into this steel cocoon: safe, calm and cosy. I know I'm in good hands.

•

We land abruptly on the roof of the Orlando Regional Medical Center, and the tranquillity evaporates the moment the door is opened. I'm whisked out of the helicopter into the bright sun and intense Florida heat and transferred onto a waiting hospital bed. Rob briefs the emergency nurses, who hurry me into the hospital.

The nurse in charge is walking beside me while I'm raced through the hallways. She asks my name and date of birth, and then asks whether I know where I am and what day it is. Thankfully I do. I'm distracted by the hellishly uncomfortable neck brace, which is not only digging into my collarbones and under my chin, but also feels like it's making the burning sensation in my neck much worse. It's blazing now — feeling more like a sharpness, as if bone shards are jabbing my flesh.

'Okay, Brad, we're going to get you straight in for an MRI,' the nurse explains.

As I'm sliding into the giant magnetic donut, I feel anxious and afraid. The MRI technician puts headphones over my ears and then closes a cage-like thing over my head. I feel like a prisoner behind bars, restrained with no freedom. Little do I know, this is just the beginning . . .

•

It's close to an hour since I crashed head-first into the landing at Lake Ronix. Throughout this whole time it has been nonstop questioning, poking, prodding and moving. So much has been happening around me that I haven't had a chance to soak in the reality of my situation. It's only now that I'm alone with my thoughts that it is starting to hit home.

I've broken my neck; I'm completely paralysed. Will I ever wakeboard again? Will I even be able to walk again? Or have sex? What the fuck! No girl is ever going to want me now. How much will all of this cost? How will I pay for it? Who is going to look after me? What sort of life could I possibly live now? I don't want to live like this . . . I don't want to live . . .

And while I'm deep in despair about the fact that I can't move my body, the MRI technician's voice comes through the headphones: 'Okay, Brad, I'm going to get started now. Each scan can take a little while and I need you to remain completely still. Please try not to move.'

REALLY?! Did he really just say that?!

I want to fucking strangle that guy!

I want to cry but at the same time I feel like I could burst out laughing. I give a slight chuckle as I fight off the tears welling in my eyes and say, 'That shouldn't be too difficult.'

The MRI starts its first scan, the loud honking, beeping and pulsating alarm-like sounds beginning to penetrate my flesh and bone to deliver images of my spinal cord, to tell us just how bad my situation is. I feel my eyelids getting heavy. As I did in the helicopter, I find comfort in my little cocoon, and the rhythmic sounds of the machine are soothing and almost hypnotic. Before long, I drift off to sleep.

•

I wake up suddenly, feeling the earth shaking around me. Startled, I open my eyes to look around but it's dark. It takes a few moments for my eyes to adjust. I'm lying on my back looking up at the ceiling — which is moving swiftly by. I'm being taken somewhere, but I don't even know where I am to begin with. I blink and squint and make out the shape of someone standing over me, pushing me in an oversized shopping cart.

Where am I? Who is this person? I feel extremely uneasy as the seconds tick by but nothing is coming back to me. I try to move, struggle and strain, but it's no use. They must have me restrained. I'm beginning to panic as every part of this unknown situation is spiralling around in my head. My entire body feels stiff, as if I have been stuck in this position for days.

By this point my eyes have adjusted enough to see that I'm being pushed down a corridor. I'm jolted as we come to a sudden stop, and the mysterious man looks at me before he turns and walks away, saying nothing, just leaving me here. A haunting moment of realisation sweeps across me — *Oh fuck, I've been kidnapped!*

I lie here, trying again to free myself from my restraints, but when I look down I can't see anything restraining me. *They must have drugged me.* Unless I've been kept captive for so long without food or water that I'm just too malnourished to move.

I've been left in a cold, dark, damp concrete tunnel, like you'd find under a football stadium. *What do they want with me? Who are they?* The thoughts and fears spiral around in my head.

I have no idea how long it has been — maybe minutes, maybe hours — but my captor emerges from the darkness. This time, I'm going to get some answers. But for some reason I go straight to begging him to let me go.

'*Pleeeeease!*' I attempt, but when I open my mouth, hardly any sound comes out. 'Please, let me go! There's been some mistake!' I mouth, not knowing if he can hear or understand me.

He ignores me, so I figure I need to step things up a bit. 'Please! Let me go! I'll give you 30 grand, if you'll just let me go!'

I have no idea where I think I'm going to find 30 grand, or even where that number came from, but there's still no response from the mystery man. I'm starting to feel like I know him, like his face is somewhat familiar, but before I can put my finger on it he's off again, into the black of the night.

•

I must've dozed off, because as I wake and open my eyes, I look down to see an apple and a banana both sitting right by the fingertips of my right hand. *Someone left me some food!* I feel a surge of hope and reach for the apple. If I can eat something, I'll get some strength back, then I can get myself out of here. But however much I stretch, my hand doesn't move any closer to the fruit. I try again, this time with some positive reinforcement. *You've got this. All you need to do is grab the apple. Just reach out and grab it.* But no matter how hard I try, no matter how much I tell myself I can do it, my hand does not move.

The man is back, and someone is with him. I plead and beg for them to let me go, but once more, my pleas are inaudible. Suddenly I think I know who the man is. *Is that . . .? It can't be . . . he's a wakeskater!* I know him, I've even hung out with him. *I've been kidnapped by wakeskaters! What the fuck?!*

I am baffled by this — what do they have against me? I've always been friendly with most people in wakeboarding. I can't wrap my head around it. What could they possibly gain from kidnapping me? They know I have next to no money.

'What do you want with me?' I try but it's hopeless. It's like I'm not even here. They don't care what I have to say. They simply turn away and disappear again. I've never felt so helpless, I've never known such vulnerability, I have never been in a situation where I'm completely powerless. But here in this corridor, in this hellhole, I'm alone and I'm terrified. My life is in someone else's hands — but whose?

My mind is exhausted from the tornado of fear and confusion. My body is utterly drained from my unsuccessful attempts to free myself. I am done. I'm ready to submit; I have nothing left. The darkness is closing in on me. This must be what death is like — cold, lonely, helpless . . .

I am done.

My eyelids are heavy. As I slowly open them, my vision gradually clears and I'm able to focus on the unfamiliar room I'm lying in. I don't know where I am or how I got here, but I feel a comforting level of calm.

The morning light through the windows above the bed illuminates the entire room with a yellowish orange glow. I soak in the soothing feeling as one of my other senses homes in on a pleasant aroma wafting through the air and into my nostrils — freshly brewed coffee. I can see movement across the hallway. Three young women wearing matching scrubs are drinking coffee. I think they must all be nurses who live together.

Clearly I'm not in my trailer at Lake Ronix. Did I go out partying last night and go home with someone? That would explain the memory loss and extreme lethargy. This isn't my bed, but it's comfortable and warm.

One of the nurses notices I'm awake so she walks over to me. She is slim and athletic-looking, with long brown hair in a ponytail. She carries herself with confidence and she's beautiful, in a unique way. It makes sense that I would have gone home with her. It wouldn't be the first time I've ended up at a beautiful stranger's house after a night out in Orlando's bars. But surely I should remember meeting this woman.

I look up at her and smile, and she returns the smile, looking at me with compassionate eyes. I go to sit up but my head feels like it weighs a thousand kilos — I can't even lift it off the pillow. There's a sharp pain in my neck and I go to groan but no sound comes out. I can't move or feel anything in my body, just a dull tingling feeling — a *buzzzzzzzzz*.

An indescribable chill runs through my body and I'm aware of a sharp, scratchy pain from a ventilator tube going through my neck into my lungs. A feeding tube runs up my nose and down the back of my throat. I see wires coming from my chest leading to monitors beside my bed.

It all comes back to me. Memories of my crash whip through my mind like a terrifying slideshow — the moment I backed out, the head-first impact, the guys dragging me out of the water, the Medevac, the MRI. Then nothing. How long ago was that? How long have I been lying here?

I look back over at the girl who just walked in. This isn't her house, and she's not some girl I met downtown last night. I'm in hospital, in the ICU, and she's my nurse.

She's crushing up some medication.

'I'm Amanda, and I'm your nurse for today,' she says.

I feel overwhelming confusion and emotion building up inside me as something hits me — *I was kidnapped by wakeskaters!* So how did I get here?

My focus shifts back to Amanda as she plugs a syringe into my feeding tube.

'It's okay,' she says reassuringly, seeing the look on my face. 'I'm just giving you something for the pain, and to help keep your temperature down. You had quite the fever last night.'

A cool sensation runs down my throat.

The tracheotomy site is itching like crazy. Instinctively, I go to scratch it with my finger but I'm met with another painful reminder of my paralysis.

Amanda finishes pushing a second syringe of meds into my tube.

'Okay, Brad, I'm all done. Hopefully that helps take the edge off. I'll be back in to check on you shortly.' She bends a black tube forward and positions the end in front on my mouth. 'Just puff into this to activate your call bell if you need anything. Oh, and your mom will be in soon too!'

That's right — Mum is here! A wave of relief washes over me as I remember. I don't know how I know, but I remember the feeling of her presence.

A tear rolls out of the corner of my eye as emotion floods in. At first it's a glimmer of happiness and comfort, but it's quickly followed abruptly by fear, guilt, grief, anger. *What the fuck have I done?! I've fucked everything up.* I realise the pain I must've caused my family and I want to roll over and scream into my pillow. My inability to move makes me feel anxious, trapped, helpless. In a panic, I try to gasp for air but I get nothing, which dials up the panic and I gasp again. *I can't breathe!* Then I hear a quiet 'click' beside me as the ventilator delivers a dose of air to my lungs.

I focus on the timing of the ventilator. 'Click' — *inhale . . . 2 . . . 3 . . . 4 . . . 5 . . . exhale . . . 2 . . . 3 . . . 4 . . .*

It's slower than my body is naturally wanting, but counting it out in my head and waiting for that click is helping to settle me down.

'Click' — *inhale . . . 2 . . . 3 . . . 4 . . . 5 . . . exhale . . . 2 . . . 3 . . . 4 . . .*

As I continue to count and breathe, my thoughts begin to slowly dissipate. My eyelids are heavy again.

I slowly drift off to sleep.

•

I awaken to see Mum sitting beside my bed. She kisses my forehead as soon as she sees I'm awake. I'm so glad to see her. She looks at me and smiles, but I can tell it's her brave face. I can barely look her in the eyes because I can see the heartache behind them. It shatters my heart to see the pain I've caused her.

'How are you feeling today?' she asks. I'm already on the verge of tears, and her question nearly breaks me but I do my best to keep the floodgates from bursting open.

'I was kidnapped last night,' I mouth to her.

'You were what?!' She is clearly confused.

Not knowing whether she was unable to read my lips or confused by my claim, I mouth again, slowly this time, *'Kiddd-naaaapped! I was fucking kidnapped by wakeskaters!'*

'What do you mean kidnapped?'

'KID-NAPPED!' I'm trying to yell it, but it's still coming out at zero decibels.

Amanda walks into the room and Mum turns to her and says, 'What's going on? He thinks he was kidnapped last night!' I can tell she doesn't believe me.

'IT ACTUALLY HAPPENED!' I mouth, but she's listening to Amanda.

I *need* Mum to understand, so I make a clicking sound with my mouth, which is the only sound I can make that is loud enough to get someone's attention.

'Why don't you believe me? *It actually happened!'* I mouth again.

Mum and Amanda are both paying attention, but when I see the way they're looking at me, it starts to sink in just how outrageous my claim must seem. But it was so real! I was there experiencing the entire thing — all the fear, the misery, the darkness. It must have happened, but then again, how could it?

My eyes begin to well up again and Mum says softly, 'I know it must seem real, but you've been here in the ICU for almost a week now, and I've been with you every possible moment.'

A week?! I can't deal with the conflict between what I know I've experienced, and what I'm being told is real. So I close my eyes and turn my head away — well, as much as my neck will allow, which isn't much.

Mum and Amanda step outside the room to talk, but I can still hear every word. Amanda explains that late the previous night the staff were moving me to the step-down unit when my fever spiked severely.

'He had a temperature of 108°F (over 42°C), which could explain his hallucinations about being kidnapped.'

'Wait, *whaaat?*' Mum responds angrily. 'What were they doing moving him in the middle of the night when I wasn't here? That's *unacceptable!*'

Amanda stammers slightly. 'I . . . I do apologise, Mrs Smeele. The doctor must've felt that your son was ready to be moved. I'll pass your feelings on to the team and make sure nothing like that is done in future without notifying you first.'

'I would appreciate that,' my mother replies firmly. Then, as her anger fades, she asks, 'What would have caused that temperature spike? Isn't that dangerously high?'

'108° is about as high as I've seen,' Amanda nods. 'It's likely to have been caused by his pneumonia, along with his body's inability to regulate temperature. Such high temperatures can definitely cause hallucinations and if prolonged, or any higher, then there's a chance of trauma to the brain. According to the notes, your son may also have experienced seizures due to the fever.'

'Oh god,' says Mum.

'His temperature was crash-cooled using medication, and a lot of ice,' Amanda goes on. 'He wasn't very responsive so there was some concern about possible brain injury, but he seems much more stable now — aside from still believing the hallucinations were real.'

•

Mum spends the entire day by my side. She's getting better at reading my lips, but I have to keep everything really simple, mouth it really slow. Sometimes I even resort to charades: 'Three words . . . First word sounds like . . .' It's frustrating, but at least I'm able to communicate with her.

She tells me everything she knows about what has happened to me, and about spinal cord injury. It's too much to process — for both of us. When I ask what the doctor told her about my injury, it's like I already know. Like I've heard it before.

'. . . a 1–2 per cent chance of regaining upper-limb function . . .'

The words rip through me, piercing my heart, pummelling my soul and crushing my already shattered spirit. What, so my walking again isn't even being considered a possibility? And 1–2 per cent chance of moving my arms might as well be zero chance.

'You shattered your C4 vertebrae and severely crushed your spinal cord — but it's not *severed*, so that's a positive!' Mum says, with a small amount of forced hope in her expression. I tear up as she runs through my diagnosis. 'You spent more than nine hours on the operating table as they stabilised your neck with two titanium alloy rods, a plate and 14 screws. 'You've also got pneumonia, which means you've got fluid in your lungs.'

It feels as if she's telling me I'm going to die — and honestly, I'm starting to wish I'd died right then at Lake Ronix. *I don't want to live like this!* But I don't say this to Mum. She's going through enough pain thanks to me.

At about 10.30 p.m. Mum tells me she's going to get some sleep. She's staying at nearby Hubbard House, which the hospital makes available to family members of ICU patients.

She kisses me on the cheek. 'I love you,' she says. 'I know you probably can't see it now, but it's all going to be okay. I hope you get some sleep and I'll see you tomorrow.'

I close my eyes and nod, then mouth back, 'I love you too.'

FOURTEEN: ICU (AKA HELL)

My solitude has a haunting feeling. The lights are off in my room but there's a glow through the curtains from the well-lit hallway and nursing station, not to mention the monitor and ventilator displays on either side of my bed. Yet I sense an overwhelming darkness coming from within me, from the truths I have not yet allowed myself to feel.

I've heard enough about spinal cord injuries before to know that they're basically permanent. I'm not going to magically get better. The black thoughts come at me: *You've completely lost your physical abilities; no more wakeboarding; no more living at Lake Ronix; no more building; no more walking or running or swimming; no more sex — FUCK! No more sex! You won't ever be able to please a woman sexually again! How could any woman want you now anyway?*

No more guitar; you can't drive; can't skate or surf; can't travel; can't party with your friends; can't even scratch an itch or pick your nose, let alone dress or feed yourself. For fuck's sake, dude, you can't even breathe on your own! You're going to have to rely on other people for EVERYTHING. You're going to be a burden on your family and friends. Your life is officially over.

This is so fucking unfair. I don't want to live like this! What's the point? I *can't* live like this — I want to die but, goddammit, I can't even kill myself! There's literally no way out — I'm trapped. There's got to be a way I can end it. It's not worth carrying on like this — nothing will ever be even remotely as good again. I need to *end it.*

While I'm lying here listing all the things I can't do any more, and trying to think of ways to end my life, a giant African American man, who must be at least 6 foot 4 (193 cm) tall, pulls back the curtain and enters the room. He's wearing scrubs so I assume he must work here. 'Mr Smeelee, I'm Daaaniel.' He speaks slowly. 'I've just come to drain your bladder.'

Oh right — add that to the list: I can't even fucking take a piss on my own any more.

Thankfully I can't feel him inserting the catheter; I just close my eyes and disconnect.

•

Seconds, minutes or hours later I wake up in a panic. It takes me a second to remember where I am, and I can't breathe. I try to cough but the ventilator won't let me, so I end up with chest convulsions. It feels like my airway is closed and I'm choking on phlegm.

I can't breathe!

The ventilator sends a breath of air my way but it hardly gets through. I'm still trying to cough and it's still not happening.

Well, I guess this might be my way out.

Another partial breath from the ventilator rattles through the thick gunk in my chest before the machine's alarm begins beeping. A few seconds later louder alarms start to sound outside the room. Two nurses burst in and turn on the lights. One of them grabs the long thin tube that's attached where the ventilator tube enters my throat. She pushes it in and I feel it scratch its way down my trachea and into my lungs. It sends me into a stronger coughing fit, and then, miraculously, the tube starts suctioning the phlegm and fluid that are blocking my airway. The nurse keeps it going, drawing the tube slowly back out, until the ventilator finally delivers a full dose of air to my lungs.

She repeats this uncomfortable process several times, until my airway is clear and most of my vitals return to normal. I still have a fever, so a nurse mixes up another concoction of Tylenol and saline. I'm completely exhausted and I'm fast asleep before she's finished injecting it through my feeding tube.

•

It's 5.30 a.m. and I'm ripped from my dreams of wakeboarding and working in paradise, and thrown into my new reality, my nightmare.

'Mr Smeele, I'm here to X-ray your chest,' says the silhouetted figure of a man standing against the dim light through the curtains. *Okay, yeah, that's cool, but why the fuck are you doing it so early?*

'Hard board sliding under you,' he says routinely, almost robotically, as he manoeuvres the X-ray board under my back. Every movement is agonising. Every small shuffle sends painful twinges through my neck.

He then positions the portable X-ray machine and zaps me. After a few moments he checks the image. 'Sorry, I'll have to do that again — your lungs are bigger than I expected,' he says, before shuffling the board lower. He adjusts the machine and zaps me again.

Sometimes I think it's lucky that I can't speak. Because if I could say what I'm thinking, I don't think I'd be making too many friends at the moment. I'm pissed off enough at my situation, let alone all the poking and prodding and pain the staff are administering. I stew in uncharacteristic silence.

I close my eyes, hoping I can find the dream I was enjoying before I was rudely awakened. Back to my paradise I go.

•

Mum is here when I wake again, which takes away a small amount of the pain from the harsh stab of realisation that comes from waking up in this place.

'I hear you had a bit of a rough night,' Mum says, obviously having been briefed. 'Did you get much sleep?'

'A little,' I mouth. I want to tell her more, but our communication is still at the beginner level.

'I've been speaking with Dawn,' she tells me. 'She's a really sweet girl. I've been keeping her updated every day and she's asking when she can come to see you.'

I'm not ready; I don't want her to see me like this. I gently shake my head and mouth, 'Not yet.'

'Okay, fair enough. I'll tell her we're not ready.'

I signal for Mum to grab the suction straw. Since I'm not able to swallow, not even my own saliva, I have to spit it into a suction straw. You don't realise how often you swallow your own saliva until you can't.

'Jeff will be here in a little while,' Mum adds. 'He's been absolutely amazing since your injury. He flew straight here and has been calling anyone and everyone to find out as much as he can about spinal cord injury and what might be able to help. And he's been helping to organise a fundraiser!'

Jeff Weatherall arrives a few hours later, and it's good to see him. 'Hey buddy, how are you feeling today?' he asks.

Does he want an honest answer? If there's anyone who can take it, it's Jeff. But I choose halfway honest and mouth, 'Feeling pretty shitty, bro.'

'I bet,' Jeff replies. 'I can't imagine what you're going through. But I'm glad you're still with us, bro!' Then he reaches for my phone and says, 'Maybe this will cheer you up a little.' He starts reading out some of the messages I didn't know were there.

He goes through text messages, emails, Facebook and Instagram messages. There are hundreds of them! Messages from people I know, and from people I don't. Pictures of me have been apparently flooding social media feeds. Beautiful messages of support that make my eyes well up. I didn't know that so many people cared.

The fundraiser Jeff's organising is set up for tomorrow night downtown. People have kindly donated heaps of auction items, and Jeff's wearing one of the tanktops he had printed to sell. It has a picture of me on the front, the same picture that people have mostly been posting. I'm standing, smiling, and I've got my arms up in the air in celebration.

'This picture represents everything people think of you, Brad,' Jeff says. 'The smile on your face — they see your strength, they see that you're a fucking champion!'

I hang out with Jeff for the rest of the afternoon. And honestly, for the first time, I'm beginning to feel like all might not be lost. I have a loving family. I have some fucking awesome friends. And I'm feeling the love from the whole wakeboarding community.

Maybe, just maybe, life could be worth fighting for.

•

Night time becomes a constant battle to keep my temperature under control. The pneumonia is to blame, and the spinal cord injury makes it worse. The nurses have been trying everything they can think of to keep it under control.

Tonight my nurse has a new idea. She produces some ice packs wrapped in thin fabric and puts the first two in my armpits. 'The body temperature should respond really quickly to cold packs under your armpits . . . and in your groin.'

Sorry, what?

But by the time I've processed the thought, she's tucking an ice pack under my scrotum.

'*Woooohh! Take it out!*' I shout (silently). Then: 'What the . . .?! I felt that! I shouldn't be able to feel that but I did!'

The nurse whips the pack back out from under my family jewels, apologising, but then says, 'That's a good thing!'

I'm thinking the same — surely that painful sensation *must* be good. My brain is receiving some signals, and of course it would be from my balls. Typical.

•

On the day of the fundraiser I get a very unexpected, but very welcome visitor. It's my friend Sunni, who I haven't seen in at least five years. Sunni used to be a pro wakeboarder but had to retire due to shoulder problems. She travelled around with Bower and me on the Australian pro tour, and I showed her around New Zealand for a while. We were close, but lost touch when she moved back to Canada. And now she has flown all the way from Canada to go to my fundraiser and visit me. She definitely puts a smile on my face, and makes sure it lasts by drawing a big smiling sun on my window, which makes me smile whenever I look at it.

Jeff is over the moon the next day when he comes to report on the fundraiser. He introduces me to the beautiful woman he's with, Kayla. I smile and raise my eyebrows in a way that says *I approve* . . . not that he needs my approval.

'Bro, it was unreal last night!' he says. 'There were so many people there and we raised loads of money! Everyone loves you so much, dude — it was really so cool to see everyone rally together for you. We're still tallying it all up but it looks like we raised about 25 grand for you!'

I'm speechless, figuratively as well as literally. My heart swells and my eyes well up as it sinks in. People did that for me. I've never felt such a surge of gratitude and just pure love.

'That's amazing, bro! I can't thank you enough!' I mouth. It takes several attempts for him to read my lips.

'Don't even mention it. And I can't take all the credit; there were so many people involved, including Kayla.' I smile at Kayla with gratitude. 'We just want to help raise as much money as possible for your recovery.' Jeff goes on to show me pictures and videos from the fundraiser — all the familiar faces, all the cool auction items, just so much love!

•

Today is the first day of physiotherapy.

I'm joined in my room by three women who begin stretching my limbs. They put some white stockings on my legs to help control my blood pressure.

'Okay Brad, we're going to sit you up and do a few exercises,' says Erika, the lead physio. 'Do you think you can do that?' I nod my head, not sure exactly what I'm in for but keen to get moving. I've been lying in this bed for over a week now.

They sit me up, and at first I feel a bit dizzy but it settles. They then turn me and lower my legs over the side of the bed. My head feels so heavy I'm struggling to hold it up as they shift me, and the ventilator tube is pulling against my trachea, but I persevere. The physios pull a table up in front of me, then lift my arms and rest them on the table. I try to balance myself using the table but my arms feel completely dead, like they're not even mine. I would completely fall over if not for the ladies holding me. I keep trying to bend my elbow, or flex my wrist, or wiggle my fingers — to move anything — but I get nothing.

The physios notice my anxiety building so they give my upper body a little extra support. 'Try to stay calm, Brad,' Erika says. 'We're just going to start slowly, okay?'

'Now,' she continues, 'I want you to focus on your shoulders. Try to roll your shoulders back, squeezing your shoulderblades together.'

I direct all my energy to my shoulders, thinking about how I would pull my shoulders back and squeeze my shoulderblades together every time I stood up on my wakeboard. I picture the rope coming tight as I strain my shoulders. My right arm slides back towards me about 5 centimetres. *Is that it?*

'Good, Brad, that's a nice start!' Erika says reassuringly. After a few more minutes of that exercise the 5 cm turns to 2 cm and then none.

For the next exercise, I'm literally just working on holding my head up, and by the end of it I'm exhausted. *How can I be exhausted from barely moving?* I'm deeply disappointed. After lying me back in bed, Erika and her assistants give me some more stretches, mainly for hands and ankles, while also showing Mum how to do them. Erika stresses the importance of regular stretching as it sends signals that could potentially reconnect, and the hands and ankles can easily tighten up if they're not stretched regularly.

From then on, Mum is stretching my ankles or my hands almost all the time she's with me. It works well for both of us, as she recently had a knee replacement and needs to do her own rehab. So as she's stretching out my calf muscle by pushing my foot up towards my shin, she's doing lunges to strengthen her new knee at the same time. We're quite a team.

•

It's late, and Mum is still here. We're waiting for some suppositories to make my bowels move — yet another little indignity resulting from this injury. I never would've thought I would miss taking a shit. But honestly, I've basically gone back to needing the same care as an infant. Needing someone to clean up my shit for me takes away all feeling of being human and I'm not ready to accept it.

Eventually Mum checks and confirms that the suppositories have done their job, so she calls for the nurse to come in and clean me up. The nurse pops her head in to say they're a bit busy right now but she'll send in a nursing assistant to sort me out soon. Half an hour passes and no one has come. Mum keeps popping her head impatiently out into the hallway. I'm doing my best to pretend this isn't happening, trying to forget that I'm lying in my own filth.

Mum presses the call bell again, then after another 20 minutes she's done sitting around waiting. 'This is getting a bit ridiculous!' she says as she storms out of the room. Next thing I hear her going off at one of the nurses. 'This is not good enough! My son has been lying in his own filth for almost an hour — you need to get him cleaned up now!'

I'm embarrassed, but within minutes they have someone there to clean me up.

•

Not being able to drink means my mouth and throat are constantly dry. I want to know why I'm not allowed to swallow, so I've been learning about the ventilator setup and how it works. In the first days after my spinal surgery, my breathing was controlled by a ventilator, through a tube that went into my mouth and down my throat into my lungs. After the doctor discovered that I had been chewing on the tube, they decided to perform a tracheotomy.

The surgeon cut a hole through the front of my neck, near where the collarbones meet, and inserted a plastic tube into my trachea. For that to work it needs to be a closed system, so they inserted a balloon in my throat and inflated it above the opening, blocking the top section of my trachea. This means the ventilator can inflate and deflate my lungs without the air leaking out through my mouth. Unfortunately, it also means my oesophagus is blocked, so I'm unable to eat or drink . . . or speak.

To combat the dry mouth, my nurse has been bringing me cups of ice to suck on, which also helps with keeping my temperature down. I love crunching the ice with my teeth and letting it liquify in my mouth. It takes major self-control to resist swallowing the water.

Occasionally, if I'm looking for a bit of flavour, I'll get the nurse to add some Gatorade for me to swish around my mouth. It tastes good at the time, but it leaves a bad aftertaste.

•

I'm getting all my nutrients through the feeding tube in my nose. A few times per day a nurse brings a bottle of thick yellowy-green liquid that they plug into the tube and then hang upside down above my bed. 'Time for your steak shake!' one of them likes to joke.

I notice my skin is flaking off onto my bed. The tanned flakes build up on the white sheets and the nurses have to brush it off the sheets every day. The line on the side of my hands where it turns from tanned skin to the white of my palm, that's where I really start to notice the change. Each day, the tan recedes more and more. The evidence of 21 back-to-back summers is disappearing by the day.

Sudden loud noises are an issue, sending shockwaves through my body. If a nurse drops her clipboard I react as if someone has just fired a gun right behind me. It's like everything gives my body a fright. I let Mum know and she does her best to prevent any sudden moves.

Tonight I can't sleep. I think I'm hot but it's hard to be sure. Hot to me is a sensation like pressure I feel in my face. It's just after midnight and I puff into my call bell to call my nurse into the room. Tonight's nurse is Letitia, a sweet young woman who's around my age. She looks on the monitor and says I have another fever over 100°F. After pulling off my top sheet and laying a cold damp cloth across my forehead she asks me if there's anything else she can do to make me more comfortable. I mouth one word: 'Ice.'

Letitia returns with a cup of ice and a blue icy-pop. She doesn't need to ask if I want it because my smile says enough. She breaks up the long tube of sugary frozen treat and mixes it in with the crushed ice, then proceeds to spoon-feed me the best thing I've tasted in weeks! My tastebuds are in heaven as I crunch it up and hold it in my mouth until it's completely melted, willing the flavour to get absorbed into my tongue before it's all suctioned away.

I have a secret that I've been keeping from the nurses — I've discovered that I can swallow small amounts of water around the balloon in my throat. It's not easy, but it feels so goddamn good on my sore throat! There have been no ill-effects so far.

Once I have finished my cup of flavoured ice, Letitia looks at me with a cheeky smile and asks if I want another. By the end of my third ice sensation, I'm beyond satisfied. I thank Letitia for my midnight treats, which seem to have helped bring my temperature down. She's one of my favourite nurses now, not just because of the icy-pops but because she sits there with me when I can't sleep, keeping me company. There's no forced conversation; she's not *trying* to cheer me up. Just sitting with me. I can tell she's got a big heart and became a nurse because she genuinely wants to help people. And tonight, she's done exactly that.

I think I can sleep now.

•

After stalling Dawn for a week, I let her know that she can come and visit. I don't know what to expect — or what she expects. I remember the conversation in which she made it clear she doesn't want a long-distance relationship, and why would she want to be with me now? I can't see why any girl would want to be with me. I would only be a burden.

•

It's 17 July, 11 days since my injury. Amanda is my nurse most days. I look forward to seeing her smile as she waltzes into my room at the start of her shift — and I like to think she looks forward to seeing me too. She generally hangs around without any real urgency to rush off to her other patients, and I enjoy her company.

Today she's wearing her hair differently — in a tidy braid down her back.

'How are you doing today, Brad?'

'I'm feeling okay, thank you,' I reply, with a rare smile. 'I like your hair today. The braid looks good!'

Her eyes, reading my lips, light up as she smiles and says, 'Aww, thank you! I could braid yours a bit later today, and give it a wash if you like?'

I like this idea!

Later in the morning the physios are back for my next therapy session.

'Hi Brad,' Erika says enthusiastically. 'How do you feel about getting out of bed today?'

I smile and mouth, 'Yes please.' One of the therapists pushes a big recliner armchair into the room and says brightly, 'We're going to transfer you into this!'

They put on my compression stockings and sit me up, positioning themselves around me for the transfer. A slide board positioned under my backside will be used to bridge me across to the chair. They get me there, but in the process the ventilator tube pops off my neck and falls to the ground. I start to panic but one of my physios grabs the tube and puts it straight back.

It feels good to be sitting upright, though I can't support myself so they stuff pillows down either side of me and strap me in.

After a little while I begin to feel light-headed and there's some weird blotchiness going on with my vision. I feel like I'm about to pass out. I look over at Erika and click my tongue to get her attention, but I don't know how to tell her. Luckily she sees it in my face and immediately reclines the back of the chair and lifts my feet up. My vision goes black for a few seconds before it starts coming back again.

After around an hour in the chair they move me back into the bed (with nice clean sheets) and notice my temperature is up. So in come the bowl of ice water and wet cloths to cool me off.

Soon Amanda returns to my room with a dry shampoo kit. I've been 11 days now without a shower or bath. I get a bed-wash every day but it's just a basic wipe-down — not the same at all. I would give anything right now to dive into the calm waters of Lake Ronix and scrub myself down . . .

I love the idea of a hair wash but 'dry shampoo' is strange. It doesn't feel like my hair is getting clean. The nurse puts a shower cap on my head and moves it around a little with the stuff inside, then that's it. But then she stands behind me and runs her fingers through my hair, combing it back in preparation for braiding, and the feeling is euphoric. It's the best thing I've felt since all of this started.

•

At the end of Amanda's shift at 3 p.m. she introduces me to her replacement, a dark-haired man named Andrew who somehow looks familiar. Instantly I can tell we're going to get along. He's a few years older than me and has a cool, confident demeanour that I find reassuring. He offers to give me a shave later in the afternoon — 'Gotta get you lookin' fresh for when your girl gets here tomorrow!' I like this guy already.

I hate to see Amanda go, but, as the cliché goes, I love to watch her leave.

Andrew returns after completing the handover of my neighbours. We're quite a mix here in the trauma ICU — from broken necks to gunshot wounds and car accidents and more. Some are still dancing with the grim reaper, but we're in the best place to dodge him. I feel like I've had my close encounter but now I'm well and truly in the clear.

As Andrew starts shaving my face, he tells me how he himself loves wakeboarding.

'We've actually got a mutual friend,' he says. 'I hear you know my friend Brian, better known as Bdahl.'

'*Yes!* Bdahl is the man!' I mouth enthusiastically. Bdahl and I became good friends at Lake Ronix. Like me, he was involved since the beginning. This mutual connection means Andrew and I become friends right away. It's bugging me how familiar he looks, even though I'm pretty certain I've never met him before.

That afternoon Oscar, my respiratory nurse, tells me, 'We're going to try to take you off the ventilator today.'

This is very exciting.

Oscar explains the process as he casually removes the ventilator tube — almost too casually considering this is the machine that's kept me alive for the past couple of weeks. But his calm approach is keeping me calm. He places an oxygen mask loosely over my open trachea and says, 'This won't actually help you with your breathing — it's just feeding you some extra oxygen because your own breaths will be smaller and your lungs won't absorb as much oxygen due to the pneumonia.'

I struggle to keep my breathing calm. Each breath is short, sharp and shallow, as if my chest is being weighed down. But slowly I begin to get it under control, focusing on one breath at a time. *Long and slow*, I think to myself. *Long and slow.*

'We'll keep going as long as you feel up to it,' Oscar tells me, not realising what he's just done. He's set me a challenge, and if there's one thing I'll grab and run with (figuratively speaking), it's a challenge.

Five minutes goes by.

'How are you feeling, dude?'

'Feels good!' I mouth, nodding my head. I still can't talk because the balloon is still inflated in my throat.

Ten minutes.

'Still feeling good, Brad?'

I nod and smile, before my expression returns to steely focus.

Fifteen minutes pass, then 20 and still going strong.

I'm breathing on my own!

At 45 minutes each breath is getting more difficult. I'm done. As Oscar reattaches the ventilator to my trachea, I'm feeling stoked. Finally I'm making progress!

'Nice job, Brad,' says Oscar. 'That was awesome! Your lungs are getting strong. Most people usually only go for five to 10 minutes the first time. We'll try again tomorrow.'

That night my temperature is up again. Andrew comes in with some cold cloths.

'A hundred and one degrees — dude, you're burning up!' he says. 'Let's get you cooled down. I don't want to see you up around 108 again!'

'Wait, you were there that night?' I ask.

'Yeah, I was. In all my years in this job I've never seen anyone who needed to be completely covered in ice, like you were. Literally only your head was showing!'

The penny drops — it suddenly hits me that Andrew looks a lot like a guy I know named Drew McGuckin — and Drew is a wakeskater! Andrew, my nurse, was my mysterious captor the night of my hallucination. It all makes sense now! I laugh at myself, slightly embarrassed that I had thought it really happened. Kidnapped by wakeskaters — hah!

•

The following morning I'm pleased to see my mum's best friend, Kerena, who arrived last night from Australia. She's here to support Mum, who has been such a pillar of support for me but who also needs someone to support her.

I can't wait for Oscar to arrive so I can go off the vent for even longer! But it turns out it's Oscar's day off so Chevonne is my respiratory nurse. I've had her once before and she's cool.

After reaching 45 minutes yesterday, the overachiever in me wants to make it to one hour today. The first five minutes cruise by, then I hit 10, 15, 20 . . .

I'm up to 30 minutes when Mum and Kerena walk through the door. Not long after, I notice that Kerena is wearing quite a strong fragrance and it's starting to make me feel a bit dizzy. At about 40 minutes off the vent my breathing becomes more restricted, like my airway is closing up. I turn and ask Chevonne to use the suction and for some reason I'm feeling unsettled by it. Then all of a sudden the room starts to spin. I turn to Chevonne and mouth the words 'I don't feel so gooooooo . . .'

Then everything goes dark.

•

Moments later I'm looking directly up at the ceiling and I'm surrounded by people looking concerned. Why is everyone staring at me like that? Mum looks terrified. They're crowding me and it's unsettling; I feel claustrophobic.

A bit later I'm told that my heart actually stopped — that I basically just died in front of my mother's eyes, which is why she looked the way she did. Apparently I was sent into the realm of nothingness for around 60 seconds, but for me it was merely a second of darkness, slightly more than a blink. There was no highlight reel of my life, no bright light, no stairway to heaven — just nothingness. For the rest of the day I contemplate life and death. How my light had been so suddenly switched off, and how easily it could've stayed that way. I would never have known. I had always pictured floating out of my own body and seeing my empty vehicle just lying below me, but it didn't happen.

•

Today's events have changed me. I have no interest in dancing with the reaper. I have decided to keep fighting, because life is starting to feel more and more worth fighting for. I don't want my light switched off yet.

•

Dawn arrived this evening, and Jeff has picked her up from the airport. She walks into the room, eyes already wet with tears. She comes straight over and kisses me, and holds her cheek against mine, then sits on the chair beside my bed, looking at me with her beautiful, tear-filled blue eyes.

'Hi baby, I'm here!' she says. 'Your mom just told me what happened today — we nearly lost you!' She reaches for my hand to hold but I can't feel her hand squeezing mine.

I can't hold back my own tears. Looking into her eyes I feel both love and pain, but the love is stronger. She keeps kissing me and telling me she loves me. I mouth those words back as she watches my lips. She reads that one easily, and, over the next hour, she gets pretty good at understanding me.

She tells me she wants to move to New Zealand to be with me and look after me, and that she wants to get married and have my babies. I'm dumbfounded. I've been convincing myself that no girl is going to want me, and then the girl I've wanted the most for the last seven years is telling me she wants it all. I'm so far beyond vulnerable right now, and this is beyond my expectations of Dawn's visit, but she's filled me up with love. A type of love I thought I'd never feel again.

She's back bright and early the next day and we spend the entire day together, talking about the future as well as the past. She makes me smile, and not just through my mouth, but from my eyes too. We make plans and she even goes as far as pondering baby names.

•

The doctors tell me the X-rays show that the fluid in my lungs has begun to lessen, which is exciting news. I have been overwhelmed with love since Dawn arrived a couple of days ago, but last night and this morning my mind has been working overtime — and not in a good way. I'm not sleeping well because my mind just won't shut off. I feel so lucky to have all these promises from Dawn, but a part of me won't let myself completely believe it. The reality is that prior to me breaking my neck, she wasn't prepared to make the small changes and sacrifices for us to be together — so why now? Why would she now want to make gigantic life changes to be with me in what's undoubtedly going to be an incredibly challenging lifestyle?

If she wouldn't move to Orlando to be with a tall, presentable, professional athlete, how come she's suddenly willing to move halfway around the world to be with a quadriplegic? I believe she truly does love me, and care about me deeply, but does she *really* know what she's getting herself into?

My overnight thoughts also swirled around the talk of babies. I don't even know if I can still have kids, and even if I can, what sort of father could I be if I can't even pick my own child up and hold them? The prospect scares the absolute shit out of me. I'm not the guy I was a few weeks ago.

When Mum and Dawn arrive, I'm not the same guy I was yesterday. I feel so low. Lower than I thought possible. The combination of spiralling downward overthinking and sheer exhaustion from lack of sleep, topped off with 15 minutes of attempting to cough my lungs up with no abs to force the cough out, has well and truly slammed me. Mum is talking to me but I don't even hear her; I don't have the energy or the will to respond. I'm just staring into space thinking about how crappy my life is — and will be hereafter. I miss Lake Ronix, I miss my trailer, I miss wakeboarding, I miss working with the team, I miss my body, my energy, my life. I feel like my soul has left me. I'm still alive . . . but completely empty.

Mum leaves Dawn and me alone, saying she's going upstairs to the small lounge she found by the café to do some more research on my options for rehab centres. I can tell she's upset but I just don't have it in me to fake a smile for her today.

Dawn does her best to cheer me up. I just feel like crying but I don't want to erupt with her here, so I do my best to hold it in. She's holding my hand and running her fingers through my hair, which soothes my whirlwind of thoughts, and soon enough I'm fast asleep.

•

I'm awoken as Erika arrives for today's physio session. I have no idea how long I've been asleep but I'm feeling marginally refreshed, and I'm comforted to see that Dawn is still here. She's just woken up from a nap too.

Each day Erika brings in different types of chairs to try out, from specialised wheelchairs to La-Z-boy recliners. My favourite part of the ritual is lying on my back on the hard flat bed after they deflate my pressure-relieving air mattress so the physios can climb on the bed to move me. I'm always positioned on one side or the other while in bed, so it feels amazing to lie flat on my back on the hard surface. It reminds me of lying on the floor of my trailer after a long hot day working and riding. I'm always overheating after sitting up so the ice-cold-flannel cool-down session is super refreshing and reminds me of getting in the water at the beginning of the New Zealand season when the water is still crispy cold. I take so much from these small, simple pleasures.

Mum and Dawn and Kerena head out to get some dinner, and Jeff arrives to hang out for a while. He tells me all about chats with his new friends Josh Wood and Barney Miller, both of whom suffered severe spinal cord injuries over 10 years ago. Barney still gets out and surfs, lying on his front and propped up on his elbows. Josh had a miraculous recovery and has completely ditched his wheelchair — Jeff shows me the front cover of Josh's book, showing him walking away from a burning wheelchair.

'Fuck yeah! That's what I'm going to do!' I mouth to Jeff. I haven't even got a wheelchair yet, but I'm already picturing it going up in flames.

By the time Dawn gets back from dinner I'm back in the mindset that I'm going to beat this thing. I'm going to work harder than I ever have to gain my movement back.

When the nurses come in to turn me from my right side to my left, I ask them to slide me a little further to the side of the bed so there's room for Dawn to get in beside me. Having her here, cuddling up to me in my weakest and most vulnerable state, gives me so much strength and fills me with hope. I don't know what that future will look like — whether it will involve walking or wakeboarding, or if Dawn will be a part of it. All I know is that right now this beautiful girl from Oklahoma is my angel.

Dawn has planned to stay for a week and we spend every possible moment together. She only leaves my room to give me privacy while the nurse is draining my bladder or when I'm being cleaned up after emptying my bowels. I don't need her around for that.

•

Later in the week some of my teammates come in to visit. There's actually a list of people wanting to see me, but Mum has been restricting the number of visitors because of my pneumonia-weakened state. Parks, Danny and Ruck wander slowly into my room, looking more like they're attending a funeral than visiting a friend. We hang out for a while, talking about the recovery that's ahead of me. Dawn acts as translator when the guys struggle to read my lips.

'I just can't wait to get my arms moving again!' I tell them.

'Yeah, B-rad,' Parks says enthusiastically. 'We all know you're no stranger to hard work — you're going to crush that rehab!'

All three of them play the guitar, with Ruck being the absolute jam master — he has a band and everything. I've always wanted to be as good as he is.

'I've been dreaming about playing the guitar again,' I tell them. 'It's going to be such a good rehab exercise to get my fingers moving again.'

The boys fall silent. Parks gently nods his head as I see a shimmer in his eye, Danny looks at the floor and Ruck — well, Ruck has never had a good poker face. When he's contemplating his reaction it's already written across his face. His eyes widen as he looks directly at me, stunned, with a dose of pity.

They all know the doctors have said I'm not likely to gain any movement back, but I refuse to believe that. I'm directing every little bit of intent towards my hands; I can practically feel the strings against my fingertips. I *know* I'm going to get them moving again. I'm going to prove the doctors wrong.

I really enjoy the guys' company. I tell them how good it is to see them again.

'It's great to see you, dude,' Parks replies. 'You're looking much better than the last time we came in.'

Wait, what? 'Have you guys been in already?'

'Yeah, man, we came and saw you a couple days after your surgery.'

'Was I awake? I honestly don't remember that!'

'Yeah, you were awake.' Parks looks confused. He's not the only one.

●

Later in the afternoon I ask Mum who else came to see me in that first week. She tells me my brother Alex flew over from London and was the first one here. 'Paul flew down from Seattle to see you. Mike Brown came from Kentucky, and most of your teammates came in too,' she says.

How do I not remember this? Maybe that temperature spike and the seizures really did cause some damage and wiped some of my memory.

Dawn's week has come to an end. It's hard to say goodbye, but she reassures me that she's going to come back as soon as she can. After smothering me with kisses, she drags herself away.

When Mum comes to see me, Kerena quite often stays outside. Mum reassures me it's only because Kerena is not here to visit me, but to support her. But I'm sure Kerena has been feeling terrible about the perfume incident, even though I don't blame her for it in the slightest. Today she gingerly enters the room behind Mum.

'No fragrance, today, Brad!' she says softly. I smile back at her and say thank you.

'Is there anything I can do for you?' she asks.

To which I respond idly, 'My scalp is so itchy, it's driving me crazy!'

She holds up her hands to show her long fingernails. 'Head scratches?' she asks.

'Yes please!'

The next half-hour is pure bliss. My itchy scalp has been driving me mad ever since I got here. An itch is only mildly inconvenient when you can scratch it, but when you can't, it's absolute torture! From then on, whenever Kerena is in the room, she's standing behind my bed treating me to the new most satisfying thing in my life: a head scratch.

•

Today I have moved rooms. I guess it's a good sign that they don't feel they need me right by the nurses' station any more, and hopefully that will mean less noise. I am gutted, however, that I have to leave Sunni's window artwork behind. I'm later told that the next patient asked for it to stay up, so I'm glad someone else is enjoying it.

Jeff comes strolling in, wearing a disposable yellow gown and gloves.

'Apparently you're contagious!' he laughs. The doctor told me earlier today that I have a hospital superbug, which is an antibiotic-resistant infection. They think it got in through the small pressure sore that has begun to form on my tailbone.

•

My closest support crew have been amazing, particularly Mum and Jeff, who have been hard at work researching my future options. From the moment Jeff received that distressing phone call from Dean, he has been on the hustle on my behalf. Aside from helping pull together the Orlando fundraiser, he quickly got in touch with our friend Becky, the lawyer who specialises in action sports who helped me get my US visa at the beginning of this year.

Becky put Jeff on to Barney and Josh, the other spinal cord injury sufferers, who provided a wealth of information. They also highlighted the ongoing costs of living with a spinal cord injury, which prompted Jeff to organise the Orlando fundraiser and start looking for other funding opportunities.

Mum's husband Gordon began looking into New Zealand's government-run Accident Compensation Corporation, to see if they cover injuries that occur overseas. It turns out they cover almost any injury that happens in New Zealand,

and injuries to Kiwis overseas *only if* those people have been away for less than six months. After telling them that I had planned on returning to New Zealand after the world championships we worked out that I would've been away from home for six months *and three days*. There are no grey areas: you're either in or you're out, and I was out.

So Mum starts looking into how things are done here in the US and whether there might be funding avenues to pursue here. Since I don't have personal insurance, she asks around to find out if I might be covered by Ronix's insurance. This leads her to an Orlando lawyer who specialises in liability claims. When I ask her about it, she just tells me not to worry about it. 'You just focus on your recovery, darling. Let me worry about this stuff.'

•

Yesterday the doctor mentioned that my bowel suppositories don't seem to be working as well as they should be, and said they were 'thinking about the options'. Would I be open to trying 'digital stimulation' to see if that might speed things up? he asks.

I don't like talking about this stuff so I nod my head, thinking digital stimulation must be some sort of new technological device or something. Worth a try, I guess.

Later on when Andrew is reading my chart he says, 'I see the doc spoke with you about trying digital stimulation.'

'Yeah — what is it?' I ask innocently.

Andrew holds up a hand and wiggles his fingers. With his other hand he points at them. 'Digits,' he says. Then he holds just one finger up and swirls it around.

Realisation — and horror — sweep across my face.

'What? *Noooo!* That's not . . . *noooo!*' I'm not down with that at all!

I half expect Andrew to laugh, but he's very professional and compassionate.

•

My lungs are still not clear of the pneumonia, despite a new vibrating chest wrap that the respiratory nurse has been trying on me to loosen all the gunk up so it can be suctioned out. So the doctor books me in for a bronchoscopy. I awaken midway through the procedure to see my own lungs being suctioned on the screen beside me, but I'm put back under the moment they notice I'm awake.

Alex Brown is back in town after being away for work.

'It's good to see you, bro,' I mouth, but his lip-reading needs work and it takes a few attempts for him to understand.

We spend the afternoon hanging out and watching the newest *Superman* movie on my tiny screen. How ironic is it that Christopher Reeve, the original movie Superman, is now the most famous person ever to suffer a high-level spinal cord injury?

Alex and I don't need to talk — we've known each other long enough that our bond goes deeper than words. At one point I glance down and notice that he's holding my hand, gently bending my fingers back and forth. Usually, holding hands with one of my best friends just simply wouldn't happen, but in this instance I'm comforted by it. He sees me looking down at our hands and breaks the silence to say, 'No homo, bro!' We both laugh.

Jesse, one of my best friends from New Zealand, has flown in to see me. He spends some of his time out on missions with Jeff — base-jumping, wakeboarding, whatever else they can get into — and the rest of the time he's here with me. Most of our time is spent binge-watching *Breaking Bad*. It's so comforting to have Jesse here.

•

After a month of not being able to speak a word, today is the day the speech therapist is going to give me my voice back. She unplugs the ventilator tube and attaches a small one-way valve in its place, then plugs the ventilator back. Meanwhile my respiratory nurse deflates the balloon in my throat. I instantly feel air rush up and out through my mouth. It's continuous — I'm not aware of air entering my lungs, but it keeps exiting up through my throat. I struggle at first to get control of it, coughing and spluttering as I learn to close my throat to let the air fill my lungs. It's the opposite of what had become autonomous my entire life: usually I'm opening my throat to inhale, now I have to go against instinct and close it. Within a couple of minutes I've found my rhythm: I close my throat to breathe in, and open it to let the air flow out.

I now have an audience of about 10 — nurses, physios and other therapists, along with Jesse and Mum. The speech therapist says, 'Okay, now we've all been looking forward to hearing that voice of yours, so why don't you start by telling us your name?'

I slowly work my way through a few more breaths, struggling to suppress an overwhelming urge to cough. Then in a low, croaky voice I say, 'Braaaad . . . Ssssssmeele.' Air rushes out my mouth as I speak so I sound like Darth Vader. The room breaks out in '*Ooohhs*' and '*Ahhhhs*' as their faces light up.

'Oh wow, it's good to hear that accent!' says my speech therapist. 'Now how do you pronounce your last name? I think we've been getting it wrong.'

'It's pronounced Smay-ler. Like 'sailor' but with an M added in,' I explain to her softly.

I can't believe this. For the next 20 minutes or so I chat away with everyone, my voice getting stronger with every sentence. I tell them how much I'm looking forward to being able to eat and drink again. 'I just want a smoothie, or an ice-cold beer!'

My therapist replies, 'Well this is definitely a step in the right direction. We'll do a swallow study in the next few days to see if you're ready to eat and drink again.'

After the room has cleared, I get Mum to dial Dawn. She answers, expecting to hear Mum's voice, but instead she hears mine. 'Hey, I'm back!'

'Oh my god, baby, it's so good to hear your voice!' I can hear her tears.

•

Today's the day of the swallow study. If I pass, I'm finally allowed to eat and drink again. For the past month my mouth has been dry, my throat so parched it's like a desert, and my tastebuds are screaming for flavour. I've already told Mum I want fruit and I want a smoothie. I've been craving that juicy flavoursome burst from biting into a grape, or a piece of melon. I've also been telling Andrew just how much I'm craving an ice-cold Stella Artois!

I'm wheeled in my bed to the radiology department and I'm sat upright. They bring out a tray with food on it — a glass of water, some yoghurt, a small fruit salad and a packet of crackers. Each food will have white barium fluid added as a dye so they can track its progress on the X-ray machine.

First, I'm to drink the whole glass of water. The first gulp is like heaven, and I finish the entire glass in one go, as ordered. Next is the yoghurt, which I get down easily. The radiologist is watching to make sure it's all going down my oesophagus and none is getting into my trachea.

'It's all looking good, Brad,' says my speech therapist. 'Now let's try the fruit.'

I've been excited for this part, but when the juices burst onto my tastebuds I'm disappointed. I can't really identify the taste. I'm not sure if it's because of the barium fluid, or the preservatives in the packaged fruit salad, or if it's just that my tastebuds are out of practice, but all I'm getting is tang, no actual taste.

I'm on to the final item. I crunch the dry cracker, but, mixed with the barium fluid it turns into a paste that sticks to the roof of my mouth. It's hard to swallow, but eventually I get it down with a little water.

The good news is that I passed. 'Congratulations Brad. You're now allowed to eat and drink again!'

I arrive back into my room to find Mum and my brother Alex, who has just arrived from London, waiting for me with a berry smoothie. By now my tastebuds have had time to sort themselves out and goddamn it's good! This one berry smoothie is everything and more.

•

A couple of hours later Andrew pops his head in after his shift finishes.

'Nice work, dude!' he says, reaching into his backpack. 'As promised, I got you that Stella!' He retrieves a bottle of Stella Artois wrapped up in an ice-pack. 'It's been in there all day so it might not be ice cold, but I hope you enjoy it. Oh, and you didn't get it from me!'

He hands the beer to my brother and leaves. Alex pops the top off the green bottle and uses the bed remote to sit me up.

I've anticipated this for too long. Alex positions the rim against my lips and tips the bottle up. It takes a few goes to get the angle right but eventually I gulp down a couple of mouthfuls. While the bubbles feel good in my throat, the experience is disappointing. My tastebuds aren't quite ready for the bitterness of beer, and it's warm . . .

•

We have been tossing around options for where I should go after I'm discharged from hospital. They have been trying to move me to a regular ward but I've been resisting — I know and like the team here and I don't want to undergo two moves.

We've narrowed it down to two options: Craig Hospital in Denver, Colorado, or Shepherd Center in Atlanta, Georgia. A representative of each has already come to meet me and talk. The two places seem pretty similar and both are crazy expensive — like $3000 a day! Since I'm likely to be there for several months, this is going to cost a shitload of money.

Mum just keeps telling me not to worry about it but I can't help it. I know there's been an incredible amount of money raised so far, with several fundraiser events and a Givealittle page, but surely nowhere near enough.

Then today we received a call from Shepherd Center offering me a *full scholarship*, meaning we would have to pay absolutely nothing! So that makes the decision pretty easy. I can tell that Mum is hugely relieved, like a great weight has been lifted off her shoulders.

Then Mum tells me that Florida Medicaid has agreed to pay for my surgery and ICU stay. I cannot believe my luck.

•

It's my last day in the Orlando Regional Medical Center and I'm excited to be moving on. Alex Brown has come to visit before I leave. We chat for a while but he seems like he's got something on his mind. After a little while Alex breaks the news to me.

'So, I wanted to get your advice on something.'

I nod for him to continue.

'Erin just told me last night that she's pregnant.'

'Wooah, dude, I was not expecting you to say that! That's . . . er, that's huge!'

Alex and Erin have not been together for long, and I know Alex was certainly not planning on having kids anytime soon.

'I know, bro,' Alex says. 'I just don't know what to do. She says she's open to talking about the options, but I know she wants to keep it. I just don't think I'm ready.'

I pause to think for a moment. 'Hey, man, I don't think many guys our age are ready to have kids; it just happens. You and I have both spent years fucking around with wakeboarding and bottle flipping and girls and partying and doing pretty much everything to avoid getting real jobs and becoming adults. So maybe, if you guys choose to keep this baby, it could be the kick in the arse you need to make you get your shit together — you know, that grown-up shit! Plus I know you'd be an awesome dad.'

Alex smiles. 'Thanks, dude! I knew you'd help me wrap my head around this.'

We keep chatting for a while longer, and eventually Alex gets up to leave.

'All the best for the move tomorrow. I'll be up to see you soon. Love you, bro.'

'Love you too, dude.'

It's totally new for me to express love to my close friends like this. Even among family growing up we rarely told each other 'I love you'. We knew it; we just never verbalised it. So as much as telling my good friend Alex that I love him feels strange, it also feels good. It feels right because my friends and family nearly lost me, so it feels important to express my deep gratitude for these people being in my life.

While I have my speaking valve in, I decide it's time to share some words with my supporters and wakeboard followers around the world. My brother holds up the phone and records as I speak my first public words since my life was flipped upside down. I thank everyone for their support, their messages and kind donations, and let them know that I'm moving up to Shepherd Center tomorrow. 'So on to stage two of this battle, and I'll keep you updated!'

After the hardest five weeks of my life I'm not even close to being done. I still have a lot of work to do to get off the ventilator, I still have pneumonia, and I still haven't had a night without a fever. I haven't gained any movement back but I am able to tolerate two hours sitting in the chair. I am learning to appreciate small signs of progress. The speaking valve has given me back my voice, and I can eat and drink again.

I'm eternally grateful to everyone who has had a hand in my care to this point. But I'm ready to get the fuck outa here!

On my 34th day I wake to my room being packed up, and soon a flight team arrives to get me ready for transport — on a stretcher bed on a Learjet! Outside the ward there's a bit of a crowd building of friends waiting to see me off. As I'm brought out of the room all my nurses are lined up along the corridor, plus my physios and a bunch of other staff who were involved in my care. Andrew is here on his day off and he's wearing one of the fundraiser tanktops! I flash a smile at them on my way by.

As we burst through the ICU doors I see around 40 of my wakeboarding friends cheering and clapping as we roll through and get straight into the elevator. I'm pissed off at the flight nurse pushing my bed for not stopping so I can spend a minute with all of these amazing people who got up early and drove to the hospital to see me off. I feel guilty that I wasn't able to give them more of my time but there's nothing I can do about it now.

When I heard we were taking a Learjet I pictured a flash private jet and I was excited. But as they're pushing my stretcher in through the door I feel like I'm being stuffed into a toothpaste tube. There's barely enough room for me, Mum and the three nurses and medics but we cram in and the door closes.

Ready for takeoff. Ready for the next chapter.

FIFTEEN: SHEPHERD CENTER

We land in Atlanta after a bumpy flight and an ambulance unloads me in front of a tall building. I'm taken up to my new temporary room in Shepherd Center's small ICU. Here I'm swarmed with admissions staff and paperwork while nurses poke and prod and check my vitals.

I'm not sure what medication I was given for the trip up here but I'm feeling very light and floaty. I'm convinced I can feel my right hand moving — it's lifting right up towards the ceiling! — but when I look, my arm is still lying by my side.

A young man walks into the room and introduces himself as my respiratory nurse (RN).

'Hi, Bradley,' he says. 'Or do you prefer Brad?'

I nod.

'Okay, so I see you've been battling pneumonia. I've got something here that will hopefully help you clear some of that fluid out of your lungs,' he tells me. 'Then I'll put a speaking valve in for you.'

My face lights up; it's so frustrating not being able to talk again after being given my voice back temporarily.

He pulls up a machine that he wheeled in with him. 'This is a cough-assist machine. What this does is fill your lungs with air, and then suction it back out. The goal is to help you cough up some of that fluid.'

The force of air coming in feels familiar, but when it sucks the air back out it forces me to cough hard, and up comes a whole pile of lung gunk. The RN removes two 10-centimetre sections of tubing that are filled with the sticky fluid, and replaces them with clean ones. We go two more rounds, filling four more sections of tubing.

'Wow, that's a lot!' says Mum. 'Better out than in.'

I agree. This is much more effective than the vibrating chest wrap and small suction tube.

'I'll come back later this afternoon and we'll see if we can get some more out before taking you off the vent,' says the RN, before plugging in a speaking valve.

An hour later I'm feeling really cold and I ask a nurse for an extra blanket.

She puts her hand on my arm. 'Bradley, you don't feel cold.' She checks my temperature. 'In fact it looks like you're a bit warm. Here, let me take the blankets off.'

'But I swear I feel cold; it doesn't make any sense,' I protest.

'Here,' she says, bringing my hand up to touch my face. 'Do you feel that?'

I feel the warmth of my hand against my cheek, but it's strange because it feels like it could be someone else's hand.

'You're warm,' the nurse explains. 'What you're feeling is called neuropathic pain. Your doctor will be in to see you tomorrow and he'll explain it to you.'

•

Late afternoon, my brother Alex arrives. He couldn't fit in the Learjet and flew up separately. My RN takes me through another round of the cough machine, then takes me off the ventilator. Once he is confident that I'm okay, a team of nurses transfer me into a La-Z-boy armchair.

I love that they're getting straight into it on day one. Sitting in a chair might not sound like rehab, but I need to build up my tolerance of sitting if I'm to progress to a wheelchair and some actual rehab in the gym. I also need to learn to control my breathing while I'm upright, which is more difficult than it sounds!

Today's rehab, though, is watching a movie with my bro. I figure if I can get right through a movie while sitting up and off the vent, then that's good progress. Alex sets up the iPad, generously sent to me by the Chris Ackerman Foundation, which came preloaded with movies. But first we go through some of the messages that have come in over the last couple of days. After 20 minutes I seem to be doing well so we put on a movie — *Captain Phillips*. I hadn't realised before we started that the film is almost two and a half hours long, so by the end of it I've lasted over three hours sitting up in the chair and breathing on my own. It's the first time off the vent since I flatlined, so it's a huge achievement and I'm feeling proud of what I've accomplished. I'm transferred back into bed for a welcome rest.

•

My doctor and his team visit the next day and he tells me about the plan ahead.

'When can I get started with rehab?' I ask him bluntly.

He explains that they want to keep me in ICU until we have the pneumonia beaten. 'We'll move you to a ward and start on your rehab program after that.' I also need more 'chair work'. 'I see you managed three hours yesterday. That's a great start. We'll have our wheelchair technician look to get you fitted for one of our chairs this week, so you can start increasing that time.'

'What about the ventilator?' I ask impatiently. 'What do I need to do to get off that?'

'In order to wean you off it completely, you're going to need to do 16 hours without it each day, for five days in a row. Then you'll do a night off the ventilator and we'll see how that goes.'

Excellent. That's all I need — a target, a goal, a focus. Sixteen hours. Let's fucking do this!

'Right now, though,' the doctor continues, 'I think it's time to get rid of that feeding tube.' He nods at a nurse, who peels the tape off my nose and slowly pulls out the long thin tube that reaches down to my stomach. It tickles and scratches as it's removed but I'm so happy to have it out that I don't care. I'm just so excited to start eating actual meals again.

The one thing he tells me that I'm really not stoked about is that they are going to fit me with a neck brace that I need to wear at all times.

'But I've gone this whole time without one at all, so why now?' I ask.

'It's a precaution, to make sure your neck is supported, especially when you're being moved around and when you're sitting up,' the doctor explains.

I hate the neck brace. It's uncomfortable and it makes me more anxious.

The next time I see him the doctor explains the neuropathic pain, and how the damage to my spinal cord may cause my nervous system to create a variety of new sensations. He offers medication to help.

•

Throughout the next week we focus on three main things: clearing the fluid from my chest, increasing my sitting tolerance, and spending more and more time off the ventilator. I make good progress on all fronts, and soon I get fitted for a hospital wheelchair. I'm not enthused about the idea, but once I'm sitting in it I actually kinda like that I can be tilted back whenever I'm feeling a little bit light-headed, and that brings my blood pressure back up without having to get transferred back to bed.

I think my problem with wheelchairs is that I don't want to *need* one. I'm going to prove the doctors wrong and walk again.

This afternoon I receive a call from a woman called Bridget who works for a wheelchair company, who tells me they want to help me out with my own wheelchair. She got my number from Jesse. I don't know exactly what she means by 'help you out' but I play along.

'We have one of our reps in the area, so we can arrange for him to come by tomorrow and take you through the options,' she says.

Tim, the Quantum Rehab rep, is a friendly guy who turns out to know Chad, so that breaks the ice a little. He flicks through a brochure and asks me to start selecting different options and colours. And while I go along with it and pick out a stealthy black-on-black theme, it feels like I'm picking out my own casket.

'So, Tim,' says Mum, cutting to the chase, 'when Brad was told that Quantum would help Brad out with a chair, what exactly does that mean?'

'I've been sent here to help you pick out a chair that Quantum would like to give to you for free,' Tim replies.

Mum, looking excited and relieved, thanks him profusely. I manage to smile and say thank you, but it's pretty clear to everyone that I'm not stoked on picking out a wheelchair, free or otherwise.

•

After a week in the ICU my pneumonia is mostly cleared up so I'm moved to a room in Ward 5. The room is spacious, with an ensuite and large windows that look out over the city of Atlanta.

That afternoon I meet Jill, one of my physios. She explains a little about the plan for getting into the gym, and then begins with some stretches. In the gym the next day she introduces me to my other physio, also helpfully named Jill.

I'm eager to get to work. All I've been thinking about and visualising is getting my arms moving. I've pictured fancy machines and gadgets that will kick-start the process, but my first session delivers a dose of reality — and more stretching. I don't know what I was expecting, but not this. This doesn't feel like work, but I'm surprisingly exhausted by the end of it. Clearly I need to lower my expectations. This is going to take longer than I thought.

I have a bad night. My nerve pains are firing — one minute I'm freezing cold and the next I feel like I'm on fire. It's strange and it's incredibly unpleasant. Like intense pins-and-needles. I'm aware that tears are rolling down my cheeks, so I puff into my call bell straw to call the nurse in. After giving me some paracetamol and another painkiller, she rolls me back on my side and the cool sensation of the tear-soaked pillow against my face brings me the only respite from the discomfort I feel through my whole body.

I just had my first actual shower in almost six weeks and it felt *so good*. It was a bit of a mission, but the moment I felt that warm water running over my head was one of the best moments since this nightmare began. It was really strange to feel the water run down my face and neck, and then feel nothing at all as it ran down my chest, like it wasn't touching my skin at all.

I've been learning to drive my wheelchair using something called a *sip and puff* control. A straw in front of my mouth operates the chair based on different pressures of sip or puff. When I want to drive, I hold the straw in my mouth and puff hard to go forward. At this stage it's set on turtle mode so I only have one single slow speed. To turn right, I puff softly. To turn left, I sip softly. And to stop, I sip hard. When I'm stationary, if I want to reverse I give a continual hard sip command. It's taking some getting used to, and I've bumped into a few things around my room.

There's also a little button mounted beside my head on the headrest. If I bump it with my head it takes me to a menu that lets me tilt the chair back. I need to tilt all the way back every half hour to relieve the pressure on my backside from sitting. The pressure sore I developed in Orlando actually seems to be getting worse.

It's beyond frustrating not being able to use my arms, but at least I have control of *something* in my life.

•

My brother Alex has returned to London and Mum has gone back to New Zealand but I'm excited that Dawn arrives today for a week. As soon as she arrives I'm showered with kisses, and she tears up to hear me speaking and see me up in a wheelchair. Although we have been speaking every night, when she left me last I was bedridden and she had to lip-read everything I said.

We spend our time talking and making plans, and if I'm in bed I get the nurses to move me across so Dawn can snuggle in with me. She's taking in everything she can to do with my injury.

I've been improving in leaps and bounds on the breathing front. I'm up to 10 hours a day without the ventilator. Dawn is excited to help me push it up to 16 hours, and today I manage 12. The next day it's 14 hours. Then on day three with Dawn beside me I hit 16 hours!

•

Today I receive an incredible surprise. I receive the latest copy of *Wakeboarding* magazine and I'm on the cover! They've used a photo taken by Flash Garrison a couple of months back at Lake Ronix. I'm stoked. It's also got signatures and messages all over it from some of my favourite riders and good friends. And if that's not cool enough, the cover-line reads:

READERS' POLL — #1 BRAD SMEELE!

I'm speechless, and tears fill my eyes as an overwhelming wave of appreciation rolls over me.

•

The doctors stop in on their morning rounds, mainly to check out my pressure sore. I'm rolled over and the doc takes a look.

'Unfortunately it doesn't look like it's improved at all. If there's no improvement in the next week we might need to try a skin graft,' he tells me. Then takes a photo to show me. It's gone from being a small split in the skin to an open, weepy wound. The doctor says they try to avoid the surgery as it doesn't always heal well. I have to be careful when in my chair to make sure I'm either sitting right up straight or tilted right back, and whenever I can I should get back into bed and lie on my side.

•

I'm back in bed for a couple of hours and back on the vent to give myself a rest after today's rehab session. Dawn is getting ready to take a shower, and is entertaining me by dancing around the room topless. She looks incredible naked and I'm reminded that my sex drive is well and truly intact. I can't stop thinking about what I wish I could do with her.

She emerges from the bathroom wearing a tanktop and some cute panties, then comes over and starts kissing me. I talk softly in her ear, suggesting she let me go down on her — or I guess it would be her going up on me. I would have suggested having sex, since I can still get hard, but I have an indwelling catheter at the moment.

She takes some convincing, then we have a quick discussion of what to do if we hear the door open, before she climbs on the bed and positions herself over me. I soon discover that one benefit of the ventilator is that I never need to pause for air! I love seeing her over the top of me.

She's just starting to get close when we hear the door open. Dawn panics, and rather than sliding down beside me and throwing the edge of the sheet over herself as planned, she perches awkwardly beside my head and looks at the nurse with a painfully embarrassed expression. The nurse apologises for 'interrupting' and leaves the room.

Dawn is mortified but I can't stop laughing.

A minute or so later and the nurse returns with a piece of paper on which is printed: PRIVACY PLEASE. DO NOT DISTURB. 'Just put this up whenever you want some privacy,' she says casually. 'I'll put it up on the door for you now.'

She closes the door behind her and I say to Dawn, 'All right, babe, back up ya get!'

But we've lost the moment and she's far too thrown to risk it again.

•

The worst part of my day is around 7–8 p.m., when the nurse comes in to do bowel duty. Dawn excuses herself. My usual nurse for these unpleasantries is Zara, one of the bubbly, fabulous black women that epitomise Atlanta. Every day she has a vastly different hairstyle, to the point that it's really confusing. Last night her hair was short and blonde, today it's long and dark, and tomorrow it might have braids with purple highlights.

Whenever a nurse starts their shift, they write their name on the whiteboard in my room. Zara always starts with a big sweeping 'Z' that covers half the board, like she's Zorro and the whiteboard marker is her sword.

Zara turns me on my side, gloves up and asks if I'm ready. I'm never ready for this. Using a squirt of numbing lube, she inserts her finger into my rectum and begins slowly swirling it around and around. I can't feel it directly, just a faint pressure. After a while it starts to give me a headache, but the real pain is to my dignity. I do my best to tune out but I can never remove myself from the horrifying reality here in this room. Somewhere between 20 to 40 minutes later, Zara tells me we're done.

When Dawn returns her presence alone is enough to lift my spirits. Looking into my eyes she sees that I'm struggling, that I'm on the verge of tears. She puts her hand on my cheek and says, 'I love you. I'm so sorry you have to go through that.' Then she plants a kiss on my lips.

She tells me she spent the whole time she was away down in the chapel praying for me. 'So many people are praying for you,' she tells me. She sees me roll my eyes. I have never believed in God and she knows that. I have received so many messages telling me that God is with me, and it's all part of God's plan, and as much as I appreciate the gesture, if this actually is God's plan then God is a dick. What sort of cruel plan is this? And does she really believe that people *praying* for me is going to heal my spinal cord?

Her eyes well up and the tears start flowing.

'It really upsets me that you're denying people's prayers,' she says. 'All those people are praying for you and you won't let them in.'

'Look, I just see it differently,' I say. 'I appreciate the gesture. I think it's incredible that so many people are thinking of me and sending love, and I'll take any positive vibes sent my way. I just don't believe there's a God that's listening to them and magically going to heal me.'

'But I *do* believe God will heal you,' Dawn says between tears, 'so I'm going to keep praying for you!'

'Thank you, baby, I appreciate it,' I reply, hoping this defuses the situation, because I know that if I were to be completely honest we would end up arguing all night. She pulls herself closer to me, her face against mine, and I can feel her tear-soaked cheeks. Physically we couldn't be closer, but I can feel the space between us beginning to grow.

•

At 10 p.m. my RN comes into the room.

'Okay Brad, that's another 16 hours — nice work,' she says. 'If you keep hitting those times we'll be able to remove this machine from your room in no time.'

She starts to attach the ventilator again.

'Can I stay off it a bit longer, please?' I ask. 'I'm not ready to go to sleep and I don't want my voice taken away just yet.'

'Okay, but the latest I can come back is midnight. Would you like me to come back then?' she asks.

'Thank you, that would be perfect!' I reply, happy to have a couple more hours talking with Dawn, and stoked to be pushing past the target set for me.

Dawn and I decide that my RN should be renamed Ursula — after Ursula from *The Little Mermaid*, who took Ariel's voice away.

When she comes back and takes mine away at midnight, I've been breathing on my own for 18 hours!

After Ursula has taken my voice, Dawn moves to her bed — an armchair that folds out into a bed on the other side of the room. This way there's less chance of her being disturbed when the nurses come in to turn me at about 3 a.m.

I'm woken up again at 6 a.m. to remove my assisted breathing and return my voice — I'm aiming for another 18 hours. And it warms my heart to see my love across the room curled up fast asleep.

●

My rehab is getting more interesting as Jill and Jill start me on some of the gym equipment. The other day I got to try a tilt table, which is like a narrow bed that I lie on and get strapped to, which then slowly tilts me up to standing. I made it to about 30 degrees before I fainted.

Today I'm being strapped into a type of stationary bike that uses electrical stimulation to tense my leg muscles in the right order to pedal the bike. It's cool to see them moving again. A motor is actually doing the work, but I love seeing the muscles tensing and contributing to the movement.

Every day in the gym I'm working tirelessly to get my arms going. There's an arm cycle that's part of the same machine as I use on my legs. I've noticed some slight flickers in my biceps so I'm putting every bit of intention to them, every bit of willpower, all of my focus. I will claim back my arms!

There can be up to 10 people using the gym when I'm there. I keep to myself most of the time, but I gradually start meeting the other spinal cord patients here on level 5. We attend classes together to learn about things like managing blood pressure, avoiding and managing pressure wounds. We learn about sex and what our injuries allow and don't allow. There's a heap of helpful information on offer.

Most of the others are younger than me, and most were injured either in car accidents or diving into shallow water. It shocks me to find out that's the second most common cause. One young girl took a gunshot wound to the spine, but the wildest back-story has to belong to a redhead who just arrived. She was in college, hanging with some friends, and some guys were goofing off some distance behind her. One guy tossed a football at a friend who tried to hit it with a golf club. The impact snapped the club and sent one end flying, impaling this girl through the back of the neck! It's like something out of a *Final Destination* movie.

It's nice getting to know everyone, but most of the others here have an injury level lower than mine, and I really struggle with the envy I feel about those who are gaining movement back, or who already have movement in their arms. One day a kid walks in wearing a turtle-shell brace on his chest and neck — I think we all feel jealous of him; it feels like he doesn't belong here. I have to remind myself that every single person here is going through the hardest time of their lives, and whether it's better or worse than my situation makes no difference to the battle they're going through.

There's a friendly kid named Jimmy who also has a C4 spinal cord injury, and he has been gaining movement back in his arms. I ask him how he did it.

'One night I was just lying in bed trying to move them,' he says, 'and after a while I got angry and gave it absolutely everything I could — I pretty much punched myself in the face!'

So that's it? Just get angry? The next time I'm lying in my bed I channel everything. I grit my teeth and tense. I struggle and fight and think about just how pissed off I am . . .

'*GrrrrrraaaaahhhHHHHHH! Fuuuccckkkk yoooouuu!*'

My arms don't budge.

•

I haven't heard much from Paul lately and I find out he's been told by Ronix's lawyer not to have any contact with me while a possible lawsuit is looming. A lawsuit? That's the first I've heard of a lawsuit. I thought my lawyer was looking at whether I could lodge a claim through Ronix's insurance. It turns out he's actually in the process of *suing* Ronix, Kilgus, Sesitec and several other parties. That would explain why I haven't heard much from Parks, Danny or Chad either — they're all part-owners in Ronix.

I know that's how they do things in this country — everyone suing everyone else — but I'm not down with it at all. I hate that this is coming between me and my mates. I talk to Mum about it and she says, 'It's ultimately your choice, but you need to think about your future, Brad. Gordon and I are still looking into ACC to see if there are any loopholes or other ways to get you covered, but we haven't found anything yet.'

I ask Dawn to dial the lawyer for me.

'Look, I don't feel comfortable with all of this,' I say.

'What are you saying?' he replies. 'Are you saying you want me to cease and desist legal action?'

'Yes . . . yes, that's what I want. I'm sorry for the trouble you went to but it just doesn't feel right,' I tell him.

I feel so relieved, like a weight has been lifted.

Mum, on the other hand, seems more stressed.

•

It's time for Dawn to fly back to Oklahoma to get back to work. After she leaves, my nurse tells me I'm going back to the ICU briefly so they can monitor me as I spend my first night off the ventilator. I'm a little nervous about it, but the next morning I'm told I did not stop breathing while asleep.

One afternoon I'm taken on a tour of the rest of the facility. Downstairs I'm shown the swimming pool for hydrotherapy, but my pressure sore needs to be healed before I can get in there.

I look at the pool in front of me and a disturbing thought crosses my mind: *This is how I could end it. All I need to do is drive my chair into the deep end and I'll sink like a rock. No more suffering. I won't have to live my whole life in a wheelchair. It will all be over.*

The thought scares me. Never in my life have I contemplated suicide, and here I am not only contemplating it, but planning it. I'm one hard puff away from ending this nightmare. But I think about Mum and Dad back home, and Dawn — and the pain it would cause them and the rest of my family and friends. I just can't do it to them.

And in any case I'm not ready to give up yet.

•

Jeff is staying with me for a few days leading up to the Wake Awards. I've had loads of visitors rolling through and today we all decide to go out into the garden to get some fresh air. This is where I escape to when I'm feeling confined, but my nurse has to come with me, pulling a cart laden with oxygen bottles and other emergency stuff.

I've recently been given two extra speeds for my chair, so with a second hard puff it accelerates to around 3 kph, which allows me to cruise down the hallway at walking pace rather than snail's pace. As we go out the door there's a long wheelchair ramp that hugs the side of the building on my left, and has a handrail on the right. I'm driving down at my slowest speed, focusing on keeping straight, but halfway down there's a slight bend and I puff lightly to turn, but obviously puff too hard. Rather than turning, my chair picks up speed and I crash into the brick side of the building.

Everyone is immediately on edge, but thankfully the only damage is some scraping on the side of the chair. When everyone sees that I'm okay we burst out laughing, including my nurse.

'A bit of whisky throttle there, bro?' Jeff laughs.

The day after I crash my loan chair, Tim arrives with my shiny new black wheelchair. I'm much more enthusiastic than when I ordered it, although I notice instantly that the black-on-black theme is thrown off by the silver wheels. I get transferred into it and he sets up my driving program to match the rental I'm used to. I don't want to make a fuss — since they're giving me the chair for free — but I mention the wheels and Tim immediately realises, and tells me he'll bring the wheels I ordered in a couple of days.

If I'm going to be in a wheelchair, I've still gotta look fly!

•

My sister and her partner arrive tomorrow, along with a television news crew from New Zealand. Jeff helps give my face a shave so I look fresh for the interview. This is more intimate than I thought Jeff and I would ever get . . . We've become ever closer friends through this. I truly appreciate everything he has done for me, from helping set up fund raisers to connecting me with other action sports athletes with spinal injuries. He's really stepped up to the plate in a big way.

The film crew get busy to record the arrival of Monique and her fiancé Jonny — they actually got engaged on their way here on an overnight stopover in Hawaii! It's so great to see them and I'm excited to have them here for the week. That first night of them being here turns out to be the first night that I don't spike a fever overnight. It's the best night's sleep I've had since my injury and I'm stoked.

That following day it's my interview. I've been trying to remain positive throughout this entire journey, even when I'm not feeling it, but the journalist's questions keep tapping away at my positive outer shell until it cracks — I crack. My eyes tear up when I'm describing the moment I woke up in the water after the crash. I don't burst into tears, but a couple escape my eyelids and roll down my cheeks.

That afternoon they film me in the gym. I've been learning to use a mouthstick stylus to operate an iPad and my phone. When I first tried it back in Orlando ICU, I hated it and refused to use it, but now after a few sessions I'm beginning to get the hang of it. My occupational therapist has set up some basic games for me to play and I'm nailing it! It takes a lot of focus and control of my neck muscles, which are still pretty weak, but I'm getting good enough to take control of my phone again.

My session is interrupted by my RN for today, a tatted-up military-looking guy.

'Hey Brad, I've got some exciting news for you!' he starts. 'Since you've been crushing your target times off the vent, and you've done your overnight in the ICU, we're taking the ventilator out of your room and your trachea tube is ready to come out too!'

Excited, I reply, 'Awesome! When?!'

'Right now, dude! You ready?'

He pulls his trolley of supplies up beside my chair. With cameras rolling, he unties my collar, then oh so casually pulls the plastic trachea tube from my throat, leaving a pinky-finger-sized hole into my trachea. It doesn't hurt coming out, just a bit of a scratchy tickle. For a moment my breathing becomes tricky but he fixes this quickly by taping a gauze dressing over it.

'The hole should close up on its own in a couple of days,' he explains. 'This means you can go anywhere in the hospital on your own, without your nurse following with the oxygen bottle cart. Congratulations, dude!' The physios and Monique and Jonny cheer and applaud as the camera rolls.

•

Jeff helps me record an acceptance speech and thank you message for the upcoming Wake Awards. Although I've known deep down that I was going to win Trick of the Year, ever since the moment I landed it in Germany, Jeff confirms the fact, so I ask if he and my brother can accept it on my behalf. In my acceptance video I do my best to come across upbeat and excited, since this is an award I've aspired to win since the awards began. But everyone knows it was the same trick that put me here in this wheelchair.

Later in the evening Zara is due to do my bowel routine and Jeff is kicking it in my room until she arrives. But when the door opens, it's not the sprightly little woman I'm expecting . . . it's a large man who introduces himself as Tyrone. My heart sinks even further when I glance at his huge hands. I look up at Jeff, whose eyes were drawn to the same place as mine. He then gives me a look that I will never forget, of pity and terror combined — a look that says, 'Oh bro, I'm so, *so* sorry for what you're about to go through,' before he leaves the room.

There's an awkward tension in the room — I can tell that Tyrone is about as enthusiastic as I am.

'Yo, dude,' he says, 'do you mind if I turn the TV on?'

'Please, I could use the distraction too!' I answer, attempting to lighten the mood.

After Tyrone has finished, Jeff comes back and asks, 'Are you doing okay after that prison rape, bro?' I can always count on Jeff to ease the tension with an inappropriate joke.

'Maybe it's a dose of my own medicine after what I've done with girls over the years,' I add, using an inappropriate joke of my own to attempt to make light of my recent traumatising experience. Because if I don't laugh, I'll cry.

•

It's Wake Awards night, and Alex has flown into Orlando to meet up with Jeff. They've also got a guy named Aaron with them, who is from the Road2Recovery Foundation. They have set up a fund for me and are there to raise people's awareness of what they do for injured action sports athletes.

Jeff Skypes me on my iPad from his laptop, while Paul FaceTimes me on my phone. With both devices mounted in front of me I have great coverage of the event — not to mention all the people the phone and laptop get passed to who want to say hi. Even Camilla is there and steals the phone for a few minutes.

At the very end of the ceremony they announce me as winner of Trick of the Year. Cannons blast confetti into the air and the whole crowd goes absolutely nuts while footage of my double tantrum to blind plays on the big screens. Jeff and Alex go up on stage to accept the award, and the entire Ronix team are on stage in support. Jeff delivers an epic speech, finishing with: 'I want you all to get on your feet and give one big *hoo-rah for B-rad!*' He holds me up high through the laptop in his hands while everyone cheers.

As amazing as the moment is, sitting here in my hospital room watching it through a couple of screens I'm hit hard with a very lonely feeling. It hurts knowing I'm not there for the most prestigious accolade of my career, where I finally receive the recognition I know I deserve. It really hurts.

Dawn flies in the following evening and is met by TV cameras as she enters the room. After the film crew are gone she and I spend the weekend together. I tell her I'll be going back to New Zealand as soon as I'm fit to get on a plane, and ask about her plans. She says she wants to stick around for a while at least, to support her brother who's about to start playing college football. That sounds like a pretty shitty reason to me. I don't know her family dynamic: all I know is that in the moment she first entered my room in ICU she told me she wanted to move to New Zealand and look after me and have my babies, and now it seems like she's backpedalling.

Some time later we're talking on the phone and she says something about not wanting to move away while her grandparents are still around. So now I have to wait for her brother to finish college and for all of her grandparents to die?

•

Dawn leaves at the end of the weekend, and Paul arrives after a big Surf Expo weekend in Orlando. He has brought me a gift — a shiny gold Wakeboard with a *B-RAD* logo on it.

'Here you go, my friend, this is the prototype for the pro model graphic we're getting made to raise money for you,' he says.

Unbelievable! 'Thank you, my friend,' I respond, awestruck by the magnificent gold glow the board emits.

It's great to have Paul here, especially after not being able to see or talk to each other while the legal shit was going on.

We chat about Lake Ronix and he tells me how much I'm missed. I tell him how much I miss it — truly, madly, deeply!

I show Paul a new trick I just discovered. If I tilt my chair all the way forward, there's a reaction in my hands — all my fingers stretch out straight for a few seconds. This is the first movement I've seen in them since my crash. I don't know what it is, or what it means, but it's got to be a good thing.

'Dude!' Paul says excitedly. 'You're such a fucking bad-arse, Brad!' He begins pounding his fist against his chest. 'Let's do this! Let's . . . fucking . . . do . . . this, Brad!'

I love that he gets so pumped up at anything I do. It's really motivating, because I struggle to find my own motivation sometimes.

I recall Paul telling me about the head injury he suffered after he came off a skateboard when he was younger. He mentions it again now.

'When I had my brain injury, my dad told me the same thing I'm about to tell you now: Don't worry about anything but your recovery. Don't worry about money — I've got you.' He's tearing up slightly. 'I fucking love you, Brad!'

I'm really touched by this. But on another level it makes me uneasy. Mum, Alex, Jeff and Dawn have all assured me that they'll look after me. It's gratifying, and it's amazing, but I want to be able to *take care of myself*, like I always have. I feel my independence has been stripped from me, so I have no option but to accept help. (And later, I'm disappointed to learn that it's just muscle spasms creating the movement in my fingers.)

I have a constant procession of visitors. Alex Brown is among them — he tells me he has a new job and is moving with Erin to Houston.

Now that I'm completely weaned off the ventilator, and Mum and Gordon have been trained in how to manage any problems that arise, I'm allowed to leave the hospital grounds. So a few of us, including the Aussies Chris-O and Brenton, venture down the road to the local Houston's Steak House, where I'm thrilled to finally get that ice-cold pint of Stella and, damn, does it taste good! The lads are equally thrilled to feed it to me, and I down almost a quarter of it without stopping. A minute later I'm super light-headed and need to tilt myself back in my chair. Thankfully my blood pressure levels out quickly and I'm able to enjoy the best meal I've had in months.

It's Dawn's birthday and I'm a bit stumped on what to get her. I can't exactly go shopping and I don't just want to order her something generic. Eventually I have an idea. Using my mouthstick and phone, I find a picture of an Air New Zealand boarding pass and download an app that allows me to manipulate it. I spend hours making every detail perfect, adding her name, the destination *Auckland NZ*, and where it says the departure time I write: 'Whenever you're ready'. I then spend all day writing out a poem for her, with the last verse saying:

Whenever you're ready, together we'll be.
Your flight to New Zealand, just leave it with me.

I send the boarding pass to her phone while we're talking, along with the poem, and then read it aloud for her.

'Look, I know you're a bit hesitant to come to New Zealand, but for your birthday I want to buy you a return ticket so you can come and check it out before you commit to moving there.'

She's blown away, and we're both excited that she's coming to visit next weekend.

During the week, Mum calls from Auckland with some amazing news: ACC has agreed to cover my injury!

'How on earth did you manage that?' I ask.

'We found out that Ronix were reimbursing you for building materials that you paid for on your New Zealand credit card. Since that money was going into your New Zealand account, it means at the time of the accident you were receiving a taxable income in New Zealand, which means you were also paying ACC levies! So you're fully covered!'

This means ACC will cover the vast majority of my costs from the moment I arrive home — from medical bills to paying for caregivers to purchasing medical equipment and more. This is *huge* and I can't believe it.

'No way! That's awesome news — well done!'

The weight has finally been lifted. Mum can now relax about my financial future, as I know it's been stressing her out. I am massively relieved.

It's crazy to think that if the Bank of America had approved a credit card for me, instead of declining it, then all of my expenses would have gone on that, and no money would have gone back to my New Zealand account. Things would be looking a whole lot different.

•

Danny and Parks come up to visit so we head outside into the garden to kick it in the autumn sun. Danny pulls out a spliff and asks if I'm up to smoking.

'Why not?' I say. 'It's been a few months so I should take it easy, plus there's the whole pneumonia deal, but I'll smoke a doobie with you guys.'

'Sorry it's not up to the B-rad standard,' Danny says. 'I've got some work to do on my rolling skills.'

It's another stinging reminder of something I enjoyed that I won't get to do any more.

Parks holds it to my lips and I take a small toke, but that's enough for me. I just enjoy the moment, sitting with my idols who became my friends, and enjoying the closest thing to normality that I've felt since this all began.

A couple of days later I have some more visitors — a crew of riders and wake industry guys have come up from Orlando. We hang out in the garden for a couple of hours, sharing stories and reminiscing. In the evening, when we're back up in my room, Sean Dishman and Jake disappear for close to half an hour. Just before they return, Josh, one of Dano's friends who lives nearby, waltzes into the room holding a stack of pizza boxes and pulling a large suitcase behind him. Josh and his girlfriend Jenna have been coming in to visit me for the last few weeks. I'd never met them before but they heard about my accident from Dano and they started visiting and bringing me home-cooked meals.

Josh lays the suitcase down and I hear it clunk. Sure enough, he opens it to reveal that it's packed full of cold beer! On one side are the craft beers, and on the other side are the standard lagers that I like, including Stella. We start to hoe into the pizza and beer, until Dish and Jake come back into the room.

'B-rad, we've got a surprise for you!' Dish says. 'But you've gotta come with us to the gym,' he adds mysteriously as he heads out the door.

'A surprise? Aww, you guys got me strippers, didn't you? That's so thoughtful — you shouldn't have!' I say jokingly, driving my chair out the door as the rest of the guys grab the pizza and beer to bring along with us.

I drive through the double doors into the gym to find a big projector screen set up.

'Welcome to the world premiere of *Prime*, my friend!' says Dish.

'Fuck yeah, dudes! I'm so pumped to see this!' I say, turning to look at them all. 'Seriously, I'm really stoked I get to watch it with you guys!'

The movie is epic — more epic than I had imagined. Kilgus did an incredible job. There are two Lake Ronix sections. I open the first, with an interview on the beach talking about how incredible the property is. Then I close the second section with my double tantrum. It's the one I landed on film about a month prior to my crash, and it finishes off the section perfectly. The gang all cheer and clap as they turn to look at me.

I'm happy with the section, for sure, and I'm really proud of all the work I did behind the scenes to make it possible, but deep down I'm beating myself up. Obviously I know that a double tantrum to blind would've been an even better hammer for it to finish on, but the section was complete without it. I'm in this wheelchair because I was too stubborn to let it go. In my mind I had to land the dub T2B — there was no option!

But clearly there was another option, and hindsight is showing it clear as day.

I don't sleep well that night. My thoughts keep swirling and stabbing at me: *You fucked your life up for a wakeboard movie! You fucked your life up for a sport! You fucked your life up because you were so fucking stubborn — look what you've done!*

•

Friday evening rolls around after a week of rehab fuelled by my frustration. I'm excited to see Dawn tonight. I've spent the last few days getting things organised for a late birthday celebration. Also, it's our last time together before I fly home to New Zealand next weekend. I've arranged for a table to be set up on the top floor of the hospital, by a window that overlooks the Atlanta skyline. There are flowers and even a bottle of wine ready to add to the table, and Zara is picking up dinner from Houston's Steak House on her way to work.

Then my phone rings and it's Dawn. I thought she would be on the plane by now.

I answer the phone to hear her crying.

'I'm *sooo* sorry,' she sobs. 'I can't get on the plane.'

'Why? What's wrong, babe? Did you miss your flight?'

She's borderline hyperventilating now. 'No, I . . . I'm still in the parking lot. I can't even get out of my car.'

'Wait, what? I don't understand. Tell me, babe, what's up?'

'I'm sorry, I can't get on the plane. I'm scared I'm going to catch Ebola.'

She bursts into tears just as I'm about to burst out laughing.

Ebola has been all over the news for the last couple of weeks after a single apparent case made it to the US, causing mass hysteria. I personally am not buying into some of the bullshit they run on Fox News.

'*Really?* Ebola? Come on, babe, get on the plane. It's fine, you're not going to catch Ebola,' I say lightly, attempting to calm her down. But it doesn't work.

For the next 20 minutes I regurgitate facts about Ebola.

'You know it's not an airborne virus, right? It only spreads through bodily fluids. You had a higher chance of dying on the drive to the airport than you do of catching Ebola on the plane. The one case in America is in Dallas and you're flying to Atlanta.'

All to no avail. She's been brainwashed. So I end the call, pissed off and hurt. Part of me thinks it's nothing to do with Ebola. She's scared to see me for what she knows will be the last time because she's never going to move away from Oklahoma.

The following day I call her. I tell her I love her, but feel we need to be realistic about this: our differing religious beliefs, the difference in how we each let things like the news affect us, and how right now I just need to surround myself with positive energy – maybe we're just not compatible. And besides, I say, the relationship clearly isn't going to work since she has no intention of moving to New Zealand.

'I do want to but I just can't leave my family,' she replies.

'I know, and that's fine,' I reply. 'I get it. I don't like it, but I get it. Look, you were my angel when I needed you the most, so I can never thank you enough. You saved me,' I say through tears, 'but we both know this is over.'

And just like that, we're done.

●

The following day I call Mum, who's coming back in a few days to take me home. I tell her about Dawn, and we agree that although she's been an amazing support these last few months, it's probably for the best.

She asks me how I'm doing, and the question triggers a response from deep within me. I'm suddenly rocked by a tidal wave of emotion. Tears stream down my cheeks and I'm almost hysterical.

'Mum, what have I done? I've completely fucked my life up!'

Throughout this whole journey since the accident I've done everything I can to remain positive — putting on a positive face to keep my friends, family and followers happy because that's the only way I knew how to keep going. I've cried a few tears from time to time but nothing more. But now I'm really crying, ugly crying. Every feeling I've pushed down and bottled up in my attempt to stay strong is now pouring out of me. I've bottled up so much that the breakup with Dawn not only made the bottle overflow, it completely shattered it. I'm a total mess.

This lasts around half an hour, while Mum does her best to console me. Eventually I pull myself together and get the nurse to wipe the snot from under my nose and dry my face. I'm emotionally exhausted, but the knot in my chest is gone. I actually feel better for having let it all out.

●

My brother Alex flies in from London to spend the last week with me before Mum arrives. Paul comes back for a couple of days too.

Two days before I leave I'm preparing to speak to a room full of trainee nurses, which I've been asked to do. Suddenly I'm not feeling so good. I begin to shiver uncontrollably but start sweating at the same time. My head is pounding. Paul calls for the nurse, who rushes in and discovers that my catheter is blocked. She sorts it out quickly but the bad news is that I have a bladder infection. I have to bail on my speech. The doctor prescribes some antibiotics and reassures me I'll still be fit to travel.

This is my first experience with autonomic dysreflexia (AD), which I learnt about in class. AD is a rapid massive spike in blood pressure and accompanying heavy sweating leading to extreme discomfort that can have serious or even fatal results. It is common after high-level spinal cord injuries, where the involuntary nervous system overreacts to various external stimuli. There can be all sorts of contributing causes, from a full bladder or bladder infection to kidney stones to pressure sores.

•

It's Saturday, 20 October 2014, and after 72 days here at Shepherd Center I'm finally heading home to New Zealand. I say goodbye to my amazing team, and we fly home, landing in Auckland feeling fresh and rested.

Driving through the arrival doors, I'm greeted by an overwhelming reception. Applause erupts from a large group of friends and family who got up early to welcome me home. I see Monique and Jonny with my nieces Maisey and Mila. There's Jordan and Emma and the entire Lewis family, Rory, Brant, Jesse and so many more — there must be 30 people here!

I see Courtney bawling her eyes out, there's my Nanna Ros, and walking towards me for a long-overdue hug is Dad. A handful of media photographers snap photos while TV cameras roll, capturing the moment when I'm reunited with him and so many others who mean the world to me.

It feels so good to be home . . .

SIXTEEN: HOME, BUT FAR FROM IT

The reality is that of course I'm not actually going home. At the airport I'm loaded into a mobility van and taken directly to Middlemore Hospital in south Auckland, where the next chapter of my journey begins.

I spend a week sleeping a lot. Jet-lag hits me hard, and I find out that my usual nerve pain medication is not available so I'm switched to another one. My body does not like the change in meds and my nerve pains become almost unbearable, like my body is being swarmed by fire ants. My fever spikes overnight and my only relief comes via my nurse Sophia, who sits by my bed and uses cold facecloths to help keep my temperature under control. After a few nights I become addicted to the feeling of cold on my forehead, even when my temperature is normal. I realise that being unable to feel anything on my skin below my shoulders, this form of touch feels satisfying, and almost seems to mask the nerve pain. That and head scratches and kisses, but I might be pushing my luck to get those from Sophia.

The one other escape I get comes one morning when I get to have a bath in a special type of bath-bed. It's still strange feeling the water over my shoulders and neck but not on the rest of my body, but it's soothing to be partially submerged again.

After the long and somewhat miserable week at Middlemore, I'm moved down the road to the Auckland Spinal Rehab Unit. It's not flash — nothing like Shepherd Center — but at least I get my own room, since I need to be isolated after picking up the hospital superbug MRSA while in the US.

The first major change is made after the doctor checks my pressure wound. Dr Suresh tells me in a direct but soft-spoken manner that they want me to stay on bed-rest until the wound is healed.

I don't like the sound of that at all — it feels like a big step backwards.

'How long do you think that will take?' I ask.

'It could be weeks, it could be months. But it's of the utmost importance that we keep the pressure off that wound until it's completely healed.' Seeing my frustration in my face, he adds, 'I understand, Brad, that it must be incredibly frustrating, but if we don't get on top of it now, it could get much worse and has the potential to keep you out of your chair for a long time.'

A few days later I'm visited by Mum's friend Susie Turner, who has helped me out at her Pilates studio over the years with conditioning my body and rehabbing after injuries. For years she's been practising something called kinesiology, which she used to help me after I hurt my shoulder a few years back.

Kinesiology is an alternative therapy that aims to use muscle monitoring (biofeedback) to detect and correct bodily imbalances caused by stress or injury, and Susie tells me she wants to do some kinesiology work with me now.

'We can work through any emotional blockages you may have, and I'll see if I can help open some of them up to clear some of your energy pathways,' she tells me. I tell her it sounds good, though I don't really understand the kinesiology thing.

'It might be something you feel you're not ready to face right now,' she says, and she's right, because I instantly feel a wall go up. What does she know about what I'm going through? Then Susie tells me about the tragedy she went through when she lost twins shortly after birth, and I realise that maybe she understands a thing or two.

She does some quick muscle testing and says, 'One of the emotional blockages this shows is that you appear to be dealing with a lot of guilt. Tell me what comes to mind.'

Hah — where do I start? I feel a lump in my throat that immediately chokes me up. 'I feel guilty for everything!' My eyes well up as I think about everyone who has donated money to help me. I feel guilty for leaving Lake Ronix unattended, for leaving Dano without a co-announcer, I feel guilty that I won't be there to guide future Kiwi wakeboarders through the US pro scene as Jeff did for me.

Then there's the guilt that comes from knowing what I'm burdening my friends and family with now — all the adjustments they have had to make so far and all the sacrifices to come. I chose to take that risk, and although I paid the biggest price, so many others are affected. That brings me to the most prominent guilty feeling . . .

'I struggle to look Mum in the eye,' I say through tears. 'Out of everyone, I've burdened her the most with this. I struggle to look her in the eye because then I see what I'm putting her through.'

'That's a very natural way to feel, Brad, but as much as it feels like it's your fault, you're not responsible for the actions or feelings of others,' Susie tells me.

'But it's my fault!' I reply. 'How am I not responsible when it's my fault?'

'Brad, a mother's love for her child is something that is wired into her. Something that you have no control over. And when a child is sick or injured or in need, a mother will do anything for them, and that includes pointless things like stress and worry. So you're not responsible for her grey hair or wrinkles, just as you have no control over the feelings and reactions of others. It's such a beautiful thing that people from all around the world feel for you and want the best for you. How incredible is it that you touched so many lives in such a way that now they want to help you? That's why they do it, that's why they support you, that's why they donate — because they love you.'

I do my best to absorb what Susie is telling me, but it's hard.

She boils it down to one thing I try to hold onto: 'You're not responsible for how others act or feel.'

Susie tells me she wants to come and see me every week. 'We're going to work through this together, and I don't see why we couldn't have you walking again within the next couple of years.'

If she believes that I can regain movement, then I'm all in!

•

We start to make my room a little more my own. We put up a poster of me wakeboarding, and move in a mini-fridge to store all the ingredients for my lunchtime smoothies, as recommended by Susie.

Brant works not far away at the Harley-Davidson dealership, so each day he comes to visit me on his lunch break. He loads all of the ingredients — coconut water, coconut oil, spinach, banana and berries, along with a dollop of a nutrition powder — into the Nutribullet and blends up my lunch. And, conveniently, Brant eats my hospital lunch.

Dad has been visiting me a lot and it's so good to spend time with him, since he was unable to get to the US. Our time together gives me a much better understanding for what he has been going through for the last 20 years with Parkinson's disease. And with my own experience, I can now understand his frustration at becoming so limited by his body, and his anger over the loss. We talk about how frustrating it is to feel like a prisoner in our own bodies.

•

The next time Susie comes to visit, she notices an A4 page that's stuck to the ceiling above my bed. On it are the seven principles of Huna.

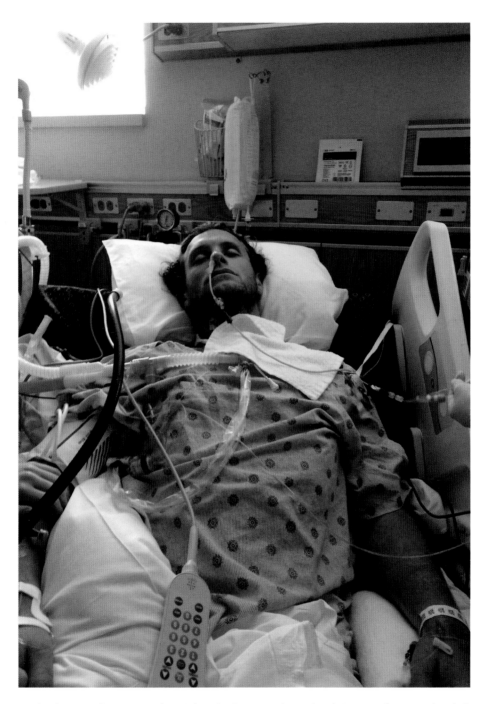

Early days in the ICU at the Orlando Regional Medical Center. I've got the full works: tubes, wires, monitors and a ventilator.

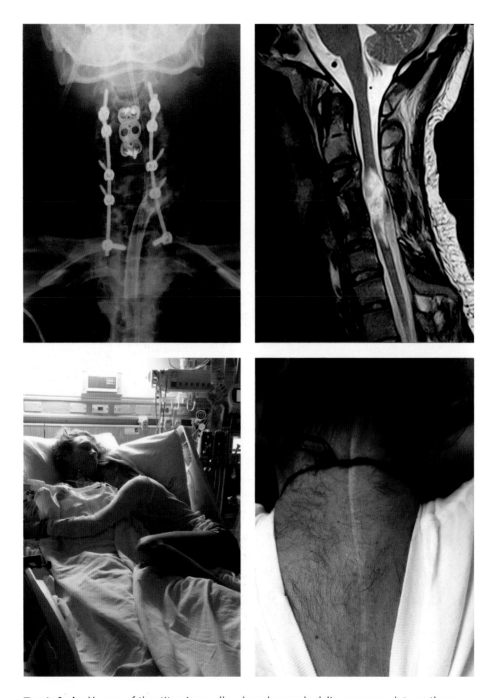

Top left An X-ray of the titanium alloy hardware holding my neck together. **Top right** An MRI showing my crushed spinal cord. **Bottom left** The angel who was by my side when I needed her the most. **Bottom right** A scar to tell the tale.

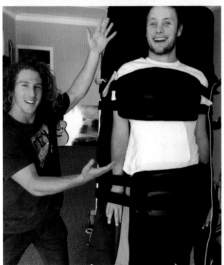

Top The crew visiting me at Shepherd Center in Atlanta for the private premiere of *Prime*, the movie by Sean Kilgus that we appeared in. **Bottom left** Standing on the tilt table alongside my mate Bob Soven. **Bottom right** What are friends for? Jesse helping me do what I can't.

Top Celebrating Deano and Amber's wedding in front of the Sydney Opera House and Harbour Bridge. **Bottom** Hosting the 2016 Wake Awards with my boy Dano the Mano (photo by Rodrigo Donoso).

Top 'Beached as' with Brant at Auckland's Piha beach (photo by Jade Whirley). **Bottom left and right** Intense rehab sessions at Nextstep in Orlando with my trainer Travis. On the left I'm using a walking frame for assisted walking (photos by Josh Letchworth).

Top Twilight hangs with team Ronix near the completed tiki tower that I started building before my accident (photo by Bryan 'Bear' Soderlind). **Bottom** 'Long hair don't care': Brant (left), me and Jesse showing off the long locks we grew for a fundraiser.

Top A return visit to the Orlando Regional Medical Center. Flight nurse Rob George is showing me the chopper that flew me in from the crash site back in 2014 (photo by Erik Ruck). **Bottom** Grounding myself among nature: a hike with friends in Auckland's Waitākere Ranges.

Top Back in the water for the first time since my accident: a pool session with the boys at Rossi's place in Orlando. **Bottom** My first freedive training session with Bob (left) and Jesse.

'Ooh I like that!' she says. 'Where did that come from?'

'My auntie sent it to me so I thought I should have it stuck somewhere I'll always see it,' I reply. I had it on my ceiling at Shepherd, too, so I've had some time to ponder on them.

Huna is the Hawaiian word for secret, and in Native Hawaiian healing practices the seven principles encapsulate ancient knowledge said to enable an individual to connect to their highest wisdom.

Susie and I talk a little about what each principle means to us.

IKE — The world is what you think it is.
What we focus our thoughts on can shape our experience. If I focus on all the positive and beautiful things in the world, then the world becomes a beautiful place to me. If I focus on the negative, my mind and my world become negative.

KALA — There are no limits, everything is possible.
I feel that this is about pushing ourselves, and not accepting limits. Susie explains that it's more about our belief systems — the beliefs that have become part of our everyday life, even if we're not conscious of them. We can be limited by those beliefs, or we can realise that most limits exist only in our minds. So if I believe the doctors when they say I'll never walk again, then I deny myself that possibility.

MAKIA — Energy flows where attention goes.
Again, this is about focusing on the things you want, on the positive, on the present and moving forward. If I spend all my time focusing on the past, and things that aren't real any more, then all that energy is wasted. If I put my energy into being grateful, then I become grateful, and gratitude is powerful.

MANAWA — Now is the moment of power.
The past is gone and there's nothing we can do to change it, and the future is unknown, so living in the present is the most powerful way to live. This motivates me to take action now, rather than delaying and procrastinating.

ALOHA — To love is to be happy.
Love is a word that I've mainly attached to relationships with women, but I realise it is so much more than that. Love is a state of truly appreciating and enjoying

something or someone. I am starting to express my love for the people in my life, because I truly appreciate them.

MANA — Power comes from within.
We have a wealth of power within us. So often we look outside ourselves for motivation when we have it within us all along. For me it is about figuring out how to tap into that inner power. The more we accept who we are and believe in ourselves, the more power we have. Understanding that I have power over my thoughts and actions gives me power over my life again.

PONO — Effectiveness is the measure of truth.
I struggled to wrap my head around this one initially, until I found some alternative wording: *Harmony is the measure of truth.* This helped me understand that it's all about doing what feels right for you. What's true for you might not be true for me, so it's about finding harmony through living out what feels right for you.

•

Before she leaves, Susie says, 'I want you to think about Manawa, about being present. I'm excited to hear how you get on.'

•

The bed-rest continues, and when I don't have any visitors I spend time on my phone, replying to messages of support from people all around the world. At around 10 p.m. one night my phone dings to tell me I have a new message. It's from Bower! We haven't spoken since long before the crash, so I call his number.

'Hey mate,' he says, 'I'm sorry it's taken this long to get in touch, but you know I've been thinking of ya without me having to plaster it all over social media. I just thought I'd let the dust settle and let the vultures stop pecking at you.'

I ask what he means by that, though I have some idea.

'You must be so sick of all these fucking people coming in to visit just to get a picture with you for their Instagram, like: *Look at how great I am visiting my crippled friend in hospital!*' he rants.

'Dude, *thank you!*' I say, feeling a sudden relief at the honesty in his scepticism. It's like he's unlocked the door to my metaphorical closet of negativity — a place where I've locked away my sceptical and negative thoughts in order to help me protect my positive shell.

My friendship with Bower has always been like this — we can go months or even years without making contact, but we both know our friendship will always be there. And he's good at cutting through the bullshit and getting to the truth. I discovered this on our first long road-trip during my first Aussie pro tour.

'I've been trying to remain so positive throughout this,' I tell him now, 'and I always do my best to look at the bright side of situations, but *fuuuck!* You're so right, it's amazing how many people came out of nowhere and suddenly gave a shit! And not just them, but sponsors and magazines too. I got fuck-all support before, but as soon as I'm hurt it's like *NOW* I'm on the cover of *Wakeboarding* mag and *NOW* I'm getting a pro model from Ronix, *NOW* I get offered financial support. Where the fuck was all this before?'

I feel myself giving vent to the deep anger and frustration at the unfairness of my situation. I do believe people have the best intentions, and I really do appreciate the support from my visitors and from the wakeboard industry, so I usually focus on the positive aspects of it all. But just this once it feels good to let the anger out. After taking a moment to draw breath, I thank my friend for allowing me to finally vent the negativity, for being so real and not talking to me like I'm precious and need protecting. Bower just talks to me like I'm the same guy I've always been, because I guess I still am.

We talk for over an hour. By the end of it I feel better for having released all the negativity that's been building — and we have some good laughs too.

●

I've been receiving a fair amount of media attention since getting home, and I allow the *Sunday Star-Times* in to interview me. They ask about the messages of support I've received, so of course I go on about how incredible it's been, but I also reveal the flipside, mentioning the messages that tell me this is all part of God's plan. I'm aware that this may offend some people. But I'm not prepared for the article appearing on the *Stuff* media website with my quote as the headline: 'If this is God's plan, then God's a dick!'

I find it pretty funny at first, but as the article starts being shared around I realise a lot of my US and global supporters may be upset, so I manage to convince them to change the headline. It took away from the message I was trying to put across, which was about my positive approach to this injury and my recovery.

Susie has a good laugh when I tell her about it all. She's not religious so I feel comfortable opening up to her. She persuades me that people send those messages from a place of love.

'They don't know what you're going through, and they don't know what to say to you, so they resort to something they know — something they believe in. Instead of letting yourself get angry about it, try to focus on the intention behind their message, which is simply to send you love.'

It makes sense. 'But how do I do that?' I ask.

'Swap out the word God with Love. Whenever someone uses the word God, just translate it in your head to love, to what you believe that entity to be, and let go of the need to debate your stance on the topic. Simply accept their love.'

Susie explains that everything I'm going through requires me to rewire my brain. The software I'm currently operating off, which I have developed throughout my whole life, is no longer compatible with my new hardware. It seems pretty daunting to have to reprogram my brain and I don't know where to start; I'm glad I have Susie to guide me through.

•

I've been thinking a lot about Morgan. At the time a photo of Dawn and me ended up on the front page of the *Herald* I knew Morgan was working with my family and friends organising a fundraiser for me. When I left New Zealand in March I had fallen for Morgan but knew there was no future as I had no plans of coming back. We kept in touch, but less and less. I never stopped caring about Morgan, but I'm painfully aware that I'm not the same guy she fell in love with.

One evening I decide to call her. She's in the South Island filming but she sounds happy to hear from me. We talk for a while, catching up on this and that. Then I say, 'I'm so sorry you found out about Dawn that way — that must've been so shitty.' I explain that there wasn't really anything to tell until Dawn was at my bedside in the ICU and suddenly became labelled as my girlfriend.

'Brad, you don't need to explain,' says Morgan. 'It did hurt, but I'm glad you had someone there for you.' We talk for around half an hour. I look forward to seeing her in about a month when she's back in Auckland.

•

It's been over a month and I'm still stuck on bed-rest. Every four hours I'm turned from side to side to keep me off my pressure sore and stop me from getting any new ones. Thankfully, it's healing well. This means I'm allowed an actual shower each day, rather than bed-washes. I've been allowed to be in my chair for an hour a day too. It's not long but it's a welcome change. Sitting upright again tanks my blood pressure at first — I need to rebuild my tolerance.

Alex has flown back home for the summer, and, to make things even better, Dean and Amber have come over from Australia for a visit. They have some exciting news: Amber is pregnant! They're rapt, and I'm so stoked for them. I feel closer to Dean than I ever have. He saved my life and we will have that connection forever.

My occupational therapist, a very attractive young woman named Megan, helps hoist me into my chair while they're with me. For whatever reason, I've been getting an erection every time I get into my chair since being on bed-rest. Usually it only lasts a minute or so. I'm not disappointed to see that it can still happen, but it's a little inconvenient today and my loose-fitting trackpants are not doing a good job at covering it up. Thankfully, the fact that I'm tilted back to allow my blood pressure to settle is hiding it from my visitors. After I tilt back upright I instantly get a light-headed feeling, so back I go again. It happens again, and when I come back up for the third time I notice that I'm still pitching a full-blown circus tent! What's going on?! My two Australian friends across the room are looking down absolutely glued to their phones.

There's only one way to approach this.

'Shit, my blood pressure is not playing ball today!' May as well address the elephant in the room: 'All the blood must be rushing elsewhere!' I say.

Dean, Amber and Alex all burst out laughing and I even see a chuckle from Megan.

'We were trying to be polite over here, mate,' Dean says. 'I was trying so hard not to laugh. No wonder you were light-headed!'

I learnt in one of the classes at Shepherd that apparently I can no longer get turned on by sight or thought, only through touch. So theoretically an attractive girl could be dancing naked in front of me but nothing would happen, whereas an overweight, middle-aged man could be washing my genitals or checking my catheter and I'd be at full attention. That could be very inconvenient . . .

•

I've finally been getting into the gym for some rehab. While I'm lying on the tilt table I'm watching several other patients going through their own rehab. I find it hard to watch others progressing without feeling incredibly envious of them.

A few days later I start to feel unwell. A rattle in my throat quickly turns into a full-blown chest infection. But I can't cough because I have zero abdominal muscle-power to help force the air out of my lungs, so I need the nurses to help by shoving my belly up into my diaphragm to help force a cough out. They have to do it hard — it's almost like a punch in the guts.

It's hard to sleep because I can't breathe properly, and I'm constantly calling the nurses to help me cough up green phlegm. At one stage I'm dozing when I'm suddenly awakened to realise I can't breathe at all — my airway is completely blocked. The nurse rushes in just in time to help me cough it up. After that I'm hooked up to a fluid drip, fitted with a tube that feeds oxygen through my nose, and they bring in a nebuliser, which creates a vapour that's supposed to help loosen the gunk so I can cough it up. A drug is added to relax my airways, and finally a cough-assist machine is brought in.

Thankfully, by afternoon my symptoms have improved, but it takes two more days to clear my lungs. It's frightening to be reminded of just how fragile I am.

•

Susie returns, this time with an assistant who is here to surrogate for me so Susie can get a reading from my body. I'm still a bit sceptical about it all, but supposedly Susie can use kinesiology to ask my body what it needs. Instead of asking me to hold my arm out, since I'm unable, she asks her assistant Dani to place her hand on mine, and Dani holds her arm out. Susie explains that she will ask a series of yes/no questions.

'Dani holds her arm out straight and strong, and as I ask the question I push down on it. If her arm drops down easily then it's a no, and if it remains strong then it's a yes.' Generally, Susie goes on, certain emotions can affect different internal organs, and she can help drain any that are overloaded, by rubbing on that area of the belly where the organ sits.

I'm well and truly sceptical now but I submit happily enough. I have nowhere else I have to be.

After she finishes up she asks how I'm getting on with the guilt stuff we worked on. I tell her I'm still having trouble forgiving myself for the effect of my accident on Mum.

She explains to me about the five stages of grief: *denial, guilt, anger, depression* and then finally *acceptance*. After she leaves, I ponder that process. I think I'm still working through guilt, though sometimes I'm angry, sometimes I'm depressed. I guess this is different to mourning a death, because that person is gone completely. Mourning the loss of myself, I'm also still around to remind myself constantly of what I've lost. It's confusing to think about.

I spend my evening messaging various girls I've reconnected with, and a couple of new faces I've met through social media. I enjoy the attention, even if some of it may be prompted by pity. It's still nice to feel wanted.

•

Tonight is the New Zealand premiere of *Prime*, but this morning I woke up with a bladder infection. I'm on an antibiotic drip but I'm told that if my fever doesn't come down they're going to send me back to Middlemore Hospital.

'I can't, please!' I beg. 'I *have* to go to this premiere tonight. I'm being picked up at six!'

It's not just the movie — it's my first chance to see all of my Kiwi friends together in one place, along with a bunch of crew from the wakeboard community who haven't seen me since before the accident. We've hired out a cinema and everything.

The doctor is unmoved by my wheedling. Unless my temperature returns to normal, it's not happening.

For the rest of the day I drink litres of water, apply cold flannels to my forehead and keep all blankets off, I'm naked with just a thin sheet covering my hips and bits. By late afternoon my temperature has come down a little, but it's still above 38°C. The doctor breaks the news that they're sending me to hospital.

I'm completely gutted, and I break down and cry.

In hospital my fever still won't break, and soon I'm at a roasting 39.5° and I'm moved to the high-dependency unit. I'm a mess: the nerve pains are ruthless, like there's acid running through my veins; my head won't stop pounding; I'm burning up and I just want it to stop. I just want it all to end. It's the longest night.

When dawn finally breaks, so does my fever and I can finally relax. I sleep for most of the day; three days later I'm moved back to the spinal unit.

•

Christmas definitely doesn't feel like Christmas. The whole family come to visit, including my Nanna and Uncle Mark, and it's nice to have them here but it's not the same as eating and drinking and playing games and swimming and laughing at Mum's place.

New Year's Eve is similar — my mates and I would usually be causing a ruckus somewhere, partying, getting drunk and stoned and chasing tail. But it's fun to be telling stories and hanging with my closest friends, even here. We ring in the new year and then Ron, an older guy who had been working here for yonks, pops his head in to tell us it's time to call it a night. I actually really like Ron. He's a bit of a grumpy old bastard but he's actually really friendly underneath. Plus he's experienced and super efficient so he's the best person to take care of anything I need.

After the crew head on their way, my room feels empty, as I do.

This is not how I imagined I would be starting 2015.

•

A week into the new year and I'm in the gym with Jesse, who's keen to watch my rehab session. I'm back on the tilt table. To date I have only managed to get up to around 60° for no longer than a minute. Today, however, I'm feeling good, and I'm motivated to smash that record. And after gradually working my way up, while convincing my little Filipino physio that I'm not going to pass out, I make it to 85°, which is as tall as it goes!

Damn it feels good to be standing tall again! I stay there for a couple of minutes — long enough for Jesse to get in for a photo standing beside me.

I'm sent in an ambulance to Auckland Hospital for surgery to have a suprapubic catheter put in. In a matter of hours it'll be *free willy* when the in-dwelling catheter is removed from my penis, and I couldn't be happier about it! The new catheter will go through my belly just below my belly button, straight into my bladder, freeing up my penis for other things . . .

I'm back to the spinal unit the next day and I'm surprised how quickly I bounce back (so to speak) from having a hole cut into me to give me a new place to pee from. I bounce back so fast that a few nights later I'm escaping my cell to go to a concert! My pressure sore is healed so I'm able to be back in my chair during the day. This will be my first time getting out to something public and social in over six months. I'm a bit nervous about being in a crowd, but I'll be with my bodyguards, Alex and Brant, and we're going with Morgan and her bestie, so I'm in good hands.

Arriving at The Powerstation, an Auckland live music venue, I'm guided through a back entrance and we find a good place for me to park in my chair, beside a pillar and before a step down to the main dance floor. As the venue packs out I'm glad to have my friends on either side keeping my safe space safe.

The lights dim, and the crowd erupts as the silhouettes of German band Milky Chance grace the stage. I feel the energy of the crowd ripple through me. And when the music starts, and the stage lights beam, so does my smile. I look over to see the faces of my friends light up and we exchange smiles and nods as they begin to dance.

I turn back to the stage to absorb the waves of ecstasy the music is sending through me — I'd forgotten how fucking beautiful music is! Especially live music, where the entire room is feeling the same energy vibrating through their cellular make-up; thousands of people all feeling the same vibe, grooving to the same rhythm.

I'm doing my best to move to the music but my main move is a rhythmic head nod, and occasionally I'll bring my shoulders in for a Stevie Wonder-style head sway. I close my eyes and let the music fill me up. It feels like a top-up for the soul, my vessel, which needs a good refill! It's doing a good job of making me forget my reality for a while — until I watch the people dancing and interacting all around me. Suddenly I just wish I could dance. I look at Morgan and wish I was dancing with her, taking her hand and cutting shapes with her. I watch my brother show off his own impressive moves. I keep trying to trick my body into moving, trying to force my way out, but I'm concreted in.

Suddenly it's like the plug is pulled and my vessel begins to drain. The more I wish I could dance, the more frustrated I'm getting that I can't move, and the more I try to move, the more trapped I feel. Every time I look at Morgan I'm reminded that I'm not good enough. She will never love me like she did this time last year — how could she? I'm breathing short and sharp as the anxiety knots itself up in my chest.

An arm reaches across in front of me and there's a drink in its hand. As if Brant sensed that I needed it, he feeds me a big drink of vodka and Red Bull that symbolically reminds me to relax and enjoy the music. So I close my eyes and tune back into the sounds. Slowly, the noise in my head is overrun by an acoustic guitar and a drumbeat and the knot begins to unravel. I pick up on the difference in how I feel and realise how true it is that I need to keep my mind focused on what makes me feel good.

MAKIA — Energy flows where attention goes.

I thought I understood the concept of that one, but feeling it in a real-life scenario makes it click that much more. If I focus on the negative of not being able to dance, or what I used to have with Morgan, then my mood is going to follow that negative trend. When I switch off my overthinking and enjoy the moment, soaking in the show in all its encapsulating sights and sounds, feel the energy in the room and ride the wave, I'm removed from my broken body and lifted up by pure energy.

Back in bed after the concert my body is still tingling. I glance up at the third Huna wisdom and smile, doing what I can to hang onto that good energy for as long as possible.

•

We've been given word that I'm to move out of the spinal unit in a couple of weeks. But where to? Mum's place is not suitable because it's completely wheelchair-unfriendly, so Mum has been on the hunt for an accessible rental home for me.

I'll also need some caregivers. ACC will cover the cost of my caregivers 24/7, unlike in the US, where most of the responsibility is dumped on the family. This means that I can still live somewhat independently, which is a huge bonus.

I meet a bunch of potential caregivers and shortlist a few.

After about a week of searching, Mum finds me a suitable home that's already set up for a wheelchair user. It won't be available for a little over a month so we need to find somewhere for me to go in the interim. Thankfully, Mum has organised me a stopover through the Laura Fergusson Trust.

•

My three-month stay at the Auckland Spinal Rehab Unit is finally up! After saying goodbye to a few of the staff who I've got to know well, I'm loaded into a mobility taxi to take me to my next temporary containment facility. It's not far from my old hood so I think I'm going to like it around here.

The moment I'm unloaded and I look around, I realise I've been here before. This place has a huge oak tree surrounded by beautiful gardens that I planted! I even installed the irrigation system. I proudly show the welcoming administrator the patched-up tarmac where I dug a trench across the driveway for the irrigation hose.

This place is so much nicer than the spinal unit. My room is more like a little apartment than a hospital room, with access from outside.

My first day in the gym I get vertical on the tilt table. My blood pressure is not holding up well but my physios have come up with a trick to keep me standing a while longer. As soon as I start feeling faint I let them know and one of them begins shaking my knees around, bending them back and forth the little amount the restraints allow. This triggers some small muscle spasms in my legs and hips which in turn raises my blood pressure a little.

It's been close to five minutes when I warn them that my BP is dropping again, even with the leg shaking, but I've stood at full tilt for a total of five minutes, so I let myself celebrate this one.

Two days later we go for it again but I push myself too far. Next thing I know I'm opening my eyes to my physios fussing over me.

'Brad, are you okay?' I hear a muffled voice underneath the ringing in my ears.

'I'm fine. Did I pass out?' I ask as the surrounding sounds of the room come back into clarity.

'Yeah, you muttered that you weren't feeling good and then before we could do anything, you were out.'

•

There's not a whole lot to do when I'm not in the gym. Mostly I hang in my room and play around on my phone. I post old wakeboarding memories, I give progress updates and positive messages out to my supporters. But most of the time I'm messaging girls. I can't let go of wanting to feel like I'm still desired.

I've been messaging Lindsay a little, and over the past few months she's been keeping me entertained with gorgeous naked photos and we've been reminiscing about the night we had together a week before my injury. However, it's only now that she reveals that she actually got pregnant after that night, but lost it through miscarriage inside the first trimester. I'm shocked. My first reaction is relief, but then I think: *What if that was my last chance to have kids?* It's a thought that lingers . . .

The caregiver agency keeps sending potential carers for me to meet, and while I've given the okay on a couple, I've turned down a bunch too. Today, while I'm in the gym, I'm meeting another possible — a Filipino guy named Kristian. I get a shock when he walks in. I had pictured this classic small Filipino, but this dude can't be far off 1.83 metres tall and his arms are covered in tattoos. I find out that he's from Naga City, where I've been, and he's into wakeboarding! And he's a registered nurse.

Well, that was an easy choice!

•

Ants is back from Europe and he's stopped in for a visit. We have a great catchup, and after hanging out for a while, he gets up to leave.

'It feels strange not being able to give you the ol' slap and pound to say hi and bye,' he says. 'Like when I got here I didn't know what to do.'

I know what he means. Not only have I lost the traditional slap-pound greeting I had with my mates, I've also lost the ability to hug people, to shake hands, to high-five, fist-pump, knuckle, shaka, the shocker, the 'rock on' devil horns, pinky promise, middle finger . . . and the ability to hold someone's hand in mine. While I've thought a lot about the loss of physical connection with women, until now I hadn't given a thought to losing something as simple as the bonding greetings with my best friends.

Ants and I decide our new greeting will be a light head-butt — similar to the traditional Māori hongi, where two people touch foreheads and press noses. So Ants leans in and knocks his forehead gently against mine before he takes off. I decide this is my new slap-pound.

•

Tomorrow I'm getting out for an entire day! I'm going to hang out with Travis Pastrana and the Nitro Circus crew, who are in the country with their world-famous action sports stunt shows. They've invited me to go down to the Franklin Farm in Tokoroa tomorrow, where they'll be practising for the show this weekend. What's more, ACC have arranged a loan van for my use until they eventually supply me with one to keep!

After my morning cares are done and I'm up in my chair, Brant and Soph arrive and we're soon on the road to Tokoroa. Soph and I have remained friends since dating a few years back and she's come to visit me often. Since she's rather handy with a camera, she's agreed to join us to film the day's action.

The place is swarming with talent, with some of the world's best dudes on dirt bikes, BMXs, skateboards, mountain bikes and even a guy that rips on a scooter.

I unload out of the van and as I'm headed to the foam pit to check out the action, Travis makes his way over and says hi. The last time I saw him I almost collected him with my board while doing a double flip over him on the mega-ramp for his upcoming film *Action Figures* — and that was only a week before my accident. He gets a little choked-up while we're talking, even though this man has likely seen more serious-injury accidents than anyone on the planet, including those he's been in himself. I think maybe it choked him up to be reminded what can happen when it all goes wrong. We catch up for a few minutes before he's pulled away for media obligations, but those few minutes mean the world to me. We could get back in the van and drive home right now and the trip would have been worth it.

We sit and watch for a few hours, Brant, Soph and I, and our eyes are treated to an incredible display of the world's best tricks being done right now. Suddenly, thunder rumbles from close by, and a storm is upon us. In less than a minute we're being pelted by buckets of large raindrops. We head for cover and I'm halfway down the ply pathway (yes, ply!) when my wheels start sliding in the wet. Brant grabs the back of my chair but he's got no grip either so we're sliding together.

Thankfully BT, the Red Bull manager, rushes in and saves the day, and I make it to the bottom safely. I'm soaked, but in that moment of complete loss of control, I was in complete control mentally. I knew there was nothing I could do, so I was simply along to enjoy the ride. I got the best adrenalin rush I've had since this all started — just your typical day with Travis and the Nitro Circus dudes.

Back in the rehab centre, my bed feels like a prison cell after my small taste of sweet freedom. I'm battling internally over whether I should be happy or sad. Today was such a surreal day and one that felt very special, but it was also such a painful reminder of what I can no longer do. Tonight, the darkness triumphs and I simply cannot stop the tears.

•

On my 28th birthday, in February 2015, I get everyone together at a bar to celebrate. Arriving at the Cavalier, I'm surrounded by friends, family and acquaintances. It's great to be surrounded by so many people who care about me but it's also somewhat overwhelming to have no ability to move around freely. I'm sat in one place looking up at everyone towering over me and it's making me feel uneasy. Things look and feel very different for a guy who used to stand tall enough to see over most crowds.

I'm pretty much stuck talking to whoever is standing beside me, which in itself gets tricky as more people crowd in and the noise level goes up and up. My vocal level is massively limited due to the lack of abdominal muscle activity and I'm struggling.

There are a lot of attractive girls here — it wouldn't be a B-rad birthday without some of Auckland's finest-looking females in attendance. Some are just friends, some I've dated, some I've made out with, some I've slept with, and maybe one or two I thought I might've ended up with. As much as I love that they're all here to celebrate with me, it's crystal clear that everything has changed. None of them look at me the way they used to. The hint of desire in their eyes, the flirting, have gone, and behind their friendly smiles it's now pity I see. My confidence is shot to shit.

Alex feeds me a big drink of my beer and I get into some of the food that's circulating, which takes my mind away from the dark hole it was about to fall into. With some help, I've moved outside onto the deck where it's a little quieter, and I enjoy a drink with the guys. There is some sense of normality in this at least.

•

There's a knock at the door and a nurse asks if I'm up for a visitor.

'Of course,' I reply, seeing that she's come with another resident, a young man in a chair similar to mine.

'Brad, I want you to meet Angus,' the nurse says, and I notice as he drives in that he's still breathing on a ventilator attached to the back of his chair. He's also driving tilted back at about 30 degrees and using his chin to control the chair.

Angus and I do our best to hold a conversation, although I rely on his nurse, Katie, to help with his answers as his voice is little more than a whisper and there's a rattly sound to his breathing. It takes me straight back to my ICU days, when the fluid in my chest rattled with every breath and I spoke with difficulty through a speaking valve attached to my ventilator.

I learn that Angus has a C2-level spinal injury, two levels higher than mine, which means he can't move anything. Angus can literally only move his facial muscles. I have an immediate sense of gratitude that I can sit somewhat upright in my chair, use my phone with a mouthstick, and breathe on my own.

Angus's story is unbelievable.

'I went to the A&E with a bad headache,' he tells me. 'The doctor checked me out and sent me home with some paracetamol, and I woke up in the ICU two weeks later like this.'

'Wait — what?' I respond. 'I don't understand.'

Katie chimes in to explain that the emergency doctor misdiagnosed Angus, who actually had an infection in his spinal fluid, which went on to cause his paralysis.

'So if it's not from a direct injury, does that mean you don't get ACC cover?' I ask.

Angus says something I have trouble picking up so Katie repeats it for him: 'It was medical misadventure, so he has different cover.'

I just can't imagine it — at least I got my injury doing something I love. I only have myself to blame. I can't imagine the utter unfairness of it being a medical fuck-up. Angus then goes on to tell me how many of his family don't bother coming to visit. He doesn't really have visits from anyone.

After they leave, I'm left feeling so bad for Angus, but most of all I just feel *sooo* grateful for what I have. Have I taken for granted how lucky I am to have such an incredibly supportive family and such amazing friends and supporters? I know I've thanked them, I know I love them, but sometimes I know I take it all for granted. Although Angus may not be able to move a muscle below his chin, he just delivered a solid smack in the face to wake me up to how fucking lucky I am.

•

A few months ago Jeff told me that the Tairua Pipe Masters is being brought back as a fundraiser event to help with my recovery. I'm tasked with finding sponsorship for the event and I've been sending emails when I can.

The event is this weekend so Brant and I road-trip down to Tairua to check out how the build is going. Kristian comes along for his first few days as my caregiver. We pull up to the contest site where the crew have been slaving away to get the rails built. Brenton is in charge. He's a qualified builder and one of the top rail riders with a good chance of winning this thing, so we flew him in for the job. He's had help from a crew of local riders and builders, mates of Devo, who used to run the event back in the day.

It's great to catch up with Jeff and Kayla. Deano and Scotty Broome have come from Oz to ride in the event, and young ripper Gunner Daft has come all the way from the US! Also here from Oz are Brenton's brother Dwayne, and Carnie. I'm so pumped to see them all.

We pull up at our accommodation, the only 'wheelchair accessible' room we could find. We soon discover that it's not exactly accessible for my big power-chair, but we make it work.

Kristian gets me up early for my morning ablutions. After waiting for an hour for my bowels to empty, he gets me ready to shower. The 'wheelchair accessible' bathroom is tiny and there's no way I can get into the shower cubicle, but thankfully the bathroom itself has a drain plug in the middle, so Kristian just places me in the shower chair outside the shower and pulls the shower hose out to sluice me down.

The whole morning routine takes longer than expected, which makes me late for my planned visit to Tairua Primary School. When I get there, Devo is keeping the kids entertained. The whole school is waiting for me in the assembly hall.

I haven't really planned a speech but I just start telling my story. I go with the flow, on a theme of encouraging the kids to pursue their dreams. After I'm done, the whole school sing 'Lean on Me', and I'm so touched that my eyes fill with tears. The rest of my day is lifted by such a cool and inspiring start to the day.

All afternoon I sit with good friends and watch the riders practise for the main event tomorrow. Having all the guys around, especially the Aussie crew, brings a feeling of such familiarity that for a moment, maybe just a few seconds, I forget how much everything has changed. In that moment I'm not worried about what my future might hold, or dwelling on all the things I can't do any more. I'm simply enjoying a beer in the company of good friends.

After a reasonably quiet night, I'm back up and ready for the main event day. As the tide rolls in, so do the crowds. By the 3 p.m. start time, the banks are packed with spectators and supporters mingling among our sponsors' marquees. Donation buckets are being taken around, and there's a brisk trade in T-shirts, hats and stickers. The music is pumping and the weather is beautiful — this thing is off to a good start!

A mic stand is placed in front of me, and Jesse is sitting beside me with a mic of his own. It feels good to be commentating the event but I notice very quickly that my voice doesn't have half the power it used to. With Jesse's help we stay the course as the guys tear up the unique jet-ski-towed rail course.

I wish I could say the event went off without a hitch, but unfortunately Kiwi rider Nick Beal was seriously injured when he slipped out on the most high-risk feature of the course. His lower leg slammed into the open end of a PVC pipe. I could see from where I sat that his leg was probably broken, but it turned out to be much worse. The PVC pipe actually severed most of his shin muscles and he had to be helicoptered to hospital.

This is the last thing anyone wanted at an event raising money for an injury recovery. A sombre feeling hangs over the event while this is all going on, but Jesse and I manage to get things back on track after the heli leaves. We're in the local bar for the awards and after-party as I announce Deano in third place, Jeff in second and Brenton as the winner! The night then ascends (descends?) into the chaotic party I expect. I sink a couple of beers and socialise with the crew, but as it becomes too crowded and too loud for me, I call it quits close to midnight.

Reflecting on the event, it's incredible to have felt such support from riders and the local community. It seems like we raised some money, but regardless of what the fundraising result may be, this has been such a successful event, except for Nick's injury, of course . . . and I've had him on my mind all evening, because all we've been told is that he's 'stable'. Thankfully, we find out later that they saved his leg.

●

At my last physio session before I leave the Laura Fergusson Trust rehab centre I'm focused on the tilt table, and I hit 20 minutes — my longest time yet!

I'm pretty chuffed with myself. What a great way to end my stay here.

SEVENTEEN: WHO AM I?
(MONDAYS WITH SUSIE)

Today I'm finally moving into my new rental home on Auckland's North Shore. It's a four-bedroom house that's wheelchair accessible, and has had a couple of other minor modifications made — ramps and wider doorways. I'm so excited to be out of the hospital system and in my own space.

With me in the master bedroom and a room for my caregiver, I've got space for a couple of roommates. One of them is Courtney! The fourth bedroom is a large one downstairs and it's semi self-contained, so I'll look to find someone — possibly even a couple — for that space.

On day one, Brant rocks up to pick up Courtney and me for a Foo Fighters gig at Mount Smart Stadium. A few days ago, while at work at Harley Davidson, Brant met lead singer and legend Dave Grohl when he and drummer Taylor Hawkins borrowed some bikes for while they were in New Zealand. Brant managed to score some tickets from them and we're even invited to meet the band before the concert!

Unfortunately, due to a lift malfunction, we miss the VIP meet and greet but I'm just stoked to be going to see one of my favourite bands live. We're seated in the disability area, which is a platform to the side of the main crowd in front of the stage, which is slightly elevated to give wheelchair users a better vantage point. My first thought is *Great, I have to sit in the 'special' area*, but it turns out to be a really good spot, with a great view and plenty of space so I'm not constantly bumped by people.

It's the best live show I've ever seen and by the end of the night I'm absolutely buzzing. While I had some moments of wishing I could be raging in the mosh pit or running around in the crowd chasing tail, I find the music pulling me into a zone where I'm completely immersed in the sights and sounds of the show. I no longer give any thought to my injury, my restrictions, my disabilities — everything is trumped by my dedication to rocking out and raging to the Foos with my good friends.

In the first few days of living in the house, my caregivers and I work on getting a routine together. It's strange to have someone with me all the time; when I ask for something it feels like I've got a servant or something, which just feels so wrong.

But this is *real life* now. This is my house, this is my life — and I have to get used to having a *babysitter* here to look after me because, well, shit, they are my hands now. I'd die of thirst or starve to death without them! Actually, if I were left with no help, the thing that would kill me would probably be the inability to take a leak. My bladder would fill beyond capacity, causing the urine to back up into my kidneys, resulting in an AD response that would start pushing my blood pressure up and up. I'd be drenched in sweat first, then my head would start pounding and my nerve pains would intensify, getting worse and worse as my systolic blood pressure soared over 200. The extreme hypertension could lead to a series of strokes until I'm dead, or a vegetable. It's spooky to think about, but that's the truth of how dependent and how vulnerable I am.

Asking a caregiver to do things for me is going to take some getting used to, and after only a few days I'm already getting frustrated trying to explain how to do this, or where to put that — how to give me a drink without spilling it down my front, how much food to put on the fork, what angle to bring it towards my mouth. Some definitely pick it up faster than others.

On day three I'm parked up on the deck in the sun. I keep myself busy replying to people's messages on social media, and of course I end up mindlessly scrolling. I have an uncomfortable feeling that I should be doing something — it sits anxiously in my chest — but there's nothing *to* do. The only way I can *do* anything independently is on my phone.

There are times I notice myself trying to avoid: times when I'm alone and I look away from my phone and I'm present in the room. I don't know what the fuck I'm supposed to be doing. It's like there's a big question mark hovering over my head. I can't do anything I used to do. I don't recognise this life — where am I? *Who* am I? Finally I work out that now, outside the hospital bubble of doctors, nurses and other wheelchair users buzzing about, it's just me, and it's a me that I don't recognise.

•

As the day goes on I'm feeling a bit off, physically. My nerve pains are a little stronger, and I'm having more frequent muscle spasms, strong enough to send a right hook across the front of my body and hit my phone mount out of the way. I don't think much of it but by late afternoon I'm feeling cold and begin shivering. Within 15 minutes my jaw is going nonstop, making my teeth chatter. Kristian, who's on shift today, wraps a hot wheat bag over my shoulders, which calms the shakes for a couple of minutes. He takes my temperature and it's slightly elevated at 37.2°, but not high enough to be of concern.

After an hour my nerve pains are much worse and my neck and jaw are starting to cramp up so I submit to the fact that I need to call an ambulance. When I'm speaking with the ambulance call centre, the woman doesn't seem to understand the urgency of the situation. I tell her it could be autonomic dysreflexia — to try to create a bit of urgency — but she has no clue what that is. It's around the time the ambos arrive that I remember back to how I felt on the morning of the *Prime* premiere. Fuck. I think I have another bladder infection.

I'm loaded into the ambulance and whisked to hospital. Mum is with me now, and although her rubbing my shoulders helps relax the cramping muscles, the shakes — which the nurse tells me are called rigors — are becoming unbearable. I beg the ED nurse for some painkillers. A doctor arrives and asks me to rank my pain level out of 10, zero being no pain, 10 being the worst pain imaginable.

I give it a seven. Usually my nerve pains are about a two. The doctor does the business and within a couple of minutes my shakes start to subside and a wave of floaty relief washes over me. I'm finally admitted with a urinary tract infection that they suspect has got into the blood. I'm put on a broad-spectrum antibiotic until the blood and urine cultures come back with more specific results.

The following morning a doctor tells me that they've found a hospital superbug in my blood.

'Oh yeah, MRSA,' I reply. 'I picked that up in hospital in the US.'

'Unfortunately this isn't MRSA, it's a different superbug called ESBL. It's caused by an *E. coli* infection and is resistant to most antibiotics. So we're going to keep you in an isolation room for a week on five-day intravenous antibiotic course.'

•

A week later I'm all better and happy to be on my way home. It's good timing too as I'm meeting with a possible new physiotherapist just two days later.

I arrive at Flexa Clinic, which is just 10 minutes from home. The building and facilities look to be top of the line, and I'm very impressed with the talent among the staff — physical attractiveness must be part of the hiring criteria! The receptionist introduces herself as Sammy before going to find the boss for me.

A few minutes later I meet Murray Hing, and we start talking through my goals. Throughout this journey I've met so many specialists and physicians, and I can tell very quickly if they're someone I want to work with. Murray's energy is infectious, and his positive attitude towards my recovery gives me confidence that he's a perfect fit for my rehab team.

'I know how driven you are,' he says, 'so I'll book you in for five days a week for two hours each session, starting Monday next week. How does that sound?'

It sounds pretty damned good to me.

Murray then introduces me to a petite young woman named Kelly who will be my primary physiotherapist.

I'm back the following Monday and eager to get started. Kelly greets me with a smile and takes me through to the clinic. She's cute and super friendly, and although she's young she quickly gains my faith in her knowledge and ability as a physio. We're joined by a second physio, a young Pakistani girl named Yumna who is also easy on the eyes.

Murray bursts into the room and begins running through instructions for the girls. He gets them to put my feet up on the massage table and remove my slippers and compression socks. 'As you can see, Brad has moderate oedema in his feet, so I want you to work on flushing that swelling through,' he says. 'I'd also like you to work on his arms — flush any swelling through and make sure all his joints stay nice and limber.' He keeps going, confidently dropping in long technical terms I don't understand, but the physios are onto it.

After the first hour we move into the studio to do some actual rehab. Yumna has another patient to see, so Murray brings in Lisa and Vianca, who almost look like they could be sisters. With the extra motivation from being surrounded by three very attractive young women, I'm directed to the first of several pieces of equipment I'll meet that morning.

By the end of the set I'm physically exhausted. I get home and after lunch I tilt my chair back and pass out into a solid afternoon nap.

•

The weeks progress and I'm at Flexa every weekday. While the clinic work is pretty repetitive, I enjoy the workouts in the studio. All the 'exercises' involve the physios moving my limbs around for me, but I'm putting in sustained effort to 'help' with the movement.

Flexa is not the only physio I go to. Twice a week I go straight from Flexa to Neuro Rehab Results where Amy, a neuro physiotherapist, focuses on specialised spinal cord injury rehab involving Functional Electrical Stimulation (FES). She sets up the FES pads on my arm, then, with my arm resting on a table with slide mats underneath to reduce friction, we work through a series of arm exercises, using the electrical stimulation to assist with the movement.

Pinpointed stimulation to my bicep causes it to tense up as if I'm flexing, and enough stim to my triceps straightens my arm out. My left arm is less responsive than my right, but I guess that's to be expected since I'm right-handed. There's nothing more frustrating than directing every bit of energy and will I possess into trying to move my arm and seeing only the slightest twitch. After exhausting my arms, we move to another exercise.

Over the weeks we work through a variety of different exercises, including sling work, where my arms are suspended in slings so I can move them around more freely. I'm also hoisted to sit on the edge of a padded table where we work to stabilise me so that I don't fall either forward or back. Thankfully Amy is ready to catch me if I start tipping.

On these back-to-back physio days I'm utterly drained by the end of it. It's strange that I get so tired from unsuccessfully trying to move, but I'm willing to do whatever it takes to get moving again. It's going to happen, I just know it!

•

I'm woken up at 7 a.m., same as every morning. I don't really have a choice these days as the caregivers are rostered on and have a timetable. Day after day it's Groundhog Day. I'm barely given the chance to wake up before my 7 a.m. meds are poured into my mouth and washed down with an entire glass of water. Then it's the bowel business.

One part I quite like about sitting on the commode chair is that its armrests are narrow enough for my fingers to droop and hang in space, so while I'm waiting, I focus on my fingers. I don't take my eyes off them as I focus in on trying to make my fingers move. I feel the strain inside my hands and forearms as my phantom fingers wiggle away beneath the skin, but on the outside they hang lifeless.

One day, after about 15 minutes of this I notice my thumb twitch. *Holy shit! Did I just do that?* It twitches again — just a small twitch, but it's something! I keep going but that's it for today.

The whole process (bowel cares, shower, getting dressed) takes about three hours.

Having someone else clean my teeth, all four of the caregivers having their own slightly different technique, is just one of a hundred frustrations I submit to every time. I'm in my chair by 10 a.m., finally ready to face the day. But Groundhog Day has a new focus now, and most mornings I get a few small twitches in my fingers.

●

It's been a rough month of news coming in. I hear that an old friend I first met at the Auckland water-ski club has taken his own life. I am devastated, as we had reconnected in the past few years and he was really enthusiastic about helping with my fundraiser. He even got his own 'Stay strong Brad' T-shirt made. I didn't know he had been struggling, and I can't help but feel like maybe I could've helped.

Then I hear that my Uncle Bart, who was living in the Philippines, has just taken his own life. And between these two shocks, I hear that two kids at the high school up the road have recently done the same thing. I feel deeply saddened by each individually, but together they have me questioning what the hell is going on. What has led those four people to each feel like that was the only way out?

I'm familiar with the feeling, so I understand on some level, but it's hard to know what was going on for them. Their trauma isn't on display like mine is. A small part of me envies their escape from the struggle, but that thought only crosses my mind for a second before I think about my friend's family, and my dad losing his brother, and the families of those two teens. I just couldn't do that.

It makes me think about how many people are struggling behind the outer shell they show.

●

At Flexa I always look forward to seeing Sammy, who greets me with a warm smile. I may have developed a bit of a crush — she's super sweet to me and we've become friends. She's always on her lunch break when I arrive, so most days we sit together in the café chatting away until one of the physios comes for me.

They've started flipping me over onto my stomach on a massage table so they can dig into my back, glutes and hamstrings. Today as usual, with Kristian's help, they hoist me onto the table using the portable hoist that travels in my van with me. I lie flat and feel my body spasm as it stretches out. Then I notice the girls acting a little strange, like they don't know what to do next. At first I assume they're just figuring out the next move in turning me over — until I glance down to see that I'm at full mast and my thin trackies are doing nothing to hide my raging erection. That explains their awkwardness.

I pretend I'm oblivious but my red cheeks must be a dead giveaway. Thankfully my unconscious excitement dissipates quickly. I need them to understand it's an involuntary reaction, so the next time it happens I break the awkwardness with a joke.

'Jeeez, I'm excited for my massage, but I didn't think I was *that* excited!'

The girls chuckle and continue as if nothing's happened.

When I'm rolled onto my stomach, my face in the hole in the massage table, it's usually not long before I fall asleep. Today is no different, but I'm just on the verge of sleep when I notice the girls have gone quiet. Then I watch as their shoes walk out of the room. A minute later Kristian comes in and breaks the news to me that I've had a bowel accident.

God damn — I want to curl up and die of embarrassment. This is the worst, most demoralising feeling. As if being stuck in a wheelchair unable to move my limbs isn't enough on its own to make me feel completely worthless — now I've just shat myself in front of my two gorgeous physios.

Since there's nothing we can do about it here, Kristian tactfully gets me hoisted back into my chair, races me home, and then it's close to an hour of hoisting, undressing, cleaning and dressing before I'm back in my chair.

Back at Flexa the next day the girls are once again their usual bubbly friendly selves, as if it never happened.

This is not my first bowel accident, and I am forever extremely nervous when hoisting or lying on my stomach. Drinking coffee and eating Indian or Mexican food can also be a problem. Sometimes I feel like the fear of having a bowel accident runs my life. If there's even the slightest chance, I'd rather stay at home.

•

Susie comes over and we just sit and chat. I'm feeling very low after shitting myself at physio and I tell Susie about it. Seeing that I'm feeling emotional, she stands beside me and puts her hand on my shoulder. Just the contact alone begins to ease my pain.

'It's the first time it's happened in front of people, and it had to be two gorgeous girls,' I tell her. 'I fucking hate that this is part of my life now — like I've regressed to being an infant. I don't even recognise myself any more — this is *not* my life.' I sob, feeling completely lost.

Susie sits and lets me rant.

'That's got to be really embarrassing for you,' she says, 'but your body is still adjusting to all of this. You need to believe me when I tell you that this won't last. You will get better at knowing the signs; your body will adjust and you'll get into a routine that will mean things like this happen much less often.'

I want to believe her, but how does she know?

'Your comment about not recognising yourself — I'd like to dig into that today,' she says. 'Obviously, so much has changed for you, and I can't imagine how tough that must be. But you are still you — you're still the exact same Brad. I'm sure it doesn't feel that way because of how much has changed, but you've still got your brain, you've still got your personality, and you've still got your beautiful face.' She chuckles, no doubt thinking of how she used to tell me my attendance at her Pilates classes 'motivated the housewives' who attended.

'It's your personality that makes you *you* — not your body, not your wakeboarding skills, not your injury and not your wheelchair,' she goes on.

'But that can't be true,' I interrupt. 'How can my body, and what I do, not be part of who I am? They are a huge part of my identity! In the past, if ever telling someone who I was, it was: "I'm a wakeboarder."'

'That's who you *thought* you were, and the story your ego told you about who you were, but that's not you. Here's an example. If an amputee came into your house right now, you wouldn't say, "Hi, it's good to see most of you today." The fact that they're missing part of their body doesn't take away from who they are. Just as the loss of the use of your body doesn't take away from who you are. Sure, your life has changed drastically, but you're still you.'

I like what she says, and I sit silently nodding. But I still feel like just a fraction of the man I used to be.

'Even if I'm still me, that doesn't change how shitty this is, and how embarrassing this stuff is for me,' I respond, still feeling sorry for myself.

'The hard part for you, I imagine, is accepting that this has happened to you — that this is what your life looks like right now,' Susie says. 'What you need to understand is that acceptance is just a choice to accept the present. It's not "I'm going to be in a wheelchair forever." You've told me about people who have contacted you saying that's what you need to accept, and telling you not to have hope, and I think that says a lot about those people. They have these fears because they can't accept the present.'

She stops talking and we sit in silence for a bit as I ponder what she's saying about acceptance.

'This is a really big thing for you,' Susie starts up again. 'A good example of accepting the present is when you made a joke to your physios about your random erection — which I'm sure they were flattered by! At first you closed your eyes and pretended it hadn't happened — that's not accepting it, and it didn't help, did it? Whereas acknowledging it and making a joke about it meant you'd accepted it and chosen to go with it. And how much easier and less embarrassing was that for you?

'You can choose to accept each moment and learn from it, or you can fight it. Accepting the present is almost like opening up a gift every single day. You never know what's in it — one day it might be something precious; another day it's a turd. You just have to work with that and find a way to be calm in the process. To be at peace with that process.

'When you can do that I feel like everything will unlock for you. Because the less resistance there is for you, the more you'll open up energetically, and I think that's when you'll have the best chance of regaining movement and walking again.'

•

I'm excited to receive a message from some of my American friends to say they're coming to New Zealand to visit after being in Melbourne for the Moomba Masters. First, three of the top women in wake — Melissa Marquardt, Nicola Butler and Ashley Leugner — drop by, and they bring me a fern as a housewarming present. I make sure to let them know I'm having a housewarming party this weekend.

A few days later my friends Colin Harrington and Bob Soven drop in. It's Friday night and I figure we should take them out. While I'm not super comfortable with going out and socialising, I've been invited to a party put on by my old modelling agency, so I figure it's probably worth taking the guys along to a party full of models.

It's no crazy raging party, but the bar is teeming with talent! I catch up with the agency staff and owners — it's the first time any of them have seen me in a wheelchair. One girl, clearly a model and clearly intoxicated, is dancing around nearby. She's unbelievably gorgeous with her dark features and light brown skin and incredible figure — I'm not surprised she's on the agency's books.

She seems like a bit of a wild child, or at least she is tonight. She's now dancing right in front of me. I do my best to dance along with her, and try to introduce myself but the music is too loud, and anyway she's in her zone. Then before I know what's happening she starts kissing me — with tongue and everything!

I have no idea why but I'm enjoying it! After our lips part she dances a little more before taking off outside.

Bob and Colin are sitting there stunned — they both start laughing and cheering for me. 'Did that really just happen?' Bob laughs.

'I guess I've still got it!' I say through a big grin, although I know the chances are I'll never see her again.

●

The following night is my housewarming party and the relatively small living area is packed in no time. I pretty much just park in one place and chat to people as they come up to me. Morgan is here and she looks really good. We talk for a while and I'd be lying if I said I didn't still hold out some hope for us in the future.

As the night progresses and a few people clear out, including Morgan, I manoeuvre my way into the kitchen where my buddy Seadon is chatting with his girlfriend, who brought a couple of friends along. He introduces me to Grace and Rosie, both absolute hotties! As is the case for most people still here at this point, they're a little drunk, but they're having a good time. Rosie shows interest in how my chair works, so I show her a few moves and accidentally run over her toes. I feel terrible and apologise profusely, but she assures me she's fine and laughs it off. I can guarantee that 280 kg of me-plus-wheelchair steamrolling over her toes can't have felt good! She's a champ for playing it off so well.

I've taken a liking to Rosie, but I know I don't have a chance. She seems interested but I guess she's just being friendly. Nevertheless, she and I continue chatting until the party is over and they're the last to leave.

To my surprise, I receive a Facebook message from her the following day:

Sorry for gate-crashing last night. It was nice to meet you and thanks for having us.

●

I'm stoked to hear from her and especially happy when she offers to bring me coffee later in the week. Rosie is tall and skinny with long straight brown hair and brown eyes. She has a small nose ring. She's a model but she's not stuck up or vain, just a very real and genuine soul. She's passionate about volleyball, and she definitely has an athlete's body! However, she's just coming back from injury so she's having a rough time not being able to do what she loves. Naturally, we connect on this topic.

While I really enjoy sipping coffee and talking with Rosie on the deck in the sun, her visit triggers something dark in me after she leaves. I find myself sitting and staring into the distance with tears in my eyes. My heart hurts and my mind is leading me down a bad path. Rosie is without a doubt a girl I would've gone for if we'd met before I became paralysed, but what kind of man could I possibly be for her now? She would never want me.

It's the same with Sammy and Lisa at physio. Thinking about them is accompanied by incredibly negative thoughts about myself. It's like every lovely woman I meet just brings stabbing reminders of what I'm not. As a 27-year-old six-foot-two professional athlete, model and builder I could build giant structures with my own two hands, perform double flips on my wakeboard, and attract beautiful women who I could please in the bedroom. Now I'm a quadriplegic with no use of my arms or legs, stripped of the ability to perform tasks of any kind. Not only can I not make love to a woman, I can't even show affection through simple physical gestures like placing my hand on the small of a girl's back as I offer to buy her a drink — or a gentle hand to the cheek as I initiate that first kiss . . .

•

A visit from Susie the next day just couldn't come at a better time. Of course she is stoked to hear that I've met a nice girl.

'See? You've still got it!'

'I don't think she's into me like that.' I shake my head. Then I explain all my negative thought processes. As I speak, my heart aches and I feel worthless.

'Look, Brad, it's totally natural for you to feel that way,' she says. 'Stop being so hard on yourself.' She explains that the huge contrast between then and now was always going to make the transition difficult.

'This will be a big thing for you to work through, because over the years you've placed so much importance on the physical, as most guys do. But you know you have so much to offer as you are now — you've got so much going for you.'

It feels like she's just saying that — it doesn't feel to me like there's much left to offer.

'We spoke last time about you being more than just your body and what you can do with it. Because you put so much importance on that before, that's where you've always felt your value lies. But what is it about you that girls have fallen in love with before? Sure, they've started with a physical attraction, but it's your personality they fall in love with. I bet that's why Rosie came to see you. And you're still hot!' she says. 'Wouldn't you rather someone love you for who you are instead of what you do and how you look?'

'Yes of course, but how do I go from feeling completely inadequate, to feeling worthy of love?' I ask. 'Because that doesn't seem possible from where I'm sitting.'

'What it comes down to is the belief behind your worth. We've talked briefly before about belief systems—'

'I don't know if I completely understand what you mean by that,' I interrupt.

'Belief systems are basically the framework on which your mind is built — your programming. They guide the decisions we make. Belief systems are beliefs that are so ingrained into us that we're not really aware of them. The best example would be religion. Each religion has certain rules that shape the way people live. Like the belief that if you're good you go to heaven and if you're bad you go to hell.

'Another example would be cultural beliefs, like in some cultures it's the children's job to look after the elderly, whereas in western society it's quite common just to put them in a home. Or look at the food of different cultures: breakfast for westerners might be toast or cereal or bacon and eggs, but in Japan a very common breakfast is rice, fish and miso soup. To each culture group, the other seems like a strange breakfast to have, but that's purely because of the beliefs ingrained in them from birth.

'There are common beliefs that you must finish school and go to college and get a good job working nine to five, five days a week; and that in order to be happy you must do all of this and make lots of money and have kids and a big house, just to fit society's image of success.

'Many beliefs have been created over time to mould and control people, including the toxic belief that we must have a particular body type in order to be considered attractive. In reality we all have flaws, we're all built differently, in our own beautiful way, and over time our bodies change. Or there's the toxic belief that money somehow equals happiness. How many miserable rich people do you know? Or happy poor people?'

I chime in here, knowing about this one first-hand. 'One of the happiest times I've had was when I was living in a trailer with no power or running water and driving a shitty $1800 Chevy Tahoe,' I laugh. 'Granted, it was on a private lake wakeboard paradise, but still . . .'

'Exactly. You haven't fallen for that one because you know that happiness comes from living a life you're passionate about,' Susie says.

'So, getting back to you, your belief system around adequacy is built primarily on the physical you. A lot of people out there, particularly young men, believe this because it's how they've been shaped — by advertising, by movies, by pornography and now by social media. But love and attraction and companionship are about so much more than that.'

I get her point, but for everyone else doesn't all of that other stuff come along with the physical parts as well? I can't add value to a relationship with things like helping out around the house — or helping raise kids. But rather than bring it up, I sit silently, absorbing what Susie is telling me.

I still have a hard time believing that someone would be attracted to me, but I decide I'll spend some time working on the belief that my attractiveness goes far beyond the physical. I'm fascinated by the idea of these belief systems, so I'm going to spend some time pondering on them.

•

My morning routine is such a process that I want my team to be as efficient as possible, and from the start I've been forced to become somewhat of a micro-manager, to make sure everything gets done right. While some caregivers get straight into the rhythm of the routine, others just don't seem to be listening because every day they're on shift I'm having to prompt them the whole way through. It's beyond frustrating to be constantly repeating myself to apparently deaf ears. It gives me a taste of what Mum had to deal with when I was growing up. The difference is that Mum couldn't fire me.

I begin cycling through caregivers as some simply don't work out. Fiona, Kristian, Edwin and Loisi remain as my core team. When they're not helping me out doing jobs around the house, my caregivers usually hang out in the staffroom, to give me some privacy. To get their attention, rather than yelling their name I use the same whistle Dad always used to get our attention as kids. I just feel like it's much less intrusive than yelling, especially when I have friends or visitors over.

I find I constantly question when I should and shouldn't bother calling for them. Obviously I need them for things like eating and drinking, driving a car or getting me dressed, but then there's the endless number of little things — adjusting the TV volume, brushing the hair out of my face, scratching my nose, picking food from between my teeth, rubbing the sleep out of my eyes, adjusting my clothes, brushing food crumbs off my T-shirt, swatting a fly or bee that wants to land on me, scratching an itch and so much more. If I asked my caregivers to help with all of these things I'd be calling out for them constantly, and I just really can't be bothered.

When I get frustrated I remind myself how lucky I am to live in New Zealand, where I actually have paid caregivers on tap. I'm also really grateful to have Courtney living with me because she's such a sweetheart and we've been friends for so long that she's become a big part of my support crew. Sometimes she just listens to my rants at the end of the day, or gives me a hug when I need it, but what I really love is when she gives me head scratches!

Susie is interested in my frustrations with my caregivers.

'It just drives me mad sometimes,' I tell her. 'As if it's not bad enough being stuck in this chair, I also have to deal with idiots with no common sense fucking up doing things for me. I know I should be grateful to have their help, but that doesn't take away from how infuriating it can be.'

Susie's take is that the frustration comes from the separation between expectation and reality.

'What you have to remember is that you did things to an incredibly high level before. You were highly skilled and did things efficiently and with intention and purpose. You did things harder, better and faster than most because of the way your brain worked, and the abilities of your body. It's like your programming is several updates ahead of most other people's. So now that you have other people doing practically everything for you, you should expect that most are not going to be as good as you, especially not when compared with doing things for yourself.'

'So you're saying I should lower my expectations?'

'I guess, in a way, yes. But what it comes down to is empathy towards your caregivers. Understanding that they don't have a pro athlete mindset, and that they're doing the best they can. Tolerance means simply understanding and having empathy for the fact that others operate differently, and the better you get at it, the less frustration you'll experience.'

•

Today I'm meeting a man who is being sent by ACC to assess how much of a lump-sum payout I will receive from them. It's a strange meeting because he's basically here to assess how fucked up my life is — the more fucked up, the higher the payout.

It doesn't take long for him to establish that I'm eligible for the maximum payout of $120,000. It's a lot of money, but it's nothing in terms of compensation for my loss. I wouldn't take $120 million to exchange my old life for this existence.

●

Morgan is over for dinner tonight. She's her usual bubbly self and as always she lifts my spirits simply by being with me. I'm grateful, because my spirit continually hangs low. Morgan's energy is infectious. It's how she's been since the night we met; in fact it was her energy that drew me to her in the first place — that and the fact that she's gorgeous! But as usual I'm in conflict. As much as I'm glad to have her as a friend, I can't help craving the relationship that we used to have. But I know that if there's to be a chance of us being together then I need to give her time.

●

Summer is coming to an end, as is the wakeboard season. The final event on the calendar is nationals, and even though it will be triggering for me, I want to go along in support and get back on the microphone.

It's hard to watch Jeff dominate the competition with a run that I reckon I would easily have beaten — although if I were competing, I guarantee Jeff would've stepped it up and pulled a winning run out of his arse to beat me. But I'm stoked to see him come back and school the rest of the field in what will most likely be his last nationals appearance.

This is also the time of year that I'd usually be getting on a flight back to Florida. Instead, I'm sitting here in my lounge, gazing emptily out the window as the cold wind blows the rain sideways onto the glass. I get lost scrolling on my phone again and it kills me to see loads of my wake friends posting on their social media that they're back in Orlando and hitting the lake. Deano, Amber, Massi and Dom are all out there riding with the team at Lake Ronix.

I just can't accept that it's all gone for me. I ache for that escape of carving through the glass-calm surface of an untouched lake, switching off from reality for those 20–30 minutes of pure rapturous freedom. For that time nothing else existed — no stress, no worries, no nagging thoughts swirling around my head. For that time the chatter was silenced and all that was left was the connection between body and mind, between my board and the water. It was a slice of freedom that brought me to a state of flow and nourished my soul.

It feels as if there's no escaping this deep, dark depression I'm in, as I approach my first winter in 11 years.

I explain to Susie how my longing for the life I had is crushing my soul. 'Seeing my friends and teammates getting back to Orlando reminds me that I'm missing out on the life I'm supposed to have. Literally everything I see when I'm out and about feels like a stab, a reminder of what I can't do — someone out running, a couple holding hands, families playing in the ocean. It's bad enough in real life, but social media makes it so much worse. I just feel like I'm missing out on everything.'

'I can understand how tough that must be,' Susie says. 'After I lost my twins, I would get upset whenever I'd see people with babies. But what you have to understand is that what other people have has nothing to do with you. Be careful with words like "supposed" and "should". All of these feelings of "I should be wakeboarding in Orlando" or "I'm missing out on the life I was supposed to have" — they're simply stories projected by the ego. If you're truly present, then nothing exists outside of the here and now. That means that although those feelings are completely understandable, they're nothing more than illusions of the ego.'

I look at her, saying nothing, letting this all sink in. It's hard.

'Because, get this,' Susie goes on. 'If you're truly present, which is accepting that here and now is the only truth, then it's actually impossible to miss out.'

I have to get her to repeat it while I try to wrap my head around it.

'I don't know if I quite get it. How am I not missing out right now when I would usually be going back to Florida? If I hadn't broken my neck I would be still living in the trailer at Lake Ronix, so how am I not missing out on that life?'

Susie responds calmly. 'Because those are just stories. We could assume that if your accident hadn't happened, you'd still be over there wakeboarding, but who's to say you wouldn't have been eaten by an alligator the next day? We can come up with all sorts of stories about where we *might* be if this or that had happened differently, but none of that is real. Does that make sense?'

'I guess so, but what about missing out in the present?' I ask. 'Like, if I was supposed to be going for a beer with my friends right now, but for whatever reason I can't go and I'm sitting here at home while they all still go, am I not missing out?'

'Is it possible for you to be in two places at once?' Susie asks rhetorically.

'Of course not.'

'Then how can you be missing out? In the present, you're here. That feeling of missing out is your ego's story of what it *thinks* would've happened had you gone.

But since you're here, and you're present. You're missing out on nothing.'

I'm still struggling so I dig some more. 'What about if I'm on FaceTime with my friends and I can literally *see* what I'm missing out on? Or if I know that they had an epic time and I was not there — how have I not missed out on that epic time?'

'Firstly, you're assuming things would've happened the same had you been there. But if another element is added or changed, we never know what effect that might've had on the situation. But regardless, if you can only be in one place, and in one time, then that is the only reality for you. Other things happening in the same time in a *different* place are not your reality. Things happening in the same place but at a different time are either in the past or the future, therefore they are not in your present reality either. That's the powerful thing about presence, Brad. So many people are caught up in past and future, and feeling like they're missing out, when in reality, if you are in a present frame of mind it's impossible. So ironically, they're actually missing out on reality by spending time feeling like they're missing out.'

Susie tells me it's a challenging thing to live completely in the present. Monks spend their entire lives working on it and generally never have it perfected. 'So don't be hard on yourself for not getting it all the time. It's a constant learning, a work in progress.'

•

I'm exhausted when it comes time to get into bed after a solid day of physio at both Flexa and Neuro. After I'm undressed and Fi turns me onto my side, she notices something on my skin.

'Brad, you've got a red patch with a hard lump forming on the bottom of your butt cheek. Wait . . . oh crap, it's the same on the other side,' she says.

'Dammit!' I say. 'Are they pressure sores?'

'There doesn't appear to be any broken skin, but there are red patches around smaller firm lumps about the size of a bottle cap underneath your sit bones — maybe from physio today?'

'Shit — yeah, you're probably right. It'll be from sitting on the plinth. Dammit! I'll get the doc to look at it tomorrow.'

My doctor seems unsure and concludes that the hardness under the skin is caused by infected hair follicles. What — infected hair follicles in the same place on both cheeks at the same time? I don't think so. There's no doubt in my mind that they're pressure-related — maybe the beginning of deep pressure wounds developing under the surface. I saw pictures of those at Shepherd, and they're the absolute last thing I want. I've heard stories of people being forced to take years of bed-rest to let bad wounds heal. So I plan to keep off my butt for a while and hope the lumps go away.

Being stuck in bed again takes me back to my time on bed-rest in the spinal unit. Long days, being turned every four hours from one side to the other. Thankfully I have a TV in my room and we get my phone set up so I can keep myself busy messaging friends.

On day three Rosie brings me a coffee and keeps me company for a few hours. Then she's back the following afternoon. It's so nice to have her company— she really is so sweet to me. I don't know what I did to deserve it. Maybe that's just who she is, or maybe it's out of pity — either way I'm happy to have her here. She lies beside me in bed and we watch movies and talk until she heads home late.

After more than three weeks of bed-rest the hard lumps are gradually reducing in size. It's incredibly boring, and my nerve pains are quite bad by the end of each long day, but at least I'm able to get up each day for a shower. I pass the time working on some designs for a range of T-shirts I plan to release, and my photo-editing skills with the mouthstick are getting better.

Thankfully Amy from Neuro Rehab is able to do home visits for my two sessions per week, so I'm not completely missing out on rehab. She hooks some electrical stimulator pads to my arm and we run through a series of arm exercises. I don't know if I can over-stress how strange and frustrating it is to feel as if I can move my arms, yet no matter how hard I try, I barely get the smallest flinch. But with the e-stim attached, Amy is able to get my arm to move. The electrical pulse contracts the muscle and creates a bit of movement, but I have no control over it. My muscle is purely responding to the stimulation.

•

One benefit of bed-rest is the amount of quality time I'm getting with Rosie, without my intimacy-blocking wheelchair in the way. As we spend more time together, I'm pleasantly surprised that she seems to be getting more comfortable, and snuggling up closer. The scent of her hair and fragrance is intoxicating and I so wish I could wrap my arms around her and pull her right in. It's strange not being able to feel her body against mine.

Later in the evening, when the movie is over, she turns to lie facing me and we talk. I share stories from my life pre-injury, and as time goes on I share my frustrations and my fears for the future. At one point she hesitantly reaches over and places her hand on the side of my neck while looking into my eyes, as if to comfort me, and then pulls herself in closer. It's hard to describe just how incredible this feels. Her hand on my neck sends tingles through my body — a wave of pleasure that I haven't felt in months. The lack of feeling in parts of my body makes her simple touch on my neck feel amazing.

But having her cuddled up into my neck, as close as she can be, brings me the most comfort I've felt since this all began. And when she breaks away from the cuddle, she lies her head on the pillow, with her hand on the back of my neck and her fingers in my hair, she's even closer than she was. I know that if there's going to be a moment to seize, then this is it. I can't initiate any movement or touch, so I pluck up my courage and say, 'Can I . . . umm, I really want to kiss you right now.'

She pauses for a second while looking into my eyes, then leans in and brings her lips to mine. The touch of her lips and her hand on my face feel beyond wonderful, and there's a sensation of butterflies, quickly giving way to frustration. Because a kiss has always been more than what happens between mouths. It leads to dynamic movement of hands and arms and body, but I have control of none of that. In fact it's a new frustration to learn that I can't even tilt my head, which is practically glued to the pillow. Any movement at all is down to Rosie. I do my best to silence those thoughts and enjoy the moment. And who knows — maybe she likes that she's in total control!

The next time Rosie comes over, she stays the night with me. She even borrows one of my T-shirts to sleep in. I love seeing her sexy long legs beneath a T-shirt that's only just long enough to cover her. We kiss a lot more, but falling asleep with her head on my pillow, with her forehead against mine, is a moment that brings me utter contentment.

•

My butt seems to be all healed up so I can get back up in the chair. It's full-on winter — rainy, cold, windy and miserable. I'm not used to having to wear so many layers, but since my body cannot regulate temperature, I have to try to figure out the right number of layers to keep me at normal temp. Too many layers and I'll overheat, and since I don't sweat, my temp would keep going up and up. If I don't have enough layers, because I don't get goosebumps my temp would continue to plummet.

Of course Susie is rapt when I tell her about Rosie.

'What did I tell you?' she says.

'Yeah, I honestly didn't expect it to happen. It kinda puts me in a bit of a predicament. I'm in love with Morgan, but at the same time I'm falling for Rosie. I don't know what to do', I tell Susie.

'That's so wonderful, Brad,' she replies. 'You deserve all the love that's coming to you. And maybe there's no decision to be made, not yet at least, so I wouldn't worry about it. Just soak in that love.'

I am worried. I feel like I have to decide between the two of them, but I have no idea how to make that call. But I drop it. Instead, I tell Susie how, although I loved being with Rosie, I was constantly feeling useless, battling the negative thoughts that took away from the enjoyment of the moment.

She talks again about being present, about trying not to get caught up in expectations based on previous experiences.

'But how do I do that?' I ask. 'It's so hard not to want what I know I have had.'

'Try to focus on enjoying the moment, and stay away from thoughts of what you think you should be doing, or wish you could do. What do you love about what is happening now?'

I know it's wise advice.

•

At the end of May I have some more visitors from the US — Paul from Ronix and Sully from Radar Skis! They're headed to a range showing for New Zealand retailers down at Lake Karāpiro and I make the road-trip down to join them.

The following night they come up to Auckland and we go out for dinner and drinks with Jesse, Rosie and a few others. I don't drink any alcohol, as I decided to stop earlier this year. The couple of times I'd had a few drinks I hadn't really enjoyed the feeling. I don't get the intoxicating effects, just worse nerve pains, so what's the point?

After dinner we all roll back to my place. I've had the downstairs set up with a couple of mattresses, and Jesse tests out the comfort of my new couch with a girl he brought with him to dinner. Rosie and I get into bed and of course we start making out straight away. Since we're getting much more comfortable being intimate, I've got better at asking for her to do things. First, I ask her to let me kiss her neck, and she happily obliges. I love hearing her change in breathing, which tells me I'm on the right track. When I get to the base of her neck I bite the collar of the T-shirt she's wearing, and start pulling and growling, like a puppy playing with its toy.

'I think this needs to come off!' I say boldly. Again, she obliges, and hot damn she looks so good naked! The most incredibly fit, slim body with perfect perky breasts, which I enjoy kissing my way down to. After a few more minutes I look up at her over me and say, 'I'd love to continue kissing my way down, but I'm going to need your help with that.'

She pauses. I can see that she wants to, but she's a little apprehensive. 'Are you sure?' she asks.

'Oh I'm positive,' I say confidently. 'I'd really love to.'

'How do I . . .? Umm, you're going to need to guide me through this,' she says nervously.

So I encourage her to shuffle up my body, while still leaning forward so I can kiss my way down her stomach. When it comes to committing to straddling my face she hesitates again. She's a bit shy, and she's concerned about hurting me, but I assure her I'll be fine. While she's positioning herself over me I grab the opportunity to kiss her inner thigh, then the other, kissing closer and closer until my tongue finally reaches its goal. Then I lose myself in her, and she very quickly relaxes into the moment. I can hear her heightened breathing and she's running her fingernails through my hair.

Several minutes later, with her legs shaking and her heavy breathing turning to moans, I feel her climax as the shakes peak and she practically collapses on top of me, just catching herself by grabbing the headboard.

'Wow,' she says, catching her breath. 'Just . . . wow!'

I love it so much that I've satisfied her. I've been so afraid that I might be completely inadequate in the bedroom, so it feels pretty damned good to still be able to do this.

She then turns the tables and has no trouble getting me aroused through physical touch. I'm nervous for her to go down on me, because my catheter tube will be all up in her face and might smell unclean. But it seems that's not an issue. Then she positions herself over me and guides me inside her.

I can't believe this is really happening — and with this absolute beauty! I'd pinch myself to see if I'm dreaming but . . . you know.

I'm very pleasantly surprised that I can feel something down there. I haven't really felt anything in that area since the ice-pack under my nuts back when I was in the ICU. But this is nothing like that — this is actually pleasant. It's not the usual sensation of first entry but it's something — and the only *pleasurable* feeling I've had below my shoulders since my injury! Among the nerve pains, there's the slightest pleasant tingle. To give some idea of how much: if the feeling of an orgasm is up around a 9/10, and normal feeling on first entry is, let's say, 7/10, then this would be about 0.2/10. Like I said, it's slight, but it's something.

I'm lying back watching her move her hips, marvelling at how sexy she is, and trying to banish the feeling that I should be doing more. I feel like a spectator — a starfish. I do my best to relax and enjoy the moment, because I really do love what's going on right now, but the frustration of not being able to participate is real. And it's no fault of Rosie's — she's doing everything to make me feel more involved, like placing my hands where I most want to put them . . . it's just my state of mind.

Rosie stops what she's doing and lies beside me with a cute and slightly mischievous smile on her face. I smile back at her and ask why she stopped. She pauses before she politely tells me that I was *exhausted*.

It's really sweet that she says this in a way that comes from a place of understanding and compassion — she doesn't want me to think she's disappointed that I lost my hard-on.

•

The next morning after Rosie leaves, Paul asks, 'Good night there, buddy?'

'You could say that,' I reply with a smile. Despite my plan to keep it cool, I can't contain myself. 'Guess who got laid last night!'

'*No . . . fucking . . . way!*' Paul explodes with excitement and starts slow-clapping, as if I'd just landed my first triple flip. The others join in. I know keeping it to myself would've been more honourable, but it's the first exciting news I've had to share in a long time!

Truth be told, before I met Rosie I'd pictured Morgan as the woman I'd first have sex with. I still love Morgan, even though we've had only friendly encounters lately. She once had my whole heart, but I feel a growing love now for Rosie also. I feel so strongly for both women.

I really don't know what to do, so I decide to consult my friends. When I take Paul and the guys across the bridge to meet up with my parents for brunch, I invite Morgan along too. As much as I feel like a dick for juggling the two like this, I want Paul to meet Morgan.

But he doesn't help at all. 'They're both incredible women, Brad. I don't blame you for being unable to decide.'

•

Susie still thinks I can have both women, but I'm pretty sure that's not actually an option.

I talk to her some more about intimacy, telling her that focusing on all the things I enjoy was even more difficult when Rosie and I were actually having sex.

'I can't get out of my own head!' I tell her. 'It's like I'm fighting my own mind for enjoyment.'

Susie introduces a really interesting analogy.

'Think about your mentality and the way you approached life before, as a type of currency, like the New Zealand dollar. Much of the value your currency had was in your physical prowess: your athleticism, your stature and appearance, the sex, partying, the skills you possessed in your hands. That's how you earned a living, how you found enjoyment, how you attracted the opposite sex, how you vented frustration and relaxed and so on.

'That's the currency you were spending in that part of your life, when that currency was valid. Now you're trying to spend the same currency and finding it's no longer valid. It's not an accepted currency any more. Does that make sense?'

'Kinda,' I say, trying to wrap my head around what she's saying. 'So it's like what you said about my programming not matching my hardware?'

She nods. 'Your life has changed, and I know you're working on accepting that. But if your mind doesn't adapt to the change, then you're trying to spend the currency that's no longer valid, and it's a currency that your life will no longer accept. That's why it feels like you're fighting your own mind to enjoy those moments. It's a challenging thing, but the only way to reduce that frustration and friction with your own mind is to either gain back the ability to do those things you did before, or to update your currency to work with your life as it is now.'

I get what she's saying, but it's easier said than done. I've always felt like if I hold onto the mindset of the way things were before, that was going to help me get back there.

However, that's clearly not working for me, so maybe it wouldn't be the worst thing for me to loosen my grip on that approach, and try to adapt so I can actually enjoy some of the good things I have in my life right now.

Susie has a quote from Viktor Frankl that helps me grasp the idea:

When we are no longer able to change a situation, we are challenged to change ourselves.

•

The continued support I've been receiving is seriously incredible, and it helps keep me motivated. The one question I struggle to answer positively is one that I'm asked almost daily. 'How's progress?' If I answered honestly I'd say, 'Non-existent,' but I don't want to throw a negative answer back at people who want to hear positive news of my recovery.

The truth is there are days where I just feel completely crushed at my lack of progress. Am I not working hard enough? I don't think I could do much more. I just have to keep going, keep pushing, and keep believing that I will one day walk and wakeboard again. But to be perfectly honest, at this stage I would happily settle for regaining the use of my arms and hands again. It would make such a difference to be able to hug people, and have a creative outlet like playing the guitar or building or fixing things.

I'm getting better at reading the word 'God' in people's messages without immediately putting up a wall. Susie is impressed.

'Look at the improvements you're making!' she says enthusiastically.

'Yeah, it still bugs me, but I've been working on adjusting my view on it,' I say. I talk about feeling like I'm not working hard enough.

'You're so used to being able to get what you want by working harder — that's how you got better at wakeboarding, how you improved your strength and returned from previous injuries. But what I really feel is that maybe it's not about doing more, better, faster. It's about allowing the course to run itself. Having faith that you're being led where you're supposed to be led.'

I feel a bit of resistance to the word faith, which Susie must notice.

'I'm not talking about religious faith. It's about believing that you're exactly where you're meant to be in this moment. Rather than trying to force what you want to happen, it's about allowing what needs to happen, to happen.'

'So are you saying I shouldn't be doing as much physio as I'm doing? Because that just seems backwards to me,' I argue.

'It's not about doing less, because there are definitely benefits to the rehab you're doing. Working for what you want generally gives you the best opportunity of getting there, but no matter how hard you work, you're not in control of the outcome. What I'm talking about is the *illusion of control*.'

'What do you mean by *illusion*?'

'We think we have control over everything in our lives but it's not the case. Besides controlling our attitude, our efforts and our actions, we really have no control over what happens in our life. We can have *influence* over certain things and people around us, but we can't control them. So we need to open ourselves up to being okay with not being in control, and have faith that it'll work out as it needs to.'

I don't agree with all of this. I get parts of what she's saying, and that I don't have control of a lot of things, but I've always felt like I'm mostly in control of my life. It somewhat blows my mind to hear that I'm not.

●

Morgan is flying to London tomorrow for about a month. I'm dropping her at the airport very early so she's staying over and we're trying to stay up until we have to leave the house at 4 a.m. We're lying in bed together — bearing in mind that we've still not been at all intimate, nothing more than friendly cuddles — but she was my date to a SCI fundraiser last week, and being this close and looking into her eyes I reckon maybe she still feels a connection. I want to have a go at finding out where I stand (or sit).

I wrote a letter to her on my phone a while ago, so at around 1 a.m. I read it to her. I tell her I don't want her to give me an answer now, but to think about it while she's away. She responds warmly, but gives no indication of a response.

I continue to spend time with Rosie while Morgan is away. She loves to come over and cook delicious and healthy meals for us, and then I get transferred onto my new couch that Dad helped me lift with extra blocks so the hoist can slide under to get me on it. It's nice to get onto the couch as I feel like I look less crippled, and it's great to snuggle up and watch movies.

When we're in bed one night I feel that I need to say something. We've been spending so much time together that I can feel a natural progression happening but I'm still unsure. So I avoid the conversation about 'us' by telling her I'm not ready.

EIGHTEEN: **FUMBLING AND FAILING**

Today Mum and I are being taken on a tour of the University of Auckland's Centre for Brain Research, which includes the Spinal Cord Injury Research Facility (SCIRF). We meet Professor Louise Nicholson and Dr Simon O'Carroll, who show us around the research labs and talk us through the current state of SCI research.

It's really encouraging to hear that they're working on a promising gene therapy project that could help break down the scar tissue like the kind that's formed in my spinal cord. It makes sense to me as it's the scar tissue that is stopping my nerves from reconnecting and blocking the signals from getting through. I've been looking into the possibility of going somewhere like Thailand or Panama for stem cell treatment, but from everything I've read it seems that stem cells are not all that effective in my situation. Even if they help the nerves to regrow, they would still be blocked by the scar tissue.

As exciting as their research sounds, it'll be at least five years before they're ready to start clinical trials. Nevertheless, as we leave I'm feeling hopeful that the future will bring a cure. Meanwhile, I'm going to keep working tirelessly in physio to get back as much movement as I can.

•

I get a message out of the blue from Josh Wood, one of the SCI guys Jeff put me onto when I first had my accident. Josh is coming to New Zealand to speak at a chiropractic convention, so I'm going to go along to hear him, and finally meet him in person.

We swing past his hotel to pick him up on the way, even though it's only a couple of hundred metres from the convention centre, because that's a fair distance for someone who walks with a cane. We pull up to the hotel and in climbs this dude with a shaved head, full sleeve and neck tattoos, wearing a black T-shirt and jeans. He looks more like he should be fronting a punk rock band than delivering a motivational speech to a bunch of chiropractors. Josh and I get a good hour to hang out before it's his time to speak, and we really hit it off.

His session opens with an intense video to set the scene, then he hobbles up onto the stage to loud applause. He first talks about his injury. He was snowboarding and had built a kicker with the intention of boosting a big air over a road gap, landing down the slope on the other side. Unfortunately he second-guessed himself right as he hit the kicker, sending him flailing through the air to land on his neck on the edge of the road. So far, so familiar.

Josh shattered his vertebrae from C4 to C7 and was completely paralysed like me. It's incredible to see him up and walking, even if he does use a cane. As he talks, I'm straight back to the ICU, to my version of those experiences. His movement started again with wiggling one toe. From there he worked with a chiropractor and a healer, along with continuous physical rehab. The whole crowd is dead silent, hanging on every word as he delivers this incredibly inspiring talk on hope and determination. I'm in tears at the end, and the audience erupts in applause.

This gets me thinking. *Maybe I could be a motivational speaker?* I have got a story to tell, although it would be a better one if I could walk up on stage like Josh did. Maybe one day I will, or maybe I won't need to in order to be a compelling speaker.

After saying goodbye to Josh I'm thinking about what parts of my story I'd tell, and what inspiring messages I would deliver. I know I've got some work to do before I'm ready, and maybe my story isn't ready to be told just yet.

I'm excited to tell Susie about all this, and she loves the idea of me helping others through sharing my story.

'I think you'd be an incredible speaker, Brad,' she says, 'and you have the opportunity to change so many people's lives. For me, the measure of a successful life is the number of lives we have a positive impact on. If you can change just *one life* for the better, then you've been successful. And look at the impact you've already had in the last year! All the people saying how inspiring you are to them. I know you loved your life as a wakeboarder, but you've got an opportunity now to reach and influence a much greater number of lives.'

Reality check: I would still rather be living my carefree wakeboarding life, parked up in my trailer at Lake Ronix this morning. But the reality is, I don't have a choice. That life is gone. The only choice I have is what I do with the life I have now. And if helping others is an option that will somehow make my own pain and suffering worthwhile, then bring it on!

I feel like I'm nearing a junction in the road. Morgan hasn't given me an answer to my question, and it's been months since I read her the letter. Although we've been hanging out more than before, and she's still her sweet, caring self, I have no idea what she's feeling.

Meanwhile I feel like I'm holding Rosie at arm's length. Why am I holding out for someone who doesn't seem sure how she feels, when Rosie, who seems to love me, should be the clear choice? Rosie didn't know me before my accident — she didn't know the six-foot-two pro wakeboarder, the confidence and charisma I had, my sexual ability. All she knows is Brad the quadriplegic, the Brad that I am now. Yet somehow she wants me anyway.

And maybe Morgan could love me for who I am now too, but she will always have an image of who I was when we first met.

The answer is staring me in the face, but still I can't bring myself to make the call.

Part of me hopes the path will become clear to me, whereas Susie, once again, tells me there's no decision to be made. As much as I can get onboard with a lot of her insight, I really don't think I'll ever understand this one, so I steer the conversation onto a tangent.

'Although I have these two beautiful women in my life, I'm struggling to feel like I'm good enough for either of them — I think that's part of the reason I'm unable to decide,' I tell her.

'Clearly you are good enough,' she says. 'Otherwise why would these girls be interested in you? Have you put much thought into the beliefs behind that statement about not being "good enough"? Where does that come from? Is there a universal standard that we all come either above or below?'

I sit silently thinking.

'Or do you think that's another illusion of the ego that we've been fooled into believing?' she goes on.

I nod, hating that I've already learnt this but it doesn't seem to be sinking in.

'Yeah, I guess it's an illusion that we buy into,' I admit. And I begin to wonder whose standards I've been feeling I need to live up to. Because although they're my own standards now, I wasn't born with them and I don't recall being taught them along the way. But I must've picked them up from somewhere.

'All there is, is a belief in yourself. If you love yourself and who you are, then what does it matter what other people think? What they think is more of a reflection on them than on you. When it comes to relationships, if you love and believe in yourself, then why would you feel like you're below some imaginary standard if someone doesn't want you for who you are? They're clearly not worth getting upset over. You want someone who wants and loves you for you. To the right person, you will always be enough,' she tells me.

'Can't argue with that!' I reply.

•

I know I've dragged this out for too long, and I've come to realise that I have subliminally tied Morgan to my past, and Rosie to my future. My memories with Morgan represent the epic, adventurous, spontaneous and fun-filled life I used to have — the life I so desperately want back. And poor Rosie has been burdened with my fears of the unknown future — my fear of being inadequate, of being a burden, of accepting my injury. Because although she has accepted me as I am, I still haven't.

So naturally I'm being pulled towards what I used to have, because I want it back, but is that really what's best for me? Or would it be healthier for me to accept that we're supposed to move forward in life?

I sit with these thoughts for the rest of the afternoon, mulling them over until the answer becomes clear. It should have been clear from the start. I know I need to let go of the past and embrace the unknown journey ahead, regardless of how scary it might seem.

I phone Rosie and awkwardly start making my way through a series of long-winded apologies and explanations. I apologise for keeping her at arm's length and for making her feel unwanted. On and on I go about clinging to my past and how it's been stopping me from moving forward. I then ask if she's free to catch up soon. I sense some hesitation in her voice, and then she tells me she's met someone else . . .

My heart sinks. And I know I deserve this after the way I've treated her.

•

Courtney is moving out, and I'm sad to see her go but I've found another friend to move in. I was introduced to Ruby by Jesse. I'm stoked to have her moving in because she's a joy to be around and will bring a good vibe to the house.

A few weeks later and I'm heading down to Brant's place in Mangakino for new year. It's my first time back there post-injury, and it took a fair bit of organising, including Brant building a ramp around the back of the house to get me up onto the deck! Of course it brings back all of the memories of good times wakeboarding, partying and bringing girls here. Brant, Ants and I have been coming here since it was a gang town with no wakeboarders, now it's a wakeboarding town with a few leftover gang members! We owned this town over the years.

Brant's old man, Kev, always spends the holidays camping at the next lake up, so his side of the bach is free for me to use, which works out perfectly as it's nice and open — plenty of room to hoist me in and out of bed, and a bathroom big enough for me to roll into.

On New Year's Eve we have an ultimate crew here ready to celebrate: besides Brant and me there's Ants and his girlfriend Helene, and Jesse. And I'm stoked that Morgan has accepted my last-minute invitation to join us.

It's not exactly a raging party, although it's a step up from last year in the spinal unit. A few other friends stop by for a drink, and although it's tempting to join in, I've been alcohol-free all year. We sit around the fire sharing stories until we reach the countdown.

'Three, two, one — happy new year!' we all shout, exchanging hugs and headbutts — and Morgan plants a kiss on my cheek.

A couple of hours later I'm hoisted into bed, and after Brant has me undressed, turned onto my side and ready to pass out, I'm very pleased when Morgan jumps into bed with me. We lie facing each other and talking, while I battle my usual demons. I do my best to calm that feeling as I want to enjoy this moment for what it is. I keep looking down at Morgan's lips, and she must sense what I want because she gives it to me — a tender and passionate kiss that I want to continue till morning.

I'm very pleasantly surprised, of course. I thought I'd screwed everything up with both Morgan and Rosie, but now here I am, starting out the new year with kisses from a girl I've wanted since the day we met. This injury sucks, but this moment right here and now has me forgetting about it and completely entranced by this sweet girl's kisses.

What a way to start the new year!

•

I spend the first few days of 2016 hanging out in Mangakino. Morgan and I seem to be on track to get back together, but I don't want to get ahead of myself so I'm just enjoying whatever it is. This is the first time I haven't had a full-time caregiver around since leaving the hospital system, so she and the guys look after me from late morning, after two local caregivers come in each morning to do my ablutions. I don't fit in the shower so I'm hosed down, scrubbed and rinsed on the deck.

On the third morning, after my shower, my morning caregivers are struggling with the little ramp Brant built to get me up the step from the deck into the house. It's a little abrupt, but it works if I tilt back and reverse in. Suddenly, my chair slams forward unexpectedly. My arms fly off the armrests and my whole upper body is hurled forward. All I see is the deck below coming at me fast, giving me barely enough time to say '*Arrggghhh fuck!*'

But somehow my lower body remains on the seat, leaving me slumped forward staring down at the deck with both arms dangling. The caregivers scramble to sit me back up, but they don't have the strength. Thankfully Ants is here in a flash to help sit my naked arse back up. My heart is racing and I'm completely mind-blown that I didn't faceplant the deck. I even braced for it, although that did nothing except make my insides flinch. The ladies are mortified and super apologetic. As they pull me carefully inside, and my pulse is slowing to its usual pace, I'm aware of a feeling that scares me somewhat.

I feel disappointed that I didn't fall . . .

I sit with that thought for most of the day. Why did I have such a self-destructive impulse? And I realise it's not because I wanted to injure myself, or have a reason to be angry at my caregivers. It's because my life before this injury was filled with falls. I'd crash into the water time and time again, sometimes getting winded, or having my brain rattled, then I'd emerge from the water to take a deep breath and shake it off. I miss falling because it made me feel alive! Falling was part of my life, but for the past 18 months I've basically been wrapped in cotton wool, without that regular rush of adrenalin.

I also realise that if I had fallen, unlike with wakeboarding I would've had zero control of the way I fell, and no way to brace, so I would have gone down face first and done who knows how much damage — broken nose, teeth knocked out, maybe further spinal damage. So, as much as I still miss the feeling of falling, I'm glad it didn't happen.

•

Fiona and I are flying to Sydney where I'm to attend Deano and Amber's wedding! It's a military exercise boarding and getting seated, but Fi manages it all well.

After settling into our hotel, I go to the bar where a bunch of tomorrow's wedding attendees are catching up for a few drinks. I'm so rapt to see some of my

Aussie friends from the good old days, and some who basically became family over the years in Orlando. And it wouldn't be the loose Aussie wakeboard crew without being kicked out of the bar for obnoxious drunken behaviour. I even have a few drinks myself.

Fi gets me suited up for the wedding, and even gives me some pretty fly-looking braids to complete the fresh look. I've been a little daunted by this next part — the ceremony is being held on the top deck of a three-storey party boat out on Sydney Harbour. There's no elevator — just two flights of 16 steps each.

Deano had warned me about this, but since his dad is also in a wheelchair, the guys are more than prepared, with a stair-climbing wheelchair! I'm transferred across using my travel sling, and Velcro straps secure me in place. Then my mates gather around and get ready to carry my 200-kg chair to the top. It takes Deano, Jeff, Dwayne Priestley, Scotty Broome, Rob Iacconi, Lachie Burgess, Daniel Watkins and Stu Wilson to do the job!

I'm then tilted back 45 degrees before the chair employs its tank-track drive system to slowly inch its way up to the top of the staircase, where I'm plonked back in my chair for the ceremony. My friends have just demonstrated to me in the most literal way possible that they're willing to carry the burden that I am. They would rather have me here, carrying my chair up and down more than 30 stairs, than not have me here. So watching one of them, one of my closest friends and a man who literally saved my life, marry his best friend and another dear friend of mine, brings a tear to my eye, as I'm overcome with gratitude and love.

After the ceremony we gather together for photos with the famous Sydney Opera House and Harbour Bridge in the background, before moving back downstairs for the speeches and dinner party. The boys feed me beers, and the girls lead me out onto the dance floor, where I do my best Stevie Wonder dance impression since I don't really have any other moves apart from spinning my chair around in circles. After watching a fireworks display put on by Luna Park we disembark close to midnight. But the party isn't over yet — we roll with a huge entourage back to the hotel where we continue to drink and celebrate at the hotel bar with the happy newlyweds.

The next morning, while a handful of us are downstairs having breakfast, Brenton, Dwayne and Hank roll in, still in their suits from last night. They've been on an all-nighter and regale us with tales of their adventures. Part of me feels like I missed out on an epic night, but to be honest I don't think I would've been able to keep up with them even in my partying prime. They're loose units!

I struggle with that feeling of missing out, and I realise I sometimes miss things I'd never have done, and I wish I could do things I never wanted to do before. It plays with my mind as we fly home.

•

'I know it makes no sense to feel like I'm missing out on things I wouldn't have done anyway,' I tell Susie, 'or things I've never done, but they're feelings that grab me all the time.'

'A lack of acceptance of our current reality will bring on a longing for things we don't have,' she explains, 'whereas acceptance of where we are — and even gratitude — means loving what we have in the present. I know it's a challenging one, but you're already getting better at it. When you had your movement, like everyone you took it for granted. But with that movement taken away, it's hard not to dwell on all the things you could do if you had it back. Even though you've never run a marathon, and never wanted to, it's very natural for you to wish for anything that symbolises movement for you.'

'That makes sense,' I say, 'but I'm so unhappy with where I am that acceptance and especially gratitude just seem impossible. I don't know how I could ever be grateful for this life.' It's the brutal truth.

'What about getting back with Morgan?' Susie asks. 'Surely that's something you are grateful for?'

'Of course I'm grateful for her, but that doesn't mean I'm grateful for my injury.'

'If you're truly grateful for something in the present moment, that gratitude must extend back through everything that brought you to that moment. Everything that has happened in your life, whether you perceived it to be good or bad, has led you to this moment. So if we're grateful now, we must be grateful for everything that got us here.'

I take a moment to think about that, because it makes total sense, but my brain also wants to disagree strongly.

'If anything in your past happened differently,' Susie goes on, 'then chances are you wouldn't be where you are today — grateful for getting back together with Morgan.'

I know she's right, but I just don't seem able to grasp this one yet. It seems impossible.

I spend a couple of weeks at home, back into the regular rehab. I'd been training so hard before I went that the break was a welcome refresher. At Neuro Rehab, Amy uses a piece of equipment that I recognise from Shepherd Center. It's the RT300 arm and leg FES cycle. I'm excited to get back on it and to see the muscles in my arms and legs working while getting them moving.

Late last year I applied to have one of these machines at home, funded by ACC. They denied my application, so I appealed, and they denied it again. After a second appeal and the third denial, most sane people would give up, but not me! I'd exhausted my appeals, but the next step was an independent review of ACC's decision.

Unfortunately, in the week leading up to the review hearing I was back in hospital with another UTI that turned septic. On the day of the hearing I managed to escape hospital and show up to face off against my ACC case manager. I sat opposite her at the table as she pulled out pages and pages of reasoning and evidence for why they wanted to supply me with a cheaper machine that only stimulates half the number of muscle groups and requires a technician to come over and plug into it to make any changes.

I had no 'evidence' but simply explained why I needed — and why it made sense for me to have — the one with 24 electrodes to stimulate six muscle groups on each side of the body. It didn't take much for the independent reviewer to see my side of the argument, since the technician costs alone would likely equal the $20k price difference after a handful of years.

A couple of weeks later I was stoked to hear I'd won, and was about to become the first person in New Zealand to have an RT300 FES cycle fully funded by ACC.

At Neuro Rehab we're getting my program set up for when my machine arrives. I love seeing my legs moving and I feel like I get a great workout from it. I especially like the arm cycle as I can use the limited movement I have in my shoulders to really dig in and feel like I'm contributing. I can't wait!

•

Morgan and I have been spending loads of time together since I got back from Sydney, and she's stayed over a few times. Our intimate moments are incredibly special and my love for her is as strong as ever. Yet my doubts remain — I constantly wish I could express myself physically, touch her and caress her body while she's on top of me. My feelings of inadequacy are eased when I'm able to give her an orgasm as she straddles me. She lies back down beside me with a big satisfied smile on her face, and then reveals that I just gave her the first orgasm she's ever had!

'What — the first from someone going down on you?' I ask.

'No, the first ever,' she replies. She tells me she's had great sensations that she *thought* was an orgasm, but she never actually knew what an orgasm was until just now.

No way! A big proud smile spreads across my face, and I feel even better about my achievement. Until it hits me that she and I dated for three months and had loads of great sex, but apparently I wasn't doing as great a job as I thought I was. Even though I've always tried to be unselfish in my lovemaking, I guess the fact that I'm no longer focusing on my own pleasure, and I gain more pleasure from making her feel good, makes me a better lover now.

Morgan and I take another trip with Brant down to his place in Mangakino at the end of January. On the first morning, Brant has gone out riding with some of our friends, and although I definitely feel like I'm missing out on the fun I used to have on the lake down here, I enjoy hanging back with Morgan and listening to good tunes as she sunbathes on the deck, especially when she decides to go topless.

The following day we catch up with the Haakma family; their two kids Morgan and Bradley (yes, really!) were two of my regular coaching students. I miss coaching a lot. After our last trip down here I decided it was time to get back on a boat. I've brought down my lightweight manual wheelchair and I figure we can get me in a boat in that, and use the tilt function to counteract the angle of the boat when it's getting up on plane.

The Haakmas have invited us out on their boat, so today is the day! Little Morgs, Mini Brad and Brant each get on the water for a ride. The feeling of the wind blowing past, the hum of the engine and the sights and smells of being out on the lake again all bring back so many memories. I love being able to give my favourite students more tips to improve their riding. Watching Brant ride again just feels so familiar, and after he's done I instinctively go to get up out of my seat for my turn. The instant reminder that I'm completely paralysed sets off a spiral of negative thoughts and I feel the emotion building as my mind starts fixating on what I've lost.

On the outside I show none of this emotion, because the idea is for this to be a good time for us all, a moment to celebrate, and I don't want to be a downer or a burden. So I *choose* to be happy, I *choose* to be positive.

It's Morgan's turn. She hasn't ridden a wakeboard since I took her to the cable two years ago, and this will be her first time behind a boat. I'm impressed, but not all that surprised when she pops up first try. The smile on her face is infectious, and spreads to my face as well, because I love teaching her and I want her to understand why I fell so in love with this sport. I share the coaching duties with Little Morgs — I give the instruction while Morgs stands on the back and demonstrates. By the end of her ride Morgan is brimming with joy. She gets back in the boat and gives me a cold wet kiss and shakes her wet hair all over me. Like she's sharing a small piece of the lake and the joy with me. I love it.

I notice that my negative feelings are no longer as strong, and the positive vibes I'm feeling have taken over. I'm reminded of a story I was sent about two wolves:

> An old Cherokee is teaching his grandson about life. 'A fight is going on inside me,' he says to the boy. 'It is a terrible fight and it is between two wolves. One is evil — he is anger, envy, sorrow, regret, greed, arrogance, self-pity, guilt, resentment, inferiority, lies, false pride, superiority and ego.'
>
> He continues, 'The other is good — he is joy, peace, love, hope, serenity, humility, kindness, benevolence, empathy, generosity, truth, compassion and faith. The same fight is going on inside you — and inside every other person too.'
>
> The grandson thinks about it for a minute and then asks his grandfather, 'Which wolf will win?'
>
> The old Cherokee replies, 'The one you feed.'

I picture the two wolves fighting inside me and I realise that today I've chosen to feed the good wolf. But the bad wolf still exists, and is still hungry, so although the good wolf has won this battle, the war is ongoing.

•

I enjoy sharing this experience with Susie when I'm back in Auckland.

'It sounds like you're not only starting to find acceptance with what is, but also finding gratitude for what is, even if the old way is wired in so deeply that sometimes it comes through instinctively,' she says. 'It's great to hear, and I'm sure you'll keep getting better and better at it. Eventually you'll become so good at living in the present, that any past beliefs, any past currency, any past wiring won't have any hold over you. Your injury will stop being something you continually look back at with regret, and you'll just be in the now with your eyes focused forward.'

She's excited about that idea but it seems a long way off to me.

'I must say it was nice to get out of my own head and actually enjoy myself,' I concede. And remembering the analogy about the wolves helped me to understand that I have a choice over how I feel — even though I'm still working on mastering that ability.'

'I'm proud of how far you've come, Brad. You're doing great!'

•

Just a couple of days after my 29th birthday my RT300 FES bike arrives! After talking my caregivers through assembling it, I sign in to my profile, which already has my programs set up, get all 24 electrodes stuck to the right muscles on my legs, glutes and lower back and I take my first ride.

The following day we rig up my arms, shoulders and upper back and I pump out a great workout. Although the only real progress I have seen is my shoulders getting a bit stronger, I enjoy my rehab sessions because I feel like I'm working towards a goal, especially when I feel wrecked after a workout. But the fact that I still can't lift my arm from the armrest, and that the slight flicker in my biceps remains the same, is extremely disheartening.

•

Towards the end of February, Morgan and I fly with Kristian to Queenstown for my sister's wedding. I'm the wedding MC, alongside my future brother-in-law's brother, Jarrad. He and I catch up and go over the plan and our speeches to make sure we're ready to nail it. In the evening, we host drinks for friends and family at the house Mum has rented on the outskirts of Queenstown. As we're having a few nibbles and drinks, Alex and Morgan and I are approached by a family friend who says to Morgan, on being introduced, 'And how do you fit into the picture?'

I pause, because we haven't put a label on our relationship yet and I don't know how to answer the question, but Alex pipes up and says, 'She's Brad's gggggrrey area,' stopping himself from saying *girlfriend* since he knows that hasn't been established. We all laugh at his save, including Morgan thankfully.

On the big day I'm feeling good and confident in my suit and tie; I've put a lot of work into the MC role. Unfortunately it's raining lightly, and my sister turns borderline bridezilla when the suggestion is made to move the wedding to a small area indoors. 'I'm not getting married inside this shitty room,' Monique says firmly, and I can't say I blame her. So we continue with the original plan to hold the ceremony in the beautiful gardens. Thankfully the rain is more of a light drizzle by the time the stunning bride walks down the aisle, and although everyone has umbrellas, it actually makes for a beautiful wedding.

I can't help wondering whether one day I might get to exchange similar vows with the gorgeous girl sitting next to me.

After the speeches and official duties are done, I'm relieved to feel that it went well and now I get on and enjoy myself.

When the dance floor is in full swing, I get Morgan to sit on my lap and I drive us into the middle of the dancing circle that's formed, and start spinning in circles and doing my best to make my chair dance, although the sip and puff controls aren't quite that responsive. While still sitting on my lap, Morgan whispers in my ear, 'You know, you can introduce me as your girlfriend if you like.'

I turn to her with a huge smile and we kiss as family and friends dance all around us. I'm filled with so much love. The party continues late into the night, and Morgan and I are both ready for sleep as soon as we're in bed. It's been a day filled with love and I feel so at peace with my girlfriend cuddled up beside me.

•

Over the next month, Morgan and I are back in Mangakino for multiple weekends. She's officially caught the wakeboarding bug, so I arrange through Dunc to get her a wakeboard for her birthday and she's over the moon. She's starting to get pretty comfortable on the water, especially now that she's got her own board.

Another weekend we go down for the North Island champs, where I'm back on the mic with Jesse. Nautique have flown in the legendary Shawn Watson, and after the contest the boys load me onto the G23 and we all head out onto the lake for a shred session with Watson, Brant and my local teammates Paul Maguire and David Stubbs.

The bad wolf is hovering as I watch the fun everyone else is having.

When I get back home, I say to Susie, 'I know you say that if I'm truly present, I can't miss out. But I was in the boat and I was present in the moment and I still felt strongly that I was missing out on the wakeboarding fun the boys were having.'

'Being present isn't just about being there,' Susie replies. 'It's about being *in the moment as you are*. So the missing out you felt was because you were using the old currency of wakeboarding Brad, who could get up and do anything. And that's *totally* understandable. But the ability to wakeboard is *not* part of the present you. It's the story your ego keeps telling you, because your ego is so wired in with the old you.'

She changes tack.

'I guess it's similar to the conversation we had about sex. You're there, and you're in it, but if you use the old currency you still feel like you're missing out. Remember, the new currency is about accepting the moment and finding gratitude for the things you love *about that moment*, like enjoying being with your good friends and watching them ride, rather than focusing on what you can't do.'

'Okay, yeah, I get that,' I say. 'So for me to become happy to be around wakeboarding again, am I supposed to forget the fun and progression and fulfilment it brought me? And the same for sex?' That seems unreasonable — and unrealistic — to me.

'It's not about forgetting the past. It's important to have fond memories to appreciate, but it's about understanding that the past is in the past. The reality is different now.'

I think about this. So presence is about everything being in the present moment, not just me being there physically. It's also about accepting and applying my current reality and abilities to the situation. 'If only' thinking is not being present, so to base our happiness on a fantasy of how we wish things were is just delusional.

I'm getting better at this, but it's a slippery thing.

●

I've been invited to host the 2016 Riders Choice Awards, Australia (RCAA). Kristian and I fly to Brisbane and rent a van to drive up the Sunshine Coast. Since it's Kristian's first overseas trip with me, and he's never driven in Australia, Brant comes along to help out.

We arrive at our accommodation in Maroochydore on the sunny coast, where the evening air feels thick and humid. Once we've got everything unloaded we head to a bar to catch up with two old friends who I haven't seen since before my accident, Christian Fitzpatrick, the man who put me in my first wakeboard film, and Josh O'Connell, a fellow Kiwi rider, who moved here with his family several years ago. The frosty cold jugs keep arriving, the memories flow and I'm starting to feel pretty buzzed up!

I sleep badly — my nerve pains are firing. By the time I wake up the following morning it's several hours later than we'd planned. I needed the sleep-in but now I'm dealing with a hangover.

Brant, Kristian and I get to the venue for the Riders Choice Awards. I catch up with Deano, who is my co-host for the awards. I was nervous about this, but now that I can see it's not a huge venue, my nerves settle. And after a quick run-through with Deano, I feel more confident.

A couple of hours later the place is packed full of riders I mostly don't know. It's wild how things change so fast in this sport. I'm honoured at the introduction I'm given, and gratified by the applause. Deano and I take turns introducing each award, and it falls to him to announce Best Trick.

I turn my chair to face the screen, as I'm excited to see the highlight reel of the best tricks over the last year. Harley Clifford features strongly and I figure he's going to take it out.

Then suddenly the screen flashes up with Parks Bonifay's video of my double tantrum to blind. *What?! Why am I nominated?* And I recall that throughout the night there have been several mentions of the fact that these awards are biennial, meaning everything from the last *two years* is counted.

'And the Best Trick winner is . . .' Deano says, 'with the double tantrum to blind, *B-raaaaaaaaad Smeele!*'

The room erupts in cheers and applause and the trophy is placed on my lap. I'm so stunned! Tears stream from my eyes as I'm overcome with emotion. I'm filled with gratitude, and love. I missed out on receiving my Trick of the Year award at Wake Awards, so this is one of the most special moments of my life. It dawns on me that this was the whole reason I was invited to host these awards. How did I not see this coming? But what a cool thing for them to have done. What a fucking cool surprise!

•

Having Brant on this trip with us was awesome. He was super helpful and since we think alike in many ways, I trust his logic and common sense, which makes life so much easier. We talk about the possibility of him becoming one of my caregivers. Since he already hangs out and looks after me so much, why not get paid for it? A couple of weeks later he quits his job at Harley-Davidson and joins my team.

My brother Alex is off back to London after spending the summer here. We've become so much closer since my accident, but it seems like his boss will bring him back each summer, so it might not be too long before I see him again.

•

I've missed Morgan so I'm excited to see her when she comes over the following day. I surprise her by being in full standing on my tilt table when she arrives, so she's able to stand with me at my full height again. It feels so good. I'm pumped for her as she's just landed a new role in a TV show. I love this girl, and I fought to get her back, but I honestly can't fathom why she came back to me. I believe her when she tells me she loves me, but is love enough to make up for the countless hurdles and barriers that come with dating someone in my position?

'I just don't get why she's with me,' I tell Susie.

Susie is patient with me, and very understanding, especially since we've gone over this stuff many times already. But it keeps coming up, especially now that Morgan and I are together. My fears around getting into a relationship have continued into the relationship itself, so getting the girl didn't rid me of the fears.

'What is it you're most afraid of, Brad?' Susie asks. 'This feeling of inadequacy will be tied into a bunch of fears. All of our emotions are rooted in either love or fear.'

'I hate that I can't hold Morgan's hand or pick her up for a big hug, and a relationship without all those little things feels kinda empty. Don't get me wrong, Morgan does well to fill that void from her end, but I just feel so useless that I can't do anything from mine. I also hate the idea that I wouldn't be able to protect her in any situation that called for it. But the main thing I'm afraid of is the idea that I might not be able to be an adequate husband or father without the ability to help out with everything that comes with those roles.'

Tears seem to be spilling from my eyes and rolling down my cheeks.

'I know it's scary to think about those things. But this is all based on your beliefs about what those roles entail. Your fear of not being able to protect her is valid, because you yourself are vulnerable, but it's also based on the belief that the man should protect the woman, which is a very archaic way of thinking.'

Okay, fair call, I guess.

'There's a lot of future thinking going on here, and you know what we've learnt about the future,' Susie says.

'I know — I shouldn't be thinking so much in the future. But I also think it's a very real fear because becoming a parent is kinda what we're here for, isn't it?' I ask.

'Ah — be aware of the belief behind that. Your fear is that you might not be able to do what you think a dad is *supposed* to do. Remember that word *supposed* comes from a belief about what you think a husband *should* be, to his wife, and what a father *should* do. Now think of how often you hear about kids growing up without a father. How often you hear of a single mum raising kids on her own. I can already tell you'll be a great father, and if some women can do it alone, then doing it with someone as compassionate, caring, loving and supportive as you are would be wonderful. You'll be more supportive than most husbands I know!' She winks at me.

'You were fortunate to have a loving father who supported you,' she goes on, 'so that's what you're basing your beliefs on, but remember that many kids don't have that.'

The business of these belief systems seems really complicated, but what it comes down to is realising that through our own experiences and things we pick up along the way, we put meaning on things that aren't necessarily the only truth.

●

A few days later I'm talking with Dad about what Susie's been teaching me about belief systems, and Dad says something that absolutely knocks it out of the park.

'Nothing has any meaning but the meaning we give it.'

●

Today is an exciting day at Neuro Rehab as we've been working on a new armrest that has a joystick hand control for my chair. Aaron, from the Quantum supplier, has been working on it since we trialled a few options, and he's back with the final product for me to try out. I'm nervous about trying to use a joystick when I have no movement in my hand, but after all our work moving my arm using slide mats, Amy reckons I might have just enough movement from my shoulder.

With my hand balanced on the T-bar joystick I find that the strength I've gained in my shoulder enables me to quite easily make my hand move side to side. Pushing forward is tricky — it takes a lot of control to isolate the right muscles and not allow the dominant ones to take over and send the joystick sideways.

Aaron tweaks the sensitivity so a smaller movement is required, and after some more practice we switch the chair on and I'm able to drive slowly around the rehab clinic! I'm a bit all over the place at first, but over the next couple of sessions I'm able to weave my way in and out of cones and around a course set out around the clinic.

The downside is that my shoulder can't handle the strain for long. After 30 minutes it's wrecked and requires the girls at physio to dig into it to release the knots. Not only that, but it's such a fine balance that if I ever lean my hand too far to either side, or pull too hard back — which I have no trouble doing — it can easily slip out of position, or even fall completely off the T-bar. And that's just in a flat clinic space. Out in the community on normal footpaths with all of their angles and bumps, my hand would surely fall off, and certain angles would prevent my fine movements completely.

So while I take enjoyment from this progression, and love showing off my driving skills to Morgan, I realise that this development is not something I can actually use until I have the ability to lift my hand back onto the joystick if needed. So I continue with the sip and puff control.

•

At the end of April I'm back in hospital with another bladder infection. It's my second time in hospital this month — a few weeks ago I was brought in by ambulance after I broke into uncontrollable rigor shakes that I couldn't settle.

Morgan is with me pretty much right through my week-long stay, keeping me company and talking and joking. This girl has a way of filling me with love even in my hardest times.

Tonight Brant is here hanging with me. Morgan has gone to get some food for me, since I refuse to eat the hospital food. She walks in with a couple of burgers and I notice immediately that she's not her usual bubbly self. She asks Brant to give us some privacy, and tells me that we need to talk. I know exactly what the problem is and I've been dreading this for the past 24 hours.

'Today I got sent a screenshot of your conversation with some girl named Caitlin,' Morgan says angrily.

She's fully justified in being angry.

Oh shit, you've really fucked up this time, Brad.

'You have every right to be angry at me, Morgan. I have no excuse. I fucked up.'

I feel the heavy weight of guilt for what I've done, knowing there's no talking my way out of this one.

To backtrack: it's not uncommon for me to get random messages from people on Instagram, predominantly women. Since my accident, I assume they're just being friendly and sympathetic. One day recently I got a message from a girl in

Canada. It was just the standard message about how inspiring I am. I gave the generic reply of 'Thank you, I appreciate the support' with a smiley face. But as the day went on, a few more messages went back and forth. I have heaps of women friends I message from time to time, and I know I need to keep the conversations from being anything more than friendly.

But the conversation with the girl in Canada continued, and over the course of a few days it progressed from friendly chat through to some light flirting, and then she started a game of Three Lies, One Truth, and I got caught up in the excitement of it and it quickly progressed to sexual truths and lies. After a week of back and forth, during which time things got pretty explicit, I told her it needed to stop because I didn't want to jeopardise my relationship with Morgan.

That was a couple of weeks ago, but it was too late. It turns out that the girl in Canada has a boyfriend who lives in New Zealand, and he knows her Instagram password. He found our chats, took screenshots of the worst parts, then found out who my girlfriend was and sent them to her. Caitlin warned me yesterday.

I apologise profusely to Morgan, trying to explain that it was purely fantasy and I put an end to it weeks ago, but I know that doesn't erase what she read. She's upset, and angry, and as we continue to discuss it, things get more and more heated. I can feel her slipping away.

'Please, Morgan, I know I fucked up and I have no good explanation. I'm an idiot but please know that it's not because I don't love you — because I really do love you! You deserve better.'

I want to reach out and take her hand, but although she's just a metre away, she might as well be miles away and there's nothing I can do. She tells me this is the third strike, and I'm a bit confused by that, because I can't think what the first two were. So I ask, and she replies, 'The first was Dawn, and the second was Rosie.'

I feel this is unfair — on both counts.

'Hang on,' I protest, 'but we weren't together for either of those! And I've already explained that the whole thing with Dawn happened unexpectedly while I was in the ICU fighting for my life. I understand how hurtful it must've been to see the picture in the paper of her cuddled up beside me, but there's no way that was a betrayal of you. You and I weren't together!'

'It doesn't matter if we were together or not — it's about how it made me feel. Although I was happy to know you had someone there to support you in your toughest time, it really hurt me because I was back here helping organise a fundraiser for you! I felt like I should've been the one who was there for you.'

'I totally understand you feeling that way. What about Rosie?' I ask. 'I was fighting to get you back and she fell for me and I couldn't help falling for her while you were stalling on answering me. I'm not blaming you for taking the time to figure out what you wanted. But again, we weren't actually together so how is that a strike against me?' I ask.

Already asked and answered — it's about how it made her feel.

And strike three is not up for debate. Especially knowing that she likely read my expressions of my deepest dirtiest desires to do all sorts of filthy things to this girl I don't even know.

Our argument gets more and more emotional until Morgan says, 'I can't do this,' and turns and walks out of the room. She may not have officially broken up with me, but we're barely hanging on by a thread. Brant comes in and says even he got a death stare on her way out. She obviously thinks he knew about it, but he didn't.

My last days in hospital are awful. I'm angry at myself, and depressed over everything. I call and message Morgan over and over but get no reply. The only thing that puts a smile on my face is a visit from my niece Maisey, who is now three and a half and more adorable than ever.

•

Getting back home I'm embarrassed to face my flatmate Ruby, who has become best friends with Morgan and I know she knows. When she sees how torn up I am over my fuck-up we have a good chat, and while she still thinks I'm an idiot, I think she also feels for me. She suggests I just give Morgan some space.

I start digging deep into my psyche to figure out why I sabotaged a relationship with someone I love and fought so hard to get. Not to excuse my behaviour, but to understand what drove it so I can learn. It's clear that my old programming was in full swing at the time. The old me was so heavily wired around the attention I received from women — the messages, photos and videos through text, Facebook or Instagram were part of the fuel that my ego thrived on and it was constant.

After I broke my neck, all that changed. I had other priorities, and I had Dawn, then Rosie, and Morgan. Online attention dwindled to the occasional random message. Meanwhile, I've been struggling with what's happened to me. I've felt so down about myself, my confidence shot to shit. My ego drew me back to the old ways, diving into Caitlin's online attention to build my self-esteem back up.

The other thing is that even before my screw-up, I didn't feel I deserved Morgan. Maybe I subconsciously destroyed our relationship because I don't really believe she would want a future with me. I'd rather kill it off now than be hurt when she inevitably does it a few months or years down the track.

As I sit here in my chair I feel trapped. Morgan won't talk to me, and I can't even *move* to help myself. The anxiety builds until I'm rocking back and forth and side to side as if I'm trying to break free. Tears roll down my face and I cannot wipe them. There have been bad times since the accident, but this is next-level. I'm overcome with grief over every part of my situation: the constant pain, the loss of movement and of my independence, the loss of Morgan, and the frustration of having full-time babysitters. Is this really what my life has become?

'*FUUUCK!*' I roar.

•

Susie agrees with my analysis of my behaviour when I pluck up the courage to tell her what I've done.

'I'm not saying it's okay,' she stresses, 'but it's understandable that you reached back into old patterns of behaviour.'

'Does it mean I didn't love Morgan enough? Because I really feel like I do.'

'Based on what you've told me, it seems like you love her deeply,' Susie says comfortingly. 'I'm sure you didn't intend to hurt Morgan—'

'It was all just fantasy,' I interrupt her. 'I never intended doing any of it. To be honest, Susie, I wonder if it's because I found being able to talk about fantasy sex — sex as it was and should be — so much easier than accepting what it is now.'

'I think the real reason you did this is not because you didn't love Morgan enough, but because you don't love yourself enough at the moment. You resorted to old currency because you felt you were lacking in yourself.'

Her words strike me directly in the heart. Because she's right.

'So how do I switch off that old way of thinking? Why can't I do it?' I ask.

'It comes down to learning to have unconditional love for yourself. Not conditional on whether girls want you for your body, not conditional on being able to move, not conditional on what the guys think is cool or what your beliefs tell you are needed for you to be deserving of love. Love yourself for everything that you are — not just the parts that you like, and that your ego approves of, but everything.

'Love yourself for facing this huge challenge every day and simply for doing your best, love yourself for your beautiful brain and the work you've been willing to put in to some really hard lessons,' she says. 'We've spoken about compassion for others, but you deserve compassion from yourself too!'

I sit and let it soak in as the tears continue to flow — from the loss of Morgan, and from this challenging idea of loving myself.

●

It's the middle of May and another winter is starting to kick in. While scrolling through social media I see that a fellow wakeboarder named Mac Rosen has had a gnarly crash in Thailand and they need to amputate his leg. Even though I lost the use of my limbs, I can't imagine what it would be like to completely lose a leg. At least I have a slim chance of gaining the use of my legs again, but he won't ever get that leg back. I send Mac a message of support and he responds the same day, saying he always looked up to me as a wakeboarder and that he's been following how strong I've been through my injury. I feel good knowing he's drawing inspiration from me in what must be an incredibly tough time.

●

My mornings sitting over the toilet seem to be taking longer and longer. It now takes up to two hours of sitting on the chair for me to be done. Furthermore, some mornings I've ended up with blood in the bowl by the end of it, and more recently there's even trickling blood that I can hear hitting the water below. I'm booked in to see a colorectal specialist, who tells me the bleeding is caused by haemorrhoids, most likely due to the amount of time I'm spending on the toilet every day.

So the next day I go back to having my bowel care routine carried out in bed. It feels borderline subhuman shitting the bed every morning. Of course my caregivers tuck bed pads under me so nothing gets on the sheets, but still . . . At least I'm no longer losing blood.

●

We're nearing the two-year anniversary of my crash. There's been nothing from Morgan in almost three months. Brant and I are chilling late one night in my lounge and we've tuned into the livestream of an action sport event called Munich Mash, which this year features big-air wakeboarding! After my injury they dropped the mega-ramp and I really hated that my crash basically singlehandedly halted that direction of the sport. But now it's back and Brant and I are watching my good buddies sending it in a really sick event that includes a few rail features as well as the mega-ramp.

Of course I can't help feeling I should be there — watching them perform makes me feel like I'm missing out. But as the camera focuses closely on the riders, I notice something that lifts my spirits no end. Dom Hernler, Nico von Lerchenfeld, Felix Georgii, Daniel Grant, Aaron Gunn, Dominik Gührs and several others have *I Ride for Brad* stickers on their boards! It instantly puts a smile on my face and makes me feel as if I'm there in spirit. God I love this community.

I flick a message through to my buddy Matty Crowhurst, who is doing the commentary on the live stream, and let him know I'm watching and that I appreciate the support. Next thing I hear Matty give me a shout-out over the coverage, and I watch as the riders slap and point to their *I Ride For Brad* stickers while standing and waiting for their scores. I feel the love from the opposite side of the world.

I sense the wolves starting to spar within me. The tears in my eyes mean the bad wolf (*envy, sorrow, regret, self-pity*) is gaining the upper hand so I consciously start feeding the good wolf. I throw slabs of meat his way in the form of gratitude that I got to be one of the pioneers of the action I'm watching on TV, the love I feel from the riders, and the stoke I feel for my friends as they advance through the rounds.

As the event continues, I feel the negative feelings fading and I'm finding more enjoyment from watching the best big-air riding in the world. Especially when I witness my Ronix brother Dom claim the win, which he shares with the good wolf!

•

I'm back at the spinal unit for my two-year review. The doctor and his team poke and prod at me, testing for sensation and voluntary movement. Then we sit and talk through the results. They break the news that there has been no change, and that they don't expect any significant change moving forward. Much as I hoped for positive news, I'm not surprised. If there had been any changes, I would surely be the first one to know.

Even though I know that generally any return of feeling or movement happens in the first two years, the statement 'We do not expect any significant change moving forward' still cuts through me. I've always fought that message with a determination to prove them wrong, but I'm starting to believe that they might be right.

I put on a brave face while they ask me about my mental state, mentioning the help I'm getting from Susie. If I tell them how I'm really feeling they'll want to put me on antidepressants. When I get home I make a video-recording in which I open up about my fears for the future, now that it looks as if my past life will be staying there. I fear the unknown, I fear the prospect of future relationships, and and I'm unsure if my biggest fear is that I may never have children, or if I am able to but incapable of being a good father. I've learnt that anniversaries have a way of overwhelming me with grief and fear. To bring myself back to the present I remind myself of the quote that's printed on one of my T-shirt designs:

Never forget yesterday, but always live for today, because you never know what tomorrow may bring, or what it could take away.

Mum comes over to find out how the review went. When I tell Mum how low I'm feeling, of course she wants to make me feel better but there's nothing she can do. Causing Mum to feel as if she's failed me makes me feel worse, which makes her feel worse, making me feel like shit.

So I try to halt the downward spiral by telling her something I know might be hard for her to hear. 'Mum, I know you feel terrible that you can't make this all better, and I know you just want to support me by talking with me about it, but it's clear that it doesn't do either of us much good when we try because we're both just too emotionally invested. But I just want you to know that I have Susie to talk to, so please know that I'll be okay.'

I hate feeling like I've stripped Mum of one of her motherly duties, but she knows Susie well, so she knows I'm in good hands. I hope that the fact that I'm taking a heavy emotional burden off Mum's shoulders means she'll be able to breathe easier.

•

I'm hanging out for Monday and my next appointment with Susie.

'I know it's the two-year anniversary of your accident, but what is it about this particular day that is so heavy for you?' she asks.

I ponder for a minute, then respond, 'I think it's just the thought that after two years of working tirelessly to regain movement, I've gained nothing. Plus, the doctor basically told me to get used to being in a chair because they don't expect any change. At Shepherd they told me if I was going to improve, it would happen within the first two years.'

'That must be hard to hear,' Susie says. 'I want to talk about this two-year mark the doctors have told you about. I'm sure there's some research behind it, but there will have been people who have regained movement after two years, so try not to put too much belief into this. It's not an absolute cut-off point.'

'Yeah, I know,' I concede. 'I don't see it as a definite; it's just shitty to hear stuff like that.'

'For the last two years you've put so much into rehab, so I can understand it must be frustrating not to see the results you're after,' Susie goes on. 'Remember we've talked before about not trying to *force* something to happen, but *allowing* it to happen. You want control, but some things you cannot control. Have faith that you're on this path for a reason, and the reason is that you're here to learn what you need to learn until things are ready to happen in their own time.'

This is such a hard one — letting go of trying to control.

'I know it's scary, but all we're really doing is letting go of the illusion of control.'

'So what do you think I should do about rehab?' I ask.

'I think it has its benefits, on top of working toward regaining movement — helping maintain muscle tone and joint flexibility and so on, but the amount you're doing must be incredibly draining and time consuming. Maybe it's not about doing more, maybe it's about doing it differently or doing it less. You've still got a life to live, Brad.'

I tell her about my conversation with Mum.

'That's beautiful that you were able to recognise that it wasn't working and talk with her about it. But what you said about taking the burden off your mum and unloading on me — I don't see it that way. Our chats are not a burden on me at all; in fact I feel I'm gaining a lot from them. It's a bit like someone struggling to lug around a 20 kg weight. Another person might choose to carry that weight because their strength will improve from the effort.'

I have a lot to absorb from today's session. There's so much to learn and work through, and quite honestly, as much as I'm beginning to grasp a lot of Susie's teachings, I'm still finding it tough to apply them to my day-to-day life.

•

I'm meeting a few friends for a beer at the local pub in Takapuna. When I drive in I see that the path through to the outdoor area, where my friends are, is cluttered with tables and chairs and people in them. As I start weaving between them, suddenly everyone starts moving their chairs and standing up to get out of the way. Mostly it's not actually necessary — there's plenty of room for me to get through — but people are making a big fuss and doing it anyway. I wish people wouldn't make me feel different and out of place. I know they mean well, and I *am* different, but I hate the way it makes me feel. I feel like a burden and I hate the attention it brings. I feel all the eyes on me and I can feel what people are thinking. They're looking at this fucking cripple and their eyes throw pity in my direction. I don't want their fucking pity — I just want to have a fucking beer with my mates!

It ended up being a good night, I tell Susie later, but I just hated being treated differently.

'Did anyone say anything about pitying you?' she asks. 'Because you don't know what people are thinking. What you *think* they are thinking is a reflection of how you feel about yourself. We've spoken about self-love, which breeds confidence. If you go into the bar not giving a fuck what people think of you, because you know you're awesome, then regardless of how many eyes are on you and what thoughts may lie behind them, it won't affect the way you feel about yourself. Does that make sense?'

'Yeah, it does. People think I'm confident but I'm not, and I really felt out of place going in there. I remember walking into that place just a few years ago feeling so confident, but this time it felt so different. There was even this one cute blonde girl who was looking at me. We kept catching each other's eye, but I didn't know if she was looking at me because she liked me, or because she was intrigued by my chair, or if she pitied me.'

'This self-love thing will take some time, but I know you'll master it. It seems like a big leap right now, and dating must be daunting, but if you keep working on unconditional self-love, then you *will* get there.'

I hope she's right, because I want to feel confident again. I'm putting a lot of faith in what she's teaching me, and I'm already noticing some small improvements in my mentality and my ability to overcome the down days more quickly. I guess we'll just keep slugging away at it.

•

In the last week I've finally received a few messages from Morgan. It's nice to open the line of communication again. At this stage I know it's not about getting her back, but just having her back in my life as a friend, because I've really missed her. At the beginning of August she messages to say she's ready to see me again, so we catch up and it's nice to see her. After I apologise again for betraying her we actually have a good time hanging out and chatting.

She reminds me that I inspired her strong drive to be an actress, and she tells me she's applying for a US visa to further her career in Los Angeles. I'm stoked for her. I tell her I'm in the process of arranging my first trip back to Florida to see my friends. I really think we have both missed having each other around. I just love having her energy around me and would much rather have her in my life as a friend than not at all.

My trip to the US is a major logistical exercise. I'm also going to Cologne, Germany, where I will be a special guest at a huge event called Wake the Line. It's the event I just missed out on qualifying for in Penrith in early 2013. It's held in a giant swimming-pool complex and is one of the most fun-looking events I've seen. Plus they're covering the flights from Orlando for me and my caregiver. The other special guest is Matt Manzari, who was a pro wakeskater who was electrocuted by 14,000 volts that melted 25 per cent of his skin and cooked some of his muscles. Freakishly, his accident was the same week as mine.

While wrestling to finish organising for the departure in a few days from now, I start feeling a bit off. I know from the symptoms that it's another bladder infection, which means at least five days in hospital. I hate having to tell the Wake the Line organisers that I'm pulling out, but of course they understand.

Air NZ is really helpful so it looks like I'll be off to Florida at least, a couple days after I get out of hospital.

•

Ruby has just moved out into her own place. I'm bummed because she's been an awesome flattie. While I'm chatting with Morgan she mentions that she's not super happy where she's currently living. So I say, 'Hey, this may seem a little bit strange when we've just recently broken up, but I love having you around as a friend, so why don't you move in here?'

I've still got feelings for her, but I've accepted that she probably won't take me back, and I think it would be cool to live with her. She thinks about it for a few days and then tells me she'd love to. She'll move in just as I'm leaving on my trip, so it'll give her a month to settle in.

•

It's the end of August and I'm on my way to the airport with my luggage, including hoist and shower chair. Fi is dropping off Brant and me, and Mum will meet us there. As we're pulling up to the airport I start getting the sweats. I only sweat when something is wrong. Within minutes the sweat is pouring down my face. Fiona checks my catheter and everything seems normal but it's hard to know for sure. Mum arrives to find me in an absolute state.

I figure it's either the catheter or I need to move my bowels, and since the catheter seems okay, I might have a bit of a process ahead of me to get me in a stable condition to fly. My head is beginning to pound and I'm struggling to verbalise my thoughts. I don't know what to do, but I know I have to make a phone call. This trip is being covered by a current affairs programme called *Seven Sharp*. They're booked on the same flight as us and will spend the next week with us in Orlando, focusing on me getting back to the site of my accident at Lake Ronix. I need to let them know the situation.

'I'd say it's about 50/50 whether I make this flight or not,' I tell reporter Michael Holland.

'Ahh, that's no good,' he replies. 'I hope you're okay. Don't stress about us, but please keep us updated.'

I try calling the airport to see if there's somewhere we could get me out of my chair but they've got nothing, so Mum quickly books a room at a nearby hotel. We rush up to the room, where Brant, Fi and Mum use the travel sling that's already under me to lift me out of the chair and onto the bed. As I lie flat I feel an instant relief come over me. Fi tells me that I've just wet myself, and that the catheter bag has gone from almost empty to completely full. It must have unblocked after I changed position. *Oh thank fuck!* I'm so relieved that it's just a catheter blockage and I don't have to go through the whole bowel process. With a quick change of clothes I'm back in my chair, and I'm stoked to call Michael and tell him we're still on.

Brant and I are in business class and I feel pretty baller, but it's hard to enjoy it without constantly thinking about the cost. I'm just not sure if I'll be able to handle anything less, especially considering it's a 12-hour flight to LA, followed by a five-hour flight to Orlando. I manage the flight pretty well, especially with the help of some medication prescribed by my doctor.

NINETEEN: **RETURN TO THE SCENE**

Landing in Orlando at 10 p.m. I'm met with that familiar hot, thick Florida air. I wait with our bags as Brant takes off to find our rental van. I'm so exhausted, I tilt my chair back and close my eyes.

'No way! *Brad?*' I hear. I open my eyes to see Kilgus standing beside me. He's just arrived from Seattle. We take a minute to catch up before he has to go. I knew I'd run into loads of people I know while I'm here, but I didn't think it would start at baggage claim.

Chad arrives to welcome us, and by the time we pull up to Lake Ronix it's after midnight and I'm absolutely shattered.

But this doesn't feel like Lake Ronix at all. We've pulled in to a different entrance on a new part of the property that was purchased last year. This gives the company the entire perimeter of the lake, and on top of that there's now an old farmhouse, which is where Brant and I will be staying.

•

I'm woken the next morning by the arrival of a girl named Krista, who I've hired to come in and do my morning routine, since Brant and I don't cross that line. It's a bit of a scramble the first morning, but the shower part is easy as we just wheel me outside and Krista hoses me down. In the Florida warmth it's actually very pleasant.

I look around and I don't recognise this place at all. I can't even see the lake from here, and with the surrounding paddocks, barns and overgrown borders it feels like I could be in fucking Wyoming — until I hear the familiar morning scream of the resident peacocks. The sound takes me straight back to mornings chilling on the SUP board in the middle of the lake.

Towards the end of my hose-down, a familiar white Chevy Tahoe rolls up the driveway and stops behind me.

'*Maaan*, that's a small penis!' says the familiar deep voice of Mike Ferraro. Krista, Ferraro and I all have a good laugh. It's good to see him again, and once I'm dressed he shows me through the massive new house that's being built facing the lake. It's a huge change from my old trailer being the only building on the property, but I can now see the main part of the lake and the beach where I used to live. It's starting to look more familiar.

After breakfast the *Seven Sharp* crew arrive and start work. They film Brant and me taking a stroll along the dirt driveway to main beach, to show him where I used to live. It's hard to believe that I last stepped out of my front door two years ago, expecting to be back in a couple of hours. The trailer's gone now. All that's left is the overgrown patch where it used to sit.

We retrace my steps that I'd take every morning to the beach. I'm feeling very nostalgic but not overly emotional. Brant and I talk about the wake park in front of us and I tell him how a lot has changed but I'm proud to see that my wall-ride still stands. (I don't like that they painted over its beautiful wood-grain finish with boring white.)

Brant is excited to have a ride and I'm stoked for him. It will always be a battle for me to accept that I can't ride here myself any more. After I show off some more of my handiwork in the storage container we take the rental van around to the back lake, almost getting stuck in the sand along the way. Brant finds a section of the beach that's overgrown with grass and firm enough to hold my chair, which is not at all designed for off-roading. With a couple of scraps of ply I can get up onto the AstroTurf around the pool.

I marvel at the completed tiki tower I had started on right before my crash. The guys did a great job and it looks almost exactly as I'd envisioned it! I'm proud of the finished product, even though I didn't get to build it myself. They've even left the string-line hanging up where I left it, marking where the first horizontal support beam should go. I'm told it's been left until I come and take it down myself! I love that my team are so supportive of my recovery, and now I'm really determined to take that string down some day.

With the TV camera in my face, my attention is then turned to the reason I'm back here: to face the source of my pain head-on — not for the camera, but for myself. The mega-ramp is now floating, unused and decaying, in the back corner, which saddens me because a bunch of us put a lot of time and energy into building it. But apparently my injury really spooked many of the team riders and the passion for the mega-ramp was lost.

After getting me to talk him through the day of the crash and how it all happened, Michael asks, 'How does it feel to be back here?'

I know he's trying to draw emotion out of me — that's his job.

'It's hard,' I say. 'I keep replaying it in my head and thinking about what I could've done differently, and I know that's not a healthy way to look at it. So that's the whole reason I'm here — to stare my demons in the face, and hopefully start to put the pain behind me.'

I try to fight back the tears, but I don't entirely succeed. Mission accomplished for the media team, but for me as well, because I know the tears are part of the healing process.

I want to let myself truly feel this moment, so after the camera crew have packed up and left I stay behind and sit looking across the patch of water where I lay floating lifeless just moments after my body was snatched from me. I try to feel whatever comes up in me — loss, grief, remorse. The heaviness of my thoughts is symbolised by darkening clouds over the mega-ramp.

But for some reason I find my pain beginning to be overpowered by the memories of so many good times here. The riding memories of course, but the ones that really bring a smile to my face are memories of long days working with the team, becoming closer mates as we all worked together. Chad's reaction after realising their entire build was not square; Deano coming in halfway through a build with some crazy left-field idea to throw a spanner in the works. We all had our moments out here, our screw-ups and wins. We were like a family.

I'm now overcome with immense gratitude for what this place and the team brought to my life. And although the moody clouds still linger over the mega-ramp, the sun peeks through and shines on me.

We move along to the starting area at the end of the pool, and I sit where I stood for the last time I could do so under my own power. I take a deep breath and let it out, feeling like I'm expelling most of the sorrow and the tension I felt building up to this day, to this huge moment. I'm so glad I've come back here to face it, and begin to work my way past the grip that it had on me.

•

An hour later I'm surrounded by my good mates and my team, including some relatively new additions. It's so cool to see the likes of Parks, Danny, Chad, Ruck, Deano, Amber, Rossi, Jake and Dallas. I'm greeted with head-bumps from everyone, and we crack open beers. Rossi welcomes me back with a beautifully rolled spliff, which reminds me that there's one rider in particular that's missing — my little bro Pratt! He parted ways with Ronix last year and moved on to ride for another company. I catch up with him later on this trip.

The spliff gets passed to me and I take a couple of puffs, forgetting for a moment that the *Seven Sharp* crew are still here with camera rolling. I flash a look that says, 'Yeah, we don't need to film this part,' and they smile and nod. I haven't smoked much since the accident, but the odd puff has helped me to relax and almost get a break from the pain and any anxiety issues. We chow down on the grilled-up burgers and hotdogs, and although this is all still very bittersweet for me I'm so happy to be back here with my crew.

•

On day three Brant drives us across to the other side of Orlando to Nextstep in Longwood, where I'm booked in for my first two-hour rehab session. The film crew are here so they capture my arrival as I roll through the front door. I am greeted by Amanda, who wheels herself around the desk to say hello and takes me in to meet the rest of the team. First there's Amanda's mother Liza, who started Nextstep (originally called Project Walk Orlando) after Amanda was in a car accident at age 18 that resulted in an incomplete paralysis at C6 level. Amanda, now 27, has been making some really promising progress through her rehab here.

We roll through to the main gym area to meet the two head trainers: Christin, a super friendly and rather attractive South African girl, and Travis, a beast of a man who looks like a football player. Travis wraps a kind of belt around my waist, and between them they transfer me onto a padded table. I'm used to a hoist and sling for transfers, but Travis just wraps his arms around me and grabs the belt as Christin picks my legs up, and 'three, two, one' and it's job done! Travis then spends an hour of the session assessing me.

'How much time have you done on a standing frame?' he asks.

'Umm, none. I have a tilt table at home, though,' I tell him.

'Okay cool,' he replies. 'You want to get up in standing?'

'Shit yeah!'

Immediately I'm super impressed with this place. For starters, the moment I arrived they picked me up and took me out of my chair, which I stayed out of for the whole session. And that's the goal, right? To get me out of this wheelchair. So that's the message they're immediately sending.

I'm plonked into the seat of a standing frame, and held straight as the handle is cranked back and forth until I'm up in full standing position. The machine — called a 'glider' — is basically like a familiar exercise machine from any gym where you push and pull the pole handles back and forth, which moves the legs forward and back in a skiing motion. But for me it's about trying to keep my upper body upright. The machine supports me at my core, but leaves the rest of my upper body free to move around.

I have no core strength to balance myself, but with my hands strapped to the handles I use my shoulder strength to stabilise myself. I struggle to find my balance at first, and being upright is starting to make me feel a bit light-headed, so I let Travis know there's a chance I might faint. But rather than sit me down, Travis begins moving the handles back and forth for me, moving my arms and legs, which brings my blood pressure back up. I continue the session by leaning my upper body backwards and forwards, really working all of the active muscles around my shoulders and upper back. By the end of the session I'm completely spent.

They plonk me back in my chair, where Brant straightens me up and gets me sorted, and I tilt myself back to rest for a moment while he brings me some water. I feel so wrecked, but I love it! 'This is exactly what I've been missing!' I proclaim, stoked to feel like I've had a good workout.

I thank Travis and the team, and head back to the lake looking forward to getting back here on Monday.

•

After a great night's sleep, we're filming today at the Orlando Watersports Complex, where the TV crew capture me sitting on the sidelines watching as people cut laps around the cable. I put the word out that I'd be here today, so anyone who wanted to catch up could meet me here, and I'm stoked to catch up with a handful of riders. At one point I'm sitting alone watching the cable go round and round when I feel someone's hands on my shoulders, and then a full-on kiss is planted on my lips — it's the unmistakably soft lips and tongue of Candice. My heart pounds with affection as I revel in the moment of this surprise passionate greeting. Her smile is even more beautiful than I remember and it's so good to see her again.

•

Day 9 is the day I've been waiting for — one of the main reasons I came back to Orlando. Today is the first day of Surf Expo, which means that tonight it's the *Wakeboarding* magazine Wake Awards!

Late afternoon Brant and I pull up into the underground vendor loading area where we're met by Josh — who visited me with his partner Jenna at Shepherd

Center. He sneaks us in through a back door and up in the service elevator to where the banquet is being held. There we meet up with Dano, who has been helping me arrange a special surprise: tonight the dream team will be back together as we co-host the awards night! We run through a rehearsal to make sure we've got it all dialled in, then I sit nervously waiting out the back, hidden from view, while all the guests pile in.

Dano begins, and after thanking sponsors he says, 'I knew tonight was going to be a tough night, with a heavy load to take on, and I wasn't sure if I'd be able to handle this thing by myself — so I knew I was going to have to bring somebody in to help out. I'm going through the Rolodex and wondering who that person might be, and only one name came to mind.'

Meanwhile I'm rolling behind a curtain and onto the small lift that will get me onto the stage. The fog machine is working overtime to add to the mystery as Europe's 'The Final Countdown' blasts out of the speakers.

'Ladies and gentlemen, he's a past Wake Awards Trick of the Year award winner, a world champion, and a readers' poll Rider of the Year. He is the one and only king of the world — *B . . . rad . . . Smeeeeele!*'

The crowd lets out a deafening cheer as I make my way across the stage. Every single person is standing. Eventually they quieten and sit down, and I begin:

I can't tell you just how much of an incredible honour it is to be here with all of you.

The past two years have been an absolute rollercoaster, and nothing short of humbling. I've learnt so much about myself, about my strengths, my weaknesses, and about patience and presence, fear and love. I've had to overcome intense levels of pain both physically and mentally, and overcome my ego. I've gone from being physically capable and totally independent, to completely relying on the people around me for everything, from eating, to brushing my teeth, to getting around, even my finances.

I wouldn't have been able to get through this without the amazing people around me — my family, my friends, and my supporters from all around the world, including many of you in this room right now. I honestly can't begin to thank you all enough! Through this difficult time in my life I've been shown so much love, and I never thought I'd say the words 'I love you' to so many dudes!

My audience burst out laughing.

But it hasn't just been me who has received such love and support from our incredible industry. Ladies and gents, please make some noise for the miracle man Matt Manzari, who has made an incredible recovery from being electrocuted just days before my accident.

Matt joins me on stage and with tears in his eyes.

You've also supported Mac Rosen, who lost his leg in a bad fall, and you supported family and friends through the sudden tragic loss of Will Green. And as tragic as all of these have been, they've also brought us all together and made us all realise how amazingly supportive our industry is.

This has also made me realise something. It wasn't just wakeboarding itself that I loved. It was the people and the lifestyle that I fell in love with. And that's why I plan to be involved in wakeboarding for a long time.

People start cheering so I raise my voice to deliver my final line:

I may not be able to wakeboard any more, but I'll always be a wakeboarder!

I receive a standing ovation and I watch people wiping away tears. This is the energy I missed when I was at Shepherd Center as Jeff and Alex received my Trick of the Year award for me. But I feel it now, and I close my eyes and truly soak in one of the most incredible moments of my entire life. This feeling is exactly what I strived for — the respect and love of my peers.

After the crowd finally quieten down, we move on with presenting the awards.

When I get a quiet moment later to reflect on the evening, a thought crosses my mind: *I can't move anything with my body — but with my voice, I have the power to move mountains.*

I store this thought away for later.

●

From the convention centre, Brant, Alex and I head downtown to Wall Street for the after-party, where we meet up with Candice and one of her good friends, who both my bro and Brant take a liking to. We have a few drinks and in no time Brant is making out with her friend. We don't spend too much longer downtown before, with Candice sitting on my lap, we head back to the van and take the ladies back to the lake. Alex stays out partying.

Brant and I show the ladies around the farmhouse before getting into bed. It reminds me of the good old days, where Brant and I would pull a couple of babes while on tour around New Zealand. But this time there's the awkward 20 minutes it takes for Brant to get me ready and hoisted into bed.

It's far from the intense and sexy undressing and tossing into bed that Candice and I last experienced, and when we're finally in bed together — the very same bed from three years ago — it's beyond frustrating not being able to make love to her the way I used to.

She calms my frustration with her kisses, and my attention is brought back to her as she makes up for my inability to move by bringing her body to my lips. She even obliges when I ask her to climb up and straddle my face so I can pleasure her, and we're both pleasantly satisfied when she collapses beside me less than five minutes later.

Still got it! I think to myself. Because although this is nothing like how I wish it could still be, I've decided I need to take the small wins — and this is a win!

It's not the only night I spend with Candice. Our connection seems even stronger than before and she wraps me up in love and passion, which I've been craving. We know we can't be together but we have a mutual love that we cherish when we can.

•

Over the next two days I mill around at Surf Expo catching up with friends. As I'm heading towards the Ronix booth I catch Paul and a couple of the reps as they're heading to lunch.

'*Duuuude!*' says Paul. 'I've never seen Wake Awards so captivated! From so quiet to so deafening. Bradley the wordsmith — I love you, man!' He pounds his chest with his fist.

After my final rehab session at Nextstep there's a get-together at Rossi's place before Brant and I fly out tomorrow. It's hot, and although the cold beers are hitting the spot, they're not quite doing enough to cool me down. My face is feeling really hot and red and I'm eyeing up the pool. It's been so long since I've been immersed in water, so I tell the boys I want to get in! Brant grabs the sling for my hoist and proceeds to lean me forward to take my T-shirt off and tuck the sling under me. He pulls on a life vest, then the guys pick me up out of my chair and carry me to the pool.

I can't feel the cool water as my body is lowered in, but I can tell that my body feels it because it causes a small spasm in my legs and torso. But the life vest is floating me too high, and also riding up around my neck, which is uncomfortable. So we ditch the life vest and the guys position themselves around me to make sure my head doesn't drop under the water.

The moment my shoulders, neck and the back of my head drop into the water is pure heaven. I even ask to be briefly dunked under to get the feeling of full immersion. It's a strange feeling — on the one hand it feels very familiar, refreshing and gratifying, but it's weird to not feel the cool liquid surrounding my body. Also, I'm aware that my body feels different — it's like I can feel it, but it's completely different to how it should feel. My nerve pains are definitely not as bad.

A huge part of me feels that I'm home again, I'm where I should be. It's as if I feel the connection not as it was, but on a molecular level — like every cell in my body is celebrating a feeling it has missed for so long. I work out later that it's been 804 days since I was last in the water. Now I'm reunited with a long-lost love.

The moment is only slightly ruined by the fact that I've got several of the boys crowded around holding onto me for dear life. But gradually, one by one, they begin to ease up and back away a little, until I'm left with just Harley hugging me from behind to keep me from simply lying flat on my back. Someone jokes about the 'bromantic' moment.

Before my swim is over, we gather together and they dunk me and all come under with me to snap a quick underwater photo. It's an awesome photo of my favourite moment of the whole trip.

●

The next day Brant and I fly to Los Angeles for a couple of weeks of rehab and catching up with folks in California. The low point of that time happens when we're stopped at a red light at an intersection waiting for an arrow to turn green, and as the lights change a car coming towards us just blasts through a red light and almost gets clipped by a vehicle coming out of the side street. It's so quick. Both Brant and I gasp and flinch, because if that car had been clipped, it would've been sent careening straight at us.

'Oh my god, we just nearly died!' I say to Brant after the car zooms past. He is wide-eyed and clearly as spooked as I am. There's literally nothing we could've done. We were inches away from death. We both let out a huge sigh of relief, and drive on cautiously.

Later, my thoughts are drawn back to this experience. In my current situation I don't have a lot of control over much of anything, and I'm beginning to accept that. But in that situation neither Brant nor I had any control at all. I think about how many people must die every day through absolutely no fault of their own, and then I'm a little confronted by the realisation that, although I flinched and gasped in the moment, I felt no fear of death.

Don't get me wrong — I don't want to die, but I don't fear it because most of the last 27 months it hasn't felt like I'm really living any more — just existing. I've always had the thought in the back of my mind that I could end it all simply by finding a pool to drive my chair into. I don't have a death wish, I have a life wish, but the thing I fear the most, much more than death, is a life without joy, without colour, without love, without progression.

I'm aware that the option is there, but the splashes of joy and love I do have are keeping me going so far.

•

I enjoy telling Susie about my trip. I ask her about my thoughts around my near-death experience.

'I think what will centre you more in a state of enjoyment, and being at peace with your situation, is to focus on those things that you can still do for enjoyment,' she says. 'Which means putting less attention on what you can't do. What you *have* and what you *can* do are the important things to focus on.'

'But aside from being thrown in the pool, what options do I have?'

'I think finding enjoyment in the smaller things is where it'll start, because if you don't adjust your currency from fun equalling wakeboarding, partying and raunchy sex, then enjoyment will pass you by. Does that make sense?'

'Ahh, back to the currency thing. Yeah, I guess you're right. I think I understand it, but I'm struggling to apply it,' I say.

'Give it time, and have faith that it'll happen at the right time for you. Just keep learning what the universe is asking you to learn right now.'

•

The vibe around the house is great now that Morgan's living here. Her infectious smile and bubbly energy are a welcome addition to the household.

I'm conflicted of course because a big part of me wants to try to get her back, but I know that if we got back together it could be a reason for her not to move away and pursue her dream. I love Morgan, and I think I'll always have love for her, but if I truly love her, then the only thing I can do is let her go.

•

At the beginning of November I get a call from Quantum — they have a new chair for me! I'm stoked as it comes with a new feature called iLevel, which allows me to elevate the seat up quite high, and which will be handy for crowded spaces like bars and concerts. Also, now I get to be eye-to-eye with people.

•

At my next session with Susie I talk about my feelings of inadequacy, which keep circling back.

'Let me ask you this,' she replies. 'How can anyone be inadequate?' She looks outside and says, 'See those two plants outside? They're the same species but one is slightly smaller than the other — is it inadequate?'

'It depends what the plants are for,' I reply.

'But that's about you and your needs, that's not about the plant,' Susie counters. 'The plant is as nature made it; it is simply what it is. Inadequacy is about a judgement, and we have to see where the judgement is coming from. Is it coming from ourselves? Or is it being projected for us so that we believe it? Either way, in the end it's just a judgement.

'Feeling inadequate is simply a fear of separation. It's a fear that if we're not good enough then we might somehow be alone. I hardly think that's a possibility for you, with the number of friends you have. So if we look at it that way, then how could you possibly be inadequate?'

'I see what you're saying, and that makes sense, but something is making it hard for me to apply it to my situation.'

'We're here to learn. Although you may not see it this way right now, you've been gifted the opportunity to explore these concepts that so many people strive to grapple with, but don't have the time or the deep need to work through them like you do. These things keep coming up for you because there's work to be done around them. And you're waking up every day and facing this stuff pretty damn fearlessly. I know there's fear in certain parts of it, but just like you've always done in your life, you're facing it. And that's all you're asked to do — to turn up and be open. It won't always be easy. But I can't imagine fear stopping you,' she says.

'Honestly, facing some of these things is scarier than hitting a mega-ramp or committing to a double flip,' I say.

'Yes, it's scary to peel back the layers and look inside. It's the ego that's scared of it, because the ego says, *I have my story and this is who I am and what I've done and this is what I'm about.* But then we get to points in our life when that story doesn't work for us any more, and the way we've gone about things doesn't work any more. That's when we get to the currency discussion. What used to work for me no longer works — that currency is no longer valid. And that can be a really scary thing because it's like you're replacing the foundations of your house.'

'So it all comes back to ego, right? These thoughts and feelings of inadequacy.'

'Feeling inadequate can *only* be the ego — the true self can't be inadequate because you are as the universe made you, just as the plant is as nature made it. The more you release those stories of who you thought you were, and change your currency, and accept the past knowing you can't change it, and accept that you can't control the future, the less the ego has control over you.

'Those are all places where we're trying to get you to live, where the ego can't live. The ego is saying Fuck you, I need to get bigger, because that's what the ego does. When something pops up that feels uncomfortable, the ego tells you not to worry about it, and tells you to get busy doing this, and there's this as well — to distract from the problem so it can feel better.

'Whereas you know you're having this uncomfortable feeling for a reason. You're here to learn some big stuff, Brad, and it *is* scary sometimes, but you've jumped off some big shit before so this is nothing!' She smiles.

'I'd much rather jump off some big shit,' I laugh.

'But this is just sitting still and thinking!'

'Yeah, that's way scarier to me! I think the inadequacy thing is definitely me seeing where I'm at, and knowing that I'm not happy where I am, and not understanding how someone else could ever want to be with me here.' I can't stop the tears now.

'Okay, that thought pulls up all that emotion. Let's sit with that thought and see where it goes. Keep it there, maybe even say it to yourself or write it down. It's important to understand how you think and feel about yourself. Not in a "poor me" kind of way, but more so you can understand yourself and what you value about yourself. I want you to really understand and be aware of your thoughts and the beliefs behind them. It's called "metacognition".

'From now on, whenever any emotion pops up, I need you to sit with it and let it run its course. If you need to cry then cry, because if you push it aside and resist it, you're not processing it. But if you learn about it, come to understand what causes it, what belief is behind it, then each time you'll get better and quicker at working through it. Eventually you will have such a great understanding of yourself and your thoughts and emotions that these feelings of inadequacy and being a burden and missing out and lack of control won't have a hold over you any more.'

'Really?' I ask, not sure whether to believe her.

'Absolutely! And I'm so excited for you to get there!'

I don't feel like I'm going to get there anytime soon.

•

Alex is over from London for the summer and has moved in with me. It's awesome to have him back. We've never lived together outside the family home, but because now we're mates it's cool to have him around.

We're spending Christmas as a family at Monique and Jonny's place this year. I always struggle at this time of year, but I put on a happy mask for everyone around me, particularly for my gorgeous nieces, who love Christmas.

I feel like a bit of a spectator as I sit back in my chair while Alex plays with the girls and their new toys. I have this deep urge to get up out of my chair and be involved. I feel envy build as I watch my brother chase Maisey and Mila around the room and pick them up and have them laughing hysterically as he flips them upside down in his arms and tickles them. I hate not being able to be the fun uncle. I hate not even being able to play with them. I'm just stuck in this chair watching the fun.

When I'm able to get out of my own head I actually enjoy the time. It's nice having Dad here with us, and my uncle and nana, Mum and Gordon, and some of Jonny's family too. When I'm not focusing on what I can't do and don't have — when I simply appreciate what I have and who I'm with — my mood shifts and I feel my spirits lift. It reminds me of a quote I saw on my feed:

Christmas is about presence, not presents. Love people, use things, not the other way around.

TWENTY: BREAKDOWNS TO BREAKTHROUGHS

I spend another New Year's Eve in Mangakino. I have a good time out on the boat, but get pretty frustrated that I can't do much while everyone else is boat-hopping and jumping in the lake. I enjoy it better when we get back out on the boat with the Haakmas and I'm able to do more coaching.

Everyone else leaves Brant's place to return to Auckland, but Brant and I have chosen to stay down longer. Every morning a couple of caregivers come in to help me get through the routine and up into my chair, before leaving us for the rest of the day. Brant gets paid to kick it with me, either at his place or out on the boat.

One night, after some local friends have been over for a few drinks, Brant puts me to bed at about 1 a.m. Since it's so late, and I have a carer arriving at 7 a.m., I tell him not to worry about coming in to turn me at the usual 3–4 a.m. as I'm sure I'll sleep right through. I have 'Hey Siri' on my phone to to call him if I wake up and need him. He turns me on my side, pulls the blankets up, sits my phone on the bedside table and then turns the lights out before wandering back to his room in the next house over.

I wake up sometime in the night feeling strong nerve pains. I'm also slightly overheating, which must've been what woke me. After trying to get back to sleep, I decide I need Brant to come and pull the duvet off to reduce my temperature. So I turn my head towards my phone and say 'Hey Siri, call Brant,' just as I've done on other nights here. But I don't hear a response from the lady in my phone, which is strange, so I try again a bit louder: 'HEY SIRI — CALL BRANT!'

Usually I would hear 'Calling Brant Hales mobile,' in response, followed by the dial tone, but there's nothing. Close to a minute later I hear the soft Australian female voice say, 'I'm sorry, I'm having trouble connecting right now. Please try again later.'

Crap! I think to myself. Why is Siri not working? I try a few other commands — 'Hey Siri, text Brant', 'Hey Siri, what time is it?' Nothing. I guess it must be about 3 a.m and it's clear that Siri doesn't want to work for me tonight. I've had troubles with her before, but never to the point where she doesn't work at all. My lifeline has failed me.

I try my best to relax and close my eyes in the hope of falling back to sleep.

After about 10 minutes of lying there I realise it's not going to happen, and I'm starting to feel my temperature rising, making my nerve pains worse. I *need* to get Brant to wake up, so I try Siri again, but she's still not interested in helping me. My next option is a long shot, but worth trying.

'*Brraaaaannnt!*' I call out, knowing the chances of him hearing me are slim, since the bach consists of two separate houses, separated by a deck.

'*Brrrrraaaaaaaannnnttt!*' I try again. But being paralysed has weakened my diaphragm, leaving me with a pretty pitiful yell. Not only that, but there are four walls between us, and Brant's hard enough to wake when he's in the next room.

Anxiety is building inside me. I take in as big a breath as possible and scream '*BRRRRAAAAANNNNTT!*'

It's dawning on me that this is futile. I'm on my own.

My nerve pains are really firing now and I feel like I'm roasting. I'm trapped in this one uncomfortable position and can't escape. I take deep breaths and exhale strongly to try to breathe my way through the pain, and it helps a tiny bit.

I keep trying Siri and Brant in vain, and suddenly I notice that the window above my bed is open. That window opens to the back fence, and there's a neighbouring house not far away — possibly even closer than Brant's room — so I yell 'HELP!' into the quiet Mangakino night. 'PLEEEEEASE, SOMEBODY HELP ME!' I wait for a response or sign that someone has heard me, but all I hear are crickets.

It's been maybe an hour. In between desperate attempts to raise help I have moments where I accept that no one is coming to save me, so I try once more to close my eyes and go back to sleep. Sometimes I seem to doze off for a few short moments until the pain and fever wake me up again.

Suddenly I remember that sometimes iPhones let you call emergency numbers even when there's no service, so I call, 'Hey Siri, call 111.' Nothing happens. 'Hey Siri, call the police.' Still nothing. *Fuuuck!*

I try calling anyone else I can think of — Kev, Mum, Tolan, the Haakmas — but Siri refuses to cooperate. I'm beginning to panic, taking out my frustration on my virtual assistant: 'Hey Siri, you piece of shit!' Then a minute later I get 'I'm sorry, I'm having trouble connecting right now . . .' which brings me a tiny bit of comedic relief.

It's still pitch black outside. I'm beginning to feel delirious — my temperature is still climbing and is feeding all sorts of crazy thoughts into my head. I've given up on screaming for help after over an hour of trying, and I've given up on Siri. The pain is now agonising — I haven't felt pain like this since I was in the high-dependency unit and my fever was through the roof.

But there's nothing I can do — I've exhausted all options of rescue. I'm left with nothing but my mind to help me overcome this, and I constantly tell myself, *Stay positive and you'll get through this.* If all else fails I know the rescue will come at 7 a.m. when my carer arrives. *Just hold on, Brad. You can hold on till help arrives,* I reassure myself, but no matter what, the pain and constant burning persist. It now feels like I've got boiling acid flowing through my veins and intense pressure building in my head.

I'm approaching full-blown panic mode now. I fight to move the covers off me but even in my determined desperation I move nothing at all. I begin hyperventilating and tears are streaming from my eyes. I manage to calm my breathing, but as the time ticks by, mere minutes feel like hours.

Eventually the pain pushes me over the edge into thinking that maybe this is it for me. I truly don't know if I've got it in me to last this out until 7 a.m., however far away that is. I've known my risk of an early death is much higher than most, and I've been aware that something like a bladder infection can turn to septicaemia, and that AD could push my BP up until my brain bleeds and I die, but I never thought my death would come from not being able to kick a fucking duvet off the bed.

I thought there would be more to my story, but I guess this is where it ends, and part of me is glad — this isn't the life I wanted anyway. I'm in agony, knocking on the door of death. In fact I'm pounding the door pleading for the reaper to let me in!

The idea of wishing for death scares the shit out of me. I check myself and the fighter inside me kicks back in: *Fuck that! This is not how you're going out!* I shove aside the death wish and reassure myself that I'll make it to 7 a.m.

The intensity of the pain causes such exhaustion that I think I sleep for a moment — maybe it was a few minutes. I get pinches of rest. I try Siri again . . . Briefly there is a moment of comfort as I hear a sweet soft Australian woman say 'I'm sorry, I'm having trouble connecting right now' and I feel she must be in the room with me.

The pitch-black blanket of darkness is beginning to lift and light begins to filter through the window. The birds are chirping and I get excited, thinking it must be almost time. I call out again for Siri, just to hear her calm voice.

'Hey Siri, are you there?' I ask.

'I'm sorry . . .' she responds kindly.

'Hey Siri, I'm in a lot of pain right now! I might die on you.'

'I'm sorry . . .'

'Hey Siri, why do those fucking birds start chirping so early?'

'I'm sorry . . .'

It's another couple of hellish hours before I finally hear the sweetest sound imaginable when a car pulls up outside.

The moment I hear the car door open I scream for help. It still feels like an age before the bedroom door slides open and I meet my saviour.

Brant is extremely apologetic when he comes into the room to find me lying on my back covered in cold towels. I tell him it's not his fault as it was my decision to not be turned in the middle of the night, and he's not responsible for Siri's failure. We decide that from now on he will always come in and turn me or at least check on me, and we'll always test my lifeline to make sure Siri is on the case.

•

I'm back in Auckland to celebrate my 30th birthday in February 2017. Having everyone I love together in one place to celebrate with me is really special to me, because I couldn't have made it this far without their support. Special days like birthdays and Christmas — and of course the anniversary of my accident — are tough for me. I do my best to get in the mood to celebrate, but this is not how I pictured my life at 30 — trapped in a wheelchair, living off the government and fund-raised money. I'd rather be living in the trailer at Lake Ronix and getting by on chump change.

A birthday highlight was going to the Guns N' Roses concert with Jesse and Brant the night before. We parked up in the disability area, with its incredible view of the stage at Western Springs Stadium, and rocked out to classics like 'Paradise City', 'Welcome to the Jungle' and 'Sweet Child o' Mine'. I'm not a diehard fan like Brant, but they put on an incredible show that left me buzzing afterwards. I love the effect music has on me. It's one thing that seems to pierce my soul and fill me with an energy that's hard to describe. Being here with my best mates is the best birthday present.

•

My routine has been feeling stagnant lately. I've pulled back to only three physio sessions a week rather than five, and ACC has cut back Neuro Rehab to once a week. Ever since coming back from the US and the amazing rehab I had there, I haven't found it so rewarding. So I begin looking at other options.

One afternoon Jesse is hanging at mine. He's been getting into becoming a 'social influencer', where brands hook him up with free stuff and pay for him to promote their product through his Instagram, and create content for them to use on their own platforms. He seems to be doing all right with it so far — he always seems to be off on adventures hiking, snowboarding, surfing, skydiving, riding his motorbike and even wakeboarding. His tattooed, muscular physique is just what those brands like.

He checks an email on his phone and finds he's just picked up another job.

'Fuck yeeeah, bro! G-shock have offered me four watches and four grand just to create four photos for them!' he says excitedly.

'Nice one, bro,' I manage, but in my head I'm thinking: *I was 'sponsored' by G-shock and they gave me three watches and not a cent over three years — and they were sponsoring me as a world-class athlete! And you get four grand and four watches for a few fucking selfies?*

•

I hate what my insane jealousy is making me feel about one of my very best friends, but it's not him personally. It's about the industry. I was at the pinnacle of my chosen sport and I really struggled to get any funding at all. It was because of that I decided I had to push myself to a level that would be impossible for sponsors to ignore. To take bigger and bigger risks in an effort to make brands open their wallets to support me. And now look at me.

Jesse sees that I'm distraught. 'You all right, bro?'

'Not really,' I say. 'Before I get into this I want you to know that this isn't about you at all — I'm stoked for you. But it fucking hurts, bro. It just seems so unfair.' I tell him my thinking, and I'm having trouble holding it together.

'Oh shit, I'm so sorry, bro. I didn't mean to upset you,' he replies.

'Dude, it's not your fault at all — it's my own ego problem.'

We talk about how the whole landscape has changed, with the switch of focus to social media, and how it's more of a timing thing that I missed out on. And I get that.

After Jesse leaves not long later, the swirling negative thoughts overtake me and I completely break down. All of this happened to me because I was trying to get noticed, to get paid — all for a stupid fucking movie, for a stupid fucking sport. I wallow in self-pity until I have no more tears to cry. I wish I could go back and undo it — I wish I could go back and tell 27-year-old Brad not to back out of that double flip.

I already know what Susie will say.

'It scared me that I could be so affected by what someone else has,' I tell her.

'Remember that envy of what others have is more of an indication that you're unhappy with *your* situation, than anything to do with what they have. There will always be people with more and people with less. So what it comes down to is learning to live with gratitude for what you do have.

'So once again maybe you need to sit with those feelings whenever envy comes up. Remind yourself that envy is a toxic emotion that does nothing positive for you, and that focusing on what you don't have will never bring you peace. And the more you sit with it, the better you'll get at understanding that,' she says, adding, 'because in a situation like that with your buddy, you have the choice of whether to be upset for yourself, or stoked that something cool happened for him. I think I know which you would prefer to feel.'

I hate that I let myself get so upset by something great happening to Jesse. I realise my reaction was selfish and took away from what should've been a moment for me to celebrate a positive for one of my best mates. I never want to feel that way again, so I take Susie's advice and decide to sit and learn from it.

•

Back at home, sitting by the window, I'm bored and back on my phone. I come across photos of Camilla, Hayley, Molly and other girls from my past. I'm hung up on this idea of wishing I could go back and change things — go back and tell past-Brad not to back out, or more likely not to go for it at all, because I already landed the trick in Germany. But why stop there? Why not go back further? Why not go right back and avoid the other injuries that set my career back? I daydream about what might have been had that momentum continued. I know I would've been the second in the world to land a 1260, and surely I would've been rewarded for that. I know I'd definitely do something to change the failed drug test at worlds that cost me $30k.

There are countless points in my career at which I could have changed course.

Would I even choose wakeboarding again? What if I had put the same devotion into rugby, or snowboarding? I realise I was always going to pick wakeboarding. I loved it so much.

I'm feeling such low self-esteem and total inadequacy, I waste hours every day exploring this idea of changing the past. I'm consumed by it. I think about what I would do differently in relation to women — who would I hold on to if I could go back? I loved so many of those beautiful girls I let go, but I just had to move on, following my dream around the world. I just had to follow my ego and my dick in pursuit of the next best thing, because no matter how good I had it, it was always about what's next that might be better. Hindsight is a bitch!

This fixation on girls from my past continues for weeks. Hours upon hours of my life each day are spent wondering about possible past futures with any of the girls I crossed paths with. My journey takes me right back to my first real, deep love, which still has a place in my heart after more than 12 years. Charlotte and I have kept in touch and remained good friends. She's still overseas working on superyachts.

I always embraced a 'no regrets' philosophy, but that's impossible for me now. I regret my accident, I regret my constant pursuit of more, and I regret letting so many incredible women go. The result of all this living in the past, of course, is that I'm increasingly miserable. My constantly beating myself up for missed opportunities sends me into a deeper depression, which is becoming more difficult to disguise with positivity.

I talk to Susie about it.

'We've spoken extensively about remaining present, and there's clearly more work to be done here,' she says, not for the first time. 'When we're not present, and we're dwelling on the past, it's easy to get caught up in what was, but we know that we'll never be able to change the past. Its only use is to enable us to learn from it so we can make better decisions now. However much you want to, you *cannot* go back to who you were before. You have to move forward and work with who you are now.

'Depression stems from existing in a past state of mind — usually lingering on feelings of regret, guilt or shame over things that have happened. We cannot be depressed when we're living in the present.'

I disagree. 'But I specifically feel depressed now, so how can it be true that depression can't live in the present?' I ask.

'You can be in a state of depression in the present, but not if your mental state is in the present. Once again it's the ego's battle with being unhappy with the way things are. You cannot concern yourself with what *was*, you must only act on what *is*. That's why living and acting with a present mindset is so important, and so powerful.'

Once again, Susie's teachings leave me sitting silently nodding absorbing the message. I feel like a bit of an idiot for continually letting myself slip into that frame of mind and needing to be re-taught this lesson.

●

My sex drive is as strong as ever. I crave the incredible sex I became so accustomed to. In my free time while parked up by the window, I've fantasised about so many of my past sexual experiences — there are so many highlights I teleport myself back to, with some of the sexiest and most beautiful women imaginable. I try to bring back the feeling I had at the time. I close my eyes and remember the visuals, the feelings, the taste, of the time when I was at my sexual peak.

Revisiting the memories gives me a fraction of that feeling, but what I've realised is that what I'm feeling is nothing more than my ego inflating, but it still makes me feel good so I keep taking myself back there. I also find myself on my go-to porn site. I select a cam girl and watch as she satisfies herself on camera for me and god knows how many other guys who are tuning in from all around the world.

Every time I'm watching porn I realise no more than a couple of minutes into it the pointlessness in what I'm doing. It's been almost three years since I last was able to orgasm, so now the whole objective is gone. I quit the website, but that doesn't stop me from coming back the next day — or even an hour later. Always just for a minute or two tops before again realising it's a fruitless pursuit. It's like my old sexual wiring is so deeply rooted that I'm subconsciously controlled by it. I hate myself for it, but I can't break the habit.

I'm embarrassed to bring it up with Susie, but she and I have spoken about pretty much everything over the past couple of years, so I dive in so we can start to work through it.

'So we're getting back into currency here,' she says. 'When you get the urge to watch porn, that's your old currency talking. There was a lot of currency in this department and it's sitting there screaming, "Spend me!" because your ego feels like it needs it. And as you said, you realise pretty quickly that you're spending old currency because it doesn't work any more.

'So you're already adjusting, which is real progress. As much as we wish we could exchange our currency instantly, for some of the bigger things that we invested the most into, like sex — for you and a huge percentage of young men — the exchange takes time. And we understand that porn is not real, right? That's not how sex is in real life. Pornography is toxic to young men and women because it gives a false impression of sex in real life. Obviously once two people are comfortable together then they're free to experiment, but the way porn is normalising violent things like choking and spanking — and worse — is very damaging in what it shows young men about the treatment of young women.'

'Yeah, I can see how it could have that effect — there's some pretty degrading stuff out there,' I say. 'So what's the value in the new currency? What should I focus on as a replacement?'

'Present currency can only be spent on what is. The new currency says your value is in more than sex, and it's asking you to learn to enjoy what you have now, which is more about finding love and meaningful connection, and I'm sure there's no shortage of girls to do that with.'

'Oh yeah, they're queuing up around the corner!'

'What's the point in having them lining up if you find a deep connection with just one of them?' she asks. 'Having loads of girls wanting you just fuels the ego's search for adequacy, but as we've previously established, you are already adequate as you are. What we truly crave is love and meaningful relationships, and all will happen as and when it's meant to in order to teach us what we're here to learn.'

It feels like I keep having to learn everything over and over again. It's frustrating, but I'm willing to keep working on it because I desperately want to find a way to be okay, and maybe eventually happy with how things are now.

•

In August I'm excited to start working with Gilly at Connect Neuro Physiotherapy. The facilities are top of the line, although her clinic space is small. Today I'm excited because I get to try out one of the coolest-looking contraptions I've ever seen — the REX exoskeleton! It's a set of robotic legs that I'll be strapped into to allow me to stand and walk. They look like something out of *Star Wars* or *Avatar*. Gilly tells me the exoskeleton is not designed for people with my level of injury, but she's impressed by my drive to improve my situation so she's agreed to let me give it a go.

It takes 20 minutes to get me securely in, with the help of one of the REX technicians, then Gilly activates the legs and the robot stands me upright. I need constant hands on so I don't tip over, because I'm not stable enough to hold myself up. I'm just excited for the walking part!

Each step is painfully slow and the movement is very robotic, but I guess my expectations were too high and the technology just isn't there yet. Regardless of this, I actually really enjoy being upright and mobile instead of being strapped to a tilt table, and static.

I work with Gilly each week on a range of exercises.

•

Later in the month I'm asked to speak at a conference of industry professionals in Rotorua. I've only done one speaking engagement before — a couple of months ago I was invited to share my story with the folks at Allied Medical, who supply my wheelchairs. But that was about 20 people, whereas this is around 100 business professionals. What the hell do I know that I can teach these people?

I don't really know much about my audience so I just write a speech about my story, and some of the lessons I've been learning along the way. It seems to go well — several audience members thank me afterwards, which feels good.

On the drive home I feel a sense of achievement that I haven't felt since the Wake Awards. I think I might pursue more speaking opportunities. My story seemed to go down well, plus I made $2000. Just like when I picked up the mic and the hammer — it's a matter of opening myself up to other opportunities along the journey. So while I'm striving to get moving again, I might as well move people with my story and make a little coin in the process.

•

Moving to doing my morning cares while lying in bed has meant there's been less bleeding, but my bowel pain has been getting worse and worse, which has been pushing my blood pressure higher and higher. Some mornings it reaches 200/110, which is dangerously high and means I'm sweating like crazy. It's getting to the point where I'm so physically wrecked at the end of an AD episode like this that I need a nap.

It's been a constant issue and I'm sick of it, so I've arranged to go back to the spinal unit so they can assess my routine and see if there's anything they can do to improve it. I'm booked in for early September. Ahead of that, I'm in today for a scan of my digestive system. As I sit in the waiting room I'm handed a glass of liquid and told I need to drink the whole thing. I scull it back, then go for the scan.

'Your colorectal specialist will be sent the results,' I'm told on the way out.

Later in the evening, Morgan and I are sitting in the lounge watching a movie when I feel a slight sweat come on. The discomfort in my abdomen is worse this evening, to the point that it's becoming extremely uncomfortable. As the sweats increase, I'm starting to think it's a blocked catheter. Suddenly I feel the sweat beading down my face so I know action needs to be taken.

The first action in this case is to make sure the catheter is not kinked in the bend at my hip, so I ask Morgan to gently pull the waistband of my pants to check for me. I would usually call a caregiver, but Morgan is always offering to help in any situation like this. So we both peer down to see that the catheter seems fine, but suddenly I notice something that Morgan (thank god) can't immediately see from her angle. My heart sinks and I'm overcome with total embarrassment because I've shit myself. And not just a small amount — this is full-on diarrhoea.

'Oh shit, stop — let go!' I tell Morgan, hoping she'll release my waistband immediately, but she doesn't. I assume she sees what I see, or at least smells it. I'm mortified.

'*Fuuuuuuuck!*' I immediately drive to my room and call Loisi in. When she pulls my waistband open more, it's a truly horrific sight — my dick and balls are drowning in muck. It's straight to the shower.

Just shoot me in the head and dispose of me, I think to myself, because *I'm just so fucking over it!*

Even after Loisi has scrubbed me all over twice, I still feel filthy, but she assures me I'm clean and begins drying me off before transferring me into bed. I've completely lost interest in the movie because I can't bear the thought of facing Morgan — I just want to crawl into a dark hole and die. I begin to weep as Loisi props me on my side to sleep. As soon as she leaves the room I burst into tears and a full-on ugly cry. I'm a 30-year-old man who needs to be cleaned up like a baby.

My life is so fucked.

The following day you bet your arse I call the radiology clinic and unleash on them for not making it clear to me that whatever they gave me to drink was designed to go straight through me. They're extremely apologetic, and I just reiterate that they need to be more aware of the needs of disabled patients.

•

When the first of September rolls around, I bid farewell to Morgan, who's boarding a plane to LA to pursue her acting career. We both know she has a huge challenge ahead of her, but I'm proud of her for committing to it, and proud to have helped inspire her to do so.

'I'm sure you guys will miss each other,' Susie says when I tell her Morgan has left. 'I think it's such a beautiful thing that you two have created such a great, loving friendship.'

'Yeah, I love the friendship we have — I'll definitely miss her. But maybe it's good that we're not living together any more, as it'll allow me to move forward,' I say, referring to my future dating life.

Then I change tack. 'You know that I've been struggling to apply the lessons you've taught me in my day-to-day life. I've been working on sitting with emotions that come up, and I'm getting better at understanding them, but I'm wondering if there's something else that's stopping me from taking on these lessons properly.'

Susie thinks for a moment, then says, 'The concept that ties into every one of the lessons we've worked through, which I know has been especially challenging for you, is acceptance. I know you have been able to apply it on occasion, but you still seem to be struggling with complete and total acceptance.'

'I think you're right, because after more than three years I still struggle to accept that this has happened to me,' I say, 'even though I know that acceptance is simply accepting what is.'

'Whereas, refusing to accept is denial,' Susie adds. 'So it sounds like there's work to be done there.'

I let out a sigh. 'Lately I feel worse than ever. Partly I think it's because of the pain issue. Since I'm going back to the spinal unit for two weeks to try to get that sorted, maybe I'll spend that time digging into the mental stuff too. And work on acceptance.'

'It's really understandable that you're struggling,' Susie says, 'because you've been working tirelessly to regain movement for three years now. That must be exhausting, for starters, but also frustrating to feel like you're not getting any closer. So let me know how you get on while you're there, and I'm happy to come out and visit if you want to chat through any of the stuff you're working on.'

Susie has been incredibly generous with her time throughout these last few years, and I'd be in a much worse position now without her. But I feel like I need to work through this next bit on my own. I need to learn to accept this, and I'm willing to go through whatever I need to go through over the next couple of weeks to achieve it.

Today I'm heading back to the Auckland Spinal Rehab Unit for two weeks, in the hope they'll be able to figure out what is causing my increasing pain and AD. Before I go, I meet up with Ants for a coffee. I tell him about the pain issues, and how I just feel like it's not allowing me to live my life.

'Are you okay, bro?' Ants asks, seeing that I'm clearly not.

'I want to say yes,' I tell him through tears, 'but I can't. I just feel like I'm constantly spinning the wheels and going fucking nowhere. And as you can see, all the emotion feels like it's bubbling up to the surface, like I've been wearing the positive mask for too long.'

'Dude, I can't even imagine what you endure on a daily basis. And honestly I wondered if maybe you've been wearing that mask for everyone else — as well as maybe yourself?'

'Yeah, I think it's a bit of both. Mainly for everyone else, but also because I thought I could fake it till I make it. But it's clear that I've got some shit I haven't addressed yet, or haven't fully processed. So, since I'm going to be stuck back in that miserable place for the next two weeks I figure it's a good time for me to work through it all. I'm taking a holiday from social media, and won't use my phone for anything besides important calls.'

Ants nods in agreement. 'That's a good idea, my bro. It sounds like it's needed, and it's great you've identified that!'

'Cheers, brother. I've got a couple of books to read on my iPad, and I might even do a little writing to work through stuff,' I say.

We finish our coffees, and before I load into the van he grabs the back of my head and holds his forehead against mine for a few seconds. 'Mad love, homie,' he says.

'Love you, my bro. See you on the flip side!' I say.

•

I'm allocated the room at the far end of the corridor, which suits me well, because I want to be away from everyone else. I'm here to heal, but first I think I might need to rip the wound open to start that process. After the nurses have done their thing — checking vitals — they leave me to it with a call button pinned to the side of the bed.

Over the last few years, Susie has taught me so many valuable lessons and given me the tools to work through everything, and I feel like I've taken most of it on-board but I just don't seem to be able to apply them properly. I've figured out through Susie's teachings that it's because I haven't yet taken the first and most important step — acceptance. I still have not accepted what has happened to me. So that's what I want to work on while I'm here.

Susie isn't the only source of valuable teaching I'm working on embracing. A few months ago I saw a TED talk by a woman named Brené Brown on vulnerability. I've watched it several times because it really hit home. She speaks about vulnerability as the core of shame and fear in one's struggle for worthiness. I know I'm struggling to feel worthy. In order to accept my worth I need to make myself vulnerable and open to acknowledging the issues I'm facing. Because Brené also speaks of vulnerability as the birthplace of joy, creativity, belonging and love.

I spend the first day mostly in tears, letting out all of the emotion I'd been holding in for the sake of everyone around me. This is my time to work on me, and I don't have to be anything for anyone else. I try using metacognition to pick up on any specific thoughts that come up — any deep judgements or beliefs about myself.

The first thing I notice is that I'm just generally resistant to the idea that this is what my life has become. I've had a lot of trouble letting go of the life I had before, in all ways, including the loss of so much that made me happy. I miss what my able body gave me — the freedom to express myself, to exercise, to travel the world and be spontaneous, to show affection. I miss sex and physical intimacy. I miss stretching in the morning and at the end of a hard day, I miss the feeling of the sand between my toes and then diving into the lake. I miss my independence. I hate relying on others when I used to be so capable. And I really miss having outlets like wakeboarding and playing the guitar.

Fuck I miss my old life! But I'm sick of this feeling.

After a while I accepted that this injury had happened to me, but I refused to accept I couldn't get my old life back. But Susie taught me that it's not a matter of accepting that this is how things will be forever: I simply need to accept that this is where I am *now*. The main thing I've had trouble accepting is that my old life is gone, but that's the reality. That's the cold hard truth. It's gone, and there's only one thing I can do about it — accept it. If I don't, then I'm in denial.

As I think about my worsening depression, I start to realise that it all links back to acceptance. I've spent three years putting every bit of effort, energy and time into rehab in the hope of regaining movement, and although I haven't got my arms working again, I have noticed improvements in my breathing, my voice, my upper body balance and muscle strength. In putting all my focus on moving my arms, I'd not taken the time to celebrate those small wins along the way.

I had one goal, and day after day I failed to get any closer to it, and I think that's at the root of my depression — my perceived lack of progress, and the feeling of constant failure. There's a point along the way when you have to accept that maybe you just can't move that big fucking rock.

It's as if I've been caught in the current of a river, and it's sweeping me into the unknown. I've been desperately swimming upstream to get back to where I was, because I loved it there. I refused to stop swimming, I refused to stop fighting, out of fear of the unknown, and fear of the loss of control. After three years of fighting I'm exhausted, and I feel like I'm drowning.

My constant swimming against the current is my refusal to let go of the past — my denial. So right now I have a choice. I can keep trying to swim back to where I was, meaning I'll surely drown, or I can stop swimming and go with the flow of the river. It's scary because I have no idea where the river is going, what lies around the corner or where it ends up. The truth is I've been terrified of where this new life may be sending me — I've been picturing a giant waterfall that sweeps me into a deep dark cave.

But that's just my fear painting that picture. The reality is I have no idea what's around the next bend, and I don't know where the river is going, and I won't until I'm there. The river is bound to have tumultuous patches, and other stretches that are calm and smooth-flowing, that's just the reality of life. But maybe after some challenging rapids and some small waterfalls, the river might open up to a beautiful and plentiful calm lake.

I know that what will bring me the most peace is being okay with not knowing, and accepting the journey for what it is. So here I am, trying to embrace the journey and learn to be okay with not knowing what lies ahead. I can't keep fighting this.

•

The following morning there are several nurses and healthcare assistants buzzing about in my room. As usual I'm turned onto my left side and the nurse takes my blood pressure to get a baseline before the suppositories are inserted. She tells me she'll check it every 15 minutes. I'm beginning to sweat as she's taking the next reading, and before my bowels even begin to move, my BP is 160/85. Sweat is now beading down my face and the discomfort is intense. At 203/107 I'm given a spray under the tongue to bring it back down a bit, and another nurse sticks a patch on my shoulder.

'This is a GTN [nitroglycerin] patch,' she tells me. 'It's a slow-release version of the spray we just gave you to help keep that BP down.'

After I'm all showered up, dressed and in my chair, I'm left in my room with my phone in front of me. I immediately tap my mouthstick on Instagram and up pops the sign-in page. I forgot for a moment that I'm on a social media holiday. It happens several more times throughout the day too, making me realise how bad this habit I have of resorting to social media for distraction is. A habit I'm hoping to break over the next two weeks.

I don't feel teary like I did yesterday, so that's a good start. After my realisations about acceptance yesterday, I've been thinking about the range of emotions that has really affected me over the past few years. I'm pretty sure fear is behind all of them.

One of the very first fears I had after my accident came within minutes of the crash, when I told Chad, 'Don't you call that fucking helicopter!' I was afraid of the financial repercussions for my family. And from then on, I've constantly feared being a burden on my friends and family. I would skip parties, events and adventures with my mates, out of fear of being a burden on them and holding my buddies back from having a good time.

I start to tear up as I think about how unfair it is that I can't just do everything for myself as I used to, and then I grit my teeth and shake my head to rattle myself out of my self-pity and back to what I've learnt. What I've learnt is from times like at Deano and Amber's wedding, when my Aussie mates carried my chair up two flights of stairs. There have been plenty of other occasions here in New Zealand and in Florida when my friends have shown that they're more than willing to carry the load because they want me around.

The people around me have proven that the burden is much less to them than I make it out to be. As Susie says, if we embrace every moment and understand that we're here to learn and gain from each moment, then my mates also have the opportunity to gain from these interactions. I'm a good friend who they enjoy having around, but they're also learning skills in problem solving — and gaining strength from carrying me! — and it all builds the camaraderie between us.

The reality is that while some things can make life more challenging, we have something to gain from every moment if we open ourselves up to the learning or the opportunity presented to us.

I sit and think on this for a while, and when I feel myself sinking into certain thoughts that bring on the burden feeling, I recruit the techniques Susie has taught me to pull myself back out. I need practice doing this for when thoughts like these come up in the future.

Susie taught me that fear is being afraid of something that *has not yet happened*, so fear is a future-based emotion. Anxiety is the body's reaction to fear. So the anxiety I sometimes feel as a result of the fear of being a burden comes from *not having a present mindset*. There are times when I may worry about being a burden in the present, but, as I proved to myself at Deano's wedding, I then have a choice: either I get upset over it, let fear take control and ruin the event for myself (and maybe others); or I choose gratitude and love for my friends for doing this for me, because they love me.

What would my friends prefer — me constantly saying things like 'Sorry about this' and 'I feel bad that . . .' or me saying things like 'Thanks for this!' and 'I feel lucky to have friends like you'? I know what I'd prefer to hear in their situation. So I guess it comes down to attitude and approach. Fear is really unhelpful.

•

The next few days of morning cares are slightly better with the GTN patch. My sweats aren't nearly as bad as it's keeping my blood pressure from skyrocketing. The doctor tells me they've decided to continue using patches and monitoring me for the rest of my stay.

'But that's just to keep my blood pressure in check. What about the actual issue that's causing it? Are you looking into that?' I ask, confused about their plan.

The doctor explains that their plan is to keep me stable; I'd need to follow up with the colorectal specialist to find out what's causing the pain.

Whaaat?! I thought that's what I was coming here for — to figure out the cause and treat it, not to put a literal patch over the problem.

This throws me. I've been a few days in here now, and on top of the usual physical discomfort, I now feel frustration that no one is doing anything to fix it. This feeds a mental discomfort — a feeling like I'm not at ease in this place or in my own skin. I feel the tension in my chest. Usually when I'm at home and I get this feeling, I distract myself by checking out social media pages, or by watching TV, or if I really need to tune out then sometimes I smoke some cannabis.

But here today, those options are unavailable — there's nothing to take my attention away from the source of my discomfort. I've done this deliberately so my problems are front and centre. I refuse to put a patch over my mental pain. So although I feel uneasy, instead I sit and deconstruct my emotions, peeling back the layers to see the belief systems behind them.

•

Fear of missing out is something that has dogged me ever since my accident. I understand Susie's teaching that it's impossible to miss out if we're living in the present, but somehow that doesn't stop me desperately wishing I could do things I no longer can.

I know that this stems from my inability to be happy with my current situation. It all comes back to acceptance. It's like I was sent one way down a fork in the river, but I'm not happy with the section of river I'm on, so I'm thinking about what might've been down that other fork: *I bet it's smoother and less difficult, I bet there's beautiful trees surrounding the river that leads to exactly where I want to go.* But no matter how much I think that, it doesn't change what I'm on. All I can do is make the most of where I am, and stop wasting time and energy yearning for where I'm not.

Fear of missing out comes from comparing my life now with what I used to have, and what others are doing. It's a huge contrast, so it's understandable that it's taking me so long to accept and adjust. In the past, before social media and before the internet, people had much less awareness of what others were up to — maybe that would have made it easier. But it's really tough to be 'present'.

So I'll keep being aware of my ego, and keep working on being present, and try to spend less time yearning for things that I don't have and punishing myself by wallowing in what others are doing. I need to live in reality, not fantasy. Part of that means strengthening my happiness around what I do have, and expanding my view of what I can do. My currency has to change. I'm sure if I can get to the point, options *will* open up for me.

I sit and ponder the possibilities that might be out there.

•

It's been a week now, and I've been spoilt with dinners that Mum and other visitors have been bringing in for me so I haven't had to rely much on hospital food. But at night while trying to sleep, I'm reminded of one of the reasons I hated being here before — it's the constant noise. The 'ding' of call bells, the occasional screams or shouts from other patients down the corridor, the bustle of things happening. But I remind myself that all these people are going through their own hell, so I do my best to be empathetic.

As much as I wanted to be secluded, today I am visited by one of the relatively new patients. When I arrived I let them know that if anyone here might benefit from chatting with me about my experience, I'd be happy to oblige. So now I'm joined by a young dude named Braden, who had an accident while playing provincial-grade rugby. His injury is a little lower than mine and he has more movement, but I'm able to share some tips and answer some questions and we get along really well.

On our third day hanging out, the nurse brings him in his manual chair, locks the brakes and leaves us to it. After an hour Braden is ready to go back to his room, but although he has arm movement, his lack of hand function means he can't unlock the brakes. He's about to call for the nurse but I say, 'Don't worry, bro, I got it.' I align my chair with his, then lift my leg-rest, make a couple of adjustments so my footrest lines up, then tilt my chair back to unlock his brake. I do the same for the other side and we're both stoked! It's the first time in years that I've been able to help someone physically. I just thought of my chair as the bobcat I used to drive at Lake Ronix and worked out a way. It's a satisfying feeling.

On another evening I'm reading my book when I hear a group of people arriving to visit the teenage boy in the room next door to mine. A guitar begins playing and they all burst into song — 'praise the lord, hallelujah' type of music. At first I roll my eyes and I'm like, *Really? Now I have to listen to this shit?* But they're actually really good at singing, all harmonising well and, leaving aside the words, the melody is beautiful. The positive vibes spread over me. I think about what that teenage boy has been going through, and I'm sure the music is lifting his spirits and helping him.

This gets me thinking about my resistance to the word 'God'. I feel differently now since I've been cultivating empathy and gained a better understanding of the importance of faith for some people. Not that I believe in God, but I now understand that people who do are simply looking for a path, same as I am. We all want to embrace the journey of life and have faith that our path has purpose. It's just that we just read it differently.

I don't believe that there's a divine creator, and that if I worship him I'll go to this perceived 'heaven'. But I do believe now that there's strength in having faith that we're on the path we're meant to be on, to learn and gain what we need to on this journey.

I don't believe that 'everything happens for a reason', as some do. Someone could see that I'm now getting into inspiring others through my public speaking, and they could say, 'See, your injury was meant to happen so you could inspire others.' I just cannot and will never believe that there's this 'God' up there who went, 'That guy Brad seems to be living a great life, but I'm going to make it so he breaks his neck and nearly dies and suffers for years so that down the track he can have a positive impact on others through motivational speaking — yeah, that's the plan!'

I think that's a load of shit. To say that my path is prewritten means that I have no choice over it. When my injury happened, I made a conscious choice to be positive and share my journey, and I chose to work with Susie to improve my mentality, and I chose to take up motivational speaking. The universe presents us with choices for us to make.

If you believe in 'God's plan' you have to believe that God plans war and injustice, and kids born into poverty who end up starving to death. This is the plan of a creator who loves us? I just don't buy it. I believe that if we really want something, we have to work for it, and I also think that some things just aren't meant for us. And I'm learning to have faith that the doors that close on us are leading us to more rewarding doors that are ready to be opened.

So I don't think I have total control of my path in life, but I also don't think it's all written out for us. Accepting accountability is important, because otherwise it's just taking on a victim mentality, where everything is happening to us as opposed to happening for us. And taking accountability for things that happen in our lives is so much better than blaming others for our mistakes.

I definitely feel like I'm on a spiritual journey, but I don't believe in the Bible. That's just man's attempt to interpret the world and control people. I believe that God can be translated as the beauty and wonders of the universe that we don't understand, and that God is love, and the connection we all have to one another. All is made from energy and matter and space, so we're all connected through those things. And if you look to the sky on a clear night, how could that not be perceived as the heavens? There's a quote I heard recently that sums up my views:

Religion is following the messenger. Spirituality is following the message.

We all simply have our beliefs in what works for us. And if the religious beliefs of the kid next door are helping guide him along his new and frightening path and bring him peace, then that's his truth. Finally, I understand the last Huna wisdom:

PONO — Effectiveness is the measure of truth.

The ego says, 'No, this is the way, this is what's right!' And empathy says, 'What's right for me may not be right for you, and that's okay.'

•

I manage to get to the end of the book I've been reading — the first book I've finished in a long time!

In my long periods of reflection I find I'm getting better at working my way out of the feelings of being a burden and missing out. I'm digging into the inadequacy stuff now.

Once again, Susie has given me ample teachings around this, but it's still not settling. With acceptance, I should be able to be at peace with what is, even if I don't like it. But I often struggle to cut through all the bullshit and toxic beliefs that I'm not good enough, especially in regard to women and relationships. I am who I am, I can only do as much as I can do, and if a girl thinks I'm not what she's looking for then why should I get upset? I'm looking for a relationship with someone who wants me for who I am, and there's no point getting upset if I don't match their criteria. It clearly wouldn't have worked anyway.

To the right person, I'll always be good enough. When it comes down to my own happiness, the only person whose opinion really matters is mine. The opinion of my family and close friends matters to me too, but they already accept me as enough.

This whole journey for me has been about learning to love myself again, and to be grateful for what I do have. Being back here in the spinal unit and meeting Braden helps lead me to a realisation. When I was at Shepherd Center I distinctly remember feeling envious of people with lower-level injuries than my C4-level injury. I would actually be jealous when I saw someone with a C5 or C6 who got their arms working to the point where they could push themselves in a manual chair. I desperately wanted to trade places.

Then, a few months later, when at Laura Fergusson, I met Angus, with his C2 spinal cord injury through medical misadventure. Seeing him on a full-time ventilator, driving with his chin and with a nurse with him at all times, really hit me. I vividly remember how incredibly grateful it made me feel for my C4 injury. At no point was I remotely grateful for my injury until I met Angus. I was also sad to hear that Angus passed away about a year later.

This gets me thinking. In both of those situations I was letting someone else's situation radically affect my happiness, and how I felt about myself and my situation. Yet absolutely nothing had changed for me. Why should what someone else has (or doesn't have) affect my happiness and the value I place on myself?

It's crazy — and we all do it! If other people have newer clothes, or a nicer car, or a bigger house, or a higher-paying job, we think less of ourselves. It could be about physical attributes too, like if someone else is taller, or slimmer, or has nicer skin or hair — or, in my case, greater physical ability — we envy them and let ourselves feel like crap by comparison. We attach all of these beliefs to their situation and assume they're happier than us.

It's worse these days with Instagram and other social media platforms. So many of us, myself included, look at other people's lives on Instagram and get fooled into thinking that what we see is a true representation of their lives. We need to remember that the content people are posting is as carefully curated as the pictures they hang on the wall.

We need to understand that there's more going on in other people's lives than what they choose to let us see.

I might assume that those spinal injury patients with more movement than me are happier and their lives better than mine, but I have no idea what's going on in their lives behind the scenes. I have no idea how they're handling what is undoubtedly the worst injury they've ever suffered. They might have more movement than I do, but do they have the supportive family I have? The wide circle of great friends? An amazing community like I have with wakeboarding? A guide like Susie?

It's so easy to get caught up in the pursuit of more because of what others have, and because of the toxic belief that more money, more things, more, more, more somehow leads to more happiness. But what it really comes down to is being happy with what we've got. Living from a place of gratitude. There's a great quote in *Way of the Peaceful Warrior* by Dan Millman, the book I just finished.

A teacher is asked if rich people are happier than poor people. He responds: 'One must become rich to be happy.'

Which at first goes against everything he's teaching, but he follows with:

'You are rich if you have enough money to satisfy all your desires. So there are two ways to be rich: You earn, inherit, borrow, beg, or steal enough money to meet all your desires; or, you cultivate a simple lifestyle of few desires; that way you always have enough money.'

Then follows the quote that really stuck with me:

The secret of happiness, you see, comes not from seeking more, but from developing the capacity to enjoy less.

If I can apply this concept to all aspects of my life, then I can reclaim my happiness.

When it comes to inadequacy, I can adjust my beliefs around where my value lies, and learn to love myself for who I am, instead of expecting myself to be more. Then I have no reason to believe that I am anything but adequate. And, just to clarify, an *expectation* to be more is different from a desire to be better or to improve. We can always work to improve and better ourselves, but we cannot *expect* ourselves to be more than we are in the present moment.

In my situation, I'm deciding that I don't want to spend my life fighting for something that may never come back, so this is where acceptance needs to kick in. That doesn't mean I've completely given up on regaining movement, but for now maybe I'll pull back on the rehab to maintenance level. If this is my life now, where I have no movement below my shoulders, then I choose to make it the best life possible. Because it's my choice.

Originally the goal was to get my movement back as that would make me happy again, but what is the core objective in that thought? To be happy. Sometimes we need to look past the means to see the end, to the core desire. Because in the end my happiness is more important than my movement.

I leave the unit after two weeks of digging deep, and I feel like I've found enough of a footing to help me begin to move forward now. Although my physical pain was not addressed, I'm glad I was willing to suffer for a while, and put in the hard work to learn about my mental pain.

I guess it's true what they say: 'Breakdowns lead to breakthroughs.' As much as I hate and regret the experience that led to this, and loathe coming back to the spinal unit, I'm actually grateful for it happening. I've had the chance to expand my perception, to gain a better understanding of myself and how I operate. I'm feeling more open and accepting of what may lie ahead and, since I love my quotes, I found one to help me embrace moving forward:

Face your past without regret, handle the present with confidence, and prepare for the future without fear.

I discover on re-entering the world that during my last days in the spinal unit another hurricane rolled through Florida. I FaceTime with Chad, who shares photos of the damage it inflicted on Lake Ronix. I'm devastated to see that my wall-ride, my pride and joy, has been destroyed. I'm gutted, but at the same time I'm impressed that it lasted this long — through three previous hurricane seasons. Truth be told, I kinda lost my attachment to it when it got painted white, but I'm still gutted to see that a huge representation of my presence at Lake Ronix has been torn to shreds. The mega-ramp also took a heavy amount of damage so they're dismantling that as well.

As much as I feel frustration and grief at the destruction, I realise it's the perfect metaphor. Because what is more out of our control than the weather? A storm will roll through and leave a path of destruction in its wake, and whatever we do to prepare for it, the storm cannot be controlled. But, as frightening as it can be, often the destruction creates room for new growth and new opportunities.

It's also unbelievably symbolic of the stage I'm at in my own life. The wall-ride stood for the old Brad, but a storm rips through and creates carnage. Then, when calm is restored, the old Brad is gone and a new and improved version is under construction.

•

In October I have some neck X-rays and MRIs done ahead of an appointment with a top neurosurgeon. The idea is to check out my hardware and, more importantly, look at the current state of the injury site on my spinal cord and look for anything that might be contributing to my AD. Because the more I ask around, the more I discover I seem to be more sensitive than most. I'm also interested, of course, in finding out my chances of recovery. Mum is coming along too.

Dr Law looks at my scans and points out something that's not quite right.

'See this here?' he says, turning his screen around so we can see, and zooming in. 'Right below the third screw down, it appears that the titanium alloy rod has snapped.'

'Woah — does that happen often?' I ask.

'I've never seen it before,' he replies.

I explain that I was told that the bottom screw on the other rod had become detached in the first year post-injury. 'So maybe the extra bit of movement from that created a weak point on the other side under the next screw up?' I suggest.

'Yeah, that's a possibility,' Dr Law concedes. 'Although it's still a very hard thing to break! But it's very unlikely that's got anything to do with the dysreflexia you're experiencing. In fact I don't think we need to do anything about that broken rod unless it becomes an issue.'

He then pulls up the MRI scans, takes a moment to look at them closely, then once again turns his screen around. And suddenly it all makes sense — not so much the pain and AD stuff, but the reason why I've had no success regaining movement. This whole time I've been trying a 'mind over matter' approach, visualising my spinal cord healing, but right now, right in front of my eyes, it's like I'm seeing the matter for the first time.

Dr Law adjusts his glasses, takes the fancy pen off his desk and uses it to point at the screen. 'See this dark grey strip running down here? That's your spinal cord. The thin white line on either side is the cerebrospinal fluid that surrounds the cord and brain. And this patch right here' — he points at the part that caught my attention — 'this is where your cord was crushed.' He pauses.

This is the first MRI on my neck since the first one in the ICU, and it definitely looks different. The grey cord disappears into a big clump of white with a few dull patches of grey through it. Until this moment, I hadn't seen just how bad I'd fucked that thing up. I'd never seen that patch where there appears to be no spinal cord remaining. It's pretty clear why none of the rehab has helped me regain the use of my arms.

'As you can see,' says Dr Law, 'you did severe damage to the cord, but it was not severed, so the white section in the middle here' — he circles the injury site — 'is actually an area of scar tissue built up where the cord was crushed. And the patches of grey are the damaged spinal cord in among that scar tissue.'

It's very confronting to see how much damage I did.

Dr Law brings up a couple of things he notices.

'With an injury like yours, particularly with the symptoms you're experiencing, we often look to make sure a cyst isn't forming in among the scar tissue. It's called syringomyelia. But thankfully there don't appear to be any signs of it here. The thing I'm seeing that is of concern is here' — he zooms in closer and points to an area of scar tissue — 'where there's only a very thin white line. This is where the cerebrospinal fluid flows past the scar tissue. If that blocks then that would become a problem, and it's possible that could already be contributing to your dysreflexia.'

'Can anything be done about the scar tissue?' I ask. 'So the spinal cord has a chance of being reconnected?' I figure the scarring is kinda like a landslide across a highway. If you clear the landslide, you can start to repair the highway.

Mum chips in to ask, 'And what would happen if it gets bigger and blocks the fluid from flowing?'

'If it got to that point, we would have to go in and create a bit of space again. The problem with that is that since the site is a crush injury, meaning the cord is crushed in among that scar tissue, anything we remove would likely cause further trauma to the remaining cord, and potentially more scar tissue. So to answer your question, Brad, unfortunately we don't have a procedure to safely remove the scar tissue without damaging the cord.'

I let this sink in for a few seconds, then ask, 'So in terms of my chance of recovering movement, the spinal unit doctor basically said it's unlikely I'll get anything back. Would you say that's accurate?'

'I would agree that it's unlikely to happen through physical rehab, particularly now that you're more than three years past the injury. But there's some incredible research going on, so with the way that's advancing, who knows what might be possible in the future. But I don't imagine there will be anything available for a number of years,' he says.

●

For the rest of the day I'm feeling pretty grim after that harsh dose of reality. I feel like Dr Law has pulled off my rose-tinted glasses. The hit is not nearly as hard as the two-year spinal review, but it is another blow. This is how it is, and likely how it'll stay.

Well, I guess that settles it — acceptance it is.

But even saying that out loud still doesn't feel right. I know it's the way forward, but it feels submissive. If this is the path for me to take, then I need something that feels stronger than acceptance. What's a more powerful approach than 'accepting' something that I perceive as a negative? I ponder on that for the rest of the evening.

The next day I'm heading to the Spinal Cord Injury Research Facility, part of the Centre for Brain Research at the University of Auckland. I'm attending a seminar on their gene therapy project focused on breaking down scar tissue around an injury site. I'm excited to hear they're making good progress, but I know I'm going to have to be patient. The research is in the early stages and these things take ages. Even getting through the clinical trial process can take a number of years. Nevertheless, I come away more optimistic than I was.

Accepting that rehab probably won't get me moving again doesn't mean I'm going to completely quit. But now that I've accepted that this is my life, I want to start living it. So I'm pulling the rehab back to 'maintenance mode'. I'll go to Flexa once a week, for physical rehab and massage work to help release the knots that I'm constantly getting in my upper traps and my neck. And I'll keep up neuro rehab once a week as well. I'll continue to use my tilt table at home, as it's good for bone density, blood pressure, bladder and bowel function and many other systems throughout the body. And the FES bike is great for maintaining muscle mass. Because even if it's not to regain movement, if a cure is discovered then I want my body to be in optimum condition to get into it. So, with maintenance mode engaged, I come back to my pursuit of happiness.

I know it's about focusing on what I can do, rather than what I can't. I want to feel confident again, so I've decided that I need to take Susie's advice and act as if I'm already confident. To me that means putting across the right vibe and image, so where better to start than my appearance? Look good, feel good, right?

Up until this point I've limited myself to clothes that are comfortable and suitable to my injury — trackpants, hoodies and Ugg boots. I decide I'm going to start dressing like I care. I'm going to splurge the few grand I earned from the couple of speaking engagements I did on some fresh gear. I start by ordering a couple of new pairs of Nike Air Force 1 shoes online, since they fit well without creating pressure points. My good friends at ilabb custom-make me some of their chinos and jeans, adding an elastic waistband and removing the back pockets so they won't give me pressure sores on my backside. They also flow me some jackets and shirts.

I keep running with my plain black or white T-shirts, but when going out for a drink with friends I enjoy throwing on a nice shirt. For winter I get myself a couple of stylish coats and scarves to keep me warm. It's not much, but I figure it's a good place to start building my confidence.

After thinking for a couple of days on how I can 'empower' acceptance, I realise that confidence is the key. How better to take something 'negative', like a mistake, or a flaw, than to own it? If the path to happiness is to begin with acceptance, and if I'm really going to embrace my life and make something of it, then *I need to fucking own it!* I need to own who I am and what my life is. And when I say own it, I mean wear it with pride. Like the way I owned being a professional wakeboarder. I don't think I'll ever *love* being quadriplegic, but if I love who I am regardless of being quadriplegic, and I love myself for everything I've faced, everything that I've overcome, then to me that's owning my situation, owning my life.

•

Pondering what things I can do to fill my life and give me fulfilment, I circle back to something I did recently that ended up being much more rewarding than I expected: motivational speaking. It gave me something I haven't felt much in the past three years — a sense of achievement (and yes, it also gave me a nice financial reward). From completing something that daunted me, and from the feeling that I was offering something of value to my audience, it made me feel I was actually contributing positively to society.

Several weeks later, in early December, there's another opportunity. I joined Toastmasters a while back, to upskill myself in public speaking, and one of the others there worked for Air New Zealand. A few weeks later I'm on stage in front of over 250 Air New Zealand employees, as the keynote speaker for their health and safety conference!

It's completely nerve-wracking but I really enjoy myself, and receive some positive feedback that really boosts my confidence. Maybe this really is something I could get into? It's strange how my adversity has become an asset in this case.

•

Mum hosts the 2017 family Christmas. I've barely been there because of the stairs, but since I got my lightweight manual chair from ACC it's actually possible. So after being slowly carried down the stairs I join the family for Christmas lunch. I remember how low I felt last Christmas and I quickly reel in any thoughts along the lines of 'I wish I could . . .' or 'I hate that I can't . . .' Instead, I bring my attention to my gratitude for the family I have, and for being able to spend Christmas with them. I focus on the joy my nieces display while opening their presents, and on what I enjoy about the day.

Being in my manual chair makes it more challenging, as I have even less control than usual and have to rely on family members to move me. I use it as a test of my ability to let go of control and embrace the moment, and I get into a good space that allows me to enjoy the day. It's a huge change from the way I felt last year.

By the end of the day I'm exhausted! And it's literally just from sitting still. But I guess it's symbolic of the journey I've been on this year. I needed to get uncomfortable in order to gain the strength I need to live this life. Too much comfort, and the need to change and improve does not reveal itself. Acknowledging and sitting with the discomfort has made me stronger and more resilient.

TWENTY-ONE: WHAT CAN I DO?

The 2018 summer is full steam ahead, and I'm battling with the heat since I don't sweat to stay cool. On my last trip to Florida I discovered the wonders of the spritzer bottle. My caregivers use a spray bottle to mist water onto my skin, which then cools me down much like sweat would.

This helps, but I still hate not being able to get out and get involved with all the summer activities with my friends. Sensing another downward spiral looming, I chat to Ants and Brant to figure out some things I *can* do. Next thing I know, we're out hiking through the Waitākere Ranges of West Auckland. I'm in my manual wheelchair, so my first struggle is having zero control. But I trust these guys, and I love that I'm out experiencing something new with them — new to my post-injury life, that is.

After I relax into the fact that I have no control, I find I enjoy myself more. I can look around at my surroundings as I'm moving through the forest, which I can't do when I'm focusing on where I'm driving my chair. So I take the opportunity to really soak it all in. I take in the pleasant aromas of being out in nature, I listen to the tūī singing amid the ambient sounds of cicadas buzzing, and I gaze at the lush greenery as the sun peers through the canopy above.

What started with feelings of frustration at my lack of control ends up being two of the most relaxing and grounding hours I've experienced in ages. Amazing. After letting go of thoughts of how this experience would have been had I not been injured, I was able to relish it as a chance to switch off from the struggle, and to simply enjoy nature with my best buds. I haven't been this present since riding my wakeboard.

Back home I feel like I've had a mental reset — my soul feels at ease. I'm excited to continue exploring what I can do.

It wouldn't be a Kiwi summer without getting among some concerts. We catch Fat Freddy's Drop, and then Foo Fighters are back. After how good it was last time, I'm not missing this one! But on the day of the concert it appears the universe is testing me because it's absolutely pouring down, and has been all day.

I feel like that kind of rain would not only drench me but also most likely kill my chair. But as I gaze out the window at the torrential rain, I think, *Fuck it! I'm not letting some rain stop me!* So we pull out some leftover pocket ponchos from back when we used to sell them as one of my side hustles to fund my career, and we use several of them to cover me and the chair.

'Let's do this!' I say, and head out into the rain.

The disability area at the concert is not undercover, and there are not many others brave enough to be here. The rain temporarily halts while Weezer open the show, but by the time the Foos take the stage we're being pelted. My hair and face are soaked, and water is getting through to my clothes, but I honestly couldn't care less, because I'm having the time of my life, rockin' out in the pouring rain with my bro and best mate.

There's something almost primal about the experience that is incredibly empowering. I remember days out in the rain as a kid, sliding down grass embankments and getting filthy and muddy and not caring one bit, completely embracing the rain. More recently we often worked in the warm Florida rain out at Lake Ronix. So now here I am, head-banging and rocking out to the best show I've ever seen, and the torrential rain is just adding to it. What was originally a negative has become a positive, because I've embraced it — because I'm owning it. I feel like a fucking rock star.

•

Even on maintenance mode, I still really enjoy my neuro rehab sessions with Gilly, especially when we use the REX exoskeleton. Gilly has asked me if I'd like to do some hydrotherapy sessions and I love the idea. Ever since getting in the pool at Rossi's place, I've wanted to be submerged again, so the sensation is incredible as I'm hoisted into the pool. Just floating feels like therapy for me, as every cell in my body is switched on by the connection to the water.

But since I'm here for actual hydrotherapy, Gilly begins with some new exercises that are made easier by my weightlessness in the water. The initial excitement that I feel from seeing my right arm moving away from my body on command is stifled by frustration when I can't seem to bring it back in. The other arm won't move away at all, but when Gilly moves it out for me, I'm able to bring it back in slightly. But we work through those movements as Gilly assists what I can't do. I'm more enthused by just being in the water than by the exercises, but I'll definitely keep at it.

In March Brant and I are back to Orlando because Chad is getting married! We have a great time catching up with the team and visiting friends around Orlando. And since I'm here for six weeks, I've also booked in some rehab sessions at Nextstep, where it's great to catch up with Amanda, Christin, Travis and the rest of the crew.

I'm only back in Auckland a few weeks before I'm off on the next trip. Again it's another wedding, but this time it's in Sydney. My good mate, Doug, from back at school has asked me to be his MC.

This event reconnects me with a few friends I haven't had much contact with since leaving school. Particularly a guy called Tim, who I've known since we were kids. We played cricket together, and later roller hockey. Tim comes up and asks, 'How are you, bro?'

I reply with the usual: 'Yeah, not bad, man. I've just been up on the Gold Coast doing some rehab, and before that was in the States doing the same and attending another wedding.'

Then I launch into telling him I'm thinking of starting a foundation. Proceeds would go to spinal injury research in the hope it can help bring about a cure faster. This is an idea I've had only recently, and I carry on explaining to Tim what I've learnt over the years about how spinal injury works, and blah blah blah—

'Sorry to cut you off, bro,' Tim says, 'and that stuff is all really interesting, but do you ever get tired of talking about it? I bet people all ask you the same things and you end up talking about the same stuff over and over.'

Woah. I didn't see *this* coming.

'What I really want to know,' Tim starts again, 'is how actually are you? Because what you're going through must be incredibly tough on you. I can't even imagine how tough, and I don't know how you do it.'

Immediately my eyes well up and I wrestle to keep the tears from spilling out.

Tim keeps going. 'Because I've been through my own challenges over the past few years, with a divorce, and of course having a son in the middle of it all, which makes it that much harder. And I've really struggled, but that seems almost trivial compared with what you're going through. Not that it's a competition, of course!'

I smile.

'Well, I can't imagine how hard the divorce must've been for you,' I say. 'Even though my situation seems tougher, it's such different stuff, and I don't have a kid involved. But thanks for asking, because it has been really hard. Like, I'm okay, but even just this last week has sucked, with a bladder infection and the constant discomfort I get from it. I get them all the time. The whole thing has been such a cunt of a challenge.'

'Wow,' says Tim, shaking his head.

'But I'm getting better. Like, a couple of years ago I was probably 10 per cent okay and 90 per cent not okay. The 10 percent was the positive outer shell that people saw. But more recently I feel like I've just passed 50/50. It's not that it's getting any easier, but I'm getting better at it.'

We continue on to talk for what might be an hour, both opening up about the struggles, the heartbreak, the real shit! The shit no one ever really talks about. And it's *sooo* fucking refreshing to talk about how life actually is, regardless of being a quad, because life can be hard in so many different ways.

This also gets me thinking about the way the 'How are you?' question can be asked and received differently. Mostly it's just part of a greeting that comes after 'Hi', with no expectation of an in-depth answer. Five people might ask it in the space of a couple of minutes when you arrive somewhere, but no one expects you to open up about how hard life has been.

It took Tim reiterating the question for me to realise that he actually did want to know. He even went two steps further: first by acknowledging the difficulty of my situation, and second by sharing that he too has his own struggles. Both were designed to give me the opportunity to lower my guard and feel comfortable sharing the real shit.

This experience has made me much more aware of how I ask that question, especially with close friends and family. I think it's something we all need to get better at — having real chats among the guys — because it's incredible how it allows us to connect on a level that brings us closer, cutting through the toxic positivity, the false narrative of how life is great. Why not be more real, more open and more vulnerable with our close friends?

I recall something Brené Brown said:

In order for connection to happen, we have to allow ourselves to be seen.

•

She also says that 'vulnerability is about having the courage to be imperfect'. I already feel like I've shared a few of my imperfections on social media(!), but if I'm to be completely authentic, then I feel I should be even more open and vulnerable, not putting across the notion that I'm strong all the time. So even though it scares me to be this open, I put up a social media post about my shitty day:

Today was a shit day — literally!

I continue on to explain what happened, then finish with:

The point of telling you this is not for pity, nor is it for attention. I'm telling you about my shit day because shit days happen. Not just to me, not just to everyone with a spinal cord injury. Shit days happen to everyone!

It's important to understand this because of the immense weight we put on our shoulders, particularly us men who are brought up to believe that we have to be strong all the time. Shit days happen and sometimes it's just life's way of telling us to take a break, to rest our minds. Sometimes we need a hug, to talk to someone, or to scream or cry.

I cried today because I felt like life was unfair. But you don't need to have a spinal cord injury for life to seem unfair. Everyone is dealing with their own life problems, big or small. Just know that you're not alone and you don't have to be strong all the time.

So in among all of the photoshopped highlight reels everyone feels the need to post, here's something real.

Just remember — it's not weak to speak.

I go to sleep not long after, and when I get on my phone the following morning I'm blown away at the response. I've received *thousands* of likes and hundreds of comments. Many have shared their own struggles, some commend me on being so open and inspiring, and others just send love my way.

I find it funny that my most engaging post so far is about shitting myself. But I guess that just proves the power there is in vulnerability. Moving forward, I decide to be more open about the struggles, and to post about the 'shit times' as well as the good stuff.

•

On my quest for getting amongst things that bring me joy, I continue with the hydrotherapy into the winter. It provides more challenges around keeping warm, but I pick up a basic wetsuit from my friends at Rip Curl, and we race me home after each session with the van heaters cranking to make sure my temperature doesn't drop too low before I can get dried and into warm clothes.

I've also been keeping an eye out for more concerts. In late June, I hear from Toby, who I met back when Brant, Ants and I did wakeboard demos for him at Rhythm & Vines. He invites me to the upcoming Sticky Fingers concert.

'Shit yeah, I'm in!' I tell him. He hooks me and a couple of friends up with tickets for the show, and when we arrive he takes us in through the side entrance and introduces us to the band members! A couple of them, Seamus and Beaker, actually take a minute to chat with me and they're really cool and genuine guys. But that's not all Toby has in store for us — we then head backstage and I get to park up on the back corner of the stage and stay there for the entire gig! It's the most amazing two-hour journey in which I almost forget about my injury and just soak up the musical experience. It's so cool that I can't resist going back the next night for round two.

I feel very fortunate to have friends like Toby. It just goes to show — we never know who we'll cross paths with along the journey, and what part that person might play in our lives in the future. It also shows how important it is to be open to what life presents.

TWENTY-TWO: **BREATH OF FRESH AIR**

In late August I board a flight to the US for — you guessed it — another wedding. Fiona and I land in Houston, where we overnight in a motel before another flight. One of the main challenges we encounter in motels is that the beds usually have no space underneath them, and this place is no exception. I need a 10-centimetre space under the bed for my hoist legs so I can be lowered on, and lifted off, the bed. So Fi goes to the front desk to see if they have anything we can use to prop the bed up, and comes back with a stack of Bibles. I shouldn't be surprised — we are in the Bible Belt, after all. I can honestly say it's the most uplifting experience I've ever had from the Bible. I'm glad religious-minded Fiona finds the comedy in it as well.

We head to Lake Ronix in time for Surf Expo, where I plan to launch a fundraiser I've been working on. Ever since my accident, Brant and I have been growing our hair long, to the point where it's now reaching right down our backs. Jesse joined us as well, but his hair is shorter than ours. The original plan was to keep growing it till I walk again, but since that doesn't seem to be happening anytime soon, we've turned it into a fundraiser, getting others onboard. By the time Expo comes around, there are more than a dozen wake athletes involved. The idea of the fundraiser is for people to vote whether we keep our hair or cut it, and we're launching at the Wake Awards! Any hair-cutting will take place on stage the next night and people will donate to support the challenge.

I'm introduced onto the stage by Dano at the beginning of the awards, where I'm joined by a handful of other long-haired riders, and I'm given the chance to speak. Halfway through my speech my blood pressure tanks and I feel like I'm about to pass out. My speech becomes mumbled and my vision begins closing in and I have no choice but to tilt my chair back mid-speech. Thankfully I come right quickly and finish my spiel.

The Wake Awards crowd are really receptive to the fundraiser, and the 24-hour voting poll starts immediately.

At the party the next night, the crowds pile in for the premiere of the new

Coalition wakeboard movie. In front of hundreds of fellow wakeboarders and enthusiasts, I get up on the mic to reveal that the votes are in and the majority have decided my hair should go. So, right here and now, my buddy Quinn takes a pair of scissors and hacks off my ponytail while the crowd cheer and roar.

I spend the rest of the night rockin' out to my buddy Sam Baker's band the Blue Footed Boobies. Besides raising some money to go towards research, I'm stoked to be rid of the ridiculously long hair. Since some of that hair was grown while I was still up and walking, the change accurately reflects my objective of cutting my attachment to my past, and leaving it where it belongs. Brant, Jesse and several others end up cutting their hair as well and we raise a decent chunk of money.

While in Orlando, of course I visit my buddy Alex and his beautiful family, which has grown by one since the last time I was here. They've recently brought a gorgeous girl named Juniper into the world, to join her big brother Brecken (whose middle name is Bradley, named after me!).

I also take the opportunity to get in some more rehab at Nextstep, and of course I've arranged another get-together with close friends at Rossi's place, because I really want to get in the pool again.

Last time the guys walked me down the steps into the pool, but this time I want to jump in with a splash! So eight of the lads crowd around me, lifting me up in the sling, and all jump in at once, taking me with them. The feeling of splashing into the water is incredible. For once I feel like I'm not being treated as if I'll break, and I appreciate my buddies for trusting me and doing this.

Now I tell them I want to hold my breath underwater. There are a couple of nervous laughs, but with some reassurance, and a little bit of figuring out how I'll signal that I need to come up, they're happy to proceed. I take a few deep breaths, and then with Danny on my left and Laz on my right, I take in one last big breath and nod that I'm ready to go under. I absolutely love the sensation of being underwater and holding my breath, especially with this group of best buds, some of whom started as my childhood heroes. With my eyes wide open I see their blurred faces looking at me for the signal to bring me up, but I feel like I could stay under for a couple of minutes. I'm happy chilling a while longer, when suddenly I'm pulled back up to the surface. I take in a deep breath as the guys start laughing and cheering around me.

'*Yeeeeeew!*' Brenton cheers.

'Oh my god, that was forever!' says Laz.

'*Hahahaaa, yeeeaah, Smeeze!*' Parks laughs.

I laugh and tell them I hadn't even given the signal to come up, but Danny says he was struggling to hold me under and needed to surface. I've got the biggest smile on my face — I haven't felt like this in over four years! We go under a couple more times and have the best time.

I can't think of a better way to finish the trip, and once I get back home I feel like I have a renewed drive to search for things I can do that will bring me enjoyment.

●

For the past six months I've been seeing a new girl on and off. It's a casual arrangement, nothing serious — she just comes over and we get into bed and have some fun. I'm attracted to her physically, and we're friends, but I'm not really interested in more than that, and she seems happy with a 'friends with benefits' arrangement. I think she's fascinated by my situation and seems determined to find out if she can break my four-year orgasm drought. She loves what I can do to get her there herself, but recently I've decided that it's not for me any more. I've enjoyed our arrangement, and the sex has been fun, but it just feels a bit empty without a proper loving connection between us. So we end things amicably.

I guess the reason is that I've been starting to feel something I haven't felt in too long — I'm starting to feel worthy again. That my injury doesn't mean I'm not worthy of love. I've worked hard on this, because no one else can make me feel adequate. Even when I had love coming in from women over the past four years, I didn't feel good enough within myself. Their love was great and beautiful in the moment, but they couldn't *make* me feel that I was good enough.

'Good enough' is a standard that I have recently reclaimed control over, because I believe that I am.

In order to have a sense of love and belonging, we need to first believe we're worthy of love and belonging.

This quote that Brené shared in her TED talk on vulnerability helped steer me towards what Susie has been guiding me towards also — a sense of belonging, a sense of worthiness. It's taken years to develop, but it's been like a slow snowball effect. Public speaking has given me a sense of purpose, a sense of worthiness, but

I was only confident enough to do that when I began to believe that my story was worthy of being shared. Confidence comes from experience, but we can only begin to gain experience by taking a leap of faith.

Thanks to everyone who has helped me over the past four-plus years, especially Susie and the things she's taught me, I finally feel worthy of love. I've learnt, through opening myself up to be fully seen, that people love me for who I am. I still don't like that my body is unable to move, but I love myself for having had the strength and tenacity to never give up. More than that, I'm proud of myself for having the courage and willingness to face the incredibly challenging journey of looking inside, peeling back the onion layers to see myself for who I truly am, and to learn to love that person.

I know that I am deserving of the love of someone else, and I have faith that I'll cross paths with that person when the time is right.

I tell Susie about this newfound feeling of self-worth, and I thank her for her help in getting me here. Of course she's super proud of me. And because I seem to be grasping everything she's taught me a lot better now, our chats don't tend to be as intense or in-depth any more, so we decide that weekly, or even fortnightly visits are not necessary now. She'll still come and see me every few weeks, or when I let her know that I'm struggling with something, but for now I feel like I'm in a pretty good space.

•

It's October and I'm heading to the local pub in Takapuna to catch up with the guys over a few beers while watching the All Blacks game against South Africa. When I arrive it's packed and I have to ask a few people to move so I can get through; once again it feels like I have loads of eyes on me. But unlike last time, when I felt like everyone was judging me, this time I just smile and say thank you as I drive past. I'm dressed in my freshest clothes, and even wearing kicks that match the coat I'm rocking, so for all I know, they might be thinking, *Damn, that dude's got style!*

I'm carrying newfound self-confidence from believing in and loving who I am, so I don't feel judgement or pity from other punters. The difference between this time and the last time I was here a couple years ago has nothing to do with anything except how I feel about myself. I think about how much I hated them for how they made me feel, but now I realise that, as Susie taught me right at the beginning, *I'm* in control of the way I feel — no one else can *make* me feel anything.

I have a great night with my friends, not only because it's a really close and exciting game of rugby, but also because we have some good chats. Ever since the discussion I had with Tim, I've felt comfortable speaking more openly among the guys, and I find they're all willing to have deeper chats. It's good to check in from time to time, to make sure we're all doing okay, and we've all become closer friends because of it.

•

November brings another hospital stay due to a bladder infection. Five days on IV antibiotics and I'm home again. A few days later I take delivery of a new toy I've been eagerly awaiting — an off-road wheelchair with tank tracks! For people with my type of injury, ACC generally provides a secondary power chair of some sort, and since they didn't even have to supply me with my everyday power chair, they were more than happy to get me an off-roader. This chair will definitely open up more possibilities — for going to the beach again, and joining Brant, Ants, Haydog and Stu at the motocross track.

Ants and Jesse are both into skydiving, I'm still on my quest to find fun activities I can do, so they reckon I might be up for a tandem jump.

'Give Jeff a call, I'm sure he'll take you!' Jesse says excitedly. Jeff is now a tandem skydive instructor and of course it turns out he is 100 per cent on board with the idea, and quickly starts brainstorming ideas and researching how to do it as safely as possible. There will be a lot of safety considerations and precautions to work through, so we start planning on me getting over to the Gold Coast in about a year's time to pull it off.

The other idea that really excites me is scuba diving. I can picture myself in that underwater world with a couple of mates swimming me around coral reefs and all sorts of sea life, so I start exploring this option. I call a dive school and they're open to the idea, but I'm told I need to get clearance from a dive doctor first. My GP refers me to a dive doctor from the local navy base and I give him a call. He asks me about my injury, and comes to the conclusion that the risks are too high.

'Breathing compressed gas underwater causes nitrogen to be absorbed into the body's fatty tissue and blood,' he says. 'This is why divers must ascend slowly, to allow the nitrogen to be released. If a diver comes up too quickly, it can cause nitrogen bubbles in the body, which can lead to tissue and nerve damage.'

I've heard about this — the bends.

'But for you,' the doctor goes on, 'I'd be wary of nitrogen bubbles forming on the scar tissue in your spinal cord. So unfortunately I am unable to give you clearance to scuba dive.'

'Did you say that those risks are caused by breathing compressed gas underwater?' I ask. 'What about one of those air pumps that sits on the surface and pumps the air to me down a hose?'

'That would come with the same risks, unfortunately,' he replies.

The problem solver in me is not about to let this doctor crush my goals.

'What if I hold my breath? Like freediving? Does that eliminate that risk of nitrogen bubbles?'

'I . . . I guess it would. But then we're dealing with a whole array of other known and unknown risks, the main one being your inability to swim. So for able-bodied divers, if something went wrong they would be able to swim themselves to the surface very quickly, whereas you wouldn't.'

Thank you, Captain Obvious, I want to respond, but instead I say, 'Yeah, I realise that — I'm just brainstorming. I'm sure there must be a way around that.'

The conversation continues back and forth and ends with him basically telling me that he wouldn't advise it. And that he can't stop me and my friends from going out and scuba diving, or freediving, but it's his job to inform me of the risks.

I'm annoyed that scuba diving is off the table. Yeah, I could just go and cowboy it, but that's not me. I'd want to do it properly. But holding my breath and freediving really spark my interest after my experience in Orlando. So the next morning, while lying in bed, I start practising holding my breath. I recall that before my accident I had a pretty decent breath-hold, my record being three and a half minutes. On my second attempt I blow past that and reach 3:45. I'm pleasantly surprised that I managed to beat my record so easily, but I guess my muscles are not using the oxygen like they would've in the past. I also really enjoy the feeling of pushing myself during a breath-hold.

Over the following weeks I keep working on it. I'm stoked when I set a new record of 4:30!

•

I've been invited to Charlotte's engagement party. It's good to see her again and to meet her fiancé, who seems like a great guy. Initially I wasn't sure whether I would attend, having spent so much time lately thinking about past relationships all the way back to Char. But now I'm glad I'm here; there's something about celebrating the engagement of my first love that helps me to leave the past where it belongs.

I'm genuinely happy for her, and that feels good. I'm left feeling confident that a love like that is in my future, and I'll just stay open until that time comes.

Over the new-year period Mum has rented a bach in Whangapoua, on the Coromandel Peninsula. I'm stoked to take my off-road chair so I can get on the beach, but most of all I'm looking forward to a nice relaxing getaway with the family, especially my little nieces. Unfortunately Alex isn't with us this year.

The house is perfect for me — all on one level and open-plan, with a big deck that wraps around. Out the back of the house is an incredible view looking up the valley into the Coromandel Range. I still struggle in situations like this, because I can't exactly get involved in the summer activities. It's unsettling, and I regularly feel the early signs of anxiety brewing. But I find the view out the back of the house is really settling for my soul, especially as the sun is setting over the peaks.

I notice that when I allow myself to simply enjoy what is in front of me, particularly something that doesn't require any involvement, like a beautiful view, then I'm much more at peace than when I'm watching something active in which I can't participate. When I'm sitting and soaking in the view, that's all I feel I'm supposed to do. So as the week continues, I work on expanding my capacity to enjoy each moment for what I can gain from it, rather than letting my thoughts drift to what I wish I could do.

Brant, Ants and his partner Helene come down to join us for a few days. They bring their one-year-old son Aksel, who provides loads of entertainment for us all, but especially for my nieces, who adore Aksel from the moment he arrives. It's cool to see Ants as a dad. He's really stepped up into fatherhood. I'm proud of him for the growth he's made over the years. Gone is the loose-unit, ADD, wakeboard drifter I first met. He's still a great friend but with a solid job as a firefighter, a beautiful partner and a rad little son.

We bring in the new year together with a few beers and yarns about old times.

I can't help but feel that 2019 will be a good year!

•

Brant and I head down to Tauranga, where we crash at his mum's place before a music festival called Bay Dreams in Mount Maunganui. Toby is running it, so once again he hooks it up for me and the guys! Jesse is going to meet us there after going surfing. We make tracks towards the festival. It's hot, there's not a cloud in the sky, so I'm really stoked for one of the silver linings of being in a wheelchair — I get to skip the queues!

The main reason we're all here is to see Tash Sultana and Sticky Fingers. Jesse meets up with a girl he's connected with on Instagram. She says hi to me and so does her tall gorgeous brunette friend as well.

'Hi, I'm Antonia!'

I introduce myself back, and she responds, 'Yeah, I know, I follow you on Insta. I think you're awesome!'

We all jam out to the soul-filling sounds of the Australian one-woman band, then continue to rock out when the Stickies come on stage. It's a much shorter show than last year, due to the back-to-back nature of the gig, but regardless, they put on a great show. Once they're done, we go in search of some shade and some drinks to cool off.

I love rolling around in my tank-track wheelchair, and the girls find us an hour or so later. As time passes, Antonia and I catch each other's eyes numerous times, and eventually she comes over and starts feeding me sips of her Smirnoff lolly water. I'm starting to think that maybe she's flirting with me, which seems unlikely, but I'm out of practice and unsure. An hour later she pulls a couple of lollipops out of her bag and offers me one, which I happily accept. A bit later, when she takes the lollipop from my mouth and puts it in hers, I begin to think, *Yeah, she's flirting with me.* I manage to pluck up the courage to ask for her number at the end of the night.

Three days later she is driving down from Auckland to join Brant and me at his place in Mangakino. When she arrives, I tell her, 'Hey, put your stuff in my room — you know, so I can protect you.' I flash a cheeky grin, and she smiles back and replies, 'Good plan. I feel safer already!'

She stays for the weekend and I teach her to wakeboard and we spend the nights together cuddled up, kissing and fooling around. We make plans for adventures together and concerts we want to go to. For each new thing we come up with, one of us will say, 'Put it on the list.' And I'm actually making a list. Before long we're spending loads of time together, and when, after two weeks, I tell her she's my girlfriend, she seems to be okay with that.

It's not all smooth sailing from the start. She is having some issues around her general happiness and says she's been feeling a bit lost, so I do my best to support her. She's gorgeous and a total sweetheart, and I'm very happy to have her in my life. But then I do something that upsets her. I had decided I'd do 100 days on my tilt table, inspired by Morgan recently starting a 100 days of sweat challenge.

When I posted my challenge, I credited Morgan for the inspiration. This upset Antonia, because Morgan is my ex. A week later I mess up again by posting a picture of Antonia and me on Instagram. She had told me that she doesn't like photos of herself on Insta, but I thought it was such a cute photo and I guess part of me wanted to brag about her. Thankfully all is good after we chat about it. I am getting better at seeing things from someone else's perspective.

Antonia and I go out for a picnic dinner on Valentine's Day. I spent all afternoon with Loisi prepping the vegetarian meal for her, with chicken on the side for me. And when she's cuddled up in my lap as we watch the sunset, I lean in and whisper in her ear, 'I love you.' I've fallen for this girl, and with everything I've learnt, I want to put my whole heart into things, and be vulnerable enough to say what I feel. I'm not afraid of being hurt; I'm more afraid of having regrets for not loving with my whole heart. Later in the night when we're lying in bed, she tells me she loves me too. And we follow that up by making love.

•

It's exactly four years since I got out of the hospital system and moved into this house. Which also means that Fiona and Loisi have been working with me for four years. In that time I've had loads of caregivers come and go. Edwin moved on after about a year, and Kristian after two and a half to pursue his goal of becoming a nurse. I've had caregivers I've asked to have replaced, and others I've liked who have moved on to other clients or other jobs for a variety of reasons. But Fi and Loisi have stayed solid and practically become family.

I still have frustrations with all my carers at times, but I cut them some slack because, like me, they're only human. Empathy, patience and tolerance — I'm getting better at all of them! With my team leader, Fiona, it just feels easy. She has the rhythm of it dialled, to the point where some of what she does just flows. When she hoists me into bed, it's smooth and graceful, almost as if she's dancing the waltz with the hoist. And Loisi, oh sweet Loisi. We have our moments of miscommunication, but she's just such a lovely human — always happy, always smiling, and a joy to have around.

Brant has been working with me for almost three years, and he's basically been a brother to me for over half my life. Like all brothers we have our moments, but it's been incredible to have my best friend as one of my caregivers. We've had loads of adventures over the years, and this whole journey has been another big, crazy adventure that has tightened our bond.

I've been working more on my breath-hold, using some training techniques sent to me by a breathing trainer, James Fletcher, who Jeff introduced me to. On 25 February I break five minutes! And I feel incredible afterwards — a real sense of achievement.

As a birthday present for Dad I bought us tickets to the Bryan Adams concert. Toby hooks us up with two extra tickets so Brant and his dad can come with us and it's a really fun night. Dad has a blast, singing along to all of the hits. It's great to see him so happy. The nursing home has recently increased his meds, which helps keep him moving but also gives him mild hallucinations. I hate seeing him struggle. He comes over for dinner at least once a week and we usually work on little projects that either he or I want done.

Dad has been my biggest inspiration throughout my life, and even more so since my injury. We have a lot in common with limited abilities and reliance on others to do stuff for us. He really is a huge part of the reason I've been able to get through something I never imagined I'd face, let alone overcome. We both know that that's life: shit happens, and we have the choice of whether to give in and let it dictate our lives, or work to turn that adversity into an asset that helps us move forward.

•

I've been getting in the water for hydrotherapy as much as possible, but Gilly is not so keen to be involved with my breath-holding. So I arrange to meet at the AUT Millennium pool one day with Jesse, who does a bit of spearfishing, and my old mate pro wakeboarder Bob Soven, who has freedive and spearfishing experience and is visiting from the US.

I have a dive mask and snorkel on and Bob starts teaching me some preparation techniques called 'breathe-ups'. It's about maximising the oxygen in my system while also remaining calm and keeping my heart rate down. 'Shake your head if you need to take a breath,' Bob instructs me.

After a handful of long, slow breaths, the boys roll me onto my front so I'm face down for a warm-up hold and to check my mask. During the next set of breathe-ups, Bob suggests we do a length of the 25-metre pool, with him and Jesse holding me. I nod my head and take one last deep breath before we start. We're in reasonably shallow water, around a metre deep, so they can semi-walk as they semi-swim me through the water. I look straight down and watch the tiles pass by beneath me. It's so relaxing, and I love the feeling of the cool water flowing past my face.

I can hear the muffled sounds of Bob and Jesse talking and laughing. 'We're halfway!' I hear Bob say. I feel incredibly focused and have no urge to breathe yet.

Soon I hear Bob say, 'Almost there!' Should we go for two?' he asks.

I'm still chilling so I nod my head.

'*Ooooh!* We're going for two lengths!' Bob yells, his excitement palpable.

'*Nooo waaay!*' says Jesse. Jesse is one of the most excitable people I know, but Bob's reaction makes Jesse sound completely chill.

I feel myself drop lower under the surface, now soaring closer to the bottom while my mind is being rinsed clean of any thoughts outside of right here in this pool, right in this moment, where I embrace the sense of calm that's washing over me.

'Three?' Bob asks jokingly as they roll me over at the end, letting out a few yahoos.

I take in a few deep recovery breaths, as the smile spreads across my face.

'Fuck, that was fun! Cheers, dudes!'

I don't know how long that was, probably no more than a couple of minutes, but that felt so good, so freeing to be doing something slightly risky and trusting the boys to have my back. They're also grinning ear to ear. As it turns out, when I felt myself drop lower in the water, that was when Bob decided to straddle my back and ride me like a horse to keep me under, while singing, 'Save a horse, ride a quadriplegic!' I love that type of humour, especially as other people find it so inappropriate.

Next we decide to time a stationary breath-hold. I get to four minutes and I'm done, so I shake my head and they pull me up.

'Dude, I think we could get you down to 100 feet,' Bob says, and I like the sound of that.

We finish by getting some photos of us together underwater with Jesse's GoPro. I'm completely buzzing — I haven't felt like this since before my accident. Bob's words are echoing in my head — '100 feet deep'. *Hmmm, that has a nice ring to it.*

The next night we go out for dinner. I did a talk at a local school today, and Bob and Jesse both made it along to listen. They both got teary-eyed, especially when the final slide was of the three of us underwater.

I bring Antonia along to dinner, and Jesse brings the girl he's currently seeing.

After dinner we stay on for a few more drinks and before I know it I'm drunker than I've been in years. But I feel like after the pool session yesterday, and the successful talk today, as well as having Bob here, there's a lot worth celebrating.

Next morning I wake with a deathly hangover and vow never to get that drunk again. But man, that was a fun night!

•

I've been doing a fair few talks lately — a handful of schools and three big corporates: a bank, an organisation of young financial professionals, and one of the biggest stud farms in the country. As much as I stress out a little preparing for each engagement, and get nervous leading up to the talk, I actually really enjoy it once I get going. I love seeing the engagement and connection in people's eyes as I tell my story, and I get so much from the people who come up to me afterwards and tell me how my story resonated with them, or how inspirational I am. Yes, I get that word 'inspirational' a lot, and sometimes I joke about being sick of it, but the truth is, I could never get sick of being called inspirational. It's one of the best compliments I could receive.

I feel so good after each speaking event and I'm riding a high as I'm heading home from each one. And the money is definitely better than wakeboarding, though of course it's not about the money — it was never the money.

•

It's the time of year when most of my wakeboard friends are getting ready for the northern-hemisphere summer to kick off. I've learnt to be okay about that and I'm no longer so affected by seeing their excited posts. I still miss it, but I understand that my path has gone in a different direction — and who knows, maybe by now I'd have moved on anyway. Many others have.

When I last weighed myself, in the middle of last year, I was shocked to see that I was 98 kg! That's heavier than I was before my accident, before I lost 20 kg of muscle. I knew I'd put on weight, but I didn't think it was that much. So I cut my portion sizes right down, ate healthier meals and less junk food, and rode my FES bike and arm cycle a bunch.

Now I'm back at the spinal unit to use their drive-on scales. I'm 87 kg! I lost 11 kg in 10 months. I'm proud of that. I just want to be healthy and feel good when I throw on one of my suits for a wedding! And I need to be conscious that in some scenarios I need my friends to lift me out of my chair, like when I'm getting in the boat or pool, so I don't want to make it any harder on them.

Antonia and I have been ticking a few things off our list but the honeymoon phase is starting to wear off a little. I love what we have, but I can't help wishing we could do more sexually, and I'm sure she does too. There are small frustrations we need to work through, but I'm sure most relationships have them.

One day she comes over after work. She's got a lot happening in her life at the moment, so we sit outside on the deck to talk. She tells me she thinks she needs to figure things out on her own — without me. She has said this before but this time she really means it. She tells me she thinks we should break up so she can focus on what's making her unhappy. I feel tears rush to my eyes as I hear her words, because I don't want us to break up, but if there's anyone who understands the need to take a step back away from everything to figure out their problems, it's me. So I say, 'It sucks to feel like I'm losing you, but I just want you to be happy. That's what's most important. I hate that we couldn't figure it out together, but I understand and just want the best for you.'

Tears are spilling down my cheeks, and she wipes them away for me. She tells me it's not me that's causing her to be unhappy, but I know being in a relationship with a quadriplegic is challenging. I understand that my life is tough, so I understand that it's not going to be for everyone. And because I love her, I'd rather she's happy without me than unhappy with me.

She thanks me for understanding, then gives me a big hug before she walks away.

Only an hour later I'm feeling okay about it, because I've really embraced having faith that it'll all work out as it's supposed to. If we're supposed to be together, we will be.

•

A week later, and just over a month out from the five-year anniversary of my accident, I've arranged an evening at the pool. This time, the plan is to go deep.

I book out a whole lane and say it's for a freedive group. I let them know we'll need to use the disability hoist, but I refrain from mentioning that a bunch of guys will be coming to sink their quadriplegic friend to the bottom of the pool.

Brant puts my wetsuit on me, then I'm hoisted back into my chair and we head off to the pools to meet the crew that I've arranged to help out. We have a quick briefing where I explain my signals and why it's important that we keep it simple, based on the 'okay' signal. Either I nod my head that I'm okay, or I shake it to say I'm either not okay, or I'm ready to come back to the surface.

'Don't point to the surface to ask if I want to go up, because if I nod, it'll just be confusing,' I explain. 'If there is any confusion, or if you're unsure, just get me to the surface and we can start again.'

I've got a handful of guys here to help — some old mates and some new friends: Brant, Jesse, Stu, Fraser, Ricky, Tim and Pete. Once I'm in the pool we use the shallows to check that my weight belt and ankle weights are enough to have me just positively buoyant. Then the guys float me to the deep end. By now Mum has arrived, and I brought Dad with me, so they're both watching nervously poolside.

We do a few practice dives to figure out equalising, and how to position me on the bottom and get me back up. We even practise popping off my weight belt to help float me back up if needed. Once I'm confident they've got it, I say, 'Okay, let's go for it!' I close my eyes and begin my breathe-ups.

'One more breath,' I soon tell them, then exhale all my air and take in one last big breath. I nod my head. I pack in a few extra gulps of air before I submerge, with Jesse and Fraser guiding me down. Fraser pinches my nose so I can equalise on the way down, until I reach the bottom where Pete, in scuba gear, awaits, and Tim is filming. Jesse and Fraser get me settled on the bottom and Jesse flashes the okay sign. I nod, and they swim back to the surface, leaving me in the hands of Pete and Tim.

•

First minute
Here at the bottom of the pool, 4.5 metres down, I feel myself easing into a very relaxed state. Any thoughts of nostalgia towards my past, or worries about the future, are far from my mind. My focus is on nothing but right here, right now. The ambient underwater sounds aid in bringing me into a near total meditative state. I simply focus on staying relaxed to keep my heart rate slow, to preserve as much oxygen as possible.

Breath work has been a huge part of my recovery from day one. All active rehab movements I've connected with the breath, using *shhhhh* breathing during the movement as I exhaled and engaged my core. I've used big breaths and controlled exhales to deal with intense pain, as well as frustration. I have also utilised big audible sighs to help release anxiety and emotional anguish. It's incredible how strong the breath is. At the start I was wholly dependent on a ventilator, and now my respiratory system is so strong that I can hold my breath for minutes on end.

While Pete has his eyes fixed on me he holds up the okay signal and I nod my head. Then Jesse swims down and holds up a single finger to indicate that I've been down for a minute. *Wow, that minute flew by!*

•

Second minute

When I think about how far I've come since I was in the ICU on a ventilator, it's impossible to think past the incredible support I've received from my friends, my family, my caregivers and the wakeboarding industry. I didn't want to survive until I realised how much support I had and just how many people were behind me. I'm overcome with gratitude for everyone who has played a part, big or small, in my recovery, because I truly would not have survived this without them. It's the greatest showing of love I've ever experienced.

Pete checks if I'm okay, and again I gently nod, as I see Stu settle to my right. He smiles and puts up a shaka sign with thumb and little finger before swimming back up.

I had an incredible life before my injury, and I'm so grateful for every experience my sport brought me. I travelled the world and became one of the best at my craft. I got to push my body and my creativity to new limits, and in doing so I had the honour of inspiring so many others. I met and worked alongside so many talented people, and made friends that I'll keep for life.

I loved deeply, and got myself into the kind of sexual entanglements that most guys only ever dream about. I have no regrets over living such an action-packed life pursuing my dream. I'm even grateful for the struggles along the way — the injuries, the setbacks, the mistakes and the financial struggles — because every single one of those experiences has built me into the resilient man I'm proud to have become.

Fraser appears from above and puts up deuces to tell me I've hit two minutes. I still feel very tranquil, totally relaxed. I nod and give him a slight grin, then feel the cool water wash across my face as he kicks his fins to swim back up.

•

Third minute

As I gaze up towards the water's surface I feel proud about what I've endured in the past five years. I survived the ICU, the spinal units, the rehab facilities and numerous further hospital stays. I'm proud of myself for giving rehab everything I had. For being brave enough to plunge inward to face my greatest fears. For having the courage to sit with those incredibly uncomfortable feelings so I could understand them. And for taking the time to work through those issues to reclaim my happiness, and reclaim my life.

Thanks to Susie's teachings, I have a much better idea of the anxiety and depression I underwent, and I know now how to process those states of mind and bring myself back to the present. I know that no amount of regret or wishing will change my past, and that the most powerful thing I can do is accept it. I can learn from it to help me make better decisions in the present. I also understand that no amount of anxiety, worry or fear will change the future. The strongest way forward is to be okay with not knowing what lies ahead for me, and to embrace and find joy in the journey.

I signal that I'm okay by nodding again to Pete in response to his gesture.

I've learnt that there's no happiness to be had from focusing on what you don't have, or can't do. Joy comes from having gratitude for what you do have, what you can do and how things are. And being grateful for how things are doesn't mean you can't work to improve your lot, but you need to separate those goals from any expectations.

The people who matter to me have shown that I'm not a burden to them, and my newfound role as a motivational speaker has shown that I can actually offer something to a lot of people through sharing my story.

I no longer fear missing out, because I keep my mind focused on what I can gain from the present. I can't do everything, but I know I'll have my own adventures. Like right here, right now, sitting 4.5 metres underwater, free from my wheelchair, free from any thoughts of what was.

In this moment I'm completely at peace.

Ricky swims down and holds up three fingers. I nod. He takes the spare regulator from Pete's shoulder and starts breathing from it so he can stay down here with us.

•

Fourth minute

My recent breakup was sad, but my having faith that it'll all work out proved the power that faith can have. In the past it would've been easy for me to let the breakup trigger a serious emotional slide, but what I have learnt about empathy and compassion allowed me to not see myself as a victim in that scenario, and to understand that Antonia's search for her own happiness is valid, and is not about me. I have found a place of confidence within myself that doesn't rely on the validation of others.

Here I am in the most vulnerable position I've been in since Deano and Chad flipped me face up after my accident. The fact that I am able to sit here and remain so calm means three things:

1. I understand and completely accept that I cannot swim unaided to the surface, and all of the risks around that.

2. I am confident in the preparation I've done, and I have faith in my ability to hold my breath, and to know my limits.

3. I have total and complete trust in my friends to bring me back to the surface when I need them to. Acceptance of that lack of control is what allows me to remain so present down here.

Ricky checks in again before he takes off back to the surface. I spot Tim swimming behind Pete, with the camera still on me.

This minute is starting to feel a lot longer than the previous three. But right as that thought crosses my mind, Jesse swims down and holds up four fingers. I nod.

•

Fifth minute

This journey has brought so many challenges, but I'm grateful for all of them because it's only through undergoing those hardships that I realised the need to address the underlying issues behind them. I'm so incredibly thankful to have had a guide like Susie to help me change my perception and understanding of everything. Her teachings have been my guide back to self-love and happiness, and I wouldn't be here without her.

I know I haven't conquered all of these challenges, and probably never will, but she's given me so many valuable tools. And I've learnt that if I'm ever really struggling, I can always ask for help, because that's never something to be ashamed of.

It's okay not to be okay sometimes.

I'm excited for what my future may hold. Now that I'm more open to possibilities, I feel like more opportunities will begin to present themselves.

Freediving, public speaking, outdoor adventures — who knows what else. As for relationships and love, I'm confident it will all work out.

I remind myself that I need to allow time for them to get me back up. I'm starting to feel the urge to breathe, but I know I have a bit more time in me. Pete holds the okay signal up, and again I nod, even though I'm feeling the struggle setting in.

I imagine Mum and Dad are probably getting concerned — it must feel like an eternity to them.

At the bottom of this pool I've found passion for life, I've found progression, and I've found an incredibly special element of trust and camaraderie with my friends. And to think, this is where I imagined ending it all. Isn't life so strangely and unpredictably beautiful?

Fraser appears with his hand open and all five fingers outstretched. Five minutes! I can't hold my breath much longer, and I'm stoked I hit my goal, so I shake my head and the guys dart into action.

I break the surface and the guys are cheering as I take in a huge breath.

Mum and Dad are wreathed in smiles.

ACKNOWLEDGEMENTS

First and foremost, I would like to acknowledge that there would be no book without Susie. I would not be where I am today without her generously gifting me her time, knowledge and guidance. Susie never charged me a cent for her time, and although it is her job and she can't do it for free for everyone, I think she knew that deep down I had it in me to take the adversity I'd been handed and use it to inspire many through sharing my story. To share far and wide the knowledge she's passed down: that was her gift to me, and to humanity.

I'd like to thank my family for their constant love and support. My father Erik, my mother Linda and stepdad Gordon, my brother Alex, my sister Monique, brother-in-law Jonny and their beautiful children Maisey, Mila and Billy. You've all helped form me over my life and I feel very fortunate to have such an incredible family.

I wouldn't be here at all without Dean Smith, Chad Sharpe, Austin Pratt, Massi Piffaretti and Spencer Norris: your swift action after my accident saved my life. And huge props to Jeff Weatherall for leading the charge and rallying the troops after my injury. I truly appreciate your support in my time of need.

To my close friends. Thank you for being there for me, for keeping it real and for keeping me in check. Thank you for not treating me any differently just because of my disability. Thank you for pushing me to be better and for trusting me to know my limits when pushing myself. Thank you for helping to bring adventure and progression to my life again.

Thank you to girlfriends and lovers, past, present and future, for surrounding me with love and connection.

I'd like to thank my caregivers for putting up with my shit, taking care of me and helping me through my day-to-day. And to all of the medical staff who have been involved in my care over the years.

I want to say a special thanks to my Ronix team who I shared many absolute dream days with at Lake Ronix. And I appreciate every sponsor who supported me along the way, every person who towed me behind their boat, let me crash on their couch or helped me out in any way throughout my career. I feel very grateful to have such an incredibly supportive community behind me in the wakeboard community.

I want to say a huge thank you to all of those who donated to my recovery; without your support, I would not be where I am today.

Of course, I owe so much to my wonderful editors, Kimberley Davis and Rachel Scott, for their help with taking my 450,000-word memoir and shaping it into a digestible book. Thank you for helping me tell my story.

But most of all, I'd like to acknowledge myself for the work I put into writing this book. For spending countless hours every day for over five years, digging deep through the bittersweet memories of the best years of my life before injury. For being willing to peel back the layers to expose any uncomfortable beliefs so I could learn from them, for the sake of healing. I have shed many tears and had plenty of frustrations throughout this process but I'm still so thankful to have had the opportunity to go through it, because it was an incredibly cathartic experience that became a big part of my healing journey.

And finally, I'd like to thank you, the reader, for taking the time to read my story. I hope you enjoyed the ride!